Macroeconomics

ANDREW B. ABEL
UNIVERSITY OF PENNSYLVANIA

BEN S. BERNANKE

DEAN CROUSHORE
UNIVERSITY OF RICHMOND

RONALD D. KNEEBONE
UNIVERSITY OF CALGARY

EIGHTH CANADIAN EDITION

VICE PRESIDENT, EDITORIAL: Anne Williams
MARKETING MANAGER: Leigh Anne Graham
CONTENT MANAGER: Madhu Ranadive
PROJECT MANAGER: Sarah Gallagher
CONTENT DEVELOPER: Cheryl Finch
PRODUCTION SERVICES: Cenveo® Publisher Services

PERMISSIONS PROJECT MANAGER: Joanne Tang
PHOTO PERMISSIONS RESEARCH: Sohail Akhter, Aptara Corporation Ltd.
TEXT PERMISSIONS RESEARCH: Anjali Singh
COVER DESIGNER: Cenveo Publisher Services
COVER IMAGE: © Bildagentur Zoonar GmbH / Shutterstock

Pearson Canada Inc., 26 Prince Andrew Place, Don Mills, Ontario M3C 2T8.

978-0-13-464635-0

1 17

Library and Archives Canada Cataloguing in Publication

Abel, Andrew B., 1952-, author
    Macroeconomics / Andrew B. Abel (University of Pennsylvania), Ben S. Bernanke, Dean Croushore (University of Richmond), Ronald D. Kneebone (University of Calgary). — Eighth Canadian edition.

Includes index.
ISBN 978-0-13-464635-0 (hardcover)

    1. Macroeconomics—Textbooks. 2. Textbooks. I. Bernanke, Ben, author II. Kneebone, Ronald D. (Ronald David), 1955-, author III. Croushore, Dean Darrell, 1956-, author IV. Title.

HB172.5.A24 2018   339   C2017-903782-X

ABOUT THE AUTHORS

ANDREW B. ABEL

The Wharton School of the
University of Pennsylvania

Ronald A. Rosenfeld Professor of Finance at The Wharton School and professor of economics at the University of Pennsylvania, Andrew Abel received his A.B. *summa cum laude* from Princeton University and his Ph.D. from the Massachusetts Institute of Technology.

He began his teaching career at the University of Chicago and Harvard University and has held visiting appointments at both Tel Aviv University and The Hebrew University of Jerusalem.

A prolific researcher, Abel has published extensively on fiscal policy, capital formation, monetary policy, asset pricing, and Social Security—as well as serving on the editorial boards of numerous journals. He has been honored as an Alfred P. Sloan Fellow, a Fellow of the Econometric Society, and a recipient of the John Kenneth Galbraith Award for teaching excellence. Abel has served as a visiting scholar at the Federal Reserve Bank of Philadelphia, as a member of the Panel of Economic Advisers at the Congressional Budget Office, and as a member of the Technical Advisory Panel on Assumptions and Methods for the Social Security Advisory Board. He is also a Research Associate of the National Bureau of Economic Research and a member of the Advisory Board of the Carnegie-Rochester–NYU Conference Series.

BEN S. BERNANKE

Brookings Institution

Ben Bernanke is currently Distinguished Fellow in Residence with the Economic Studies Program at the Brookings Institution. From February 2006 to January 2014, he was Chairman of the Board of Governors of the Federal Reserve System. Before that, he served as Chair of the President's Council of Economic Advisors from June 2005 to January 2006 and was a Governor of the Federal Reserve System from August 2002 to June 2005. Prior to his work in public service, he was the Howard Harrison and Gabrielle Snyder Beck Professor of Economics and Public Affairs at Princeton University. He received his B.A. in economics from Harvard University *summa cum laude*—capturing both the Allyn Young Prize for best Harvard undergraduate economics thesis and the John H. Williams prize for outstanding senior in the Economics Department. Like coauthor Abel, he holds a Ph.D. from the Massachusetts Institute of Technology.

Bernanke began his career at the Stanford Graduate School of Business in 1979. In 1985 he moved to Princeton University, where he served as chair of the Economics Department from 1995 to 2002. He has twice been visiting professor at MIT and once at New York University, and has taught in undergraduate, M.B.A., M.P.A., and Ph.D. programs. He has authored more than 60 publications in macroeconomics, macroeconomic history, and finance.

Bernanke has served as a visiting scholar and advisor to the Federal Reserve System. He is a Guggenheim Fellow and a Fellow of the Econometric Society. He has also been variously honored as an Alfred P. Sloan Research Fellow, a Hoover Institution National Fellow, a National Science Foundation Graduate Fellow, and a Research Associate of the National Bureau of Economic Research. He has served as editor of the *American Economic Review*.

DEAN CROUSHORE

Robins School of Business,
University of Richmond

Dean Croushore is professor of economics and Rigsby Fellow at the University of Richmond. He received his A.B. from Ohio University and his Ph.D. from Ohio State University.

Croushore began his career at Pennsylvania State University in 1984. After teaching for 5 years, he moved to the Federal Reserve Bank of Philadelphia, where he was vice president and economist. His duties during his 14 years at the Philadelphia Fed included heading the macroeconomics section, briefing the bank's president and board of directors on the state of the economy and advising them about formulating monetary policy, writing articles about the economy, administering two national surveys of forecasters, and researching current issues in monetary policy. In his role at the Fed, he created the Survey of Professional Forecasters (taking over the defunct ASA/NBER survey and revitalizing it) and developed the Real-Time Data Set for Macroeconomists.

Croushore returned to academia at the University of Richmond in 2003. The focus of his research in recent years has been on forecasting and how data revisions affect monetary policy, forecasting, and macroeconomic research. Croushore's publications include articles in many leading economics journals and a textbook on money and banking. He is associate editor of several journals and visiting scholar at the Federal Reserve Bank of Philadelphia.

RONALD D. KNEEBONE

Department of Economics and the
School of Public Policy, University of Calgary

Professor of Economics at the University of Calgary, Ron Kneebone received his B.A. in economics and political science before earning a Ph.D. in economics from McMaster University.

Kneebone began his academic career at Wilfrid Laurier University. He joined the faculty at the University of Calgary in 1989. He has taught courses in economic principles and intermediate and senior undergraduate macroeconomic theory, as well as macroeconomic theory at the Ph.D. level. He has been recognized as a superior teacher in the Department of Economics eight times and has twice won the Faculty of Social Sciences Distinguished Teacher Award.

Kneebone is a former associate editor of *Canadian Public Policy/Analyse de Politiques*, Canada's foremost journal examining economic and social policy. He is currently Director of Economic & Social Policy Research and Director of the Master of Public Policy Program in The School of Public Policy.

Kneebone's research interests lie mainly in the macroeconomic aspects of public finances. He has published articles on the problems for government budget financing associated with the three-level structure of Canadian government, on the history of government fiscal and monetary relations in Canada, and on the characteristics of Canadian government fiscal policy choices. More recently he has published research on issues related to homelessness and social assistance policies. For joint work, he was awarded the Douglas Purvis Memorial Prize for the best published work in Canadian public policy in 1999/2000.

BRIEF CONTENTS

CONTENTS

Summary Tables

Key Diagrams

Applying Macroeconomics to the Real World

Symbols Used in This Book

A	productivity
B	government debt
$BASE$	monetary base
C	consumption
CA	current account balance
CU	currency in circulation
DEP	bank deposits
E	worker effort
G	government purchases
I	investment
INT	net interest payments
K	capital stock
KA	capital account balance
M	money supply
MC	marginal cost
MPK	marginal product of capital
MPN	marginal product of labour
$MRPN$	marginal revenue product of labour
N	employment, labour
$\overline{N}$	full-employment level of employment
NFP	net factor payments
NM	non-monetary assets
NX	net exports
P	price level
P^e	expected price level
$PVLC$	present value of lifetime consumption
$PVLR$	present value of lifetime resources
R	real seignorage revenue
RES	bank reserves
S	national saving
S_{pvt}	private saving
S_{govt}	government saving
T	taxes
TR	transfers
V	velocity
W	nominal wage
Y	total income or output
$\overline{Y}$	full-employment output
a	individual wealth or assets
c	individual consumption; consumption per worker
cu	currency–deposit ratio
d	depreciation rate
e	real exchange rate
$\overline{e}_{nom}$	nominal exchange rate
g	growth rate of GDP
e_{nom}	official value of nominal exchange rate
i	nominal interest rate
i^m	nominal interest rate on money
k	capital–labour ratio
n	growth rate of labour force
p_K	price of capital goods
r	expected real interest rate
r^w	world real interest rate
$r_{a\text{-}t}$	expected after-tax real interest rate
res	reserve–deposit ratio
s	individual saving; saving rate
t	income tax rate
u	unemployment rate
$\overline{u}$	natural unemployment rate
uc	user cost of capital
w	real wage
y	individual labour income; output per worker
π	inflation rate
π^e	expected inflation rate
η_Y	income elasticity of money demand
τ	effective tax rate

PREFACE

I became involved in the writing of this textbook for two reasons. One is that, although writing a textbook is hard, it can also be rewarding. It is a wonderful feeling to receive notes from students and instructors telling me that they felt they learned a lot from the book and that it changed or clarified how they understand macroeconomic events. The second reason is that, as an instructor, I found existing textbooks either were too advanced and narrow in presentation, or cast ideas and concepts in a way that was so simple that they inaccurately represented the issues students were observing in the real world on a daily basis. I wanted a textbook that did a better job of balancing the need for theoretical rigour with the need to explain events as they were observed in reality. The opportunity to modify the U.S. edition of *Macroeconomics* to better describe and evaluate macroeconomic events in ways relevant to Canadian students gave me the chance to be involved in the writing of the textbook I wanted to teach from.

NEW AND UPDATED COVERAGE

What is taught in intermediate economics courses—and how it is taught—has changed substantially in recent years. Previous editions of *Macroeconomics* played a major role in these developments. The eighth Canadian edition tightens its focus on the critical issues of macroeconomics, and introduces changes to better fit with how instructors teach intermediate macroeconomics.

Key changes with this edition include:

- *The Fiscal Policy Multiplier.* New with this edition we include, in Chapter 12, a detailed discussion of the size of the fiscal policy multiplier. This issue has gained considerable attention in part because, in a very low interest rate environment, monetary policy loses some of its ability to influence real outcome. Many governments have responded by emphasizing the use of fiscal policy as a way of stimulating a stagnating economy. This new discussion draws on multiplier calculations in the appendix to Chapter 12 to examine under what conditions one might expect the fiscal policy multiplier to be large or small.

- *The Laffer Curve.* With this edition, Chapter 15 now includes a discussion of the Laffer Curve, the relationship between tax revenue and tax rates. Our discussion explains the logic of the Laffer Curve and also directs attention to recent empirical work that tests whether, in fact, tax rates could be lowered as a way of increasing tax revenue.

- *Measuring GDP.* New approaches taken by Statistics Canada to measure GDP required a significant revision of Chapter 2. The new approach used to measure GDP by summing incomes is explained and is illustrated with recent data taken from the national accounts.

In addition, this edition has updated existing discussions of the effects of oil price shocks, the measures and consequences of government debt, the changing nature of foreign investment, the lessons learned from the 2007–2009 financial crisis for the regulation of the financial sector, and much more. In short, the eighth Canadian edition of *Macroeconomics* is tighter, more focused, and better designed to support instructors in making the most effective presentation of the macroeconomic models emphasized in intermediate macroeconomics courses.

FEATURES

In the eighth Canadian edition of *Macroeconomics*, we have added—and subtracted—material to keep the text focused and up-to-date while building on the strengths that underlie the book's lasting appeal, including:

- ***Real-world applications.*** A perennial challenge for instructors is to help students make active use of the economic ideas developed in the text. The rich variety of applications in this book shows by example how economic concepts can be put to work in explaining real-world issues, such as increasing wage inequality, the productivity slowdown, sources of international financial crises, and alternative approaches to making monetary policy. *The eighth Canadian edition has updated the best applications of previous editions but has also removed applications that are less relevant and of less interest to current students.*

  The ultimate test of a model or theory is its practical relevance. We dedicate a significant portion of each chapter to showing how the theory can be applied to real events and issues. Thus, we present additional information and topics designed to enhance students' understanding of the economic theories presented in that chapter in boxes entitled "A Closer Look" or "Applications." Examples include changes to housing prices on consumption spending (Chapter 4), comparing Canadian and foreign levels of direct investment (Chapter 5), and discussing the issues and complications involved in measuring the size of government debt (Chapter 15). Throughout the book we have provided the source of all data we presented in graphs and tables. Providing this information enables instructors and students to update tables and figures and to find their own data series to answer questions related to those discussed in the text.

- ***Broad modern coverage.*** From its conception, *Macroeconomics* has responded to students' desires to investigate and understand a wider range of macroeconomic issues than permitted by the course's traditional emphasis on short-run fluctuations and stabilization policy. This book provides a modern treatment of these traditional topics but also gives in-depth coverage of other important macro issues, such as the determinants of long-run economic growth, international trade and capital flows, labour markets, and the political and institutional framework of policymaking. This comprehensive coverage also makes the book a useful tool for instructors with differing views about course coverage and topic sequence.

- ***Reliance on a set of core economic ideas.*** Although we cover a wide range of topics, we avoid developing a new model or theory for each issue. Instead, we emphasize the broad applicability of a set of core economic ideas (such as the production function, the trade-off between consuming today and saving for tomorrow, and supply–demand analysis). Using these core ideas, we build a theoretical framework that encompasses all the macroeconomic analyses presented in the book: long-run and short-run, open economy and closed economy, and classical and Keynesian.

- *A balanced presentation.* Macroeconomics is full of controversies, many of which arise from the split between classicals and Keynesians (of the old, new, and neo- varieties). Sometimes, the controversies overshadow the broad common ground shared by the two schools. We emphasize that common ground.

    First, we pay greater attention to long-run issues (on which classicals and Keynesians have less disagreement). Second, we develop the classical and Keynesian analyses of short-run fluctuations within a single overall framework, in which we show that the two approaches differ principally in their assumptions about how quickly wages and prices adjust. Where differences in viewpoint remain—for example, in the search versus efficiency-wage interpretations of unemployment—we present and critique both perspectives. This balanced approach exposes students to all the best ideas in modern macroeconomics. At the same time, an instructor of either classical or Keynesian inclinations can easily base a course on this book.

- *Innovative pedagogy.* The eighth Canadian edition, like its predecessors, provides useful tools to help students study, understand, and retain the material. Described in more detail later in the Preface, these tools include Summary tables, Key Diagrams, Key Terms, and Key Equations to aid students in organizing their study; and three types of problems for practice and to develop understanding.

A FLEXIBLE ORGANIZATION

The basic structure of the text is unchanged from previous editions. In Part I (Chapters 1 and 2), we introduce the field of macroeconomics and discuss issues of measurement. In Part II (Chapters 3–7), we focus on long run issues, including productivity, saving, investment, growth, and inflation. We devote Part III (Chapters 8–12) to the study of short-run economic fluctuations and stabilization policy. Finally, although we discuss macroeconomic policy throughout the book, in Part IV (Chapters 13–15) we look at issues and institutions of policymaking in greater detail. In the Appendix at the end of the book, we review useful algebraic and graphical tools.

We recognize that instructors have different preferences about what to include in their courses and that their choices may be constrained by their students' backgrounds and the length of the term. The text is designed to be flexible in accommodating these different needs. In planning how to use *Macroeconomics* in your course, you might find the following suggestions useful:

- *Core chapters.* We recommend that every course include these six chapters:

    Chapter 1   Introduction to Macroeconomics
    Chapter 2   The Measurement and Structure of the Canadian Economy
    Chapter 3   Productivity, Output, and Employment
    Chapter 4   Consumption, Saving, and Investment
    Chapter 7   The Asset Market, Money, and Prices
    Chapter 9   The *IS–LM–FE* Model: A General Framework for Macroeconomic Analysis

Chapters 1 and 2 provide an introduction to macroeconomics, including national income accounting. The next four chapters on the list make up the analytical core of the book: Chapter 3 introduces the labour market, Chapters 3 and 4 together develop the goods market, and Chapter 7 discusses the asset market. Chapter 9 combines the three markets into a general equilibrium model usable for short-run analysis (in either classical or Keynesian mode).

To a syllabus containing the above six chapters, the instructor can add various combinations of other chapters according to the course focus. The following are some possible choices:

- **International macroeconomic issues.** Most instructors will want to add two open-economy chapters to the six chapters listed. Chapter 5 discusses saving, investment, and the trade balance in both small and large open economies with full employment. Chapter 10 discusses exchange-rate determination and macroeconomic policy in an open-economy model in which short-run deviations from full employment are possible. Each of these chapters directly follows its closed-economy partner.

- **Short-run, fixed price focus.** Instructors who prefer to emphasize short-run issues (business cycle fluctuations and stabilization policy) within the context of a fixed price model can omit Chapter 6 without loss of continuity. They could also go directly from Chapters 1 and 2 to Chapters 8 and 9, which introduce business cycles and the *IS–LM–FE* framework. Although the presentation in Chapters 8 and 9 is self-contained, it will be helpful for instructors who skip Chapters 3–7 to provide some background and motivation for the various behavioural relationships and equilibrium conditions.

- **Short-run, flexible price focus.** Instructors who want to build on the short-run model can deepen their analysis by adding Chapters 11 and 12. In these chapters the role of price expectations is introduced into the classical and the Keynesian models, allowing for examination of the implications of rational expectations for stabilization policies.

- **Classical emphasis.** For instructors who want to teach the course with a modern classical emphasis, Chapter 11 provides a self-contained presentation of classical business cycle theory. Other material of interest includes the Friedman–Phelps interpretation of the Phillips curve (Chapter 13), the role of credibility in monetary policy (Chapter 14), and Ricardian equivalence with multiple generations (Chapter 15).

- **Keynesian emphasis.** Instructors who prefer a Keynesian emphasis can omit Chapter 11 (classical business cycle analysis); however, they will find it useful to first present those sections of Chapter 11 that introduce and discuss the implications of the theory of rational expectations. As noted, if a short-run focus is preferred, Chapter 5 (full-employment analysis of the open economy) and Chapter 6 (long-term economic growth) may also be omitted without loss of continuity.

LEARNING AIDS

The text contains many features aimed at helping students understand, apply, and retain important concepts:

- **Detailed, colour graphs.** The book is liberally illustrated with *data graphs*, which emphasize the empirical relevance of theory, and *analytical graphs*, which guide students through the development of model and theory in a well-paced, step-by-step manner. Both types of graphs include descriptive captions that summarize the details of events shown in the graph. Our use of colour in analytical graphs is demonstrated in Figure 3.9, which shows the effects of a shifting curve on a set of endogenous variables. Note that the original curve is in black, and its new position is in teal, with arrows indicating the direction of the shift. A teal "shock box" indicates the reason for the shift, and a grey "result box" lists the main effects of the shock on endogenous variables. We consistently use these and similar conventions to make it easier for students to gain a clear understanding of the analysis.

- **Key Diagrams.** Key Diagrams, a unique study feature found at the end of selected chapters, are self-contained descriptions of the most important analytical graphs in the book (see the list in the Contents for their locations). For each Key Diagram we present the graph (the production function, Chapter 3, or the *IS–LM–FE* diagram, Chapter 9, for example) and define and describe its elements in words and equations. We then present an analysis of what the graph reveals and discuss the factors that shift the curves in the graph.

- **Summary tables.** Throughout the book summary tables compile the main results of analyses. These summary tables reduce the amount of time the student must spend learning and writing results, allowing a greater concentration on understanding and applying these results.

- **End-of-chapter review materials.** To facilitate review, at the end of each chapter the student will find a chapter summary, covering the chapter's main points; a list of key terms, with page references; an annotated list of key equations; and review questions for self-testing.

- **End-of-chapter problems.** An extensive set of problems for practice and review (more than 160 in all) includes *numerical problems*, which have explicit numerical solutions and are especially useful for checking students' understanding of basic relationships and concepts; and *analytical problems*, which ask students to use or extend theories qualitatively. Answers are provided in the Instructor's Manual.

- **Review of useful analytical tools.** Although we use no mathematics beyond high school algebra, some students will find helpful a review of the main analytical tools used in the book. The Appendix (at the end of the text) succinctly discusses functions of one and several variables, graphs, slopes, exponents, and formulas for finding the growth rates of products and ratios.

- **Glossary.** The Glossary at the end of the text includes definitions of all key terms (set in boldface in the chapters and listed at the end of each chapter) and refers the student to the page on which the term is fully defined and discussed.

SUPPLEMENTS

The following instructor supplements are available for downloading from a password-protected section of Pearson Canada's online catalogue (*http://catalogue.pearsoned.ca*). Navigate to your book's catalogue page to view a list of those supplements that are available. See your local sales representative for details and access.

- ***Instructor's Manual:*** This manual contains valuable resources including teaching notes, suggested topics for class discussion, and solutions to all end-of-chapter problems.

- ***Computerized Test Bank:*** Pearson's computerized test banks allow instructors to filter and select questions to create quizzes, tests, or homework. Instructors can revise questions or add their own, and may be able to choose print or online options. These questions are also available in Microsoft Word format.

- ***PowerPoint Presentations:*** PowerPoint presentations offer an outline of the key points for each chapter.

- ***Image Library:*** This image library consists of all figures from the text.

ACKNOWLEDGMENTS

These days a textbook is not the lonely venture of its author or co-authors but is the joint project of dozens of skilled and dedicated people. We extend special thanks to Megan Farrell, Acquisitions Editor; Leigh Anne Graham, Director Product Marketing; and Cheryl Finch, Content Developer. Each of these people contributed greatly to the project. We also thank many others at Pearson Canada and in the United States for their effort and craft.

We benefited from the advice of numerous colleagues at universities across Canada, the Bank of Canada, and Statistics Canada who patiently directed us to data sources and research studies. We appreciate the contributions of reviewers and colleagues who offered valuable comments on succeeding drafts of the book in all eight editions thus far:

REVIEWERS

Iris Au
University of Toronto

Patrick Coe
Carleton University

Alison Coffin
Memorial University

Anupam Das
Mount Royal University

Alexander Gainer
University of Alberta

Philippe Ghayad
Dawson College

Mustapha Ibn Boamah
University of New Brunswick

Robert J. McKeown
University of Toronto

Amy Peng
Ryerson University

Gabriela Sabau
Memorial University

Rizwan Tahir
McMaster University

Andrew Wong
University of Alberta

Ayoub Yousefi
King's University College at Western University

We are grateful to Mark Gertler, Rick Mishkin, and Steve Zeldes for valuable assistance with the first U.S. edition, and to reviewers of the U.S. editions. We are also grateful to several cohorts of students at the University of Pennsylvania, Princeton University, and the University of Calgary who—not entirely of their own free will but none the less very graciously—assisted us in the development of this textbook.
    Last and most important, we thank our families for their patience and support. We dedicate this book to them.

Philadelphia   A.B.A.

Princeton   B.S.B.

Calgary   R.D.K.

Chapter 1

Introduction to Macroeconomics

1.1 What Macroeconomics Is About

Macroeconomics is the study of the structure and performance of national economies and of the policies that governments use to try to affect economic performance. The issues that macroeconomists address include the following:

- *What determines a nation's long-run economic growth?* In 1870, income per capita in Norway was smaller than in Argentina. But today, income per capita is more than twice as high in Norway as in Argentina. Why do some nations' economies grow quickly, providing their citizens with rapidly improving living standards, while other nations' economies are relatively stagnant?

- *What causes a nation's economic activity to fluctuate?* After 17 years of strong economic growth, the Canadian economy began to falter in 2008. By the end of 2009, output in Canada had fallen by 2% from its level at the end of 2007. Even if they grow on average, why do economies sometimes experience sharp short-run fluctuations, lurching between periods of prosperity and periods of hard times?

- *What causes unemployment?* During the 1930s, one-fifth of the workforce in Canada was unemployed. A decade later, during World War II, less than 2% of the workforce was unemployed. Why does unemployment sometimes reach very high levels? Why, even during times of relative prosperity, is a significant fraction of the workforce unemployed?

- *What causes prices to rise?* The rate of inflation in Canada crept steadily upward during the 1970s, and reached 11% per year in the early 1980s before dropping to 3% per year in the mid-1980s, and to less than 2% per year in the early 1990s. Germany's inflation experience has been much more extreme: Although Germany has earned a reputation for low inflation in recent decades, following its defeat in World War I, it experienced an 18-month period (July 1922–December 1923) during which prices rose by a factor of several billion! What causes inflation, and what can be done about it?

- *How does being part of a global economic system affect nations' economies?* According to many observers, economic growth in Canada in the 1990s was boosted by rapid growth abroad, which added to the demand for Canadian products. On the other hand, in 2007 a crisis began to develop in the U.S. financial market that would quickly impact the Canadian economy by threatening the stability of Canadian financial institutions and causing a significant fall in Canadian exports. How do economic links between nations, such as international trade and borrowing, affect the performance of individual economies and the world economy as a whole?

- *Can government policies be used to improve a nation's economic performance?* Governments raise a great deal of revenue by taxing individuals and firms. We as citizens have deemed it appropriate that the government spend that revenue on goods and services. These include national defence, police, and education. How do government decisions about how to raise revenue—for example, by income taxes versus by borrowing—affect the overall economy? How do government spending choices—for example, on infrastructure as opposed to income support for the elderly—affect the economy? How should economic policy be conducted in order to keep the economy as prosperous and stable as possible?

Macroeconomics seeks to offer answers to such questions, which are of great practical importance and are constantly debated by politicians, the press, and the public. In the rest of this section, we consider these key macroeconomic issues in more detail.

LONG-RUN ECONOMIC GROWTH

If you've ever travelled in a developing country, you probably couldn't help but observe the difference in living standards relative to those of such countries as Canada. The problems of inadequate food, shelter, and health care experienced by the poorest citizens of rich nations often represent the average situation for the people of a developing country. From a macroeconomic perspective, the difference between rich nations and developing nations may be summarized by saying that rich nations have, at some point in their history, experienced extended periods of rapid economic growth but that poorer nations either have never experienced sustained growth or have had periods of growth offset by periods of economic decline.

In part, the long-term growth of the Canadian economy is the result of a rising population, which has meant a steady increase in the number of available workers. But another significant factor is the increase in the amount of output that can be produced with a given amount of labour. The amount of output produced per unit of labour input—for example, per worker or per hour of work—is called **average labour productivity**. Average labour productivity, defined in this case as output per employed worker, has changed a great deal over time. In 2016, for example, the average Canadian worker produced nearly six times as much output as the average worker in 1921, despite working fewer hours over the course of the year. Because today's typical worker is so much more productive, Canadians enjoy a significantly higher standard of living than would have been possible 96 years ago.

The rates of growth of output and, particularly, of output per worker ultimately determine whether a nation will be rich or poor; therefore, understanding what determines growth is one of the most important goals of macroeconomics. Unfortunately, explaining why economies grow is not easy. Why, for example, did resource-poor Japan and South Korea experience growth rates that transformed them in a generation or two from war-torn nations to industrial powers, whereas several resource-rich nations of Latin America and Africa have had erratic or even negative growth in recent years? Although macroeconomists have nothing close to a complete answer to the question of what determines rates of economic growth, they do have some ideas to offer. In Chapter 6, we will present a model that economists use to try to better understand why over the course of many decades some economies grow faster than others. As rising output is closely correlated with improved living standards, it is small wonder that this area of study has been a focus of macroeconomists for a long time.[1]

BUSINESS CYCLES

The history of Canadian output is one of steady growth when measured over the long term but growth that is sometimes interrupted by short periods of slower (and sometimes negative) growth and short periods of more rapid growth. These periods of slower than normal and faster than normal growth are known by economists as *business cycles*: short, but sometimes sharp, contractions and expansions in economic activity.[2]

The most volatile period in the history of Canadian output was between 1914 and 1945, a period marked by two world wars and the two deepest recessions in Canadian history, the second of which was so severe that it is known as the Great Depression. During the Great Depression the unemployment rate in Canada exceeded 20%, a level of unemployment not experienced since. But even relatively mild downturns in the economy, known as recessions, mean hard economic times for many people. Not surprisingly, recessions are a major concern for politicians; after all, almost every politician wants to be re-elected, and his or her chances are better if the country's economy is expanding rather than contracting.

Macroeconomists put a lot of effort into trying to determine what causes business cycles and deciding what can or should be done about them. In Chapter 8 we describe the features of business cycles in Canada, and in Chapters 9–12 we compare different macroeconomic explanations for cyclical fluctuations. Using those explanations as a guide, we also evaluate the policy options that are available for mitigating the negative effects of the business cycle.

UNEMPLOYMENT AND PRICE INSTABILITY

The hard economic times suffered by people over the course of a business cycle are felt in many ways, both personal and economic. At a macroeconomic level, the economic costs are often measured by two key variables: unemployment and price instability.

---

[1] In Chapters 6 and 8 we will look at data describing Canada's economic growth over more than a century. In Chapter 8 we will also look at data describing average labour productivity over the past half-century.
[2] A more exact definition is given in Chapter 8, where we also provide the dates when contractions and expansions have started and ended in Canada.

By an increase in **unemployment** we mean an increase in the number of people who are available and actively seeking employment but who are unable to find a job. Finding oneself unable to earn a living and support one's family is an obvious and serious hardship. Less obvious, perhaps, is the hardship suffered when the economy experiences volatility in the rate of growth in prices. Price instability can take either of two forms. **Inflation** is an ongoing increase in the prices of goods and services. **Deflation** is an ongoing decrease in prices. Canadians who lived through the high rates of inflation (in excess of 10% per year) during the 1970s and an older generation who lived during the Great Depression and saw prices (and wages) fall by 6% per year know that there are significant costs to be borne. So policymakers continually guard against the threat of prolonged periods of deflation, such as Japan has experienced since the 1990s, and the opposite threat of runaway inflation, such as that observed in recent years in countries like Zimbabwe, where prices have risen so quickly that economists have labelled it "hyperinflation."

We look closely at the determinants of unemployment and inflation, and the relationship between the two, in Chapter 13. To better our understanding of inflation, in Chapter 7 we examine the role of money and the crucial role of financial institutions in the economy.

THE INTERNATIONAL ECONOMY

Today, every major economy is an **open economy**, or one that has extensive trading and financial relationships with other national economies. (A **closed economy** does not interact economically with the rest of the world.) Macroeconomists study patterns of international trade and borrowing to better understand the links among national economies. For example, an important topic in macroeconomics is how international trade and borrowing relationships can help transmit business cycles from country to country.

The Canadian economy has always been heavily dependent on international trade in goods and services. Being able to sell goods abroad (that is, to **export**) is an advantage to Canadian manufacturers, as they are able to grow far larger than they would were they dependent on selling only to the relatively small Canadian market. Being able to buy goods from other countries (to **import**) is a great advantage for Canadian consumers, who are as a result able to choose from the best the world has to offer. Imagine how much poorer Canadians would be without the ability to purchase fresh fruit imported from Mexico during the winter months, or how much poorer Canadian wheat farmers would be without the ability to grow amounts of wheat far in excess of Canadian needs and export the rest of their crop to other countries.

The value of goods and services that Canadian firms export and the value of goods and services Canadians import need not be the same. When the value of exports exceeds the value of imports, a **trade surplus** exists. When the opposite occurs, when value of imports exceeds the value of exports, a **trade deficit** exists. An important influence on the trade balance is the **exchange rate**. The exchange rate is the number of Canadian dollars that can be purchased with one unit of foreign currency. Although exchange rates are quoted between many currencies, the Canada–U.S. exchange rate is the most important to Canada because of the very large volume of trade between the two countries.

The development of the Canadian economy has been heavily influenced by the free flow of financial capital across international borders. During the 1870s, when

Canada was building intercontinental railways and the infrastructure of a new country, and again during the 1950s and 1960s, when the Canadian economy was growing quickly thanks to external demand for our natural resources, it was the savings of foreigners that was funding these investments. More recently, Canadian savers have benefited from being able to invest in fast-growing countries such as China and India.

The long-term impact of international trade and the inflow and outflow of financial capital on the Canadian economy is the focus of Chapter 5. The role of trade and financial flows (including the crucial role played by exchange rates) in the Canadian business cycle is the subject of Chapter 10.

MACROECONOMIC POLICY

A nation's economic performance depends on many factors, including its natural and human resources, its capital stock (buildings and machines), its technology, and the economic choices made by its citizens, both individually and collectively. Another important factor affecting economic performance is the set of macroeconomic policies pursued by the government.

Macroeconomic policies attempt to affect the performance of the economy as a whole. The two major types of macroeconomic policies are fiscal policy and monetary policy. **Fiscal policy**, which is determined at the federal, provincial, and municipal levels, concerns government spending and taxation. **Monetary policy**, which is under the control of a government institution known as the central bank, affects short-term interest rates and the growth rate of the nation's money supply. In Canada, the central bank is the Bank of Canada.

The fiscal policy choices made by governments play a huge role in our daily lives. These choices determine, for example, the level and type of taxes we pay. As well, these choices matter for determining who pays these taxes: What share of taxes is paid by high-income Canadians and what share, if any, is paid by those with low incomes? Fiscal policy choices also matter for funding health care, education, and social assistance. Finally, fiscal policy choices involve decisions about the size of government deficits (the imbalance between government spending and revenues) and debt (the accumulation of annual budget imbalances). Fiscal policy choices—along with the constraint put on those choices by the reluctance of Canadians to pay taxes and the critical importance of interest rates for indebted governments—are the focus of Chapter 15. Fiscal policy choices are central to our discussion in Chapters 9–12 as well because these choices may matter for how our governments respond to the business cycle.

The choices made by the Bank of Canada with respect to monetary policy are also important to our daily lives. The interest rate paid on a student loan, car loan, or mortgage is determined by monetary policy. So too is the rate of return earned on savings toward retirement. The crucial role of monetary policy choices in ensuring the stability of financial institutions—and so protecting the savings of households—was highlighted during the world financial crisis of 2007–2009. For reasons like these, most macroeconomists agree that monetary policy plays a pivotal role in determining the success of a modern industrialized economy such as Canada's. Developing an understanding of monetary policy is the focus of Chapters 7 and 14. And, like fiscal policy, monetary policy choices are central to our discussion in Chapters 9–12 because these choices may matter for how our governments respond to the business cycle.

AGGREGATION

Macroeconomics is one of two broad areas within the field of economics, the other being microeconomics. Macroeconomics and microeconomics have many basic economic ideas and methods in common; the difference between them is the level at which the economy is studied. Microeconomists focus on individual consumers, workers, and firms, each of whom is too small to have an impact on the national economy. Macroeconomists ignore the fine distinctions among the many different kinds of goods, firms, and markets that exist in the economy and, instead, focus on national totals. For example, in their analyses, macroeconomists don't care whether consumers are buying an iPhone or a Samsung Galaxy, beef or chicken, Pepsi or Coke. Instead, they add consumer expenditures on all goods and services to get an overall total called aggregate consumption. The process of summing individual economic variables to obtain economywide totals is called **aggregation**. The use of aggregation and the emphasis on aggregate quantities, such as aggregate consumption, aggregate investment, and aggregate output, are the primary factors that distinguish macroeconomics from microeconomics.

1.2 WHAT MACROECONOMISTS DO

How do macroeconomists use their skills, and what do they do with all the data they gather and the theories they develop? Besides teaching economics, macroeconomists engage in a wide variety of activities, including forecasting, macroeconomic analysis, and basic research.

MACROECONOMIC FORECASTING

Many people believe that economists spend most of their time trying to forecast the performance of the economy. In fact, except for a relatively small number of forecasting specialists, forecasting is a minor part of what macroeconomists do. One reason macroeconomists don't emphasize forecasting is that on the whole, they're not terribly good at it! Although short-range forecasters have some success, long-range forecasting is difficult, not only because our understanding of how the economy works is imperfect but also because of the impossibility of taking into account *all* the factors—many of them not strictly economic—that might affect future economic trends. Here are some questions that a forecaster, in trying to project the course of the economy, might have to try to answer: What oil price will the Organization of the Petroleum Exporting Countries (OPEC) decide on at its next meeting? Will there be a severe drought in agricultural regions, with adverse effects on food quantities and prices? When will new technologies that are being developed come to market? Because answers to such questions are highly uncertain, macroeconomic forecasters rarely offer a single prediction. Instead, they usually combine a "most likely" forecast with "optimistic" and "pessimistic" alternative scenarios.

Does the fact that macroeconomics can't be used to make highly accurate forecasts of economic activity mean that it's a pointless field of study? Some people may think so, but that's really an unreasonable standard. Meteorology is an example of a field in which forecasting is difficult (will it *definitely* be nice this weekend?) but in which there is also a lot of useful knowledge (meteorologists helped discover the depletion of the earth's ozone layer and pointed out its dangers). Similarly, cardiologists cannot usually predict if or when a patient will have a heart attack—they can only talk about probabilities. Like meteorologists and doctors, economists deal with a system whose complexity makes gaining a thorough understanding difficult and forecasting the system's behaviour even more difficult. Rather than predicting what will happen, most macroeconomists are engaged in analyzing and interpreting events as they happen (macroeconomic analysis) or in trying to understand the structure of the economy in general (macroeconomic research).

MACROECONOMIC ANALYSIS

Macroeconomic analysts monitor the economy and think about the implications of current economic events. Many analysts are employed in the private sector, such as in banks or large corporations. Private sector analysts try to determine how general economic trends will affect their employers' financial investments, their opportunities for expansion, the demand for their products, and so on.

The public sector, which in Canada includes the federal, provincial, and municipal governments, the Bank of Canada, and international agencies such as the World Bank and the International Monetary Fund, also employs many macroeconomic analysts. The main function of public sector analysts is to assist in policymaking—for example, by writing reports that assess various macroeconomic problems and by identifying and evaluating possible policy options. Among Canadian policymakers, the officials who set monetary policy may call on the aid of economists employed by the Bank of Canada, and federal and provincial cabinets have the advice of the professional staffs of numerous departments and agencies. Economic policymakers also often go outside the government to seek the advice of macroeconomists from business or academia.

If a country has many well-trained macroeconomic analysts, as is true in Canada, does that mean its macroeconomic policies will always be intelligent and far-sighted? The answer, unfortunately, is no. Because of the complexity of the economy, macroeconomic policy analysis, like macroeconomic forecasting, is often difficult and uncertain. Perhaps even more important, though, *politicians, not economists, usually make economic policy*. Politicians are typically less concerned with the abstract desirability of a policy than with the policy's immediate effects on their constituents. Thus, in recent years, international talks intended to reduce trade barriers have sometimes failed because the governments of many developed countries found it politically inadvisable to reduce high subsidy payments to their farmers—despite economists' nearly universal opposition to both trade barriers and farm price support payments.

Although the technical advice provided by macroeconomic analysts isn't the sole basis on which macroeconomic policy is made, such advice is probably necessary for making good policy decisions, especially if dramatic changes are being considered. In recent years, for example, a number of countries in Eastern Europe have undertaken significant and successful reforms of their economies, reforms that have been guided by the advice of macroeconomic analysts to open markets to trade, to minimize tax rates and inflation, and so on. In Venezuela and Zimbabwe, on the other hand, radical changes have been introduced despite those changes being universally dismissed by macroeconomic analysts as harmful to those nations' economies.

MACROECONOMIC RESEARCH

Macroeconomic research takes an amazing variety of forms, from abstract mathematical analysis to psychological experimentation to massive number-crunching projects in which supercomputers are used to process large amounts of economic data. Nevertheless, the goal of all macroeconomic research is to make general statements about how the economy works. The general insights about the economy gained from successful research form the basis for the analyses of specific economic problems, policies, or situations.

How is macroeconomic research carried out? As in many other fields, macroeconomic research proceeds primarily through the formulation and testing of theories. An **economic theory** is a set of ideas about the economy that has been organized in a logical framework. Most economic theories are developed in terms of an **economic model**, which is a simplified description of some aspect of the economy, usually expressed in mathematical form. Economists evaluate an economic model or theory by applying four criteria:

1. Are its assumptions reasonable and realistic?

2. Is it understandable and manageable enough to be used in studying real problems?

3. Does it have implications that can be tested by **empirical analysis**? That is, can its implications be evaluated by comparing them with data obtained in the real world?

4. When the implications and the data are compared, are the implications of the theory consistent with the data?

For a theory or model—of any type, not just economic—to be useful, the answer to each of these questions must be yes. Unfortunately, though, economists may not always agree in their evaluation of a particular model, which means that controversies about the best way to model a given economic situation sometimes persist.

We present a summary of the main steps in developing and testing an economic theory or model in A Closer Look 1.1 (p. 9).

At the heart of any economic theory are descriptions of how our economic *actors*—households, firms, and government—make the choices they do. For example, what prompts members of a household to offer to work a certain number of hours per day but not more or less than that, and what motivates a firm to hire additional workers? These are questions we examine in Chapter 3. How does a change in income, interest rates, or wealth influence the decision of how many goods and services to purchase? What does this mean for saving? Why does a firm choose to invest in new machinery or factories? These questions are the focus of Chapter 4. What motivates government to raise or lower taxes and how does the Bank of Canada respond to increases in inflation? Chapters 14 and 15 look at these important issues.

Having developed an economic theory that summarizes how economic actors are predicted to respond to changes in their economic environment, a macroeconomist is able to conduct experiments. For the most part, macroeconomists are not allowed to run experiments in the manner of physicists or chemists. That is, we're not allowed to conduct experiments on our "subjects" because they are human beings and companies as opposed to the molecules and atoms that are the subject

A CLOSER LOOK 1.1

DEVELOPING AND TESTING AN ECONOMIC THEORY

To illustrate the process of developing and testing an economic theory, suppose that we want to develop a theory that explains the routes people take when they commute from home to work and back. Such a theory would be useful, for example, to a traffic planner who is concerned about how a proposed housing development will affect traffic patterns. Here are the steps we would take:

STEP 1. State the research question.
EXAMPLE: What determines traffic flows in the city during rush hours?

STEP 2. Make provisional assumptions that describe the economic setting and the behaviour of the economic factors. These assumptions should be simple yet capture the most important aspects of the problem.
EXAMPLE: The setting is described by the map of the city. The assumption about behaviour is that commuters choose routes that minimize driving time.

STEP 3. Work out the implications of the theory.
EXAMPLE: Use the map of the city to plot a route that minimizes driving time between home and place of work.

STEP 4. Conduct an empirical analysis to compare the implications of the theory with the data.
EXAMPLE: Conduct a survey of commuters to identify (1) home locations, (2) work locations, and (3) routes taken to work. Then, see whether the routes predicted by the model are generally the same as those reported in the commuter survey.

STEP 5. Evaluate the results of your comparisons.

If the theory fits the data well: Use the theory to predict what would happen if the economic setting or economic policies change.
EXAMPLE: Use the minimum-driving-time assumption to evaluate the traffic effects of a new housing development by figuring out which routes the residents of the development are likely to take.

If the theory fits the data poorly: Start from scratch with a new model. Repeat steps 2–5.
EXAMPLE: Change the provisional behavioural assumption to the following: Commuters choose the route that minimizes the distance they must drive (not the time they spend driving).

If the theory fits the data moderately well: Either make do with a partially successful theory or modify the model with additional assumptions and then repeat steps 3–5.
EXAMPLE: A possible modification of the minimum-driving-time assumption is that commuters will choose more scenic over less scenic routes, if driving time is not increased by more than, a certain number of minutes. To test the model with this modified assumption, you must determine which routes are more scenic (those that pass a lake) and which are less scenic (those that pass a garbage dump).

of experiments in physics and chemistry.[3] Instead, macroeconomists conduct their experiments using their economic models. In fact, we'll be conducting many such experiments in this book.

The experiments conducted by macroeconomists are called **comparative static experiments**. They are conducted in the following way. *First*, the economic model is assumed to be in **equilibrium**. That is to say, we begin by

---

[3] Having said that, microeconomists are sometimes allowed to run experiments on humans. From 1974 to 1979 economists were let loose to run an experiment (called MINCOME) in which the residents of the town of Dauphin, Manitoba, were given the opportunity to participate in an economic experiment: a family with no income would receive a payment equal to 60% of a measure of poverty. The aim of the experiment was to determine how this unconditional income might affect people's decision about how much to work and how it might affect poverty levels. For an interesting discussion and analysis of this experiment, see Evelyn Forget, "The Town with No Poverty: The Health Effects of a Canadian Guaranteed Annual Income Field Experiment," *Canadian Public Policy*, Volume 37, No. 3, September 2011, pp. 283–305.

assuming a situation in which the quantities demanded and supplied are equal in all markets. Thus, households and firms are consuming and producing, working and employing, and saving and investing amounts they deem optimal given their incomes and profits. *Second*, we change the value of one variable in the model, a variable whose value is not affected by changes in other variables in the model. This might be, for example, a change in weather conditions affecting wheat yields or the discovery of a giant new oil field in Mexico that will compete with Canadian production. Economists refer to events such as these as **shocks**. To the extent that fiscal and monetary policy choices are unexpected by households and firms and are not in turn influenced by how households and firms respond, these too can be considered to be shocks to the economy. *Third*, we observe how our macroeconomic model responds to the shock. In particular, we observe how the shock alters the equilibrium to which households and firms adjust. In this way, we determine how the particular shock we introduced into the model affects the choices of households and firms and so affects the whole economy. We will use comparative static experiments throughout this book in order to determine how unexpected events, and the possible fiscal and monetary policy responses to those events, impact the economy.

1.3 WHY MACROECONOMISTS DISAGREE

Over the years, the efforts of thousands of analysts, data collectors, and researchers have greatly enhanced the understanding of macroeconomic phenomena. Yet, no matter what the macroeconomic issue, the news media seem to be able to find an economist to argue either side of it. Why do macroeconomists appear to disagree so much?[4]

To a certain extent, the amount of disagreement among macroeconomists is exaggerated by the tendency of the public and the media to focus on the most difficult and controversial issues. In addition, the very fact that economic policy and performance are of such broad interest and concern contributes to the intensity of debate. More than controversies in many other fields, debates in macroeconomics tend to take place in public rather than in the seminar room or the laboratory. Although important disagreements among macroeconomists certainly exist, there are also many areas of substantial agreement in macroeconomics.

We can provide an insight into why macroeconomists disagree by drawing the important distinction between positive and normative analyses of economic policy. A **positive analysis** of an economic policy examines the economic consequences of a policy but does not address the question of whether those consequences are desirable. A **normative analysis** of policy tries to determine whether a certain policy *should* be used. For example, if an economist is asked to evaluate the effects on the economy of a 5% rise in the income tax, the response involves a positive analysis. But if asked whether the income tax *should* be raised 5%, the economist's response requires a normative analysis. This normative analysis will involve not only the economist's objective, scientific understanding of how the economy works but also personal value judgments—for example, about the appropriate size of the government sector or the amount of income redistribution that is desirable.

---

[4] Not only do macroeconomists often seem to disagree with each other, but they're also sometimes accused of not being able to agree with themselves. U.S. president Harry Truman expressed the frustration of many policymakers when he said he wanted a one-handed economist—one who wouldn't always say, "On the one hand ...; on the other hand ..."

Economists may agree on the positive analysis of a question yet disagree on the normative part because of differences in values. Value differences are, of course, common in other fields as well: Physicists, for example, may be in perfect agreement on what would happen *if* a nuclear bomb were detonated (a positive analysis), but physicist "hawks" and physicist "doves" may disagree strongly about whether nuclear weapons *should* be deployed (a normative question).

Disagreement may occur on positive issues, however, and these differences are important in economics. In macroeconomics, there have always been many schools of thought, each with a somewhat different perspective on how the economy works; one example is monetarism, which we discuss in this book. However, the most important—and enduring—disagreements on positive issues in macroeconomics involve the two schools of thought called the classical approach and the Keynesian approach.

CLASSICALS VERSUS KEYNESIANS

The classical approach and the Keynesian approach are the two major intellectual traditions in macroeconomics. We discuss the differences between the two approaches briefly here, and in much greater detail later in the book.

The Classical Approach

The origins of the classical approach go back more than two centuries, at least to the famous Scottish economist Adam Smith. In 1776, Smith published his classic work, *The Wealth of Nations*, in which he proposed the concept of the "invisible hand." The idea of the **invisible hand** is that if there are free markets and individuals conduct their economic affairs in their own best interests, the overall economy will work well. As Smith put it, in a market economy, individuals, while pursuing their own self-interest, seem to be led by an invisible hand to maximize the general welfare of everyone in the economy.

However, we must not overstate what Smith claimed: To say that an invisible hand is at work does *not* mean that no one in a market economy will be hungry or dissatisfied; free markets cannot insulate a nation from the effects of drought, war, or political instability. Nor does the invisible-hand idea rule out the existence of great inequalities between the rich and the poor: In Smith's analysis, the initial distribution of wealth among people was accepted as a given. The invisible-hand idea says that given a country's resources (natural, human, and technological) and its initial distribution of wealth, the use of free markets will make people as economically well off as possible.

The validity of the invisible-hand idea depends on a key assumption: The various markets in the economy, including financial markets, labour markets, and markets for goods and services, must function smoothly and without impediments, such as minimum wages and interest rate ceilings. In particular, wages and prices must adjust rapidly enough to maintain equilibrium in all markets. In markets where quantity demanded exceeds quantity supplied, prices must rise to bring the market into equilibrium. In markets where more of a good is available than people want to buy, prices must fall to bring the market into equilibrium.

Wage and price flexibility is crucial to the invisible-hand idea because in a free-market system, changes in wages and prices are the signals that coordinate the actions of people in the economy. To illustrate, suppose that war abroad disrupts foreign oil production. This drop in supply will drive up the price of oil. A higher oil price will make it profitable for domestic oil suppliers to pump more oil and to drill more wells. The higher price will also induce domestic consumers to conserve oil and to switch to alternative sources of energy. Increased demand for alternative energy sources will raise their prices and stimulate *their* production, and so on. Thus, in the absence of such impediments as government-imposed price controls, the adjustment of prices helps the free-market economy respond in a constructive and coordinated way to the initial disruption of supplies.

The classical approach to macroeconomics builds on Smith's basic assumptions that people pursue their own economic self-interests and that prices adjust reasonably quickly to achieve equilibrium in all markets. With these two assumptions as a basis, followers of the classical approach attempt to construct models of the macroeconomy that are consistent with the data and that can be used to answer the questions raised at the beginning of this chapter.

The use of the classical approach carries with it some strong policy implications. Because the classical assumptions imply that the invisible hand works well, classical economists often argue (as a normative proposition) that the government should have, at most, a limited role in the economy. As a positive proposition, classical economists also often argue that government policies will be ineffective or counterproductive at achieving their stated goals. Thus, for example, most classicals believe that the government should not actively try to eliminate business cycles.

The Keynesian Approach

Compared with the classical approach, the Keynesian approach is relatively recent. The book that introduced it, *The General Theory of Employment, Interest and Money*, by British economist John Maynard Keynes, appeared in 1936—160 years after Adam Smith's *The Wealth of Nations*. In 1936, the world was suffering through the Great Depression. Unprecedentedly high rates of unemployment had afflicted most of the world's economies for years, and the invisible hand of free markets seemed completely ineffective. From the viewpoint of 1936, the classical theory appeared to be seriously inconsistent with the data, creating a need for a new macroeconomic theory. Keynes provided this theory.

In his book, Keynes offered an explanation for persistently high unemployment.[5] He based this explanation on an assumption about wage and price adjustment that was fundamentally different from the classical assumption. Instead of assuming that wages and prices adjust rapidly to achieve equilibrium in each market, as in the classical tradition, Keynes assumed that wages and prices adjust slowly. Slow wage and price adjustment meant that markets could be out of equilibrium—with quantities demanded not equal to quantities supplied—for long periods of time. In the Keynesian theory, unemployment can persist because wages and prices do not adjust quickly enough to equalize the number of people firms want to employ with the number of people who want to work. While adherents of the Keynesian approach recognize that wages and prices will eventually adjust to equate demand and supply, they believe that this adjustment might be slow to occur. The famous quotation of John Maynard Keynes, that "in the long run we're all dead," makes the point that it might not be good government policy

---

[5] Actually, Keynes presented a number of explanations of unemployment in his book, and debate continues about "what Keynes really meant." Our interpretation of what Keynes meant is the one adopted by his major followers.

to wait for that eventual adjustment in wages and prices. He therefore proposed that governments take actions to alleviate the unemployment resulting from the slow adjustment of wages and prices.

Keynes's proposed solution to high and persistent unemployment was to have the government increase its purchases of goods and services, thus raising the demand for output. Keynes argued that this policy would reduce unemployment because in order to meet the higher demands for their products, businesses would have to employ more workers. In addition, Keynes suggested, the newly hired workers would have more income to spend, creating another source of demand for output that would raise employment further. More generally, in contrast to classicals, Keynesians tend to be skeptical about the ability of the invisible hand to maintain equilibrium at every point in time. They believe that disequilibrium may persist, and that this provides the rationale for governments to possibly intervene in the economy to speed adjustment and so improve macroeconomic performance.

A UNIFIED APPROACH TO MACROECONOMICS

In writing this book, we needed a strategy to deal with the fact that there are two major macroeconomic schools of thought. One strategy would have been to emphasize one of the two schools of thought and to treat the other only briefly. The problem with that strategy is that it wouldn't expose you to the full range of ideas and insights that make up modern macroeconomics. Alternatively, we might have presented the two approaches separately and then compared and contrasted their conclusions, but then you would have missed the opportunity to explore the large common ground shared by the two schools of thought.

Our choice was to take an approach to macroeconomics that is as balanced and unified as possible. In keeping with this unified approach, all our analyses in this book—whether of economic growth, business cycles, inflation, or policy, and whether classical or Keynesian in spirit—are based on a single economic model, or on components or extensions of the basic model. This economic model, which draws heavily from both the classical and Keynesian traditions, has the following characteristics:

1. *Individuals, firms, and the government interact in goods markets, asset markets, and labour markets.* We have already discussed the need for aggregation in macroeconomics. In the economic model of this book, we follow standard macroeconomic practice and aggregate all the markets in the economy into three major markets: the market for goods and services, the asset market (in which assets, such as stocks, bonds, and real estate, are traded), and the labour market. We show how participants in the economy interact in each of these three markets and how these markets relate to each other and the economy as a whole.

2. *The model's macroeconomic analysis is based on the analysis of individual behaviour.* Macroeconomic behaviour reflects the behaviours of many individuals and firms interacting in markets. To understand how individuals and firms behave, we take a "bottom-up" approach and begin our analysis at the level of individual decision making (as in A Closer Look 1.1, p. 9, where we discuss a model of individual choices about the route to take to work). The insights gained are then used for studying the economy as a whole.

The guiding principle in analyzing the behaviour of individuals and firms is the assumption that they *try to maximize their own economic satisfaction, given their needs, desires, and resources.* Although the founder of classical economics, Adam Smith, emphasized this assumption, it is generally accepted by Keynesians and classicals alike, and it is used in virtually all modern macroeconomic research.

3. Although Keynesians reject the classical assumption that wages and prices quickly adjust to achieve equilibrium even in the short term, *Keynesians and classicals agree that in the long term, prices and wages fully adjust to achieve equilibrium in the markets for goods, assets, and labour.* Because complete flexibility of wages and prices in the long term is not controversial, we examine the long-term behaviour of the economy (Chapters 3–7) before discussing short-term issues associated with business cycles (Chapters 8–12).

4. *The basic model that we present may be used with either the classical assumption that wages and prices are flexible or the Keynesian assumption that wages and prices are slow to adjust.* This aspect of the model allows us to compare classical and Keynesian conclusions and policy recommendations within a common theoretical framework.

CHAPTER SUMMARY

1. Macroeconomics is the study of the structure and performance of national economies and the policies that governments use to try to affect economic performance. Important topics in macroeconomics include the determinants of long-run economic growth, business cycles, unemployment, inflation, international trade and lending, and macroeconomic policy.

2. Because macroeconomics covers the economy as a whole, macroeconomists ignore the fine distinctions among different kinds of goods, firms, or markets and focus on national totals, such as aggregate consumption. The process of adding individual economic variables to obtain economywide totals is called aggregation.

3. The activities engaged in by macroeconomists include (in addition to teaching) forecasting, macroeconomic analysis, and macroeconomic research.

4. The goal of macroeconomic research is to be able to make general statements about how the economy works. Macroeconomic research makes

progress toward this goal by developing economic theories and testing them empirically— that is, by seeing whether they are consistent with data obtained from the real world. A useful economic theory is based on reasonable and realistic assumptions, is easy to use, has implications that can be tested in the real world, and is consistent with the data and the observed behaviour of the real-world economy.

5. A positive analysis of an economic policy examines the economic consequences of the policy but does not address the question of whether those consequences are desirable. A normative analysis of a policy tries to determine whether the policy should be used. Disagreements among macroeconomists may arise because of differences in normative conclusions, the result of differences in personal values and beliefs, and differences in the positive analysis of a policy proposal.

6. The classical approach to macroeconomics is based on the assumptions that individuals and firms act in their own best interests and that

wages and prices adjust quickly to achieve equilibrium in all markets. Under these assumptions, the invisible hand of the free-market economy works well, with only a limited scope for government intervention in the economy.

7. The Keynesian approach to macroeconomics assumes that wages and prices do not adjust rapidly, and thus the invisible hand may not work well in the short term. Keynesians argue that because of slow wage and price adjustment, unemployment may remain high for a long time. Keynesians are usually more inclined than classicals are to believe that government intervention in the economy may help improve economic performance.

KEY TERMS

aggregation, p. 6
average labour productivity, p. 2
closed economy, p. 4
comparative static experiments, p. 9
deflation, p. 4
economic model, p. 8
economic theory, p. 8
empirical analysis, p. 8
equilibrium, p. 9
exchange rate, p. 4
export, p. 4
fiscal policy, p. 5
import, p. 4
inflation, p. 4
invisible hand, p. 11
macroeconomics, p. 1
monetary policy, p. 5
normative analysis, p. 10
open economy, p. 4
positive analysis, p. 10
shocks, p. 10
trade deficit, p. 4
trade surplus, p. 4
unemployment, p. 4

REVIEW QUESTIONS

1. How have total output and output per worker changed over time in Canada? How have these changes affected the lives of typical Canadians?
2. What is a business cycle? How does the unemployment rate behave over the course of a business cycle? Does the unemployment rate ever reach zero?
3. Define *inflation* and *deflation*.
4. Define a *budget deficit*. How does it differ from a *budget surplus*?
5. What is meant by *aggregation*? Why is aggregation important for macroeconomic analysis?
6. List the principal professional activities of macroeconomists. What role does macroeconomic research play in each of these activities?
7. What steps are involved in developing and testing an economic theory or model? What are the criteria for a useful theory or model?
8. Might two economists agree about the effects of a particular economic policy but disagree about the desirability of implementing the policy? Explain your answer.
9. Compare the classical and Keynesian views on the speed of wage and price adjustment. What are the important consequences of the differences in these views?

NUMERICAL PROBLEMS

1. Here are some macroeconomic data for the country of Oz for the years 2011 and 2012.

	2011	2012
Output	12 000 tonnes of potatoes	14 300 tonnes of potatoes
Employment	1000 workers	1100 workers
Unemployed	100 workers	50 workers
Total labour force	1100 workers	1150 workers
Prices	2 spuds/tonne of potatoes	2.5 spuds/tonne of potatoes

As the data suggest, Oz produces only potatoes, and its monetary unit is the spud. Calculate each of the following macroeconomic variables for Oz, being sure to give units.

a. Average labour productivity in 2011 and 2012.
b. The growth rate of average labour productivity between 2011 and 2012.
c. The unemployment rate in 2011 and 2012.
d. The inflation rate between 2011 and 2012.

2. Go to the Statistics Canada website (*www.statcan.gc.ca*) and find "National Economic Accounts." Opening that link takes you to another link on Gross Domestic Product. There you will find data on the value of Gross Domestic Product (a measure of total output), Exports of Goods and Services, and Imports of Goods and Services for the latest year. Now open the link on "Government Financial Statistics." There

you will find data on federal government net financial debt (how much the government owes).

a. Calculate the ratio of exports to GDP, the ratio of imports to GDP, and the ratio of the trade balance to GDP for the most recent year data are available.

b. Calculate the ratio of federal government net financial debt to GDP for the most recent year data are available.

ANALYTICAL PROBLEMS

1. Can average labour productivity fall, even though total output is rising? Can the unemployment rate rise, even though total output is rising?

2. Prices were much higher in Canada in 2013 than in 1914. Does this fact mean that people were economically better off in 1914? Why, or why not?

3. State a theory for why people vote for a specific political party that could potentially satisfy the criteria for a useful theory given in the text. How would you go about testing your theory?

4. Which of the following statements are positive in nature and which are normative?

a. A tax cut will raise interest rates.

b. A reduction in the payroll tax would primarily benefit poor and middle-class workers.

c. Payroll taxes are too high.

d. A cut in the payroll tax would improve the federal government's popularity ratings.

e. Payroll taxes should not be cut unless capital gains taxes are cut also.

5. In 1993, the debate heated up in Canada about the North American Free Trade Agreement (NAFTA), which proposed reducing barriers to trade (such as taxes on, or limits to, imports) among Canada, the United States, and Mexico. Some people strongly opposed the agreement, arguing that an influx of foreign goods under NAFTA would disrupt the Canadian economy, harm domestic industries, and throw Canadian workers out of work. How might a classical economist respond to these concerns? Would you expect a Keynesian economist to be more or less sympathetic to these concerns than a classical economist? Why?

6. What point was economist John Maynard Keynes trying to make when he noted that "in the long run we're all dead"? How does it provide justification for a greater role for government intervention in the economy?

Chapter 2

The Measurement and Structure of the Canadian Economy

Measurement is a crucial part of scientific study. Accurate measurement is essential for making new discoveries, evaluating competing theories, and predicting future events or trends. During the first half of the 20th century, painstaking research on national accounting showed that careful economic measurement is not only possible but also necessary for any serious understanding of the economy. This research transformed economics from a field in which scholars relied on informal observations and broad generalizations to one in which numbers and statistical analysis play an essential role.

In this chapter, we present some of the conceptual and practical issues involved in measuring the macroeconomy. We focus on the national income accounts, a framework for measuring economic activity that is widely used by economic researchers and analysts. Learning about the national income accounts will familiarize you with some useful economic data. In addition, because the national income accounts are set up in a logical way that mirrors the structure of the economy, working through these accounts is an important first step toward understanding how the macroeconomy works. When you finish this chapter, you will have a much clearer understanding of the relationships that exist among key macroeconomic variables and among the different sectors of the economy.

2.1 NATIONAL INCOME ACCOUNTING: THE MEASUREMENT OF PRODUCTION, INCOME, AND EXPENDITURE

The **national income accounts** are an accounting framework used in measuring current economic activity. Almost all countries have some form of official national income accounts. In this section, we discuss the basic idea that underlies national income accounting. We then show how the national income accounts are used in measuring economic activity in Canada and other countries.

The national income accounts are based on the idea that the amount of economic activity that occurs during a period of time can be measured in terms of

1. the amount of output produced, excluding output used up in intermediate stages of production (the product approach);

2. the incomes received by the producers of output (the income approach); and

3. the amount of spending by the ultimate purchasers of output (the expenditure approach).

Each approach gives a different perspective on the economy. However, the fundamental principle underlying national income accounting is that, except for such problems as incomplete or misreported data, *all three approaches give identical measurements of the amount of current economic activity*.

We can illustrate why these three approaches are equivalent by an example. Imagine an economy with only two businesses, called AppleInc and JuiceInc. AppleInc owns and operates apple orchards. It sells some of its apples directly to the public. It sells the rest of its apples to JuiceInc, which produces and sells apple juice. The following table shows the transactions of each business during a year:

AppleInc Transactions

Wages paid to AppleInc employees	$15 000
Taxes paid to government	5000
Revenue received from sale of apples	35 000
Apples sold to public	10 000
Apples sold to JuiceInc	25 000

(*Note:* After-tax profit of AppleInc = revenue − costs − taxes = $15 000)

JuiceInc Transactions

Wages paid to JuiceInc employees	$10 000
Taxes paid to government	2000
Apples purchased from AppleInc	25 000
Revenue received from sale of apple juice	40 000

(*Note:* After-tax profit of JuiceInc = revenue − costs − taxes = $3000)

AppleInc pays $15 000 per year in wages to workers to pick apples, and it sells these apples for $35 000 ($10 000 worth of apples to households and $25 000 worth of apples to JuiceInc). Thus, AppleInc's profit before taxes is $35 000 − $15 000 = $20 000. Because AppleInc pays taxes of $5000, its after-tax profit is $15 000.

JuiceInc buys $25 000 of apples from AppleInc and pays wages of $10 000 to workers to process the apples into apple juice. It sells the apple juice for $40 000, so its profit before taxes is $5000 ($40 000 − $25 000 − $10 000). After paying taxes of $2000, its after-tax profit is $3000. What is the total value, measured in dollars, of the economic activity generated by these two businesses? The product approach, income approach, and expenditure approach are three different ways of arriving at the answer to this question; all yield the same answer.

1. The **product approach** measures economic activity by adding the market values of goods and services produced, excluding any goods and services used up in intermediate stages of production. This approach makes use of the value-added concept. The **value added** of any producer is the value of its output minus the value of the inputs it purchases from other producers. The product approach computes economic activity by summing the value added of all producers.

In our example, AppleInc produces output worth $35 000 and JuiceInc produces output worth $40 000. However, measuring overall economic activity by simply adding $35 000 and $40 000 would "double count" the $25 000 of apples that JuiceInc purchased from AppleInc and processed into juice. To avoid this double counting, we sum value added rather than output: Because JuiceInc processed apples worth $25 000 into a product worth $40 000, JuiceInc's value added is $15 000 ($40 000 − $25 000). AppleInc does not use any inputs purchased from other businesses, so its value added equals its revenue of $35 000. Thus, total value added in the economy is $35 000 + $15 000 = $50 000.

2. The **income approach** measures economic activity by adding all income received, including wages, taxes (the government's income), and after-tax profits (the income of the owners of AppleInc and JuiceInc). The incomes generated in the example are as follows:

Incomes Received

Wage income ($15 000 at AppleInc; $10 000 at JuiceInc)	$25 000
Taxes ($5000 from AppleInc; $2000 from JuiceInc)	7000
Profits ($15 000 at AppleInc; $3000 at JuiceInc)	18 000
Total income	$50 000

The income approach concludes that the value of economic activity is $50 000, the same amount determined by the product approach.

3. Finally, the **expenditure approach** measures activity by adding the amount spent by all ultimate users of output. In this example, households are ultimate users of apples. JuiceInc is not an ultimate user of apples because it sells the apples (in processed, liquid form) to households. Thus, ultimate users purchase $10 000 of apples from AppleInc and $40 000 of apple juice from JuiceInc for a total of $50 000, the same amount computed in both the product and the expenditure approaches.[1]

WHY THE THREE APPROACHES ARE EQUIVALENT

That the product, income, and expenditure approaches all give the same answer is no accident. The logic of these three approaches is such that they must *always* give the same answer.

To see why, first observe that the market value of goods and services produced in a given period is *by definition* equal to the amount that buyers must spend to purchase them. JuiceInc's apple juice has a market value of $40 000 only because that is what people are willing to spend to buy it. The market value of a good or service and the spending on that good or service are always the same, so the product approach (which measures market values) and the expenditure approach (which measures spending) must give the same measure of economic activity.[2]

---

[1] In the example, each business also purchases labour services from employees, but as these services are used in production, they are not counted as services purchased by ultimate users.

[2] Our explanation implicitly assumes that everything produced is sold. What if a firm produces some goods that it cannot sell? As we demonstrate shortly, the national income accounts treat unsold goods as though they were purchased by the firm from itself; that is, accumulation of unsold goods in inventory is treated as part of expenditure. Thus, expenditure and production remain equal even if some goods remain unsold.

Next, observe that what the seller receives must equal what the buyers spend. The seller's receipts in turn equal the total income generated by the economic activity, including the incomes paid to workers and suppliers, taxes paid to the government, and profits (whatever is left over). Thus, total expenditure must equal total income generated, implying that the expenditure and income approaches must also produce the same answer. Finally, as both product value and income equal expenditure, they also must be equal.

Because of the equivalence of the three approaches, over any specified time period

$$\text{total production} = \text{total income} = \text{total expenditure}, \qquad (2.1)$$

where production, income, and expenditure are all measured in the same units (for example, in dollars). Equation (2.1) is called the **fundamental identity of national income accounting** and forms the basis for national income accounting. (An identity is an equation that is true by definition.) In Section 2.2, we show how this fundamental identity is used in measuring current economic activity for the economy as a whole.

2.2 GROSS DOMESTIC PRODUCT

The broadest measure of aggregate economic activity, as well as the best-known and most often used, is **gross domestic product**, or GDP. As in the example in Section 2.1, a country's GDP may be measured by the product approach, the expenditure approach, or the income approach. Although the three approaches arrive at the same value for GDP, each views GDP differently. Using all three approaches gives a more complete picture of an economy's structure than any single approach could.

THE PRODUCT APPROACH TO MEASURING GDP

The product approach defines a nation's GDP as the market value of final goods and services newly produced within a nation during a fixed period of time. In working through the various parts of this definition, we discuss some practical issues that arise in measuring GDP.

Market Value

Goods and services are counted in GDP at their market values, that is, at the prices at which they are sold. The advantage of using market values is that it allows adding the production of different goods and services. Imagine, for example, that you want to measure the total output of an economy that produces 7 cars and 100 pairs of shoes. Adding the number of cars and the number of pairs of shoes to get a total output of 107 wouldn't make much sense because cars and shoes are not of equal economic value. But suppose that each car sells for $10 000 and each pair of shoes sells for $60. Taking these market-determined prices as measures of relative economic values, you can calculate the value of cars produced as $70 000 (7 × $10 000) and the value of shoes produced as $6000 (100 × $60). The total market value of production, or GDP, is $70 000 + $6000 = $76 000. Using market values to measure production makes sense because it takes into account differences in the relative economic importance of different goods and services.

A problem with using market values to measure GDP is that some useful goods and services are not sold in formal markets. Ideally, GDP should be adjusted upward to reflect the existence of these goods and services. However, because of the difficulty of obtaining reliable measures, some nonmarket goods and services are simply ignored in the calculation of GDP. Homemaking and child-care services performed within the family without pay, for example, are not included in GDP, although homemaking and child care that are provided for pay (for example, by professional housecleaners or by private daycare centres) are included. Similarly, because the benefits of clean air and water are not bought and sold in markets, actions to reduce pollution or otherwise improve environmental quality are not usually reflected in GDP (measures of the environmental impact of producing GDP are, however, available from Statistics Canada; see A Closer Look 2.1, p. 22).

Some nonmarket goods and services are partially incorporated in official GDP measures. An example is activity that takes place in the so-called underground economy. The **underground economy** includes both legal activities hidden from government record keepers (to avoid payment of taxes or compliance with regulations, for example) and illegal activities, such as drug dealing, prostitution, and (in some places) gambling. Statistics Canada regularly adjusts GDP figures to include estimates of the underground economy's size (currently estimated at roughly 3% of GDP). Because cash is the favoured means of payment for off-the-books transactions, one clue to the size of the underground economy is the amount of cash in circulation.

Important components of economic activity that are not sold in markets include some services provided by government, such as national defence, police and fire protection, and public education. The fact that the services of the Canadian Armed Forces, for example, are not sold in markets implies a lack of market value to use when calculating that portion of government's contribution to GDP. The solution that has been adopted is to value government services at their cost of production. Thus, the contribution of national defence to GDP equals what the government pays by way of soldiers' salaries, the costs of military equipment, and so on.

Newly Produced Goods and Services

As a measure of current economic activity, GDP includes only goods or services that are newly produced within the current period. GDP excludes purchases or sales of goods that were produced in previous periods. Thus, although the market price paid for a newly constructed house would be included in GDP, the price paid in the sale of a used house is not counted in GDP. (The value of the used house would have been included in GDP for the year it was built.) However, the value of the services of the real estate agent involved in the sale of the used house is part of GDP because those services are provided in the current period.

Final Goods and Services

Goods and services produced during a period of time may be classified as either intermediate goods and services or final goods and services. **Intermediate goods and services** are those used up in the production of other goods and services *in the same period that they themselves were produced.* For example, flour that is produced and then used to make bread in the same year is an intermediate good. The trucking company that delivers the flour to the bakery provides an intermediate service.

A CLOSER LOOK 2.1

Natural Resources, the Environment, and the National Income Accounts

A good deal of Canada's economic well-being is due to its substantial stocks of natural resources—its freshwater lakes and rivers, timber, oil, natural gas, uranium, potash, and so on. Many people are employed in industries that use these natural resources as inputs and so enjoy income that is based on their exploitation. However, the exploitation of natural resources also produces costs that are difficult to measure accurately. For example, our well-being is affected by both the air pollution that is a by-product of natural gas production and the warm houses we enjoy in winter thanks to our natural gas furnaces. Unfortunately, while we can value the warm house—natural gas is traded in markets and so its value can be accurately measured—it is much more difficult to accurately measure the value of the reduced air quality that results from the production of natural gas. This is because there is no market for air quality and so no market price is paid for using it. In the absence of market prices for air and water quality, these valued resources will not be used appropriately.

An important first step in designing markets that might price natural resources appropriately is to produce data describing the stock of natural resources, their economic value, and the impact of their exploitation on the environment. In the early 1990s, Statistics Canada developed a system of environmental and resource accounts and has been working since then to refine and improve those accounts. Statistics Canada's system of environmental and resource accounts provides information on the stock of natural resources, the use of those resources, and the pollutants produced by their exploitation.

The natural resource stock accounts measure quantities and dollar values of natural resources and the annual change in these amounts. These accounts provide the basis for a measure of Canada's natural resource wealth. Unfortunately, these amounts are tricky to measure. To understand why, one must recognize that, for example, the stock of oil in Canada is by no means known for certain. How much oil might be under Canada's still largely unexplored Arctic islands? How much oil might be extracted from oil fields in Alberta if better technology were available to enhance recovery? Similarly, how much timber has been destroyed in British Columbia as a result of the pine beetle infestation, and how much cod is there off the coast of Newfoundland and Labrador? These are complex questions that Statistics Canada deals with by including in its accounts only resource stock quantities that are known to exist with a high degree of certainty. An example of the data produced in the natural resource stock accounts comes from Statistics Canada Table 153-0122, where it is reported that established natural gas reserves in Canada fell from 1898 billion cubic metres at the beginning of 1995 to 1593 billion cubic metres at the end of 2004. The table also reports that, thanks to some large additions to established reserves, the stock of natural gas has since increased to 1953 billion cubic metres by the end of 2013.

The material and energy flow accounts also report the intensity of resource use—how much energy is used per dollar of production. Thus, Table 153-0115 reports that, in 2012, motor vehicle manufacturing used 6.2 gigajoules of energy per thousand dollars of production while crop and animal production used 10.7 gigajoules of energy per thousand dollars of production. Thus, relative to the value of their respective outputs, in 2012 farming used considerably more energy than automobile manufacturing.

In providing data like these, Statistics Canada is making available the information required by policymakers to focus attention on environmental issues and to design effective mechanisms to price natural resources appropriately.

Final goods and services are those goods and services that are not intermediate. Final goods and services are the end products of a process. For example, bread produced by the bakery is a final good, and a shopper's bus ride home from the bakery is a final service. Because the purpose of economic activity is the production of final goods and services, with intermediate goods being but a step along the way, only final goods and services are counted in GDP.

Sometimes the distinction between intermediate goods and final goods is subtle. For example, is a new lathe sold to a furniture manufacturer an intermediate good or a final good? Although the lathe is used to produce other goods, it is not used up during the year. Therefore, it is not an intermediate good; it is a final good. In particular, the lathe is an example of a type of final good called a capital good. Other more general examples of capital goods include factory equipment, office equipment, and factories and office buildings themselves. A **capital good** is a good that is itself produced (this rules out natural resources, such as land) and is used to produce other goods; however, unlike an intermediate good, a capital good is not used up in the same period that it is produced. The preparers of the national income accounts decided to classify capital goods as final goods and, thus, to include their production in GDP. Their reasoning was that the addition to productive capacity that new capital goods represent is an important purpose of economic activity.

Another subtle distinction between intermediate and final goods arises in the treatment of inventory investment. **Inventories** are stocks of unsold finished goods, goods in process, and raw materials held by firms. Inventory investment is the amount by which inventories increase during the year.[3] For example, suppose that a baker began the year with $1000 worth of flour in her storeroom, and at the end of the year she's holding $1100 worth of flour. The difference between her beginning and ending stocks, or $100 worth of flour, equals the baker's inventory investment during the year. Even though the ultimate purpose of the baker's flour is for making bread, her increase in inventory represents production of flour that is not used up during the year. As in the case of capital goods, inventory investment is treated as a final good and, thus, is part of GDP because increased inventories on hand imply greater productive capacity in the future.

In the AppleInc/JuiceInc example, we showed that total economic activity could be measured by summing the value added (value of output minus value of purchased inputs) for each producer. The advantage of the value-added technique is that it automatically includes final goods and excludes intermediate goods from the measure of total output. If you go back to that example, you'll see that by summing the value added of the two companies, we obtained a measure of economic activity that included the value of final sales of the two businesses to the public, but that excluded the intermediate goods (unprocessed apples) sold to JuiceInc by AppleInc.

GNP versus GDP

Until fairly recently, many economists focused on a measure of economic activity known as gross national product (GNP) rather than on GDP. The difference between GNP and GDP concerns the treatment of output produced by capital and labour working outside its home (domestic) country. Specifically, **gross national product** is the market value of final goods and services newly produced *by domestic factors of production* during the current period (as opposed to production taking place within a country, which is GDP).

When Canadian capital and labour—also called factors of production—are used abroad, they produce output and earn income. This output and income are included in Canadian GNP but not in Canadian GDP because they do not represent

---

[3] When inventories decline during the year, inventory investment is negative.

production taking place within Canada. So, for example, the value of roads built by a Canadian construction company in Saudi Arabia, as measured by the fees that the construction company receives from the Saudi government, is counted in Canadian GNP but not in Canadian GDP. Similarly, when foreign capital or labour is used in Canada, the output produced and the income earned are part of Canadian GDP (because the production occurs within Canada) but not of Canadian GNP (they are counted in the foreign country's GNP instead). For example, the portion of the value of Japanese cars built in Canada that is attributable to Japanese capital and management counts in Japanese GNP and Canadian GDP, but not in Canadian GNP.

We define **net factor payments from abroad** (*NFP*) to be income paid to domestic factors of production by the rest of the world, minus income paid to foreign factors of production by the domestic economy. Using this concept, we express the relationship between GDP and GNP as

$$\text{GDP} + NFP = \text{GNP}. \tag{2.2}$$

For Canada, GDP and GNP give slightly different measures of economic activity. For example, in 2015, Canadian GDP was $1983 billion and Canadian GNP was $1956 billion, a difference of just over 1%. When foreign firms invest in Canada, the interest and profits they earn count in GDP but not in GNP. The distinction between GNP and GDP is more important for such countries as Egypt and Turkey that have many citizens working abroad. The reason is that remittances sent home by workers abroad are part of a country's GNP but not its GDP.

THE EXPENDITURE APPROACH TO MEASURING GDP

A different perspective on the components of GDP is obtained by looking at the expenditure side of the national income accounts. The expenditure approach measures GDP as total spending on final goods and services produced within a nation during a specified period of time. Four major categories of spending are added to get GDP: consumption, investment, government purchases of goods and services, and net exports of goods and services. In symbols,

$$Y = \text{GDP} = \text{total production (or output)}$$
$$= \text{total income}$$
$$= \text{total expenditure;}$$
$$C = \text{consumption;}$$
$$I = \text{investment;}$$
$$G = \text{government purchases of goods and services;}$$
$$NX = \text{net exports of goods and services.}$$

With these symbols, we express the expenditure approach to measuring GDP as

$$Y = C + I + G + NX. \tag{2.3}$$

Equation (2.3), like Eq. (2.1), is one of the basic relationships in macroeconomics. Equation (2.3) is called the **income–expenditure identity** because it states that income Y equals total expenditure $C + I + G + NX$. Recent Canadian data for the four categories of spending, along with some major subcategories, are given in Table 2.1. As you read the rest of this section, you should look at Table 2.1 to get some feel for the relative sizes of different components of spending in the Canadian economy.

TABLE 2.1

Expenditure Approach to Measuring GDP in Canada, 2015

	Billions of Dollars	Percentage of GDP
Private consumption expenditures (C)	**1139.9**	**57.5**
Household final consumption expenditure	1111.6	56.0
durable goods	138.9	7.0
semi-durable goods	79.1	4.0
non-durable goods	265.9	13.4
services	627.7	31.6
Non-profit institutions serving household's consumption expenditure	28.3	1.4
Investment (I)	**468.7**	**23.6**
Private sector gross fixed capital formation	382.7	19.3
residential structures	144.4	7.3
non-residential structures, machinery, and equipment	201.8	10.2
intellectual property products	33.4	1.7
non-profit institutions serving household's gross fixed capital formation	3.1	0.2
Government gross fixed capital formation	79.9	4.0
Investment in inventories	6.1	0.3
General government final consumption expenditure (G)	**419.8**	**21.2**
Net exports (NX)	**−45.8**	**−2.3**
exports	625.4	31.5
imports	671.2	33.8
Statistical discrepancy	**0.7**	**0.03**
Total (equals GDP)	**1983.3**	**100.0**

Source: Adapted from Statistics Canada CANSIM Table 380-0064, 2015. This does not constitute an endorsement by Statistics Canada of this product. Values may not sum exactly due to rounding.

Consumption

Consumption is spending by domestic households on final goods and services, including those produced abroad.[4] It is the largest component of expenditure, usually accounting for about 60% of GDP in Canada. Consumption expenditures include spending in four categories:

1. *Durable goods,* which are long-lived items, such as motor vehicles, furniture, and appliances (but not houses, which are classified under investment)

2. *Semi-durable goods,* which are shorter-lived goods, such as clothing

3. *Nondurable goods,* such as food and utilities

4. *Services,* such as health care, financial services, rent, and restaurant meals.

---

[4] Later, we subtract imports to get total spending on the goods and services produced in the domestic economy.

These expenditures are identified in a separate category when they are made at non-profit institutions.

Investment

Investment includes both spending for new capital goods, called *fixed capital investment*, and increases in firms' inventory holdings, called *inventory investment*. Fixed capital investment is made by governments as well as by the private sector. This type of government spending, therefore, is included in I rather than G. Fixed capital investment by the private sector occurs in the form of physical structures but also in the form of products that are the result of intellectual property research and development.

Like consumption, investment includes spending on foreign-produced goods. Overall, fixed capital investment in Canada is usually about one-quarter of GDP.

As we've mentioned, increases in inventories are included in investment spending, regardless of why inventories rose. In particular, if a firm produces goods that it cannot sell, the resulting rise in inventories counts as investment by the firm. For the purposes of national income accounting, the firm has, in effect, purchased the unsold goods from itself. This accounting rule is useful because it guarantees that production and expenditure will always be equal in the national income accounts. Anything that is produced must by definition either be bought by a customer or "purchased" by the firm itself.

Government Purchases of Goods and Services

Government purchases of goods and services, which include any expenditure by the government for a currently produced good (other than capital goods) or service, foreign or domestic, is the third major component of spending. Government purchases in Canada recently have been about one-fifth of GDP. Government purchases include those made by federal, provincial, municipal, and territorial governments.

Not all cheques written by governments are for purchases of goods and services. **Transfers**, a category that includes transfers between levels of government as well as government payments to individuals in the form of public pensions, unemployment insurance benefits, welfare payments, and so on, are payments by governments that are not made in exchange for currently produced goods or services. As a result, they are excluded from the government purchases category and are not counted in GDP as calculated by the expenditure approach. Similarly, interest payments on the national debt are not counted as part of government purchases.

Net Exports

Net exports are exports minus imports. As discussed in Chapter 1, exports are the goods and services produced within a country that are purchased by foreigners; imports are the goods and services produced abroad that are purchased by a country's residents. Net exports are positive if exports are greater than imports and negative if imports exceed exports.

Exports are added to total spending because they represent spending (by foreigners) on final goods and services produced in a country. Imports are subtracted from total spending because consumption, investment, and government purchases

TABLE 2.2

Income Approach to Measuring GDP in Canada, 2015

	Billions of Dollars	Pecentage of GDP
Compensation of employees	1024.3	51.6
Plus Gross operating surplus	510.2	25.7
Plus Gross mixed income	232.2	11.7
Plus Taxes less subsidies on production	85.4	4.3
Plus Taxes less subsidies on products and imports	131.8	6.6
Equals Income-based Gross Domestic Product (GDP)	1983.9	100.0
Plus Statistical discrepancy	−0.7	−0.04
Equals Gross Domestic Product (GDP)	1983.3	100.0

Source: Adapted from Statistics Canada CANSIM Table 380-0063, 2015. This does not constitute an endorsement by Statistics Canada of this product.

Values may not sum exactly due to rounding.

are defined to include imported goods and services. Subtracting imports ensures that total spending, $C + I + G + NX$, reflects spending only on output produced in the country. For example, an increase in imports may mean that Canadians are buying cars produced in Korea instead of cars produced in Canada. For fixed total spending by domestic residents, therefore, an increase in imports lowers spending on domestic production. As we can see from Table 2.2, although exports and imports are separately large parts of total expenditures, their difference, net exports, is often quite small.

THE INCOME APPROACH TO MEASURING GDP

The third and final way to measure GDP is the income approach. It calculates GDP by adding the incomes received by producers, including profits, and taxes paid to the government.

See Table 2.2 for recent Canadian data on this approach for measuring GDP.

1. *Compensation of employees.* This is the total remuneration, in cash or in kind, payable by an enterprise to an employee in return for work done. As you can see from Table 2.2, compensation of employees is easily the largest component of the income approach to measuring GDP.

2. *Gross operating surplus.* This is the income earned from the production of goods and services that is paid to the owners of incorporated companies. These owners include corporations, governments, households, and non-profit institutions, and their ownership is typically in the form of stock shares upon which they earn dividends and other sorts of investment income. This is the second largest component of the income approach.

3. *Gross mixed income.* This is the income paid to unincorporated enterprises. Because it is difficult to separate payments made to employees from payments made to owners of the unincorporated enterprise, these two types of income are combined and is referred to as "mixed income."

4. *Taxes less subsidies on production.* These are taxes (less subsidies received) that companies pay on the use of labour, machinery, buildings, or other assets used in the production of goods and services.

5. *Taxes less subsidies on products and imports.* This defines taxes payable after a product is produced and sold in Canada or imported from abroad.

By summing these components of the income approach we arrive at an estimate of income-based GDP. A final category, called *statistical discrepancy*, identifies the difference between Statistics Canada's estimates of GDP from the expenditure approach and its estimate from the income approach. The discrepancy is added to the income approach so that the two estimates coincide.

Private Sector and Government Sector Income

In this section, we have measured economic activity as the sum of all the incomes received in an economy. Sometimes, however, economists need to know how much of total income was received by the private sector (households and businesses) and how much accrues to the government sector, which, in Canada, consists of federal, provincial, territorial, and municipal governments. For example, in trying to predict the demand for consumer goods, focusing on the income available to the private sector might be more useful than focusing on the income of the economy as a whole.

The income of the private sector, known as **private disposable income**, measures the amount of income the private sector has available to spend. In general, as for an individual family, the disposable income of the private sector as a whole equals income received from private sector activities, plus payments received by the private sector from the government, minus taxes paid to the government. The precise definition is

$$\text{private disposable income} = Y + NFP + TR + INT - T, \qquad (2.4)$$

where

$$
\begin{aligned}
Y &= \text{gross domestic product (GDP);} \\
NFP &= \text{net factor payments from abroad;} \\
TR &= \text{transfers received from the government;} \\
INT &= \text{interest payments on the government's debt;} \\
T &= \text{taxes.}
\end{aligned}
$$

As you can see from Eq. (2.4), private disposable income equals private sector income earned at home (GDP) and abroad (net factor payments from abroad, NFP)[5] plus payments to the private sector from the government sector (transfers, TR, and interest on the government debt, INT); minus taxes paid to the government, T.

The part of GNP that is not at the disposal of the private sector is the net income of the government sector. The government's net income equals taxes paid by the private sector, T, minus transfer and interest payments from the government to the private sector (transfers, TR, and interest payments on the government debt, INT):

$$\text{net government income} = T - TR - INT. \qquad (2.5)$$

Adding Eqs. (2.4) and (2.5) yields the sum of private disposable income and net government income, $Y + NFP$, which is gross national product.

---

[5] Note that the sum of incomes earned at home and abroad, GDP + NFP, equals GNP.

2.3 SAVING AND WEALTH

If you wanted to assess the economic situation of a household, the current income of the household would be an important piece of information. However, someone with a high current income is not necessarily better off economically than someone with a low current income. For example, a retired tycoon who has no current earnings but owns real estate worth $10 million is probably economically better off than a newly graduated doctor with a high salary but heavy debts left over from medical school. To determine how well off a household is, in addition to knowing current income, you also need to know what the household owns (its assets) and owes (its liabilities). The difference between assets and liabilities is called **wealth**.

As for a household, the economic well-being of a country depends not only on its income but also on its wealth. The wealth of an entire nation is called **national wealth**.

An important determinant of wealth is the rate of saving: A family that puts aside a quarter of its income each month will accumulate wealth much more quickly than a family that spends all its income. Similarly, the rate at which national wealth increases depends on the rate at which individuals, businesses, and governments in the economy save. Thus, rates of saving and wealth accumulation are closely related.

In this section, we present some concepts of aggregate saving and wealth and examine the relationships among them. Our main interest here is measurement. Such questions as what determines the rate of saving in a country are covered in later chapters.

MEASURES OF AGGREGATE SAVING

In general, the **saving** of any economic unit is the unit's current income minus its spending on current needs. The saving rate of an economic unit is its saving divided by its income. From a macroeconomic perspective, three important measures of saving are private saving, government saving, and national saving. Summary table 1 (p. 31) outlines the definitions of each measure.

Private Saving

The saving of the private sector, known as **private saving**, equals private disposable income minus consumption. Using the definition of private disposable income from Eq. (2.4), we have

$$S_{\text{pvt}} = \text{private disposable income} - \text{consumption}$$

$$= (Y + NFP - T + TR + INT) - C, \tag{2.6}$$

where S_{pvt} is private saving. Consumption is subtracted from private disposable income to obtain private saving because consumption represents the private sector's spending to meet current needs. Investment, although part of private sector spending, is not subtracted from private disposable income because capital goods are purchased to enhance future productive capacity rather than to satisfy current needs. The private saving *rate* is private saving divided by private disposable income.[6]

---

[6] A measure of aggregate saving that you may hear reported and discussed is *personal saving*, which is the saving of the household portion of the private sector. Personal saving differs from private saving by excluding saving done within businesses. However, because businesses are owned and controlled by households, it makes little economic sense to distinguish between the portion of private saving done within households and the portion done within businesses. Thus, we focus on private rather than personal saving.

Government Saving

Government saving equals net government income minus government purchases of goods and services, G. With the definition of net government income from Eq. (2.5), government saving, S_{govt}, is

$$S_{govt} = \text{net government income} - \text{government purchases}$$

$$= (T - TR - INT) - G. \qquad (2.7)$$

If you think of government purchases as the government's spending to meet current needs, this definition of government saving fits the general definition of saving. In reality, though, some goods that the government purchases—roads and government buildings, for example—are not used up during the year and, thus, are available to satisfy future needs. The national income accounts of Canada distinguish these longer-lived government purchases from spending to meet current needs. We thus define government saving to be net government income less current government spending, but without subtracting government investment.[7]

Another, probably more familiar, name for government saving is the government budget surplus. The government **budget surplus** equals government revenue minus government expenditure. **Government revenue** equals tax revenue, T. **Government expenditures** are the sum of government purchases of goods and services, G, transfers, TR, and interest payments on government debt, INT. Thus, the government budget surplus equals $T - (G + TR + INT)$, which, as you can see from Eq. (2.7), is the same as government saving.

When government revenue is less than government expenditure, the difference between expenditures and revenue is known as the government **budget deficit**. Thus, when the government runs a budget deficit, with its expenditure greater than its revenue, government saving is negative.

National Saving

National saving, or the saving of the economy as a whole, equals private saving plus government saving. Using the definitions of private and government saving, Eqs. (2.6) and (2.7), we obtain national saving, S:

$$S = S_{pvt} + S_{govt}$$

$$= (Y + NFP - T + TR + INT - C) + (T - TR - INT - G) \qquad (2.8)$$

$$= Y + NFP - C - G.$$

Equation (2.8) shows that national saving equals the total income of the economy, $Y + NFP$ (which equals GNP), minus spending to satisfy current needs (consumption, C, and government purchases, G).

THE USES OF PRIVATE SAVING

How is private saving in an economy put to use? Here we show that private saving is used to fund new capital investment, provide the resources the government needs to finance its budget deficits, and acquire assets from or lend to foreigners.

---

[7] A similar argument suggests that expenditures on cars and other long-lived consumer durables should not be subtracted from disposable income in the calculation of private saving, although in practice they are subtracted.

SUMMARY 1

MEASURES OF AGGREGATE SAVING

Saving Measure	Definition and Formula
Private saving	Private disposable income less consumption $S_{\text{pvt}} = (Y + NFP - T + TR + INT) - C$
Government saving	Government revenue less government expenditure $S_{\text{govt}} = T - (G + TR + INT)$
National saving	Private saving plus government saving; also GNP $(Y + NFP)$ less consumption and government purchases $S = S_{\text{pvt}} + S_{\text{govt}} = Y + NFP - C - G$

To derive an important identity that illustrates the uses of private saving, we first use the income–expenditure identity (Eq. 2.3) and substitute $C + I + G + NX$ for Y in the expression for national saving (Eq. 2.8):

$$S = (C + I + G + NX) + NFP - C - G.$$

Simplifying the above expression, we obtain

$$S = I + (NX + NFP). \tag{2.9}$$

The expression for national saving in Eq. (2.9) contains the term $NX + NFP$, which is the sum of net exports and net factor payments, and is called the current account balance, CA.[8]

The **current account balance** equals payments received from abroad in exchange for currently produced goods and services (including factor services), minus the analogous payments made to foreigners by the domestic economy. As we have seen, NFP is negative in Canada, reflecting the fact that foreigners receive more by way of interest and profits due to their ownership of Canadian factors of production than Canadians receive due to their ownership of foreign factors of production. Substituting CA for $NX + NFP$ in Eq. (2.9), we obtain

$$S = I + CA. \tag{2.10}$$

We now have an expression for national saving, S; our goal is an expression for private saving, S_{pvt}. Equation (2.8) shows that private saving, S_{pvt}, equals national saving, S, minus government saving, S_{govt}. Then, subtracting S_{govt} from both sides of Eq. (2.10), we get

$$S_{\text{pvt}} = I + (-S_{\text{govt}}) + CA, \tag{2.11}$$

where $-S_{\text{govt}}$ is the government budget deficit.

Equation (2.11) is another important macroeconomic identity, called the **uses-of-saving identity**. It states that an economy's private saving is used in three ways:

1. *Investment (I).* Firms borrow from private savers to finance the construction and purchase of new capital (including residential capital) and inventory investment.

---

[8] Actually, the current account balance also includes a term called *transfers*, which measures transfers between countries, such as private gifts or official foreign aid (see Chapter 5). In our analysis, we generally ignore this term.

2. *The government budget deficit (−S$_{govt}$).* When the government runs a budget deficit (so that S_{govt} is negative and $-S_{govt}$ is positive), it must borrow from private savers to cover the difference between spending and revenue.

3. *The current account balance (CA).* When the Canadian current account balance is positive, foreigners' receipts of payments from Canada are not sufficient to cover the payments they make to Canada. To make up the difference, foreigners must either borrow from Canadian private savers or sell to Canadian savers some of their assets, such as land, factories, stocks, and bonds. Thus, financing the current account balance is a use of a country's private saving.

In contrast, when the Canadian current account balance is negative, as it was during much of the postwar period, Canadian receipts of payments from foreigners are not sufficient to cover Canadian payments to foreigners. To offset this excess of payments over receipts, Canada must borrow from foreigners or sell to foreigners some Canadian assets. In this case, foreigners use their saving to lend to Canada or to acquire Canadian assets.[9]

RELATING SAVING AND WEALTH

Saving is a key economic variable because it is closely related to the rate of wealth accumulation. In the rest of this section, we discuss the relationship of saving and wealth. To do so, however, we must first introduce the concept of stocks versus flows.

Stocks and Flows

The economic variables we have discussed so far in this chapter—such as GDP and the various types of expenditure, income, and saving—are measured per unit of time (for example, per quarter or per year). For instance, annual GDP figures measure the economy's production per year. Variables that are measured per unit of time are called **flow variables**.

In contrast, some economic variables, called **stock variables**, are defined at a point in time. Examples of stock variables are the amount of money in your bank account on September 15 of this year and the total value of all houses in Canada on January 1, 2014.

In many applications, a flow variable is the rate of change in a stock variable. A classic example is a bathtub with water flowing in from a faucet. The amount of water in the tub at any moment is a stock variable. The units of a stock variable (litres, in this case) do not have a time dimension. The rate at which water enters the tub is a flow variable; its units (litres per minute) have a time dimension. In this case, the flow is equal to the rate of change of the stock.

Wealth and Saving as Stock and Flow

Saving and wealth are related to each other in much the same way that the flow and stock of water in a bathtub are related. The wealth of any economic unit, also called net worth, is its assets (the things that it owns, including IOUs from other economic units) minus its liabilities (what it owes to other units). Wealth is

---

[9] The current account and its relationship to international borrowing and lending are discussed in greater detail in Chapter 5.

measured in dollars at a point in time and is a stock variable. Saving is measured in dollars per unit of time and is a flow variable. Because saving takes the form of an accumulation of assets or a reduction in liabilities (for example, if saving is used to pay off debts), it adds to wealth just as water flowing into a bathtub adds to the stock of water.

National Wealth

National wealth is the total wealth of the residents of a country. National wealth consists of two parts: (1) the country's domestic physical assets, such as its stock of capital goods and land;[10] and (2) its net foreign assets. The **net foreign assets** of a country equal the country's foreign assets (foreign stocks, bonds, and factories owned by domestic residents) minus its foreign liabilities (domestic physical and financial assets owned by foreigners). Net foreign assets are part of national wealth because they represent claims on foreigners that are not offset by foreigners' claims on the domestic economy.

Domestic financial assets held by domestic residents are not part of national wealth because the value of any domestic financial asset is offset by a domestic financial liability. For example, a chequing account held by a Canadian in a Canadian bank is an asset for the depositor but a liability for the bank; it, thus, does not represent wealth for the economy as a whole. In contrast, a Canadian's chequing account in a foreign bank has no corresponding domestic liability (it is a liability of a foreigner) and so is part of Canadian national wealth.

National wealth can change in two ways over time. First, the value of the existing assets or liabilities that make up national wealth may change. Thus, an increase in the value of Canadian farmland raises Canadian national wealth, as does an increase in the value of foreign stocks held by Canadians. The wearing out or depreciation of physical assets, which corresponds to a fall in the value of those assets, reduces national wealth.

The second way that national wealth can change is through national saving. Over any particular period of time, with the value of existing assets and liabilities held constant, each extra dollar of national saving adds a dollar to national wealth. That is,

$$S = I + CA,$$

which you will recognize as Eq. (2.10). This equation shows that national saving has two uses: (1) to increase the stock of domestic physical capital through investment, I, and (2) to increase the nation's stock of net foreign assets by lending to foreigners or acquiring foreign assets in an amount equal to the current account balance, CA. But each dollar by which domestic physical assets or net foreign assets increase is a dollar by which national wealth increases. Thus, as we claimed, increases in national saving increase national wealth dollar for dollar. As in the example of water flowing into a bathtub, the more rapid the flow of national saving, the more quickly the stock of national wealth will rise. On the other hand, an increase in the government budget deficit that is only partially offset by increased private saving would lead to a fall in $I + CA$ and, therefore, a fall in future wealth.

[10] In principle, national wealth should also include the value of the skills and training of the country's residents—what economists call human capital. In practice, because of measurement problems, human capital is not usually included in measures of national wealth.

2.4 Real GDP, Price Indexes, and Inflation

All the key macroeconomic variables that we have discussed so far in this chapter—GDP, the components of expenditure and income, national wealth, and saving—are measured in terms of current market values. Such variables are called **nominal variables**. The advantage of using market values to measure economic activity is that it allows summing of different types of goods and services.

However, a problem with measuring economic activity in nominal terms arises if you want to compare the values of an economic variable—GDP, for example—at two different points in time. If the current market value of the goods and services included in GDP changes over time, you cannot tell whether this change reflects changes in the quantities of goods and services produced, changes in the prices of goods and services, or a combination of these factors. For example, a large increase in the current market value of GDP might mean that a country has greatly expanded its production of goods and services, or it might mean that the country has experienced inflation, which has raised the prices of goods and services.

REAL GDP

Economists have devised methods for breaking down changes in nominal variables into the part owing to changes in physical quantities and the part owing to changes in prices. Consider the numerical example in Table 2.3, which gives production and price data for an economy that produces two types of goods: computers and bicycles. The data are presented for two different years. In year 1, the value of GDP is $46 000 (5 computers worth $1200 each and 200 bicycles worth $200 each). In year 2, the value of GDP is $66 000 (10 computers worth $600 each and 250 bicycles worth $240 each), which is 43.5% higher than the value of GDP in year 1. This 43.5% increase in nominal GDP does not reflect either a 43.5% increase in physical output or a 43.5% increase in prices. Instead, it reflects changes in both output and prices.

TABLE 2.3
Production and Price Data

	Year 1	Year 2	Percentage change from Year 1 to Year 2
Product (Quantity)			
Computers	5	10	+100%
Bicycles	200	250	+25%
Price			
Computers	$1200/computer	$600/computer	−50%
Bicycles	$200/bicycle	$240/bicycle	+20%
Value			
Computers	$6000	$6000	0
Bicycles	$40 000	$60 000	+50%
Total	$46 000	$66 000	+43.5%

How much of the 43.5% increase in nominal output is attributable to an increase in physical output? A simple way to remove the effects of price changes, and thus to focus on changes in quantities of output, is to measure the value of production in each year by using the prices from some base year. For this example, let's choose year 1 as the base year. Using the prices from year 1 ($1200 per computer and $200 per bicycle) to value the production in year 2 (10 computers and 250 bicycles) yields a value of $62 000, as shown in Table 2.4. We say that $62 000 is the value of real GDP in year 2, measured using the prices of year 1.

In general, an economic variable that is measured by the prices of a base year is called a **real variable**. Real economic variables measure the physical quantity of economic activity. Specifically, **real GDP**, also called *constant-dollar GDP*, measures the physical volume of an economy's final production using the prices of a base year. **Nominal GDP**, also called *current-dollar GDP*, is the dollar value of an economy's final output measured at current market prices. Thus, nominal GDP in year 2 for our example is $66 000, which we computed earlier using current (that is, year 2) prices to value output.

What is the value of real GDP in year 1? Continuing to treat year 1 as the base year, use the prices of year 1 ($1200 per computer and $200 per bicycle) to value

TABLE 2.4

Calculation of Real Output with Alternative Base Years

Calculation of real output with base year = Year 1

	Current quantities		Base-year prices			
Year 1						
Computers	5	×	$1200	=		$6000
Bicycles	200	×	$200	=		$40 000
					Total =	**$46 000**
Year 2						
Computers	10	×	$1200	=		$12 000
Bicycles	250	×	$200	=		$50 000
					Total =	**$62 000**

Percentage growth of real GDP = ($62 000 − $46 000)/$46 000 = **34.8%**

Calculation of real output with base year = Year 2

	Current quantities		Base-year prices			
Year 1						$3000
Computers	5	×	$600	=		$48 000
Bicycles	200	×	$240	=		**$51 000**
					Total =	
Year 2	10		$600			$6000
Computers	250	×	$240	=		$60 000
Bicycles		×		=		**$66 000**
					Total =	

Percentage growth of real GDP = ($66 000 + $51 000)/$51 000 = **29.4%**

production. The production of 5 computers and 200 bicycles has a value of $46 000. Thus, the value of real GDP in year 1 is the same as the value of nominal GDP in year 1. This result is a general one: Because current prices and base-year prices are the same in the base year, real and nominal values are always the same in the base year. Specifically, real GDP and nominal GDP are equal in the base year.

Now we're prepared to calculate the increase in the physical production from year 1 to year 2. Real GDP is designed to measure the physical quantity of production. Because real GDP in year 2 is $62 000 and real GDP in year 1 is $46 000, output, as measured by real GDP, is 34.8% higher in year 2 than in year 1.

PRICE INDEXES

We have seen how to calculate the portion of the change in nominal GDP owing to a change in physical quantities. We now turn our attention to the change in prices by using price indexes. A **price index** is a measure of the average level of prices for some specified set of goods and services, relative to the prices in a specified base year. For example, the **GDP deflator** is a price index that measures the overall level of prices of goods and services included in GDP and is defined by the formula

$$real\ GDP = nominal\ GDP/GDP\ deflator.$$

The GDP deflator is the amount by which nominal GDP must be divided, or "deflated," to obtain real GDP. In our example, we have already computed nominal GDP and real GDP, so we can now calculate the GDP deflator by rewriting the preceding formula as

$$GDP\ deflator = nominal\ GDP/real\ GDP.$$

In year 1 (the base year in our example), nominal GDP and real GDP are equal, so the GDP deflator equals 1.[11]

This result is an example of the general principle that the GDP deflator always equals 1 in the base year. In year 2, nominal GDP is $66 000 (see Table 2.3) and real GDP is $62 000 (see Table 2.4), so the GDP deflator in year 2 is $66 000/$62 000 = 1.065, which is 6.5% higher than the value of the GDP deflator in year 1. Thus, the overall level of prices, as measured by the GDP deflator, is 6.5% higher in year 2 than in year 1.

The measurement of real GDP and the GDP deflator depends on the choice of a base year.

The Consumer Price Index

The GDP deflator measures the average level of prices of goods and services included in GDP. The **consumer price index**, or CPI, measures the prices of consumer goods. Unlike the GDP deflator, which is calculated quarterly, the CPI is available monthly. Statistics Canada constructs the CPI by sending people out each month to find the current prices of a fixed list, or "basket," of consumer goods and services, including many specific items of food, clothing, housing, and fuel. The CPI for that month is then calculated as the current cost of the basket of consumer items divided by the cost of the same basket of items in the base year.[12]

The calculation of the consumer price index requires the use of a base year. If a base year—say 2002—is chosen and then never changed, the basket of goods

[11] The GDP deflator is often multiplied by 100, so that it equals 100 rather than 1.00 in the base year.
[12] As with the GDP deflator, the CPI is often multiplied by 100, so base-year prices equal 100 rather than 1.00.

and services established for the base year would eventually become outdated compared with the goods and services that people are actually consuming today. (Not only do people change their buying patterns—switching, for example, from beef to chicken—but some goods on the market today did not even exist in 2002.) This problem suggests that the base year should be updated occasionally, so that the base-year basket of goods and services better resembles the basket of goods and services that consumers choose in the current year. A Closer Look 2.2 discusses another concern with using the CPI to measure prices.

Inflation

An important variable that is measured with price indexes is the rate of inflation. The rate of inflation equals the percentage rate of increase in the price index per period. Thus, if the CPI rises from 100 in one year to 105 the next, the rate of inflation between the two years is $(105 - 100)/100 = 5/100 = 0.05 = 5\%$ per year. If in the third year the CPI is 112, the rate of inflation between the second and third years is $(112 - 105)/105 = 7/105 = 0.0667 = 6.67\%$ per year. More generally, if P_t is the price level in period t and P_{t+1} is the price level in period $t + 1$, the rate of inflation between t and $t + 1$, or π_{t+1}, is

$$\pi_{t+1} = \frac{(P_{t+1} - P_t)}{P_t} = \frac{\Delta P_{t+1}}{P_t},$$

where ΔP_{t+1}, or $P_{t+1} - P_t$, represents the change in P_t.

Figure 2.1 shows the Canadian inflation rate for 1945–2015, based on the CPI as the measure of the price level. Canada experienced high bouts of inflation following World War II and the Korean War in the early 1950s. During the remainder

FIGURE 2.1

THE INFLATION RATE IN CANADA, 1945–2015

Here, inflation is measured as the annual percentage change in the CPI. Inflation fell after the Korean War, then rose during the 1960s and 1970s, before falling sharply in the 1980s and again in the 1990s. Since 1989, the Bank of Canada has imposed targets designed to keep inflation between 1% and 3% per year.

Source: Statistics Canada, CANSIM, 2015. Reproduced and distributed on an "as is" basis with the permission of Statistics Canada.

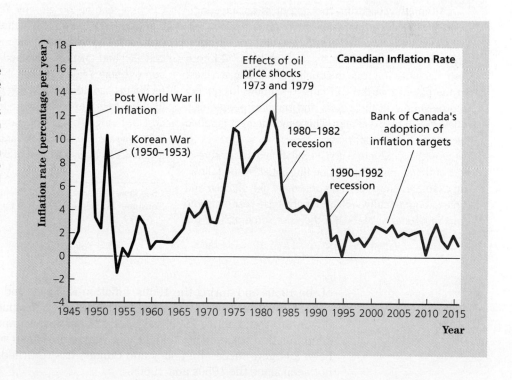

A CLOSER LOOK 2.2

DOES CPI INFLATION OVERSTATE INCREASES IN THE COST OF LIVING?

In recent years, economists have debated the accuracy of official inflation measures. In Canada, inflation, as measured by the CPI, may overstate true increases in the cost of living by up to 0.6 percentage points each year.*

In other words, if the official inflation rate is 1%, the true inflation rate may well be only 0.6% per year. While this difference may seem small, its cumulative effect may be large. In the United States, a government commission concluded that this bias may be as much as 1.1 percentage points per year.

Why might increases in the CPI overstate the actual rate at which the cost of living rises? One reason is the difficulty that government statisticians face in trying to measure changes in the quality of goods. For example, if the design of an air conditioner is improved so that it can put out 10% more cold air without an increased use of electricity, then a 10% increase in the price of the air conditioner should not be considered inflation; although paying 10% more, the consumer is also receiving 10% more cooling capacity. However, if government statisticians fail to account for the improved quality of the air conditioner and simply note its 10% increase in price, the price change will be incorrectly interpreted as inflation.

Although measuring the output of an air conditioner is not difficult, for some products (especially services) quality change is hard to measure. For example, by what percentage does the availability of 24-hour cash machines improve the quality of banking services? To the extent that the CPI fails to account for quality improvements in the goods and services people use, inflation will be overstated. This overstatement is called the *quality adjustment bias*.

Another problem with CPI inflation as a measure of cost of living increases can be illustrated by the following example. Suppose that consumers like chicken and turkey about equally well and in the base year consume equal amounts of each. But then, for some reason, the price of chicken rises sharply, leading consumers to switch to eating turkey almost exclusively. Because consumers are about equally satisfied with chicken and turkey, this switch does not make them significantly worse off; their true cost of living has not been affected much by the rise in the price of chicken. However, the official CPI, which measures the cost of buying the base-year basket of goods and services, will register a significant increase when the price of chicken skyrockets. Thus, the rise in the CPI exaggerates the true increase in the cost of living. The problem is that the CPI is based on the assumption that consumers purchase a basket of goods and services that is fixed over time, ignoring the fact that consumers can (and do) substitute cheaper goods or services for more expensive ones. This source of overstatement of the true increase in the cost of living is called the *substitution bias*.

If official inflation measures do, in fact, overstate true inflation, there are important implications. First, if cost of living increases are overstated, then increases in important quantities, such as real family income (the purchasing power of a typical family's income), are correspondingly understated. As a result, the bias in the CPI may lead to too gloomy a view of how the Canadian economy has done over the past few decades. Second, some government payments (such as pension benefits) and taxes are indexed to the CPI. If CPI inflation overstates true inflation, then some public pension recipients have been receiving greater benefit increases than necessary to compensate them for increases in the cost of living. Third, monetary policy that targets the inflation rate (see Chapters 7 and 14) may have to adjust for the CPI's overstatement of the true inflation rate.

_____

* See James Rossiter, "Measurement Biases in the Canadian Consumer Price Index," *Bank of Canada Working Paper 2005–39*, 2005.

of the 1950s and during the 1960s, inflation was subdued. A big jump in oil prices caused inflation to spike upward in the 1970s, but since then it has been on a downward trend. Since 1989, the Bank of Canada has imposed targets designed to keep inflation between 1% and 3% per year. As you can see in Figure 2.1, this has been a largely successful policy and Canada has returned to low rates of inflation not seen since the 1950s and 1960s.

2.5 Interest Rates

Interest rates are another important—and familiar—type of economic variable. An **interest rate** is a rate of return promised by a borrower to a lender. If, for example, the interest rate on a $100, one-year loan is 8%, the borrower has promised to repay the lender $108 one year from now, or $8 interest plus repayment of the $100 borrowed.

As we discuss in more detail in Chapter 4, there are many interest rates in the economy. Interest rates vary according to who is doing the borrowing, how long the funds are borrowed for, and other factors. There are also many assets in the economy, such as shares of corporate stock, that do not pay a specified interest rate but do pay their holders a return; for shares of stock the return comes in the form of dividends and capital gains (increases in the stock's market price). The existence of so many different assets, each with its own rate of return, has the potential to greatly complicate the study of macroeconomics. Fortunately, however, most interest rates and other rates of return tend to move up and down together. For purposes of macroeconomic analysis, we usually speak of "the" interest rate, as if there were only one. If we say that a certain policy causes "the" interest rate to rise, for example, we mean that interest rates and rates of return, in general, are likely to rise.

Real versus Nominal Interest Rates

Interest rates and other rates of return share a measurement problem with nominal GDP: An interest rate indicates how quickly the nominal or dollar value of an interest-bearing asset increases over time, but it does not reveal how quickly the value of the asset changes in real, or purchasing-power, terms. Consider, for example, a savings account with an interest rate of 4% per year that has $300 in it at the beginning of the year. At the end of the year, the savings account is worth $312, which is a relatively good deal for the depositor if inflation is zero; with no inflation, the price level is unchanged over the year, and $312 buys 4% more goods and services than the initial $300 did a year earlier. If inflation is 4%, however, what cost $300 a year earlier now costs $312, and in real terms the savings account is worth no more today than it was a year ago.

To distinguish changes in the real value of assets from changes in nominal value, economists frequently use the concept of the real interest rate. The **real interest rate** (or real rate of return) on an asset is the rate at which the real value or purchasing power of the asset increases over time. To distinguish them from real interest rates, we refer to conventionally measured interest rates, such as those reported in the newspaper, as nominal interest rates. The **nominal interest rate** (or nominal rate of return) tells us the rate at which the nominal value of an asset increases over time. The symbol for the nominal interest rate is i.

The real interest rate is related to the nominal interest rate and the inflation rate:

$$\text{real interest rate} = \text{nominal interest rate} - \text{inflation rate} \qquad (2.12)$$
$$= i - \pi$$

We derive and discuss Eq. (2.12) further at the end of the book in the Appendix, Section A.7.[13] For now, consider again the savings account paying 4% interest. If

---

[13] Equation (2.12) is an approximation, rather than an exact relationship. This approximation holds most closely when interest rates and inflation rates are not too high.

FIGURE 2.2

NOMINAL AND REAL INTEREST
RATES IN CANADA, 1951–2015

The nominal interest rate shown is the interest rate on three- to five-year Government of Canada bonds. The real interest rate is measured as the nominal interest rate minus the average inflation rate (using the CPI) over the current and previous two years. The real interest rate was unusually low (actually negative) in the mid-1970s. In the early 1980s, both nominal and real interest rates were very high. Since that time both nominal and real rates have fallen.

Source: Statistics Canada, CANSIM II, 2015. Reproduced and distributed on an "as is" basis with the permission of Statistics Canada.

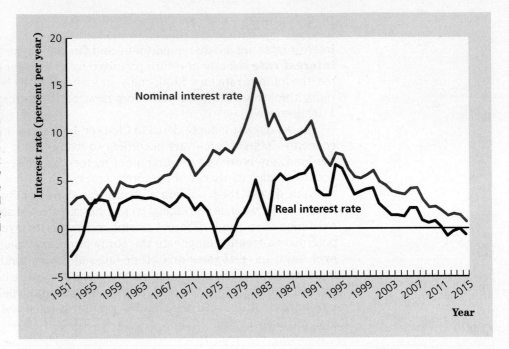

the inflation rate is zero, the real interest rate on that savings account is the 4% nominal interest rate minus the 0% inflation rate, or 4%. A 4% real interest rate on the account means that the depositor will be able to buy 4% more goods and services at the end of the year than at the beginning. But if inflation is 4%, the real interest rate on the savings account is the 4% nominal interest rate minus the 4% inflation rate, or 0%. In this case, the purchasing power of the account is no greater at the end of the year than at the beginning.

Nominal and real interest rates for Canada for 1951–2015 are shown in Figure 2.2. The real interest rate was unusually low in the mid-1970s; indeed, it was negative, which means that the real values of interest-bearing assets were actually declining over time. Both nominal and real interest rates rose to record highs in the early 1980s. Throughout the 1990s inflation remained more or less constant while nominal interest rates fell. As a result, real interest rates have fallen gradually over time.

The Expected Real Interest Rate

Usually, when you borrow, lend, or make a bank deposit, the nominal interest rate is specified in advance. But what about the real interest rate? For any nominal interest rate, Eq. (2.12) states that the real interest rate depends on the rate of inflation over the period of the loan or deposit, say, a year. However, the rate of inflation during the year cannot generally be determined until the year is over. Thus, at the time that a loan or deposit is made, the real interest rate that will be received is uncertain.

Because borrowers, lenders, and depositors don't know what the actual real interest rate will be, they must make their decisions about how much to borrow, lend, or deposit on the basis of the real interest rate they expect to prevail. They know the nominal interest rate in advance, so the real interest rate they expect depends on what they think inflation will be. The **expected real interest rate** is the nominal interest rate minus the expected rate of inflation, or

$$r = i - \pi^e, \tag{2.13}$$

where r is the expected real interest rate and π^e is the expected rate of inflation.

Comparing Eqs. (2.13) and (2.12), you can see that if people are correct in their expectations—so that expected inflation and actual inflation turn out to be the same—the expected real interest rate and the real interest rate actually received will be the same.

The expected real interest rate is the correct interest rate to use for studying most types of economic decisions, such as people's decisions about how much to borrow or lend. However, a problem in measuring the expected real interest rate is that economists don't generally know exactly what the public's expected rate of inflation is. Economists use various means to measure expected inflation. One approach is to survey the public and simply ask what rate of inflation people expect. A second method is to assume that the public's expectations of inflation are the same as publicly announced government or private forecasts. A third possibility is to assume that people's inflation expectations are an extrapolation of recently observed rates of inflation. Unfortunately, none of these methods is perfect, so the measurement of the expected real interest rate always contains some error.

How people and firms form expectations about the future is clearly important. When considering a 10-year mortgage loan, for example, a nominal interest rate of 5% might look attractive or not depending on what you think will be the rate of inflation. An expected rate of inflation of 4% suggests a real interest rate of only 1% while an expected rate of inflation of just 2% implies a real rate of interest of 3%. On a $300 000 mortgage, the difference in these two real interest rates over 10 years is equivalent to over $63 000 in inflation-adjusted dollars. Thinking carefully about the future therefore pays off! We will see more examples of the importance of making accurate forecasts of the future in the coming chapters. It turns out that understanding how people and firms form expectations about the future is as important an issue for macroeconomists as it is for households and firms.

CHAPTER SUMMARY

1. The national income accounts are an accounting framework used in measuring current economic activity. The national income accounts measure activity in three ways: the product approach, the expenditure approach, and the income approach. Although each gives the same value for current economic activity, all three approaches are used because each gives a different perspective on the economy.

2. Gross domestic product (GDP) is the broadest measure of aggregate economic activity occurring during a specified period of time. The product approach measures GDP by adding the market values of final goods and services newly produced in an economy; this approach is implemented by summing the value added by all producers. The expenditure approach measures GDP by adding the four categories of spending: consumption, investment, government purchases, and net exports. The income approach measures GDP by adding all the incomes, including taxes and profits, generated by economic activity.

3. The income of the private sector (domestic households and businesses) is called private disposable income. Private disposable income equals income received from private sector activities (GDP plus net factor payments from abroad, or GNP) plus payments received from the government (transfers and interest on government debt) minus taxes paid to the government. The net income of the government sector equals taxes collected minus transfer payments and interest paid on government debt. Private disposable income and net government income sum to GNP, which is the income of all domestic factors of production.

4. Saving is the portion of an economic unit's current income that it does not spend to meet current needs. Saving by the private sector, called private saving, equals private disposable income minus consumption. Government saving, which is the same as the government budget surplus, equals the government's net income minus its purchases of goods and services; equivalently, government saving equals government revenue minus government spending. National saving is the sum of private saving and government saving; it equals GDP plus net factor payments from abroad minus consumption and government purchases.

5. The uses-of-saving identity states that private saving equals the sum of investment, the government budget deficit, and the current account balance. Equivalently, national saving equals the sum of investment and the current account balance.

6. The national wealth of a country equals its physical assets, such as capital, plus its net foreign assets. National wealth increases in two ways: through changes in the value of existing assets and through national saving. National saving adds to national wealth because national saving is used either for investment, thus adding to physical capital, or for lending to foreigners an amount that equals the current account balance, which increases the country's net foreign assets.

7. Nominal GDP is the value of an economy's final output measured at current market prices. Real GDP is a measure of the physical volume of the economy's final output. Real GDP equals nominal GDP divided by the GDP deflator.

8. A price index is a measure of the current price level relative to a base year. The GDP deflator measures the overall price level of goods and services included in GDP. The consumer price index (CPI) measures the price level of a basket of consumer goods. The rate of inflation is the percentage rate of change of the price level, measured by percentage rate of change of a price index, such as the GDP deflator or the CPI.

9. An interest rate is a rate of return promised by a borrower to a lender. The nominal interest rate is the rate at which the nominal value of an interest-bearing asset increases over time. The real interest rate, or the nominal interest rate minus the rate of inflation, is the rate at which the value of an asset grows in real, or purchasing-power, terms. Borrowing and lending decisions are based on the expected real interest rate, which is the nominal interest rate less the expected rate of inflation.

KEY TERMS

budget deficit, p. 30
budget surplus, p. 30
capital good, p. 23
consumer price index, p. 36
consumption, p. 25
current account balance, p. 31
expected real interest rate, p. 41
expenditure approach, p. 19
final goods and services, p. 22
flow variables, p. 32
fundamental identity of
    national income accounting, p. 20
GDP deflator, p. 36
government expenditures, p. 30
government purchases, p. 26
government revenue, p. 30
government saving, p. 30
gross domestic product, p. 20
gross national product, p. 23
income approach, p. 19
income–expenditure identity, p. 24
interest rate, p. 39
intermediate goods and services, p. 21
inventories, p. 23
investment, p. 26
national income accounts, p. 17
national saving, p. 30
national wealth, p. 29
net exports, p. 26
net factor payments from abroad, p. 24
net foreign assets, p. 33
nominal GDP, p. 35

KEY EQUATIONS

$$\text{Total production} = \text{total income} = \text{total expenditure} \tag{2.1}$$

The fundamental identity of national income accounting states that the same measure of total economic activity is obtained whether activity is measured by the production of final goods and services, the amount of income generated by the economic activity, or the expenditure on final goods and services.

$$Y = C + I + G + NX \tag{2.3}$$

According to the income expenditure identity, total income or product or output, Y, equals the sum of the four types of expenditure: consumption, C, investment, I, government purchases, G, and net exports, NX.

$$S_{\text{pvt}} = (Y + NFP - T + TR + INT) - C \tag{2.6}$$

Private saving equals private disposable income less consumption, C. Private sector disposable income equals gross domestic product, Y, plus net factor payments from abroad, NFP, plus transfers, TR, and interest, INT, received from the government, less taxes paid, T.

$$S_{\text{govt}} = (T - TR - INT) - G \tag{2.7}$$

Government saving equals government revenue from taxes, T, less expenditures for transfers, TR, interest on the national debt, INT, and government purchases, G. Government saving is the same as the government budget surplus and is the negative of the government budget deficit.

$$S = S_{\text{pvt}} + S_{\text{govt}} = Y + NFP - C - G \tag{2.8}$$

National saving, S, is the sum of private saving and government saving. Equivalently, national saving equals gross domestic product, Y, plus net factor payments from abroad, NFP, less consumption, C, and government purchases, G.

$$S = I + CA \tag{2.10}$$

National saving, S, has two uses: to finance investment, I, and to lend to foreigners (or to acquire foreign assets) an amount that equals the current account balance, CA. The current account balance equals the increase in net foreign assets.

$$S_{\text{pvt}} = I + (-S_{\text{govt}}) + CA \tag{2.11}$$

According to the uses-of-saving identity, private saving is used to finance investment spending, I, to provide the government with the funds it needs to cover its budget deficit, $-S_{\text{govt}}$, and to lend to foreigners (or to acquire foreign assets) an amount that equals the current account balance, CA.

$$r = i - \pi^e \tag{2.13}$$

The expected real interest rate, r, equals the nominal interest rate, i, minus expected inflation π^e.

REVIEW QUESTIONS

1. What are the three approaches to measuring economic activity? Why do they give the same answer?
2. Why are goods and services counted in GDP at market value? Are there any disadvantages or problems in using market values to measure production?
3. What is the difference between intermediate and final goods and services? In which of these categories do capital goods, such as factories and machines, fall? Why is the distinction between intermediate and final goods important for measuring GDP?
4. List the four components of total spending. Why are imports subtracted when GDP is calculated in the expenditure approach?
5. Define private saving. How is private saving used in the economy? What is the relationship between private saving and national saving?
6. What is national wealth, and why is it important? How is national wealth linked to national saving?
7. For the purposes of assessing an economy's growth performance, which is the more important statistic: real GDP or nominal GDP? Why?
8. Describe how the GDP deflator and CPI inflation are calculated. What are some reasons that CPI inflation may overstate true inflation?
9. Explain the differences among the nominal interest rate, the real interest rate, and the expected real interest rate. Which interest rate concept is the most important for the decisions made by borrowers and lenders? Why?

NUMERICAL PROBLEMS

1. After a boat rescues everyone else from Gilligan's Island, the Professor and Gilligan remain behind, afraid of getting shipwrecked again with the same bunch of people. The Professor grows coconuts and catches fish. Last year he harvested 1000 coconuts and caught 500 fish. He values one fish as worth two coconuts. The Professor gave 200 coconuts to Gilligan in exchange for help in the harvest, and he gave Gilligan 100 fish in exchange for collecting worms for use in fishing. The Professor stored 100 of his coconuts in his hut for consumption at some future time. He also used 100 fish as fertilizer for the coconut trees, as he must every year to keep the trees producing. Gilligan consumed all his coconuts and fish.

   In terms of fish, what is the GDP of Gilligan's Island? What are consumption and investment? What are the incomes of the Professor and Gilligan?

2. National income and product data are generally revised. What effects would the following revisions have on consumption, investment, government purchases, net exports, and GDP?

   a. It is discovered that consumers bought $600 million more furniture than previously thought. This furniture was manufactured in Quebec.

   b. It is discovered that consumers bought $600 million more furniture than previously thought. This furniture was manufactured in Sweden.

   c. It is discovered that businesses bought $600 million more furniture than previously thought. This furniture was manufactured in Quebec.

   d. It is discovered that businesses bought $600 million more furniture than previously thought. This furniture was manufactured in Sweden.

3. ABC Computer Company has a $20 000 000 factory in Kanata. During the current year, ABC builds $2 000 000 worth of computer components. ABC's costs are labour, $1 000 000; interest on debt, $100 000; and taxes, $200 000.

   ABC sells all its output to XYZ Supercomputer. Using ABC's components, XYZ builds four supercomputers at a cost of $800 000 each ($500 000 worth of components, $200 000 in labour costs, and $100 000 in taxes per computer). XYZ has a $30 000 000 factory. XYZ sells three of the supercomputers for $1 000 000 each; at year's end, it has not sold the fourth. The unsold computer is carried on XYZ's books as an $800 000 increase in inventory.

   a. Calculate the contributions to GDP of these transactions, showing that all three approaches give the same answer.

   b. Repeat part (a), but now assume that in addition to its other costs, ABC also paid $500 000 for imported computer chips.

4. For each of the following transactions, determine the contribution to the current year's GDP. Explain the effects on the product, income, and expenditure accounts.

   a. On January 1, you purchase 10 sheets of plywood at $20 per sheet. The lumber store purchased the plywood the previous week at a wholesale price (transportation included) of $15 per sheet.

   b. Colonel Hogwash purchases a West Vancouver mansion for $1 000 000. The broker's fee is 6%.

   c. A homemaker enters the workforce, taking a job that will pay $20 000 over the year. The homemaker must pay $8000 over the year for professional child-care services.

   d. The Japanese build an auto plant in Quebec for $100 000 000, using only local labour and materials. (*Hint:* The auto plant is a capital good produced by Canadians and purchased by the Japanese.)

   e. You are informed that you have won $3 000 000 in Lotto 6/49, to be paid to you, in total, immediately.

   f. The lottery corporation pays you an additional $5000 fee to appear in a TV commercial publicizing the provincial lottery.

   g. Discount Car Rentals replaces its rental fleet by buying $100 000 000 worth of new cars from General Motors. It sells its old fleet to a consortium of used-car dealers for $40 000 000. The consortium resells the used cars to the public for a total of $60 000 000.

5. You are given the following information about an economy:

Gross private domestic investment	40
Government purchases of goods and services	30
Gross national product (GNP)	200
Current account balance	−20
Taxes	60
Government transfer payments	25
Interest payments from the government (all to domestic households)	15
Factor income from the rest of the world	7
Factor payments to the rest of the world	9

Find the following, assuming that government investment is zero:

   a. Consumption

   b. Net exports

   c. GDP

   d. Net factor payments

   e. Private saving

f. Government saving

g. National saving

6. Consider an economy that produces only three types of fruit: apples, oranges, and bananas. In the base year (a few years ago), the production and price data were as follows:

Fruit	Quantity	Price
Apples	3000 bags	$2 per bag
Bananas	6000 bunches	$3 per bunch
Oranges	8000 bags	$4 per bag

In the current year, the production and price data are as follows:

Fruit	Quantity	Price
Apples	4000 bags	$3 per bag
Bananas	14 000 bunches	$2 per bunch
Oranges	32 000 bags	$5 per bag

a. Find nominal GDP in the current year and in the base year. What is the percentage increase since the base year?

b. Find real GDP in the base year and in the current year. By what percentage does real GDP increase from the base year to the current year?

c. Find the GDP deflator for the current year and the base year. By what percentage does the price level change from the base year to the current year?

d. Would you say that the percentage increase in nominal GDP in this economy since the base year is due more to increases in prices or increases in the physical volume of output?

7. For the consumer price index values shown, calculate the rate of inflation in each year from 1930 to 1933. What is unusual about this period, relative to recent experience?

Year	1929	1930	1931	1932	1933
CPI	14.2	14.0	12.7	11.5	10.9

8. Hy Marks buys a one-year government bond on January 1, 2010, for $500. He receives principal plus interest totalling $545 on January 1, 2011. Suppose that the CPI is 200 on January 1, 2011, and 214 on January 1, 2012. This increase in prices is more than Hy had anticipated; his guess was that the CPI would be at 210 by the beginning of 2011.

Find the nominal interest rate, the inflation rate, the real interest rate, Hy's expected inflation rate, and Hy's expected real interest rate.

9. The GDP deflator in Econoland is 200 on January 1, 2010. The deflator rises to 242 by January 1, 2012, and to 266.2 by January 1, 2013.

a. What is the annual rate of inflation over the two-year period between January 1, 2010, and January 1, 2012? In other words, what constant yearly rate of inflation would lead to the price rise observed over those two years?

b. What is the annual rate of inflation over the three-year period from January 1, 2010, to January 1, 2013?

c. In general, if P_0 is the price level at the beginning of an n-year period, and P_n is the price level at the end of that period, show that the annual rate of inflation π over that period satisfies the equation $(1 + \pi)^n = (P_n/P_0)$.

ANALYTICAL PROBLEMS

1. After giving birth to her first child, Paula must decide whether to stay at home to raise her child or return to her paid employment in industry and pay a childminder to care for her child. How does her decision affect the size of GDP?

2. If ABC Ltd., a Canadian firm, produces widgets in a factory it has built in Mexico, the market value of those widgets is added to Canada's GNP but not to Canada's GDP. Explain why.

3. Consider a closed economy with a single telephone company, Calls-R-Us. The residents of the country make two million phone calls per year and pay $3 per phone call. One day, a new phone company, Cheap-Call, enters the market and charges only $2 per phone call. All the residents immediately stop using Calls-R-Us and switch to CheapCall. They still make two million phone calls per year. The executives of CheapCall are proud of their market share. They post billboards stating "Our country has increased its national saving by $2 million per year by switching to CheapCall." Comment on the accuracy of the statement on the billboards.

4. Economists have tried to measure the GDPs of virtually all the world's nations. This problem asks you to think about some practical issues that arise in that effort.

a. Before the collapse of the Soviet system, the economies of the Soviet Union and Eastern Europe were centrally planned. One aspect of central planning is that most prices are set by the government. A government-set price may be too low in that people want to buy more of the good at the fixed price than there are supplies available; or the price may be too high so that large stocks of the good sit unsold on store shelves. During the past several years, central planning has been largely eliminated in Eastern Europe and the former Soviet Union, but government price-setting has not been completely abandoned. For example, Russia still keeps energy prices well below market-clearing levels.

What problem does government control of prices create for economists attempting to measure a country's GDP? Suggest a strategy for dealing with this problem.

b. In very poor agricultural countries, many people grow their own food, make their own clothes, and provide services for each other within a family or village group. Official GDP estimates for these countries are often extremely low, perhaps just a few hundred dollars per person. Some economists have argued that the official GDP figures underestimate these nations' actual GDPs. Why might this be so? Again, can you suggest a strategy for dealing with this measurement problem?

Chapter 3

Productivity, Output, and Employment

In Chapter 2, we discussed the measurement of several economic variables used to gauge the economy's health. The measurement of economic performance is a prelude to the main objective of macroeconomics: *to understand how the economy works*. Understanding how the economy works requires a shift from economic *measurement* to economic *analysis*.

In Part II of this book, which begins with this chapter, we have two main goals. The first is to analyze the factors that affect the longer-term performance of the economy, including the rate of economic growth, productivity, and living standards; the long-run levels of employment and unemployment; saving and capital formation; and the rate of inflation; among others.

The second goal is to develop a theoretical model of the macroeconomy that you can use to analyze the economic issues covered in this book and others that you may encounter in the future. As outlined in Chapter 1, our model is based on the assumption that individuals, firms, and the government interact in three composite markets: the labour market (covered in this chapter), the goods market (Chapter 4), and the asset market (Chapter 7). In developing and using this model in Part II, we generally assume that the economy is at full employment, with quantities supplied and demanded equal in each of the three major markets. Since we're focusing on the long-term behaviour of the economy, this assumption is a reasonable one. In Part III, in which we explore business cycles, we allow for the possibility that quantities supplied and demanded may not be equal in the short run.

This chapter begins the discussion of how the economy works with what is perhaps the most fundamental determinant of economic well-being in a society: the economy's productive capacity. Everything else being equal, the greater the quantity of goods and services an economy can produce, the more people will be able to consume in the present and the more they will be able to save and invest for the future.

The first section of the chapter shows that the amount of output an economy produces depends on two factors: (1) the quantities of inputs (such as labour, capital, and raw materials) utilized in the production process; and (2) the **productivity** of the inputs; that is, the effectiveness with which they are used. As discussed in Chapter 1, an economy's productivity is basic to determining living standards. In this chapter, we show how productivity affects people's incomes by helping determine how many workers are employed and how much they receive in wages.

Of the various inputs to production, the most important (as measured by share of total cost) is labour. For this reason, we spend most of the chapter analyzing the labour market, using the tools of supply and demand. We first consider the factors that affect how much labour employers demand and workers supply and then look at the forces that tend to bring the labour market into equilibrium. Equilibrium in the labour market determines wages and employment; in turn, the level of employment, together with the quantities of other inputs (such as capital) and the level of productivity, determines how much output an economy produces.

Our basic model of the labour market rests on the assumption that the quantities of labour supplied and demanded are equal so that all labour resources are fully utilized. In reality, however, some fraction of workers is always unemployed. The latter part of the chapter introduces unemployment and looks at the relationship between the unemployment rate and the amount of output produced in the economy.

3.1 How Much Does the Economy Produce? The Production Function

Every day the business news reports many economic variables that influence the economy's performance—the rate of consumer spending, the value of the dollar, the gyrations of the stock market, the growth rate of the money supply, and so on. All of these variables are important. However, no determinant of economic performance and living standards is more basic than the economy's physical capacity to produce goods and services. If an economy's factories, farms, and other businesses all shut down for some reason, other economic factors would not mean much.

What determines the quantity of goods and services that an economy can produce? A key factor is the quantity of inputs—such as capital goods, labour, raw materials, land, and energy—that producers in the economy use. Economists refer to inputs to the production process as **factors of production**. All else being equal, the greater the quantities of factors of production used, the more goods and services are produced. Of the various factors of production, the two most important are capital (factories and machines, for example) and labour (workers). Hence we focus on these two factors in discussing an economy's capacity to produce goods and services. In modern economies, however, output often responds strongly to changes in the supply of other factors, such as energy or raw materials. Later in this chapter, the Application "Output, Employment, and the Real Wage During Oil Price Shocks" (p. 72) discusses the effects on the economy of a disruption in oil supplies.

The quantities of capital and labour (and other inputs) used in production do not completely determine the amount of output produced. Equally important is how effectively these factors are used. For the same stocks of capital and labour, an economy with superior technologies and management practices, for example, will produce more output than an economy without those strengths.

The effectiveness with which capital and labour are used may be summarized by a relationship called the production function. The **production function** is a mathematical expression relating the amount of output produced to quantities of capital and labour utilized. A convenient way to write the production function is

$$Y = AF(K, N) \tag{3.1}$$

where
  Y = real output produced in the current period
  A = a number measuring overall productivity

K = the capital stock, or quantity of capital, used in the current period
N = the number of workers employed in the current period
F = a function relating output Y to capital K and labour N.

The production function in Eq. (3.1) applies both to an economy as a whole (where Y, K, and N refer to the economy's output, capital stock, and number of workers) and to an individual firm, in which case Y, K, and N refer to the firm's output, capital, and number of workers.

According to Eq. (3.1), the amount of output Y that an economy (or firm) can produce during any period of time depends on the size of the capital stock K and the number of workers N. The symbol A in Eq. (3.1), which multiplies the function $F(K, N)$, is a measure of the overall effectiveness with which capital and labour are used. We refer to A as **total factor productivity**, or simply productivity. Note that for any values of capital and labour, an increase in productivity A of, say, 10% implies a 10% increase in the amount of output that can be produced. Thus, increases in productivity A correspond to improvements in production technology

APPLICATION

THE PRODUCTION FUNCTION AND PRODUCTIVITY GROWTH IN CANADA

Empirical studies show that the relationship between output and inputs in the Canadian economy is described reasonably well by the following production function[1]:

$$Y = AK^{0.3}N^{0.7}. \tag{3.2}$$

The production function in Eq. (3.2) is a specific example of the general production function in Eq. (3.1), in which we set the general function $F(K, N)$ equal to $K^{0.3}N^{0.7}$. (Note that this production function contains exponents; if you need to review the properties of exponents, see the Appendix, Section A.6.)

Equation (3.2) shows how output Y relates to the use of factors of production, to capital K and labour N, and to productivity A in Canada. Table 3.1 presents data on these variables for the Canadian economy for 1981 to 2015. Columns (1), (2), and (3) show output (real GDP), capital stock, and labour for each year. Real GDP and the capital stock are measured in billions of 2007 dollars, and labour is measured in millions of employed workers. Column (4) shows the Canadian economy's productivity for each year.

Output, capital, and labour in Table 3.1 are measured directly, but there is no way to measure productivity directly. Instead, the productivity index A shown in column (4) is measured indirectly by assigning to A the value necessary to satisfy Eq. (3.2). Specifically, for each year A is determined by the formula $A = Y/(K^{0.3}N^{0.7})$, which is just another way of writing Eq. (3.2). In 2015, for example, Table 3.1 reports that $Y = 1757$, $K = 1910$, and $N = 17.9$; therefore, the value of A for 2015 is $1752/[(1910)^{0.3}(17.9)^{0.7}]$, or $A = 24.13$. Calculating productivity in this

---

[1] This type of production function is called a Cobb–Douglas production function. Cobb–Douglas production functions take the form $Y = AK^aN^{1-a}$, where $0 < a < 1$. Under certain conditions, the parameter a in the Cobb–Douglas production function corresponds to the share of income received by owners of capital, whereas labour receives a share of income equal to $1 - a$. Thus, observing the actual shares of income received by capital and labour provides a way of estimating the parameter a.

TABLE 3.1

The Production Function for Canada, 1981–2015

Production function: $Y = AK^{0.3}N^{0.7}$

Year	(1) Real GDP, Y (Billions of 2007 dollars)	(2) Capital, K (Billions of 2007 dollars)	(3) Labour, N (Millions of workers)	(4) Total Factor Productivity, A^*	(5) Growth in Total Factor Productivity (% change in A)
1981	780	891	11.3	18.61	
1982	755	915	10.9	18.27	−1.8
1983	775	928	11.0	18.59	1.7
1984	822	941	11.3	19.29	3.8
1985	865	960	11.7	19.76	2.4
1986	889	974	12.0	19.79	0.2
1987	930	991	12.3	20.23	2.2
1988	970	1019	12.7	20.48	1.2
1989	993	1047	13.0	20.48	0.0
1990	993	1072	13.1	20.24	−1.1
1991	973	1091	12.9	19.97	−1.3
1992	982	1097	12.7	20.26	1.4
1993	1006	1101	12.8	20.66	2.0
1994	1055	1114	13.1	21.28	3.0
1995	1082	1127	13.3	21.48	1.0
1996	1099	1140	13.4	21.60	0.6
1997	1149	1167	13.7	22.10	2.3
1998	1193	1193	14.0	22.41	1.4
1999	1259	1221	14.4	23.08	3.0
2000	1328	1250	14.8	23.76	2.9
2001	1348	1280	14.9	23.75	−0.1
2002	1387	1301	15.3	23.92	0.7
2003	1413	1326	15.7	23.82	−0.4
2004	1456	1362	15.9	24.07	1.0
2005	1503	1414	16.1	24.35	1.2
2006	1539	1474	16.4	24.35	0.0
2007	1574	1530	16.8	24.23	−0.5
2008	1589	1588	17.0	23.96	−1.1
2009	1539	1607	16.7	23.39	−2.4
2010	1584	1652	17.0	23.64	1.1
2011	1633	1707	17.2	23.88	1.0
2012	1659	1768	17.4	23.80	−0.3
2013	1698	1825	17.7	23.89	0.3
2014	1742	1879	17.8	24.19	1.3
2015	1757	1910	17.9	24.13	−0.2

* Total factor productivity is calculated by the formula $A = Y/(K^{0.3}N^{0.7})$

Source: Statistics Canada, 2016.

way ensures that the production function relationship, Eq. (3.2), is satisfied exactly for each year.

The levels of the productivity index A reported in Table 3.1 depend on the units in which output, capital, and labour are measured—for example, the values of A would change if we measured workers in thousands rather than millions—and, thus, are hard to interpret. In contrast, the year-to-year growth rates of the productivity measure shown in column (5) are units-free and are, therefore, easier to work with. A close look at the productivity growth rates shown in Table 3.1 emphasizes two points.

First, productivity growth can vary sharply from year to year. Most strikingly, productivity in Canada fell 1.8% in 1982, a deep recession year, then rose 1.7% in 1983 and 3.8% in 1984, a period of economic recovery. More recently, the recession that struck Canada and much of the world's industrialized countries beginning in 2007 resulted in large falls in productivity in 2008 and 2009. Productivity normally falls in recessions and rises in recoveries, but explanations for its behaviour over the business cycle are controversial. We return to this issue in Part III of this book, which is devoted to business cycles.

Second, since 1981, productivity in Canada has been growing relatively slowly, averaging 0.8% per year during the 1981–2015 period. This result is notably less than in the 1950–1970 period, when productivity growth exceeded 2% a year.[2] This trend is bad news for the economy because the rate of productivity growth is closely related to the rate of improvement of living standards. Chapter 6 discusses the relationship between productivity and living standards in greater detail.

or to any other change in the economy that allows capital and labour to be utilized more effectively.

THE SHAPE OF THE PRODUCTION FUNCTION

The production function in Eq. (3.1) can be shown graphically. The easiest way to graph it is to hold one of the two factors of production, either capital or labour, constant and then graph the relationship between output and the other factor.[3] Suppose that we use the Canadian production function for the year 2015 and hold labour N at its actual 2015 value of 17.9 million workers (see Table 3.1). We also use the actual 2015 value of 24.13 for A. The production function (Eq. 3.2) becomes

$$Y = AK^{0.3}N^{0.7} = (24.13)(K^{0.3})(17.9^{0.7}) - 182.14K^{0.3}.$$

This relationship is graphed in Figure 3.1, with capital stock K on the horizontal axis and output Y on the vertical axis. With labour and productivity held at their 2015 values, the graph shows the amount of output that could have been produced in that year for any value of the capital stock. Point A on the graph shows the situation that actually occurred in 2015: The value of the capital stock ($1910 billion) appears on the horizontal axis, and the value of real GDP ($1757 billion) appears on the vertical axis.

---

[2] Other countries have also experienced slower productivity growth since the mid-1970s, as discussed further in Chapter 6.
[3] To show the relationship among output and both factors of production simultaneously would require a three-dimensional graph.

FIGURE 3.1

THE PRODUCTION FUNCTION

RELATING OUTPUT AND CAPITAL

This production function shows how much output the Canadian economy could produce for each level of Canadian capital stock, holding labour and productivity at 2015 levels. Point *A* corresponds to the actual 2015 output and capital stock. The production function has diminishing marginal productivity of capital: Raising the capital stock by $100 billion in order to move from point *B* to point *C* raises output by $168 billion, but adding another $100 billion in capital to go from point *C* to point *D* increases output by only $115 billion.

Source: *Statistics Canada, The Production Function of Canada* 1981–2015. Reproduced and distributed on an "as is" basis with the permission of Statistics Canada.

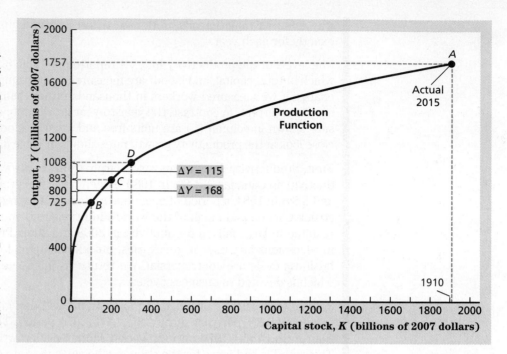

The Canadian production function graphed in Figure 3.1 shares two properties with most production functions:

1. *The production function slopes upward from left to right.* The slope of the production function tells us that as the capital stock increases, more output can be produced.

2. *The slope of the production function becomes flatter from left to right.* This property implies that although more capital always leads to more output, it does so at a decreasing rate.

Before discussing the economics behind the second property of the production function, we can illustrate it numerically using Figure 3.1. Suppose that we are initially at point *B*, where the capital stock is $100 billion. Adding $100 billion in capital moves us to point *C*, where the capital stock is $200 billion. How much extra output has this expansion in capital provided? The difference in output between points *B* and *C* is $168 billion ($893 billion output at *C* minus $725 billion output at *B*). This extra $168 billion in output is the benefit from raising the capital stock from $100 billion to $200 billion, with productivity and employment held constant.

Now, suppose that starting at *C*, we add another $100 billion of capital. This new addition of capital takes us to *D*, where the capital stock is $300 billion. The difference in output between *C* and *D* is only $115 billion ($1008 billion output at *D* minus $893 billion output at *C*), which is less than the $168 billion increase in output between *B* and *C*. Thus, although the second $100 billion of extra capital raises total output, it does so by less than did the first $100 billion of extra capital. This result illustrates that the production function rises less steeply between points *C* and *D* than between points *B* and *C*.

The Marginal Product of Capital

The two properties of the production function are closely related to a concept known as the marginal product of capital. To understand this concept, let us suppose that we start from some given capital stock K and increase the capital stock by some amount ΔK (other factors held constant). This increase in capital would cause output Y to increase by some amount ΔY. The **marginal product of capital**, or MPK, is the increase in output produced resulting from a one-unit increase in the capital stock. Because ΔK additional units of capital permit the production of ΔY additional units of output, the amount of additional output produced per additional unit of capital is $\Delta Y/\Delta K$. Thus, the marginal product of capital is $\Delta Y/\Delta K$.

The marginal product of capital $\Delta Y/\Delta K$ is the change in the variable on the vertical axis of the production function graph (ΔY) divided by the change in the variable on the horizontal axis (ΔK), which you might recognize as a slope. As explained in the Appendix, Section A.2, the slope of a curve at a particular point is equal to the slope of a *tangent* drawn to touch the curve at that point. This means that for small changes in the capital stock K, the MPK can be measured by the slope of a line drawn tangent to the production function. Using Figure 3.1 and a ruler to draw tangents to points B and D, for example, you can confirm that MPK grows smaller as the capital stock K grows larger.

With this understanding of MPK and how its size is related to the slope of tangents drawn to the production function, we can restate the two properties of the production function listed earlier.

1. *The marginal product of capital is positive.* Whenever the capital stock is increased, more output can be produced. Because the marginal product of capital is positive, the production function slopes upward from left to right.

2. *The marginal product of capital declines as the capital stock is increased.* Because the marginal product of capital is the slope of the production function, the slope of the production function decreases as the capital stock is increased. As Figure 3.1 shows, the slope of the production function at point D, where the capital stock is 300, is smaller than the slope at point B, where the capital stock is 100. Thus, the production function becomes flatter from left to right.

The tendency for the marginal product of capital to decline as the amount of capital in use increases is called the **diminishing marginal productivity** of capital. The economic reason for diminishing marginal productivity of capital is as follows: When the capital stock is low, there are many workers for each machine, and the benefits of increasing capital further are great; but when the capital stock is high, workers already have plenty of capital to work with, and little benefit is to be gained from expanding capital further. For example, in a business's call centre in which there are many more staff members than workstations (phones and computer terminals), each workstation is constantly being utilized and the staff must waste time waiting for a free workstation. In this situation, adding extra workstations leads to increased output. However, if there are already as many workstations as staff members, so that workstations are often idle and there is no waiting for a workstation to become available, little additional output can be obtained by adding yet another workstation.

The Marginal Product of Labour

In Figure 3.1, we graphed the relationship between output and capital implied by the 2015 Canadian production function, holding constant the amount of labour. Similarly, we can look at the relationship between output and labour, holding constant the quantity of capital. Suppose that we fix capital K at its actual 2015 value

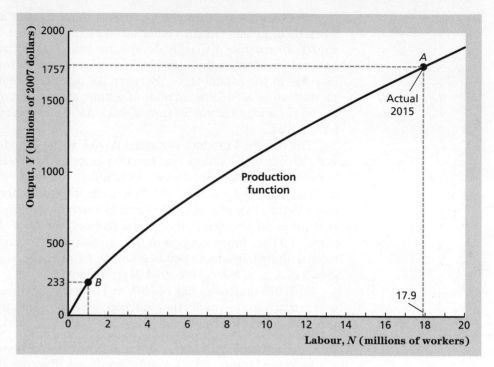

of $1910 billion and hold productivity A at its actual 2015 value of 24.13 (see Table 3.1, p. 57). The production function (Eq. 3.2) becomes

$$Y = AK^{0.3}N^{0.7} = (24.13)(1910K^{0.3})(N^{0.7}) = 232.76N^{0.7}.$$

This relationship is shown graphically in Figure 3.2. Point A, where $N = 17.9$ million workers and $Y = \$1757$ billion, corresponds to the actual 2015 values.

Although it is somewhat harder to see in Figure 3.2 than it is in Figure 3.1, by using a ruler to draw tangents to points B and A, for example, you can confirm that *MPN* grows smaller as the capital stock N grows larger.[4] As in the case of capital, increases in the number of workers raise output but do so at a diminishing rate. Thus, the principle of diminishing marginal productivity also applies to labour, and for similar reasons: The greater the number of workers already using a fixed amount of capital and other inputs, the smaller the benefit (in terms of increased output) of adding even more workers.

The **marginal product of labour**, or *MPN*, is the additional output produced by each additional unit of labour, $\Delta Y/\Delta N$. As with the marginal product of capital, for small increases in employment, the *MPN* can be measured by the slope of the line tangent to a production function that relates output and labour. In Figure 3.2, when employment equals 1 million workers, the *MPN* equals the slope of the line tangent to the production function at point B; and when employment is 17.9 million workers, the *MPN* is the slope of the line that touches the production function at point A. Because of the diminishing marginal productivity of labour, the slope of the production function relating output to labour is greater at B than at A, and the production function flattens from left to right.

---

[4] Because N is raised to the power of 0.7 but K is raised to the power of 0.3, the production function relating output and labour is not as sharply bowed as the production function relating output and capital.

SUPPLY SHOCKS

The production function of an economy does not usually remain fixed over time. Economists use the term **supply shock**—or, sometimes, *productivity shock*—to refer to a change in an economy's production function.[5] A positive, or beneficial, supply shock raises the amount of output that can be produced for given quantities of capital and labour. A negative, or adverse, supply shock lowers the amount of output that can be produced for each capital–labour combination.

Real-world examples of supply shocks include changes in the weather, such as a drought or an unusually cold winter; inventions or innovations in management techniques that improve efficiency, such as minicomputers or statistical analysis in quality control; and changes in government regulations, such as anti-pollution laws, that affect the technologies or production methods used. Another important real-world example concerns the ease and efficiency with which firms can access financial capital to facilitate their day-to-day operations. The recession in Canada and much of the rest of the world that began in 2007 stemmed from a financial crisis that severely restricted firms' access to financial capital and thus their ability to finance their operations. As a consequence, even with the same number of machines (capital) and workers (labour), firms were unable to produce as much output as before. The crisis in financial markets, then, precipitated a severe productivity shock. All these shocks are reflected in changes in productivity, A, which we measured for Canada in Table 3.1.

Figure 3.3 shows the effects of an adverse supply shock on the production function relating output and labour. The negative supply shock pivots the production

FIGURE 3.3

AN ADVERSE SUPPLY SHOCK THAT LOWERS THE *MPN*

An adverse supply shock is a downward pivot of the production function. For any level of labour, the amount of output that can be produced is now less than before. The adverse shock reduces the slope of the production function at every level of employment. This corresponds to a decrease in the multiplying factor A in Eq. (3.1).

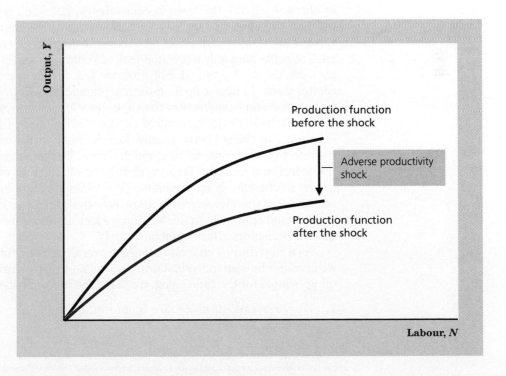

[5] The term *shock* is a slight misnomer. Not all changes in the production function are sharp or unpredictable, although many are.

function downward so that less output can be produced for specific quantities of labour and capital. In addition, the supply shock shown reduces the slope of the production function so that the output gains from adding a worker (the marginal product of labour) are lower at every level of employment.[6] Similarly, a beneficial supply shock makes possible the production of more output with given quantities of capital and labour and, thus, pivots the production function upward.[7]

The diagram of the production function, whether relating the amount of output produced to the amount of capital utilized (as in Figure 3.1) or to the amount of labour employed (as in Figure 3.2), is one of the key diagrams of macroeconomic analysis. Understanding the relationships described by these diagrams—the concept of marginal product, the assumption of diminishing marginal products of labour and of capital, and the implications of supply (or productivity) shocks—is key to understanding much of what is to come. It is key not only to understanding long-run economic performance—the subject of Part II of this book—but also for understanding business cycles and macroeconomic policy—the subject of Part III.

3.2 THE DEMAND FOR LABOUR

We have shown that the amount of output produced by a country, or by a firm, depends on both productivity and the quantities of inputs used in the production process. In Section 3.1 our focus was on productivity—its measurement and factors such as supply shocks that cause it to change. In this section, we examine what determines the quantities of inputs that producers use. Recall that the two most important inputs are capital and labour. The capital stock in an economy changes over time as a result of investment by firms and the scrapping of worn-out or obsolete capital. However, because the capital stock is long-lived and has been built up over many years, new investment and the scrapping of old capital only slowly have a significant effect on the overall quantity of capital available. Thus, for analyses spanning only a few quarters or years, economists often treat the economy's capital stock as fixed. For now, we follow this practice and assume a fixed capital stock. In taking up long-term economic growth in Chapter 6, we drop this assumption and examine how the capital stock evolves over time.

In contrast to the amount of capital, the amount of labour employed in the economy can change fairly quickly. For example, firms may lay off workers or ask them to work overtime without much notice. Workers may quit or decide to enter the workforce quickly. Thus, year-to-year changes in production can often be traced to changes in employment. To explain why employment changes, for the remainder of this chapter we focus on how the labour market works, using a supply and demand approach. In this section we look at labour demand, and in Section 3.3 we discuss factors affecting labour supply.

As a step toward understanding the overall demand for labour in the economy, we consider how an individual firm decides how many workers to employ. To keep things simple for the time being, we make the following assumptions:

1. *Workers are all alike.* We ignore differences in workers' aptitudes, skills, ambition, and so on.

---

[6] Logically, an adverse supply shock need not always reduce the marginal products of labour and capital; for example, the production function could make a parallel downward shift. However, thinking of an adverse supply shock reducing marginal products as being the normal case seems reasonable. A pivot of the production function like that shown in Figure 3.3 would occur if there were a decline in total factor productivity A, for example.

[7] The effects of supply shocks on the production function relating output and capital would be similar.

2. *Firms view the wage of the workers they hire as being determined in a competitive labour market and not set by the firms themselves.* For example, a competitive firm that wants to hire machinists knows that it must pay the going local wage for machinists if it wants to attract qualified workers. The firm then decides how many machinists to employ.

3. *In making the decision about how many workers to employ, a firm's goal is to earn the highest possible level of profit* (the value of its output minus its costs of production, including taxes). The firm will demand the amount of labour that maximizes its profit.

To figure out the profit-maximizing amount of labour, the firm must compare the costs and benefits of hiring each additional worker. The cost of an extra worker is the worker's wage, and the benefit of an extra worker is the value of the additional goods or services the worker produces. As long as the benefits of additional labour exceed the costs, hiring more labour will increase the firm's profits. The firm will continue to hire additional labour until the benefit of an extra worker (the value of extra goods or services produced) equals the cost (the wage).

THE MARGINAL PRODUCT OF LABOUR AND LABOUR DEMAND: AN EXAMPLE

Let's make the discussion of labour demand more concrete by looking at The Clip Joint, a small business that grooms dogs. The Clip Joint uses both capital, such as clippers, tubs, and brushes, and labour to produce its output of groomed dogs.

The production function that applies to The Clip Joint appears in Table 3.2. For given levels of productivity and the capital stock, it shows how The Clip Joint's daily

TABLE 3.2

The Clip Joint's Production Function

(1) Number of Workers, N	(2) Number of Dogs Groomed, Y	(3) Marginal Product of Labour, MPN	(4) Marginal Revenue Product of Labour, $MRPN = MPN \times$ (when $P = \$10$ per grooming)
0	0		
		11	$110
1	11		
		9	$90
2	20		
		7	$70
3	27		
		5	$50
4	32		
		3	$30
5	35		
		1	$10
6	36		

output of groomed dogs, column (2), depends on the number of workers employed, column (1). The more workers The Clip Joint has, the greater its daily output is.

The *MPN* of each worker at The Clip Joint is shown in column (3). Employing the first worker raises The Clip Joint's output from 0 to 11, so the *MPN* of the first worker is 11. Employing the second worker raises The Clip Joint's output from 11 to 20, an increase of 9, so the *MPN* of the second worker is 9; and so on. Column (3) also shows that as the number of workers at The Clip Joint increases, the *MPN* falls so that labour at The Clip Joint has diminishing marginal productivity. The more workers there are on the job, the more they must share the fixed amount of capital (tubs, clippers, brushes) and the less benefit there is to adding yet another worker.

The marginal product of labour measures the benefit of employing an additional worker in terms of the extra *output* produced. A related concept, the **marginal revenue product of labour**, or *MRPN*, measures the benefit of employing an additional worker in terms of the extra *revenue* produced. To calculate the *MRPN*, we need to know the price of the firm's output. If The Clip Joint receives $10 for each dog it grooms, the *MRPN* of the first worker is $110 per day (11 additional dogs groomed per day at $10 per grooming). More generally, the marginal revenue product of an additional worker equals the price of the firm's output, *P*, times the extra output gained by adding the worker, *MPN*:

$$MRPN = P \times MPN. \tag{3.3}$$

At The Clip Joint the price of output *P* is $10 per grooming, so the *MRPN* of each worker, column (4), equals the *MPN* of the worker, column (3), multiplied by $10.

Now, suppose that the wage *W* that The Clip Joint must pay to attract qualified workers is $80 per day. (We refer to the wage *W*, when measured in the conventional way in terms of today's dollars, as the nominal wage.) How many workers should The Clip Joint employ in order to maximize its profits? To answer this question, The Clip Joint compares the benefits and costs of employing each additional worker. The benefit of employing an additional worker, in dollars per day, is the worker's marginal revenue product *MRPN*. The cost of an additional worker, in dollars per day, is the nominal daily wage *W*.

Table 3.2 shows that the *MRPN* of the first worker is $110 per day, which exceeds the daily wage of $80, so employing the first worker is profitable for The Clip Joint. Adding a second worker increases The Clip Joint's profit as well because the *MRPN* of the second worker ($90 per day) also exceeds the daily wage. However, employing a third worker reduces The Clip Joint's profit because the third worker's *MRPN* of $70 per day is less than the $80 daily wage. Therefore, The Clip Joint's profit-maximizing level of employment at $80/day—equivalently, the quantity of labour demanded by The Clip Joint—is two workers.

In finding the quantity of labour demanded by The Clip Joint, we measured the benefits and costs of an extra worker in nominal, or dollar, terms. If we measure the benefits and costs of an extra worker in real terms, the results are the same. In real terms, the benefit to The Clip Joint of an extra worker is the number of extra groomings that the extra worker provides, which is the marginal product of labour, *MPN*. The real cost of adding another worker is the **real wage**, which is the wage measured in terms of units of output. Algebraically, the real wage, *w*, equals the nominal wage, *W*, divided by the price of output, *P*.

In this example, the nominal wage *W* is $80 per day and the price of output *P* is $10 per grooming, so the real wage *w* equals ($80 per day)/($10 per grooming), or 8 groomings per day. To find the profit-maximizing level of employment, The

Clip Joint compares this real cost of an additional worker with the real benefit of an additional worker, the *MPN*. The *MPN* of the first worker is 11 groomings per day, which exceeds the real wage of 8 groomings per day, so employing this worker is profitable. The second worker should also be hired, as the second worker's *MPN* of 9 groomings per day also exceeds the real wage of 8 groomings per day. However, a third worker should not be hired, as the third worker's *MPN* of 7 groomings per day is less than the real wage. The quantity of labour demanded by The Clip Joint is, therefore, two workers, which is the same result we got when we compared costs and benefits in nominal terms.

This example shows that when the benefit of an additional worker exceeds the cost of an additional worker, the firm should increase employment in order to maximize profits. Similarly, if at the firm's current employment level the benefit of the last worker employed is less than the cost of the worker, the firm should reduce employment. Summary table 2 compares benefits and costs of additional labour in both real and nominal terms. In the choice of the profit-maximizing level of employment, comparison of benefits and costs in real or nominal terms is equally valid.

A CHANGE IN THE WAGE

The Clip Joint's decision to employ two workers was based on a nominal wage of $80 per day. Now suppose that for some reason the nominal wage needed to attract qualified workers drops to $60 per day. How will the reduction in the nominal wage affect the number of workers that The Clip Joint wants to employ?

To find the answer, we can compare costs and benefits in either nominal or real terms. Let's make the comparison in real terms. If the nominal wage drops to $60 per day while the price of groomings remains at $10, the real wage falls to ($60 per day)/($10 per grooming), or 6 groomings per day. Column (3) of Table 3.2 shows that the *MPN* of the third worker is 7 groomings per day, which is now greater than the real wage. Thus, at the lower wage, expanding the quantity of labour demanded from two to three workers is profitable for The

SUMMARY 2

COMPARING THE BENEFITS AND COSTS OF CHANGING THE AMOUNT OF LABOUR

TO MAXIMIZE PROFITS, THE FIRM SHOULD	INCREASE EMPLOYMENT IF	DECREASE EMPLOYMENT IF
Real terms	$MPN > w$ $(MPN > W/P)$	$MPN < w$ $(MPN < W/P)$
Nominal terms	$P \times MPN > W$ $(MRPN > W)$	$P \times MPN < W$ $(MRPN < W)$

MPN = marginal product of labour
P = price of output
$MRPN$ = marginal revenue product of labour = $P \times MPN$
W = nominal wage
w = real wage = W/P

Clip Joint. However, the firm will not hire a fourth worker because the *MPN* of the fourth worker (5 groomings per day) is less than the new real wage (6 groomings per day).

This example illustrates a general point about the effect of the real wage on labour demand: All else being equal, *a decrease in the real wage raises the amount of labour demanded. Similarly, an increase in the real wage decreases the amount of labour demanded.*

THE MARGINAL PRODUCT OF LABOUR AND THE LABOUR DEMAND CURVE

Using The Clip Joint as an example, we showed the negative relationship between the real wage and the quantity of labour that a firm demands. Figure 3.4 shows in more general terms how the link between the real wage and the quantity of labour demanded is determined. The amount of labour *N* is on the horizontal axis. The *MPN* and the real wage, both of which are measured in goods per unit of labour, are on the vertical axis. The downward-sloping curve is the *MPN* curve; it relates the marginal product of labour, *MPN*, to the amount of labour employed by the firm, *N*. The *MPN* curve slopes downward because of the diminishing marginal productivity of labour. The horizontal line represents the real wage faced by firms in the labour market, which the firms take as given. Here, the real wage is w^*.

For any real wage w^*, the amount of labour that yields the highest profit (and therefore the amount of labour demanded) is determined at point *A*, the intersection of the real wage line and the *MPN* curve. At *A*, the quantity of labour demanded is N^*. Why is N^* a firm's profit-maximizing level of labour input? At employment levels of less than N^*, the marginal product of labour exceeds the real

FIGURE 3.4

THE DETERMINATION OF LABOUR DEMAND

The amount of labour demanded is determined by locating the point on the *MPN* curve at which the *MPN* equals the real wage rate; the amount of labour corresponding to that point is the amount of labour demanded. For example, when the real wage is w^*, the *MPN* equals the real wage at point *A* and the quantity of labour demanded is N^*. The labour demand curve, *ND*, shows the amount of labour demanded at each level of the real wage. The labour demand curve is identical to the *MPN* curve.

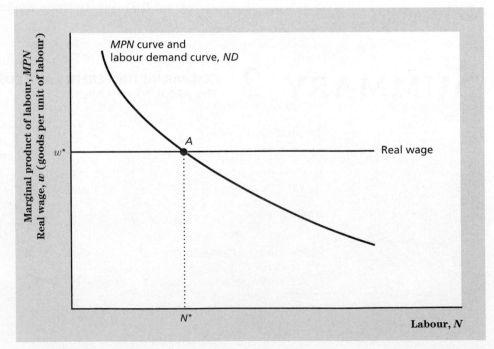

wage (the *MPN* curve lies above the real wage line); thus, if the firm's employment is initially less than N^*, it can increase its profit by expanding the amount of labour it uses. Similarly, if the firm's employment is initially greater than N^*, the marginal product of labour is less than the real wage ($MPN < w^*$) and the firm can raise profits by reducing employment. Only when employment equals N^* will the firm be satisfied with the number of workers it has. More generally, for any real wage, the profit-maximizing amount of labour input—labour demanded—corresponds to the point at which the *MPN* curve and the real wage line intersect.

The graph of the relationship between the amount of labour demanded by a firm and the real wage the firm faces is called the *labour demand curve*. Because the *MPN* curve also shows the amount of labour demanded at any real wage, *the labour demand curve is the same as the MPN curve*, except that the vertical axis measures the real wage for the labour demand curve and the marginal product of labour for the *MPN* curve.[8] Like the *MPN* curve, the labour demand curve slopes downward, indicating that the quantity of labour demanded falls as the real wage rises.

This labour demand curve is more general than that in the example of The Clip Joint in a couple of ways that are worth mentioning. First, we referred to the demand for labour and not specifically to the demand for workers, as in The Clip Joint example. In general, labour N can be measured in various ways—for example, as total hours worked, total weeks worked, or the number of employees—depending on the application. Second, although we assumed in the example that The Clip Joint had to hire a whole number of workers, the labour demand curve shown in Figure 3.4 allows labour N to have any positive value, whole or fractional. Allowing N to take any value is sensible because people may work fractions of an hour.

FACTORS THAT SHIFT THE LABOUR DEMAND CURVE

Because the labour demand curve shows the relation between the real wage and the amount of labour that firms want to employ, changes in the real wage are represented as movements *along* the labour demand curve. Changes in the real wage do not cause the labour demand curve to shift. The labour demand curve shifts in response to factors that change the amount of labour firms want to employ *at any given level of the real wage*. For example, we showed earlier in this chapter that beneficial or positive supply shocks are likely to increase the *MPN* at all levels of labour input, and adverse or negative supply shocks are likely to reduce the *MPN* at all levels of labour input. Thus, a beneficial supply shock shifts the *MPN* curve upward and to the right and raises the quantity of labour demanded at any given real wage; an adverse supply shock does the reverse.

The effect of a supply shock on The Clip Joint's demand for labour can be illustrated by imagining that the proprietor of The Clip Joint discovers that playing New Age music soothes the dogs. It makes them more cooperative and doubles the number of groomings per day that the same number of workers can produce. This technological improvement gives The Clip Joint a new production function, as described in Table 3.3. Note that doubling total output doubles the *MPN* at each employment level.

---

[8] Recall that the real wage and the *MPN* are measured in the same units, goods per unit of labour.

TABLE 3.3

The Clip Joint's Production Function after a Beneficial Productivity Shock

(1) Number of Workers, N	(2) Number of Dogs Groomed, Y	(3) Marginal Product of Labour, MPN	(4) Marginal Revenue Product of Labour, $MRPN = MPN \times P$ (when $P = \$10$ per grooming)
0	0		
		22	$220
1	22		
		18	$180
2	40		
		14	$140
3	54		
		10	$100
4	64		
		6	$ 60
5	70		
		2	$ 20
6	72		

The Clip Joint demanded two workers when faced with the original production function (Table 3.2, p. 57) and a real wage of 8 groomings per day. Table 3.3 shows that the productivity improvement increases The Clip Joint's labour demand at the given real wage to four workers because the MPN of the fourth worker (10 groomings per day) now exceeds the real wage. The Clip Joint will not hire a fifth worker, however, because this worker's MPN (6 groomings per day) is less than the real wage.

The effect of a beneficial supply shock on a labour demand curve is shown in Figure 3.5. The shock causes the MPN to increase at any level of labour input, so the MPN curve shifts upward and to the right. Because the MPN and labour demand curves are identical, the labour demand curve also shifts upward and to the right, from ND^1 to ND^2 in Figure 3.5. When the labour demand curve is ND^2, the firm hires more workers at any real wage level than when the labour demand curve is ND^1. Thus, worker productivity and the amount of labour demanded are closely linked. A reduction in payroll taxes (such as employer contributions to Employment Insurance) would have the same effect as a beneficial supply shock. This tax change would raise the after-tax marginal product of labour and, so, shift the labour demand curve to the right.

Another factor that may affect labour demand is the size of the capital stock. Generally, an increase in the capital stock K—by giving each worker more machines or equipment to work with—raises workers' productivity and increases the MPN at any level of labour. Hence an increase in the capital stock will cause the labour demand curve to shift upward and to the right, raising the amount of labour that a firm demands at any particular real wage.[9]

---

[9] An increase in the capital stock may reduce the demand for labour if the new capital substitutes for the use of labour. For example, the installation of automatic elevators reduced the marginal product of elevator operators and, thus, the demand for these workers.

FIGURE 3.5

THE EFFECT OF A BENEFICIAL SUPPLY SHOCK ON LABOUR DEMAND

A beneficial supply shock that raises the *MPN* at every level of labour shifts the *MPN* curve upward and to the right. Because the labour demand curve is identical to the *MPN* curve, the labour demand curve shifts upward and to the right from ND^1 to ND^2. For any real wage, firms demand more labour after a beneficial supply shock.

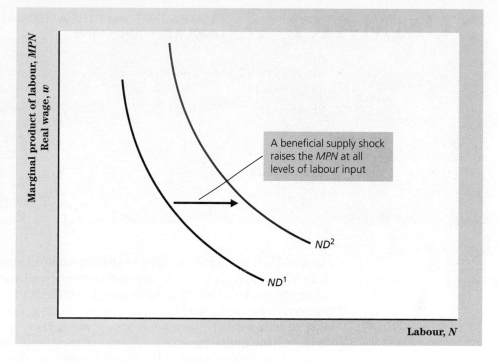

AGGREGATE LABOUR DEMAND

So far, we have focused on the demand for labour by an individual firm, such as The Clip Joint. For macroeconomic analysis, however, we usually work with the concept of the **aggregate demand for labour**, or the sum of the labour demands of all the firms in an economy.

Because the aggregate demand for labour is the sum of firms' labour demands, the factors that determine the aggregate demand for labour are the same as for an individual firm. Thus, the aggregate labour demand curve looks the same as the labour demand curve for an individual firm (see Figure 3.4, p. 60). Like the firm's labour demand curve, the aggregate labour demand curve slopes downward, showing that an increase in the economywide real wage reduces the total amount of labour that firms want to use. Similarly, a beneficial supply shock or an increase in the aggregate capital stock shifts the aggregate labour demand curve upward and to the right; an adverse supply shock or a drop in the aggregate capital stock shifts it downward and to the left. The factors affecting aggregate labour demand are listed for convenience in Summary table 3.

It is important to remember when reviewing Summary table 3 (and similar summary tables that will appear in this and other chapters) that when we discuss the effect of a change in productivity on the position of the aggregate labour demand curve, we are making the assumption that the change in productivity is the only change that has occurred. In particular, we assume there has been no change in the capital stock. Similarly, when we discuss the effect of a change in the capital stock on the position of the aggregate labour demand curve, we are making the assumption that the change in the capital stock is the only change that has occurred: We assume productivity is unchanged. Thus, in Summary table 3 we say that, *all else equal*, an increase in productivity causes the labour demand curve to shift to the right. In the

SUMMARY 3   FACTORS THAT SHIFT THE AGGREGATE LABOUR DEMAND CURVE

ALL ELSE EQUAL, AN INCREASE IN	CAUSES THE LABOUR DEMAND CURVE TO SHIFT	REASON
Productivity	Right	Beneficial supply shock increases *MPN* and shifts *MPN* curve up and to the right.
Capital stock	Right	Higher capital stock increases *MPN* and shifts *MPN* curve up and to the right.

real world it is rare for economists to observe such "all else equal" changes. Factors that shift the aggregate labour demand curve often change simultaneously. If both the capital stock and productivity change, it is difficult to identify which change was responsible for the shift of the labour demand curve. For that reason, economists must perform what are often referred to as *thought experiments* in which they ask what is usually only a hypothetical question: How would the value of one economic variable change in response to the change in just one other variable? Summary table 3 presents the results of two such thought experiments.

3.3 THE SUPPLY OF LABOUR

The demand for labour is determined by firms, but the supply of labour is determined by individuals or members of a family making a joint decision. Each person of working age must decide how much (if at all) to work in the wage-paying sector of the economy versus non–wage-paying alternatives, such as taking care of the home and children, going to school, or being retired. The **aggregate supply of labour** is the sum of the labour supplied by everyone in the economy.

Recall that in determining how much labour to demand, firms compare the costs and benefits of hiring additional workers. Similarly, in deciding how much to work, an individual weighs the benefits against the costs of working. Beyond any psychological satisfaction gained from having a job, the principal benefit of working is the income earned, which can be used to buy necessities and luxuries. The principal cost of working is that it involves time and effort that are no longer available for other activities. Economists use the term **leisure**[10] for all off-the-job activities, including eating, working around the house, spending time with family and friends, and so on. To make themselves as well off as possible, individuals choose to supply labour up to the point at which the income obtained from working an extra hour just makes up for the extra hour of leisure they have to forgo.

THE INCOME–LEISURE TRADE-OFF

To illustrate how the trade-off between income and leisure affects the labour supply decision, let's look at an example. Consider a tennis instructor named Ace who

---

[10] The term *leisure* does not imply that all off-the-job activities (housework or schoolwork, for example) are "leisurely"!

offers tennis lessons. After paying taxes and job-related expenses, Ace can earn $35 per hour, which we will call his (after-tax) nominal wage rate. Ace enjoys a reputation as an outstanding tennis instructor and could work as many hours per year as he chooses. He is reluctant to work too much, however, because every day he spends teaching tennis means one less day available to devote to his real passion, skydiving. The decision Ace faces is how many hours to work this year—or, in other words, how much labour to supply.

Ace approaches this question by asking himself: Economically speaking, what really makes me happy? After a little reflection, Ace concludes that his level of happiness, or *utility*, depends on the amount of goods and services he consumes and on the amount of leisure time he has available to jump out of airplanes. His question can, therefore, be recast as follows: How much should I work this year so as to obtain the highest possible level of utility?

To find the level of labour supply that maximizes his utility, Ace must compare the costs and benefits of working an extra hour. The cost of an extra hour of work is the loss of an hour of leisure; this cost can be measured as the loss in utility that Ace experiences when he must work for an hour instead of skydive. The benefit of working an extra hour is an increase of $35 in income, which allows Ace to enjoy more consumption.

If the benefit of working an extra hour (the utility gained from extra income) exceeds the cost (the utility lost by reducing leisure), Ace should work the extra hour. In fact, he should continue to increase his time at work until the utility he receives from the additional income of $35 just equals the loss of utility associated with missing an hour of leisure. Ace's labour supply at that point is the one that maximizes his utility.[11] Using the idea that the labour supply decision results from a trade-off of leisure against income, we can discuss factors that influence the amount of labour supplied by Ace.

REAL WAGES AND LABOUR SUPPLY

The real wage is the amount of real income that a worker receives in exchange for giving up a unit of leisure (an hour, a day, or a week, for example) for work. It is an important determinant of the quantity of labour that is supplied.

Generally, an increase in the real wage affects the labour supply decision in two ways. First, an increase in the real wage raises the benefit (in additional real income) of working an additional hour and, thus, tends to make the worker want to supply more labour. The tendency of workers to supply more labour in response to a higher reward for working is called the **substitution effect of a higher real wage** on the quantity of labour supplied.

Second, an increase in the real wage makes workers effectively wealthier because, for the same amount of work, they now earn a higher real income. Someone who is wealthier will be better able to afford additional leisure and, as a result, will supply less labour. The tendency of workers to supply less labour in response to becoming wealthier is called the **income effect of a higher real wage** on the quantity of labour supplied. Note that the substitution and income effects of a higher real wage operate in opposite directions, with the substitution effect tending to raise the quantity of labour supplied and the income effect tending to reduce it.

---

[11] Not everyone can choose his or her labour supply as flexibly as Ace; for example, some jobs are available for 40 hours a week or not at all. Nevertheless, by choosing to work overtime, part time, or at a second job, or by varying the number of family members who are working, households do have a significant amount of latitude over how much labour to supply.

A Pure Substitution Effect: A One-Day Rise in the Real Wage

We can illustrate the substitution effect by supposing that after some consideration, Ace decides to work 48 hours per week, by working eight hours per day for six days each week. He leaves every Wednesday free to go skydiving. Although Ace could work and earn $35 per hour each Wednesday, his highest utility is obtained by taking leisure on that day instead.

Now imagine that one Tuesday, an eccentric tennis player calls Ace and requests a lesson on Wednesday to help him prepare for a weekend amateur tournament. He offers Ace his regular wage of $35 per hour, but Ace declines, explaining that he plans to go skydiving on Wednesday. Not willing to take no for an answer, the tennis player then offers to pay Ace $350 per hour for an all-day lesson on Wednesday. When Ace hears this offer to work for 10 times his usual wage rate, he thinks: "I don't get offers like this one every day. I'll go skydiving some other day, but this Wednesday I'm going to work."

Ace's decision to work rather than skydive (that is, to substitute labour for leisure) on this particular Wednesday represents a response to a very high reward, in terms of additional income, that each additional hour of work on that day will bring. His decision to work the extra day results from the substitution effect. Because receiving a very high wage for only one day does not make Ace substantially wealthier, the income effect of the one-day wage increase is negligible. Thus, the effect of a one-day increase in the real wage on the quantity of labour supplied by Ace is an almost pure example of the substitution effect.

A Pure Income Effect: Winning the Lottery

In addition to skydiving, Ace enjoys playing the provincial lottery. As luck would have it, a week after spending the Wednesday teaching the eccentric tennis player, Ace wins $300 000 in the lottery. Ace's response is to reduce his workweek from six to five days, because the additional $300 000 of wealth enables him to afford to take more time off from work—and so he does. Because the lottery prize has made him wealthier, he reduces his labour supply. As the lottery prize does not affect the current reward for giving up an hour of leisure to work—Ace's real wage is still $35 per hour—there is no substitution effect. Thus, winning the lottery is an example of a pure income effect.

Another example of a pure income effect is an increase in the expected future real wage. Suppose that the aging tennis pro at the posh country club in Ace's community announces that he will retire the following year, and the country club agrees to hire Ace beginning one year from now. Ace will earn $50 per hour (after taxes) for as many hours as he wants to teach tennis.[12] Ace recognizes that this increase in his future wage has effectively made him wealthier by increasing the future income he will receive for any given amount of labour supplied. Looking at his lifetime income, Ace realizes that he is better able to afford leisure today. That is, the increase in the future real wage has an income effect that leads Ace to reduce his current labour supply. Because this increase in the future wage does not change Ace's current wage and, thus, does not affect the current reward for giving up an hour of leisure to work an additional hour, there is no substitution effect on Ace's current labour supply. Thus, the increase in the future real wage has a pure income effect on Ace's labour supply.

---

[12] We assume that zero inflation is expected over the next year, so the $50 per hour wage rate in the following year is an increase in Ace's real wage rate as well as an increase in his nominal wage rate.

The Substitution Effect and the Income Effect Together: A Long-Term Increase in the Real Wage

The aging tennis pro at the country club quits suddenly, and the country club asks Ace to start work immediately. Ace accepts the offer and earns $50 per hour (after taxes) for as many hours as he wants to teach tennis.

In his new job, will Ace work more hours or fewer hours than he did before? In this case, the two effects work in opposite directions. On the one hand, because the reward for working is greater, Ace will be tempted to work more than he did previously. This tendency to increase labour supply in response to a higher real wage is the substitution effect. On the other hand, at his new, higher wage, Ace can pay for food, rent, and skydiving expenses by working only three or four days each week, so he is tempted to work less and spend more time skydiving. This tendency to reduce labour supply because he is wealthier is the income effect.

Which effect wins? One factor that will influence Ace's decision is the length of time he expects his new, higher wage to last. The longer the higher wage is expected to last, the larger its impact on Ace's lifetime resources and the stronger the income effect. Thus, if Ace expects to hold the new job until he retires, the income effect is strong (he is much wealthier) and he is more likely to reduce the amount of time he works. In contrast, if Ace believes that the job may not last very long, the income effect is weak (the increase in his lifetime resources is small) and he may choose to work more so as to take advantage of the higher wage while he can. In general, the longer an increase in the real wage is expected to last, the larger the income effect and the more likely that the quantity of labour supplied will be reduced.

Empirical Evidence on Real Wages and Labour Supply

Because of conflicting income and substitution effects, there is some ambiguity about how a real wage change will affect labour supply. What is the empirical evidence?

Research on labour supply generally shows that the aggregate amount of labour supplied rises in response to a temporary increase in the real wage but falls in response to a permanent increase in the real wage. The finding that a temporary increase in the real wage raises the amount of labour supplied confirms the substitution effect: If the reward for working rises for a short period, people will take advantage of the opportunity to work more. The result that a permanent increase in the real wage lowers the aggregate amount of labour supplied indicates that for long-lived increases in the real wage the income effect outweighs the substitution effect: If permanently higher wages make workers much better off, they will choose to work less. The size of these effects depends on a person's family situation (married or not, whether the family has children or older parents to care for, and so on) and the tax rate (which determines how much income can be kept after taxes are paid).

THE LABOUR SUPPLY CURVE

We have discussed how the amount of labour supplied by an individual depends on the current and expected future real wage rates. The *labour supply curve* of an individual worker relates the amount of labour supplied to the current real wage, with other factors (including the expected future real wage) held constant.

FIGURE 3.6

THE LABOUR SUPPLY CURVE OF AN INDIVIDUAL WORKER

The horizontal axis shows the amount of labour that a worker will supply for any given current real wage on the vertical axis. The labour supply curve slopes upward, indicating that, with other factors including the expected future real wage held constant, an increase in the current real wage raises the amount of labour supplied.

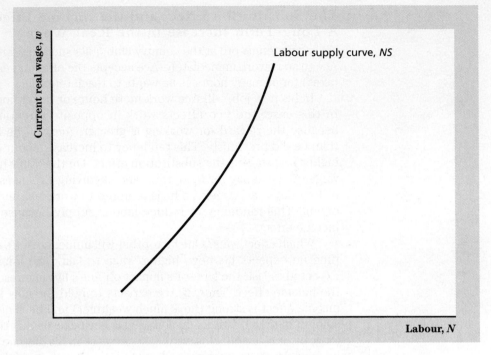

Figure 3.6 is a graph of a typical labour supply curve. The current real wage is measured on the vertical axis, and the amount of labour supplied is measured on the horizontal axis. The labour supply curve slopes upward because an increase in the current real wage leads to an increase in the amount of labour supplied.

FACTORS THAT SHIFT THE LABOUR SUPPLY CURVE

Any factor that changes the amount of labour supplied at a given level of the current real wage shifts the labour supply curve. Specifically, any factor that increases the amount of labour supplied at a given level of the real wage shifts the labour supply curve to the right, and any factor that decreases the amount of labour supplied at a given level of the real wage shifts the labour supply curve to the left. We have already discussed how an increase in wealth (say, from winning the lottery) has a pure income effect that reduces the amount of labour supplied at a given real wage. Thus, as shown in Figure 3.7, an increase in wealth shifts the labour supply curve to the left. We also have discussed how an increase in the expected future real wage has a pure income effect that reduces the amount of labour supplied at a given real wage. Figure 3.7 also depicts the response of the labour supply curve to an increase in the expected future real wage.

AGGREGATE LABOUR SUPPLY

As we mentioned earlier, the aggregate supply of labour is the total amount of labour supplied by everyone in the economy. Just as the quantity of labour

FIGURE 3.7

THE EFFECT ON LABOUR SUPPLY OF AN INCREASE IN WEALTH

An increase in wealth reduces the amount of labour supplied at any real wage. Therefore, an increase in wealth causes the labour supply curve to shift to the left. Similarly, an increase in the expected future real wage, which has the effect of making the worker wealthier, reduces the amount of labour supplied at any given current real wage and shifts the labour supply curve to the left.

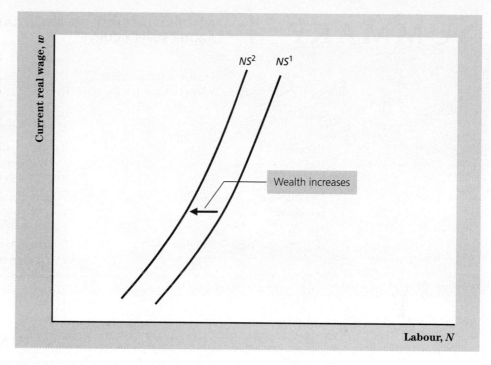

supplied by an individual rises when the person's current real wage rises, the aggregate quantity of labour supplied increases when the economywide real wage rises. An increase in the current economywide real wage raises the aggregate quantity of labour supplied for two reasons. First, when the real wage rises, people who are already working may supply even more hours—by offering to work overtime, by changing from part time to full-time work, or by taking a second job. Second, a higher real wage may entice some people who are not currently in the labour force to decide to look for work. Because higher current real wages induce people to want to work more, the aggregate labour supply curve—which shows the relation between the aggregate amount of labour supplied and the current real wage—slopes upward.

Factors other than the current real wage that change the amount of labour people want to supply cause the aggregate labour supply curve to shift. Summary table 4 lists the factors that shift aggregate labour supply. We discussed the first two factors in the table—wealth and the expected future real wage—when we considered the individual's labour supply decision. Aggregate labour supply will also increase if, all else equal, the country's working-age population increases (for example, because of an increased birth rate or immigration), or if changes in the social or legal environment cause a greater proportion of the working-age population to enter the labour force (increased labour force participation). For example, evolving attitudes about the role of women in society contributed to a large increase in the number of women in the Canadian labour market from the late 1960s to the mid-1990s; and the elimination of mandatory retirement in many fields might increase the participation rates of older workers.

SUMMARY 4

FACTORS THAT SHIFT THE AGGREGATE LABOUR SUPPLY CURVE

ALL ELSE EQUAL, AN INCREASE IN	CAUSES THE LABOUR SUPPLY CURVE TO SHIFT	REASON
Wealth	Left	Increase in wealth increases amount of leisure workers can afford.
Expected future real wage	Left	Increase in expected future real wage increases amount of leisure workers can afford.
Working-age population	Right	Increased number of potential workers increases amount of labour supplied.
Participation rate	Right	Increased number of people wanting to work increases amount of labour supplied.

3.4 LABOUR MARKET EQUILIBRIUM

Equilibrium in the labour market requires that the aggregate quantity of labour demanded equal the aggregate quantity of labour supplied. The basic supply–demand model of the labour market is summarized in Figure 3.8. Labour market equilibrium is represented graphically by the intersection of the aggregate labour demand curve *ND* and the aggregate labour supply curve *NS* at point *E*. The equilibrium of labour demand and labour supply determines a level of employment and a real wage that satisfies both sides of the labour market: labour suppliers (workers) and labour demanders (firms). The real wage at that equilibrium is just

FIGURE 3.8

LABOUR MARKET EQUILIBRIUM

The quantity of labour demanded equals the quantity of labour supplied at point *E*. The equilibrium real wage is $\overline{w}$, and the corresponding equilibrium level of employment is $\overline{N}$, the full-employment level of employment.

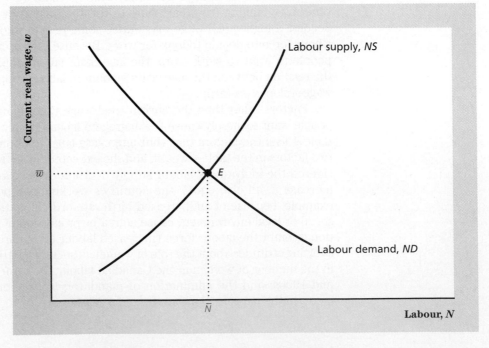

sufficient that workers receive exactly the compensation they require for them to surrender leisure. At the equilibrium real wage, firms have hired a sufficient number of workers such that the marginal benefit of the last worker hired exactly equals the marginal cost of hiring that worker.

If the real wage did not simultaneously satisfy both sides of the labour market, there would be disequilibrium. In disequilibrium, the level of employment is not sustainable because one side of the labour market—either labour demanders or labour suppliers—is unhappy with it. Either firms are unable to equate the marginal cost to the marginal benefit of the last worker hired, or workers are finding that they are unable to equate the value of their leisure to the real wage. In responding to their dissatisfaction with the current level of employment, workers and firms cause the real wage to adjust until such time as we establish equilibrium at a point such as E in Figure 3.8.

Whether, and how quickly, the market adjusts to establish equilibrium is central to much of macroeconomic analysis. For that reason, the supply–demand model of the labour market summarized in Figure 3.8 is one of the key diagrams of macroeconomic analysis. An assumption we introduce here is that the real wage adjusts to balance labour supply and labour demand. Thus, if labour supply is less than labour demand, firms competing for scarce workers bid up the real wage, whereas if many workers are competing for relatively few jobs, the real wage will tend to fall. All economists accept this description of labour market adjustment. They differ only with respect to how quickly this adjustment occurs. Since our focus in this, Part II of the text, is on long-run economic performance, it is appropriate for us to assume that the real wage has adjusted to equate labour demand and labour supply. This assumption describes what is called the *classical model of the labour market*. In Part III of the text, when we turn our attention to explaining short-run economic fluctuations, we will return to the model of labour demand and supply to show the implications of assuming that the wage is slow to adjust to equate labour demand and labour supply.

In the classical model of the labour market, the equilibrium level of employment, achieved after the complete adjustment of wages and prices, is known as the **full-employment level of employment**, $\overline{N}$. The corresponding market-clearing real wage is $\overline{w}$.

Factors that shift either the aggregate labour demand curve or the aggregate labour supply curve affect both the equilibrium real wage and the full-employment level of employment. An example of such a factor is a temporary adverse supply, or productivity shock. A temporary adverse supply shock—because of, say, a spell of unusually bad weather—decreases the marginal product of labour at every level of employment. As Figure 3.9 shows, this decrease causes the labour demand curve to shift to the left, from ND^1 to ND^2. Because the supply shock is temporary, however, it is not expected to affect future marginal products or the future real wage, so the labour supply curve does not shift. Equilibrium in the labour market moves from point A to point B. Thus, the model predicts that a temporary supply shock will lower both the current real wage (from $\overline{w}_1$ to $\overline{w}_2$) and the full-employment level of employment (from $\overline{N}_1$ to $\overline{N}_2$).

The classical supply–demand model of the labour market has the virtue of simplicity and is quite useful for studying how economic disturbances or changes in economic policy affect employment and the real wage. However, a significant drawback of this basic model is that it cannot be used to study unemployment. Because it assumes that any worker who wants to work at the equilibrium real wage can find a job, the model implies zero unemployment, which never occurs. We discuss unemployment later in this chapter, but in the meantime we will continue to use the classical supply–demand model of the labour market.

FIGURE 3.9

EFFECTS OF A TEMPORARY
ADVERSE SUPPLY SHOCK ON
THE LABOUR MARKET

An adverse supply shock that lowers the marginal product of labour
(see Figure 3.3, p. 55) reduces the
quantity of labour demanded at
any real wage level. Thus, the
labour demand curve shifts left,
from ND^1 to ND^2, and the labour
market equilibrium moves from
point A to point B. The adverse
supply shock causes the real wage
to fall from $\bar{w}_1$ to $\bar{w}_2$ and reduces
the full-employment level of
employment from $\bar{N}_1$ to $\bar{N}_2$.

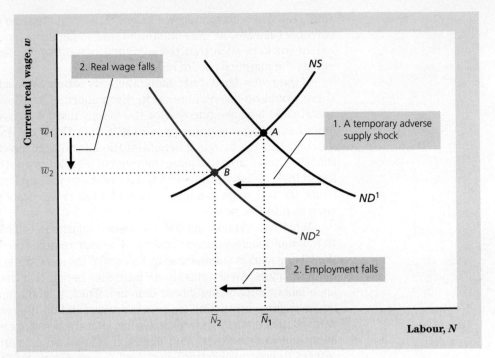

APPLICATION

OUTPUT, EMPLOYMENT, AND THE REAL WAGE DURING OIL PRICE SHOCKS

Oil has for many years been an important input into industrial production. Figure 3.10 shows how the industrial price of petroleum sold in Canada, measured both in nominal and in real 2007 dollars, has fluctuated from 1886 to 2016. The real price of petroleum has historically been the subject of wide swings. At various times over the past 130 years, the real price has shot upward and plummeted downward. Price fixing by oil producers has been the major reason for price increases. This was the case in 1903 when Shell and Standard Oil controlled the world market for oil between them; in the late 1920s when the so-called "Seven Sisters" (Shell, BP, Gulf, Texaco, Chevron, Mobil, and Exxon) agreed to limit competition; and in 1973, 1979, and 1998 when the Organization of the Petroleum Exporting Countries (OPEC) curtailed production so as to drive up price. Prices have plummeted when major new oil fields have been discovered. In particular, following the discovery of the East Texas field in 1931, discoveries of large oil fields in the Middle East in 1938, and the discovery of the Leduc field in Alberta in 1947, the real price of oil fell to all-time lows in the 1950s and 1960s. Political turmoil in the Middle East and in other major oil-producing countries such as Nigeria and Venezuela has also contributed to the volatility in oil prices. That turmoil, plus the rapid growth of countries like India and China, is generally understood to have fuelled the increase in the world demand for oil and is in large part behind the dramatic price increases between 2000 and 2014. Since that time, however, a new production process called "fracking" has enabled the development of new sources of oil and this has resulted in another large fall in the price.

FIGURE 3.10

NOMINAL AND REAL PRICES OF OIL, 1886–2016

This figure shows the price of a barrel of oil available in Edmonton. The nominal price is divided by the GDP price deflator for Canada to produce the real price. Note how price increases are associated with industry concentration and with efforts by producers to fix price. Price decreases are associated with important new discoveries of oil pools and with the collapse of price fixing arrangements.

Sources: Authors' calculations.

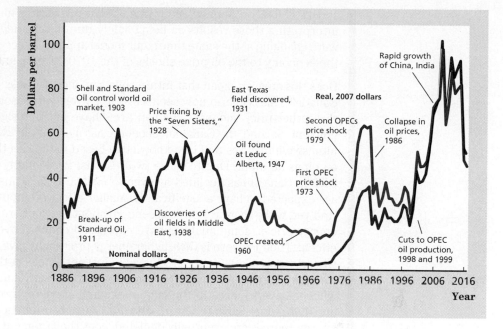

In Canada, oil price increases benefit oil-producing firms and their employees, as well as governments (such as those of Alberta, Saskatchewan, and Newfoundland and Labrador) that earn significant amounts of revenue from oil royalties. Periodic collapses in oil prices similarly harm these same groups. The reverse is true for firms and their employees that use oil as an input into their production process. Increases in oil prices increase the cost of production, causing such firms to cut back on energy use. As a result, less output is produced at any particular levels of capital and labour. Since more firms in Canada use petroleum as an input in the production process than produce oil as an output, increases in energy prices have generally been viewed as an adverse supply shock for the Canadian economy as a whole.

In recent years, however, high oil prices have prompted a huge expansion in both the number and size of firms extracting oil from Alberta's oil sands, and have provided the incentives for firms to pursue efforts to extract oil off the coast of Newfoundland and Labrador. These investments have resulted in remarkable employment growth in Alberta and elsewhere—in this sense, it may be the case that the dramatic increase in oil prices since 1998 has acted as a beneficial demand shock to the Canadian economy.

How important have shocks to oil prices been to the Canadian economy? When the first OPEC oil price shocks occurred in 1973 and 1979, they struck a Canadian economy that had grown reliant on the low prices of oil during the 1950s and 1960s. Canadian firms were paying little attention to energy conservation and relied on oil-intensive production processes. As a result, the OPEC price shocks imposed large costs on firms using oil as an input; they represented large adverse supply shocks to the Canadian economy.

Our analysis predicts that an adverse supply shock will lower labour demand, reducing employment and the real wage as well as reducing the supply of output. In Canada, the economy went into recession following the 1973, 1979, and 2008 oil shocks.[13] Real output and employment fell in all cases. While care must be taken in interpreting these results as being solely due to oil price shocks (other factors were changing at the same time), our model appears to account for the response of the economy to the oil price shocks of the 1970s, 1980s, and 1990s.

Does this analysis mean that future spikes in energy prices will cause recessions in Canada? This scenario now seems less likely for two reasons. First, in response to the earlier price shocks, Canadian firms have become significantly more energy efficient. Second, the Canadian economy has also shifted away from heavy, energy-intensive industries and into knowledge-based industries that rely far less heavily on oil as an input. Due to these two reasons, total energy use as a percentage of GDP in Canada has declined by over 25% since 1978. Thus, increases in oil prices are expected to have a significantly smaller effect on input costs than previously. And yet, while there is now less concern about the short-run impacts of changes in energy prices, some analysts have expressed concern over possible longer-term effects. Their concern is that higher energy prices may give rise to "Dutch disease," whereby growth in energy-producing industries comes at the expense of manufacturing industries. According to this view, manufacturing industries in Ontario and Quebec have suffered in the face of expanding energy projects in Newfoundland and Labrador, Saskatchewan, and particularly Alberta. When non-renewable energy sources are eventually depleted, goes the argument, the country will be left without either the energy sector or a manufacturing sector. The evidence of the "Dutch disease" phenomenon in Canada has, however, proved difficult to find.[14]

APPLICATION

TECHNOLOGICAL CHANGE AND WAGE INEQUALITY

Because many families have little income other than wage income, trends in real wages have important implications for the standard of living of a large segment of society. During the 25 years after World War II, real wages in Canada grew strongly. Since about 1970, however, overall real wage growth has slowed considerably. What's more, real wages have become more unequal, with wages of the best-paid workers continuing to rise at a faster rate than those of the worst-paid workers.

Trends in income inequality are illustrated in Table 3.4. The table shows, for selected years, the percentages of employed people (including part-time workers) earning incomes of less than $40 000 per year, between $40 000 and $59 999 per year, and over $60 000 per year, measured in constant (2011) dollars. The table also breaks these percentages down by sex.

If real wages were growing for all groups, then the percentage of people earning under $40 000 per year would decline steadily. Instead, we see that the percentage of those earning under $40 000 has remained more or less constant since 1980. The percentage of people earning in the middle bracket—between $40 000 and $59 999

---

[13] In Chapter 8 we present data describing the extent of these recessions and the impact they had on a number of macroeconomic variables.

[14] For a recent contribution to this debate, see Stephen Gordon, "The Canadian Manufacturing Sector, 2002–2008: Why Is It Called Dutch Disease?," *SPP Research Papers*, The School of Public Policy, Volume 6, Issue 26, September 2013.

TABLE 3.4

Wage Inequality Since 1980

Constant (2011) dollar earnings, all workers

	Under $40 000			$40 000–$59 999			Over $60 000		
	Women (%)	Men (%)	Both sexes (%)	Women (%)	Men (%)	Both sexes (%)	Women (%)	Men (%)	Both sexes (%)
1980	83.1	46.3	61.5	12.4	26.4	20.6	4.5	27.3	17.9
1990	78.9	52.7	64.6	14.4	20.8	17.9	6.7	26.3	17.4
2000	74.5	52.6	62.8	15.4	19.8	17.8	10.1	27.6	19.5
2010	69.0	53.8	61.0	16.6	17.1	16.9	14.5	29.1	22.2

Source: Statistics Canada, Wage Inequality Since 1980, 2016. Reproduced and distributed on an "as is" basis with the permission of Statistics Canada.

per year—has declined steadily, while the percentage of people earning over $60 000 per year has increased substantially.

The experiences of men and women differ quite considerably. The percentage of women earning less than $40 000 per year has fallen substantially while the percentage of men earning this amount has increased. On the other hand, the percentage of women earning between $40 000 and $59 999 per year has increased while the percentage of men earning in this income bracket has fallen. The most dramatic difference between the sexes is with respect to those earning in excess of $60 000 per year: The percentage of women earning incomes in this bracket has increased by more than three times while the percentage of men earning in this bracket has increased only slightly.

The figures in Table 3.4 suggest that the ratio of women's wages to men's wages—sometimes called the earnings ratio—has risen steadily. Wage inequality between the sexes has therefore declined. Most explanations of this trend focus on changes in labour supply, particularly the increased participation of women in the full-time labour force. While an increase in labour supply tends to lower the real wage, increased full-time job experience tends to raise the real wage by raising productivity.

The explanations offered by most economists for the increase in the percentage of those earning higher incomes tend to focus on the pattern of technological change. In particular, they argue that technological change during the past two decades has been *skill-biased*, meaning that it has raised the productivity of highly trained or educated workers more than that of the less skilled. For example, some new manufacturing techniques rely considerably more on worker initiative and problem solving than did the traditional assembly-line approach and, thus, require better-skilled workers. Computerization is another development that has, in many cases, increased the productivity of more skilled workers while squeezing out those without the education or training to use this new tool effectively. It is interesting to note that the evidence presented in Table 3.4 suggests that women, more than men, have benefited from changes that reward skill-biased technological change.

Figure 3.11 illustrates the labour market effects of a skill-biased technological change. Here, we drop the simplifying assumption made earlier that all workers are

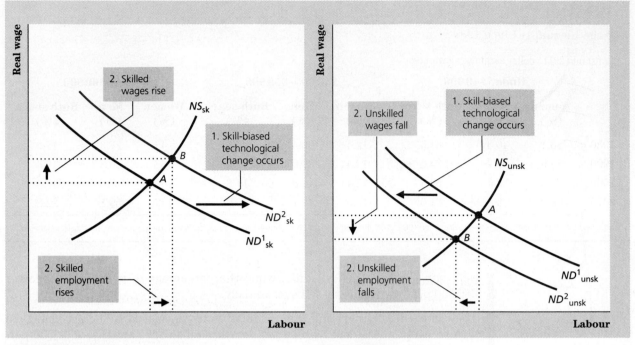

(a) Skilled workers   **(b) Unskilled workers**

FIGURE 3.11

THE EFFECTS OF SKILL-BIASED TECHNOLOGICAL CHANGE ON WAGE INEQUALITY

The supply and demand for skilled labour is shown in (a), and the supply and demand for unskilled labour is shown in (b). The initial equilibrium is shown as point A in both parts. Because skilled workers have a higher MPN than unskilled workers, their real wage is higher. A skill-biased technological change increases the MPN of skilled workers relative to the MPN of unskilled workers. A rise in the MPN of skilled workers raises the demand from ND^1_{sk} to ND^2_{sk} in (a). If the MPN of unskilled workers actually falls, demand for unskilled labour falls, from ND^1_{unsk} to ND^2_{unsk} in (b). At the new equilibrium, point B in both parts, the wages of skilled workers have risen relative to those of unskilled workers.

identical and instead allow for two types of workers, skilled and unskilled.[15] Supply and demand for each type of worker are shown separately, with the market for skilled workers shown in Figure 3.11(a) and the market for unskilled workers shown in Figure 3.11(b). The supply of each type of worker reflects the number of people in the labour force with each level of skills. For simplicity, and to focus on the effects of a skill-biased technological change, we ignore population growth and changing participation rates and assume that the labour supply curves are fixed. The demand for each type of worker depends on the MPN of that type of worker, assuming a given capital stock and assuming a given number of employed workers of the other type.

The initial labour demand curves are ND^1_{sk} in Figure 3.11(a) and ND^1_{unsk} in Figure 3.11(b), and the initial labour market equilibrium is at point A in both parts. The real wages of skilled workers are higher than those of unskilled workers (that is, the equilibrium real wage at point A in Figure 3.11(a) is higher than the equilibrium real wage at point A in Figure 3.11(b)). This difference reflects the higher MPN and lower supply of skilled workers relative to unskilled workers.

---

[15] With two types of workers, there are three factors of production: capital, skilled labour, and unskilled labour. The production function thus becomes $Y = AF(K, N_{sk}, N_{unsk})$, where N_{sk} is the number of skilled and N_{unsk} the number of unskilled workers employed. A skill-biased technological change changes the function F so that the marginal product of skilled workers rises relative to the marginal product of unskilled workers.

A skill-biased technological change, such as the introduction of computers, raises the *MPN* of skilled workers (who can accomplish more with the aid of a computer than they could without one) but reduces the *MPN* of unskilled workers (who do not have the training to be productive in a computerized workplace). Because the *MPN* curve and the demand curve for labour are the same, this technological change raises the demand for skilled workers (from ND^1_{sk} to ND^2_{sk} in Figure 3.11(a)), but reduces the demand for unskilled workers (from ND^1_{unsk} to ND^2_{unsk} in Figure 3.11(b)). At the new equilibrium, at point *B* in both parts, skilled workers' real wages and employment have risen, and the wages and employment of the unskilled have fallen. The increased wage inequality predicted by this analysis is consistent with the facts. It also appears to be true that the fraction of employment composed of skilled workers has increased, while the fraction composed of unskilled workers has decreased.[16]

FULL-EMPLOYMENT OUTPUT

By combining labour market equilibrium and the production function, we can determine how much output firms want to supply. **Full-employment output**, $\overline{Y}$, sometimes called *potential output*, is the level of output that firms in the economy supply when wages and prices have fully adjusted. Equivalently, full-employment output is the level of output supplied when aggregate employment equals its full-employment level $\overline{N}$. Algebraically, we can define full-employment output $\overline{Y}$ by using the production function, Eq. (3.1):

$$\overline{Y} = AF(K, \overline{N}) \qquad (3.4)$$

Equation (3.4) shows that, for constant capital stock K, full-employment output is determined by two general factors: the full-employment level of employment $\overline{N}$ and the production function relating output to employment.

Anything that changes either the full-employment level of employment $\overline{N}$ or the production function will change full-employment output $\overline{Y}$. For example, an adverse supply shock that reduces the *MPN* (see Figure 3.9, p. 72) works in two distinct ways to lower full-employment output:

1. The adverse supply shock lowers output directly, by reducing the quantity of output that can be produced with any fixed amounts of capital and labour. This direct effect can be thought of as a reduction in the productivity measure *A* in Eq. (3.4).

2. The adverse supply shock reduces the demand for labour and, thus, lowers the full-employment level of employment $\overline{N}$, as Figure 3.9 shows. A reduction in $\overline{N}$ also reduces full-employment output $\overline{Y}$, as Eq. (3.4) confirms.

---

[16] A complication not shown in Figure 3.11 arises if workers expect the skill bias of technological change to be permanent. In that case, skilled workers expect both their current and future wages to rise, which shifts their labour supply curve to the left; expected declines in the future wage of the unskilled shifts their labour supply curve to the right. This complication may reverse the predictions of the analysis about employment, but it only reinforces the main conclusion drawn here, that skilled workers' wages rise relative to those of unskilled workers. A second complication is that unskilled workers may respond to lower relative wages by acquiring skills through training. This response would reduce the supply of unskilled labour and increase the supply of skilled labour, reducing wage inequality. This adjustment seems to be very slow, however.

3.5 UNEMPLOYMENT

Our classical model of the labour market, which relies on supply–demand analysis, is useful for studying the wage rate and the level of employment in an economy and for showing how these variables are linked to output and productivity. However, this model of the labour market is based on the strong assumption that when the labour market is in equilibrium, all workers who are willing to work at the prevailing wage are able to find jobs. In reality, of course, not everyone who would like to work has a job; there is always some unemployment. The existence of unemployment implies that, at any time, not all of society's labour resources are actively involved in producing goods and services.

We discuss the problem of unemployment several times in this book, notably in Chapter 13. Here, we introduce the topic by presenting some basic facts about unemployment and then turning to a preliminary economic analysis of it.

MEASURING UNEMPLOYMENT

In order to estimate the unemployment rate in Canada, each month Statistics Canada surveys about 54 000 households. Each person over 15 years old in the surveyed households is assigned to one of three categories:

1. *Employed*, if the person worked full time or part time during the past week (or was on sick leave, on vacation, or on strike)

2. *Unemployed*, if the person was without work during the past week, had actively sought work in the past four weeks, and was available for work

3. *Not in the labour force*, if the person did not work during the past week and did not look for work during the past four weeks (examples are full-time students, retirees, and homemakers)

Table 3.5 shows the number of people in each category in 2016. In that year there were, on average, 18.1 million employed and 1.4 million unemployed workers. The **labour force** consists of all employed and unemployed workers, so on

TABLE 3.5

Employment Status of the Canadian Adult Population, 2016

Category	Number (millions)	Share of Labour Force %	Share of Adult Population %
Employed workers	18.1	92.8	61.1 (employment ratio)
Unemployed workers	1.4	7.2 (unemployment rate)	4.7
Labour force (employed + unemployed workers)	19.5	100.0	65.9 (participation rate)
Not in labour force	10.1		34.1
Adult population (labour force + not in labour force)	29.6		100.0

Data are seasonally adjusted.
Source: Adapted from Statistics Canada, 2017. This does not constitute an endorsement by Statistics Canada of this product.

average in 2016, it totalled 19.5 million workers (18.1 million employed plus 1.4 million unemployed). The working-age population in 2016 was 29.6 million, which leaves 10.1 million adults not in the labour force (total adult population of 29.6 million less 19.5 million in the labour force).[17]

Useful measures of the labour market include the unemployment rate, the participation rate, and the employment ratio. The **unemployment rate** is the fraction of the labour force that is unemployed. During 2016, the unemployment rate averaged 7.2% (1.4 million unemployed divided by 19.5 million in the labour force).

The fraction of the working-age population in the labour force is the **participation rate**. Of the 29.6 million working-age people in Canada in 2016, 19.5 million were in the labour force, so the participation rate was 65.9%. In contrast, the participation rate in 1976 was 61.5%. The increase is due in part to a rise in the participation rate of women, from 45% to 64%. During the same period, the participation rate of men fell from 78% to 72%.

The **employment ratio** is the employed fraction of the working-age population. In 2016, the employment rate was 61.1% (18.1 million employed divided by the working-age population of 29.6 million). With an employment ratio of 61.1%, 38.9% of the adult population was not employed in 2016. Of this 38.9%, 4.7% reflected unemployment and the remaining 33.7% reflected people not in the labour force. Thus, a large majority of working-age people who are not employed at any given time are not in the labour force rather than unemployed.

CHANGES IN EMPLOYMENT STATUS

The labour market is in a constant state of flux. Even when the unemployment rate remains unchanged from one month to the next, during the month hundreds of thousands of Canadian workers become unemployed and hundreds of thousands become employed.

Figure 3.12, based on research by Stephen Jones of McMaster University and Craig Riddell of the University of British Columbia, shows how workers

FIGURE 3.12

CHANGES IN EMPLOYMENT STATUS IN A TYPICAL MONTH

The arrow between two boxes represents a change from one employment status to another; the label on the arrow shows the number of people in one status who switched to the other status in a typical month, during the period 1990–1994. For example, the arrow from the unemployed box to the employed box shows that 326 346 unemployed workers (21.8% of the unemployed) became employed the following month. The arrow from the employed box to the unemployed box shows that 195 690 employed workers (1.5% of the employed) became unemployed during the following month.

Source: Data from Stephen R.G. Jones and W. Craig Riddell, "Gross Flows of Labour in Canada and the United States," *Canadian Public Policy*, February 1998, pp. 103–120.

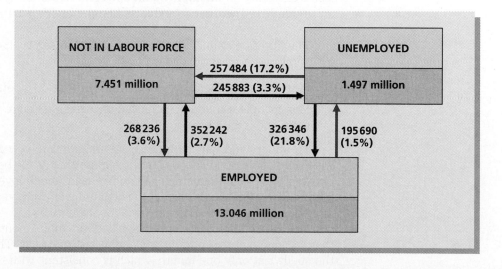

[17] The population and labour force data reported in Table 3.5 are measured in millions of people. For ease of presentation, values reported in the table have been rounded to the nearest 100 000 people. This results in some slight rounding errors in the calculations presented in this and following paragraphs.

change their employment status (that is, whether they are employed, unemployed, or not in the labour force) in a typical month. The arrow linking each pair of boxes represents a change from one employment status to another, and the number on the arrow shows the number of people in one status who switch to the other status in a typical month. Thus, for example, the arrow from the employed box to the unemployed box has the label 195 690, indicating that 195 690 of employed workers in a typical month will become unemployed by the following month. Typically, fewer than half of all those becoming unemployed have lost their jobs, while the remainder are job leavers or are entering or re-entering the labour force.

What are the employment prospects of an unemployed worker? Figure 3.12 shows that 21.8% of the unemployed people in a typical month will be employed the following month and that 17.2% of the unemployed people will be out of the labour force the next month. The remaining 61% of the unemployed people will still be unemployed the following month. Of the 17.2% of the unemployed who leave the labour force each month, some are **discouraged workers**, or people who have become so discouraged by lack of success at finding a job that they stop searching. Other unemployed workers leave the labour force to engage in some activity outside the labour market, such as homemaking or going to school.

HOW LONG ARE PEOPLE UNEMPLOYED?

Of the 61% of those unemployed in a typical month who remain unemployed the following month, some may remain unemployed for a considerable period of time. The period of time that an individual is continuously unemployed is called an **unemployment spell**. The length of time that an unemployment spell lasts is called its **duration**. The duration of an unemployment spell determines, in large part, the degree of hardship suffered by an unemployed worker. At one extreme, a one-week unemployment spell will cost a worker a week's pay but will probably not seriously affect the worker's standard of living. At the other extreme, an unemployment spell that lasts for several months may force an unemployed worker to exhaust his or her life savings or to sell the car or house.

The duration of unemployment spells in Canada is characterized by two seemingly contradictory statements:

1. Most unemployment spells are of short duration, about two months or less.

2. Most people who are unemployed on a given date are experiencing unemployment spells with long duration.

To understand how both these statements can be true, consider an economy with 100 people in the labour force. Suppose that at the beginning of every month, two workers become unemployed and remain unemployed for one month before finding a new job. In addition, at the beginning of every year, four workers become unemployed and remain unemployed for the entire year.

In this example, there are 28 spells of unemployment during a year: 24 spells that last one month, and four spells that last one year. Thus, 24 of 28, or 86%, of the spells last only one month, which is consistent with the first statement: Most spells are short.

How many people are unemployed on a given day, say, on May 15? There are six unemployed workers on May 15: two unemployed workers who began one-month spells of unemployment on May 1, and four unemployed workers who began one-year spells of unemployment on January 1. Thus, four of six, or 67%, of the workers unemployed on May 15 are experiencing one-year spells of unemployment, which is consistent with the second statement: Most people who are unemployed on a given date are experiencing long spells of unemployment.[18]

WHY THERE ARE ALWAYS UNEMPLOYED PEOPLE

Even when the economy is growing vigorously and many new jobs are being created, some people remain unemployed. Why is unemployment apparently a permanent feature of the economy? Here, we discuss frictional unemployment and structural unemployment, two types of unemployment that always exist in the labour market and, thus, prevent the unemployment rate from ever reaching zero.

Frictional Unemployment

The labour market is characterized by a great deal of searching on the part of both workers and firms. Unemployed workers search for suitable jobs, and firms with vacancies search for suitable workers. If all workers were identical and all jobs were identical, these searches would be short and easy: Unemployed workers would simply have to find firms that had vacancies, and they would immediately be hired. The problem, of course, is that neither jobs nor workers are identical. Workers vary in their talents, skills, experience, goals, geographic location (and willingness to move), and in the amount of time and energy they are willing to commit to their job. Similarly, jobs vary in the skills and experience required, working conditions, location, hours, and pay. Because of these differences, an unemployed worker may search for several weeks or more before finding a suitable job; similarly, a firm may search for a considerable time before it is able to hire a suitable worker.

The unemployment that arises as workers search for suitable jobs and firms search for suitable workers is called **frictional unemployment**. Because the economy is dynamic, with jobs continually being created and destroyed and workers continually entering and exiting the labour force, there is always some frictional unemployment as workers are matched with appropriate jobs.

Structural Unemployment

In addition to those suffering long spells of unemployment, many people are chronically unemployed. Although their unemployment spells may be broken by brief periods of employment or being out of the labour force, workers who are **chronically unemployed** are unemployed a large part of the time. Long spells of unemployment and chronic unemployment cannot be attributed primarily to the

[18] The average duration of an unemployment spell varies over time and by region of the country. It also varies by age and sex. See Statistics Canada, CANSIM II Table 282–0048 for data on the average duration of unemployment by province, by age, and by sex.

matching process. People in these situations do not seem to search for work very intensively and do not generally find stable employment. The long-term and chronic unemployment that exists even when the economy is not in a recession is called **structural unemployment**.

Structural unemployment occurs for two primary reasons. First, unskilled or low-skilled workers are often unable to obtain desirable, long-term jobs. The jobs available to them typically offer relatively low wages and little chance for training or advancement. Most directly related to the issue of structural unemployment is the fact that jobs held by low-skilled workers often do not last long. After a few months, the job may end or the worker may quit or be fired, thus entering another spell of unemployment. Some workers with low skill levels eventually get enough training or experience to obtain more secure, long-term jobs. Because of such factors as inadequate education, discrimination, and language barriers, however, some unskilled workers never make the transition to long-term employment and remain chronically unemployed.

The second source of structural unemployment is the reallocation of labour from industries that are shrinking, or regions that are depressed, to areas that are growing. When industries find that their product is no longer in demand (for example, buggy whip manufacturers) or that they are no longer competitive (for example, Canadian garment producers who lost much of the market to overseas manufacturers), workers in these industries lose their jobs. At the same time, some industries will be growing (for example, health-care providers and computer software developers). To prevent unemployment from rising, workers who lose jobs in declining industries must be matched somehow with jobs in growing industries. This matching may involve a long period of unemployment, especially if workers need to relocate to another city or province or be trained for a new job.

The Natural Rate of Unemployment

Because of the combination of frictional and structural unemployment, an economy's unemployment rate is never zero, even when the economy is at its full-employment level. The rate of unemployment that prevails when output and employment are at the full-employment level is called the **natural rate of unemployment**, $\overline{u}$. The natural rate of unemployment reflects unemployment owing to frictional and structural causes. Although there is no single official measure of the natural rate of unemployment, many economists believe that the natural rate was roughly 5% during the 1960s, increased gradually to about 8% in the 1980s, then fell to between 6% and 7% by 2007. The financial crisis that precipitated the recession suffered by most industrialized countries during 2007–2009 is feared by many analysts to have pushed the natural rate of unemployment upward, reversing this long-term trend. Chapter 13 discusses the reasons for changes in the natural rate.

As output fluctuates around its full-employment level, the unemployment rate fluctuates around the natural rate. The difference between the actual unemployment rate and the natural rate of unemployment is called **cyclical unemployment**. Specifically, cyclical unemployment $= u - \overline{u}$, where u is the actual unemployment rate and $\overline{u}$ is the natural rate. Cyclical unemployment is positive whenever the economy's output and employment are below full-employment levels; it is negative when output and employment exceed full-employment levels.

CHAPTER SUMMARY

1. The production function tells us the amount of output that can be produced with any given quantities of capital and labour. The production function can be graphed as a relationship between output and capital, holding labour fixed, or as a relationship between output and labour, holding capital fixed. In either case, the production function slopes upward, implying that greater use of capital or labour leads to more output. A shift in the production function, which indicates a change in the amount of output that can be produced with given amounts of capital and labour, is called a supply shock.

2. The extra output that can be produced when the capital stock is increased by one unit, with labour held constant, is called the marginal product of capital (MPK). In a graph of the production function relating output to capital, the MPK can be measured as the slope of the production function. The MPK falls as the capital stock increases, reflecting the diminishing marginal productivity of capital. Similarly, the marginal product of labour (MPN) is the extra output that can be produced when labour increases by one unit, with capital held constant. The MPN—which can be measured as the slope of the production function relating output to labour—falls as employment rises, indicating that labour also has diminishing marginal productivity.

3. To maximize profits, firms demand labour to the point that the marginal revenue product of labour ($MRPN$) equals the nominal wage, W; or, equivalently, to the point that the MPN equals the real wage, w.

4. The labour demand curve is identical to the MPN curve. Because an increase in the real wage causes firms to demand less labour, the labour demand curve slopes downward. Factors that increase the amount of labour demanded at any real wage, such as a beneficial supply shock or an increase in the capital stock, shift the labour demand curve to the right. Aggregate labour demand is the sum of the labour demands of firms in the economy.

5. An individual's decision about how much labour to supply reflects a comparison of the benefit and cost of working an additional hour. The benefit of working an additional hour is the additional real income earned, which can be used to increase consumption. The cost of working an extra hour is the loss of an hour's leisure. An individual's happiness, or utility, is maximized by supplying labour to the point where the cost of working an extra hour (the utility lost because of reduced leisure) equals the benefit (the utility gained because of increased income).

6. An increase in the real wage has competing substitution and income effects on the amount of labour supplied. The substitution effect of a higher real wage increases the amount of labour supplied, as the worker responds to the increased reward for working. The income effect reduces the amount of labour supplied, as the higher real wage makes the worker wealthier and, thus, able to afford more leisure. The longer an increase in the real wage is expected to last, the stronger the income effect. Thus, a temporary increase in the real wage will increase the amount of labour supplied. A permanent increase in the real wage will increase the amount of labour supplied by a smaller amount than a temporary increase in the real wage of the same size, however, and may even lead to a decrease in the amount of labour supplied.

7. The labour supply curve relates the amount of labour supplied to the current real wage. The labour supply curve slopes upward, indicating that an increase in the current real wage—with other factors, including the expected future real wage, held fixed—raises the amount of labour supplied. Factors that decrease the quantity of labour supplied at the current real wage and, thus, shift the labour supply curve to the left include an increase in wealth and an increase in the expected future real wage. Aggregate labour supply, which is the sum of labour supplies of the individuals in the economy, is also influenced by changes in the working-age population

and social or legal factors that affect the number of people participating in the labour market.

8. The classical supply–demand model of the labour market is based on the assumption that the real wage adjusts relatively quickly to equalize the quantities of labour demanded and supplied. The equilibrium level of employment, which arises when wages and prices in the economy have fully adjusted, is called the full-employment level of employment. Fluctuations in employment and the real wage are the result of factors that shift the labour supply curve and/or the labour demand curve.

9. Full-employment output, or potential output, is the amount of output produced when employment is at its full-employment level. Increases in the full-employment level of employment or beneficial supply shocks increase the full-employment level of output.

10. Working-age people without jobs are classified as unemployed if they looked for work during the preceding four weeks; they are classified as not in the labour force if they have not been looking for work. The labour force consists of all employed workers plus all unemployed workers. The unemployment rate is the fraction of the labour force that is unemployed.

11. Frictional unemployment reflects the time required for potential workers to find suitable jobs and for firms with vacancies to find suitable workers. Structural unemployment—long-term and chronic unemployment that exists even when the economy is not in recession—occurs because some workers do not have the skills needed to obtain long-term employment or because of delays in reallocating workers from economically depressed areas to those that are growing. Frictional and structural unemployment together account for the natural rate of unemployment, which is the unemployment rate that exists when employment is at its full-employment level. Cyclical unemployment is the excess of the actual unemployment rate over the natural rate of unemployment.

KEY DIAGRAM 1
The Production Function

The production function indicates how much output an economy or a firm can produce with any given quantities of capital and labour.

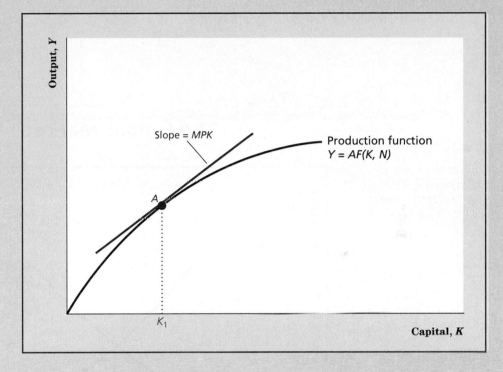

DIAGRAM ELEMENTS

- The production function graphed here has the amount of output produced, Y, on the vertical axis and the quantity of capital used, K, on the horizontal axis, with labour, N, held constant. It can also be drawn as a relationship between output and labour, with capital held constant. The production function relating output to labour looks similar to the graph shown here.

- The equation for the production function is $Y = AF(K, N)$, where A (total factor productivity, or simply productivity) measures how effectively the economy uses capital and labour.

ANALYSIS

- The production function slopes upward, reflecting the fact that an increase in the quantity of capital will allow more output to be produced.

- The production function becomes flatter from left to right, implying that the larger the capital stock already is, the less extra output is gained by adding another unit of capital. The fact that extra capital becomes less productive as the capital stock grows is called diminishing marginal productivity of capital.

- With labour held constant, if an increase in capital of ΔK leads to an increase in output of ΔY, then $\Delta Y/\Delta K$ is called the marginal product of capital, or MPK. The MPK is measured graphically by the slope of the line tangent to the production function. For example, in the diagram, the MPK when the capital stock is K_1 equals the slope of the line tangent to the production function at point A.

FACTORS THAT SHIFT THE CURVES

- Any change that allows more output to be produced for given quantities of capital and labour—a beneficial supply shock—shifts the production function upward. Examples of beneficial supply shocks include new inventions and improved management techniques.

• Any change that reduces the amount of output that can be produced for given quantities of capital and labour—an adverse supply shock—shifts the production function downward. Examples of adverse supply shocks include bad weather and the depletion of natural resources.

KEY DIAGRAM 2

The Labour Market

An economy's level of employment and the real wage are determined in the labour market.

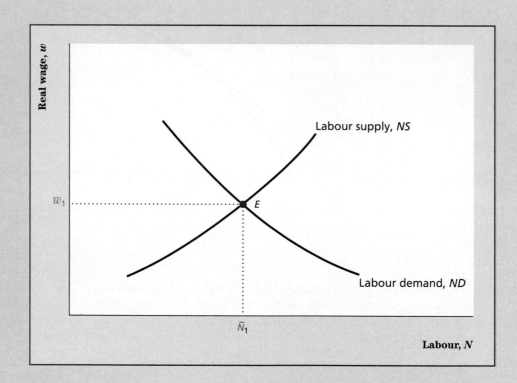

DIAGRAM ELEMENTS

• The current real wage, w, is on the vertical axis, and the level of employment, N, is on the horizontal axis. The variable N may also represent alternative measures of labour, such as total hours worked.

• The labour demand curve, ND, shows the amount of labour that firms want to employ at each current real wage. The labour demand curve slopes downward because firms find hiring more labour profitable when the real wage falls. The labour demand curve for an individual firm is the same as the MPN curve, which shows the marginal product of labour at each level of employment.

• The labour supply curve, NS, shows the amount of labour offered by workers at each current real wage. The labour supply curve slopes upward because an increase in the current real wage, with other factors held constant, increases the amount of labour supplied.

ANALYSIS

- Equilibrium in the labour market occurs when the quantity of labour demanded equals the quantity of labour supplied. In the figure, equilibrium employment is $\overline{N}_1$, and the equilibrium real wage is $\overline{w}_1$. The equilibrium level of employment, which occurs after wages and prices have fully adjusted, is called the full-employment level of employment.

FACTORS THAT SHIFT THE CURVES

- Any factor that increases the amount of labour demanded at a given current real wage shifts the labour demand curve to the right. Such factors include an increase in the marginal product of labour at any given level of employment and an increase in the capital stock. (See Summary table 3 on p. 64.)

- Any factor that increases the amount of labour supplied at a given current real wage shifts the labour supply curve to the right. Such factors include a decline in wealth, a drop in the expected future real wage, a rise in the working-age population, and an increase in labour force participation. (See Summary table 4 on p. 70.)

KEY TERMS

aggregate demand for labour, p. 63
aggregate supply of labour, p. 64
chronically unemployed, p. 81
cyclical unemployment, p. 82
diminishing marginal productivity, p. 53
discouraged workers, p. 80
duration, p. 80
employment ratio, p. 79
factors of production, p. 48
frictional unemployment, p. 81
full-employment level of employment, p. 71
full-employment output, p. 77
income effect of a higher real wage, p. 65
labour force, p. 78
leisure, p. 64
marginal product of capital (MPK), p. 53
marginal product of labour (MPN), p. 54
marginal revenue product of labour (MRPN), p. 58
natural rate of unemployment, p. 82
participation rate, p. 79
production function, p. 48
productivity, p. 47
real wage, p. 58
structural unemployment, p. 82
substitution effect of a higher real wage, p. 65
supply shock, p. 55
total factor productivity, p. 49
unemployment rate, p. 79
unemployment spell, p. 80

KEY EQUATIONS

$$Y = AF(K, N) \qquad (3.1)$$

The production function indicates how much output Y can be produced for given quantities of capital K and labour N and for a given level of total factor productivity A.

$$\overline{Y} = AF(K, \overline{N}) \qquad (3.4)$$

Full-employment output $\overline{Y}$ is the quantity of output supplied by firms when wages and prices have fully adjusted, and employment equals its equilibrium value $\overline{N}$.

REVIEW QUESTIONS

1. What is a production function? What are some factors that can cause a nation's production function to shift over time? What do you have to know besides an economy's production function to know how much output the economy can produce?
2. The production function slopes upward, but its slope declines from left to right. Give an economic interpretation of each of these properties of the production function.
3. Define marginal product of capital, or *MPK*. How can the *MPK* be shown graphically?
4. Explain why the profit-maximizing level of employment for a firm occurs when the marginal revenue product of

labour equals the nominal wage. How can this profit-maximizing condition be expressed in real terms?

5. What is the *MPN* curve? How is the *MPN* curve related to the production function? How is it related to labour demand?

6. Use the concepts of income effect and substitution effect to explain why a temporary increase in the real wage increases the amount of labour supplied, but a permanent increase in the real wage may decrease the quantity of labour supplied.

7. What two variables are related by the aggregate labour supply curve? What are some factors that cause the aggregate labour supply curve to shift?

8. Define full-employment output. How is full-employment output affected by an increase in labour supply? by a beneficial supply shock?

9. Why is the classical model of the labour market discussed in this chapter not very useful for studying unemployment?

10. Define the following: *labour force*, *unemployment rate*, *participation rate*, and *employment ratio*.

11. Define *unemployment spell* and *duration*. What are the two seemingly contradictory facts about unemployment spells? Why are the two facts not actually contradictory?

12. What is frictional unemployment? Why is a certain amount of frictional unemployment probably necessary in a well-functioning economy?

13. What is structural unemployment? What are the two principal sources of structural unemployment?

14. Define *the natural rate of unemployment* and *cyclical unemployment*. What does negative cyclical unemployment mean?

NUMERICAL PROBLEMS

1. The following data give real GDP, Y, capital, K, and labour, N, for the Canadian economy in various years:

Year	Y	K	N
1960	223	225	5.9
1970	368	352	7.9
1980	577	498	11.1
1990	768	650	13.1

Units and sources are the same as in Table 3.1 on page 50.
Assume that the production function is $Y = A K^{0.3} N^{0.7}$.

a. How much did Canadian total factor productivity grow between 1960 and 1970? between 1970 and 1980? between 1980 and 1990?

b. What happened to the marginal product of labour between 1960 and 1990? Calculate the marginal product numerically as the extra output gained by adding one million workers in each of the two years. (The data for employment, N, are measured in millions of workers, so an increase of one million workers is an increase of 1.0.)

2. An economy has the production function

$$\overline{Y} = 0.2(K + \sqrt{N}).$$

In the current period $K = 100$ and $N = 100$.

a. Graph the relationship between output and capital, holding labour constant at its current value. What is the *MPK*? Does the marginal productivity of capital diminish?

b. Graph the relationship between output and labour, holding capital constant at its current value. Find the *MPN* for an increase of labour from 100 to 110. Compare this result with the *MPN* for an increase in labour from 110 to 120. Does the marginal productivity of labour diminish?

3. Acme Widget Inc., has the following production function:

Number of Workers	Number of Widgets Produced
0	0
1	8
2	15
3	21
4	26
5	30
6	33

a. Find the *MPN* for each level of employment.

b. Acme can get $5 for each widget it produces. How many workers will it hire if the nominal wage is $38? if it is $27? if it is $22?

c. Graph the relationship between Acme's labour demand and the nominal wage. How does this graph differ from a labour demand curve? Graph Acme's labour demand curve.

d. With the nominal wage fixed at $38, the price of widgets doubles from $5 each to $10 each. What happens to Acme's labour demand and production?

e. With the nominal wage fixed at $38 and the price of widgets fixed at $5, the introduction of a new automatic widget maker doubles the number of widgets that the same number of workers can produce. What happens to labour demand and production?

f. What is the relationship between your answers to part (d) and part (e)? Explain.

4. The marginal product of labour (measured in units of output) for a certain firm is

$$MPN = A(100 - N),$$

where A measures productivity and N is the number of labour hours used in production. The price of output is \$2 per unit.

a. If $A = 1.0$, what will be the demand for labour if the nominal wage is \$10? if it is \$20? Graph the demand curve for labour. What is the equilibrium real wage if the supply of labour is fixed at 95?

b. Repeat part (a) for $A = 2.0$.

5. Consider an economy in which the marginal product of labour MPN is $MPN = 309 - 2N$, where N is the amount of labour used. The amount of labour supplied, NS, is given by $NS = 22 + 12w + 2T$, where w is the real wage and T is a lump-sum tax levied on individuals.

a. Use the concepts of income effect and substitution effect to explain why an increase in lump-sum taxes will increase the amount of labour supplied.

b. Suppose that $T = 35$. What are the equilibrium values of employment and the real wage?

c. With T remaining equal to 35, the government passes minimum-wage legislation that requires firms to pay a real wage greater than or equal to 7. What are the resulting values of employment and the real wage?

6. Suppose that the production function is

$$Y = 9K^{0.5}N^{0.5}.$$

With this production function, the marginal product of labour is

$$MPN = 4.5K^{0.5}N^{-0.5}.$$

The capital stock is

$$K = 25.$$

The labour supply curve is

$$NS = 100[(1 - t)w]^2,$$

where w is the real wage rate, t is the tax rate on labour income, and hence

$$(1 - t)w$$

is the after-tax real wage rate.

a. Assume that the tax rate on labour income, t, equals zero. Find the equation of the labour demand curve. Calculate the equilibrium levels of the real wage and employment, the level of full-employment output, and the total after-tax wage income of workers.

b. Repeat part (a) under the assumption that the tax rate on labour income, t, equals 0.6.

c. Suppose that a minimum wage of $w = 2$ is imposed. If the tax rate on labour income, t, equals zero, what are the resulting values of employment and the real wage? Does the introduction of the minimum wage increase the total income of workers, taken as a group?

7. Consider an economy with 500 people in the labour force. At the beginning of every month, five people lose their jobs and remain unemployed for exactly one month; one month later, they find new jobs and become employed. In addition, on January 1 of each year, 20 people lose their jobs and remain unemployed for six months before finding new jobs. Finally, on July 1 of each year, 20 people lose their jobs and remain unemployed for six months before finding new jobs.

a. What is the unemployment rate in this economy in a typical month?

b. What fraction of unemployment spells lasts for one month? What fraction lasts for six months?

c. What is the average duration of an unemployment spell?

d. On any particular date, what fraction of the unemployed are suffering a long spell (six months) of unemployment?

8. You are given the following data on the unemployment rate and output:

Year	1	2	3	4
Unemployment rate	8%	6%	7%	5%
Output	950	1030	1033.5	1127.5

a. Assume that the natural rate of unemployment is 6% and that $(\overline{Y} - Y)/\overline{Y} = 2(u - \overline{u})$. Find the full-employment level of output in each year.

b. Calculate the growth rate of full-employment output in years 2, 3, and 4 by using the values for full-employment output that you found in part (a).

9. Consider an economy that initially has a labour force of 2000 workers. Of these workers, 1900 are employed and each works 40 hours per week. Ten units of output are produced by each hour of labour.

a. What is the total number of hours worked per week in the economy? What is the total output per week in the economy? What is the unemployment rate?

b. The economy enters a recession. Employment falls by 4%, and the number of hours per week worked by each employed worker falls by 2.5%. In addition, 0.2% of the labour force becomes discouraged at the prospect of finding a job and leaves the labour force. Finally, suppose that whenever total hours fall by 1%, total output falls by 1.4%.

After the recession begins, what is the size of the labour force? How many workers are unemployed and what is the unemployment rate? What is the total output per week in the economy?

ANALYTICAL PROBLEMS

1. a. A technological breakthrough raises a country's total factor productivity A by 10%. Show how this change affects the graphs of both the production function relating output to capital and the production function relating output to labour.

b. Show that a 10% increase in A also increases the MPK and the MPN by 10% at any level of capital and labour. (*Hint:* What happens to ΔY for any increase in capital ΔK or for any increase in labour ΔN?)

c. Can a beneficial supply shock leave the MPK and MPN unaffected? Show graphically.

2. How would each of the following affect the current level of full-employment output? Explain.

a. A large number of immigrants enter the country.

b. Energy supplies become depleted.

c. New teaching techniques improve the educational performance of high school students.

d. A new law mandates the shutdown of some unsafe forms of capital.

3. During the 1980s and 1990s, the average rate of unemployment in Europe was high. Some economists claimed that this rate was in part the result of "real wage rigidity," a situation in which unions kept real wages above their market-clearing levels.

a. Accepting for the sake of argument that real wages were too high in Europe in the 1980s and 1990s, show how this would lead to unemployment (a situation where people who would like to work at the going wage cannot find jobs).

b. What is the effect of real wage rigidity on the output actually supplied by firms, relative to the output they would supply if there were no real wage rigidity?

4. How would each of the following affect Helena Handbasket's supply of labour?

a. The value of Helena's home triples in an unexpectedly hot real estate market.

b. Originally an unskilled worker, Helena acquires skills that give her access to a higher-paying job. Assume that her preferences about leisure are not affected by the change in jobs.

c. A temporary income tax surcharge raises the percentage of her income that she must pay in taxes, for the current year only. (Taxes are proportional to income in Helena's country.)

5. Suppose that under a new law all businesses must pay a tax equal to 6% of their sales revenue. Assume that this tax is not passed on to consumers. Instead, consumers pay the same prices after the tax is imposed as they did before. What is the effect of this tax on labour demand? If the labour supply curve is unchanged, what will be the effect of the tax on employment and the real wage?

6. Can the unemployment rate and the employment ratio rise during the same month? Can the participation rate fall at the same time that the employment ratio rises? Explain.

Chapter 4

Consumption, Saving, and Investment

Chapter 3 focused on some of the factors determining the amount of output produced, or *supplied*, in the economy. This chapter considers the factors that underlie the economywide *demand* for goods and services. In other words, we move from examining how much is produced to examining how that production is used.

Recall from Chapter 2 that aggregate demand (spending) in the economy has four components: the demand for consumer goods and services by households (consumption), the demand for new capital goods by firms and governments (investment), government purchases of goods and services, and the net demand for domestic goods by foreigners (net exports). Because the levels of government purchases and investment are determined primarily by the political process, macroeconomic analysis usually treats these components of spending as given. For this chapter, we also assume that the economy is closed so that net exports are zero (we drop the closed-economy assumption in Chapter 5). That leaves two major components of spending—consumption and private investment—to be discussed in this chapter. Section 4.1 presents the factors that determine how much households choose to consume, and Section 4.2 looks at the decision by firms about how much to invest.

We have said that this chapter is about the aggregate demand for goods and services. However, we could just as easily say that it is about a seemingly very different (but equally important) topic: the determination of saving and capital formation. Studying the aggregate demand for goods and services is the same as studying the factors that determine saving and capital formation for the following reasons: First, saving is simply what is left after an economic unit (say, a household) decides how much of its income to consume. Thus, the decision about how much to consume is the same as the decision about how much to save. Second, investment spending is part of the aggregate demand for goods and services, but it also represents the acquisition of new capital goods by firms; and so, in studying investment spending, we are also looking at the factors that lead an economy to acquire new factories, machines, and housing. In effect, we do two things at once in this chapter:

- We explore the determinants of the aggregate demand for goods, which prepares you for future discussions of topics such as the role of spending fluctuations in business cycles.

- While exploring aggregate demand, we also examine the factors affecting saving and capital formation, which prepares you for future discussions of the sources of economic growth and other issues.

In making many economic decisions, including those we consider in this chapter, people must trade off the present against the future. In deciding how much to consume and save, for example, a household must weigh the benefits of enjoying more consumption today against the benefits of putting aside some of its income as saving for consumption in the future. Similarly, in deciding how much to invest, a firm's manager must determine how much to spend today in order to increase the firm's productive capacity one, five, or even twenty years from now. In making these trade-offs, households and firms must take into account their expectations about the future of the economy, including expectations about government policy. In Chapters 9–12 where we examine complete models of the economy, these considerations will take on a central role.

In Chapter 3 we asked, "What forces act to bring the labour market into equilibrium?" We close this chapter by asking the same question for the goods market. The goods market is in equilibrium when the quantity of goods and services that producers want to supply (discussed in Chapter 3) equals the quantity of goods and services demanded by households, firms, and the government (discussed in this chapter). Equivalently, the goods market is in equilibrium when desired saving in the economy equals desired investment. We show that the real interest rate plays a key role in bringing the goods market into equilibrium.

4.1 Consumption and Saving

We begin consideration of the demand for goods and services by discussing the factors that affect consumer spending. Because consumption spending by households is, by far, the largest component of the demand for goods and services— accounting for about 60% of total spending—changes in consumers' willingness to spend have major implications for the behaviour of the economy.

Besides the sheer size of consumption spending, another reason to study consumption is that the individual's or household's decision about how much to consume is closely linked to another important economic decision, the decision about how much to save. Indeed, for given levels of disposable income, the decision about how much to consume and the decision about how much to save are really the same decision. For example, a student with a part-time job that pays $4000 per year after taxes might decide to spend $3700 per year on clothes, food, entertainment, and other consumption. If she does consume this amount, her saving will automatically be $300 ($4000 − $3700) per year. Equivalently, she might decide to save $300 per year. If she succeeds in saving $300, her consumption is automatically $3700 ($4000 − $300) per year. Because the decision about how much to consume and the decision about how much to save are actually two sides of the same coin, we analyze them together.

From a macroeconomic perspective, we are interested in the aggregate, or national, levels of consumption and saving. We define the national level of *desired consumption*, C^d, as the aggregate quantity of goods and services that households want to consume, given income and other factors that determine households' economic opportunities. We will analyze desired consumption and its response to various factors, such as income and interest rates, by examining the consumption decisions of individual households. The aggregate level of desired consumption,

C^d, is obtained by adding up the desired consumption of all households. Thus, any factor that increases the desired consumption of individual households will increase C^d, and any factor that decreases the desired consumption of individual households will decrease C^d.

Just as a household's consumption decision and saving decision are closely linked, a country's desired consumption is closely linked to its desired national saving. Specifically, *desired national saving*, S^d, is the level of national saving that occurs when aggregate consumption is at its desired level. Recall from Chapter 2, Eq. (2.8) that if net factor payments from abroad (*NFP*) equal zero (as must be true in a closed economy), then national saving, S, equals $Y - C - G$, where Y is output, C is consumption, and G is government purchases. Because desired national saving, S^d, is the level of national saving that occurs when consumption equals its desired level, we obtain an expression for desired national saving by substituting desired consumption, C^d, for consumption, C, in the definition of national saving. This substitution yields

$$S^d = Y - C^d - G. \tag{4.1}$$

We can gain insight into the factors that affect consumption and saving at the national level by considering how consumption and saving decisions are made at the individual level. An explanation of how individuals make their consumption and savings decisions is provided in the following section; a much more formal analysis of this decision-making process is available on the Companion Website (*www.pearsoned.ca/abel*).

THE CONSUMPTION AND SAVING DECISION OF AN INDIVIDUAL

Let's consider the case of Prudence, a bookkeeper for the Spectacular Eyeglasses Company. Prudence earns $20 000 per year after taxes. Hence she could, if she chose, consume $20 000 worth of goods and services every year. Prudence, however, has two other options.

First, she can save by consuming less than $20 000 per year. Why should Prudence consume less than her income allows? The reason is that she is thinking about the future. By consuming less than her current income, she'll accumulate savings that will allow her, at some time in the future, to consume more than her income. For example, Prudence may expect her income to be very low when she retires; by saving during her working life, she'll be able to consume more than her income during retirement. Indeed, the desire to provide for retirement is an important motivation for saving in the real world.

Alternatively, Prudence could consume more than her current income by borrowing or by drawing down previously accumulated savings. If she borrows $5000 from a bank, for example, she could consume as much as $25 000 worth of goods and services this year, even though her income is only $20 000. Consuming more than her income is enjoyable for Prudence, but the cost to her is that at some future time, when she must repay the loan, she will have to consume less than her income.

If Prudence consumes less today, she'll be able to consume more in the future, and vice versa. In other words, she faces a trade-off between current consumption and future consumption. The rate at which Prudence trades off current and future consumption depends on the real interest rate prevailing in the economy. Suppose that Prudence can earn a real interest rate of r per year on her saving and, for simplicity, suppose that if she borrows, she must pay the same real interest rate r on the loan. These assumptions imply that Prudence can trade one unit of current (this year's) consumption for $1 + r$ units of future (next year's) consumption. For example, suppose Prudence reduces her consumption today by one dollar, thereby increasing her saving by one dollar. Because she earns a real interest rate of r on her saving, the dollar she saves today will be worth $1 + r$ dollars one year from now.[1] Under the assumption that Prudence uses the extra $1 + r$ dollars to increase her next year's consumption, she has effectively traded one dollar's worth of consumption today for $1 + r$ dollars of consumption a year from now.

Similarly, Prudence can trade $1 + r$ real dollars of future consumption for one extra dollar of consumption today. She does so by borrowing and spending an extra dollar today. In a year, she'll have to repay the loan with interest, a total of $1 + r$ dollars. Because she has to repay $1 + r$ dollars next year, her consumption next year will be $1 + r$ dollars less than it would be otherwise. So, the "price" to Prudence of one dollar's worth of extra consumption today is $1 + r$ dollars' worth of consumption in the future.

The real interest rate, r, determines the relative price of current consumption and future consumption. Given this relative price, how should Prudence choose between consuming today and consuming in the future? One extreme possibility would be for her to borrow heavily and consume much more than her income today. The problem with this strategy is that after repaying her loan, Prudence would be able to consume almost nothing in the future. The opposite, but equally extreme, approach would be for Prudence to save nearly all of her current income. This strategy would allow her to consume a great deal in the future, but at the cost of near-starvation today.

Realistically, most people would choose neither of those extreme strategies but would instead try to avoid sharp fluctuations in consumption. The desire to have a relatively even pattern of consumption over time—avoiding periods of very high or very low consumption—is known as the **consumption-smoothing motive**. Because of her consumption-smoothing motive, Prudence will try to spread her consumption spending more or less evenly over time rather than bingeing in one period and starving in another.

Next, we'll see how the consumption-smoothing motive guides Prudence's behaviour when changes occur in some important determinants of her economic well-being, including her current income, her expected future income, and her wealth. As we consider each of these changes, we will hold constant the real interest rate r and, hence, the relative price of current consumption and future consumption. Later, we'll discuss what happens if the real interest rate changes.

EFFECT OF CHANGES IN CURRENT INCOME

Current income is an important factor affecting consumption and saving decisions. To illustrate, suppose that Prudence receives a one-time bonus of $3000 at work, which increases her current year's income by $3000. (We ignore income taxes; equivalently, we can assume that the bonus is actually larger than $3000 but that after paying her taxes, Prudence finds that her current income has

---

[1] We are assuming that there is zero inflation over the coming year, so that $1 purchases the same amount of real goods in each period. Alternatively, we could say that since the real interest rate is r, each *real* dollar Prudence saves today will be worth $1 + r$ *real* dollars one year from now.

increased by $3000.) What will she do with this extra income? Prudence could splurge and spend the entire bonus on a trip to Hawaii. If she spends the entire bonus, her current consumption will increase by $3000, but because she hasn't increased her saving, her future consumption will be unchanged. Alternatively, she could save the entire bonus, leaving her current consumption unchanged but using the bonus plus the interest it earns to increase her consumption in the future. Because of the consumption-smoothing motive, however, Prudence is unlikely to follow either of these extreme strategies. Instead, she'll spend part of the bonus (increasing current consumption) and save the rest (enabling her to increase future consumption as well).

The portion of her bonus that Prudence spends will depend on such factors as her willingness to defer gratification and her assessment of her current and future needs. We define Prudence's **marginal propensity to consume**, or MPC, as the fraction of additional current income that she consumes in the current period. Because Prudence consumes some but not all of her extra income, her MPC will be between zero and one. Suppose, for example, that Prudence has an MPC equal to 0.4, so that she consumes 0.4, or 40%, of an increase in current income. Then, when she receives a $3000 bonus, Prudence will increase her current consumption by $(0.4)(\$3000) = \$1200$. Because the part of income that is not consumed is saved, her saving also increases by the amount of $3000 − $1200 = $1800.

The marginal propensity to consume also applies to declines in current income. For example, if Prudence were temporarily laid off from her bookkeeping job so that her current year's income decreased by $4000, she would reduce both her consumption and her saving. If we assume that her marginal propensity to consume remains 0.4, she would reduce her consumption by $(0.4)(\$4000) = \$1600$, and her saving would, therefore, have to diminish by $4000 − $1600 = $2400.

Aggregate income and consumption reflect the decisions of millions of individuals and households, so that the lessons we learned from thinking about the case of Prudence also apply at the macroeconomic level. Just as an increase in Prudence's income caused her to consume more, we would expect an increase in aggregate output (income) Y to lead to an increase in aggregate desired consumption, C^d, as well. Because marginal propensities to consume are less than 1, however, the increase in C^d will be less than the increase in Y. As not all of the increase in Y is spent, desired national saving S^d will also rise when Y rises.

EFFECT OF CHANGES IN EXPECTED FUTURE INCOME

Today's consumption decisions may depend not only on current income but also on the income one expects to earn in the future. For example, an individual who is currently not employed but who has a contract to begin a high-paying job in three months will probably consume more today than another unemployed individual with no job prospects.

To illustrate the effect of changes in expected future income, suppose that instead of receiving the $3000 bonus during the current year, Prudence learns that she'll receive a $3000 bonus (after taxes) next year. The promise of the bonus is legally binding, and Prudence has no doubt that she'll receive the extra income next year. How will this information affect her consumption and saving in the current year?

Because her current income is unaffected, Prudence could leave her current consumption and saving unchanged, waiting until she actually receives the bonus to increase her consumption. If her decisions are guided by a consumption-smoothing motive, however, she'll prefer to use the bonus to increase her current consumption as well as her future consumption. She can increase her current consumption, despite the fact that her current income remains unchanged, by reducing her current saving (she could even "dissave," or have negative current saving, with current consumption exceeding current income, by using her accumulated assets or by borrowing). Suppose, for example, that Prudence decides to consume $1000 more this year. Because her current income is unchanged, Prudence's $1000 increase in current consumption is equivalent to a $1000 reduction in current saving.

The $1000 reduction in current saving will reduce Prudence's available resources in the next year, relative to the situation in which her saving is unchanged, by $1000(1 + r)$. For example, if the real interest rate is 0.05, cutting current saving by $1000 reduces Prudence's available resources next year by $1000(1.05) = 1050. Overall, her available resources next year will increase by $3000 because of the bonus but will decrease by $1050 because of reduced current saving, giving a net increase in resources of $3000 − $1050 = 1950, which can be used to increase consumption next year or in the following years. Effectively, Prudence can use the increase in her expected future income to increase consumption both in the present and in the future.

To summarize, an increase in an individual's expected future income is likely to lead that person to increase current consumption and decrease current saving. The same result applies at the macroeconomic level: If people expect that aggregate output and income, Y, will be higher in the future, current desired consumption, C^d, should increase and current desired national saving, S^d, should decrease.

This discussion suggests that expectations about the future are important. But how do economists measure those expectations? One way is to simply asked them. See A Closer Look 4.1, "Surveying Households," for a discussion of a new approach being used by the Bank of Canada to measure household's expectations.

How do economists determine people's expectations about the future? One way is to simply asked them. See A Closer Look 4.1, "Surveying Households," for a discussion of a new approach being used by the Bank of Canada to measuring household's expectations.

A CLOSER LOOK 4.1

SURVEYING HOUSEHOLDS

People's decisions—economic and otherwise—depend on what they expect the future to bring. In other words, how people anticipate the future affects the decisions they make in the present. As discussed above—and as we will discuss further in this and future chapters—because the rate of inflation people expect to observe in the future influences current wage negotiations, price setting, and financial contracting for investment, it is one of the main drivers of current inflation. This makes policy-makers particularly interested in measuring expectations about inflation and

the values of other economic variables. To that end, the Bank of Canada recently launched a quarterly survey to measure the expectations of Canadian households. The survey, known as the Canadian Survey of Consumer Expectations (CSCE), started to collect information in the fourth quarter of 2014. Results from the survey are expected soon.

The CSCE is a major innovation because it contains information not previously collected regularly from Canadian consumers. The survey of consumers will complement surveys of businesses conducted by the

Conference Board of Canada in its Survey of Business Confidence and the Bank of Canada in its Business Outlook Survey (BOS).

One set of questions asked in the CSCE has to do with expectations of inflation. Respondents are asked to provide their estimate of the likelihood that the rate of inflation will fall between certain ranges over the next 12 months. An interesting part of the design of the CSCE is that it will provide measures of inflation expectations held by households in different demographic groups. Preliminary analysis of the CSCE results find that inflation expectations to be higher among less-educated, lower-income, and younger households. Other questions investigate households' expectations about income, interest rates, house prices, and the ability to make debt payments.

The information contained in the CSCE will provide policy-makers with timely information about the current financial situation of Canadian households and information describing how households anticipate their financial situation will change. The hope is that by monitoring expectations of future outcomes, policy-makers will be able to formulate more effective public policy.

EFFECT OF CHANGES IN WEALTH

Another factor that affects consumption and saving is wealth. Recall from Chapter 2 that the wealth of any entity, such as a household or an entire nation, equals its assets minus its liabilities.

To see how consumption and saving respond to an increase in wealth, suppose that while cleaning out her attic, Prudence finds a stock certificate for 50 shares of stock in a pharmaceutical company. Prudence's grandmother bought this stock for her when she was born, and Prudence didn't know about it. She immediately calls her broker and learns that the stock is now worth $3000. This unexpected $3000 increase in Prudence's wealth has the same effect on her available resources as the $3000 increase in current income that we examined earlier. As in the case involving an increase in her current income, Prudence will use her increase in wealth to increase her current consumption by an amount smaller than $3000 so that she can use some of the additional $3000 to increase her future consumption. Because Prudence's current income isn't affected by finding the stock certificate (she doesn't cash it in), the increase in her current consumption is matched by a decrease in current saving of the same size. In this way, an increase in wealth increases current consumption and reduces current saving. The same line of reasoning leads to the conclusion that a decrease in wealth reduces current consumption and increases saving.

Much of the wealth owned by individuals is in the form of financial assets such as mutual funds, bonds, and equities. These financial assets are owned indirectly as a result of individuals participating in employer-sponsored pension plans (which in turn own mutual funds, bonds, and equities), and directly as a result of individuals purchasing such assets as a way of saving for retirement. Owning wealth in the form of mutual funds, bonds, and equities exposes individuals to the ups and downs of the stock market. As a consequence we should expect that changes in the stock market, because they affect wealth, ought to have an influence on consumption spending. The other major form in which individuals hold their wealth is housing. A booming (or crashing) housing market, like the ups and downs of the stock market, should therefore also have an influence on consumption. The influence of these sources of fluctuations in wealth on consumption is explored in the following Application: "Stock Market Wealth, Housing Wealth, and Consumer Spending."

APPLICATION

STOCK MARKET WEALTH, HOUSING WEALTH, AND CONSUMER SPENDING

On October 19, 1987, stock prices took their largest-ever one-day plunge in Canada. On that day, now known as Black Monday, the Toronto Stock Exchange's composite index of 300 stock prices (TSE 300) lost 407 points, an amount equal to 11.3% of its value. Although estimates differ, about $100 billion (measured in 1987 dollars) in financial wealth—equal in value to more than two months of GDP—was lost through declining stock values from August to December 1987. While perhaps none have been as dramatic as Black Monday, since 1987 the TSE (renamed the TSX in 2001) has exhibited a number of other large swings in value. Between September 2002 and October 2007, for example, the TSX increased by 136% before falling 44% to February 2009. These fluctuations in stock prices had considerable impact on those households holding their wealth in the form of stocks.

Household wealth held in the form of housing tends to fluctuate less dramatically than wealth held in the stock market but can nonetheless be subject to large changes. For example, the price of new housing in Canada increased by over 10% per quarter in 2006 but then, three years later, fell by roughly 3% per quarter in 2009. Although less frequent and smaller than fluctuations in the stock market, it is fluctuations such as these that have recently alarmed economists and to governments. Their alarm is due not only to the potential effect this may have on the largest component of national income—consumption—but also to its possible contagion effect. That is, those who carry large mortgages may, should house prices fall by a large amount, choose to abandon their homes and their mortgage debt. The effect this has on the rest of the financial market is a topic we will consider in a later chapter.

Research at the Bank of Canada shows that the effect on consumers' spending of changes in wealth is significantly different depending on whether the change arises from a change in wealth held in the form of housing or wealth held in the form of financial assets.[2] This research shows that the average Canadian household increases its spending by 5.7 cents for every dollar increase in housing wealth but that consumption spending is not measurably influenced by changes in stock market wealth.

The researchers offer a number of explanations for this result. First, while only about one-third of Canadian households own stocks, approximately two-thirds of households own their own homes. Thus, changes in housing prices will influence the consumption choices of many more consumers than will changes in stock prices. Second, stock prices are far more volatile than are housing prices. As a result, while households may shrug off large changes in stock prices as likely to be reversed in relatively short order, they are likely to judge changes in housing prices as more or less permanent. Third, in Canada, increases in wealth arising from increases in housing prices are exempt from capital gains taxation while increases in wealth arising from increases in stock prices are often subject to taxation.[3] For

---

[2] See Lise Pichette, "Are Wealth Effects Important for Canada?," *Bank of Canada Review*, Spring 2004.

[3] The exception is an increase in wealth due to increases in stock prices when stocks are held in a Registered Retirement Savings Plan (RRSP).

all these reasons we might expect that consumers' spending choices would be more strongly influenced by changes in wealth arising from changes in housing prices than from fluctuations in stock prices.

The sensitivity of consumption to housing wealth reported in the Bank of Canada study—consumption increases by 5.7 cents for every dollar increase in housing wealth—is quite important. If we suppose the average house price in Canada is $350 000, then a 20% decrease in house prices ($70 000) translates into a decrease in consumption spending of $4000 per year, or about $330 per month. The potential for a sudden fall in housing prices to have such a large impact on consumption spending—and by extension a large impact on the whole economy—is the reason why many analysts express concern over the possibility of a housing price "bubble" that may one day burst.

EFFECT OF CHANGES IN THE REAL INTEREST RATE

We've seen that the real interest rate is the price of current consumption in terms of future consumption. We held the real interest rate fixed when we examined the effects of changes in current income, expected future income, and wealth. Now we'll let the real interest rate vary and examine the effect on current consumption and saving.

How would Prudence's consumption and saving change in response to an increase in the real interest rate? Her response to such an increase reflects two opposing tendencies. On the one hand, because each real dollar of saving in the current year grows to $1 + r$ real dollars next year, an increase in the real interest rate means that each dollar of current saving will have a higher payoff in increased future consumption. This increased reward for current saving tends to increase saving.

On the other hand, a higher real interest rate means that Prudence can achieve any future savings target with a smaller amount of current saving. For example, suppose she's trying to accumulate $1400 to buy a new laptop computer next year. An increase in the real interest rate means that any current saving will grow to a larger amount by next year, so the amount she needs to save this year to reach her goal of $1400 is lower. Because she needs to save less to reach her goal, she can increase her current consumption and, thus, reduce her saving.

The two opposing effects described above are known as the substitution effect and the income effect of an increase in the real interest rate. The **substitution effect of the real interest rate on saving** reflects the tendency to reduce current consumption and increase future consumption as the price of current consumption, $1 + r$, increases. In response to an increase in the price of current consumption, consumers *substitute* away from current consumption, which has become relatively more expensive, toward future consumption, which has become relatively less expensive. The reduction in current consumption implies that current saving increases. Thus, the substitution effect implies that current saving increases in response to an increase in the real interest rate.

The **income effect of the real interest rate on saving** reflects the change in current consumption that results when a higher real interest rate makes a consumer richer or poorer. For example, if Prudence has a savings account and hasn't borrowed any funds, she is a recipient of interest payments. She, therefore, benefits from an increase in the real interest rate because her interest income increases.

With a higher interest rate, she can afford to have the same levels of current and future consumption as before the interest rate change, and she would have some additional resources to spend. These extra resources are effectively the same as an increase in her wealth, so she will increase both her current and her future consumption. Thus, for a saver, who is a recipient of interest payments, the income effect of an increase in the real interest rate is to increase current consumption and reduce current saving. The income and substitution effects of an increase in the real interest rate work in opposite directions, with the income effect reducing saving and the substitution effect increasing saving.

The income effect of an increase in the real interest rate is different for a payer of interest, such as a borrower. An increase in the real interest rate increases the amount of interest payments that a borrower must make, thereby making the borrower unable to afford the same levels of current and future consumption as before. The borrower has effectively suffered a loss of wealth as a result of the increase in the real interest rate, and responds to this decline in wealth by reducing both current and future consumption. The reduction in current consumption means that current saving increases (that is, borrowing decreases). Hence, for a borrower, the income effect of an increase in the real interest rate is to increase saving. Both the substitution effect and the income effect of an increase in the real interest rate increase the saving of a borrower.

Let's summarize the effect of an increase in the real interest rate. For a saver, who is a recipient of interest, an increase in the real interest rate tends to increase saving through the substitution effect but to reduce saving through the income effect. Without additional information, we can't say which of these two opposing effects is larger. For a borrower, who is a payer of interest, both the substitution effect and the income effect operate to increase saving. Consequently, the saving of a borrower unambiguously increases.

What is the effect of an increase in the real interest rate on national saving? Because the national economy is composed of both borrowers and savers, and because, in principle, savers could either increase or decrease their saving in response to an increase in the real interest rate, economic theory can't answer this question. Since economic theory doesn't indicate whether national saving increases or decreases in response to an increase in the real interest rate, we must rely on empirical studies that examine this relationship using actual data. Unfortunately, interpretation of the empirical evidence from the many studies done continues to inspire debate. The most widely accepted conclusion seems to be that an increase in the real interest rate reduces current consumption and increases saving, but that this effect isn't very strong.

It is worth remarking that identifying the response of national saving to a change in the real interest rate is also complicated by the fact that there are many different types of interest rates, and changes in some of these interest rates may affect national saving differently than changes in others. See A Closer Look 4.2, "Interest Rates," for a discussion of these different types of interest rates and their relationships to one another.

Taxes and the Real Return to Saving

In discussing the real return that savers earn, we haven't yet mentioned an important practical consideration: Interest earnings (and other returns on savings) are taxed. Because part of interest earnings must be paid as taxes, the real return earned by savers is actually less than the difference between the nominal interest rate and expected inflation.

A useful measure of the returns received by savers that recognizes the effects of taxes is the *expected after-tax real interest rate*. To define this concept, we let i represent the nominal interest rate and t the rate at which interest income is taxed. In Canada, for example, most interest earnings are taxed as ordinary income, so t is the income tax rate. Savers retain a fraction $(1 - t)$ of total interest earned, so that the after-tax nominal interest rate, received by savers after payment of taxes, is $(1 - t)i$. The **expected after-tax real interest rate**, r_{a-t}, is the after-tax nominal interest rate minus the expected inflation rate π^e, or

$$r_{a-t} = (1 - t)i - \pi^e. \tag{4.2}$$

The expected after-tax real interest rate is the appropriate interest rate for consumers to use in making consumption and saving decisions because it measures the increase in the purchasing power of their saving after payment of taxes.

A CLOSER LOOK 4.2

INTEREST RATES

Although in our theoretical discussions we refer to "the" interest rate, as if there were only one, there are actually many different interest rates, each of which depends on the identity of the borrower and the terms of the loan. Here are some of the many interest rates observed in November of 2006, 2007, 2008, and 2009.

	2006	2007	2008	2009
Target overnight rate	4.25%	4.50%	2.25%	0.25%
Prime rate (1 month)	4.31	4.74	2.53	0.36
3-month Treasury bill	4.18	3.91	1.70	0.22
6-month Treasury bill	4.17	3.96	1.62	0.28
1-year Treasury bill	4.12	3.95	1.61	0.48
5-year Canada bond	3.85	3.91	2.48	2.41
7-year Canada bond	3.87	3.97	2.87	2.74
10-year Canada bond	3.94	4.07	3.36	3.25
3-month commercial paper	4.30	4.84	2.68	0.39

Source: Data from Selected Canadian and International Interest Rates including Bond Yields and Interest Arbitrage, Bank of Canada http://www.bankofcanada.ca/rates/interest-rates/selected-historical-interest-rates/.

The target overnight rate is the centre of the central bank's target range for the overnight rate, which, in turn, is the interest rate at which chartered banks make short-term loans to one another. The target overnight rate is the key indicator of monetary policy, which we describe in more detail in Chapter 14. The prime rate is

the basic rate that chartered banks and trust companies charge on loans to their best customers. These first two rates are called administered rates, while the other rates vary continuously as financial market conditions change. Treasury bills and Canada bonds are debt of the federal government, and commercial paper is a debt of a private issuer.

The interest rates charged on these different types of loans need not be the same. One reason for this variation is differences in the risk of non-repayment, or default. Federal government debt is believed to be free from default risk, but there is always a chance that a business, bank, or province may not be able to repay what it borrowed. Lenders charge risky borrowers extra interest to compensate themselves for the risk of default. Thus, the prime rate and the commercial paper rate are higher than they would be if there were no default risk. Note that the three-month commercial paper rate was greater than the three-month Treasury bill rate in all four years.

A second factor affecting interest rates is the length of time for which the funds are borrowed. The relationship between the life of a bond (its *maturity*) and the interest rate it pays is called the *yield curve*. The accompanying figure shows the yield curve in November of 2006, 2007, 2008, and 2009 using the yields on federal government bonds of various

(continued)

maturities, as given in the table. What does the shape of the yield curve indicate?

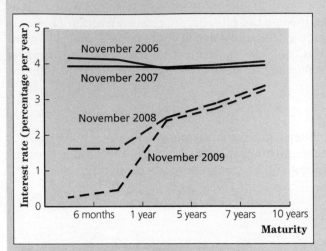

Since 2000, the interest rate paid on long-term bonds has exceeded that paid on six-month Treasury bills by about 1.5 percentage points. The yield curve in November 2008 was therefore typical of that historical average. A yield curve steeper than this—where the interest rate paid on long-term bonds exceeds that on six-month Treasury bills by more than 1.5 percentage points—is generally interpreted as a signal that buyers and sellers of bonds expect the economy to expand in the near future. A yield curve flatter than this is generally interpreted as a signal that bond market participants expect the economy to slow down. Should the yield curve flatten, as it did in November 2007, this is judged to be a signal of uncertainty among bond market participants about the future state of the economy. Some may be expecting an economic expansion and so expect interest rates to rise in the future. Some may be expecting an economic contraction and so expect that interest rates will need to fall in the future. As the description of a flat yield curve suggests, a downward sloping (or "inverted") yield curve—where the interest rate paid on long-term bonds is less than that paid on six-month Treasury bills, such as observed in November 2006—is generally interpreted as a signal that buyers and sellers of bonds are more or less in agreement that they expect the economy to contract in the near future. The four yield curves in the figure above tell an interesting story about how bond market participants judged the state of the Canadian economy leading up to the recession that began in early 2008. By late 2006 (inverted yield curve), market participants deemed it likely that the economy would contract in the near future. This didn't happen, and so a year later, in November 2007 (flat yield curve), there was somewhat more uncertainty about the likelihood of a contraction, even though the onset of recession was in fact just months away. By the middle of the recession (November 2008) the yield curve had regained its usual upward slope, suggesting that market participants expected the economy to soon recover. Finally, by November 2009, when the Bank of Canada was announcing the end of the recession, the steepened yield curve indicated that bond market participants expected further expansion in the economy.

Although the levels of various interest rates are typically quite different—the exception is the case of a flat yield curve, as in November 2007—interest rates go up and down together most of the time. Thus, nearly all the interest rates discussed here decreased between 2006 and 2009. As a general rule, interest rates tend to move together; therefore, we usually refer to "the" interest rate as if there were only one.

Table 4.1 shows how to calculate the after-tax nominal interest rate and the expected after-tax real interest rate. Note that given the nominal interest rate and expected inflation, a reduction in the tax rate on interest income increases the nominal and real after-tax rates of return that a saver receives. Thus, by reducing the rate at which it taxes interest, the government can increase the real rate of return earned by savers and (possibly) increase the rate of saving in the economy. The stimulation of saving is one of the motivations for tax provisions, such as Registered Retirement Savings Plans (RRSPs), which allow savers to shelter part of their interest earnings from taxes and, thus, earn higher after-tax rates of return. Unfortunately, because economists disagree about the effect of higher real interest rates on saving, the effectiveness of RRSPs and similar tax breaks for saving is also in dispute.

TABLE 4.1
Calculating After-Tax Interest Rates

i = nominal interest rate = 5% per year
π^e = expected inflation rate = 2% per year

Example 1
t = tax rate on interest income = 30%
After-tax nominal interest rate = $(1 - t)i = (1 - 0.30)5\% = 3.5\%$
Expected after-tax real interest rate = $(1 - t)i - \pi^e = (1 - 0.30)5\% - 2\% = 1.5\%$

Example 2
t = tax rate on interest income = 20%
After-tax nominal interest rate = $(1 - t)i = (1 - 0.20)5\% = 4\%$
Expected after-tax real interest rate = $(1 - t)i - \pi^e = (1 - 0.20)5\% - 2\% = 2\%$

FISCAL POLICY

We have just demonstrated how government tax policies can affect the real return earned by savers and thus, perhaps, the saving rate. However, even when government fiscal policies—its decisions about spending and taxes—are not intentionally directed at affecting the saving rate, these policies have important implications for the amount of consumption and saving that take place in the economy. Although understanding the links between fiscal policy and consumer behaviour requires some difficult economic reasoning, these links are so important that we introduce them here. We discuss several of these issues further in this book, particularly in Chapter 15.

To make the discussion of fiscal policy effects as straightforward as possible, we take the economy's aggregate output Y as a given. That is, we ignore the possibility that the changes in fiscal policy we consider affect the aggregate supply of goods and services. This assumption is valid if the economy is at full employment (as we are assuming throughout Part II of this book) and if the fiscal policy changes do not significantly affect the capital stock or labour supply. Later, we review the fixed-output assumption and discuss both the classical and Keynesian views about how fiscal policy changes can affect output.

In general, fiscal policy affects *desired consumption, C^d*, primarily by affecting households' current and expected future incomes. More specifically, fiscal changes that increase the tax burden on the private sector, either by raising current taxes or by leading people to expect that taxes will be higher in the future, will cause people to consume less.

For a given level of output Y, government fiscal policies affect desired national saving S^d, or $Y - C^d - G$, in two basic ways. First, as we just noted, fiscal policy can influence desired consumption: For any levels of output Y and government purchases G, a fiscal policy change that reduces desired consumption C^d by one dollar will at the same time raise desired national saving S^d by one dollar. Second, for any levels of output and desired consumption, increases in government purchases directly lower desired national saving, as is apparent from the definition of desired national saving, $S^d = Y - C^d - G$.

To illustrate these general points, we consider how desired consumption and desired national saving would be affected by two specific fiscal policy changes: an increase in government purchases and a tax cut.

Government Purchases

Suppose that current government purchases G increase by $1 billion, say, because the government increases defence spending. Assume that this increase in G is temporary so that plans for future government purchases are unchanged. (Analytical Problem 5 at the end of this chapter looks at the case of a permanent increase in government purchases.) For any level of output Y, how will this change in fiscal policy affect desired consumption and desired national saving in the economy?

Let us start by finding the effect of the increased government purchases on consumption. As already mentioned, changes in government purchases affect consumption because they affect private sector tax burdens. Suppose, for example, that the government pays for the extra $1 billion in defence spending by raising current taxes by $1 billion. For given total (before-tax) output Y, this tax increase implies a $1 billion decline in consumers' current (after-tax) incomes. We know that consumers respond to a decline in their current incomes by reducing consumption, although by less than the decline in current income.[4] So, in response to the $1 billion tax increase, consumers might reduce their current consumption by $600 million.

What happens to consumption if the government doesn't raise current taxes when it increases its purchases? The analysis in this case is more subtle. If the government does not raise current taxes, it will have to borrow the $1 billion to pay for the extra spending. The government will have to repay the $1 billion it borrows, plus interest, sometime in the future, implying that future taxes will have to rise. If taxpayers are clever enough to understand that increased government purchases today mean higher taxes in the future, households' expected future (after-tax) incomes will fall, and again they will reduce desired consumption. For the sake of illustration, we can imagine that they again reduce their current consumption by $600 million, although the reduction in consumption might be less if some consumers don't understand that their future taxes are likely to rise. What about the effects on desired national saving? The increase in government purchases affects desired national saving, or $Y - C^d - G$, directly by increasing G and indirectly by reducing desired consumption C^d. In our example, the increase in government purchases reduces desired consumption by $600 million, which by itself would raise national saving by $600 million. However, this effect is outweighed by the increase in G of $1 billion so that overall desired national saving $Y - C^d - G$ falls by $400 million, with output Y held constant.[5] More generally, because the decline in desired consumption can be expected to be less than the initial increase in government purchases, a temporary increase in government purchases will lower desired national saving.

To summarize, for the current level of output Y, we conclude that a temporary increase in government purchases reduces both desired consumption and desired national saving.

Taxes

Now, suppose that government purchases G remain constant but that the government reduces current taxes T by $1 billion. To keep things as simple as possible, we suppose that the tax cut is a *lump sum*, giving each taxpayer the same amount

---

[4] Recall that the marginal propensity to consume out of current income is positive but less than 1.

[5] Note that national saving would fall by even more than $400 million if consumers ignored the prospect of future tax increases and thus did not reduce their current consumption.

(think of the country's 10 million taxpayers receiving $100 each). With government purchases G and output Y held constant, desired national saving $Y - C^d - G$ will change only if desired consumption C^d changes. So the question is, How will desired consumption respond to the cut in current taxes?

Again the key issue is how the tax cut will affect people's current and expected future incomes. The $1 billion current tax cut directly increases current (after-tax) incomes by $1 billion, so the tax cut should increase desired consumption (by somewhat less than $1 billion). However, the $1 billion current tax cut should also lead people to expect *lower* after-tax incomes in the future. The reason is that because the government hasn't changed its spending, to cut taxes by $1 billion today it must also increase its current borrowing by $1 billion. Because the extra $1 billion of government debt will have to be repaid with interest in the future, future taxes will have to be higher, which in turn implies lower future disposable incomes for households. All else being equal, the decline in expected future incomes will cause people to consume less today, offsetting the positive effect of increased current income on desired consumption. Thus, in principle, a current tax cut—which raises current incomes but lowers expected future incomes—could either raise or lower current desired consumption.

Interestingly, some economists argue that the positive effect of increased current income and the negative effect of decreased future income on desired consumption should exactly cancel so that the overall effect of a current tax cut on consumption is zero! The idea that tax cuts do not affect desired consumption and (therefore) also do not affect desired national saving[6] is called the **Ricardian equivalence proposition**.[7]

The Ricardian equivalence idea can be briefly explained as follows (see Chapter 15 for a more detailed discussion). In the long run, all government purchases must be paid for by taxes. Thus, if the government's current and planned purchases don't change, a cut in current taxes can affect the *timing* of tax collections but (advocates of Ricardian equivalence emphasize) not the ultimate tax burden borne by consumers. A current tax cut with no change in government purchases doesn't really make consumers any better off (any reduction in taxes today is balanced by tax increases in the future), so they have no reason to respond to the tax cut by changing their desired consumption.

Although the logic of the Ricardian equivalence proposition is sound, many economists question whether it is applicable in practice. Most of these skeptics argue that even though the proposition predicts that consumers will not increase consumption when taxes are cut, in reality, lower current taxes will likely lead to increased desired consumption and, thus, reduced desired national saving. One reason why consumption may rise after a tax cut is that many, perhaps most, consumers don't understand that increased government borrowing today is likely to lead to higher taxes in the future. Thus, consumers may simply respond to the current tax cut, as they would to any other increase in current income, by increasing their desired consumption.

---

[6] In this example, private disposable income rises by $1 billion, so if desired consumption doesn't change, desired private saving rises by $1 billion. However, the government deficit also rises by $1 billion because of the tax cut, so government saving falls by $1 billion. Therefore, desired national saving—private saving plus government saving—does not change.

[7] The argument was first advanced by the 19th-century economist David Ricardo, although he expressed some reservations about its applicability to real-world situations. The word *equivalence* refers to the idea that if Ricardian equivalence is true, taxes and government borrowing have equivalent effects on the economy.

The effects of a tax cut on consumption and saving may be summarized as follows: According to the Ricardian equivalence proposition, with no change in current or planned government purchases, a tax cut does not change desired consumption and desired national saving. However, the Ricardian equivalence proposition may not apply if consumers fail to take account of possible future tax increases in their planning; in that case, a tax cut will increase desired consumption and reduce desired national saving.

The factors that affect consumption and saving are listed in Summary table 5.

4.2 INVESTMENT

Let's now turn to a second major component of spending: investment spending by firms. Like consumption and saving decisions, the decision about how much to invest depends largely on expectations about the economy's future. Investment also shares with saving and consumption the idea of a trade-off between the present and the future. In making a capital investment, a firm commits its current resources (which could otherwise be used, say, to pay increased dividends to shareholders) to increasing its capacity to produce and earn profits in the future.

Recall from Chapter 2 that *investment* refers to the purchase or construction of capital goods, including residential and non-residential buildings, machines and equipment used in production, and additions to inventory stocks. From a macroeconomic perspective, there are two main reasons to study investment behaviour. First, more so than the other components of aggregate spending, investment

SUMMARY 5   DETERMINANTS OF DESIRED NATIONAL SAVING

ALL ELSE EQUAL, AN INCREASE IN	CAUSES DESIRED NATIONAL SAVING TO	REASON
Current output, Y	Rise	Part of the extra income is saved to provide for future consumption.
Expected future income	Fall	Anticipation of future income raises current desired consumption, lowering current desired saving.
Wealth	Fall	Some of the extra wealth is consumed, which reduces saving for given income.
Expected real interest rate, r	Probably rise	An increased return makes saving more attractive, probably outweighing the fact that less must be saved to reach a specific savings target.
Government purchases, G	Fall	Higher government purchases directly lower desired national saving.
Taxes, T	Remain unchanged or rise	Saving does not change if consumers take into account an offsetting future tax cut; saving rises if consumers do not take into account a future tax cut and thus reduce current consumption.

spending fluctuates sharply over the business cycle, falling in recessions and rising in booms. Even though investment is only about one-sixth of GDP, in a typical recession, half or more of the total decline in spending is reduced investment spending. Hence, explaining the behaviour of investment is important for understanding the business cycle, which we explore further in Part III.

The second reason for studying investment behaviour is that investment plays a crucial role in determining the long-run productive capacity of the economy. Because investment creates new capital goods, a high rate of investment means that the capital stock is growing quickly. As discussed in Chapter 3, capital is one of the two most important factors of production (the other is labour). All else being equal, output will be higher in an economy that has invested rapidly and, thus, built up a large capital stock than in an economy that has not acquired much capital.

THE DESIRED CAPITAL STOCK

To understand what determines the amount of investment, we must consider how firms decide how much capital they want. If firms attempt to maximize profit, as we assume, a firm's **desired capital stock** is the amount of capital that allows the firm to earn the largest expected profit. Managers can determine the profit-maximizing level of the capital stock by comparing the costs and benefits of using additional capital—a new machine, for example. If the benefits outweigh the costs, expanding the capital stock will raise profits. But if the costs outweigh the benefits, the firm should not increase its planned capital stock and may even want to reduce it. As you might infer from this brief description, the economic logic underlying a firm's decision about how much capital to use is similar to the logic of its decision about how many workers to employ, discussed in Chapter 3.

In real terms, the benefit to a firm of having an additional unit of capital is the marginal product of capital, MPK. Recall from Chapter 3 that the MPK is the increase in output that a firm can obtain by adding a unit of capital, holding constant the firm's workforce and other factors of production. Because lags occur in obtaining and installing new capital, the expected *future* marginal product of capital, MPK^f, is the benefit from increasing investment today by one unit of capital. This expected future benefit must be compared with the expected cost of using that extra unit of capital, or the user cost of capital.

The User Cost of Capital

To make the discussion of the user cost of capital more concrete, let's consider the case of Tony's Bakery Inc., a company that produces specialty cookies. Tony, the bakery's owner-manager, is considering investing in a new solar-powered oven that will allow him to produce more cookies in the future. If he decides to buy such an oven, he must also determine its size. In making this decision, Tony has the following three items of information:

1. A new oven can be purchased in any size at a price of $1000 per cubic metre, measured in real (base-year) dollars.

2. Because the oven is solar powered, using it does not involve energy costs. The oven also does not require maintenance expenditures.[8] However, the oven

---

[8] These assumptions simplify the example. If there were operating costs, such as fuel and maintenance costs, we would subtract them from the expected future marginal product of capital when calculating the benefit of using the machine.

becomes less efficient as it ages: With each year that passes, the oven produces 10% fewer cookies. Because of this depreciation, the real value of an oven falls 10% per year. For example, after one year of use, the real value of the oven is $900 per cubic metre.

3. Tony can borrow (from a bank) or lend (to the government, by buying a one-year government bond) at the prevailing expected real interest rate of 8% per year.

In calculating the user cost of capital, we use the following symbols (the numerical values are from the example of Tony's Bakery):

$$p_K = \text{real price of capital goods (\$1000 per cubic metre)}$$
$$d = \text{rate at which capital depreciates (10\% per year)}$$
$$r = \text{expected real interest rate (8\% per year)}$$

The **user cost of capital** is the expected real cost of using a unit of capital for a specified period of time. For Tony's Bakery, we consider the expected costs of purchasing a new oven, using it for a year, then selling it. The cost of using the oven has two components: a depreciation cost and an interest cost.

In general, the **depreciation** cost of using capital is the value lost as the capital wears out. Because of depreciation, after one year the oven that Tony pays $1000 per cubic metre for when new will be worth only $900 per cubic metre. The $100-per-cubic-metre loss that Tony suffers over the year is the depreciation cost of using the oven. Even if Tony does not sell the oven at the end of a year, he suffers this loss because at the end of the year, the asset's (the oven's) economic value will be 10% less.

The interest cost of using capital equals the expected real interest rate times the price of the capital. As the expected real interest rate is 8%, Tony's interest cost of using the oven for a year is 8% of $1000 per cubic metre, or $80 per cubic metre. To see why the interest cost is a cost of using capital, imagine first that Tony must borrow the funds necessary to buy the oven; in this case, the interest cost of $80 per cubic metre is the interest he pays on the loan, which is obviously part of the total cost of using the oven. Alternatively, if Tony uses profits from the business to buy the oven, he gives up the opportunity to use those funds to buy an interest-bearing asset, such as a government bond. For every $1000 that Tony puts into the oven, he is sacrificing $80 in interest that he would have earned by purchasing a $1000 government bond. This forgone interest is a cost to Tony of using the oven. Thus, the interest cost is part of the true economic cost of using capital, whether the capital's purchase is financed with borrowed funds or with the firm's own retained profits.

The user cost of capital is the sum of the depreciation cost and the interest cost. The interest cost is rp_K, the depreciation cost is dp_K, and the user cost of capital, uc, is

$$uc = rp_K + dp_K = (r + d)p_K. \tag{4.3}$$

In the case of Tony's Bakery,

$$uc = 0.08(\$1000 \text{ per cubic metre}) + 0.10(\$1000 \text{ per cubic metre})$$
$$= \$180 \text{ per cubic metre.}$$

Thus, Tony's user cost of capital is $180 per cubic metre per year.

FIGURE 4.1

DETERMINATION OF THE
DESIRED CAPITAL STOCK

The desired capital stock (50 cubic metres of oven capacity in this example) is the capital stock that maximizes profits. When the capital stock is 50 cubic metres, the expected future marginal product of capital MPK^f is equal to the user cost of capital uc. If the MPK^f is larger than uc, as it is when the capital stock is 40 cubic metres, the benefit of extra capital exceeds the cost, and the firm should increase its capital stock. If the MPK^f is smaller than uc, as it is at 60 cubic metres, the cost of extra capital exceeds the benefit, and the firm should reduce its capital stock.

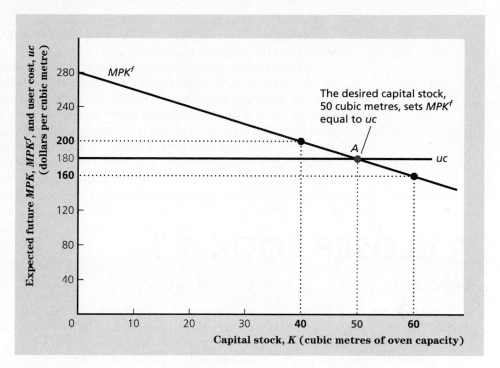

Determining the Desired Capital Stock

Now we can find a firm's profit-maximizing capital stock, or desired capital stock. A firm's desired capital stock is the capital stock at which the expected future marginal product of capital equals the user cost of capital.

Figure 4.1 shows the determination of the desired capital stock for Tony's Bakery. The capital stock K, expressed as cubic metres of oven capacity, is measured along the horizontal axis. Both the MPK^f and the user cost of capital are measured along the vertical axis.

The downward-sloping curve shows the value of the MPK^f for different sizes of the capital stock K; at each level of K, the MPK^f equals the expected real value of the extra cookies that could be produced if oven capacity were expanded an additional cubic metre. The MPK^f curve slopes downward because the marginal product of capital falls as the capital stock is increased (we discussed reasons for the diminishing marginal productivity of capital in Chapter 3). The user cost (equal to $180 per cubic metre in the example) does not depend on the amount of capital and is represented by a horizontal line.

The amount of capital that maximizes the expected profit of Tony's Bakery is 50 cubic metres, represented by point A in Figure 4.1. At A, the expected benefit of an additional unit of capital, MPK^f, equals the user cost, uc. For any amount of oven capacity of less than 50 cubic metres, Tony's Bakery could increase its expected profit by increasing oven capacity. For example, Figure 4.1 shows that at a planned capacity of 40 cubic metres, the MPK^f of an additional cubic metre is $200 worth of cookies per year, which exceeds the $180 expected cost of using the additional cubic metre of capacity. Starting from a planned capacity of 40 cubic metres, if Tony adds an extra cubic metre of capacity, he will gain an additional $200 worth of future output while incurring only $180 in expected future costs. Thus, expanding beyond 40 cubic metres is profitable for Tony. Similarly, Figure 4.1 shows that at an oven capacity of more than 50 cubic metres, the expected future marginal product of

---

capital, MPK^f, is less than the user cost, uc; in this case, Tony's Bakery could increase expected profit by reducing its capital stock. Only when $MPK^f = uc$ will the capital stock be at the level that maximizes expected profit.

As mentioned earlier, the determination of the desired capital stock is similar to the determination of the firm's labour demand, described in Chapter 3. Recall that the firm's profit-maximizing level of employment is the level at which the marginal product of labour equals the wage. Analogously, the firm's profit-maximizing level of capital is the level at which the expected future marginal product of capital equals the user cost, which can be thought of as the "wage" of capital (the cost of using capital for one period). The desired capital stock can be derived in other ways as well. In A Closer Look 4.3, "Investment and the Stock Market," we discuss the relationship of the desired capital stock to stock prices.

A CLOSER LOOK 4.3

INVESTMENT AND THE STOCK MARKET

Fluctuations in the stock market can have important macroeconomic effects. Changes in stock prices may cause households to change how much they consume and save (see the Application "Stock Market Wealth, Housing Wealth, and Consumer Spending," p. 99). Similarly, economic theory suggests that rises and falls in the stock market should lead firms to change their rates of capital investment in the same direction. The relationship between stock prices and firms' investment in physical capital is captured by the "q theory of investment," developed by the late James Tobin of Yale University, who was a Nobel laureate.

Tobin argued that the rate of investment in any particular type of capital can be predicted by looking at the ratio of the capital's market value to its replacement cost. When this ratio, often called "Tobin's q," is greater than 1, it is profitable to acquire additional capital because the value of capital exceeds the cost of acquiring it. Similarly, when Tobin's q is smaller than 1, the value of capital is less than the cost of acquiring it, so it is not profitable to invest in additional capital.

Because much of the value of firms comes from the capital they own, we can use the stock market value of a firm as a measure of the market value of the firm's capital stock. If we let V be the stock market value of a firm, K be the amount of capital the firm owns, and p_K be the price of new capital goods, then for an individual firm,

$$\text{Tobin's } q = \frac{V}{p_K K},$$

where $p_K K$ is the replacement cost of the firm's capital stock. If the replacement cost of capital isn't changing

much, a boom in the stock market (an increase in V) will cause Tobin's q to rise for most firms, leading to increased rates of investment. Essentially, when the stock market is high, firms find it profitable to expand.

Empirically, researchers have found that investment in new capital goods does tend to rise when the stock market rises and to fall when the market falls, although the relationship isn't always strong. Part of the problem is that, in practice, stock prices reflect many assets besides capital, such as the patents a firm holds or the reputation of a firm's products. Thus, changes in stock prices are imperfect measures of the changes in the market value of capital.

Although it may seem different, the q theory of investment is very similar to the theory of investment discussed in this chapter. In the theory developed in this chapter we identified three main factors affecting the desired capital stock: the expected future marginal product of capital, MPK^f; the real interest rate, r; and the purchase price of new capital, p_K. Each of these factors also affects Tobin's q: (1) An increase in the expected marginal product of capital tends to increase the expected future earnings of the firm, which raises the stock market value of the firm and thus increases q; (2) a reduction in the real interest rate also tends to raise stock prices (and hence q), as financial investors substitute away from low-yielding bonds and bank deposits and buy stocks instead; and (3) a decrease in the purchase price of capital reduces the denominator of the q ratio and thus increases q. Because all three types of change increase Tobin's q, they also increase the desired capital stock and investment, as predicted by our analysis in this chapter.

FIGURE 4.2

A DECLINE IN THE REAL
INTEREST RATE RAISES THE
DESIRED CAPITAL STOCK

For the Tony's Bakery example, a decline in the real interest rate from 8% to 6% reduces the user cost, *uc*, of a cubic metre of oven capacity from $180 to $160 per cubic metre and shifts the user cost line down from uc^1 to uc^2. The desired capital stock rises from 50 (point *A*) to 60 (point *C*) cubic metres of oven capacity. At 60 cubic metres, the MPK^f and the user cost of capital again are equal, at $160 per cubic metre.

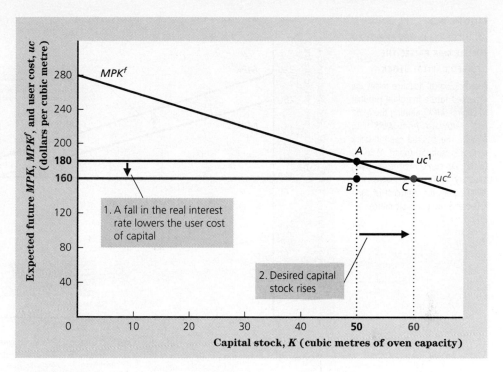

CHANGES IN THE DESIRED CAPITAL STOCK

Any factor that shifts the MPK^f curve or changes the user cost of capital changes the firm's desired capital stock. For Tony's Bakery, suppose that the real interest rate falls from 8% to 6%. If the real interest rate r is 0.06 and the depreciation rate d and the price of capital p_K remain at 0.10 and $1000 per cubic metre, respectively, the decline in the real interest rate reduces the user cost of capital $(r + d)p_K$ from $180 per cubic metre to $(0.06 + 0.10)\$1000$ per cubic metre, or $160 per cubic metre.

This decline in the user cost is shown as a downward shift of the user cost line, from uc^1 to uc^2 in Figure 4.2. After that shift, the MPK^f at the original desired capital stock of 50 cubic metres (point *A*), or $180 per cubic metre, exceeds the user cost of capital, now $160 per cubic metre (point *B*). Tony's Bakery can increase its profit by raising planned oven capacity to 60 cubic metres, where the MPK^f equals the user cost of $160 per cubic metre (point *C*). This example illustrates that a decrease in the expected real interest rate—or any other change that lowers the user cost of capital—increases the desired capital stock.

Technological changes that affect the MPK^f curve also affect the desired stock of capital. Suppose that Tony invents a new type of cookie dough that requires less baking time, allowing 12.5% more cookies to be baked daily. Such a technological advance would cause the MPK^f curve for ovens to shift upward by 12.5% at each value of the capital stock. Figure 4.3 shows this effect as a shift of the MPK^f curve from MPK^{f1} to MPK^{f2}. If the user cost remains at $180 per cubic metre, the technological advance causes Tony's desired capital stock to rise from 50 to 60 cubic metres. At 60 cubic metres (point *D*), the MPK^f again equals the user cost of capital. In general, with the user cost of capital held constant, an increase in the expected future marginal product of capital at any level of capital raises the desired capital stock.

FIGURE 4.3

AN INCREASE IN THE EXPECTED
FUTURE *MPK* RAISES THE
DESIRED CAPITAL STOCK

A technological advance raises the
expected future marginal product
of capital, *MPK^f*, shifting the *MPK^f*
curve upward from *MPK^{f1}* to
MPK^{f2}. The desired capital stock
increases from 50 (point *A*) to 60
(point *D*) cubic metres of oven
capacity. At 60 cubic metres, the
MPK^f equals the user cost of capital *uc* at \$180 per cubic metre.

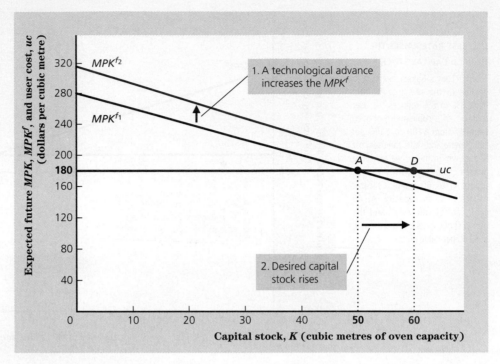

Taxes and the Desired Capital Stock

So far, we have ignored the role of taxes in the investment decision. But Tony is interested in maximizing the profit his firm gets to keep after paying taxes. Thus, he must
take into account taxes in evaluating the desirability of an additional unit of capital.

Suppose that Tony's Bakery pays 20% of its revenues in taxes. In this case,
extra oven capacity that increases the firm's future revenues by, say, \$200 will
raise Tony's after-tax revenue by only \$160, with \$40 going to the government. To
decide whether to add this extra capacity, Tony should compare the after-tax
MPK^f of \$160—not the before-tax *MPK^f* of \$200—with the user cost. In general, if
τ is the tax rate on firm revenues, the after-tax future marginal product of capital
is $(1 - \tau)MPK^f$. The desired capital stock is the one for which the after-tax future
marginal product equals the user cost, or

$$(1 - \tau)MPK^f = uc.$$

Dividing both sides of this equation by $1 - \tau$, we obtain

$$MPK^f = \frac{uc}{1 - \tau} = \frac{(r + d)p_K}{1 - \tau} \qquad (4.4)$$

In Eq. (4.4), the term $uc/(1 - \tau)$ is called the **tax-adjusted user cost of
capital**. The tax-adjusted user cost of capital shows how large the before-tax
future marginal product of capital must be for a firm to willingly add another unit
of capital. An increase in the tax rate τ raises the tax-adjusted user cost and, thus,
reduces the desired stock of capital.

To derive the tax-adjusted user cost, we assumed that taxes are levied as a
proportion of firms' revenues. However, actual corporate taxes in Canada and
other countries are much more complicated. Firms generally pay taxes on their

profits rather than on their revenues, and the part of profit that is considered taxable may depend on how much the firm invests. For example, when a firm purchases some capital, it is allowed to deduct part of the purchase price of the capital from its taxable profit in both the year of purchase and in subsequent years. By reducing the amount of profit to be taxed, these deductions, known as *depreciation allowances*, allow the firm to reduce its total tax payment.

Another important tax provision, which was used from 1975 to 1987 in Canada, is the investment tax credit. An *investment tax credit* permits the firm to subtract a percentage of the purchase price of new capital directly from its tax bill. So, for example, if the investment tax credit is 10%, a firm that purchases a $15 000 piece of equipment can reduce its taxes by $1500 (10% of $15 000) in the year the equipment is purchased.

Economists summarize the many provisions of the tax code affecting investment by a single measure of the tax burden on capital called the **effective tax rate**. Essentially, the idea is to ask what tax rate, τ, on a firm's revenue would have the same effect on the desired capital stock as would the actual provisions of the tax code. The hypothetical tax rate that answers this question is the effective tax rate. Changes in the tax law that, for example, raise the effective tax rate are equivalent to an increased tax on firm revenue and a rise in the tax-adjusted user cost of capital. Thus, all else being equal, an increase in the effective tax rate lowers the desired capital stock.

Table 4.2 shows effective tax rates on capital for the G7 countries over the period 2005–2015, as calculated by Philip Bazel and Jack Mintz writing for the School of Public Policy at the University of Calgary. From inspection of the table, you can see that governments in Canada have been successful in their effort to reduce the effective tax rate on capital investment not only absolutely but also relative to other countries. The effective tax rate in Canada in 2015 is nearly half what it was in 2005, and over that same period Canada moved from having one of the highest tax rates among G7 countries to having one of the lowest.

FROM THE DESIRED CAPITAL STOCK TO INVESTMENT

Now let us look at the link between a firm's desired capital stock and the amount it invests. In general, the capital stock (of a firm or of a country) changes over time through two opposing channels. First, the purchase or construction of new capital

TABLE 4.2
Effective Tax Rates on Capital Investment (%), G7 Countries, 2005–2015

Country	2005	2010	2015
Canada	38.8%	19.9%	20.0%
Germany	33.8	24.3	23.8
Italy	32.5	27.2	8.3
United States	35.2	34.6	34.6
United Kingdom	29.7	28.7	22.9
Japan	45.8	45.8	42.1
France	35.1	33.7	36.1

Source: 2015 Tax Competitiveness Report: Canada is Losing its Attractiveness", The School of Public Policy, *SPP Research Papers*, Volume 9, Issue 37, November 2016.

goods increases the capital stock. We have been calling the total purchase or construction of new capital goods that takes place each year *investment*, but its precise name is **gross investment**. Second, the capital stock depreciates or wears out, which reduces the capital stock.

Whether the capital stock increases or decreases over the course of a year depends on whether gross investment is greater or less than depreciation during the year; when gross investment exceeds depreciation, the capital stock grows. The change in the capital stock over the year—or, equivalently, the difference between gross investment and depreciation—is **net investment**.

We express these concepts algebraically with the following symbols:

I_t = gross investment during year t,

K_t = capital stock at the beginning of year t, and

K_{t+1} = capital stock at the beginning of year $t + 1$ (equivalently, at the end of year t).

Net investment, the change in the capital stock during period t, equals $K_{t+1} - K_t$. The amount of depreciation during year t is dK_t, where d is the fraction of capital that depreciates each year. The relationship between net and gross investments is

$$\text{net investment} = \text{gross investment} - \text{depreciation};$$
$$K_{t+1} - K_t = I_t - dK_t. \tag{4.5}$$

In most but not all years, gross investment is larger than depreciation so that net investment is positive and the capital stock increases. Figure 4.4 shows the behaviour since 1926 of gross and net investments in Canada, expressed as percentages of GDP; the difference between gross and net investments is depreciation. Note the occasional large swings in both gross and net investments and the negative rates of net investment that occurred in several years during the Great Depression of the 1930s and World War II.

FIGURE 4.4

GROSS AND NET INVESTMENTS, 1926–2015

The figure shows private gross and net investments in Canada since 1926 as percentages of GDP. During some years of the Great Depression and World War II, net investment was negative, implying that the private capital stock was shrinking.

Source: Adapted from Statistics Canada, 2017. This does not constitute an endorsement by Statistics Canada of this product.

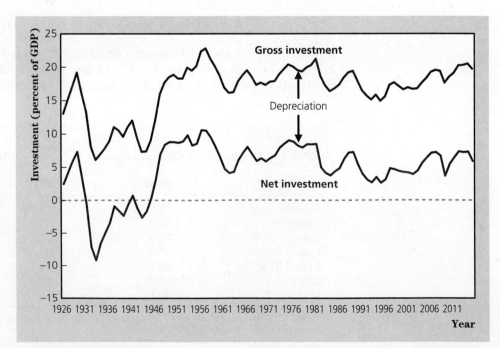

We can use Eq. (4.5) to illustrate the relationship between the desired capital stock and investment. First, rewriting Eq. (4.5) gives

$$I_t = K_{t+1} - K_t + dK_t$$

which states that gross investment equals net investment plus depreciation.

Now, suppose that firms use information available at the beginning of year t about the expected future marginal product of capital and the user cost of capital in order to determine the desired capital stock K^* they want by the end of year t (beginning of year $t + 1$). For the moment, suppose also that capital is easily obtainable so that firms can match the actual capital stock at the end of year t, K_{t+1}, with the desired capital stock K^*. Substituting K^* for K_{t+1} in the preceding equation yields

$$I_t = K^* - K_t + dK_t. \tag{4.6}$$

Equation (4.6) shows that firms' gross investment, I_t, during a year has two parts: (1) the desired net increase in the capital stock over the year, $K^* - K_t$; and (2) the investment needed to replace worn-out or depreciated capital, dK_t. The amount of depreciation that occurs during a year is determined by the depreciation rate and the initial capital stock. However, the desired net increase in the capital stock over the year depends on the factors—such as taxes, interest rates, and the expected future marginal product of capital—that affect the desired capital stock. Indeed, Eq. (4.6) shows that any factor that leads to a change in the desired capital stock K^* results in an equal change in gross investment I_t.

Lags and Investment

The assumption just made, that firms can obtain capital quickly enough to match actual capital stocks with desired levels each year, is not realistic in all cases. Although most types of equipment are readily available, a skyscraper or a nuclear power plant may take years to construct. Thus, in practice, a $1 million increase in a firm's desired capital stock may not translate into a $1 million increase in gross investment within the year; instead, the extra investment may be spread over several years as planning and construction proceed. Despite this qualification, factors that increase firms' desired capital stocks also tend to increase the current rate of investment. Summary table 6 brings together the factors that affect investment.

SUMMARY 6 DETERMINANTS OF DESIRED INVESTMENT

ALL ELSE EQUAL, AN INCREASE IN	CAUSES DESIRED INVESTMENT TO	REASON
Real interest rate, r	Fall	The user cost increases, which reduces desired capital stock.
Effective tax rate	Fall	The tax-adjusted user cost increases, which reduces desired capital stock.
Expected future MPK	Rise	The desired capital stock increases.

INVESTMENT IN INVENTORIES AND HOUSING

Our discussion so far has emphasized what is called business fixed investment, or investment by firms in structures (such as factories and office buildings) and equipment (such as drill presses and jetliners). However, there are two other components of investment spending: inventory investment and residential investment. As discussed in Chapter 2, inventory investment equals the increase in firms' inventories of unsold goods, unfinished goods, or raw materials. During business cycles, inventory investment is the most volatile component of investment spending. Residential investment is the construction of housing, such as single-family homes, condominiums, or apartment buildings.

Fortunately, the concepts of future marginal product and the user cost of capital, which we used to examine business fixed investment, apply equally well to inventory investment and residential investment. Consider, for example, a new-car dealer trying to decide whether to increase the number of cars she normally keeps on her lot from 100 to 150, that is, to make an inventory investment of 50 cars. The benefit of having more cars to show is that potential car buyers will have a greater variety of models to select from and may not have to wait for delivery, enabling the car dealer to sell more cars. The increase in sales commissions the car dealer expects to make, measured in real terms and with the same sales force, is the expected future marginal product of the increased inventory. The cost of holding more cars reflects (1) depreciation of the cars sitting on the lot, and (2) the interest the car dealer must pay on the loan obtained to finance the higher inventory. The car dealer will make the inventory investment if the expected benefits of increasing her inventory, in increased sales, are at least as great as the interest and depreciation costs of adding 50 cars. This principle is the same one that applies to business fixed investment.

We can also use this same approach to analyze residential investment. The expected future marginal product of an apartment building, for example, is the real value of rents that can be collected from the tenants, minus taxes and operating costs. The user cost of capital for an apartment building during a year is its depreciation, or loss of value from wear and tear, plus the interest cost (reflected in mortgage payments, for example). As for other types of capital, constructing an apartment building is profitable only if its expected future marginal product is at least as great as its user cost.

4.3 GOODS MARKET EQUILIBRIUM

In Chapter 3, we demonstrated that the quantity of goods and services supplied in an economy depends on the level of productivity—as determined, for example, by the technology used—and on the quantity of inputs, such as the capital and labour used. In this chapter, we have discussed the factors that affect the demand for goods and services, particularly the demand for consumption goods by households and the demand for investment goods by firms. But how do we know that the amount of goods and services consumers and investors want to buy will be the same as the amount producers are willing to provide? Putting the question another way, What economic forces bring the goods market into equilibrium, with quantities demanded equal to quantities supplied? In this section, we show that the real interest rate is the key economic variable whose adjustments help bring the quantities of goods supplied and demanded into balance; thus, a benefit of our analysis is an explanation of what determines interest rates. Another benefit is that by adding the analysis of goods market equilibrium to the analysis of labour market equilibrium in Chapter 3, we take another large step toward constructing a complete model of the macroeconomy.

The goods market is in equilibrium when the aggregate quantity of goods supplied equals the aggregate quantity of goods demanded. (For brevity, we refer only to *goods* rather than to *goods and services*, but services are always included.) Algebraically, this condition is

$$Y = C^d + I^d + G. \qquad (4.7)$$

The left-hand side of Eq. (4.7) is the quantity of goods Y supplied by firms, which is determined by the factors discussed in Chapter 3. The right-hand side of Eq. (4.7) is the aggregate demand for goods. If we continue to assume no foreign sector, so that net exports are zero, the quantity of goods demanded is the sum of desired consumption by households, C^d, desired investment by firms, I^d, and government purchases, G.[9] Equation (4.7) is called the goods market equilibrium condition.

The goods market equilibrium condition is different in an important way from the income–expenditure identity for a closed economy, $Y = C + I + G$ (this identity is Eq. 2.3, with $NX = 0$). The income expenditure identity is a relationship between actual income (output) and actual spending, which, by definition, is always satisfied. In contrast, the goods market equilibrium condition does not always have to be satisfied. For example, firms may produce output faster than consumers want to buy it so that undesired inventories pile up in firms' warehouses. In this situation, the income–expenditure identity is still satisfied (because the undesired additions to firms' inventories are counted as part of total spending—see Chapter 2); however, the goods market would not be in equilibrium because production exceeds *desired* spending (which does *not* include the undesired increases in inventories). Although in principle the goods market equilibrium condition need not always hold, strong forces act to bring the goods market into equilibrium fairly quickly.

A different, but equivalent, way to write the goods market equilibrium condition emphasizes the relationship between desired saving and desired investment. To obtain this alternative form of the goods market equilibrium condition, we first subtract $C^d + G$ from both sides of Eq. (4.7):

$$Y - C^d - G = I^d.$$

The left-hand side of this equation, $Y - C^d - G$, is desired national saving, S^d (see Eq. 4.1). Thus, the goods market equilibrium condition becomes

$$S^d = I^d. \qquad (4.8)$$

This alternative way of writing the goods market equilibrium condition says that the goods market is in equilibrium when desired national saving equals desired investment.

Because saving and investment are central to many issues we present in this book, and because the desired-saving-equals-desired-investment form of the goods market equilibrium condition is often easier to work with, we utilize Eq. (4.8) in most of our analyses. However, we emphasize once again that Eq. (4.8) is equivalent to the condition that the supply of goods equals the demand for goods, Eq. (4.7).

---

[9] We assume that G always equals the level desired by the government and so do not distinguish between desired and actual G.

FIGURE 4.5

GOODS MARKET EQUILIBRIUM

Goods market equilibrium occurs when desired national saving equals desired investment. In the figure, equilibrium occurs when the real interest rate is 6% and both desired national saving and desired investment equal 100. If the real interest rate were, say, 3%, desired investment (150) would not equal desired national saving (85), and the goods market would not be in equilibrium. Competition among borrowers for funds would then cause the real interest rate to rise until it reached 6%.

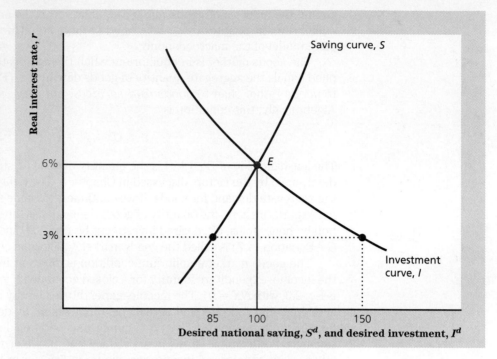

THE SAVING–INVESTMENT DIAGRAM

For the goods market to be in equilibrium, then, the aggregate supply of goods must equal the aggregate demand for goods, or equivalently, desired national saving must equal desired investment. We demonstrate in this section that adjustments of the real interest rate allow the goods market to attain equilibrium.[10]

The determination of goods market equilibrium can be shown graphically with a saving–investment diagram (Figure 4.5). The real interest rate is measured along the vertical axis, and national saving and investment are measured along the horizontal axis. The saving curve, S, shows the relationship between desired national saving and the real interest rate. The upward slope of the saving curve reflects the empirical finding (see Section 4.1) that a higher real interest rate raises desired national saving. The saving curve is drawn for given levels of current output Y, expected future output, wealth, government purchases G, and taxes T. A change in any of these variables will cause the saving curve to shift. The investment curve, I, shows the relationship between desired investment and the real interest rate. The investment curve slopes downward because a higher real interest rate increases the user cost of capital and, thus, reduces desired investment. The investment curve is drawn for given levels of the effective tax rate and expected future marginal product of capital. A change in either of these variables will cause the investment curve to shift.

Goods market equilibrium is represented by point E, at which desired national saving equals investment, as required by Eq. (4.8). The real interest rate corresponding to E (6% in this example) is the only real interest rate that clears the goods market. When the real interest rate is 6%, both desired national saving and desired investment equal 100.

---

[10] Strictly speaking, we should refer to the *expected real interest rate* rather than simply the *real interest rate*. The two are the same if expected inflation and actual inflation are equal.

How does the goods market come to equilibrium at E, where the real interest rate is 6%? Suppose instead that the real interest rate is 3%. As Figure 4.5 shows, when the real interest rate is 3%, the amount of investment that firms want to do (150) exceeds desired national saving (85). With investors wanting to borrow more than savers want to lend, the "price" of saving—the real interest rate that lenders receive—will be bid up. The return to savers will rise until it reaches 6%, where desired national saving and desired investment will be equal. Similarly, if the real interest rate exceeds 6%, the amount that savers want to lend will exceed what investors want to borrow, and the real return paid to savers will be bid down. Thus, adjustments of the real interest rate, in response to an excess supply or excess demand for saving, bring the goods market into equilibrium.

Although Figure 4.5 shows goods market equilibrium in terms of equal saving and investment, keep in mind that an equivalent way to express goods market equilibrium is that the supply of goods, Y, equals the demand for goods, $C^d + I^d + G$, Eq. (4.7). Table 4.3 illustrates this point with a numerical example consistent with the values shown in Figure 4.5. Here the assumption is that output Y and government purchases G are fixed at values of 450 and 150, respectively. Desired consumption C^d and desired investment I^d depend on the real interest rate. Desired consumption depends on the real interest rate because a higher real interest rate raises desired saving, which necessarily reduces desired consumption. Desired investment depends on the real interest rate because an increase in the real interest rate raises the user cost of capital, which lowers desired investment.

In the example in Table 4.3, when the real interest is 6%, desired consumption $C^d = 200$. Therefore, desired national saving $S^d = Y - C^d - G = 450 - 200 - 150 = 100$. Also, when the real interest rate is 6%, desired investment $I^d = 100$. As desired national saving equals desired investment when $r = 6\%$, the equilibrium real interest rate is 6%, as in Figure 4.5.

Note, moreover, that when the real interest rate is at the equilibrium value of 6%, the aggregate supply of goods, Y, which is 450, equals the aggregate demand for goods, $C^d + I^d + G = 200 + 100 + 150 = 450$. Thus, both forms of the goods market equilibrium condition, Eqs. (4.7) and (4.8), are satisfied when the real interest rate equals 6%.

Table 4.3 also illustrates how adjustments of the real interest rate bring about equilibrium in the goods market. Suppose that the real interest rate is initially 3%. Both components of private sector demand for goods (C^d and I^d) are higher when the real interest rate is 3% than when it is 6%. The reason is that consumers save less and firms invest more when real interest rates are relatively low. Thus, at a real interest rate of 3%, the demand for goods ($C^d + I^d + G = 215 + 150 + 150 = 515$)

TABLE 4.3

Components of Aggregate Demand for Goods: An Example

Desired Aggregate

Real Interest Rate, r	Output, Y	Desired Consumption, C^d	Desired Investment, I^d	Government Purchases, G	National Saving, $S^d = Y - C^d - G$	Demand for Goods, $C^d + I^d + G$
3%	450	215	150	150	85	515
6%	450	200	100	150	100	450

is greater than the supply of goods ($Y = 450$). Equivalently, at a real interest rate of 3%, Table 4.3 shows that desired investment ($I^d = 150$) exceeds desired saving ($S^d = 85$). As Figure 4.5 shows, an increase in the real interest rate to 6% eliminates the disequilibrium in the goods market by reducing desired investment and increasing desired national saving. An alternative explanation is that the increase in the real interest rate eliminates the excess of the demand for goods over the supply of goods by reducing both consumption demand and investment demand.

Figure 4.5 is a key diagram of macroeconomic analysis. As we noted previously, saving and investment are central to many issues we present in this book, and this simple diagram shows how these key variables are brought into equilibrium. We noted earlier that the saving curve is drawn for given values of current output Y, expected future output, wealth, government purchases G, and taxes T, and that the investment curve is drawn for given levels of the effective tax rate and expected future marginal product of capital. We can, therefore, use this diagram to show how a change in any of these variables, by causing changes in the positions of the saving and investment curves, cause changes to three key macroeconomic variables: the interest rate r, desired national saving S^d, and desired investment I^d. This is the subject of the next two sections.

Shifts of the Saving Curve

For any real interest rate, a change in the economy that raises desired national saving shifts the saving curve to the right, and a change that reduces desired national saving shifts the saving curve to the left. (Summary table 5 on p. 108 lists the factors affecting desired national saving.)

A shift of the saving curve leads to a new goods market equilibrium with a different real interest rate and different amounts of saving and investment. Figure 4.6 illustrates the effects of a decrease in desired national saving—resulting, for example, from a temporary increase in current government purchases. The initial

FIGURE 4.6

A DECLINE IN DESIRED SAVING

A change that reduces desired national saving, such as a temporary increase in current government purchases, shifts the saving curve to the left, from S^1 to S^2. The goods market equilibrium point moves from E to F. The decline in desired saving raises the real interest rate, from 6% to 7%, and lowers saving and investment, from 100 to 85.

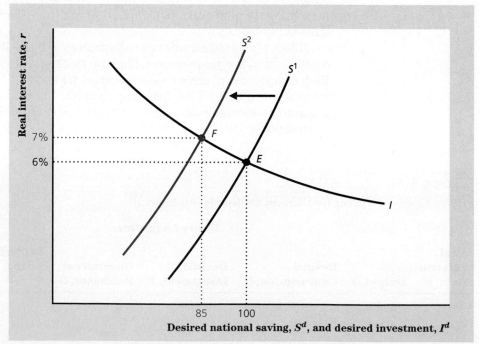

equilibrium point is at E, where (as in Figure 4.5) the real interest rate is 6% and desired national saving and desired investment both equal 100. When current government purchases increase, the resulting decrease in desired national saving causes the saving curve to shift to the left, from S^1 to S^2. At the new goods market equilibrium point, F, the real interest rate is 7%, reflecting the fact that at the initial real interest rate of 6% the demand for funds by investors now exceeds the supply of saving.

Figure 4.6 also shows that in response to the increase in government purchases, national saving and investment both fall, from 100 to 85. Saving falls because of the initial decrease in desired saving, which is only partially offset by the increase in the real interest rate. Investment falls because the higher real interest rate raises the user cost of capital that firms face. When increased government purchases cause investment to decline, economists say that investment has been *crowded out*. The crowding out of investment by increased government purchases occurs, in effect, because the government is using more real resources, some of which would otherwise have gone into private investment.

Shifts of the Investment Curve

Like the saving curve, the investment curve can shift. For any real interest rate, a change in the economy that raises desired investment shifts the investment curve to the right, and a change that lowers desired investment shifts the investment curve to the left. (See Summary table 6 on p. 117 for the factors affecting desired investment.)

The effects on goods market equilibrium of an increase in desired investment are shown in Figure 4.7. Suppose that a new invention or, at the aggregate level, an economic reform in an emerging market economy raises the expected future marginal product of capital. The increase in desired investment shifts the investment curve to the right, from I^1 to I^2, changing the goods market equilibrium point from E to G. The real interest rate rises from 6% to 8% because the increased demand

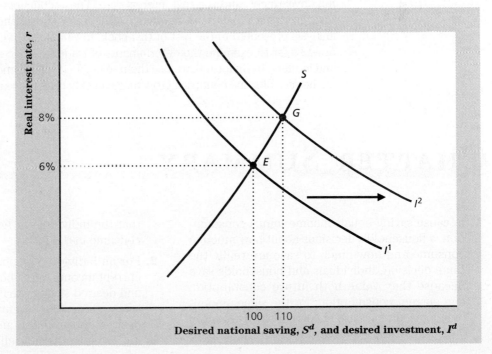

FIGURE 4.7

AN INCREASE IN DESIRED INVESTMENT

A change in the economy that increases desired investment, such as an invention that raises the expected future *MPK*, shifts the investment curve to the right, from I^1 to I^2. The goods market equilibrium point moves from E to G. The real interest rate rises from 6% to 8%, and saving and investment also rise, from 100 to 110.

Desired national saving, S^d, and desired investment, I^d

for investment funds causes the real interest rate to be bid up. Saving and investment also increase, from 100 to 110, with the higher saving reflecting the willingness of savers to save more when the real interest rate rises.

Before leaving this discussion, it is worth remarking that while we have interpreted the key diagram of this chapter, Figure 4.5, as showing how the interest rate is determined in a single closed economy, it can also be interpreted as showing how the interest rate in world markets is determined. Thus, Eq. (4.7) can be interpreted as indicating that the goods market equilibrium for the world economy requires that the quantity of goods demanded is the sum of desired consumption by all households in the world, desired investment by all firms in the world, and purchases by all governments in the world. Similarly, Eq. (4.8) demonstrates that, in equilibrium, desired world saving must equal desired world investment. The saving curve, S, and the investment curve, I, in Figure 4.5 are the diagrammatic versions of Eqs. (4.7) and (4.8), and they express the determination of the market-clearing interest rate in world financial markets.

Given that interpretation, you might find it interesting to review the discussion of shifts in the saving and investment curves and relate what these shifts mean for interest rates in the world economy. For example, if we suppose that the temporary increase in spending by governments involved in wars in Afghanistan and Iraq has had a noticeable impact on world saving, then, as shown in Figure 4.6, this spending has led to an increase in the world interest rate and a decrease in desired world investment and saving. Similarly, if we suppose that the adoption of free market policies by governments in China, India, and elsewhere over the past 20 years has increased the average level of expected future marginal product of capital, MPK, in the world, then, as shown in Figure 4.7, these policies have also led to an increase in the world real interest rate and increases in desired world investment and saving.

In these last two chapters, we have presented supply–demand analyses of the labour and goods markets and developed tools needed to understand the behaviour of various macroeconomic variables, including employment, the real wage, output, saving, investment, and the real interest rate. These concepts—and a few more developed in the study of asset markets in Chapter 7—form the basis for the economic analysis presented in the rest of this book. In Chapter 5, we use the concepts developed so far to examine the determinants of trade flows and international borrowing and lending. In Chapter 6, we use them to tackle the fundamental question of why the economies of some countries grow more quickly than those of other countries.

CHAPTER SUMMARY

1. Because saving equals income minus consumption, a household's decisions about how much to consume and how much to save are really the same decision. Individuals and households save because they value both future consumption and current consumption; for the same amount of income, an increase in current saving reduces current consumption but increases the amount that the individual or household will be able to consume in the future.

2. For an individual or household, an increase in current income raises both desired consumption and desired saving. Analogously, at the national level, an increase in current output raises both desired consumption and desired national saving. At both the household and national levels,

an increase in expected future income or in wealth raises desired consumption; however, because these changes raise desired consumption without affecting current income or output, they cause desired saving to fall.

3. An increase in the real interest rate has two potentially offsetting effects on saving. First, a higher real interest rate increases the price of current consumption relative to future consumption (each unit of current consumption costs $1 + r$ units of forgone future consumption). In response to the increased relative price of current consumption, people substitute future consumption for current consumption by saving more today. This tendency to increase saving in response to an increase in the relative price of current consumption is called the substitution effect of the real interest rate on saving. Second, a higher real interest rate increases the wealth of savers by increasing the interest payments they receive, while reducing the wealth of borrowers by increasing the amount of interest they must pay. By making savers wealthier, an increase in the real interest rate leads savers to consume more and reduce their saving; however, because it makes borrowers poorer, an increase in the real interest rate causes borrowers to reduce their consumption and increase their saving. The change in current consumption that results because a consumer is made richer or poorer by an increase in the real interest rate is called the income effect of the real interest rate on saving.

   For a saver, the substitution effect of an increase in the real interest rate (which tends to boost saving) and the income effect (which tends to reduce saving) work in opposite directions, so that the overall effect is ambiguous. For a borrower, both the substitution effect and the income effect of a higher real interest rate act to increase saving. Overall, empirical studies suggest that an increase in the real interest rate increases desired national saving and reduces desired consumption, but not by very much.

   The real interest rate that is relevant to saving decisions is the expected after-tax real interest rate, which is the real return that savers expect to earn after paying a portion of the interest they receive in taxes.

4. With total output held constant, a temporary increase in government purchases reduces desired consumption. The reason is that higher government purchases imply increases in present or future taxes, which makes consumers feel poorer. However, the decrease in desired consumption is smaller than the increase in government purchases, so that desired national saving, $Y - C^d - G$, falls as a result of a temporary increase in government purchases.

5. According to the Ricardian equivalence proposition, a current lump-sum tax cut should have no effect on desired consumption or desired national saving. The reason is that if there is no change in current or planned government purchases, a tax cut that increases current income must be offset by future tax increases that lower expected future income. If consumers do not take account of expected future tax changes, however, the Ricardian equivalence proposition will not hold, and a tax cut is likely to raise desired consumption and lower desired national saving.

6. The desired capital stock is the level of capital that maximizes expected profits. At the desired capital stock, the expected future marginal product of capital equals the user cost of capital. The user cost of capital is the expected real cost of using a unit of capital for a period of time; it is the sum of the depreciation cost (the loss in value because the capital wears out) and the interest cost (the interest rate times the price of the capital good).

7. Any change that reduces the user cost of capital or increases the expected future marginal product of capital increases the desired capital stock. A reduction in the taxation of capital, as measured by the effective tax rate, also increases the desired capital stock.

8. Gross investment is spending on new capital goods. Gross investment minus depreciation (worn-out or scrapped capital) equals net investment, or the change in the capital stock. Firms invest in order to achieve their desired level of capital stock; when the desired capital stock increases, firms invest more.

9. The goods market is in equilibrium when the aggregate quantity of goods supplied equals the aggregate quantity of goods demanded, which (in a closed economy) is the sum of desired consumption, desired investment, and government

purchases of goods and services. Equivalently, the goods market is in equilibrium when desired national saving equals desired investment. For any given level of output, the goods market is brought into equilibrium by changes in the real interest rate.

10. The determination of goods market equilibrium, for any supply of output Y is represented graphically by the saving–investment diagram. The saving curve slopes upward because empirical evidence suggests that a higher real interest rate raises desired saving. The investment curve slopes downward because a higher real interest rate raises the user cost of capital, which lowers firms' desired capital stocks and, thus, the amount of investment they do. At constant output, changes in variables that affect desired saving or investment shift the saving or investment curves and change the real interest rate that clears the goods market.

KEY DIAGRAM 3

Saving–Investment

In an economy with no foreign trade, the goods market is in equilibrium when desired national saving equals desired investment. Equivalently, the goods market is in equilibrium when the aggregate quantity of goods supplied equals the aggregate quantity of goods demanded.

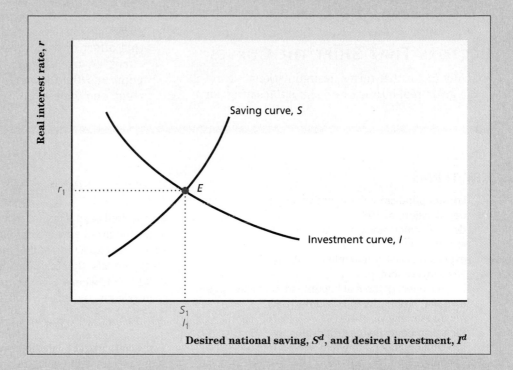

DIAGRAM ELEMENTS

- The real interest rate r is on the vertical axis; desired national saving S^d and desired investment I^d are on the horizontal axis.

- The saving curve, S, shows the level of desired national saving at each real interest rate. The saving curve slopes upward because a higher real interest rate increases the reward for saving and causes households to save more. (Empirically, this effect outweighs the tendency of a higher real interest rate to lower saving by reducing the amount of saving necessary to reach any specified target.) The saving curve is drawn for given levels of current output Y, expected future output, wealth, government purchases G, and taxes T. A change in any of these variables will cause the saving curve to shift. Desired national saving is defined as $S^d = Y - C^d - G$, where Y is output, C^d is desired consumption, and G is government purchases.

- The investment curve, I, shows the amount that firms want to invest in new capital goods at each real interest rate. The investment curve slopes downward because a higher real interest rate raises the user cost of capital and thus lowers the amount of capital that firms want to use. The investment curve is drawn for given levels of the effective tax rate and expected future marginal product of capital. A change in either of these variables will cause the investment curve to shift.

ANALYSIS

- Goods market equilibrium requires that desired national saving equal desired investment, or $S^d = I^d$.

- Goods market equilibrium occurs in the diagram at point E, where the saving curve and investment curve intersect. At E, desired national saving equals S_1, desired investment equals I_1, and $S_1 = I_1$. The real interest rate at E, r_1, is the real interest rate that clears the goods market.

- An alternative way to express the goods market equilibrium condition is as follows: The quantity of goods supplied, Y, equals the quantity of goods demanded by households, C^d, firms, I^d, and the government, G, or $Y = C^d + I^d + G$. As $S^d = Y - C^d - G$, this condition is equivalent to $S^d = I^d$.

FACTORS THAT SHIFT THE CURVES

- Any factor that raises desired national saving at a given real interest rate shifts the saving curve

to the right; similarly, any factor that lowers desired national saving shifts the saving curve to the left. Factors that affect desired national saving are listed in Summary table 5 (p. 108). Similarly, factors that change desired investment for a given real interest rate shift the investment curve; see Summary table 6 (p. 117) for factors that affect desired investment. Shifts of either curve change the goods market equilibrium point and thus change national saving, investment, and the real interest rate.

KEY TERMS

consumption-smoothing motive, p. 94
depreciation, p. 108
desired capital stock, p. 107
effective tax rate, p. 113
expected after-tax real interest rate, p. 101
gross investment, p. 114
income effect of the real interest rate on saving, p. 99
marginal propensity to consume, p. 95
net investment, p. 114
Ricardian equivalence proposition, p. 105
substitution effect of the real interest rate on saving, p. 99
tax-adjusted user cost of capital, p. 112
user cost of capital, p. 108

KEY EQUATIONS

$$S^d = Y - C^d - G \tag{4.1}$$

Desired national saving, S^d, is the level of national saving that occurs when consumption is at its desired level. Equation (4.1) is obtained by substituting desired consumption C^d for actual consumption C in the definition of national saving.

$$r_{a-t} = (1 - t)i + \pi^e \tag{4.2}$$

The expected after-tax real interest rate, r_{a-t}, is the after-tax nominal interest rate, $(1 - t)i$, minus the expected rate of inflation π^e. The expected after-tax real interest rate is the real return earned by a saver when a portion t of interest income must be paid as taxes.

$$uc = rp_K + dp_K = (r + d)p_K \tag{4.3}$$

The user cost of capital, uc, is the sum of the interest cost, rp_K, and the depreciation cost, dp_K, where d is the depreciation rate and p_K is the price of a new capital good.

$$MPK^f = \frac{uc}{1 - \tau} = \frac{(r - d)P_K}{1 - \tau} \tag{4.4}$$

The desired capital stock, or the capital stock that maximizes the firm's expected profits, is the capital stock for which the expected future marginal product of capital, MPK^f, equals the tax-adjusted user cost of capital, $uc/(1 - \tau)$, where τ is the tax rate on firm revenues (equivalently, the effective tax rate).

$$Y = C^d + I^d + G \tag{4.7}$$

The goods market equilibrium condition says that the goods market is in equilibrium when the aggregate quantity of goods supplied, Y, equals the aggregate quantity of goods demanded, $C^d + I^d + G$.

$$S^d = I^d \tag{4.8}$$

Another way of stating the goods market equilibrium condition is that desired national saving, S^d, must equal desired investment, I^d. This equation is equivalent to Eq. (4.7).

REVIEW QUESTIONS

1. Given income, how are consumption and saving linked? What is the basic motivation for saving?
2. How are desired consumption and desired saving affected by increases in current income, expected future income, and wealth?
3. Use the concepts of income effect and substitution effect to explain why the effect on desired saving of an increase in the expected real interest rate is potentially ambiguous.
4. What effect does a temporary increase in government purchases—for example, to fight a war—have on desired consumption and desired national saving for a constant level of output? What is the effect on desired

national saving of a lump-sum tax increase? Why is the effect of a lump-sum tax increase controversial?

5. What are the two components of the user cost of capital? Explain why each is a cost of using a capital good.

6. What is the desired capital stock? How does it depend on the expected future marginal product of capital, the user cost of capital, and the effective tax rate?

7. What is the difference between gross investment and net investment? Can gross investment be positive when net investment is negative?

8. Give two equivalent ways of describing equilibrium in the goods market. Use a diagram to show how goods market equilibrium is attained.

9. Explain why the saving curve slopes upward and the investment curve slopes downward in the saving–investment diagram. Give two examples of changes that would shift the saving curve to the right, and two examples of changes that would shift the investment curve to the right.

NUMERICAL PROBLEMS

1. A consumer is making saving plans for this year and next. She knows that her real income after taxes will be $25 000 in both years. Any part of her income saved this year will earn a real interest rate of 10% between this year and next year. Currently, the consumer has no wealth (no money in the bank or other financial assets), and no debts. There is no uncertainty about the future.

   The consumer wants to save an amount this year that will allow her to (1) make university tuition payments next year equal to $6300 in real terms; (2) enjoy exactly the same amount of consumption this year and next year, not counting tuition payments as part of next year's consumption; and (3) have neither assets nor debts at the end of next year.

   a. How much should the consumer save this year? How much should she consume?
   How are the amounts that the consumer should save and consume affected by each of the following changes (taken one at a time, with other variables held at their original values)?

   b. Her current income rises from $25 000 to $27 100.

   c. The income she expects to receive next year rises from $25 000 to $27 100.

   d. During the current year she receives an inheritance of $525 (an increase in wealth, not income).

   e. The expected tuition payment for next year rises from $6300 to $7350.

   f. The real interest rate rises from 10% to 25%.

2. Hula hoop fabricators cost $100 each. The Hi-Ho Hula Hoop Company is trying to decide how many of these machines to buy. HHHHC expects to produce the following number of hoops each year for each level of capital stock shown:

Number of Fabricators	Number of Hoops Produced per Year
0	0
1	100
2	150
3	180
4	195
5	205
6	210

Hula hoops have a real value of $1 each. HHHHC has no other costs besides the cost of fabricators.

   a. Find the expected future marginal product of capital (in terms of dollars) for each level of capital. The MPK^f for the third fabricator, for example, is the real value of the extra output obtained when the third fabricator is added.

   b. If the real interest rate is 12% per year and the depreciation rate of capital is 20% per year, find the user cost of capital (in dollars per fabricator per year). How many fabricators should HHHHC buy?

   c. Repeat part (b) for a real interest rate of 8% per year.

   d. Repeat part (b) for a 40% tax on HHHHC's sales revenues.

   e. A technical innovation doubles the number of hoops a fabricator can produce. How many fabricators should HHHHC buy when the real interest rate is 12% per year? 8% per year? Assume that there are no taxes and that the depreciation rate is still 20% per year.

3. You have just taken a job that requires you to move to a new city. In relocating, you face the decision of whether to buy or rent a house. A suitable house costs $200 000 and you have saved enough for the down payment. The (nominal) mortgage interest rate is 10% per year, and you can also earn 10% per year on savings. Interest earnings on savings are taxable, and you are in a 30% tax bracket. Interest is paid or received, and taxes are paid on the last day of the year. The expected inflation rate is 5% per year.

The cost of maintaining the house (replacing worn-out roofing, painting, and so on) is 6% of the value of the house. Assume that these expenses are also paid entirely on the last day of the year. If the maintenance is done, the house retains its full real value. There are no other relevant costs or expenses.

a. What is the expected after-tax real interest rate on the home mortgage?

b. What is the user cost of the house?

c. If all you care about is minimizing your living expenses, at what (annual) rent level would you be indifferent between buying a house and renting a house of comparable quality? Rent is also paid on the last day of the year.

4. Consider a firm that faces the following expected future marginal product of capital:

$$MPK^f = 1000 - 2K,$$

where MPK^f is the expected future marginal product of capital and K is the capital stock. The price of capital, p_K, is 1000, the real interest rate, r, is 10%, and the depreciation rate, d, is 15%.

a. What is the user cost of capital?

b. What is the value of the firm's desired capital stock?

c. Now suppose that the firm must pay a 50% tax on its revenue. What is the value of the desired capital stock?

d. Now suppose that in addition to the 50% tax rate on revenue, the firm can take advantage of a 20% investment tax credit, which allows it to reduce its taxes paid by 20% of the value of new capital purchased. What is the firm's desired capital stock now? (*Hint:* An investment tax credit effectively reduces the price of capital to the firm.)

5. An economy has full-employment output of 900, and government purchases are 200. Desired consumption and desired investment are as follows:

Real Interest Rate (%)	Desired Consumption	Desired Investment
2	610	150
3	600	140
4	590	130
5	580	120
6	570	110

a. Why do desired consumption and desired investment fall as the real interest rate rises?

b. Find desired national saving for each value of the real interest rate.

c. If the goods market is in equilibrium, what are the values of the real interest rate, desired national

saving, and desired investment? Show that both forms of the goods market equilibrium condition, Eqs. (4.7) and (4.8), are satisfied at the equilibrium. Assume that output is fixed at its full-employment level.

d. Repeat part (c) for the case in which government purchases fall to 160. Assume that the amount people desire to consume at each real interest rate is unchanged.

6. An economy has full-employment output of 600. Government purchases, G, are 120. Desired consumption and desired investment are

$$C^d = 360 - 200r + 0.10Y, \text{ and } I^d = 120 - 400r,$$

where Y is output and r is the real interest rate.

a. Find an equation relating desired national saving S^d to r and Y.

b. Using both versions of the goods market equilibrium condition, Eqs. (4.7) and (4.8), find the real interest rate that clears the goods market. Assume that output equals full-employment output.

c. Government purchases rise to 144. How does this increase change the equation describing desired national saving? Show the change graphically. What happens to the market-clearing real interest rate?

7. Suppose that the economywide expected future marginal product of capital is $MPK^f = 20 - 0.02K$, where K is the future capital stock. The depreciation rate of capital, d, is 20% per period. The current capital stock is 900 units of capital. The price of a unit of capital is 1 unit of output. Firms pay taxes equal to 50% of their output. The consumption function in the economy is $C = 100 + 0.5Y - 200r$, where C is consumption, Y is output, and r is the real interest rate. Government purchases equal 200, and full-employment output is 1000.

a. Suppose that the real interest rate is 10% per period. What are the values of the tax-adjusted user cost of capital, the desired future capital stock, and the desired level of investment?

b. Now consider the real interest rate determined by goods market equilibrium. This part of the problem will guide you to this interest rate.

i. Write the tax-adjusted user cost of capital as a function of the real interest rate r. Also write the desired future capital stock and desired investment as functions of r.

ii. Use the investment function derived in part (i) along with the consumption function and government purchases to calculate the real interest rate that clears the goods market. What are the goods market-clearing values of consumption, saving, and investment? What are the tax-adjusted user cost of capital and the desired capital stock in this equilibrium?

ANALYTICAL PROBLEMS

1. Use the saving–investment diagram to analyze the effects of the following on national saving, investment, and the real interest rate. Explain your reasoning.
   a. Consumers become more future-oriented and, thus, decide to save more.
   b. The government announces a large, one-time bonus payment to farmers because of a drought. The bonus will be financed by additional taxes levied on the general population over the next five years.
   c. The government introduces an investment tax credit (offset by other types of taxes, so total tax collections remain unchanged).
   d. A large number of accessible oil deposits are discovered, which increases the expected future marginal product of oil rigs and pipelines. It also causes an increase in expected future income.

2. A country loses much of its capital stock to a war.
   a. What effects should this event have on the country's current employment, output, and real wage?
   b. What effect will the loss of capital have on desired investment?
   c. The effects on desired national saving of the wartime losses are ambiguous. Give one reason for desired saving to rise and one reason for it to fall.
   d. Assume that desired saving does not change. What effect does the loss of capital have on the country's real interest rate and the quantity of investment?

3. Analyze the following:
   a. The effects of a temporary increase in the price of oil (a temporary adverse supply shock) on current output, employment, the real wage, national saving, investment, and the real interest rate. Because the supply shock is temporary, you should assume that the expected future *MPK* and households' expected future incomes are unchanged. Assume

throughout that output and employment remain at full-employment levels (which may change).
   b. The effects of a permanent increase in the price of oil (a permanent adverse supply shock) on current output, employment, the real wage, national saving, investment, and the real interest rate. Show that in this case, unlike the case of a temporary supply shock, the real interest rate need not change. (*Hint:* A permanent adverse supply shock lowers the current productivity of capital and labour, just as a temporary supply shock does. In addition, a permanent supply shock lowers both the expected future *MPK* and households' expected future incomes.)

4. Economists often argue that a temporary increase in government purchases, say, for military purposes, will crowd out private investment. Use the saving–investment diagram to illustrate this point, explaining why the curve(s) shift. Does it matter whether the temporary increase in military spending is funded by taxes or by borrowing?

   Alternatively, suppose that the temporary increase in government purchases is for infrastructure (roads, sewers, bridges) rather than for military purposes. The government spending on infrastructure makes private investment more productive, increasing the expected future *MPK* at each level of the capital stock. Use the saving–investment diagram to analyze the effects of government infrastructure spending on current consumption, national saving, investment, and the real interest rate. Does investment by private firms get crowded out by this kind of government investment? If not, what kind of spending, if any, does get crowded out? Assume that there is no change in current productivity or current output and assume also (for simplicity) that households do not expect a change in their future incomes.

5. "A permanent increase in government purchases has a larger effect than a temporary increase of the same amount." Use the saving–investment diagram to evaluate this statement, focusing on effects on consumption, investment, and the real interest rate for a fixed level of output. (*Hint:* The permanent increase in government purchases implies larger increases in current and future taxes.)

Chapter 5

Saving and Investment in the Open Economy

With virtually no exceptions, modern economies are open economies, which means that they engage in international trade of goods and services and in international borrowing and lending. Economic openness is of tremendous benefit to the average person. Because Canada is an open economy, Canadian consumers can enjoy products from around the world (Japanese cars, Italian shoes, and Irish woollens) and Canadian businesses can find new markets abroad for their products (potash, wheat, and engineering services). Similarly, the internationalization of financial markets means that Canadian savers have the opportunity to purchase German government bonds or shares in Taiwanese companies as well as domestic assets, and Canadian firms that want to finance investment projects can borrow in London or New York as well as in Toronto or Montreal.

Beyond the economic diversity and opportunity it creates, economic openness carries another important implication: In an open economy, a *country's spending need not equal its production in every period*, as would be required in a closed economy with no foreign trade and no international borrowing and lending. In particular, by importing more than they export and borrowing from abroad to pay for the difference, the residents of an open economy can temporarily spend more than they produce.

The ability of an open economy to spend more than it produces is both an opportunity and a potential problem. For example, by borrowing abroad, Canada was able to finance an excess of imports over exports during the mid-1970s. As a result, Canadians enjoyed higher levels of consumption, investment, and government purchases than they could have otherwise. At the same time, however, they incurred foreign debts that may be a future burden to the Canadian economy.

Why do countries sometimes borrow abroad to pay for an excess of imports over exports but at other times export more than they import and lend the difference to other countries? Why doesn't each country just balance its books and import as much as it exports each year? As this chapter explains, the fundamental determinants of a country's trade position are the country's saving and investment decisions. Thus, although the issues of trade balances and international lending introduced here may seem at first to be unrelated to the topics covered in Chapter 4, the two sets of questions actually are closely related.

To explore how desired national saving and desired investment help determine patterns of international trade and lending, we extend the idea of goods market equilibrium, described by the saving–investment diagram, to include a foreign sector. We show that, unlike the situation in a closed economy, in an open economy, desired national saving and desired investment do not have to be equal. Instead, we show that when a country's desired national saving exceeds its desired investment, the country will be a lender in the international capital market and will have a current account surplus. Similarly, when a country's desired national saving is less than its desired investment, the country will be an international borrower and will have a current account deficit.

By emphasizing saving and investment, this chapter develops an important theme of this part of the book. However, in order to focus on the role of saving and investment, we ignore some other factors that also influence international trade and lending. The most important of these factors is the exchange rate, or the rate at which domestic currency can be exchanged for foreign currency. We discuss exchange rates and their role in the open economy fully in Chapter 10.

5.1 BALANCE OF PAYMENTS ACCOUNTING

Examining the factors that affect international trade and lending first requires an understanding of the basics of balance of payments accounting. The **balance of payments accounts**, which are part of the national income accounts discussed in Chapter 2, are the record of a country's international transactions. As you read this section, you should refer to Table 5.1, which presents Canadian balance of payments data for 2015; note that some of the numbers are positive and others are negative. To sort out which international transactions are entered with a plus sign and which are entered with a minus sign, keep the following principle in mind: Any transaction that involves a flow of funds *into* Canada is a *credit* item and is entered with a plus sign; any transaction that involves a flow of funds *out of* Canada is a *debit* item and is entered with a minus sign. We illustrate this principle as we discuss the various components of the balance of payments accounts.

THE CURRENT ACCOUNT

The **current account** measures a country's trade in currently produced goods and services, along with net transfers between countries. For convenience, we divide the current account into three separate components: (1) net exports of goods and services, (2) investment income from assets abroad, and (3) current transfers.

Net Exports of Goods and Services

We discussed the concept of net exports, *NX*, or exports minus imports, as part of the expenditure approach to measuring GDP in Chapter 2. Here, we point out that net exports are often divided into two categories: merchandise (goods) and services.

Merchandise consists of currently produced goods, such as American soybeans, French perfume, Brazilian coffee, and Japanese cars. When a Canadian buys a Japanese car, for example, the transaction is recorded as a merchandise import for Canada (a debit item for Canada, because funds flow out of Canada to pay for the car) and a merchandise export for Japan (a credit item for Japan because funds flow into Japan to pay for the car). The difference between a country's merchandise exports and its merchandise imports is called the **merchandise trade balance**, or simply the trade balance. The merchandise trade balance receives a lot of attention from the public and the press. This attention does not seem entirely warranted, however, because merchandise trade is only one component of the current account.

Internationally traded services include transportation, tourism, insurance, education, and financial services, among others. When a Canadian family spends a week's vacation in Mexico, for example, the family's expenditures for accommodations, food, sightseeing tours, and so on are counted in the Canadian current account as an import of tourism services (a debit item for Canada because funds are flowing out of the country). The family's expenditures count as an export of tourism services for Mexico (a credit item in the Mexican current account). Similarly, when a foreign student attends a university in Canada, the tuition payments are included as an export of services for Canada and an import of services for his or her home country.

Investment Income from Assets Abroad

Investment income received from assets abroad includes interest payments, dividends, royalties, and other returns that residents of a country receive from assets (such as bonds, stocks, or patents) that they own outside their own country. For example, the interest that a Canadian saver receives from a French government bond he or she owns, or the profits a Canadian company receives from a foreign subsidiary, are income receipts from assets abroad. These are credit items in the current account because the receipts are payments from foreigners to domestic residents.

Payment of investment income to foreign owners of assets in a country are debit items because they represent funds that flow out of the country. *Net* investment income from assets abroad equals investment income received from assets abroad minus investment income paid to foreign owners of domestic assets.

For Canada, net investment income from abroad is quantitatively almost the same as net factor payments from abroad, *NFP*, discussed in Chapter 2. The difference between the two concepts is that net factor payments from abroad also include wages and salaries of Canadians working outside the country, less the wages and salaries of foreigners working in Canada. In practice, the wage and salary component of *NFP* is very small, so we ignore it and treat *NFP* and net investment income from abroad as equivalent concepts.

Current Transfers

Current transfers are payments from one country to another that do not correspond to the purchase of any good, service, or asset. Examples are official foreign aid (a payment from one government to another), pension payments, or a gift of money from a resident of one country to family members living in another country. When Canada makes a transfer to another country, the amount of the transfer is a debit item because funds flow out of Canada. A country's current transfers equal transfers received by the country minus transfers flowing out of the country. The negative value of current transfers in Table 5.1 shows that Canada was a net payer of transfers to other countries.

TABLE 5.1

Canada's Balance of International Payments, 2015 (billions of dollars)

CURRENT ACCOUNT

Net exports			**−47.4**
Exports		622.8	
Goods	523.6		
Services	99.2		
Imports		−670.2	
Goods	−547.3		
Services	−122.9		
Net investment income from abroad (NFP)			**−13.3**
Income receipts on investments		90.6	
Income payments on investments		−103.9	
Current transfers			**−5.0**
Current Account Balance (*CA*)			**−65.7**
CAPITAL AND FINANCIAL ACCOUNT			
Increase in Canadian-owned assets abroad			**−209.1**
(capital outflow)			
Canadian official reserve assets		−10.9	
Other Canadian assets		−198.2	
Increase in foreign-owned assets in Canada			**264.3**
(capital inflow)			
Financial account			**55.2**
Capital account			**−0.1**
Capital and Financial Account Balance (*KA*)			**55.1**
Statistical discrepancy			**10.5**

Source: Adapted from Statistics Canada, 2017. This does not constitute an endorsement by Statistics Canada of this product.

Current Account Balance

Adding all the credit items and subtracting all the debit items in the current account yields a number called the **current account balance**. If the current account balance is positive—with the value of credit items exceeding the value of debit items—the country has a current account surplus. If the current account balance is negative—with the value of debit items exceeding the value of credit items—the country has a current account deficit. As Table 5.1 shows, in 2015, Canada had a $65.7 billion current account deficit, equal to the sum of net exports ($NX = -$47.4 billion), net investment income from abroad ($NFP = -$13.3 billion), and current transfers (−$5.0 billion).

THE CAPITAL ACCOUNT

Not all transactions with foreign countries are tallied in the current account. If a Japanese investor purchases a 10-year-old vacation house in Canmore, Alberta, for example, the purchase is *not* included in the current account of either Canada or Japan. The reason is that the current account includes only the trade of currently produced goods and services. A 10-year-old house is an existing asset rather than a currently produced good or service, so its sale is not part of the current account.

Trade between countries in existing assets, either real (direct investment) or financial (portfolio investment), is recorded in the **capital and financial account**. When the home country sells an asset to another country, the transaction is recorded as a **financial inflow** for the home country and as a credit item in the capital account. So, for example, if a Canadian bond is sold to Italian investors, the transaction is counted as a capital inflow to Canada and as a credit item in the Canadian capital account. (Why is a capital inflow a credit item? Because when a Canadian sells an asset to a foreigner, funds flow into Canada.) Similarly, when the home country buys an asset from abroad—say, a Canadian obtains a Swiss bank account—the transaction is a **financial outflow** from the home country (Canada in this example) and a debit item in the home country's capital account (funds are flowing out of Canada).

The capital and financial account is divided into two parts called the financial account and the capital account. The financial account records direct and portfolio investment, while the capital account records migrants' funds, inheritances, and transactions in intellectual property, such as patents. Economists usually refer to the capital and financial account simply as the **capital account** (even though most of the transactions involved are in the financial account), and we will follow this usage here.

The **capital account balance** equals the value of capital inflows (credit items) minus the value of capital outflows (debit items). When residents of a country sell more assets to foreigners than they buy from foreigners, the capital account balance is positive, creating a capital account surplus. When residents of the home country purchase more assets from foreigners than they sell, the capital account balance is negative, creating a capital account deficit. Table 5.1 shows that in 2015, Canadians increased their holdings of foreign assets by $209.1 billion, while foreigners increased their holdings of Canadian assets by $264.3 billion. Thus, the financial account balance was the difference: $55.2 billion. There was an added capital outflow in the form of migrants' funds and purchases of Canadian intellectual property of $0.1 billion, so the capital and financial account balance was $55.1 billion. Thus, in 2015, Canada experienced a net capital inflow or capital account surplus.

The Official Settlements Balance

In Table 5.1, one set of capital account transactions, transactions in official reserve assets, has been listed separately. These transactions differ from other capital account transactions in that they are conducted by central banks (such as the Bank of Canada), which are the official institutions that determine national money supplies. Held by central banks, **official reserve assets** are assets, other than domestic money or securities, that can be used in making international payments. Historically, gold was the primary official reserve asset, but now the official reserves of central banks also include government securities of major industrialized economies, foreign bank deposits, and special assets created by the International Monetary Fund (an international agency that facilitates trade and financial relationships among countries).

Central banks can change the quantity of official reserve assets they hold by buying or selling reserve assets on open markets. For example, the Bank of Canada could increase its reserve assets by using dollars to buy gold. According to Table 5.1 (see the line "Canadian official reserve assets"), in 2015, the Canadian central bank purchased $10.9 billion of official reserve assets.[1]

---

[1] Remember that a positive number in the capital account indicates a capital inflow, or a sale of assets. A negative number in the capital account indicates a capital outflow, or purchase of assets.

The **official settlements balance**—also called the **balance of payments**—is the net increase (domestic less foreign) in a country's official reserve assets. A country that increases its net holdings of reserve assets during a year has a balance of payments surplus, and a country that reduces its net holdings of reserve assets has a balance of payments deficit.

For the issues we discuss in this chapter, the balances on current account and capital account play a much larger role than the balance of payments. The macroeconomic significance of the balance of payments is explained in Chapter 10, when we discuss the determination of exchange rates.

THE RELATIONSHIP BETWEEN THE CURRENT ACCOUNT AND THE CAPITAL ACCOUNT

The logic of balance of payments accounting implies a close relationship between the current account and the capital account. Except for errors arising from problems of measurement, *in each period, the current account balance and the capital account balance must sum to zero*. That is, if

$$CA = \text{current account balance,}$$

$$KA = \text{capital account balance,}$$

then

$$CA + KA = 0. \tag{5.1}$$

The reason that Eq. (5.1) holds is that every international transaction involves a swap of goods, services, or assets between countries. The two sides of the swap always have offsetting effects on the sum of the current and capital account balances, $CA + KA$. Thus, the sum of the current and capital account balances must equal zero.

Table 5.2 helps clarify this point. Suppose that a Canadian buys an imported British sweater, paying $75 for it. This transaction is an import of goods to Canada and, thus, reduces the Canadian current account balance by $75. However, the British exporter who sold the sweater now holds $75. What will he or she do with it? There are several possibilities, any of which will offset the effect of the purchase of the sweater on the sum of the current and capital account balances.

The Briton may use the $75 to buy a Canadian product, say, a telephone. This purchase is a $75 export for Canada. This Canadian export together with the original import of the sweater into Canada results in no net change in the Canadian current account balance CA. The Canadian capital account balance KA has not changed, as no assets have been traded. Thus, the sum of CA and KA remains the same.

A second possibility is that the Briton will use the $75 to buy a Canadian asset, say, a bond issued by a Canadian corporation. The purchase of this bond is a capital inflow to Canada. This $75 increase in the Canadian capital account offsets the $75 reduction in the Canadian current account caused by the original import of the sweater. Again, the sum of the current and capital account balances, $CA + KA$, is unaffected by the combination of transactions.

Finally, the Briton may decide to go to his or her bank and trade the dollars for British pounds. If the bank sells these dollars to another Briton for the purpose of buying Canadian exports or assets, or if it buys Canadian assets itself, one of the previous two cases is repeated. Alternatively, the bank may sell the dollars to the Bank of Canada in exchange for pounds. But in giving up $75 worth of British

---

TABLE 5.2

Why the Current Account Balance and the Capital Account Balance Sum to Zero: An Example (balance of payments data refer to Canada)

Case I: Canada Imports $75 Sweater from Britain;
Britain Imports $75 Telephone from Canada

Current Account	
Exports	+$75
Imports	−$75
Current account balance, CA	0
Capital Account	
No transaction	
Capital account balance, KA	0
Sum of current and capital account balances, $CA + KA$	0

Case II: Canada Imports $75 Sweater from Britain;
Britain Buys $75 Bond from Canada

Current Account	
Imports	−$75
Current account balance, CA	−$75
Capital Account	
Capital inflow	+$75
Capital account balance, KA	+$75
Sum of current and capital account balances, $CA + KA$	0

Case III: Canada Imports $75 Sweater from Britain;
Bank of Canada Sells $75 of British Pounds to British Bank

Current Account	
Imports	−$75
Current account balance, CA	−$75
Capital Account	
Capital inflow (reduction in Canadian official reserve assets)	+$75
Capital account balance, KA	+$75
Sum of current and capital account balances, $CA + KA$	0

---

pounds, the Bank of Canada reduces its holdings of official reserve assets by $75, which counts as a capital inflow. As in the previous case, the capital account balance rises by $75, offsetting the decline in the current account balance caused by the import of the sweater.[2]

This example shows why, conceptually, the current account balance and capital account balance must always sum to zero. In practice, problems in measuring international transactions prevent this relationship from holding exactly. The amount that would have to be added to the sum of the current and capital account balances

---

[2] In this case, the balance of payments falls by $75, reflecting the Bank's loss of official reserves. We did not consider the possibility that the Briton would just hold $75 in Canadian currency. As dollars are an obligation of Canada, the Briton's acquisition of dollars would be a credit item in the Canadian capital account, which would offset the effect of the sweater import on the Canadian current account.

for this sum to reach its theoretical value of zero is called the **statistical discrepancy**. As Table 5.1 shows, in 2015 the statistical discrepancy was $10.5 billion.

NET FOREIGN ASSETS AND THE BALANCE OF PAYMENTS ACCOUNTS

In Chapter 2, we defined the net foreign assets of a country as the foreign assets held by the country's residents (including, for example, foreign stocks, bonds, or real estate) minus the country's foreign liabilities (domestic physical and financial assets owned by foreigners). Net foreign assets are part of a country's national wealth, along with the country's domestic physical assets, such as land and the capital stock. The total value of a country's net foreign assets can change in two ways: (1) the value of existing foreign assets and foreign liabilities can change, as occurs when stock held by a Canadian in a foreign corporation increases in value or the value of Canadian farmland owned by a foreigner declines; and (2) the country can acquire new foreign assets or incur new foreign liabilities.

What determines the quantity of new foreign assets that a country can acquire? In any period, *the net amount of new foreign assets that a country acquires equals its current account surplus*. For example, suppose a country exports $10 billion more in goods and services than it imports and, thus, runs a $10 billion current account surplus (assuming that net investment income from abroad and current transfers are both zero). The country must then use this $10 billion to acquire foreign assets or reduce foreign liabilities. In this case, we say that the country has undertaken net foreign lending of $10 billion.

Similarly, if a country has a $10 billion current account deficit, it must cover this deficit either by selling assets to foreigners or borrowing from foreigners. Either action reduces the country's net foreign assets by $10 billion. We describe this situation by saying that the country has engaged in net foreign borrowing of $10 billion.

Equation (5.1) emphasizes the link between the current account and the acquisition of foreign assets. Because $CA + KA = 0$, if a country has a current account surplus, it must have an equal capital account deficit. In turn, a capital account deficit implies that the country is experiencing capital outflows, or a net increase in holdings of foreign assets. Similarly, a current account deficit implies a capital account surplus and a decline in the country's net holdings of foreign assets. Summary table 7 presents some equivalent ways of describing a country's current account position and its acquisition of foreign assets.

In evaluating the significance of a country's foreign assets or debt, you must remember that net foreign assets are only one component of national wealth, the other being domestic physical assets. If national wealth is growing at a healthy rate overall, there is not much reason to be concerned if one of its components is falling. For example, if a country were to incur large foreign debts in order to build up its capital stock, and if the new capital were highly productive, the foreign debt would not be an economic burden. Canada's current account deficit of the mid-1950s can be viewed in this light. In the mid-1950s, investment accounted for a large share of output, and Canadian output and wealth grew rapidly.

From 1999 to 2008, Canada ran current account surpluses. Over that period, Canada's national wealth was being supplemented by increases in net foreign assets—or, more precisely, decreased foreign debt. From 2009 to 2015, Canada ran current account deficits, and these deficits have pushed the value of foreign debt back up.

SUMMARY 7

EQUIVALENT MEASURES OF A COUNTRY'S INTERNATIONAL TRADE AND LENDING

EACH ITEM DESCRIBES THE SAME SITUATION

A current account surplus of $10 billion

A capital account deficit of $10 billion

Net acquisition of foreign assets of $10 billion

Net foreign lending of $10 billion

Net exports of $10 billion (if net factor payments, *NFP*, and current transfers equal zero)

5.2 GOODS MARKET EQUILIBRIUM IN AN OPEN ECONOMY

We are now ready to investigate the economic forces that determine international trade and borrowing. In the remainder of this chapter, we demonstrate that a country's current account balance and foreign lending are closely linked to its domestic spending and production decisions. Understanding these links first requires developing the open-economy version of the goods market equilibrium condition.

In Chapter 4, we derived the goods market equilibrium condition for a closed economy. We showed that this condition can be expressed either as desired national saving equals desired investment or, equivalently, as the aggregate supply of goods equals the aggregate demand for goods. With some modification, we can use these same two conditions to describe goods market equilibrium in an open economy.

Let's begin with the open-economy version of the condition that desired national saving equals desired investment. In Chapter 2, we derived the national income accounting identity (Eq. 2.9):

$$S = I + CA = I + (NX + NFP). \tag{5.2}$$

Equation (5.2) is a version of the uses-of-saving identity. It states that national saving S has two uses: (1) to increase the nation's stock of capital by funding investment I, and (2) to increase the nation's stock of net foreign assets by lending to foreigners (recall that the current account balance CA equals the amount of funds that the country has available for net foreign lending). Equation (5.2) also reminds us that (assuming no current transfers) the current account CA is the sum of net exports NX and net factor payments from abroad NFP.

Because Eq. (5.2) is an identity, it must always hold (by definition). For the economy to be in goods market equilibrium, actual national saving and investment must also equal their desired levels. If actual and desired levels are equal, Eq. (5.2) becomes

$$S^d = I^d + CA = I^d + (NX + NFP), \tag{5.3}$$

where S^d and I^d represent desired national saving and desired investment, respectively. Equation (5.3) is the goods market equilibrium condition for an open economy, in which the current account balance CA equals net lending to foreigners, or capital outflows. Hence Eq. (5.3) states that *in goods market equilibrium in an open economy, the desired amount of national saving* S^d *must equal the desired amount of domestic investment* I^d *plus the amount lent abroad CA.* Note that the closed-economy equilibrium condition is a special case of Eq. (5.3), with $CA = 0$.

In general, net factor payments *NFP* are determined by past investments and are not much affected by current macroeconomic developments. If, for simplicity, we assume that net factor payments *NFP* are zero, the current account equals net exports and the goods market equilibrium condition, Eq. (5.3), becomes

$$S^d = I^d + NX. \tag{5.4}$$

Equation (5.4) is the form of the goods market equilibrium condition that we will work with. Under the assumption that net factor payments are zero, we can refer to the term *NX* interchangeably as net exports or as the current account balance.

As for the closed economy, we can also write the goods market equilibrium condition for the open economy in terms of the aggregate supply and aggregate demand for goods. In an open economy, where net exports *NX* are part of the aggregate demand for goods, this alternative condition for goods market equilibrium is

$$Y = C^d + I^d + G + NX, \tag{5.5}$$

where Y is output, C^d is desired consumption spending, and G is government purchases. This way of writing the goods market equilibrium condition is equivalent to the condition in Eq. (5.4).[3]

We can rewrite Eq. (5.5) as

$$NX = Y - (C^d + I^d + G). \tag{5.6}$$

Equation (5.6) states that in goods market equilibrium, the amount of net exports a country sends abroad equals the country's total output (gross domestic product), Y, less total desired spending by domestic residents, $C^d + I^d + G$. Total spending by domestic residents is called **absorption**. Thus, Eq. (5.6) states that an economy in which output exceeds absorption will send goods abroad ($NX > 0$) and have a current account surplus and that an economy that absorbs more than it produces will be a net importer ($NX < 0$), with a current account deficit.

5.3 SAVING AND INVESTMENT IN A SMALL OPEN ECONOMY

To show how saving and investment are related to international trade and lending, we first present the case of a small open economy, such as Canada. A **small open economy** is an economy that is too small to affect the world real interest rate. The **world real interest rate** is the real interest rate that prevails in the international capital market, the market in which individuals, businesses, and governments borrow and lend across national borders. Because changes in saving and investment in the small open economy are not large enough to affect the world real interest rate, this interest rate is fixed in our analysis. Later in this chapter, we consider the case of an open economy, such as the U.S. economy, that is large enough to affect the world real interest rate.

---

[3] To see that Eq. (5.5) is equivalent to Eq. (5.4), subtract $C^d + G$ from both sides of Eq. (5.5) to obtain $Y - C^d - G = I^d + NX$. The left-hand side of this equation equals desired national saving S^d, so it is the same as Eq. (5.4).

We will further assume that financial markets in our small open economy are fully accessible to borrowers and savers who live elsewhere in the world, and that financial markets in the rest of the world are fully accessible to borrowers and savers who live in the small open economy. We assume, in other words, that markets for financial capital are open to all savers and borrowers regardless of where they live. We discuss all the implications of this assumption fully in Chapter 10, but for now we rely on only one: In a small open economy with open financial markets, the domestic real interest rate will adjust in the long run to equal the (expected) world real interest rate.[4],[5] The logic of why this should be so is clear: If the world real interest rate is r^w, the domestic real interest rate must be r^w as well, as no domestic borrower with access to the international capital market would pay more than r^w to borrow, and no domestic saver with access to the international capital market would accept less than r^w to lend.

APPLICATION

DOMESTIC AND FOREIGN INTEREST RATES

The United States is the largest economy in the world, and Canada's financial markets are more closely integrated with those in the United States than with any other country. As a result, when Canadian borrowers and savers consider interest rates in countries other than Canada, it is typically U.S. interest rates they consider. The lines in Figure 5.1 show nominal interest rates paid on comparable assets issued by governments in Canada and the United States. The bars represent the difference between the Canadian interest rate and the U.S. interest rate. Note that the interest rates in the two countries move together. Given the close integration of Canadian and American financial markets, this pattern is what we expect. If Canadian savers can receive a higher interest rate on a comparable U.S. asset, they will purchase the U.S. asset. In doing so, they will force Canadian borrowers to offer interest rates comparable to those in the United States.

It is important to note, however, that there exists a difference in the two interest rates, and that this difference has varied over time. We will discuss these issues fully in Chapter 10, but for now it is enough to say that interest rates will tend to differ on comparable assets if there are considerations other than interest rates that affect the expected rate of return earned on a domestic versus foreign asset. For example, purchasing a foreign financial asset usually involves transaction fees one would not need to pay when purchasing a domestic asset. With all else equal, then, a foreign asset will need to pay a higher interest rate to be comparable to a domestic asset. Countries may also differ in their tax treatments on interest income, and this may cause savers to prefer the assets of one country over another, even though they pay the same before-tax rate of interest. Before-tax interest

---

[4] As we discussed in Chapter 2, the real interest rate is the correct interest rate to use for studying most types of economic decisions, such as people's decisions about how much to borrow or lend. The real interest rate that one realizes from saving, or pays when borrowing, depends on the rate of inflation over the period of the deposit or loan, and is consequently not known in advance. For this reason, people's decisions about how much to borrow or lend are based on the *expected* real rate of interest.

[5] For simplicity, we ignore such factors as differences in risk or taxes that might cause the domestic real interest rate to differ from the world real interest rate. These issues are discussed in the Application "Domestic and Foreign Interest Rates" and again in Chapter 10.

FIGURE 5.1

INTEREST RATES IN CANADA AND THE UNITED STATES

The graph shows nominal interest rates paid on Canadian and U.S. government three-month Treasury bills and the difference between them. Note that the Canadian interest rate tends to move with changes in the U.S. interest rate. This reflects the fact that Canadian savers are able to freely choose between owning Canadian and U.S. financial assets. Note as well that the gap between Canadian and U.S. interest rates was considerably larger between 1975 and 1995 than it had been either before or after. This suggests that some influence unique to that period was causing savers to demand that Canadian borrowers offer a more attractive interest rate to compensate them for purchasing Canadian assets. We return to this issue in Chapter 10.

Source: Adapted from Statistics Canada, 2017. This does not constitute an endorsement by Statistics Canada of this product.

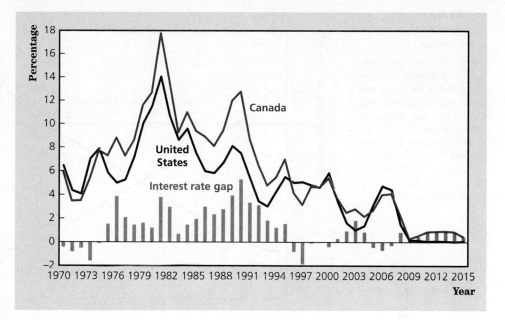

rates will need to adjust to account for these differences in tax treatment. Political turmoil too may affect the size of the interest rate gap, if such turmoil causes savers to question the ability or motivation of foreign borrowers to repay borrowed money. Thus, many analysts believe that the election in 1976 of the Parti Québécois, a political party advocating the separation of Quebec from Canada, was responsible for a widening of the gap between interest rates in Canada and the United States. In Chapter 10 we provide another explanation for persistent differences in interest rates across countries, an explanation that relates to exchange rate expectations.

Our discussion in this Application, along with the information in Figure 5.1, has pertained to nominal interest rates. We have indicated that in a small open economy like Canada, a similar relationship should hold for real interest rates. This is a more difficult relationship to illustrate because, as we discussed in Chapter 2, the real interest rate is given by the difference between the nominal rate and the expected rate of inflation, and economists generally do not know exactly what the public's expected rate of inflation is. The methods economists use to measure expected inflation always contain some error, making it difficult to measure the expected rate of inflation and, hence, the real interest rate.

As with the closed economy, we can describe the goods market equilibrium in a small open economy by using the saving–investment diagram. In what follows, then, we again make use of one of our key diagrams. First introduced in Chapter 4 and used to examine goods market equilibrium in a closed economy, here we adapt the diagram to examine the same issue in a small open economy. In Figure 5.2, goods market equilibrium in a closed economy would be represented by point *E*, the intersection of the curves. The equilibrium real interest rate in the closed economy would be 4% (per year), and national saving and investment would be

FIGURE 5.2

A SMALL OPEN ECONOMY THAT
LENDS ABROAD

The graph shows the saving–
investment diagram for a small
open economy. The country faces a
fixed world real interest rate of
6%. At this real interest rate,
national saving is $5 billion (point
B) and investment is $1 billion
(point A). The part of national saving not used for investment is lent
abroad, so foreign lending is
$4 billion (distance AB).

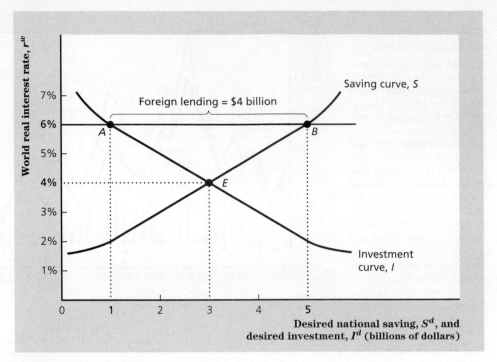

$3 billion (per year). In an open economy, however, desired national saving need
not equal desired investment. If the small open economy faces a fixed world real
interest rate r^w higher than 4%, desired national saving will be greater than desired
investment. For example, if r^w is 6%, desired national saving is $5 billion and
desired investment is $1 billion, so desired national saving exceeds desired invest-
ment by $4 billion.

Can the economy be in equilibrium when desired national saving exceeds
desired investment by $4 billion? In a closed economy, it could not. The excess
saving would have no place to go, and the real interest rate would have to fall to
bring desired saving and desired investment into balance. However, in the open
economy, the excess $4 billion of saving can be used to buy foreign assets. This
capital outflow uses up the excess national saving so that there is no disequilibrium. Instead, the goods market is in equilibrium with desired national saving of
$5 billion, desired investment of $1 billion, and net foreign lending of $4 billion
(see Eq. 5.4 and recall that net exports NX and net foreign lending are the same).

Alternatively, suppose that the world real interest rate r^w is 2% instead of 6%.
As Figure 5.3 shows, in this case desired national saving is $1 billion and desired
investment is $5 billion, meaning that desired investment exceeds desired saving
by $4 billion. Now firms desiring to invest will have to borrow $4 billion in the international capital market. Is this also a goods market equilibrium? Yes it is, because
desired national saving ($1 billion) again equals desired investment ($5 billion)
plus net foreign lending (−$4 billion). Indeed, a small open economy can achieve
goods market equilibrium for any value of the world real interest rate. All that is
required is that net foreign lending equal the difference between the country's
desired national saving and its desired investment.

A more detailed version of the example illustrated in Figures 5.2 and 5.3 is
presented in Table 5.3. As shown in the top panel, we assume that in this small

FIGURE 5.3

A SMALL OPEN ECONOMY THAT BORROWS ABROAD

The same small open economy shown in Figure 5.2 now faces a fixed world real interest rate of 2%. At this real interest rate, national saving is $1 billion (point *C*) and investment is $5 billion (point *D*). Foreign borrowing of $4 billion (distance *CD*) makes up the difference between what investors want to borrow and what domestic savers want to lend.

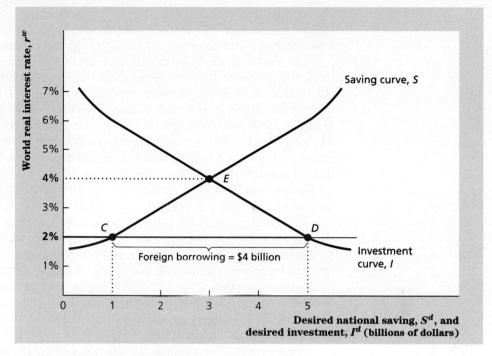

country gross domestic product Y is fixed at its full-employment value of $20 billion and government purchases G are fixed at $4 billion. The middle panel shows three possible values for the world real interest rate r^w and the assumed levels of desired consumption and desired investment at each of these values of the real interest rate. Note that higher values of the world real interest rate imply lower

TABLE 5.3

Goods Market Equilibrium in a Small Open Economy: An Example (Billions of Dollars)

Given

Gross domestic product, Y	20
Government purchases, G	4

Effect of real interest rate on desired consumption and investment

	(1)	(2)	(3)
(1) World real interest rate, r^w (%)	2	4	6
(2) Desired consumption, C^d	15	13	11
(3) Desired investment, I^d	5	3	1

Results

(4) Desired absorption, $C^d + I^d + G$	24	20	16
(5) Desired national saving, $S^d = Y - C^d - G$	1	3	5
(6) Net exports, $NX = Y -$ desired absorption	−4	0	4
(7) Desired foreign lending, $S^d - I^d$	−4	0	4

Note: We assume that net factor payments, *NFP*, equal zero.

levels of desired consumption (because people choose to save more) and lower desired investment. The bottom panel shows the values of various economic quantities implied by the assumed values in the top two panels.

The equilibrium in this example depends on the value of the world real interest rate r^w. Suppose that $r^w = 6\%$, as shown in Figure 5.2. Column (3) of Table 5.3 shows that, if $r^w = 6\%$, desired consumption C^d is \$11 billion (row 2) and that desired investment I^d is \$1 billion (row 3). With C^d at \$11 billion, desired national saving, $Y - C^d - G$, is \$5 billion (row 5). Desired net foreign lending, $S^d - I^d$, is \$4 billion (row 7)—the same result illustrated in Figure 5.2. If $r^w = 2\%$, as in Figure 5.3, column (1) of Table 5.3 shows that desired national saving is \$1 billion (row 5) and that desired investment is \$5 billion (row 3). Thus, desired foreign lending, $S^d - I^d$, equals −\$4 billion (row 7)—that is, foreign borrowing totals \$4 billion. Again, the result is the same as that illustrated in Figure 5.3.

An advantage of working through the numerical example in Table 5.3 is that we can also use it to demonstrate how the goods market equilibrium, which we have been interpreting in terms of desired saving and investment, can be interpreted in terms of output and absorption. Suppose again that $r^w = 6\%$, giving a desired consumption C^d of \$11 billion and a desired investment I^d of \$1 billion. Government purchases G are fixed at \$4 billion. Thus, when r^w is 6%, desired absorption (the desired spending by domestic residents), $C^d + I^d + G$, totals \$16 billion (row 4, column 3).

In goods market equilibrium, a country's net exports—the net quantity of goods and services that it sends abroad—equal gross domestic product Y minus desired absorption (Eq. 5.6). When r^w is 6%, Y is \$20 billion and desired absorption is \$16 billion so that net exports NX are \$4 billion. Net exports of \$4 billion imply that the country is lending \$4 billion abroad, as in Figure 5.2. If the world real interest rate drops to 2%, desired absorption rises (because people want to consume more and invest more) from \$16 billion to \$24 billion (row 4, column 1). Because in this case absorption (\$24 billion) exceeds domestic production (\$20 billion), the country has to import goods and services from abroad ($NX = -\$4$ billion). Note that desired net imports of \$4 billion imply net foreign borrowing of \$4 billion, as shown in Figure 5.3.

THE EFFECTS OF SUPPLY SHOCKS IN A SMALL OPEN ECONOMY

It is useful to recall that in the saving–investment diagram, the saving curve is drawn for given values of current output Y, expected future output, wealth, government purchases G, and taxes T, all of which are determinants of desired national saving. Similarly, the investment curve is drawn for given levels of the effective tax rate and expected future marginal product of capital, the determinants of desired national investment. The saving–investment diagram can therefore be used to determine the effects of any economic disturbance that causes a change in desired national saving (and, hence, the position of the saving curve, S) or a change in desired national investment (and, hence, the position of the investment curve, I). Briefly, any change that increases desired national saving relative to desired investment at a given world real interest rate will increase net foreign lending, the current account balance, and net exports (which are all equivalent).[6] A decline in

---

[6] Remember that we are assuming that net factor payments from abroad and net transfers are zero so that net exports equal the current account balance.

FIGURE 5.4

A TEMPORARY ADVERSE SUPPLY SHOCK IN A SMALL OPEN ECONOMY

Curve S^1 is the initial saving curve and curve I^1 is the initial investment curve of a small open economy. With a fixed world real interest rate of r^w, national saving equals the distance OB and investment equals distance OA. The current account surplus (equivalently, net foreign lending) is the difference between national saving and investment, shown as distance AB. A temporary adverse supply shock lowers current output and causes consumers to save less at any real interest rate, which shifts the saving curve left, from S^1 to S^2. National saving decreases to distance OD, and the current account surplus decreases to distance AD.

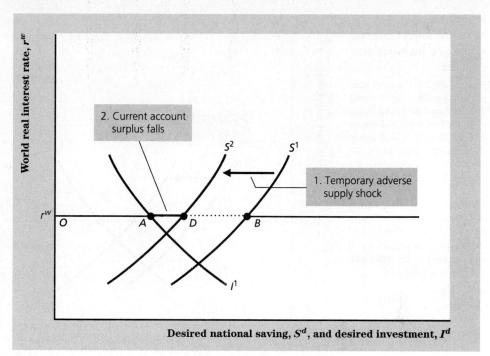

desired national saving relative to desired investment reduces those quantities. Let's look at two examples that arise frequently in various countries.

Example 1: A Temporary Adverse Supply Shock

Suppose that a small open economy is hit with a severe drought—an adverse supply shock—that temporarily lowers output. The effects of the drought on the nation's saving, investment, and current account are shown in Figure 5.4. The initial saving and investment curves are S^1 and I^1. For the world real interest rate r^w, initial net foreign lending (equivalently, net exports or the current account balance) is distance AB.

The drought brings with it a temporary decline in income. A drop in current income causes people to reduce their saving at any prevailing real interest rate, so the saving curve shifts left, from S^1 to S^2. If the supply shock is temporary, as we have assumed, the expected future marginal product of capital is unchanged. As a result, desired investment at any real interest rate is unchanged, and the investment curve does not shift. The world real interest rate is given and does not change.

In the new equilibrium, net foreign lending and the current account have shrunk to distance AD. The current account shrinks because the country saves less and thus is not able to lend abroad as much as before.

In this example we assumed that the country started with a current account surplus, which is reduced by the drought. If, instead, the country had begun with a current account deficit, the drought would have made the deficit larger. In either case, the drought reduces (in the algebraic sense) net foreign lending and the current account balance.

As in Figure 5.4, the small open economy's initial national saving and investment curves are S^1 and I^1. At the fixed world real interest rate of r^w, there is an initial current account surplus equal to the distance *AB*. An increase in the expected future marginal product of capital (MPK^f) shifts the investment curve right, from I^1 to I^2, causing investment to increase from *OA* to distance *OF*. The current account surplus, which is national saving minus investment, decreases from distance *AB* to distance *FB*.

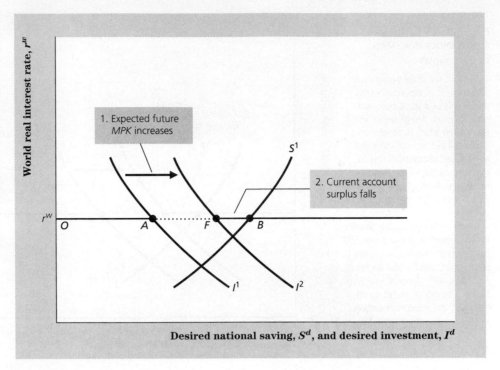

Desired national saving, S^d, and desired investment, I^d

Example 2: An Increase in the Expected Future Marginal Product of Capital

Suppose that technological innovations increase the expected future marginal product MPK^f of current capital investments. The effects on a small open economy are shown in Figure 5.5. Again, the initial national saving and investment curves are S^1 and I^1 so that the initial current account surplus equals distance *AB*.

An increase in the MPK^f raises the capital stock that domestic firms desire to hold so that desired investment rises at every real interest rate. Thus, the investment curve shifts right, from I^1 to I^2. The current account and net foreign lending shrink to length *FB*. Why does the current account fall? Given that building capital has become more profitable in the home country, more of the country's output is absorbed by domestic investment, leaving less to send abroad.[7]

APPLICATION

GLOBALIZATION AND THE CANADIAN ECONOMY

We opened this chapter by noting that virtually without exception, modern economies are open economies engaged in international trade of goods and services and in international borrowing and lending. This is certainly true of Canada. The Canadian economy has historically been an important part of the world trading community, and has historically been reliant upon foreign investment to develop its natural resources.

---

[7] A possibility we have neglected so far is that technological innovations also cause savers to expect a higher future income, which would reduce current saving at every level of the world real interest rate. A leftward shift of the saving curve would further reduce the current account balance. This in turn would only reinforce the effect on the country's current account of the rightward shift of the investment curve, so for simplicity we continue to ignore this potential change in desired saving.

Over the past 30 years, the whole world—including Canada—has grown even more open to trade in goods and services and to international borrowing and lending. Canada's increased openness to international trade stems from its signing of free trade agreements with the United States, with the United States and Mexico, and, most recently, with the European Union.[8] In Europe, the lowering of trade barriers that resulted from the signing of the Maastricht Treaty by members of the European Union (EU) in 1992 and the adoption of the euro as the common currency of many European countries had similar effects on trade and financial flows in those countries. Finally, the growing adoption of free market policies by China and India since the later 1980s has sparked dramatic increases in trade between those countries and the rest of the world. In short, the openness of countries to international trade and to the free movement of financial capital—what has come to be called *globalization*—has increased quite significantly over the past 20 years.

Globalization has certainly had impacts on the world's economy. Some Canadians have suggested that globalization has gone too far, and that perhaps restrictions should be applied—if not to stop the process of Canada's integration into the world economy, then at least to slow it down.

An issue that has often been of concern to Canadians is the effect of globalization on foreign ownership. The worry is that foreigners are buying up Canadian firms, and that this may have negative effects on the Canadian economy. In particular, should foreigners take a controlling interest in the management of Canadian firms, they may make employment and investment decisions that are harmful to Canada's interests.

To gain an understanding of this issue, we begin by examining some facts. *Direct investments* are those in which investors have a significant influence on the management of the firm in which they have invested. What are known as *portfolio investments* are those in which investors' purchase of shares in the firm is not such to gain influence on the management of the firm. Concerns about globalization are usually directed toward direct investment, and so we focus our attention there.

Figure 5.6 presents data on the stock of foreign direct investment (FDI)—the amount of direct investment by foreigners in Canada—and the stock of Canadian direct investment abroad (CDIA)—the amount of direct investment by Canadians in other countries. The difference between the two, the excess of FDI over CDIA, is shown by the bars. All of these data are presented as a percentage of GDP.

Figure 5.6 shows that foreign direct investment in Canada has historically been quite significant. After falling to a low of 18% of GDP in 1985, FDI has since increased; by 2015 the stock of FDI in Canada was equal to 39% of GDP.

The increase in FDI associated with the increased integration of world financial markets over the past 30 years is often identified as a source of concern for those worried that globalization is resulting in a "sell-out of Canada." Interestingly, however, Canadian direct investment abroad (CDIA) has increased even more quickly. Globalization has given spark to a dramatic increase in Canadian ownership and control of foreign firms, so much so that by 1997, and for the first time in Canada's history, the stock of CDIA exceeded the stock of FDI. Since 1997, Canadian ownership and control of foreign firms has exceeded foreign ownership and control of Canadian firms

---

[8] Canada signed the Canada–U.S. Free Trade Agreement in 1989, and in 1994 signed the North American Free Trade Agreement (NAFTA) with the United States and Mexico. In early 2017, Canada signed the Comprehensive Economic and Trade Agreement (CETA) with the European Union.

FIGURE 5.6

**INTERNATIONAL DIRECT
INVESTMENT, 1961–2015**

The lines in the figure show the dollar value of the stock of foreign direct investment in Canada (FDI) and the stock of Canadian direct investment abroad (CDIA), both expressed as a percentage of Canada's GDP. The bars measure the difference in these series: Net foreign direct investment. Increased globalization has encouraged non-residents to increase their ownership and control of Canadian firms but has also, and to a much greater extent, encouraged Canadians to increase their ownership and control of foreign firms.

Source: Adapted from Statistics Canada, 2017. This does not constitute an endorsement by Statistics Canada of this product.

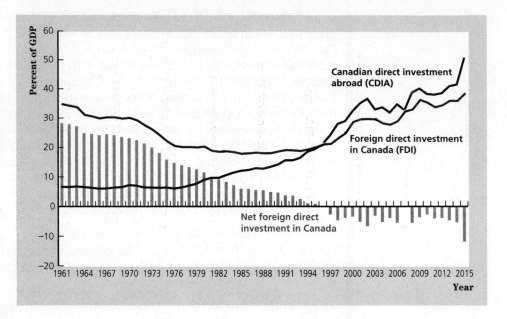

by an amount averaging 4.5% of Canada's GDP. This marks a dramatic turnaround from the 1960s, when FDI exceeded CDIA by an average of 25% of GDP.

The increased openness of international financial markets is a result of countries' easing their regulatory burdens and reducing taxes that discriminate against non-residents. Direct investment abroad by Canadians benefits Canada by providing domestic savers with a broader range of investment opportunities, by increasing the market share of Canadian companies, and by expanding export opportunities. It also benefits those countries that received Canadian direct investment, since Canadian financial capital is used to finance expansions of their industry. Moreover, foreign direct investment in Canada by non-residents benefits Canada by providing competition for Canadian firms and by importing foreign innovations, research, and knowledge. For all these reasons, analysts such as Jack Mintz and Andrey Tarasov stress that Canada should embrace and encourage the increased flows of both FDI and CDIA that have resulted from globalization rather than consider limitations to them.[9] Wherever you stand on these issues, it is interesting to remember that the question of the costs and benefits of foreign ownership cut both ways; Canadians now own a larger amount of foreign companies than foreigners own of Canadian companies.

5.4 SAVING AND INVESTMENT IN LARGE OPEN ECONOMIES

Although the model of a small open economy facing a fixed real interest rate is appropriate for studying many of the countries in the world, it is not the right model to use for analyzing the world's largest developed economies. The problem is that significant changes in the saving and investment patterns of a major economy can

---

[9] "Canada Is Missing Out on Global Capital Market Integration," C. D. Howe Institute *e-Brief*, August 21, 2007.

and do affect the world real interest rate, which violates the assumption made for the small open economy that the world real interest rate is fixed. Fortunately, we can readily adapt the analysis of the small open economy to the case of a **large open economy**, that is, an economy large enough to affect the world real interest rate. To do so we will again turn to the saving–investment diagram, a key diagram first introduced in Chapter 4 and used there to examine goods market equilibrium in a closed economy. In Section 5.3 we adapted this diagram to examine goods market equilibrium in a small open economy. In this section we adapt it once again, this time to examine goods market equilibrium in a large open economy.

To begin, let's think of the world as comprising only two large economies: (1) the home or domestic economy, and (2) the foreign economy (representing the economies of the rest of the world combined). Figure 5.7 shows the saving–investment diagram that applies to this case. Figure 5.7(a) shows the saving curve S and the investment curve I of the home economy. Figure 5.7(b) displays the saving curve S_{For} and the investment curve I_{For} of the foreign economy. These saving and investment curves are just like those for the small open economy.

Instead of taking the world real interest rate as given, as we did in the model of a small open economy, we determine the world real interest rate within the model for a large open economy. What determines the value of the world real interest rate? Remember that for the closed economy, the real interest rate was set by the

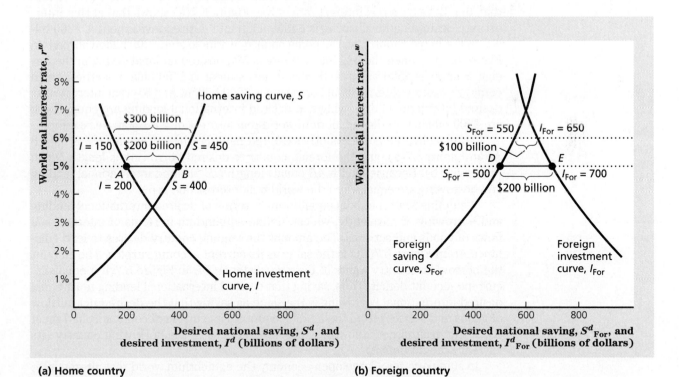

(a) Home country

(b) Foreign country

FIGURE 5.7

THE DETERMINATION OF THE WORLD REAL INTEREST RATE WITH TWO LARGE OPEN ECONOMIES

The equilibrium world real interest rate is the real interest rate at which desired international lending by one country equals desired international borrowing by the other country. In the figure, when the world real interest rate is 5%, desired international lending by the home country is $200 billion ($400 billion desired national saving less $200 billion desired investment, or distance AB), which equals the foreign country's desired international borrowing of $200 billion ($700 billion desired investment less $500 billion desired national saving, or distance DE). Thus, 5% is the equilibrium world real interest rate. Equivalently, when the interest rate is 5%, the current account surplus of the home country equals the current account deficit of the foreign country (both are $200 billion).

condition stating that the amount savers want to lend must equal the amount investors want to borrow. Analogously, in the case of two large open economies, *the world real interest rate will be such that desired international lending by one country equals desired international borrowing by the other country.* At this real interest rate, desired world saving equals desired world investment.

To illustrate the determination of the equilibrium world real interest rate, we return to Figure 5.7. Suppose, arbitrarily, that the world real interest rate r^w is 6%. Does this rate result in a goods market equilibrium? Figure 5.7(a) shows that at a 6% real interest rate, in the home country, desired national saving is $450 billion and desired investment is $150 billion. Because desired national saving exceeds desired investment by $300 billion, the amount that the home country would like to lend abroad is $300 billion.

To find how much the foreign country wants to borrow, we turn to Figure 5.7(b). When the real interest rate is 6%, desired national saving is $550 billion and desired investment is $650 billion in the foreign country. Thus, at a 6% real interest rate, the foreign country wants to borrow $100 billion ($650 billion less $550 billion) in the international capital market. Because this amount is less than the $300 billion the home country wants to lend, 6% isn't the real interest rate that is consistent with equilibrium in the international capital market.

At a real interest rate of 6%, desired international lending exceeds desired international borrowing, so the equilibrium world real interest rate must be less than 6%. Let's try a real interest rate of 5%. Figure 5.7(a) shows that at that interest rate desired national saving is $400 billion and desired investment is $200 billion in the home country, so the home country wants to lend $200 billion abroad. In Figure 5.7(b), when the real interest rate is 5%, desired national saving in the foreign country is $500 billion and desired investment is $700 billion, so the foreign country's desired international borrowing is $200 billion. At a 5% real interest rate, desired international borrowing and desired international lending are equal (both are $200 billion), so the equilibrium world real interest rate is 5% in this example.

Graphically, the home country's desired lending when r^w equals 5% is length *AB* in Figure 5.7(a), and the foreign country's desired borrowing is length *DE* in Figure 5.7(b). Because length *AB* equals length *DE*, desired international lending and borrowing are equal when the world real interest rate is 5%.

We defined international equilibrium in terms of desired international lending and borrowing. Equivalently, we can define equilibrium in terms of international flows of goods and services. The amount the lending country desires to lend (distance *AB* in Figure 5.7(a)) is the same as its current account surplus. The amount the borrowing country wants to borrow (distance *DE* in Figure 5.7(b)) equals its current account deficit. Thus, saying that desired international lending must equal desired international borrowing is the same as saying that the desired net outflow of goods and services from the lending country (its current account surplus) must equal the desired net inflow of goods and services to the borrowing country (its current account deficit).

In summary, for a large open economy the equilibrium world real interest rate is the rate at which the desired international lending by one country equals the desired international borrowing of the other country. Equivalently, it is the real interest rate at which the lending country's current account surplus equals the borrowing country's current account deficit.

Unlike the situation in a small open economy, for large open economies, the world real interest rate is not fixed but will change when desired national saving or desired investment changes in either country. Generally, any factor that increases desired international lending relative to desired international borrowing at the initial world real interest rate causes the world real interest rate to fall. Similarly, a change that reduces desired international lending relative to desired international borrowing at the initial world real interest rate will cause the world real interest rate to rise.

5.5 THE TWIN DEFICITS

The late 1980s and early 1990s in Canada were characterized by large government budget deficits and large current account deficits. Were these two phenomena related? Many economists and other commentators argue that they were, suggesting that, in fact, the budget deficit was the primary cause of the current account deficit. Those supporting this view often use the phrase *twin deficits* to convey the idea that the government budget deficit and the current account deficit were closely linked. Not all economists agree with this interpretation, however; some argue that the two deficits were largely unrelated. In this section, we briefly discuss what the theory has to say about this issue.

THE CRITICAL FACTOR: THE RESPONSE OF NATIONAL SAVING

In theory, the issue of whether there is a link between the government budget deficit and the current account deficit revolves around the following proposition: An increase in the government budget deficit will raise the current account deficit only if the increase in the budget deficit reduces desired national saving.

Let's first look at why the link to national saving is crucial. Figure 5.8 shows the case of the small open economy. The world real interest rate is fixed at r^w. We

FIGURE 5.8

THE GOVERNMENT BUDGET DEFICIT AND THE CURRENT ACCOUNT IN A SMALL OPEN ECONOMY

An increase in the government budget deficit affects the current account only if the increased budget deficit reduces national saving. Initially, the saving curve is S^1 and the current account surplus is distance AB. If an increase in the government deficit reduces national saving, the saving curve shifts left, from S^1 to S^2. With no change in the effective tax rate on capital, the investment curve I doesn't move. Thus, the increase in the budget deficit causes the current account surplus to decrease from distance AB to distance AC. In contrast, if the increase in the budget deficit has no effect on national saving, the current account is also unaffected and remains equal to distance AB.

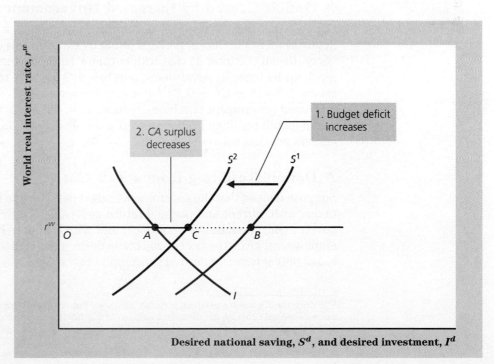

draw the initial saving and investment curves S^1 and I so that, at the world real interest rate r^w, the country is running a current account surplus, represented by length AB. Now, suppose that the government budget deficit rises. For simplicity, we assume throughout this section that the change in fiscal policy doesn't affect the tax treatment of investment so that the investment curve doesn't shift. Hence, as Figure 5.8 shows, the government deficit increase will change the current account balance only if it affects desired national saving.

The usual claim made by supporters of the twin-deficits idea is that an increase in the government budget deficit reduces desired national saving. If it does, the increase in the government deficit shifts the desired national saving curve left, from S^1 to S^2. The country still has a current account surplus, now equal to distance AC, but it is less than the original surplus AB.

We conclude that in a small open economy an increase in the government budget deficit reduces the current account balance by the same amount that it reduces desired national saving. By reducing saving, the increased budget deficit reduces the amount that domestic residents want to lend abroad at the world real interest rate, thus lowering capital outflows. Equivalently, reduced national saving means that a greater part of domestic output is absorbed at home; with less output to send abroad, the country's current account falls. Similar results hold for the large open economy (you are asked to work out this case in Analytical Problem 4 at the end of the chapter).

THE GOVERNMENT BUDGET DEFICIT AND NATIONAL SAVING

Let's now turn to the link between the budget deficit and saving and consider two cases: a budget deficit arising from an increase in government purchases, and a deficit arising from a cut in taxes.

A Deficit Caused by Increased Government Purchases

Suppose that the source of the government budget deficit is a temporary increase in government purchases, perhaps owing to a war. In this case, there is no controversy. Recall (Chapter 4) that with output Y held constant at its full-employment level, an increase in government purchases G directly reduces desired national saving, $S^d = Y - C^d - G$.[10,11] Because economists agree that a deficit owing to increased government purchases reduces desired national saving, they also agree that a deficit resulting from increased government purchases reduces the nation's current account balance.

A Deficit Resulting from a Tax Cut

Suppose instead that the government budget deficit is the result of a cut in current taxes, with current and planned future government purchases unchanged. With government purchases G unchanged and with output Y held constant at its full-employment level, the tax cut will cause desired national saving, $S^d = Y - C^d - G$, to fall only if it causes desired consumption C^d to rise.

Will a tax cut cause people to consume more? As we discussed in Chapter 4, believers in the Ricardian equivalence proposition argue that a lump-sum tax change (with current and future government purchases held constant) will not affect desired consumption or desired national saving. These economists point out that a cut in taxes today forces the government to borrow more to pay for its current purchases; when this extra borrowing plus interest is repaid in the future, future taxes will have to rise. Thus, although a tax cut raises consumers' current after-tax incomes, the tax cut creates the need for higher future taxes and lowers the after-tax incomes that consumers can expect to receive in the future. Overall, according to this argument, a tax cut does not benefit consumers and, thus, will not increase their desired consumption.

If the Ricardian equivalence proposition is true, a budget deficit resulting from a tax cut will have no effect on the current account because it does not affect desired national saving. However, as we noted in Chapter 4, many economists argue that—despite the logic of Ricardian equivalence—in practice, many consumers do respond to a current tax cut by consuming more. For example, consumers simply may not understand that a higher deficit today makes higher taxes tomorrow more likely. If for any reason consumers do respond to a tax cut by consuming more, the deficit resulting from a tax cut will reduce national saving and, thus, will also reduce the current account balance.

Debate over the twin-deficits hypothesis continues, in part because the evidence of its existence is not always observed in all countries and during all periods of time. What we can say for sure (because it is implied by the uses-of-saving identity, Eq. 2.11 on p. 32) is that if an increase in the government budget deficit is not offset by an equal increase in private saving, the result must be a decline in domestic investment, a rise in the current account deficit, or both.

CHAPTER SUMMARY

1. The balance of payments accounts consist of the current account and the capital account. The current account records trade in currently produced goods and services, investment income from assets held abroad, and transfers between countries. The capital account records trade in existing assets, both real and financial.

2. In the current account, exports of goods and services, receipts of investment income from assets held abroad, and transfers received from abroad count as credit (plus) items. Imports of goods and services, payments of investment income to foreigners holding assets in the home country, and transfers sent abroad are debit (minus) items in the current account. The current account balance, CA, equals the value of credit items less debit items in the current account. Setting net factor payments and net transfers to zero makes the current account balance the same as net exports, NX. The capital account balance, KA, is the value of assets sold to foreigners (capital inflows) minus the value of assets purchased from foreigners (capital outflows).

3. In each period, except for measurement errors, the current account balance and the capital account balance must sum to zero. The reason is that any international transaction amounts to a swap of goods, services, or assets between countries; the two sides of the swap always have offsetting effects on the sum of the current account and capital account balances.

4. In an open economy, goods market equilibrium requires that the desired amount of national saving equal the desired amount of domestic investment plus the amount the country lends abroad. Equivalently, net exports must equal the country's output (gross domestic product) less desired total spending by domestic residents (absorption).

5. A small open economy faces a fixed real interest rate in the international capital market. In goods market equilibrium in a small open economy, national saving and investment equal their desired levels at the prevailing world real interest rate; foreign lending, net exports, and the current account all equal the excess of national saving over investment. Any factor that increases desired national saving or reduces desired investment at the world real interest rate will increase the small open economy's foreign lending (equivalently, its current account balance).

6. The levels of saving and investment of a large open economy affect the world real interest rate. In a model of two large open economies, the equilibrium real interest rate in the international capital market is the rate at which desired international lending by one country equals desired international borrowing by the other country. Equivalently, it is the rate at which the lending country's current account surplus equals the borrowing country's current account deficit. Any factor that increases desired national saving or reduces desired investment at the initial interest rate for either large country will increase the supply of international loans relative to the demand and cause the world real interest rate to fall.

7. Whether budget deficits cause current account deficits is the subject of disagreement. In theory, and if we assume no change in the tax treatment of investment, an increase in the government budget deficit will raise the current account deficit only if it reduces national saving. Economists generally agree that an increase in the budget deficit caused by a temporary increase in government purchases will reduce national saving, but whether an increase in the budget deficit caused by a tax cut reduces national saving is controversial.

KEY DIAGRAM 4

National Saving and Investment in a Small Open Economy

This open-economy version of the saving–investment diagram shows the determination of national saving, investment, and the current account balance in a small open economy that takes the world real interest rate as given.

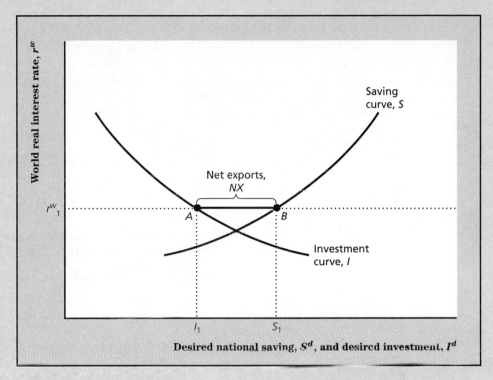

DIAGRAM ELEMENTS

- The world real interest rate is measured on the vertical axis, and the small economy's desired national saving S^d and desired investment I^d are measured on the horizontal axis.

- The world real interest rate r^w is fixed, as indicated by the horizontal line.

- The saving curve S and the investment curve I are the same as in the closed-economy saving–investment diagram, Key Diagram 3 (p. 125).

ANALYSIS

- Goods market equilibrium in a small open economy requires that desired national saving equal desired investment plus net exports (Eq. 5.4). In the diagram, when the world real interest rate

is r^w_1, desired national saving is S_1 and desired investment is I_1. The country's net exports NX and current account balance CA, or $S_1 - I_1$, is distance AB. Equivalently, distance AB, the excess of desired national saving over desired investment, is the amount that the small open economy is lending abroad, or its capital account deficit.

FACTORS THAT SHIFT THE CURVES

- Anything that increases desired national saving in the small open economy, for a fixed value of the world real interest rate, shifts the saving curve right. Factors that shift the saving curve right (see Summary table 5, p. 106) include

  – an increase in current output, Y,
  – a decrease in expected future output,
  – a decrease in wealth,

– a decrease in current government purchases, G, and
– an increase in current taxes, T, if Ricardian equivalence doesn't hold and taxes affect saving.

• Anything that increases desired investment at the prevailing real interest rate shifts the investment curve right. Factors that shift the investment curve right (see Summary table 6, p. 115) include an increase in the expected future marginal product of capital, MPK^f, and a decrease in the effective tax rate on capital.

• An increase in desired national saving shifts the saving curve right and raises net exports and the current account balance. Equivalently, an increase

in desired national saving raises the country's net foreign lending, which equals its capital account deficit. Similarly, an increase in desired investment shifts the investment curve right and lowers net exports, the current account balance, net foreign lending, and the capital account deficit.

• An increase in the world real interest rate r^w raises the horizontal line in the diagram. Because an increase in the world real interest rate increases national saving and reduces investment, it raises net foreign lending, net exports, the current account surplus, and the capital account deficit.

KEY DIAGRAM 5

National Saving and Investment in Large Open Economies

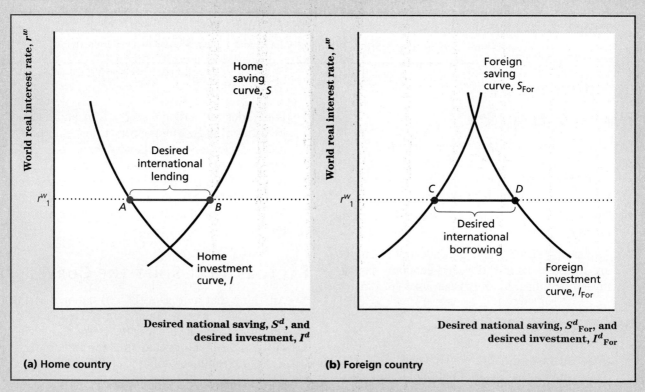

(a) Home country

(b) Foreign country

This diagram shows the determination of national saving, investment, and the current account balance in large open economies—economies large enough to affect the world real interest rate.

DIAGRAM ELEMENTS

- The figure consists of two saving–investment diagrams, one for the home country and one for the foreign country (representing the rest of the world).

- The world real interest rate r^w, measured on the vertical axis, is the real interest rate faced by both countries in the international capital market.

- The saving and investment curves in the home country (S and I) and in the foreign country (S_{For} and I_{For}) are the same as the saving and investment curves presented before (Key Diagram 3, p. 125, and Key Diagram 4).

ANALYSIS

- This case differs from the case of the small open economy (Key Diagram 4) in that the world real interest rate r^w is determined within the model, not given.

- Goods market equilibrium for large open economies requires that the desired international lending of one country equal the desired international borrowing of the other. Equivalently, because a country's international lending equals its current account balance, goods market equilibrium requires that one country's current account surplus equal the other country's current account deficit.

- The world real interest rate adjusts to achieve goods market equilibrium. In the diagram r^w_1 is the equilibrium world real interest rate, because at that interest rate the home country's desired international lending (its desired national saving less desired investment, or distance AB) equals the foreign country's desired international borrowing (its desired investment less desired national saving, or distance CD).

FACTORS THAT SHIFT THE CURVES

- The saving and investment curves in the two countries are shifted by the same factors as in Key Diagram 3, p. 125, and Key Diagram 4, p. 155.

- The world real interest rate changes when desired national saving or desired investment changes in either country. Any change that increases desired international lending relative to desired international borrowing at the initial world real interest rate will cause the world real interest rate to fall to restore equilibrium in the international capital market. Changes that increase desired international lending relative to desired international borrowing include an increase in desired national saving or a decrease in desired investment in either country. Similarly, a decrease in desired national saving or an increase in desired investment in either country reduces desired international lending relative to desired international borrowing and raises the world real interest rate.

KEY EQUATIONS

$$CA + KA = 0 \qquad (5.1)$$

Except for problems of measurement, the current account balance, CA, and the capital account balance, KA, always sum to zero. The reason is that every international transaction involves a swap of goods, services, or assets, and the two sides of the swap always have offsetting effects on $CA + KA$.

$$S^d = I^d + NX \qquad (5.4)$$

The goods market equilibrium condition in an open economy holds that desired national saving, S^d, must equal desired investment, I^d, plus the amount lent abroad. The amount lent abroad equals the current account balance, which (if we assume that net factor payments and transfers are zero) also equals net exports, NX.

$$NX = Y - (C^d + I^d + G) \qquad (5.6)$$

An alternative way of writing the goods market equilibrium condition, this equation states that net exports must equal the country's output, Y, less its desired absorption, $C^d + I^d + G$.

REVIEW QUESTIONS

1. List the categories of credit items and debit items that appear in a country's current account. What is the current account balance? What is the relationship between the current account balance and net exports?

2. What is the key difference that determines whether an international transaction appears in the current account or the capital account?

3. A Canadian publisher sells $200 worth of books to a resident of Brazil. By itself, this item is a credit item in the Canadian current account. Describe some offsetting transactions that could ensure that the Canadian current and capital account balances would continue to sum to zero.

4. How do a country's current and capital account balances affect its net foreign assets? If country A has greater net foreign assets per citizen than does country B, is country A necessarily better off than country B?

5. Explain why, in a small open economy, (a) national saving does not have to equal investment, and (b) output does not have to equal absorption.

6. Generally, what types of factors will cause a small open economy to run a large current account deficit and thus borrow abroad? More specifically, what two major factors contributed to heavy LDC borrowing in the 1970s?

7. In a world with two large open economies, what determines the world real interest rate? What relationship between the current accounts of the two countries is satisfied when the world real interest rate is at its equilibrium value?

8. How does an increase in desired national saving in a large open economy affect the world real interest rate? How does an increase in desired investment affect it? Why do changes in desired saving or investment in large open economies affect the world real interest rate while changes in desired saving or investment in small open economies do not?

9. Under what circumstances will an increase in the government budget deficit affect the current account balance in a small open economy? In the cases in which the current account balance changes, by how much does it change?

10. What are the twin deficits? What is the connection between them?

NUMERICAL PROBLEMS

1. Here are some balance of payments data (without pluses and minuses):

Merchandise exports, 100
Merchandise imports, 125
Service exports, 90
Service imports, 80
Investment income receipts from assets, 110
Investment income payments on assets, 140
Transfers from home country to other countries, 10
Increase in home country's ownership of assets abroad, 160
Increase in foreign ownership of assets in home country, 200
Increase in home reserve assets, 30
Increase in foreign reserve assets, 35

Find the merchandise trade balance, net exports, the current account balance, the capital account balance, the official settlements balance, and the statistical discrepancy.

2. In a small open economy, output (gross domestic product) is $25 billion, government purchases are $6 billion, and net factor payments from abroad are zero. Desired consumption and desired investment are related to the world real interest rate in the following manner:

World Real Interest Rate	Desired Consumption	Desired Investment
5%	$12 billion	$3 billion
4%	$13 billion	$4 billion
3%	$14 billion	$5 billion
2%	$15 billion	$6 billion

For each value of the world real interest rate, find national saving, foreign lending, and absorption. Calculate net exports as the difference between output and absorption. What is the relationship between net exports and foreign lending?

3. In a small open economy,

desired national saving, S^d = \$10 billion + (\$100 billion)r^w;

desired investment, I^d = \$15 billion − (\$100 billion)r^w;

output, Y = \$50 billion;

government purchases, G = \$10 billion;

world real interest rate, r^w = 3%.

a. Find the economy's national saving, investment, current account surplus, net exports, desired consumption, and absorption.
b. Owing to a technological innovation, the country's desired investment rises by \$2 billion at each level of the world real interest rate. Repeat part (a).

4. Consider two large open economies, the home economy and the foreign economy. In the home country the following relationships hold:

desired consumption, C^d = 320 + 0.4(Y − T) − 200r^w;

desired investment, I^d = 150 − 200r^w;

output, Y = 1000;

taxes, T = 200;

government purchases, G = 275.

In the foreign country the following relationships hold:

desired consumption, C^d_{For} = 480 + 0.4(Y_{For} − T_{For}) − 300r^w;

desired investment, I^d_{For} = 225 − 300r^w;

output, Y_{For} = 1500;

taxes, T_{For} = 300;

government purchases, G_{For} = 300.

a. What is the equilibrium interest rate in the international capital market? What are the equilibrium values of consumption, national saving, investment, and the current account balance in each country?
b. Suppose that in the home country government purchases increase by 50–325. Taxes also increase by 50 to keep the deficit from growing. What is the new equilibrium interest rate in the international capital market? What are the new equilibrium values of consumption, national saving,

investment, and the current account balance in each country?

5. Consider a world with only two countries, which are designated the home country (H) and the foreign country (F). Output equals its full-employment level in each country. You are given the following information about each country:

Home Country

Consumption:	$C_H = 100 + 0.5Y_H − 500r$
Investment:	$I_H = 300 − 500r$
Government purchases:	$G_H = 155$
Full-employment output:	$\overline{Y}_H = 1000$

Foreign Country

Consumption:	$C_F = 225 + 0.7Y_F − 600r$
Investment:	$I_F = 250 − 200r$
Government purchases:	$G_F = 190$
Full-employment output:	$\overline{Y}_F = 1200$

a. Write national saving in the home country and in the foreign country as functions of the world real interest rate r.
b. What is the equilibrium value of the world real interest rate?
c. What are the equilibrium values of consumption, national saving, investment, the current account balance, and absorption in each country?

6. A small island nation is endowed with indestructible coconut trees. These trees live forever and no new trees can be planted. Every year \$1 million worth of coconuts fall off the trees and can be eaten locally or exported to other countries. In past years, the island nation ran current account surpluses and capital account deficits, acquiring foreign bonds. It now owns \$500 000 of foreign bonds. The interest rate on these bonds is 5% per year. The residents of the island nation consume \$1 025 000 per year. What are the values of investment, national saving, the current account balance, the capital account balance, net exports, GDP, and GNP in this country?

ANALYTICAL PROBLEMS

1. Explain how each of the following transactions would enter the Canadian balance of payments accounts. Discuss only the transactions described. Do not be concerned with possible offsetting transactions.
a. The Canadian government sells military equipment to a foreign government.
b. A London bank sells yen to, and buys Canadian dollars from, a Swiss bank.

   c. The Bank of Canada sells yen to, and buys dollars from, a Swiss bank.

   d. A Canadian bank receives the interest on its loans to Brazil.

   e. A Canadian collector buys some modern art from a collection in Japan.

   f. A Canadian oil company buys insurance from Lloyds of London to insure its oil rigs in the Beaufort Sea.

   g. A Canadian company borrows from a U.S. bank.

2. For each transaction described in Analytical Problem 1 that by itself changes the sum of the Canadian current account balance, *CA*, and the Canadian capital account balance, *KA*, give an example of an offsetting transaction that would leave *CA* + *KA* unchanged.

3. A large country imposes capital controls that prohibit foreign borrowing and lending by domestic residents. Analyze the effects on the country's current account balance, national saving, and investment, and on domestic and world real interest rates. Assume that before the capital controls were imposed, the large country was running a capital account surplus.

4. Section 5.5 showed that for a small open economy, an increase in the government budget deficit raises the current account deficit only if it affects desired national saving in the home country. Show that this result is also true for a large open economy. Then assume that an increase in the government budget deficit does affect desired national saving in the home country. What effects will the increased budget deficit have on the foreign country's current account, investment in both countries, and the world real interest rate?

5. How would each of the following affect national saving, investment, the current account balance, and the real interest rate in a large open economy?

   a. An increase in the domestic willingness to save (which raises desired national saving at any given real interest rate).

   b. An increase in the willingness of foreigners to save.

   c. An increase in foreign government purchases.

   d. An increase in foreign taxes (consider both the case in which Ricardian equivalence holds and the case in which it does not hold).

6. Suppose that in Canada and in the United States, the interest rates on government bonds of identical maturity and risk are 8% and 6%, respectively. Assuming savers are indifferent between owning Canadian or U.S. bonds, what would we expect to happen to the interest rates on these bonds? Explain how this would happen.

7. Herb lives in Calgary. When it was time to shop for the best interest rate on a mortgage, Herb checked out interest rates at all of the major lending institutions. Just to be on the safe side, for every lending institution, Herb checked the interest rates available at a branch in Toronto with the rate available at branches in Calgary. He found that in every case the interest rates were identical. Explain why Herb should have known this.

8. Analyze the effects on a large open economy of a temporary adverse supply shock that hits only the foreign economy. Discuss the impact on the home country's national saving, investment, and current account balance—and on the world real interest rate. How does your answer differ if the adverse supply shock is worldwide?

9. The chief economic adviser of a small open economy makes the following announcement: "We have good news and bad news. The good news is that we have just had a temporary beneficial productivity shock that will increase output; the bad news is that the increase in output and income will lead domestic consumers to buy more imported goods, and our current account balance will fall." Analyze this statement, taking as given that a beneficial productivity shock has indeed occurred.

10. The world is made up of only two large countries: Eastland and Westland. Westland is running a large current account deficit and often appeals to Eastland for help in reducing this current account deficit. Currently, the government of Eastland purchases $10 billion of goods and services, and all these goods and services are produced in Eastland. The finance minister of Eastland proposes that the government purchase half of its goods from Westland. Specifically, the government of Eastland will continue to purchase $10 billion of goods, but $5 billion will be from Eastland and $5 billion will be from Westland. The finance minister gives the following rationale: "Both countries produce identical goods, so it doesn't really matter to us which country produced the goods we purchase. Moreover, this change in purchasing policy will help reduce Westland's large current account deficit." What are the effects of this change in purchasing policy on the current account balance in each country and on the world real interest rate? (*Hint:* What happens to net exports by the private sector in each country after the government of Eastland changes its purchasing policy?)

Chapter 6
Long-Run Economic Growth

A country's ability to provide improving standards of living for its people depends crucially on its long-run rate of economic growth. Over a long period of time, even an apparently small difference in the rate of economic growth can translate into a large difference in the income of the average person.

Compare, for example, the historical experiences of Australia and Japan. In 1870, real GDP per person was more than four times greater in Australia than in Japan, as the data on national growth performances in Table 6.1 show. Indeed, of 16 major economies considered by British economist Angus Maddison in his important research on long-run growth (and from whose work the data in Table 6.1 are taken), Australia was the richest and Japan the poorest in 1870. Australia's economy did not stand still after 1870. Over the next 140 years, according to Maddison's data, Australian real GDP per person grew by an average of 1.5% per year, so that by 2010 the real income of the average Australian was more than seven times higher than it had been in 1870. However, during the same period, Japanese real GDP per person grew at an average rate of 2.4% per year, reaching a level in 2010 that was nearly 30 times larger than it had been in 1870.

The Japanese growth rate of 2.4% per year may not seem dramatically greater than the Australian growth rate of 1.5% per year. Yet, by 1990, Japan, which had been far poorer than Australia a century earlier, had surpassed its Pacific neighbour in real per capita GDP by a margin of 10%. Sluggish growth in Japan allowed Australia to retake the lead by 1998 and to establish a lead of more than 15% by 2010. Other, similar comparisons can be drawn from Table 6.1; compare, for example, the long-term growth performance of the United Kingdom against that of Canada or Sweden. Note, however, that even those countries that grew relatively slowly have dramatically increased their output per person during the past century.

Although the comparisons highlighted by Table 6.1 span a long period of time, a change in the rate of economic growth can have important effects over even a decade or two. For example, since about 1973, Canada and other industrialized countries have experienced a sustained slowdown in their rates of growth. Between 1947 and 1973, total (not per capita) real GDP in Canada grew by about 5% per year, but between 1973 and 2015, Canada's real GDP grew by only 2.6% per year. To appreciate the significance of this slowdown, imagine that the 1947–1973

TABLE 6.1

Economic Growth in Eight Major Countries, 1870–2010

| Country | Levels of Real GDP per Capita | | | | Annual Growth Rate |
	1870	1913	1950	2010	1870–2010
Australia	3273	5157	7412	25 584	1.5%
Canada	1695	4447	7291	24 941	1.9
France	1876	3485	5186	21 477	1.7
Germany	1839	3648	3881	20 661	1.7
Japan	737	1387	1921	21 935	2.4
Sweden	1662	3096	6739	25 306	2.0
United Kingdom	3190	4921	6939	23 777	1.4
United States	2445	5301	9561	30 491	1.8

Note: Figures are in U.S. dollars at 1990 prices, adjusted for differences in the purchasing power of the various national currencies.

Source: Data from J. Bolt and J. L. van Zanden, "The First Update of the Maddison Project; Re-Estimating Growth Before 1820," Maddison Project Working Paper 4, 2013, available at *www.ggdc.net/maddison*.

growth trend had continued—that is, suppose that real GDP in Canada had continued to grow at 5% per year instead of at the 2.6% per year rate actually achieved. Then, in 2015 the Canadian real GDP would have been more than twice its actual value—a bonus of $2718 billion, or $75 500 per person (in 2007 dollars).

No one understands completely why economies grow, and no one has a magic formula for inducing rapid growth. Indeed, if such a formula existed, there would be no poor countries. Nevertheless, economists have gained useful insights about the growth process. In this chapter, we identify the forces that determine the growth rate of an economy over long periods of time and examine various policies that governments use to try to influence the rate of growth. Once again, saving and investment decisions play a central role in the analysis. Along with changes in productivity, the rates at which a country saves and invests—and, thus, the rate at which it accumulates capital goods—are important factors in determining the standard of living that the country's people can attain.

6.1 THE SOURCES OF ECONOMIC GROWTH

An economy's output of goods and services depends on the quantities of available inputs, such as capital and labour, and on the productivity of those inputs. The relationship between output and inputs is described by the production function, introduced in Chapter 3:

$$Y = AF(K, N). \tag{6.1}$$

The relationship defined by Eq. (6.1) is that total output Y depends on the economy's use of capital K, labour N, and total factor productivity A.

If inputs and productivity are constant, the production function states that output will also be constant—there will be no economic growth. For the quantity of output to grow, either the quantity of inputs must grow or productivity must improve or both. The relationship between the rate of output growth and the rates of input growth and productivity growth is

$$\frac{\Delta Y}{Y} = \frac{\Delta A}{A} + a_K \frac{\Delta K}{K} + a_N \frac{\Delta N}{N},$$ (6.2)

where

$$\frac{\Delta Y}{Y} = \text{rate of output growth;}$$

$$\frac{\Delta K}{K} = \text{rate of capital growth;}$$

$$\frac{\Delta N}{N} = \text{rate of labour growth;}$$

$$\frac{\Delta A}{A} = \text{rate of productivity growth;}$$

a_K = elasticity of output with respect to capital;
a_N = elasticity of output with respect to labour.

In Eq. (6.2) the elasticity of output with respect to capital, a_K, is the percentage increase in output resulting from a 1% increase in the capital stock, and the elasticity of output with respect to labour, a_N, is the percentage increase in output resulting from a 1% increase in the amount of labour used. The elasticities a_K and a_N are both numbers between 0 and 1 that must be estimated from historical data.[1]

Equation (6.2), called the **growth accounting equation**, is the production function (Eq. 6.1) written in growth rate form. Some examples will be helpful for understanding the growth accounting equation.

Suppose that a new invention allows firms to produce 10% more output for the same amount of capital and labour. In terms of the production function, Eq. (6.1), for constant capital and labour inputs, a 10% increase in productivity A raises output Y by 10%. Similarly, from the growth accounting equation, Eq. (6.2), if productivity growth $\Delta A/A$ equals 10% and capital and labour growth are zero, output growth $\Delta Y/Y$ will be 10%. Thus, the production function and the growth accounting equation give the same result, as they should.

Now, suppose that firms' investments cause the economy's capital stock to rise by 10% ($\Delta K/K = 10\%$) while labour input and productivity remain unchanged. What will happen to output? The production function shows that if the capital stock grows, output will increase. However, because of the diminishing marginal productivity of capital (see Chapter 3), the extra capital will be less productive than that used previously, so the increase in output will be less than 10%. Diminishing marginal productivity of capital is the reason that the growth rate of capital, $\Delta K/K$, is multiplied by a factor less than 1 in the growth accounting equation. For Canada this factor, a_K, the elasticity of output with respect to capital, is about 0.3. Thus, the growth accounting equation, Eq. (6.2), indicates that a 10% increase in the capital stock, with labour and productivity held constant, will increase Canadian output by about 3%, or (0.3)(10%).

Similarly, the elasticity of output with respect to labour a_N is about 0.7 in Canada. Thus, according to Eq. (6.2), a 10% increase in the amount of labour used ($\Delta N/N = 10\%$), with no change in capital or productivity, will raise Canadian output by about 7%, or (0.7)(10%).[2]

---

[1] Elasticities and growth rate formulas such as Eq. (6.2) are discussed further in the Appendix, Sections A.3, A.6, and A.7.

[2] Chapter 3 examined the production function for the Canadian economy, $Y = AK^{0.3}N^{0.7}$. In that production function, called a Cobb–Douglas production function, the exponent on the capital stock K, 0.3, equals the elasticity of output with respect to capital, and the exponent on the quantity of labour input N, 0.7, equals the elasticity of output with respect to labour. See the Appendix, Section A.7.

GROWTH ACCOUNTING

According to Eq. (6.2), output growth $\Delta Y/Y$ can be divided into three parts:

1. that resulting from productivity growth, $\Delta A/A$,
2. that resulting from increased capital inputs, $a_K \Delta K/K$, and
3. that resulting from increased labour inputs, $a_N \Delta N/N$.

Growth accounting measures empirically the relative importance of these three sources of output growth. A typical growth accounting analysis involves the following four steps (see Table 6.2 for a summary and numerical example):

- *Step 1.* Obtain measures of the growth rates of output, $\Delta Y/Y$, capital, $\Delta K/K$, and labour, $\Delta N/N$, for the economy over any period of time. In the calculation of growth rates for capital and labour, more sophisticated analyses make adjustments for

TABLE 6.2

The Steps of Growth Accounting: A Numerical Example

Step 1. Obtain measures of output growth, capital growth, and labour growth over the period to be studied.

Example:

$$\text{Output growth} = \frac{\Delta Y}{Y} = 40\%;$$

$$\text{Capital growth} = \frac{\Delta K}{K} = 20\%;$$

$$\text{Labour growth} = \frac{\Delta N}{N} = 30\%.$$

Step 2. Using historical data, obtain estimates of the elasticities of output with respect to capital and labour, a_K and a_N.

Example: $a_K = 0.3$ and $a_N = 0.7.$

Step 3. Find the contributions to growth of capital and labour.

Example: $\text{Contribution to output growth of growth in capital} = a_K \frac{\Delta K}{K} = (0.3)(20\%) = 6\%;$

$\text{Contribution to output growth of growth in labour} = a_N \frac{\Delta N}{N} = (0.7)(30\%) = 21\%.$

Step 4. Find productivity growth as the residual (the part of output growth not explained by capital or labour).

Example: $\text{Productivity growth} = \frac{\Delta A}{A} = \frac{\Delta Y}{Y} - a_K \frac{\Delta K}{K} - a_N \frac{\Delta N}{N}$
$$= 40\% - 6\% - 21\% = 13\%.$$

In this example of growth accounting, the calculations demonstrate that over the time period considered output grew by 40%. Growth in the capital stock accounted for 6 percentage points of that growth, growth in the labour force accounted for 21 percentage points, and productivity growth accounted for the remaining 13 percentage points of output growth.

changing quality as well as quantity of inputs. For example, to obtain a quality-adjusted measure of N, an hour of work by a skilled worker is counted as more labour than an hour of work by an unskilled worker. Similarly, to obtain a quality-adjusted measure of K, a machine that can turn 50 bolts a minute is treated as being more capital than a machine that can turn only 30 bolts a minute.

- *Step 2.* Estimate values for the elasticities a_K and a_N from historical data. Keep in mind the estimates for Canada of 0.3 for a_K and 0.7 for a_N.

- *Step 3.* Calculate the contribution of capital to economic growth as $a_K \Delta K/K$ and the contribution of labour to economic growth as $a_N \Delta N/N$.

- *Step 4.* The part of economic growth assignable to neither capital growth nor labour growth is attributed to improvements in total factor productivity. The rate of productivity change $\Delta A/A$ is calculated from the formula

$$\frac{\Delta A}{A} = \frac{\Delta Y}{Y} - a_K \frac{\Delta K}{K} - a_N \frac{\Delta N}{N},$$

which is the growth accounting equation, Eq. (6.2), rewritten with $\Delta A/A$ on the left-hand side. Thus, the growth accounting technique treats productivity change as a residual, that is, the portion of growth not otherwise explained.[3]

APPLICATION

GROWTH ACCOUNTING AND THE EAST ASIAN "MIRACLE"

Several East Asian countries—sometimes called the East Asian tigers—exhibited remarkable rates of economic growth during the final third of the 20th century. Between 1966 and 1991, Hong Kong averaged real GDP growth of more than 7% per year, and between 1966 and 1990, Singapore, South Korea, and Taiwan averaged real GDP growth of more than 8% per year. An 8% annual growth rate sustained over 25 years translates into a level of real output nearly seven times as high at the end of the period as at the beginning. These countries were hit by a severe financial crisis in the late 1990s, which slowed their GDP growth—and even caused negative GDP growth in some cases. Nevertheless, the East Asian miracle remains an interesting example to economists, political leaders, and businesspeople who would like to find a way to create similar miracles in their own countries.

What caused the East Asian miracle? To address this question, Alwyn Young of the University of Chicago applied growth accounting in a particularly careful study of East Asian growth.[4] Young used a variety of data sources to develop comprehensive measures of the growth of output, capital, and labour for Hong Kong, Singapore, South Korea, and Taiwan. He found that to a surprising degree, the rapid economic growth of these East Asian economies resulted from rapid growth in capital and labour inputs rather than improvements in total factor productivity. For example,

[3] The growth accounting method for calculating productivity growth is similar to the method we used to find productivity growth in Section 3.1, where we also determined productivity growth as the part of output growth not explained by increases in capital and labour. The differences are that growth accounting uses the growth accounting equation, which is the production function in growth rate form, instead of using the production function directly, as we did in Chapter 3; and growth accounting analyses usually adjust measures of capital and labour for changes in quality, which we did not do in Chapter 3.

[4] "The Tyranny of Numbers: Confronting the Statistical Realities of the East Asian Growth Experience," *Quarterly Journal of Economics*, August 1995, pp. 641–680.

all four countries experienced remarkable increases in labour force participation rates as well as general population growth. Similarly, extremely high rates of national saving (in some cases, enforced by government regulations) led to rapid growth in capital stocks.

After accounting for increases in inputs, Young found that rates of growth in productivity in the four East Asian countries were not as high as many people had thought: 2.3% for Hong Kong, 1.7% for South Korea, 2.6% for Taiwan, and only 0.2% for Singapore! These are good rates of productivity growth (except for Singapore's) but not "miraculous" rates; for example, over approximately the same period, Italy enjoyed productivity growth of about 2% per year.

As we discuss in detail in this chapter, the declining marginal productivity of capital makes it very difficult to sustain growth over the very long term by increasing inputs alone. At some point, only advances in productivity can keep an economy on a path of rapid growth. Thus, an implication of Young's research is that (even without the Asian financial crisis) the rapid growth in East Asia may have run out of steam on its own. Furthermore, the rapid growth of the East Asian tigers is unlikely to resume, unless those countries can find ways to stimulate growth in productivity.

Since Young's research, a new Asian "tiger" has appeared on the scene: China. For the past two decades China has experienced very high rates of economic growth. Young's research and the economic model we discuss in this chapter suggest that, just like the East Asian tigers, the "miraculous" rates of growth in China over the past two decades are unlikely to continue. Indeed, signs of slowdown are starting to appear.

Growth Accounting and the Productivity Slowdown

What does growth accounting say about the sources of Canadian economic growth? Table 6.3 summarizes some of the research, much of it originated by Harvey Lithwick of Carleton University.

The last entry in column (3) shows, for example, that over the 1926–1956 period, output grew at an average rate of 3.9% per year. According to these measurements, the growth of labour accounted for output growth of 0.6% per year. The growth of labour, in turn, resulted primarily from an increase in population, an increase in the percentage of the population in the labour force, and higher educational levels, which raised workers' skills. (Offsetting these trends to a degree was a decline in the number of hours worked per person.) The growth of the capital stock also accounted for output growth of 0.6% per year. So, together, labour and capital growth contributed 1.2% per year to the 3.9% per year average growth rate of output for the period.

The difference between total growth (3.9%) and the amount of growth attributed to capital and labour growth (1.2%) from 1926 through 1956 is 2.7%. By the growth accounting method, this remaining 2.7% per year of growth is attributed to increases in productivity. Thus, increased quantities of factors of production and improvements in the effectiveness with which those factors were used both played important roles in Canadian growth after 1926.

Data for periods after 1956 are given in columns (4)–(6) of Table 6.3. They show rapid output growth during 1962–1973, which has slowed since. Comparing column (4) with column (5), for 1974–1986, or with column (6), for 1987–2015, shows that a significant amount of the decline in output growth can be accounted for by a decline in productivity growth.

TABLE 6.3

Sources of Economic Growth in Canada (percent per year)

	(1) 1891–1910	(2) 1910–1926	(3) 1926–1956
Source of Growth			
Labour growth	1.8	1.0	0.6
Capital growth	0.8	0.3	0.6
Total input growth	2.6	1.3	1.2
Productivity growth	0.8	1.2	2.7
Total output growth	**3.4**	**2.5**	**3.9**

	(4) 1962–1973	(5) 1974–1986	(6) 1987–2015
Source of Growth			
Labour growth	2.2	1.6	1.0
Capital growth	1.5	0.9	0.7
Total input growth	3.7	2.5	1.7
Productivity growth	1.6	0.9	0.7
Total output growth	**5.3**	**3.4**	**2.4**

Source: Based on the following: 1891–1956: N. Harvey Lithwick, *Economic Growth in Canada: A Quantitative Analysis*, 2nd ed., Toronto: University of Toronto Press, 1970; 1962–2015: Statistics Canada, CANSIM series v1078498, v246119, v3860085, and Labour Force Historical Review, 2004.

The finding of a significant slowdown in productivity growth beginning in the early 1970s has been confirmed by many studies, both for Canada and for other industrialized countries. The fact that the initial slowdown in productivity growth was so widespread across industrial economies and so closely timed to the early 1970s suggests a common cause, and in fact there has been considerable research trying to pinpoint that cause. One explanation that has been offered is that there has not been a slowdown at all; rather, what appears to be a productivity slowdown is actually the result of a measurement error. By failing to adequately measure the increase in quality of certain capital inputs—computers, in particular—statisticians have understated true productivity growth.

Another explanation that has been offered is that the productivity slowdown was sparked by the large increase in oil prices that occurred in the 1970s as a result of the actions of the OPEC oil cartel. The idea here is that as companies responded to high oil prices by using less energy, the amount of output they could produce with the same amount of capital and labour declined, reducing productivity. This explanation seems particularly plausible because not only is the timing right—the decline in productivity growth appears to have begun in earnest at the same time as energy prices increased—but the oil price idea also explains why all major industrial countries experienced a slowdown at about the same time. Unfortunately, this explanation seems difficult to reconcile with the failure of productivity growth to surge when oil prices fell quite dramatically in real terms in the 1980s (recall Figure 3.10 on p. 73).

Other explanations for the productivity slowdown since 1973 have been offered, but none have proven entirely satisfactory. Indeed, the lack of a convincing argument suggests the possibility of another explanation: The relatively high rate of productivity growth experienced during the 1950s and 1960s was an anomaly, and the slowdown that began in the 1970s simply reflects the return of a long-term normal rate of productivity growth. If we emphasize this interpretation, then our focus needs to turn to explaining the abnormally fast productivity growth of the 1950s and 1960s.

6.2 GROWTH DYNAMICS: THE NEOCLASSICAL GROWTH MODEL

Although growth accounting provides useful information about the sources of economic growth, it does not completely explain a country's growth performance. Because growth accounting takes the economy's rates of input growth as given, it cannot explain why capital and labour grow at the rates they do. The growth of the capital stock, in particular, is the result of the myriad saving and investment decisions of households and firms. By taking the growth of the capital stock as given, the growth accounting method leaves out an important part of the story.

In this section, we take a closer look at the dynamics of economic growth, or how the growth process evolves over time. In doing so, we drop the assumption made in Chapter 3 that the capital stock is fixed and study the factors that cause the economy's stock of capital to grow. Our analysis is based on a famous model of economic growth developed in the late 1950s by Nobel laureate Robert Solow of MIT and Trevor Swan of the Australian National University, called the **neoclassical growth model**.[5] This model has become the basic framework for most subsequent research on growth; for this reason, the diagram we use to examine the implications of the model is one of the key diagrams of macroeconomic analysis. Besides clarifying how capital accumulation and economic growth are interrelated, the Solow–Swan model is useful for examining three basic questions about growth:

1. What is the relationship between a nation's long-run standard of living and such fundamental factors as its saving rate, its population growth rate, and its rate of technical progress?

2. How does a nation's rate of economic growth evolve over time? Will economic growth stabilize, accelerate, or stop?

3. Do economic forces exist that will ultimately allow poorer countries to catch up with the richest countries in terms of living standards?

SETUP OF THE MODEL

The growth model examines an economy as it evolves over time. In order to analyze the effects of labour force growth as well as changes in capital, we assume that the population is growing and that at any particular time a fixed share of the population is of working age. For any year t,

$$N_t = \text{the number of workers available.}$$

We assume that the population and workforce both grow at fixed rate n. So, if $n = 0.05$, the number of workers in any year is 5% greater than in the previous year.

[5] For simplicity, we shall often refer to the neoclassical growth model simply as the growth model. The original articles are by Robert M. Solow, "A Contribution to the Theory of Economic Growth," *Quarterly Journal of Economics*, February 1956, pp. 65–94; and Trevor W. Swan, "Economic Growth and Capital Accumulation," *Economic Record*, November 1956, pp. 334–361.

At the beginning of each year t, the economy has available a capital stock K_t. (We demonstrate shortly how this capital stock is determined.) During each year t capital, K_t, and labour, N_t, are used to produce the economy's total output, Y_t. Part of the output produced each year is invested in new capital or in replacing worn-out capital. We further assume that the economy is closed and that there are no government purchases,[6] so the uninvested part of output is consumed by the population. If

Y_t = output produced in year t,

I_t = gross (total) investment in year t, and

C_t = consumption in year t,

the relationship among consumption, output, and investment in each year is

$$C_t = Y_t - I_t. \tag{6.3}$$

Equation (6.3) states that the uninvested part of the economy's output is consumed.

Because the population and the labour force are growing in this economy, focusing on output, consumption, and the capital stock per worker is convenient. Hence we use the following notation:

$$y_t = \frac{Y_t}{N_t} = \text{output per worker in year } t;$$

$$c_t = \frac{C_t}{N_t} = \text{consumption per worker in year } t;$$

$$k_t = \frac{K_t}{N_t} = \text{capital stock per worker in year } t.$$

The capital stock per worker, k_t, is also called the **capital–labour ratio**. An important goal of the model is to understand how output per worker, consumption per worker, and the capital–labour ratio change over time.[7]

The Per-Worker Production Function

In general, the amount of output that can be produced by specific quantities of inputs is determined by the production function. Earlier we introduced the production function as a relationship between total output Y, the total quantities of capital and labour units K and N, and the level of total factor productivity A. In order to emphasize that each of these determinants of growth is defined for a particular time period we write the production function as

$$Y_t = A_t F(K_t, N_t). \tag{6.4}$$

Dividing through by N_t and using the relationships defined in the previous section, we can also write the production function in per-worker terms as

$$y_t = A_t f(k_t). \tag{6.5}$$

---

[6] Analytical Problem 3 at the end of this chapter adds government purchases to the model. The required modifications to the model are minor and they do not change the key lessons to be learned from the model. For this reason we choose to ignore government purchases when setting up the model, even though later in the chapter we discuss public policies and the impact they have on long-run economic growth.

[7] For purposes of analysis, discussing output and consumption per worker is more convenient than discussing output and consumption per member of the population as a whole. Under the assumption that the workforce is a fixed fraction of the population, anything we say about the growth rate of output or consumption per worker will also be true of the growth rate of output or consumption per member of the population.

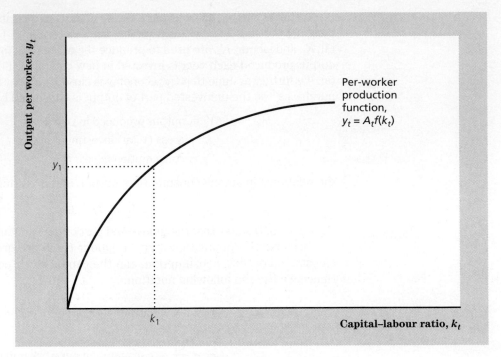

Equation (6.5) indicates that, in each year t, output per worker y_t depends on the amount of available capital per worker k_t and on the level of total factor productivity A_t.[8] Here, we use the symbol f instead of F for the production function to emphasize that the measurement of output and capital is in per-worker terms.

The per-worker production function is graphed in Figure 6.1. The capital–labour ratio (the amount of capital per worker) k_t is measured on the horizontal axis, and output per worker y_t is measured on the vertical axis. The production function slopes upward from left to right because an increase in the amount of capital per worker allows each worker to produce more output. As with the standard production function, the bowed shape of the per-worker production function reflects the diminishing marginal product of capital. Thus when the capital–labour ratio is already high, an increase in the capital–labour ratio has a relatively small effect on output per worker.

Steady States

One of the most striking conclusions obtained from the neoclassical growth model is that in the absence of productivity growth the economy reaches a steady state in the long run. A **steady state** is a situation in which the economy's output per worker, consumption per worker, and capital stock per worker are constant—that is, in the steady state, y_t, c_t, and k_t do not change over time. (Remember that y_t, c_t, and k_t are all ratios measuring total output (Y_t), consumption (C_t), and capital (K_t) relative to the size of the workforce (N_t). In a steady state, then, Y_t, C_t, and K_t all grow at the rate n, the rate of growth of the workforce.) To explain how the growth

---

[8] To write the production function in the form of Eq. (6.5) requires the assumption of constant returns to scale, which means that an equal percentage increase in both capital and labour inputs results in the same percentage increase in total output. So, for example, with constant returns to scale, a 10% increase in both capital and labour raises output by 10%. In terms of the growth accounting equation, Eq. (6.2), constant returns to scale requires that $a_K + a_N = 1$. See Analytical Problem 6 at the end of this chapter.

model works, we first examine the characteristics of a steady state and then discuss how the economy might attain it.

Let's begin by looking at investment in a steady state. In general, gross (total) investment in year t, I_t, is devoted to two purposes: (1) replacing worn-out or depreciated capital, and (2) expanding the size of the capital stock. If d is the capital depreciation rate, or the fraction of capital that wears out each year, the total amount of depreciation in year t is dK_t. The amount by which the capital stock is increased is net investment. What is net investment in a steady state? Because capital per worker, K_t/N_t, is constant in a steady state, the total capital stock grows at the same rate as the labour force, that is, at rate n. Net investment is therefore nK_t in a steady state.[9] To obtain steady-state investment, we add net investment nK_t and depreciation dK_t:

$$I_t = (n + d)K_t \text{ (in a steady state).} \tag{6.6}$$

Equation (6.6), then, defines the amount of total investment I_t that must be made in order for the economy to remain in a steady state; the amount of investment I_t must be sufficient each year to replace capital lost to depreciation d and to accumulate new capital sufficiently quickly to keep up with population growth n.

To obtain steady-state consumption (output less investment), we substitute Eq. (6.6) for Eq. (6.3):

$$C_t = Y_t - (n + d)K_t \text{ (in a steady state).} \tag{6.7}$$

Equation (6.7) measures consumption, output, and capital as economywide totals rather than in per-worker terms. To put them in per-worker terms, we divide both sides of Eq. (6.7) by the number of workers N_t, recalling that $c_t = C_t/N_t$, $y_t = Y_t/N_t$, and $k_t = K_t/N_t$. Then we use the per-worker production function, Eq. (6.5), to replace y_t with $A_t f(k_t)$ and obtain

$$c = Af(k) - (n + d)k \text{ (in a steady state).} \tag{6.8}$$

Equation (6.8) shows the relationship between consumption per worker c and the capital–labour ratio k in the steady state. Because consumption per worker and the capital–labour ratio are constant in the steady state, we dropped the time subscripts, t.

Equation (6.8) shows that an increase in the steady-state capital–labour ratio k has two opposing effects on steady-state consumption per worker c. First, an increase in the steady-state capital–labour ratio raises the amount of output each worker can produce for a given level of productivity, $Af(k)$. Second, an increase in the steady-state capital–labour ratio also increases the amount of output per worker that must be devoted to investment, $(n + d)k$. More goods devoted to investment leaves fewer goods to consume.

Figure 6.2 shows the trade-off between these two effects. In Figure 6.2(a), different possible values of the steady-state capital–labour ratio k are measured on the horizontal axis. The curve is the per-worker production function, $y = Af(k)$, as in Figure 6.1. The straight line shows steady-state investment per worker, $(n + d)k$. Equation (6.8) indicates that steady-state consumption per worker c equals the height of the curve $Af(k)$ minus the height of the straight line $(n + d)k$. Thus, consumption per worker is the height of the shaded area.

The relationship between consumption per worker and the capital–labour ratio in the steady state is shown more explicitly in Figure 6.2(b). For each value of

---

[9] Algebraically, net investment in year t is $K_{t+1} - K_t$. If total capital grows at rate n, then $K_{t+1} = (1 + n)K_t$. Substituting for K_{t+1} in the definition of net investment, we find that net investment $= (1 + n)K_t - K_t = nK_t$ in a steady state.

FIGURE 6.2

THE RELATIONSHIP OF CONSUMPTION PER WORKER TO THE CAPITAL–LABOUR RATIO IN THE STEADY STATE

(a) For each value of the capital–labour ratio, k, steady-state output per worker, y, is given by the per-worker production function, $Af(k)$. Steady-state investment per worker, $(n + d)k$, is a straight line with slope $n + d$. Steady-state consumption per worker, c, is the difference between output per worker and investment per worker (the shaded area). For example, if the capital–labour ratio is k_G, steady-state consumption per worker is c_1.

(b) For each value of the steady-state capital–labour ratio, k, steady-state consumption per worker, c, is derived in (a) as the difference between output per worker and investment per worker. Thus, the shaded area in (b) corresponds to the shaded area in (a). Note that starting from a low value of the capital–labour ratio, an increase in the capital–labour ratio raises steady-state consumption per worker. However, starting from a capital–labour ratio greater than k_G, an increase in the capital–labour ratio actually lowers consumption per worker. When the capital–labour ratio equals k_{max}, all output is devoted to investment, and steady-state consumption per worker is zero. The steady state at which consumption per worker is maximized, k_G in this diagram, is known as the Golden Rule steady state.

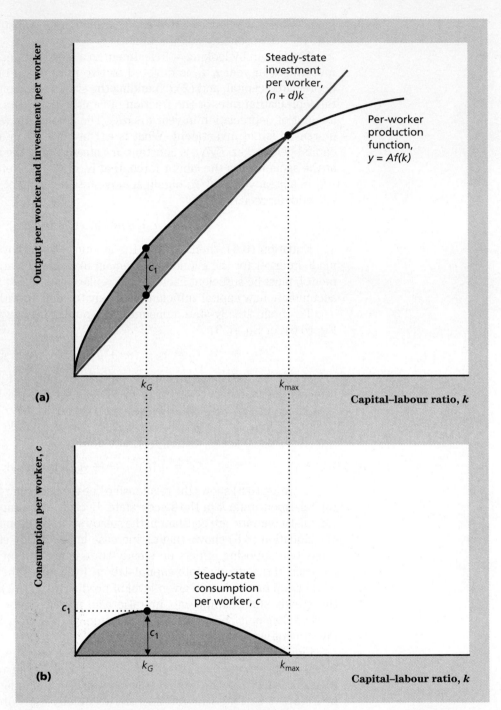

the steady-state capital–labour ratio k, steady-state consumption c is the difference between the production function and investment in Figure 6.2(a). Note that starting from low and medium values of k (values less than k_G in Figure 6.2(b)), increases in the steady-state capital–labour ratio lead to greater steady-state consumption per worker. The level of the capital–labour ratio that maximizes consumption per worker in the steady state, shown as k_G in Figure 6.2, is known as the

Golden Rule capital–labour ratio. The reason for the name given to this capital–labour ratio will become apparent later on.[10]

As Figure 6.2(b) demonstrates, for high values of k (values greater than k_G), increases in the steady-state capital–labour ratio result in lower steady-state consumption per worker. This occurs because so much investment is needed to maintain the high level of capital per worker. In the extreme case, where $k = k_{\max}$ in Figure 6.2, all output has to be devoted to replacing and expanding the capital stock, leaving nothing left to consume!

Later in this chapter we will examine public policies that might be used to move the economy to a new steady state. But already we have derived an important result: Policies focused solely on increasing capital per worker, k (and, hence, output per worker, y) may do little to increase the consumption possibilities of the country's citizens, c. If such policies are to increase consumption possibilities the economy must be at a capital–labour ratio that is below the Golden Rule capital–labour ratio.

In any economy in the world today, could a higher capital stock lead to less consumption in the long run? An empirical study of seven advanced industrial countries concluded that the answer is no. Even for high-saving Japan, further increases in capital per worker would lead to higher steady-state consumption per worker.[11] Thus, in our analysis, we will always assume that an increase in the steady-state capital–labour ratio raises steady-state consumption per worker.

Reaching the Steady State

Our discussion of steady states leaves two loose ends. First, we need to say something about why an economy like the one we describe here will eventually reach a steady state, as we claimed earlier. Second, we have not yet shown which steady state the economy will reach; that is, we would like to know the steady-state level of consumption per worker and the steady-state capital–labour ratio that the economy will eventually attain.

To tie up these loose ends, we need one more piece of information: the rate at which people save. To keep things as simple as possible, suppose that saving in this economy is proportional to current income:

$$S_t = sY_t, \tag{6.9}$$

where S_t is national saving[12] in year t, and s is the saving rate, which we assume to be constant. Because a \$1 increase in current income raises saving, but by less than \$1 (see Chapter 4), we take s to be a number between 0 and 1. Equation (6.9) ignores some other determinants of saving discussed in earlier chapters, such as the real interest rate. However, including these other factors wouldn't change our basic conclusions, so for simplicity we omit them.

In every year, national saving S_t equals investment I_t. Therefore,

$$sY_t = (n + d)K_t \text{ (in a steady state),} \tag{6.10}$$

where the left-hand side of Eq. (6.10) is saving (see Eq. 6.9) and the right-hand side of Eq. (6.10) is steady-state investment (see Eq. 6.6). As in Chapter 4, saving

---

[10] Readers familiar with calculus might try to use Eq. (6.7) to show that at the Golden Rule level of the capital–labour ratio the marginal product of capital equals $n + d$. In terms of Figure 6.2(a), the Golden Rule capital–labour ratio can be found by finding that value of k where the slopes of the two lines are equal.

[11] See Andrew B. Abel, N. Gregory Mankiw, Lawrence H. Summers, and Richard J. Zeckhauser, "Assessing Dynamic Efficiency: Theory and Evidence," *Review of Economic Studies*, January 1989, pp. 1–20.

[12] With no government in this model, national saving and private saving are the same.

equals investment (which implies a real interest rate), but we now study the dynamic evolution of the economy as the capital stock changes.

Equation (6.10) shows the relation between total output Y_t and the total capital stock K_t that holds in the steady state. To determine steady-state capital per worker, we divide both sides of Eq. (6.10) by N_t. We then use the production function, Eq. (6.5), to replace y_t with $Af(k)$:

$$sAf(k) = (n + d)k \text{ (in the steady state).} \qquad (6.11)$$

Equation (6.11) indicates that saving per worker $sAf(k)$ equals steady-state investment per worker $(n + d)k$. Because the capital–labour ratio k is constant in the steady state, we again drop the subscripts t from the equation.

With Eq. (6.11), we can now determine the steady-state capital–labour ratio that the economy will attain, as shown in Figure 6.3. The capital–labour ratio is measured along the horizontal axis. Output, saving, and investment per worker are measured on the vertical axis.

The uppermost bowed curve is the per-worker production function discussed earlier. The lower bowed curve is new. This is the per-worker saving function $sAf(k)$, and it shows that an increase in the capital–labour ratio implies higher output per worker and, thus, more saving per worker. The per-worker saving function has the same general shape as the per-worker production function because saving per worker equals the per-worker production function $Af(k)$ multiplied by the fixed saving rate s.

The straight line in Figure 6.3 represents steady-state investment per worker $(n + d)k$. The steady-state investment line slopes upward because as the capital–labour ratio rises, more investment per worker is required to replace depreciating capital and equip new workers with the same high level of capital.

According to Eq. (6.11), the steady-state capital–labour ratio must ensure that saving per worker and steady-state investment per worker are equal. The one level

FIGURE 6.3

DETERMINING THE CAPITAL–LABOUR RATIO IN THE STEADY STATE

The steady-state capital–labour ratio, k^*, is determined by the condition that saving per worker, $sAf(k)$, equals steady-state investment per worker, $(n + d)k$. The steady-state capital–labour ratio k^* corresponds to point X, where the saving curve and the steady-state investment line cross. From any starting point, eventually the capital–labour ratio reaches k^*. If the capital–labour ratio happens to be below k^*, say, at k_1, saving per worker, $sAf(k_1)$, exceeds the investment per worker, $(n + d)k_1$, needed to maintain the capital–labour ratio at k_1. As this extra saving is converted into capital, the capital–labour ratio will rise, as indicated by the arrows. Similarly, if the capital–labour ratio is greater than k^*, say, at k_2, saving per worker, $sAf(k_2)$, is too low relative to the investment per worker, $(n + d)k_2$, needed to maintain the capital–labour ratio at k_2. As a result, the capital–labour ratio will fall until it adjusts to k^*.

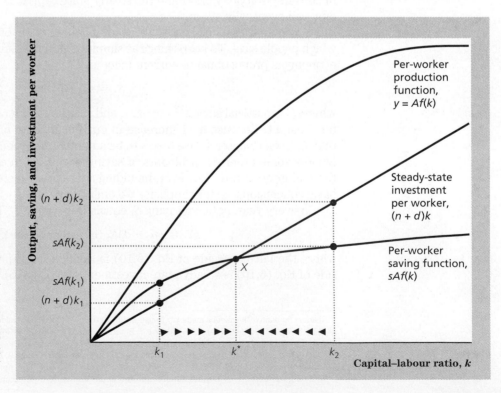

of the capital–labour ratio for which this condition is satisfied is shown in Figure 6.3 as k^*, the value of k at which the saving curve and the steady-state investment line cross. For any other value of k, saving and investment will not be equal in the steady state. Thus, given values of the rate of population and workforce growth n, the level of productivity A, and the rate of saving s, k^* is the only possible steady-state capital–labour ratio for this economy. It's important to note that when capital per worker is k^*, the amount people choose to save will just equal the amount of investment necessary to keep capital per worker at k^*. When the economy's capital–labour ratio reaches k^*, it will remain there forever unless there is a change in the saving rate s, the rate of population growth n, or the level of productivity A.

But is there any reason to believe that the capital–labour ratio will ever reach k^* if it starts at some other value? Yes, there is. Suppose that the capital–labour ratio happens to be less than k^*; for example, it equals k_1 in Figure 6.3. When capital per worker is k_1, the amount of saving per worker, $sAf(k_1)$, is greater than the amount of investment needed to keep the capital–labour ratio constant, $(n + d)k_1$. When this extra saving is converted into capital, the capital–labour ratio will rise. As indicated by the arrows, the capital–labour ratio will increase from k_1 toward k^*.

If capital per worker is initially greater than k^*—for example, if k equals k_2 in Figure 6.3—the explanation of why the economy converges to a steady state is similar. If the capital–labour ratio exceeds k^*, the amount of saving that is done will be less than the amount of investment that is necessary to keep the capital–labour ratio constant. (In Figure 6.3, when k equals k_2, the saving curve lies below the steady-state investment line.) Thus, the capital–labour ratio over time will fall from k_2 toward k^*, as indicated by the arrows. Output per worker will also fall until it reaches its steady-state value.

We are now in a position to add all the ingredients of our model of economic growth into one key diagram. Figure 6.4(a) graphs two bowed relationships showing how output per worker $y = Af(k)$ and saving per worker $sAf(k)$ vary with the capital–labour ratio. It also shows the steady-state per-worker investment line $(n + d)k$. As we have just seen, the economy always adjusts to that capital–labour ratio where saving per worker equals steady-state investment per worker. In Figure 6.4 this steady state occurs at capital–labour ratio k^*. Figure 6.4(b) graphs the relationship between values of steady-state consumption per worker and the capital–labour ratio. As discussed previously, consumption per worker—our measure of living standards—is maximized at the Golden Rule steady state k_G. Consistent with empirical evidence, Figure 6.4 has been drawn to show an economy with a steady-state capital–labour ratio that is below the Golden Rule level.

With the unique steady-state capital–labour ratio k^*, we can also find steady-state output and consumption per worker. From the per-worker production function, Eq. (6.5), if the steady-state capital–labour ratio is k^*, steady-state output per worker y^* is

$$y^* = Af(k^*).$$

From Eq. (6.8), steady-state consumption per worker, c^*, equals steady-state output per worker, $Af(k^*)$, minus steady-state investment per worker, $(n + d)k^*$:

$$c^* = Af(k^*) - (n + d)k^*.$$

In terms of Figure 6.4(a), the steady-state value of output per worker y^* is measured by the vertical distance from the horizontal axis to the per-worker production function at steady-state capital–labour ratio k^* (distance YZ). The steady-state value of investment per worker $(n + d)k^*$ is measured by the vertical distance

FIGURE 6.4

IDENTIFYING THE STEADY STATE AND THE GOLDEN RULE STEADY STATE

Panel (a) shows a per-worker production function, a per-worker saving function, and a steady-state per-worker investment line. The position of these curves reflects assumptions about the size of the productivity parameter, A, the saving rate, s, the rate of depreciation, d, and the rate of population growth, n. Given those values, the steady state occurs at capital–labour ratio k^*. Panel (b) shows the amounts of consumption per worker that can be realized for various savings rates, s, given values of the productivity parameter, A, the rate of depreciation, d, and the rate of population growth, n. The Golden Rule steady state is identified as capital–labour ratio k_G while the steady state that results with savings rate s is identified as k^*.

Note that the scale of the vertical axis in panel (b) is exaggerated in order to more clearly show values of consumption per worker, c.

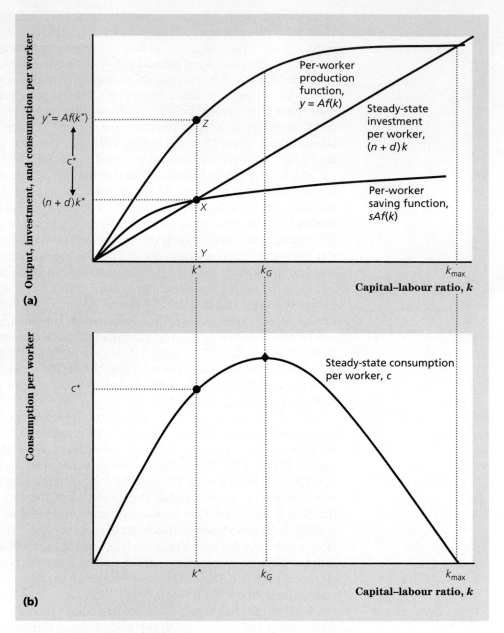

from the horizontal axis to the per-worker investment function at steady-state capital–labour ratio k^* (distance YX). As we noted above, since in a steady state national saving equals steady-state investment, distance YX also measures national saving in steady state. Finally, the steady-state value of consumption per worker c^* is measured as the vertical distance between the per-worker production function and the per-worker investment function measured at the steady-state capital–labour ratio k^* (distance XZ).

In Figure 6.4(b), the steady-state value of consumption per worker c^* is measured by the vertical distance from the horizontal axis to the steady-state per-worker consumption curve. This distance is equal to distance XZ identified in Figure 6.4(a). (Note that the scale of the vertical axis in panel (b) is exaggerated in order to more clearly show values of consumption per worker, c.) Consumption per worker $c*$ is less than that which could be achieved were the economy at the Golden Rule steady state k_G. The diamond on the steady-state per-worker consumption curve identifies the maximum level of consumption per worker that can be achieved for current values of n, d, and A and so identifies the location of the Golden Rule steady-state capital–labour ratio.

To this point we have shown that the economy will always adjust toward a steady state. In countries like Canada, those steady states tend to be the ones below the economy's Golden Rule steady state. What we would like to do next is to use this key diagram to gain a better understanding of how certain key variables influence our standard of living, as measured by consumption per worker. Figure 6.4 shows a steady state for given values of total factor productivity A, saving rate s, and rate of population growth n. By changing any of these values, we change the position of one or more of the curves in our key diagram and so change the position of the steady state. How these changes affect our living standards is the subject of the next section.

THE FUNDAMENTAL DETERMINANTS OF LONG-RUN LIVING STANDARDS

What determines how well off the average person in an economy will be in the long run? If we measure long-run well-being by the steady-state level of consumption per worker, we can use the growth model to answer this question. Here, we discuss three factors that affect long-run living standards: the saving rate, population growth, and productivity growth (see Summary table 8).

The Saving Rate

According to the neoclassical growth model, a higher saving rate implies higher living standards in the long run. This will be illustrated using our key diagram, reproduced as Figure 6.5. Figure 6.5(a) presents graphs of the per-worker production function, the per-worker savings function, and the steady-state per-worker investment function, all drawn for given values of the rate of population and workforce

SUMMARY 8

THE FUNDAMENTAL DETERMINANTS OF LONG-RUN LIVING STANDARDS

ALL ELSE EQUAL, AN INCREASE IN	CAUSES LONG-RUN OUTPUT, CONSUMPTION, AND CAPITAL PER WORKER TO	REASON
The saving rate, s	Rise	Higher saving allows for more investment and a larger capital stock.
The rate of population growth, n	Fall	With higher population growth more output must be used to equip new workers with capital, leaving less output available to increase consumption or capital per worker.
Productivity	Rise	Higher productivity directly increases output; by raising incomes, it also raises saving and the capital stock.

FIGURE 6.5

THE EFFECT OF AN INCREASED SAVING RATE ON THE STEADY-STATE CAPITAL–LABOUR RATIO

An increase in the saving rate causes the per-worker saving curve to pivot upward. The point where saving per worker equals steady-state investment per worker moves from point X to point Y in panel (a). Over time, the steady-state capital–labour ratio rises from k_1^* to k_G. In panel (b) we see that the rise in the capital–labour ratio causes consumption per worker to increase over time from c_1 to c_G. In the short term, however, consumption per worker falls because at the initial capital–labour ratio, increases in saving and investment leave less output available for current consumption. Thus, the long-term gain in living standards comes at the cost of short-term pain.

Note that the scale of the vertical axis in panel (b) is exaggerated in order to more clearly show values of consumption per worker, c.

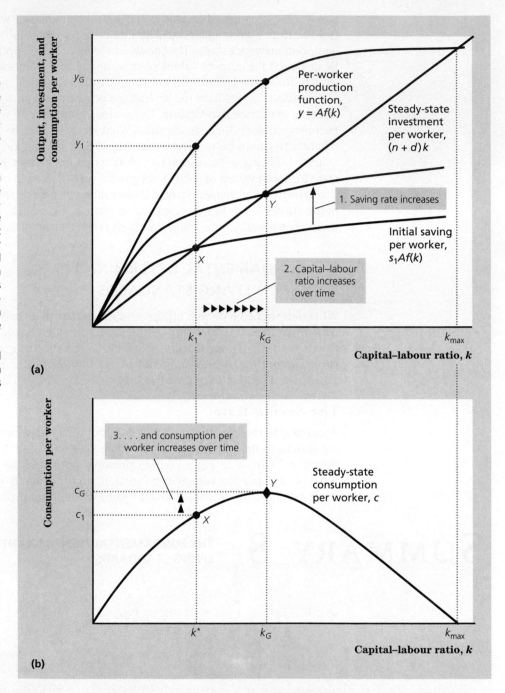

growth rate n, the level of total factor productivity A, and the rate of saving s_1. As usual, steady state in this economy corresponds to the intersection of the saving curve and the investment line (point X). This occurs at capital–labour ratio k_1^*. Figure 6.5(b) shows how the steady-state value of consumption per worker—our measure of living standards—varies by the size of the capital–labour ratio. Where we find the maximum value of consumption per worker—identified by the diamond on the steady-state per-worker consumption curve—identifies the Golden Rule capital–labour ratio k_G. Consistent with empirical evidence indicating that in advanced industrial economies steady-state capital–labour ratios tend to fall below the Golden Rule level, the figure shows that consumption per worker c_1 is less than the amount attainable were the economy at the Golden Rule capital–labour ratio c_G.

In a situation like this, it is potentially good public policy for the government to introduce legislation that would have the effect of moving the economy toward the Golden Rule capital–labour ratio k_G. Suppose that the government introduces policies that strengthen the incentives for saving, and that as a result the country's saving rate rises from s_1 to a higher rate s_G, a saving rate consistent with moving the economy to the Golden Rule steady state. The increased saving rate raises saving at every level of the capital–labour ratio. Graphically, the saving curve pivots upward. The new steady-state capital–labour ratio k_G corresponds to the intersection of the new saving curve and the investment line (point Y in Figure 6.5(a)). By moving the economy to the Golden Rule capital–labour ratio, the policy has also increased living standards, as measured by the steady-state value of consumption per worker, from c_1 to c_G (point Y in Figure 6.5(b)).

If enacting legislation that has the effect of moving the economy toward the Golden Rule capital–labour ratio increases living standards, why is this not common practice? Later in this chapter, when we discuss policy changes that were designed to do this, we'll see that these efforts have often been met with considerable resistance. But why would there be resistance to policies designed to increase living standards?

To understand why there might be opposition to such policies, it is important to emphasize that the adjustment of the economy from one capital–labour ratio to another may require a substantial length of time. While it is true that the adjustment from capital–labour ratio $k_1{}^*$ to the Golden Rule capital–labour ratio k_G will cause living standards to rise in the long run, in the short run there is a price to be paid: An increase in the saving rate initially causes consumption per worker to fall. This decline occurs because at the initial capital–labour ratio, increases in saving and investment leave less output available for current consumption. Living standards must, therefore, fall in the short term in order to make available those resources that are needed to expand the capital stock and so set the stage for higher living standards in the long run. Society's choice of a saving rate should take into account this trade-off between current and future consumption.

Economists often refer to such policy choices as involving "short-term pain for long-term gain." Understanding the nature of this trade-off suggests why policymakers can find it difficult to advocate such policies. Politicians are elected for relatively short terms (four to five years in Canada), and a policy that increases the saving rate imposes costs on current voters in the form of lower present consumption. While it is true that consumption levels will increase in the future, will the prospect of this long-term gain be enough for current voters to view favourably policies that will impose short-term pain? The trade-off between current and future generations suggests the source of the label "Golden Rule" steady state: To reach it, the current generation is being asked to obey the biblical Golden Rule, "Do to others as you would have them do to you" (Matthew 7:12).

It is worth noting the effect on the rate of output growth of a policy to increase the saving rate. As the capital–labour ratio increases from $k_1{}^*$ to k_G, output per worker, y, also increases (we slide up the per-worker production function). Since $y = Y/N$, and since N is growing at rate n, then during the period of adjustment from $k_1{}^*$ to k_G it must be the case that Y is growing at a rate greater than n. Thus, a policy to increase the saving rate results in a temporary growth spurt that causes output to grow at a rate greater than that experienced in the steady state.

Population Growth

A second fundamental determinant of long-run living standards is the rate of population growth. In many developing countries, a high rate of population growth is considered a major problem, and reducing it is an important policy goal. In China, for example, a "one-child" policy was introduced in 1979 as a way of slowing the rate of population growth and encouraging economic development. Conversely, in many more developed countries, a declining rate of population growth is considered a problem. What is the relationship between population growth and a country's level of development, as measured by output, consumption, and capital per worker?

The growth model's answer to this question can be illustrated using our key diagram, reproduced as Figure 6.6. Figure 6.6(a) shows an economy with a population and workforce growth rate n_1, a level of productivity A, and a rate of saving s. As usual, steady state in this economy corresponds to the intersection of the saving curve and the investment line (point X). This occurs at capital–labour ratio k_1^*. Figure 6.6(b) shows how steady-state consumption per worker—our measure of living standards—varies by the size of the capital–labour ratio. Consumption per worker is maximized at the Golden Rule capital–labour ratio k_G. Figure 6.6(b) shows that in the current steady state, consumption per worker c_1 is less than the amount attainable were the economy at the Golden Rule capital–labour ratio c_G. Now, suppose that the rate of population growth, which is the same as the rate of labour force growth, rises from an initial level of n_1 to n_2. What happens?

An increase in the population growth rate means that workers are entering the labour force more rapidly than before. These new workers must be equipped with capital. Thus, to maintain the same steady-state capital–labour ratio, the amount of investment per current member of the workforce must rise. Algebraically, the rise in n increases steady-state investment per worker from $(n_1 + d)k$ to $(n_2 + d)k$ where $n_2 > n_1$. This increase in the population growth rate causes the steady-state investment line to pivot up and to the left, as its slope rises from $(n_1 + d)$ to $(n_2 + d)$.

The pivot of the steady-state investment line does two things. First, it means the new steady state is at point Y and capital–labour ratio k_2^*. Second, the pivot reduces the difference between the production function and the investment line and so reduces consumption per worker at every capital–labour ratio. The steady-state consumption per worker curve is now shown by the blue line in panel (b) and the new steady state is shown at point Y on that curve.

Thus, the growth model implies that increased population growth will lower living standards. The basic problem is that when the workforce is growing rapidly, a large part of current output must be devoted to providing capital for the new workers to use. This result suggests that policies to reduce population growth will indeed improve living standards.

While a high rate of population growth is often identified as a problem for developing countries, in many developed countries, such as Italy, Japan, and Russia, the opposite is often claimed: that they suffer from too low a rate of population growth. Were it not for its high rate of immigration, many economists believe that Canada would suffer from this problem as well.

How can too low a rate of population growth be a problem for developed countries? To understand why, remember that an assumption in the growth model is that the proportion of the total population that is of working age is fixed. In the model, then, a decrease in the population growth rate means no change in the ratio of

FIGURE 6.6

THE EFFECT OF A HIGHER
POPULATION GROWTH RATE
ON THE STEADY-STATE
CAPITAL–LABOUR RATIO

An increase in the population growth rate causes the steady-state investment per worker line to pivot upward. The point where saving per worker equals steady-state investment per worker shifts from point X to point Y in panel (a). As a consequence, the steady-state capital–labour ratio will over time fall from k_1^* to k_2^*. The increase in the population growth rate reduces the difference between the production function and the investment line and so reduces consumption per worker at every capital–labour ratio. The steady-state consumption per-worker curve is now shown by the blue line in panel (b). The fall in the steady-state capital–labour ratio causes consumption per worker to fall from c_1 to c_2, as shown in panel (b). A higher rate of population growth therefore results in a fall in living standards.

Note that the scale of the vertical axis in panel (b) is exaggerated in order to more clearly show values of consumption per worker, c.

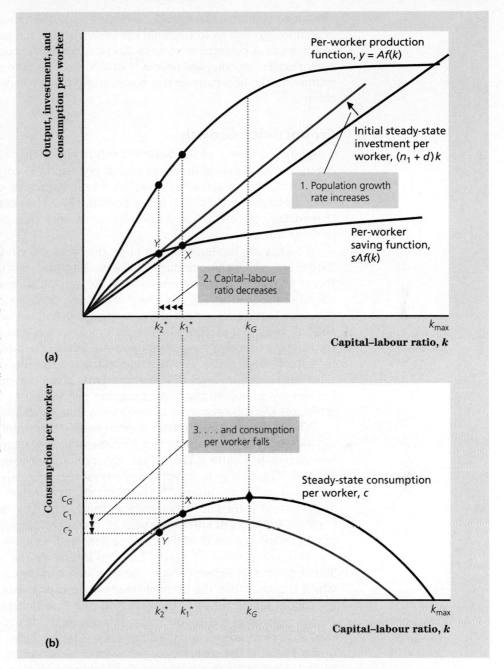

working-age people to retirees. But what if the decrease in the population growth rate is associated with a change in the age composition of the population? In Canada, the combination of a declining birth rate and the fact that baby boomers (those born between 1946 and 1964) are nearing retirement age means that the ratio of working-age people to retirees will be unusually low for about the next 20–40 years. This development raises concerns about the ability of those working to afford the tax payments necessary to finance pensions and health-care costs. The policy goal for developed countries like Canada, therefore, is not so much to increase the rate of population growth as to maintain the proportion of the total population that is of working age. A potential solution to this problem is to encourage increased immigration of skilled, working-age people.[13] In this way, the ratio of working-age people to retirees can be held more or less constant even as the baby-boom generation grows older.

Productivity Growth

A significant aspect of the basic growth model is that ultimately, the economy reaches a steady state in which output per capita is constant. But in the introduction to this chapter, we described how Japanese output per person was 30 times larger by 2010 than it had been in 1870! How can the model account for that sustained growth? The answer has to do with changes in the rate of productivity growth.

To examine the implications of productivity growth for long-run living standards, we will again employ our key diagram, reproduced as **Figure 6.7**. Figure 6.7(a) shows an economy with a rate of population and workforce growth n, a level of productivity A_1, and a rate of saving s. Steady state in this economy corresponds to the intersection of the saving curve and the investment line (point X), and this occurs at capital–labour ratio k_1^*. Figure 6.7(b) shows how steady-state consumption per worker—our measure of living standards—varies by the size of the capital–labour ratio. The diamond on the steady-state consumption curve identifies the maximum level of living standards given current values of n, s, and A. In the current steady state, consumption per worker c_1 is less than the amount attainable were the economy at the Golden Rule capital–labour ratio.

The effect of a productivity improvement—the result, say, of a new technology—causes the value of total factor productivity A to increase. This change affects two curves in Figure 6.7(a). First, the per-worker production function pivots upward. This occurs because at any prevailing capital–labour ratio each worker can produce more output.[14] The second curve affected by the productivity improvement is the per-worker saving function $sA_1 f(k)$. As saving per worker is a constant fraction s of output per worker, the per-worker saving function must also pivot upward as a result of the improvement in productivity.

The new per-worker saving function intersects the steady-state investment line at point Y in Figure 6.7(a). The new steady-state capital–labour ratio is k_2^*, which is higher than the original steady-state capital–labour ratio k_1^*. Over time the capital–labour ratio will increase toward k_2^*, as indicated by the arrows.

As a result of the productivity improvement, steady-state consumption per worker rises at every capital–labour ratio. This is shown in Figure 6.7(b) by the upward pivot of the steady-state per-worker consumption curve. The Golden Rule capital–labour ratio also increases. The maximum level of consumption per worker now available following the productivity improvement is identified by the diamond

---

[13] This, in fact, seems to be part of Canada's immigration policy. In 2012, 54% of adult immigrants to Canada had 13 or more years of education and 83% of all immigrants were younger than 45 years of age. To learn more about the economic and other characteristics of immigrants to Canada, see the publication *Facts and Figures*, available from the Citizenship and Immigration Canada website at *www.cic.gc.ca*.

[14] A productivity improvement corresponds to a beneficial supply shock, as explained in Chapter 3. A fall in productivity is represented in the model by a lower value for A. A fall in productivity would cause the per-worker production function to pivot downward because at any capital–labour ratio k, less output y could be produced. A reduction in productivity corresponds to an adverse supply shock.

FIGURE 6.7

THE EFFECT OF A PRODUCTIVITY IMPROVEMENT ON THE STEADY-STATE CAPITAL–LABOUR RATIO

In the growth model, a productivity improvement is represented by an increase in parameter A. As a result, a productivity improvement causes two curves in panel (a) to pivot upward: the per-worker production function $Af(k)$ and the per-worker saving function $sAf(k)$. The point where saving per worker equals steady-state investment per worker shifts from point X to point Y and the corresponding steady-state capital–labour ratio rises from $k_1{}^*$ to $k_2{}^*$. Because it enables capital and labour to be used more productively, a productivity improvement also means that fewer resources need to be devoted to maintaining any capital–labour ratio. As a result, the amount of consumption per worker available at any steady state also increases. This is shown in panel (b) by the upward pivot in the steady-state per-worker consumption curve c. As the steady-state capital–labour ratio increases, so too does consumption per worker, as shown by the arrows. Thus, a productivity improvement raises the capital–labour ratio and increases living standards.

Note that the scale of the vertical axis in panel (b) is exaggerated in order to more clearly show values of consumption per worker, c.

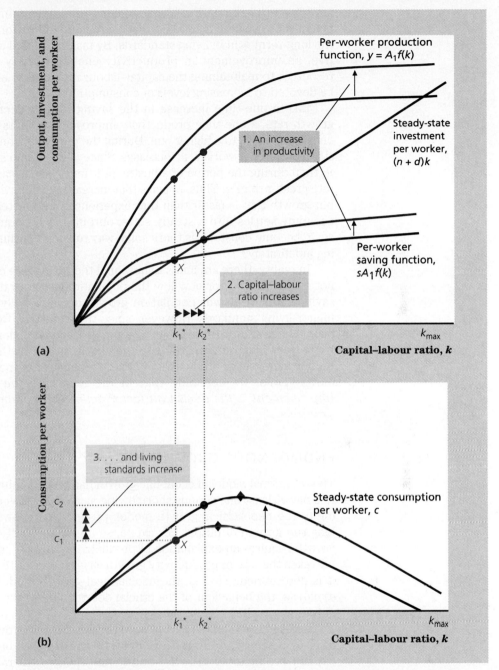

on the new blue steady-state per-worker consumption curve. Note that as a result of the productivity improvement the Golden Rule steady state now occurs at a higher capital–labour ratio and defines a higher level of consumption per worker. Over time, consumption per worker rises from c_1 to c_2, as indicated by the arrows.

Overall, a productivity improvement raises steady-state output and consumption per worker in two ways. First, it directly increases the amount that can be produced at any capital–labour ratio. Second, as Figure 6.7 shows, by raising the supply of saving, a productivity improvement also causes the long-run capital–labour ratio to rise. Thus, a productivity improvement has a doubly beneficial impact on the standard of living. Making productivity improvements even more beneficial to society is the fact that there is no "short-term pain" associated with the long-term gain in living standards. By making capital and labour more productive, an improvement in productivity enables society to devote fewer of its resources to maintaining the capital–labour ratio and so allows those resources to be devoted to increasing levels of consumption.

Like a one-time increase in the saving rate or decrease in the population growth rate, a one-time productivity improvement shifts the economy only from one steady state to a higher one. During the period of transition to the new steady state, output per worker, y, increases. Since $y = Y/N$, and since N is growing at rate n, then during the period of adjustment it must be the case that Y is growing at a rate greater than n. Thus, policies that increase productivity result in a rate of output growth that is faster than that experienced in the steady state. But when the economy settles into a steady state, output and consumption per worker once again become constant. Is there some way to keep consumption per worker growing indefinitely?

In reality, there are limits to how high the saving rate can rise (it certainly cannot exceed 100%!) or how low the population growth rate can fall. Thus, higher saving rates or slower population growth are not likely sources of continually higher living standards. However, since the Industrial Revolution, if not before, people have shown remarkable ingenuity in becoming more and more productive. In the very long run, according to the neoclassical growth model, only these continuing increases in productivity hold the promise of perpetually better living standards. Thus, we conclude that in the long run, *the rate of productivity improvement is the dominant factor determining how quickly living standards rise.*

ENDOGENOUS GROWTH THEORY

The traditional model of economic growth has proved quite useful, but it nevertheless has at least one serious shortcoming as a model of economic growth. According to the neoclassical growth model, productivity growth is the only source of long-run growth of output per capita, so a full explanation of long-run economic growth requires an explanation of productivity growth. The model, however, simply takes the rate of productivity growth as given rather than trying to explain how it is determined. That is, the neoclassical growth model *assumes*, rather than *explains*, the behaviour of the crucial determinant of the long-run growth rate of output per capita.

In response to this shortcoming of the neoclassical growth model, a new branch of growth theory, **endogenous growth theory**, has been developed to try to explain productivity growth—and hence the growth rate of output—*endogenously*, or *within the model*.[15] As we will see, an important implication of endogenous growth theory is that a country's long-run growth rate depends not only on exogenous productivity growth (as implied by the neoclassical growth model), but also on its rate of saving and investment.

[15] Two important early articles in endogenous growth theory are Paul Romer, "Increasing Returns and Long-Run Growth," *Journal of Political Economy*, October 1986, pp. 1002–1037; and Robert E. Lucas, Jr., "On the Mechanics of Economic Development," *Journal of Monetary Economics*, July 1988, pp. 3–42. A more accessible description of endogenous growth theory is in Paul Romer, "The Origins of Endogenous Growth," *Journal of Economic Perspectives*, Winter 1994, pp. 3–22.

Here we present a simple endogenous growth model in which the number of workers remains constant, a condition implying that the growth rate of output per worker is simply equal to the growth rate of output. Our simple endogenous growth model is based on the aggregate production function

$$Y = AK, \tag{6.12}$$

where Y is aggregate output and K is the aggregate capital stock. The parameter A in Eq. (6.12) is a positive constant. According to the production function in Eq. (6.12), each additional unit of capital increases output by A units, regardless of how many units of capital are used in production. Because the marginal product of capital, equal to A, does not depend on the size of the capital stock K, the production function in Eq. (6.12) does not imply diminishing marginal productivity of capital. The assumption that the marginal productivity is constant, rather than diminishing, is a key departure from the neoclassical growth model.

Endogenous growth theorists have provided a number of reasons to explain why, for the economy as a whole, the marginal productivity of capital may not be diminishing. One explanation emphasizes the role of **human capital**, the economist's term for the knowledge, skills, and training of individuals. As economies accumulate capital and become richer, they devote more resources to "investing in people," through improved nutrition, schooling, health care, and on-the-job training. This investment in people increases the country's human capital, which, in turn, raises productivity. If the physical capital stock increases while the stock of human capital remains fixed, there will be diminishing marginal productivity of physical capital, as each unit of physical capital effectively works with a smaller amount of human capital. Endogenous growth theory argues that as an economy's physical capital stock increases, its human capital stock tends to increase in the same proportion. Thus, when the physical capital stock increases, each unit of physical capital effectively works with the same amount of human capital, so the marginal productivity of capital need not decrease.

A second rationalization of a constant marginal productivity of capital is based on the observation that in a growing economy, firms have incentives to undertake research and development (R&D) activities. These activities increase the stock of commercially valuable knowledge, including new products and production techniques. According to this R&D-focused explanation, increases in capital and output tend to generate increases in technical know-how, and the resulting productivity gains offset any tendency for the marginal productivity of capital to decline.

Having examined why a production function like Eq. (6.12) might be a reasonable description of the economy as a whole, once such factors as increased human capital and research and development are taken into account, we work out the implications of this equation. As in the neoclassical growth model, we assume that national saving, S, is a constant fraction s of aggregate output, AK, so that $S = sAK$. In a closed economy, investment must equal saving. Recall that total investment equals net investment (the net increase in the capital stock) plus depreciation, or $I = \Delta K + dK$. Therefore, setting investment equal to saving, we have

$$\Delta K + dK = sAK. \tag{6.13}$$

Next, we divide both sides of Eq. (6.13) by K and then subtract d from both sides of the resulting equation to obtain the growth rate of the capital stock:

$$\frac{\Delta K}{K} = sA - d. \tag{6.14}$$

Because output is proportional to the capital stock, the growth rate of output equals the growth rate of the capital stock. Therefore, Eq. (6.14) implies

$$\frac{\Delta Y}{Y} = sA - d. \tag{6.15}$$

Equation (6.15) shows that in the endogenous growth model, the growth rate of output depends on the saving rate s. As we are assuming that the number of workers remains constant over time, the growth rate of output per worker equals the growth rate of output given in Eq. (6.15) and, thus, depends on the saving rate s. The result, that the saving rate affects the long-run growth rate of output, stands in sharp contrast to the results of the neoclassical growth model, in which the saving rate does not affect the long-run growth rate. Saving affects long-run growth in the endogenous growth framework because in that framework, higher rates of saving and capital formation stimulate greater investment in human capital and R&D. The resulting increases in productivity help spur long-run growth. In summary, in comparison to the neoclassical growth model, the endogenous growth model places greater emphasis on saving, human capital formation, and R&D as sources of long-run growth.

Work on the endogenous growth model continues because the approach appears promising in at least two dimensions. First, this theory attempts to explain, rather than assume, the economy's rate of productivity growth. Second, it shows how the long-run growth rate of output may depend on such factors as the country's saving rate, which can be affected by government policies. Many economists working in this area are optimistic that endogenous growth theory will yield further insights into the creative processes underlying productivity growth, while providing lessons that might be applied to help the poorest nations of the world achieve substantially higher standards of living.

ECONOMIC GROWTH AND THE ENVIRONMENT

The growth models studied so far—both the neoclassical growth model and the endogenous growth model—do not have a lot to say about the relationship between economic growth and the environment. An accusation often levelled at those promoting growth-enhancing policies is that economic growth leads to environmental degradation. What does research on this question suggest?

Gene Grossman and Alan Krueger, of Princeton University, have shown that while in poor countries increases in GDP are often associated with declines in environmental quality, once GDP reaches a certain threshold environmental quality begins to improve.[16] Thus, graphing environmental quality against GDP per capita gives a graph with a U shape; environmental quality initially falls but later rises as economic growth proceeds. The optimistic conclusion one can draw from this evidence is that cities and countries with poor air quality today may enjoy better air quality in the future as their GDP rises. Certainly evidence from China over the past three decades supports this claim. Following the adoption of pro-growth policies during the 1980s, air quality in China's major cities was sacrificed in a drive toward faster economic growth. After decades of rapid growth and fast-rising incomes, however, the Chinese government is today embarking on a significant

---

[16] "Economic Growth and the Environment," *Quarterly Journal of Economics,* April 1995, pp. 353–377.

effort to improve air quality and address other environmental concerns, including the possible use of a market-based pollution permit trading system. As suggested by the response of the government in China, and as confirmed by most researchers, a strong public policy response is likely required to find the right balance between economic growth and environmental quality.

6.3 GOVERNMENT POLICIES TO RAISE LONG-RUN LIVING STANDARDS

Increased growth and a higher standard of living in the long run are often cited by political leaders as primary policy goals. Let's examine government policies that may be useful in raising a country's long-run standard of living. (A Closer Look 6.1 discusses whether the form of government—democratic or nondemocratic—affects the long-run growth rate of an economy.)

POLICIES TO AFFECT THE SAVING RATE

The neoclassical growth model suggests that the rate of national saving is a principal determinant of long-run living standards. However, this conclusion does not necessarily mean that policymakers should try to force the saving rate upward. Recall from our discussion of Figure 6.5 (p. 180) that an increase in the saving rate imposes "short-term pain for long-term gain." That is, an increase in the saving rate results in a fall in living standards in the short term in order to make available resources needed to expand the capital stock and so set the stage for higher living standards in the long run. If markets are working well and public policies do not discriminate either for or against the decision to save, then the saving rate freely chosen by individuals should be the one that optimally balances the benefit of saving more (higher living standards in the future) against the cost of saving more (lower living standards in the short term).

In contrast to those who suggest that saving decisions are best left to individuals and the free market, some analysts think there are reasons to suggest that the saving decisions currently being made are not optimal; that Canadians save too little and that public policy should be aimed at raising the saving rate. With regard to Figure 6.5, these analysts argue that public policy should be used to increase the saving rate and in so doing move the economy from point X to point Y.

What policies can be used to increase saving? If saving were highly responsive to the real interest rate, tax changes that increased the real return that savers received would be effective. For example, some economists advocate taxing households on how much they consume rather than on how much they earn, thereby exempting from taxation the income that is saved and so increasing the after-tax real rate of return on saving. This is the rationale for economists' recommendations to governments to reduce their reliance on income taxes in favour of consumption taxes such as the federal government's goods and services tax (the GST) or the shared federal–provincial sales tax known as the harmonized sales tax (HST). Unfortunately, as we noted in Chapter 4 ("Effect of Changes in the Real Interest Rate," p. 101), although saving appears to increase when the expected real return available to savers rises, most studies find this response to be small. For example, during the 1980s, the tax rate on investment earnings fell for upper-income Canadians, with little effect on the saving rate. Thus, there may not be much scope for policies to influence the level of private saving by affecting the real after-tax interest rate.

A CLOSER LOOK 6.1

ECONOMIC GROWTH AND DEMOCRACY

Economic growth is an important social goal, but it is certainly not the only one. Most people also highly value political freedom and a democratic political process. Are these goals conflicting or mutually supporting? If the citizens of poor countries succeed in achieving democracy, as many did during the 1980s and early 1990s, can they expect to enjoy faster economic growth as well? Or does increased political freedom involve economic sacrifice?

There are several reasons to believe that democracy may promote growth. Relative to dictatorships, democratic governments that command popular support might be expected to be more stable, to be less likely to start wars, and to have better relations with the advanced industrial nations, most of which are democracies. Constitutional protections of both human and property rights should increase the willingness of both foreigners and residents to invest in the country, and freedoms of speech and expression are probably essential for the full development of a nation's educational and scientific potential. However, the ability of a democratic government to undertake unpopular but necessary economic reforms or make other tough choices may be hampered by pressures of interest groups or fluctuations of public opinion. Similarly, a dictatorial government may be better able than a democratic one to enforce a high national saving rate and keep government spending under control.

What does empirical evidence show about the relationship between democracy and economic growth? On the face of it, the answer seems clear: In the latter half of the 20th century, countries like the United States, Canada, and those in Western Europe with their free markets and democracy flourished, while the Soviet Union and countries of Eastern Europe with their centrally planned economies and dictatorships failed. Democracy and economic growth therefore seem closely linked. However, the link would not seem to be terribly strong: India and China are two of the fastest growing economies in the world, but one is a democracy while the other is a one-party state.

A more direct empirical test of the relationship between democracy and economic growth is to examine the growth performance of countries that experienced sharp changes in their level of democracy. Jenny Minier, of the University of Miami, identified 13 countries that experienced sharp increases in democracy and 22 countries that experienced sharp decreases in democracy during the period 1965–1987.[*]

To get a clear measure of the impact of changes in the level of democracy on the subsequent rate of economic growth, for each change in the level of democracy Minier formed a control group of countries. She chose the control groups so that prior to the change in democracy, the levels of income per capita and of democracy were the same in the control group as in the country undergoing the change. She found that over the five-year period following an increase in democracy, countries experienced economic growth that averaged almost 2%, compared with growth of –1% in the control groups. Countries that experienced a decrease in democracy had economic growth of almost 8% in the five-year period following the change, compared with almost 15% growth in the control groups. Thus, relative to the control groups, increases in democracy tended to increase economic growth, and decreases in democracy tended to decrease economic growth.

These findings were strengthened by Minier's examination of growth in the 15-year period following a change in the level of democracy. Countries that increased democracy experienced economic growth of 32% in the 15 years after a change (compared with 6% growth for the control groups), and countries that decreased democracy saw their economies grow by less than 8% in the 15 years after the change (compared with 35% for the control groups).

---

[*]Jenny A. Minier, "Democracy and Growth: Alternative Approaches," *Journal of Economic Growth*, September 1998, pp. 241–266.

An alternative and more direct way to increase the national saving rate is to *require* people to increase the amount they save. Proposals for such an approach were prompted by the financial crisis of 2008–2009 that resulted in the failure or near-failure of a significant number of private pension plans. The apparent exposure of people's pension savings to the ups and downs of financial markets prompted the federal government to consider proposals to significantly expand the government-guaranteed Canada Pension Plan (CPP) by increasing the payroll taxes Canadians pay as contributions to that plan.[17] A problem with such an approach, however, is that people may simply reduce other forms of saving because they can rely more heavily on the government-backed CPP. This suggests that a government wishing to increase national saving might need to do so in the most direct way possible: by increasing the amount the government saves.

Recall from Chapter 2 that government saving is measured by the difference between what governments collect in tax revenue and what they spend. By reducing government spending or increasing tax revenue, governments increase government saving and, hence, national saving. Canadians are familiar with such a policy: During the 1990s Canadian governments at all levels initiated serious efforts to cut their spending. This policy reduced their deficits (or, equivalently, increased their saving) and so increased national saving. As predicted by our examination of Figure 6.5, the policy of deficit reduction was initially met by resistance as it introduced "short-term pain" in the form of cuts to government programs. After that initial reluctance, Canadians seemingly became convinced of the wisdom of avoiding large government deficits. Most likely this is because a period of strong economic growth followed the period of deficit reduction. Very recently, however, and in response to an economic slowdown, the federal government has introduced a long-term plan to maintain sizable annual deficits and add a significant amount to government debt. This change in direction is defended by supporters who argue the borrowed money is being used to increase infrastructure and so increase the productivity of economic activity. The potential for public investment in infrastructure to increase productivity is discussed in the next section. The decision to fund productivity-enhancing investments in infrastructure with borrowing that lowers national saving raises the question of whether Canadians will realize a net benefit from these conflicting policies.

POLICIES TO RAISE THE RATE OF PRODUCTIVITY GROWTH

Of the factors affecting long-run living standards, the rate of productivity growth may well be the most important in that—according to the neoclassical growth model—only ongoing productivity growth can lead to continuing improvement in output and consumption per worker. Government policy can attempt to increase productivity in several ways.[18]

Improving Infrastructure

Some research findings suggest a significant link between productivity and the quality of a nation's infrastructure—its highways, bridges, utilities, dams, airports, and other publicly owned capital. This research finds that public spending on infrastructure is most effective at promoting productivity when it serves to complement

---

[17] For a discussion and evaluation of this proposal, see Jonathan Kesselman, "Expanding Canada Pension Plan Retirement Benefits: Assessing Big CPP Proposals," *SPP Research Papers*, Volume 3, Issue 6, The School of Public Policy, University of Calgary, October 2010.

[18] For a useful review of how public policies might increase productivity, see Andrew Sharpe, "Lessons for Canada from International Productivity Experience," *International Productivity Monitor*, No. 14, Spring 2007, pp. 20–37.

the activities of the private sector. Thus, for example, by lowering transportation costs, public spending on highways increases the productivity of private trucking firms and stimulates tourism. But, of course, improving infrastructure also yields social benefits. For example, public spending on highways provides citizens easy access to mountain parks and beaches and lowers the price of goods shipped by road, benefits enjoyed by taxpayers while not necessarily increasing the productivity of private firms. Recognition of these dual effects of public infrastructure spending is behind recent public policies to encourage what are known as *public–private partnerships*. So-called PPP initiatives reflect a recognition that many public infrastructure projects are complementary to the activities of private firms, and that the firms should therefore play a more prominent role in the financing of such projects than might have previously been the case.

Building Human Capital

Recent research findings point to a strong connection between productivity growth and human capital. Governments affect human capital through educational policies, worker training or relocation programs, health programs, and in other ways. Specific programs should be examined carefully to see whether benefits exceed costs, but a case may be made for greater commitment to human capital formation as a way to fight the productivity slowdown.

One crucial form of human capital, which we have not yet mentioned, is entrepreneurial skill. People with the ability to build successful new businesses or to bring a new product to market play key roles in economic growth. Productivity growth may increase if the government were to remove unnecessary barriers to entrepreneurial activity (such as excessive red tape) and give people with entrepreneurial skills greater incentives to use those skills productively.

Encouraging Research and Development

Governments also may be able to stimulate productivity growth by affecting rates of scientific and technical progress. The Canadian government directly supports much basic scientific research (through its research councils, for example). Most economists agree with this type of policy because the benefits of scientific progress, like those of human capital development, spread throughout the economy. Basic scientific research, therefore, may be a good investment from society's point of view, even if no individual firm finds such research profitable. Some economists would go further and say that even more applied, commercially oriented research deserves government aid.

Is there scope for policies to promote R&D in Canada? The evidence on this matter is mixed.[19] In 1963, total R&D spending was equal to just under 1% of GDP. This grew more or less steadily until it reached a maximum of 2% of GDP in 2004. Since then, total R&D spending has slowly fallen so that by 2015 it was equal to just under 1.6% of GDP. Interestingly, the share of total R&D spending by government has fallen more or less steadily since 1963 and today accounts for only about one-quarter of all R&D spending. The remaining three-quarters of R&D spending comes from the private sector.

Despite the growth in total R&D spending over the past four decades, R&D expenditures in Canada are a smaller proportion of GDP than in any other G7

---

[19] Data on R&D expenditures, by donor and by recipient, are available from Statistics Canada, CANSIM Table 358-0001.

country. On this evidence, some commentators have argued that R&D expenditures, both public and private, should be more strongly encouraged.

One way of encouraging increases in R&D spending by the private sector is for the government to offer tax incentives. Economists Ken McKenzie and Natalia Sershun of the University of Calgary maintain that tax subsidies provide significant inducements to increase private sector R&D expenditures.[20] However, not all economists are convinced. They point to what are already generous levels of taxpayer support for private sector R&D and conclude that the case for still further subsidies is weak.

Industrial Policy

Beyond support for basic science and technology, an aggressive approach that has been proposed for encouraging technological development is industrial policy. Generally, **industrial policy** is a growth strategy in which the government—using taxes, subsidies, or regulation—attempts to influence the country's pattern of industrial development. More specifically, some advocates of industrial policy argue that the government should subsidize and promote "high-tech" industries in order to try to achieve or maintain national leadership in technologically dynamic areas.

The idea that the government should try to determine the country's mix of industries is controversial. Economic theory and practice suggest that under normal circumstances the free market can allocate resources well without government assistance. Thus, advocates of industrial policy must explain why the free market fails in the case of high technology. Two possible sources of market failure that have been suggested are borrowing constraints and spillovers.

Borrowing constraints are limits imposed by lenders on the amounts that individuals or small firms can borrow. Because of borrowing constraints, private companies, especially start-up firms, may have difficulty obtaining enough financing for some projects. Development of a new supercomputer, for example, is likely to require heavy investment in research and development and involve a long period during which expenses are high and no revenues are coming in.

Spillovers occur when a given company's innovation—say, the development of an improved computer memory chip or medical scanner—stimulates a flood of related innovations and technical improvements by other companies and industries. The innovative company may thus enjoy only some of the total benefits of its breakthrough while bearing the full development cost. Without a government subsidy (argue advocates of industrial policy), such companies may not have a sufficiently strong incentive to innovate.

These theoretical arguments for government intervention assume that the government is skilled at picking "winning" technologies and that its decisions about which industries to subsidize would be free from purely political considerations. However, both assumptions are questionable. A danger of industrial policy is that the favoured industries would be those with the most powerful political supporters rather than those with the most economic promise.

Market Policy

Possibly the most important productivity-related policies a society and its government can establish are those having to do with the extent to which government will

---

[20] "Taxation and R&D: An Investigation of the Push and Pull Effects," *Canadian Public Policy*, Volume 36, No. 3, 2010, pp. 307–324.

restrict the free operation of markets—what we call **market policy**. At the most basic level, a society and its government must make a choice between rigidly government-controlled markets on the one hand and completely unfettered markets on the other. Thus, societies must choose between communism and capitalism and, hence, choose whether to respect property rights. This choice is not black and white, of course, as there are many shades of market policy between the extremes of communism and unfettered capitalism.

Where a society chooses to stand along this spectrum is determined by how it chooses to deal with certain outcomes that result from the respect (or denial) of property rights. Economists favour respect for property rights and a reliance on free markets to allocate resources and goods because these choices maximize the efficient use of resources and so maximize consumption possibilities for citizens. However, it is common for economists to identify reasons why it may be desirable for government to interfere with the free operation of markets. Thus, markets may evolve in such a way that production becomes highly concentrated and monopolies or oligopolies result. In these cases, resources are not used efficiently and governments are encouraged to regulate or police concentrated markets.[21] Even if not unduly concentrated, free markets may also produce outcomes that a society may deem unattractive, and this may lead to demands that those markets be regulated. This is the case, for example, with the allocation of medical services, where the free market solution of allocating goods and services to the highest bidder is not judged to be desirable. For this reason, in almost all countries the market for the provision of medical services is regulated in some way.

Social Insurance

The efficient operation of free markets involves the reallocation of labour and capital from dying firms and industries to new, more efficient firms and industries. The efficient operation of markets, therefore, involves the dislocation of resources, including human resources. In the face of such dislocations, societies sometimes choose to interfere with the unfettered operation of markets by providing social insurance. Examples here include providing employment insurance and social assistance, the purpose of which is to provide income during a period of transition from unemployment to re-employment.[22]

The choice to regulate or otherwise interfere in the operation of markets is often thought to imply a trade-off between efficiency and equity. For example, the redistribution of income creates incentives for people—both those who are taxed and those who receive the income transfer—to work less hard and for shorter periods than they would were it not for the income transfer. The gain in equity thus comes at the cost of efficiency. A growing collection of research suggests, however, that this conclusion should be resisted. For example, Harold Alderman and Ruslan Yemtsov, writing for the World Bank,[23] emphasized that experience has shown that a well-designed social "safety net" is important for redistributing the gains from economic growth and necessary to win support for growth-enhancing public policies in the first place. Thus, citizens may vote in

---

[21] In Canada, this is the mandate of the federal government's Competition Bureau. To learn more about the mandate and operation of the Competition Bureau, visit its website at *www.competition.ic.gc.ca*.

[22] Such provisions are not limited to unemployed workers. Governments often choose to share in the private costs of adjusting to new market conditions by aiding in the re-employment of capital. This is the rationale for accelerated depreciation allowances, tariffs, and certain tax incentives.

[23] "How Can Safety Nets Contribute to Economic Growth?," *The World Bank Economic Review*, Volume 28, No. 1, June 2013, pp. 1–20.

favour of growth-enhancing policies only if they are convinced that they will be "caught" by a comprehensive social safety net should growth cause them to be disadvantaged. The literature that Alderman and Yemtsov summarize indicates that well-designed redistributive policies are an integral part of policies to promote growth, and that increases in growth may require, rather than be discouraged by, increases in social insurance.

CHAPTER SUMMARY

1. Economic growth is the principal source of improving standards of living over time. Over long periods, even small differences in growth rates can have a large effect on nations' standards of living.

2. Growth accounting is a method for breaking total output growth into the portions resulting from growth in capital inputs, growth in labour inputs, and growth in productivity. All three factors have contributed to long-run economic growth in Canada. However, the slowdown in output growth after 1973 in Canada (and in other countries) primarily reflects a sharp decline in productivity growth. This decline is in turn the result of various factors, including slower technical progress and increased oil prices.

3. The neoclassical growth model examines the interaction of growth, saving, and capital accumulation over time. It predicts that in the absence of productivity growth the economy will reach a steady state in which output, consumption, and capital per worker are constant.

4. According to the growth model, each of the following leads to higher output, consumption, and capital per worker in the long run: an increase in the saving rate, a decline in the population growth rate, and an increase in productivity.

5. Endogenous growth theory attempts to explain, rather than assume, the economywide rate of productivity growth. One strand of this approach emphasizes the formation of human capital, including the acquisition of skills and training by workers. A second strand focuses on research and development activity by firms. Endogenous growth theorists argue that because growth in capital and output engenders increased human capital and innovation, the marginal productivity of capital may not be diminishing for the economy as a whole. An implication of this theory is that the saving rate can affect the long-run rate of economic growth.

6. Government policies to raise long-run living standards include raising the rate of saving and increasing productivity. Possible ways of increasing productivity involve investing in public capital (infrastructure), encouraging the formation of human capital, and increasing research and development. A more aggressive strategy is industrial policy, in which the government uses subsidies and other tools to influence the pattern of industrial development and, in particular, to stimulate high-tech industries. Critics of this approach contend that in practice, the government cannot successfully pick and subsidize only "winning" technologies. The most important source of productivity gains is via the effective use of market policies. Market policies include the choice between free and regulated markets and the choice between free trade and protectionism.

KEY DIAGRAM 6

The Neoclassical Growth Model

The neoclassical growth model is used to show how living standards, as measured by consumption per worker, are affected by changes in the rate of saving s, the rate of population growth n, and the level of productivity A.

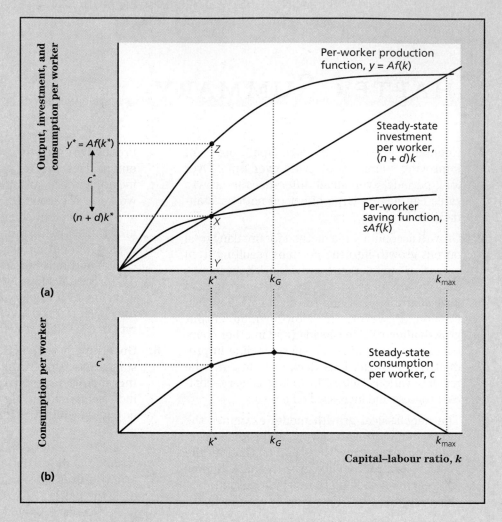

DIAGRAM ELEMENTS

- The diagram in panel (a) graphs two bowed relationships showing how output per worker $y = Af(k)$ and saving per worker $sAf(k)$ vary with the capital–labour ratio. It also shows the steady-state per-worker investment line $(n + d)k$. For assumed values of the saving rate s, the rate of population growth n, and the level of productivity A, the diagram identifies the steady-state capital–labour ratio k^* where saving per worker equals steady-state investment per worker.

- The diagram in panel (b) graphs the relationship between values of steady-state consumption per worker and the capital–labour ratio. Steady-state consumption per worker—our measure of living standards—is maximized at the Golden Rule steady state k_G. Consistent with empirical evidence, the two diagrams are drawn to show an economy with a steady-state capital–labour ratio that is below the Golden Rule level.

ANALYSIS

- The slope of the per-worker production function measures the marginal product of capital *MPK*. It is bowed due to diminishing *MPK*, a property of production functions discussed in Chapter 3.

- The per-worker saving function is also bowed because it is simply the per-worker production function multiplied by saving rate *s*, which is a constant fraction.

- The steady-state per-worker investment line has a slope determined by the rate of population growth *n* and the rate of capital depreciation *d*.

- The height of the steady-state per-worker consumption function is determined by the vertical distance between the steady-state per-worker investment line and the per-worker production function. Its maximum value identifies the Golden Rule capital–labour ratio for given values of the saving rate *s*, the rate of population growth *n*, and the level of productivity *A*.

- The steady-state capital–labour ratio is found where the per-worker saving function intersects the steady-state per-worker investment line.

FACTORS THAT SHIFT THE CURVES

- We use this key diagram to show the effect on the standard of living of changes in the saving rate *s*, the rate of population growth *n*, and the level of productivity *A*.

- An increase in the saving rate *s* causes the per-worker saving function to pivot upward. As a result, the steady-state capital–labour ratio increases and moves closer to the Golden Rule steady-state value.

- An increase in the rate of population growth *n* causes the steady-state investment line to pivot up. As a result, the steady-state capital–labour ratio falls and moves further away from the Golden Rule steady-state value.

- An increase in the level of productivity *A* causes the per-worker production function, the per-worker saving function, and the steady-state per-worker consumption function to pivot upward. The steady-state capital–labour ratio increases, and so too does the Golden Rule steady-state capital–labour ratio.

KEY TERMS

KEY EQUATIONS

$$\frac{\Delta Y}{Y} = \frac{\Delta A}{A} + a_K \frac{\Delta K}{K} + a_N \frac{\Delta N}{N} \quad (6.2)$$

The growth accounting equation states that output growth, $\Delta Y/Y$, depends on the growth rate of productivity, $\Delta A/A$, the growth rate of capital, $\Delta K/K$, and the growth rate of labour, $\Delta N/N$. The elasticity of output with respect to capital, a_K,

gives the percentage increase in output that results when capital increases by 1%. The elasticity of output with respect to labour, a_N, gives the percentage increase in output that results when labour increases by 1%.

$$y_t = A_t f(k_t) \quad (6.5)$$

For any year t, the per-worker production function relates output per worker, y_t, to the level of total factor productivity A_t and to capital per worker (also called the capital–labour ratio), k_t.

$$c = Af(k) - (n + d)k \quad (6.8)$$

Steady-state consumption per worker c equals steady-state output per worker $Af(k)$ minus steady-state investment per worker $(n+d)k$. Steady-state output per worker is determined by per-worker production $Af(k)$, where k is the steady-state capital–labour ratio. Steady-state investment per worker has two parts: equipping new workers with the per-worker capital stock, nk, and replacing worn-out or depreciated capital, dk.

$$sAf(k) = (n + d)k \quad (6.11)$$

The steady state is determined by the condition that saving per worker $sAf(k)$ equals steady-state investment per worker $(n + d)k$. Saving per worker equals the saving rate s times output per worker $Af(k)$.

$$Y = AK \qquad (6.12)$$

Endogenous growth theory replaces the assumption of diminishing marginal productivity of capital with the assumption that the marginal productivity of capital is independent of the level of the capital stock. In the production function relating aggregate output Y to the aggregate capital stock K in Eq. (6.12), the marginal product of capital is constant and equal to the parameter A.

$$\frac{\Delta Y}{Y} = sA - d \qquad (6.15)$$

In an endogenous growth model, the growth rate of output is determined endogenously by the saving rate, s. An increase in the saving rate increases the growth rate of output.

REVIEW QUESTIONS

1. According to the growth accounting approach, what are the three sources of economic growth? From what basic economic relationship is the growth accounting approach derived?
2. Of the three sources of growth identified by growth accounting, which one is primarily responsible for the slowdown in Canadian economic growth after 1973? What explanations have been given for the decline in this source of growth?
3. According to the neoclassical growth model, if there is no productivity growth, what will happen to output per worker, consumption per worker, and capital per worker in the long run?
4. True or false? The higher the steady-state capital–labour ratio is, the more consumption each worker can enjoy in the long run. Explain your answer.
5. What effect should each of the following have on long-run living standards, according to the neoclassical growth model?
   a. An increase in the saving rate.
   b. An increase in the population growth rate.
   c. A one-time improvement in productivity.
6. What two explanations of productivity growth does endogenous growth theory offer? How does the production function in an endogenous growth model differ from the production function in the neoclassical growth model?
7. What types of policies are available to a government that wants to promote economic growth? For each

type of policy you identify, explain briefly how the policy is supposed to work, and list its costs or disadvantages. How might endogenous growth theory change our thinking about the effectiveness of various pro-growth policies, such as increasing the saving rate?

NUMERICAL PROBLEMS

1. Two economies, Hare and Tortoise, each start with a real GDP per person of $5000 in 1950. Real GDP per person grows 3% a year in Hare and 1% a year in Tortoise. In the year 2000, what will be real GDP per person in each economy? Make a guess first; then use a calculator to get the answer.
2. Over the past 20 years, an economy's total output has grown from 1000 to 1300, its capital stock has risen from 2500 to 3250, and its labour force has increased from 500 to 575. All measurements are in real terms. Calculate the contributions to economic growth of growth in capital, labour, and productivity
   a. assuming that $a_K = 0.3$ and $a_N = 0.7$;
   b. assuming that $a_K = 0.5$ and $a_N = 0.5$.
3. For a particular economy, the following capital input K and labour input N were reported in four different years:

Year	K	N
1	200	1000
2	250	1000
3	250	1250
4	300	1200

The production function in this economy is

$$Y = K^{0.3}N^{0.7},$$

where Y is total output.
   a. Find total output, the capital–labour ratio, and output per worker in each year. Compare year 1 with year 3, and year 2 with year 4. Can this production function be written in per-worker form? If so, write algebraically the per-worker form of the production function.
   b. Repeat part (a) but assume now that the production function is $Y = K^{0.3}N^{0.8}$.
4. Use the data from Table 6.1 (p. 164) to calculate annual growth rates of GDP per capita for each country listed over the period 1950–1998. (*Note:* The annual growth rate z will satisfy the equation $(1 + z)^{48} = \text{GDP}_{1998}/\text{GDP}_{1950}$. To solve this equation for z using a calculator, take logs of both sides of the equation.) You will find that Germany and Japan, two countries that suffered extensive damage in World

War II, had the two highest growth rates after 1950. Give a reason, based on the analysis of the growth model, for these countries' particularly fast growth during this period.

5. An economy has the per-worker production function

$$y_t = 3k_t^{0.5},$$

where y_t is output per worker and k_t is the capital–labour ratio. The depreciation rate is 0.1, and the population growth rate is 0.05. Saving is

$$S_t = 0.3Y_t,$$

where S_t is total national saving, and Y_t is total output.
   a. What are the steady-state values of the capital–labour ratio, output per worker, and consumption per worker?

   The rest of the problem shows the effects of changes in the three fundamental determinants of long-run living standards.
   b. Repeat part (a) for a saving rate of 0.4 instead of 0.3.
   c. Repeat part (a) for a population growth rate of 0.08 (with a saving rate of 0.3).
   d. Repeat part (a) for a production function of

   $$y_t = 4k_t^{0.5}.$$

   Assume that the saving rate and population growth rate are at their original values.

6. Consider a closed economy in which the population grows at the rate of 1% per year. The per-worker production function is $y = 6\sqrt{k}$, where y is output per worker and k is capital per worker. The depreciation rate of capital is 14% per year.
   a. Households consume 90% of income and save the remaining 10% of income. There is no government spending. What are the steady-state values of capital per worker, output per worker, consumption per worker, and investment per worker?
   b. Suppose that the country wants to increase its steady-state value of output per worker. What steady-state value of the capital–labour ratio is needed to double the steady-state value of output per worker? What fraction of income would households have to save to achieve a steady-state level of output per worker that is twice as high as in part (a)?

7. Both population and the workforce grow at the rate of $n = 1\%$ per year in a closed economy. Consumption is $C = 0.5(1-t)Y$, where t is the tax rate on income and Y is total output. The per-worker production function is $y = 8\sqrt{k}$, where y is output per worker and k is the capital–labour ratio. The depreciation rate of

capital is $d = 9\%$ per year. Suppose for now that there are no government purchases and the tax rate on income is $t = 0$.
   a. Find expressions for national saving per worker and the steady-state level of investment per worker as functions of the capital–labour ratio, k. In the steady state, what are the values of the capital–labour ratio, output per worker, consumption per worker, and investment per worker?
   b. Suppose that the government purchases goods each year and pays for these purchases using taxes on income. The government runs a balanced budget in each period and the tax rate on income is $t = 0.5$. Repeat part (a) and compare your results.

ANALYTICAL PROBLEMS

1. According to the neoclassical growth model, how would each of the following affect consumption per worker in the long run (that is, in the steady state)? Explain.
   a. The destruction of a portion of the country's capital stock in a war.
   b. A permanent increase in the rate of immigration (which raises the overall population growth rate).
   c. A permanent increase in energy prices.
   d. A temporary rise in the saving rate.
   e. A permanent increase in the fraction of the population in the labour force (the population growth rate is unchanged).

2. An economy is in a steady state with no productivity change. Because of an increase in acid rain, the rate of capital depreciation rises permanently.
   a. According to the neoclassical growth model, what are the effects on steady-state capital per worker, output per worker, consumption per worker, and the long-run growth rate of the total capital stock?
   b. In an endogenous growth model, what are the effects on the growth rates of output, capital, and consumption of an increase in the depreciation rate of capital?

3. This problem adds the government to the growth model. Suppose that a government purchases goods in the amount of g per worker every year; with N_t workers in year t, total government purchases are gN_t. The government has a balanced budget so that its tax revenue in year t, T_t, equals total government purchases. Total national saving S_t is

$$S_t = s(Y_t - T_t),$$

where Y_t is total output and s is the saving rate.

a. Graphically show the steady state for the initial level of government purchases per worker.

b. Suppose that the government permanently increases its purchases per worker. What are the effects on the steady-state levels of capital per worker, output per worker, and consumption per worker? Does your result imply that the optimal level of government purchases is zero?

4. In a Solow–Swan-type economy, total national saving S_t is

$$S_t = sY_t - hK_t.$$

The extra term, $-hK_t$, reflects the idea that when wealth (as measured by the capital stock) is higher, saving is lower. (Wealthier people have less need to save for the future.)

Find the steady-state values of per-worker capital, output, and consumption. What is the effect on the steady state of an increase in h?

5. Two countries are identical in every way except that one has a much higher capital–labour ratio than the other. According to the neoclassical growth model, which country's total output will grow more quickly? Does your answer depend on whether one country or the other is in a steady state? In general terms, how will your answer be affected if the two countries are allowed to trade with each other?

6. Suppose that total capital and labour both increase by the same percentage amount so that the amount of capital per worker k does not change. Writing the production function in per-worker terms, $y = f(k)$, requires that this increase in capital and labour must not change the amount of output produced per worker y. Use the growth accounting equation to show that equal percentage increases in capital and labour will leave output per worker unaffected only if $a_K + a_N = 1$.

7. An economy has a per-capita production function $y = Ak^a h^{1-a}$, where A and a are fixed parameters, y is per-worker output, k is the capital–labour ratio, and h is human capital per worker, a measure of the skills and training of the average worker. The production function implies that for a given capital–labour ratio, increases in average human capital raise output per worker.

The economy's saving rate is s, and all saving is used to create physical capital, which depreciates at rate d. Workers acquire skills on the job by working with capital; the more capital with which they have to work, the more skills they acquire. We capture this idea by assuming that human capital per worker is always proportional to the amount of capital per worker, or $h = Bk$, where B is a fixed parameter.

Find the long-run growth rates of physical capital, human capital, and output in this economy.

8. *Luddites* was a name given to a group of skilled textile workers (known as *croppers*) who, in the early 1800s in England, would break into textile mills and smash the new mechanized textile looms they feared would put them out of work. Since that time, the term *Luddites* has often been applied to any group that tries to halt technological advances. Using the neoclassical growth model, show the effect of a technological advance that increases productivity.

a. Show how the technological advance affects living standards both immediately and after the economy adjusts to a new steady state.

b. How can the concerns of the Luddites be represented in a diagram?

c. During the adjustment to the new steady state, is the rate of growth in output greater than, less than, or equal to the rate of growth experienced in the steady state? Explain.

Chapter 7

The Asset Market, Money, and Prices

Chapters 3 and 4 discussed the labour market and the goods market, two of the three markets in our model of the macroeconomy. In this chapter, we consider the third market, the asset market. By *asset market* we mean the entire set of markets in which people buy and sell real and financial assets, including, for example, gold, houses, stocks, and bonds.

A type of asset that has long been believed to have special macroeconomic significance is money. *Money* is the economist's term for assets that can be used in making payments, such as cash and chequing accounts. One reason why money is important is that most prices are expressed in units of money, such as dollars, yen, or euros. Because prices are measured in money terms, understanding the role of money in the economy is basic to studying issues related to the price level, such as inflation and its causes. In addition, many economists believe that the amount of money in the economy affects real economic variables, such as output and employment. If it does, then it may be possible to use monetary policy to promote stable output growth and fight unemployment, as we discuss in Part III.

Because money is such an important asset, it is the focus of our discussion of the asset market. The first part of the chapter explains what money is and why people choose to hold it. We show that a person's decision about how much money to hold (his or her money demand) is part of a broader decision about how to allocate wealth among the various assets that are available. We then bring together the demand for money and the supply of money (which is determined by the central bank) to analyze equilibrium in the asset market. This analysis demonstrates that the price level in an economy is closely related to the amount of money in the economy. Thus, high rates of inflation—that is, rapid increases in prices—are likely when the money supply is growing rapidly.

7.1 WHAT IS MONEY?

In economics, the meaning of the term *money* is different from its everyday meaning. People often say *money* when they mean *income* or *wealth*, as in "That job pays good money," or "Her family has a lot of money." In economics, however, **money** refers specifically to assets that are widely used and accepted as payment. Historically, the forms of money have ranged from beads and shells to gold and silver—and even to cigarettes.[1] In modern economies, the most familiar forms of money are coins and paper money, or currency. Another common form of money is chequable deposits, or bank accounts on which cheques can be written for making payments.

THE FUNCTIONS OF MONEY

Since the earliest times, almost all societies—from the most primitive to the most sophisticated and with many types of political and economic systems—have used money. Money has three useful functions in an economy: It is a medium of exchange, a unit of account, and a store of value.

Medium of Exchange

In an economy with no money, trading takes the form of barter, or the direct exchange of certain goods for other goods. Even today some people belong to barter clubs, in which members swap goods and services among themselves. Generally, though, barter is an inefficient way to trade, because finding someone who has the item you want and is willing to exchange that item for something you have is both difficult and time-consuming. In a barter system, if one of the authors of this book wanted a restaurant meal, he would first have to find a restaurateur willing to trade his special of the day for an economics lecture—which might not be easy to do.

Money makes searching for the perfect trading partner unnecessary. In an economy that utilizes money, the economics professor does not have to find a restaurant owner who is hungry for knowledge. Instead, he can first exchange his economics lecture to students (and taxpayers) for money and then use the money to buy a meal. In functioning as a **medium of exchange**, or a device for making transactions, money permits people to trade at less cost in time and effort. Having a medium of exchange also raises productivity by allowing people to specialize in economic activities at which they are most skilled. In an economy with money, specialized producers have no problem trading their goods or services for the things they need. In a barter economy, though, the difficulty of trading would leave people no choice but to produce most of their own food, clothing, and shelter. Thus, in a barter economy, the opportunity to specialize is greatly reduced.

Unit of Account

As a **unit of account**, money is the basic unit for measuring economic value. In Canada, for example, virtually all prices, wages, asset values, and debts are expressed in dollars. Having a single, uniform measure of value is convenient. For example, pricing all goods in Canada in dollars—instead of some goods being priced in yen, some in gold, and some in Canadian Pacific shares—simplifies comparison among different goods.

The medium-of-exchange and unit-of-account functions of money are closely linked. Because goods and services are most often exchanged for money (the medium-of-exchange function), expressing economic values in money terms (the unit-of-account function) is natural. Otherwise, we could just as well express economic

---

[1] Cigarettes were used as money in prisoner-of-war (POW) camps during World War II. The fact that some prisoners valued goods more than others meant that gains from trade were available, but an alternative to money as a medium of exchange had to be found. Cigarettes weren't perfect in this role—cigarettes used as money couldn't be smoked!—but they proved to be the best alternative available.

values in terms of, say, bushels of wheat. However, the medium of exchange and the unit of account are not always the same. In countries with high and erratic inflation, for example, fluctuating currency value makes money a poor unit of account because prices must be changed frequently. In such cases, economic values are commonly stated in terms of a more stable unit of account, such as U.S. dollars or ounces of gold, even though transactions may continue to be carried out in the local currency.

Store of Value

As a **store of value**, money is a way of holding wealth. An extreme example is a miser who keeps his or her life's savings in cash under the mattress. But even someone who spends his or her cash wages 15 minutes after receiving them is using money as a store of value for that short period.

In most cases, only money functions as a medium of exchange or a unit of account, but any asset—for example, stocks, bonds, or real estate—can be a store of value. As these other types of assets normally pay the holder a higher return than money does, why do people use money as a store of value? The answer is that money's usefulness as a medium of exchange makes it worthwhile to hold, even though its return is relatively low.

MEASURING MONEY: THE MONETARY AGGREGATES

Money is defined as those assets that are widely used and accepted in payment. This definition suggests a hard-and-fast line between assets that should be counted as money and those that should not. Actually, the distinction between monetary assets and nonmonetary assets is not so clear. For example, should funds held in a money market account be considered money? There are typically restrictions on how frequently one can access such an account or interest penalties to be paid for withdrawing funds. In this case the funds in the money market account are not nearly as convenient as cash. Should the funds be considered money? There is no definitive answer.

Because assets differ in their "moneyness," no single measure of the amount of money in the economy—or the money stock, as it's often called—is likely to be completely satisfactory. For this reason, in most countries, economists and policymakers use several different measures of the money stock. These official measures are known as **monetary aggregates**. The various monetary aggregates differ in how narrowly they define the concept of money. Table 7.1 presents details on the composition of three monetary aggregates defined by the Bank of Canada: M1+, M2, and M3.

The M1+ Monetary Aggregate

The most narrowly defined official money measure, **M1+**, consists primarily of currency and balances held in chequing accounts. More precisely, M1+ is made up of currency held by the public and chequable deposits in personal and non-personal accounts. Personal chequing accounts include interest-bearing chequable deposits, such as daily interest chequing accounts, while non-personal accounts are held by firms. M1+ is perhaps the closest counterpart to the theoretical definition of money because all its components are actively used and widely accepted for making payments.

As usual, one way to bring the astronomical numbers in Table 7.1 down to earth is to divide by the population. In November 2016, the Canadian population was about 36.3 million, so the stock of currency per person was $2151 ($78.1 billion divided by

TABLE 7.1

The Canadian Monetary Aggregates (November 2016)

M1+	**$797.2 billion**
Currency	$78.1 billion
Chequable deposits	$686.2 billion
M2	**$1488.7 billion**
M1+	$797.2 billion
Personal savings deposits	$642.3 billion
Non-personal demand and notice deposits	$51.0 billion
M3	**$2226.0 billion**
M2	$1488.7 billion
Non-personal term deposits	$319.6 billion
Foreign currency deposits of residents	$430.1 billion

Source: Statistics Canada, 2016. Reproduced and distributed on an "as is" basis with the permission of Statistics Canada.

36.3 million). Perhaps while looking inside their wallets and turning their pockets inside-out most people would think this to be a surprisingly large number. One explanation lies in the fact that currency is used extensively in the underground economy, either to conduct illegal transactions or to hide legal transactions from tax collectors. The figure is significantly larger in the United States because a good deal of U.S. currency is held abroad. People in countries that are politically or economically unstable hold U.S. currency because it's a relatively secure store of value.

The M2 and M3 Monetary Aggregates

Everything in M1+ plus other assets that are somewhat less "moneylike" comprise **M2**. The additional assets in M2 are personal and non-personal non-chequable deposits. As cheques cannot be written on these deposits, they are less convenient as a medium of exchange and so a little less "moneylike," making M2 a more broadly defined measure of the money supply than M1+. The additional assets in **M3** include non-personal term deposits held by businesses. Term deposits pay a higher interest rate but cannot be withdrawn for a specified period without penalty. Once again, therefore, assets included in M3 are less convenient to use as a medium of exchange than assets in either M1+ or M2, making M3 a still more broadly defined measure of the money supply. Note that M3 includes, under the category "foreign currency deposit of residents," the value of assets such as U.S.-dollar accounts held by Canadians. While these cannot be used directly for making purchases, because these assets can be quickly and cheaply converted into currency or chequable deposits, economists include them in the broader measures of money.

THE MONEY SUPPLY

The **money supply** is the amount of money available in an economy.[2] In modern economies, the money supply is partly determined by the central bank—in Canada, the Bank of Canada.

---

[2] The terms *money supply* and *money stock* are used interchangeably.

For simplicity, we can assume that the Bank of Canada sets the money supply. In fact, the Bank influences the money supply indirectly by influencing short-term interest rates. A detailed explanation of how central banks control the money supply raises issues that would take us too far afield at this point, so we defer that discussion to Chapter 14. To grasp the basic idea, however, let's consider the simple hypothetical situation in which the only form of money is currency. In this case, to increase the money supply, the central bank only needs to increase the amount of currency in circulation. How can it do so?

One way—which is close to what happens in practice—is for the central bank to use newly minted currency to buy financial assets, such as government bonds, from the public. In making this swap, the public increases its holdings of money, and the amount of money in circulation rises. When the central bank uses money to purchase government bonds from the public, thus raising the money supply, it is said to have conducted an *open-market purchase*.

To reduce the money supply, the central bank can make this trade in reverse, selling government bonds that it holds to the public in exchange for currency. After the central bank removes this currency from circulation, the money supply is lower. When the central bank sells government bonds to the public to reduce the money supply, the transaction is an *open-market sale*. Open-market purchases and sales are together called **open-market operations**.

In addition to buying government bonds from the public, the central bank can increase the money supply by buying newly issued government bonds directly from the government itself. For example, if a country's treasury needs $1 billion to pay for some new highways, it might give an IOU for $1 billion (government bonds) to the central bank in exchange for $1 billion in newly minted currency. The treasury then gives the $1 billion of currency to the road builders. After the treasury has distributed this currency, the amount of money in circulation—the money supply—will be higher by $1 billion. Effectively, this second way of increasing the money supply amounts to the government financing its expenditures by printing money.[3] This practice is most common in developing countries with limited sources of tax revenue or in countries racked by war or natural disaster, in which government spending often greatly exceeds the amount that can be raised through taxes.[4]

For the rest of this chapter, we assume that the economy has a money supply of M dollars, which is determined by the central bank. The term M may represent M1+, M2, or some other measure of money. For the purpose of developing the theoretical model, which measure of money M refers to doesn't matter.

7.2 PORTFOLIO ALLOCATION AND THE DEMAND FOR ASSETS

Our next goal is to understand how people determine the amount of money they choose to hold. We begin by considering the broader question of how people allocate their wealth among the many different assets that are available, of which money is only one example.

---

[3] In Chapter 2, we said that the portion of government spending not covered by taxes had to be borrowed from the private sector. Is this still true when the government has the option of paying for its spending by printing money? Yes; for national income accounting purposes, the Bank of Canada is treated as part of the private sector. So, when the government sells government bonds to the Bank in exchange for currency, it is still technically borrowing from the private sector.

[4] While raising revenue without the need to raise taxes sounds terribly attractive, it has some serious drawbacks. The effects of financing government spending through money creation are discussed further in Chapter 15.

A consumer, a business, a pension fund, a university, or any other holder of wealth must decide how to distribute that wealth among many types of assets. The set of assets that a holder of wealth chooses to own is called a *portfolio*. The decision about which assets and how much of each asset to hold is called the **portfolio allocation decision**.

The portfolio allocation decision can be complex. Many people make their living by giving financial advice to holders of wealth, and a major branch of economics, called financial economics, is devoted largely to the study of the portfolio allocation decision. But, fundamentally, only three characteristics of assets matter for the portfolio allocation decision: expected return, risk, and liquidity.

EXPECTED RETURN

The rate of return to an asset is the rate of increase in its value per unit of time. For example, the return on a bank account is the interest rate on the account. The return on a share of stock is the dividend paid by the stock plus any increase in the stock's price. Clearly, a high return is a desirable feature for an asset to have: All else being equal, the higher the return a wealth holder's portfolio provides, the more consumption he or she can enjoy in the future for any given amount of saving done today.

Of course, the return on an asset is not always known in advance. Stock prices may go up or down, for example. Thus, holders of wealth must base their portfolio allocation decisions on **expected returns**, or their best guesses about returns on assets. Everything else being equal, the higher an asset's expected return (after subtracting taxes and fees such as brokers' commissions), the more desirable the asset is and the more of it holders of wealth will want to own.[5]

RISK

The uncertainty about the return an asset will earn relates to the second important characteristic of assets—riskiness. An asset or a portfolio of assets has high **risk** if there is a significant chance that the actual return received will be very different from the expected return. An example of a risky asset is a share in a start-up gene-splicing company that will be worthless if the company fails but will triple in value if the company succeeds. Because most people do not like risk, they hold risky assets only if the expected return is higher than that on relatively safe assets, such as government bonds.

LIQUIDITY

Besides risk and return, a third characteristic, liquidity, affects the desirability of assets. The **liquidity** of an asset is the ease and speed with which it can be exchanged for goods, services, or other assets. Because it is accepted directly in payment, money is a highly liquid asset. An example of an illiquid asset is your automobile: Time and effort are required to exchange a used car for other goods and services; you must find someone interested in buying the car and arrange legal transfer of ownership. Between liquid money and illiquid autos are many assets, such as stocks and bonds, of intermediate liquidity. A share of stock, for example,

---

[5] For the purpose of comparing expected returns among assets, returns may be expressed in either real or nominal terms. For any expected rate of inflation, if asset A's nominal return is 1% higher than asset B's nominal return, asset A's expected real return (its nominal return minus expected inflation) will also be 1% higher than asset B's expected real return.

cannot be used directly to pay for groceries as cash can, but stock can be transformed into cash with a short delay and at the cost of a broker's fee.

In addition to making transactions easier and cheaper, liquidity provides flexibility to the holder of wealth. A liquid asset can easily be disposed of if there is an emergency need for funds or if an unexpectedly good financial investment opportunity arises. Thus, everything else being equal, the more liquid an asset is, the more attractive it will be to holders of wealth.

TIME TO MATURITY

Financial securities have a fourth and final key characteristic, which is their time to maturity. **Time to maturity** is the amount of time until a financial security matures and the security's owner is repaid his or her principal. Considering time to maturity is especially relevant for all types of bonds, as a saver can purchase bonds that will mature at any time: in one day, one week, one month, one year, or in 30 years.

Savers compare the rates of return on bonds with differing times to maturity to see which is expected to give them the highest return. Thus, a saver might compare the choice of two savings plans. Plan A involves buying a one-year bond at 6% and then, when it matures in a year, replacing it with another one-year bond. Plan B involves buying a two-year bond that pays 7% in each year. Assuming these bonds are equivalent in all other respects, the choice of which savings plan to adopt depends on what the saver believes will happen to the interest rate paid on one-year bonds a year from now. If the interest rate on one-year bonds is expected to remain at 6% next year, then savings Plan B is the more attractive; the interest rate on the two-year bond (7%) exceeds the interest rate paid on the one-year bond in both years. If, on the other hand, the interest rate on one-year bonds is expected to increase next year to 9%, then Plan A is now preferred. That is, the average return on Plan A is 7.5% (6% in the first year and 9% in the second year for an average return of 7.5%).

The idea that investors compare the returns on bonds with differing times to maturity to see which is expected to give them the highest return underlies the **expectations theory of the term structure** of interest rates. *Term structure* refers to the fact that bonds similar in all respects except their terms to maturity have different rates of return. In equilibrium, according to the expectations theory, Plans A and B, which involve holding bonds with different terms to maturity over the same two-year period, should yield the same expected return; that is, the interest rate on a two-year bond should equal the average interest rate expected on two successive one-year bonds, so that a saver doesn't prefer one plan over another. More generally, the expected rate of return on an N-year bond should equal the average of the expected rates of return on one-year bonds during the current year and the $N - 1$ succeeding years.

Although the expectations theory of the term structure of interest rates is a useful starting point, it cannot explain why we observe that, on average, the interest rates on long-term bonds generally exceed the interest rates on short-term bonds. (See the graph of the yield curve on p. 224, which illustrates the term structure of interest rates.) When short-term interest rates are expected to be higher in the future than the current short-term rate, the expectations theory predicts that the long-term interest rate will exceed the short-term interest rate. However, when short-term interest rates are expected to be lower in the future than the current short-term rate, the theory predicts, as described above, that the long-term interest rate will be lower than the short-term interest rate. To see why long-term interest rates usually exceed short-term interest rates, we need to take account of the fact that longer-term bonds are riskier than shorter-term bonds because the prices of long-term bonds are more sensitive to changes in the interest rate. Because savers do not like risk, they must be compensated for holding longer-term bonds. The result is what is called a **term premium**: an interest rate on long-term bonds that is somewhat higher than the expectations theory would suggest.

If we add the term premium to the expectations theory, we have a more complete theory of how interest rates vary with time to maturity. For example, suppose the interest rate on a one-year bond today is 5% per year, the interest rate on a one-year bond one year from now is expected to be 6% per year, and the term premium on a two-year bond is 0.75% per year. Then, in equilibrium, the interest rate on a two-year bond should equal the average interest rate on the one-year bonds, which equals (5% + 6%)/2 = 5.5%, plus the term premium, 0.75%, or 6.25%.

TYPES OF ASSETS AND THEIR CHARACTERISTICS

What types of assets do people hold, and how do the characteristics of those assets differ? Though there are many different assets, we will consider a few that are the most popular: money, bonds, stocks, houses, and consumer durable goods.

We have already seen in Section 7.1 that there are different types of money. All types of money usually have a low expected rate of return compared with other assets. Money also usually does not have much risk, although there is always some risk that inflation will be higher than expected, so that the real return on holding money might turn out to be lower than expected. But money is very liquid compared with other assets; indeed, its liquidity is generally the defining characteristic of what we call money. Because of its liquidity, money's time to maturity is generally very short. However, some assets included in M2, such as term deposits, may have a longer time to maturity and are not very liquid.

Bonds are financial securities that are sometimes called fixed-income securities because they promise to pay bondholders specific amounts on specific dates. People often choose to hold bonds issued by the Canadian government because these bonds have very little risk of default. Bonds issued by corporations are similar, but there is always some chance that a corporation will go bankrupt and fail to pay the interest or repay the principal it owes to its bondholders. Thus, bonds offer a higher expected return than money, but the return is riskier. Many bonds, especially those sold by the Canadian government, are very liquid, as an owner can easily sell his or her bond quickly and with low transactions costs. However, some corporate bonds are not very liquid, especially in bad economic times, and it may be difficult to sell them without a high cost. Bonds are issued in a variety of times to maturity.

Stocks represent ownership in a company. Most stocks pay periodic dividends to shareholders, but the dividend payments are not guaranteed. When the economy is weak and the company is not doing well, it may even stop paying dividends altogether for a time. Prices of stocks rise and fall every day, so the overall return to a shareholder consists of the dividends received plus any capital gain resulting from an increase in the price of the stock less any capital loss resulting from a decrease in the price of the stock. Because dividends and, especially, stock prices can change unpredictably, stocks are subject to a substantial amount of risk. Stocks in large companies are sold in very liquid markets, but when you buy or sell a stock there is a delay of several days for the transaction to clear and payment to be made. Most stocks do not have maturity dates, so the time to maturity is infinite.

Although most large companies are owned by shareholders, who can readily buy and sell shares of stock in organized stock exchanges such as the Toronto Stock Exchange (TSX), many small businesses are directly owned by one or a few people. These businesses, which are directly owned by their proprietors, are not incorporated and do not issue stock that can be traded on exchanges. Because there are no marketable shares of stock in these companies it is difficult for the owners to quickly sell ownership in them, so this ownership is very illiquid. Indeed, because there are no marketable shares, it is difficult to measure accurately the value of the ownership stake in these companies. The return to the owners of the company takes the form of profits earned by the company plus any opportunity that they may someday sell the company.

For most homeowners, housing is their largest asset. The returns to owning a house come in two forms: (1) the benefits to the household in terms of shelter net of maintenance costs and property taxes, and (2) the change in the value of the house (or the land it sits on) over time. Unfortunately, many people have at various times come to the mistaken belief that there is no risk in holding their wealth as housing. As we discuss in the Application "The U.S. Housing Crisis and Its Aftermath," this notion was exposed as being not only false but also dangerous for the economy when a precipitous fall in housing prices in the United States, exacerbated by lax financial regulations, contributed to a very serious financial crisis that quickly spread to Canada and other industrialized countries. Compared with other assets, housing is very illiquid—it may take months or years for a homeowner to sell his or her home, especially in a recession. However, the availability of home equity loans and home equity lines of credit permits households to quickly borrow money against a portion of the value of their house. There is, of course, no specified time to maturity on housing, as it is not a financial security.

Households also hold some of their wealth in the form of consumer durable goods, such as automobiles, furniture, and appliances. As in the case of housing, durable goods provide services (such as transportation) over a period of time but may also require maintenance expenditures and will depreciate over time. There is some risk to the value of consumer durables, and it may be difficult and costly to sell them, as the market for consumer durables is not as well developed as the market for stocks and bonds. Thus, consumer durables are not very liquid and, like housing, have no specified time to maturity.

Households must determine what mix of these various assets is ideal for them. Wealthier households generally purchase more financial assets (stocks and bonds) as a percentage of their total wealth than do poorer households. Many households will also put aside funds for retirement by holding assets in pension funds, which hold stocks, bonds, and types of money (such as money market mutual funds). Of course, their mix of different assets will typically change over time; younger households commit most of their savings toward the purchase of their first home, while older households target the purchase of financial assets in preparation for retirement.

ASSET DEMANDS

Typically, there is a trade-off among the three characteristics that make an asset desirable: a high expected return, safety (low risk), and liquidity. For example, a safe and liquid asset, such as a chequing account, is likely to have a low expected return. The essence of the portfolio allocation decision is determining which assets, taken together, achieve the wealth holder's preferred combination of expected return, safety, and liquidity.

The amount of each particular asset that a holder of wealth desires to include in her portfolio is called her demand for that asset. Because all wealth must be held as some type of asset, the sum of a wealth holder's asset demands must equal her total wealth. For example, suppose you have wealth of $10 000 and decide to hold $5000 in stock, $4000 in bonds, and $1000 in cash. The sum of your three asset demands must equal your total wealth of $10 000.

APPLICATION

THE U.S. HOUSING CRISIS AND ITS AFTERMATH

Many people at various times have come to believe that there is no risk in holding their wealth as housing. This mistaken belief was reinforced during the late 1990s and most of the 2000s when housing prices in the United States and in Canada (and in many other countries) increased quickly and for a prolonged period. The rapid increase in the value of housing wealth made people anxious to secure mortgages at the very limit of their ability to afford them. In part they did so because they felt that if anything should go wrong—say, they lost their job, or the interest rate on their mortgage increased—they could always sell the house at a sizeable profit. Unfortunately, when an unexpected downturn in housing prices occurred in late 2007 in the United States and in late 2008 in Canada, the risk of home ownership turned out to be much higher than previously thought.

Figure 7.1 shows the year-over-year percentage increase in house prices in Canada and the United States from 1993Q1 to 2016Q3. Over the entire period, house prices increased by an average of 2.4% per year in Canada and 3.4% per year in the United States. However, as the figure shows, these averages hide some dramatic swings in year-over-year changes in prices. From the beginning of 2000 to the end of 2006,

FIGURE 7.1

INCREASE IN HOUSE PRICES FROM ONE YEAR EARLIER, 1993–2016

The figure shows quarterly data on the percentage increase in house prices from one year earlier in Canada and the United States. Over the entire period shown in the figure, house prices increased by an average of 2.4% per year in Canada and 3.4% per year in the United States. During this period, however, were times of much faster growth in house prices and also times of falling prices. Periods of unusually rapid increases concern policymakers, who worry that Canadians might become overly reliant on rising prices to secure ever larger mortgages.

Source: Data from the Federal Housing Finance Agency, *www.fhfa. gov* and Bank of Canada, *www.bankofcanada.ca.*

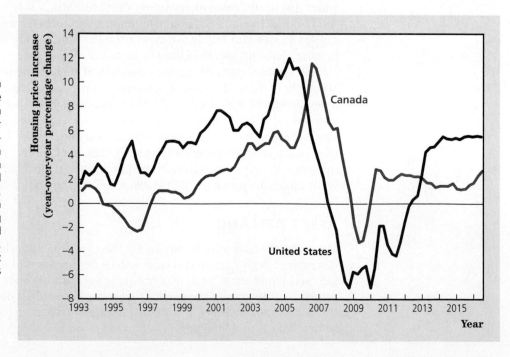

house prices increased by an average of 4.9% per year in Canada and 7.8% per year in the United States. These numbers represented strong rates of return on wealth and, not surprisingly, attracted buyers to the housing market. The resulting housing boom in the United States would prove to have long-reaching implications for world financial markets. What happened?

As housing prices moved higher and higher in the early 2000s in the United States, many people in that country found themselves unable to afford to buy a home because their monthly mortgage payments would be too high relative to monthly income. But as housing prices increased rapidly—in excess of 11% per year in 2005, for example—mortgage lenders began making loans to people who did not meet normal, or "prime," lending standards. These underqualified people were known as sub-prime borrowers. The sub-prime mortgage market grew rapidly. To compensate the lenders for the additional risk and potential costs of lending to sub-prime borrowers, the interest rate on sub-prime mortgages was higher than that on conventional, or prime, mortgages. In many cases, sub-prime lenders even dispensed with the usual income verification for borrowers, further subjecting themselves to the risk that borrowers would not be able to repay. In addition, some loans had creative features that gave the appearance that the borrower could afford to make the monthly payments, at least for a while. For instance, most sub-prime loans were adjustable-rate loans with a low initial interest rate that would increase after two or three years.

Why were lenders willing to offer these risky loans to sub-prime borrowers, and why were borrowers willing to take on these very risky obligations? To a large degree, the answer is that they expected house prices to continue to rise rapidly for the foreseeable future, just as they had in the recent past. Both borrowers and lenders thought they were insulated from risk because, even if the worst happened and borrowers could not repay their mortgages, the price of the house would have increased sufficiently that it could be sold for an amount in excess of the amount of the mortgage. Of course, this could be true only if house prices continued to rise substantially.

In 2005, as mortgage interest rates in the United States began to rise, the rate of increase in house prices began to slow. In 2006, defaults on sub-prime mortgages began to increase as the interest rates on sub-prime mortgages started to be adjusted upward following the initial period of low rates. More and more borrowers could no longer afford their mortgage payments and began to default. As defaults occurred in increasing numbers, banks started to tighten their lending standards; by mid-2007, they were making few if any sub-prime mortgage loans. But that in turn reduced the demand for houses, thus causing the increase in house prices to be even smaller. Eventually, prices actually began to fall in 2008, as shown in Figure 7.1.

Falling house prices in the United States caused a surprising variety of problems at both the micro and macro levels. Thousands of households that had bought houses with sub-prime mortgages lost their homes to foreclosure when they could not make their monthly payments. Homeowners often found themselves owning homes whose value had fallen below the amount they owed on their mortgages, giving them reason to simply stop making mortgage payments and allow their homes to be repossessed by the mortgage lender. The mortgage lender, usually a bank, would often have to sell the repossessed house for far less than the outstanding mortgage. Financial institutions lost billions of dollars on such deals.

What is most surprising about the problems in the U.S. mortgage market is that the impact was felt far more broadly. It turns out that most banks had sold bundles of their sub-prime mortgages in the form of mortgage-backed securities (MBSs), and investors in MBSs suffered large losses. When the losses began to materialize, investors trying all at once to bail out of such investments drove prices to very low levels. Financial institutions that had purchased MBSs were now suffering huge losses. Since many buyers of MBSs were from outside the United States, these losses spread internationally.

There had been signs early in 2007 that the U.S. financial system was in trouble. On February 27, 2007, the Federal Home Loan Mortgage Corporation[6] announced that it would no longer buy sub-prime mortgages. In April, a leading lender of sub-prime mortgages in the United States fell into bankruptcy. By August, short-term interest rates had jumped dramatically upward, reflecting questions regarding the value of the widely held MBSs. Financial institutions soon became wary of lending to one another; they were unsure who held risky MBSs and so was at risk of default. Firms reliant on the ability to borrow in order to finance their day-to-day operations quickly found it next to impossible to find a financial institution willing to lend to them. Borrowing and lending froze, followed by bankruptcies and fast-rising unemployment. Between October 2007 and February 2009 the U.S. stock market had fallen by more than 49% (as measured by the Dow Jones Industrial Index). Canada was not immune to the crisis that had begun in the United States—over the same period, the Toronto Stock Exchange (TSX) index fell by more than 44%. Financial markets around the world were seemingly under threat of collapse, and major firms were declaring bankruptcy. (Heretofore the largest carmaker in the world, General Motors, declared bankruptcy on June 1, 2009, as part of a restructuring that involved governments in Canada, the United States, and Ontario taking significant ownership shares.) World leaders and heads of the world's major central banks met to coordinate massive interventions designed to stabilize global financial markets. Although by the end of 2009 the worst of the financial crisis had passed, in its wake lay widespread bankruptcy, large government deficits, high unemployment rates, and the prospect of a long period of painful economic recovery.

While the definitive history of these recent events has yet to be written, many analysts emphasize that a major contributing factor was a failure of effective regulation in U.S. financial markets generally and the U.S. mortgage market in particular. Those who have studied the financial crisis have suggested that Canadian financial institutions avoided the worst of the financial crisis because regulation of the mortgage market by the Bank of Canada and the Office of the Superintendent of Financial Institutions (OSFI) discouraged the proliferation of sub-prime mortgages and thereby the development of MBSs, the complex financial instruments designed to make them more palatable to lenders. These stricter regulations meant that the sub-prime mortgage market remained small in Canada—equal to about 5% of mortgages versus 22% in the United States[7] For that reason, as the world considers what can be done to avoid a repeat of the 2007–2009 financial crisis, a good deal of attention is being paid to the regulations that guide the Canadian financial market.

This is not to say, however, that economists are unconcerned about the Canadian housing market. While the evidence shown in Figure 7.1 suggests that annual

[6] Popularly known as "Freddie Mac," this is a private company supported by the U.S. government and tasked with providing mortgages with advantageous interest rates and low down payments.
[7] For an accessible discussion of the differences in Canadian and U.S. housing market regulations, see James MacGee, "Not Here? Housing Market Policy and the Risk of a Housing Bust," *C.D. Howe Institute e-brief*, August 31, 2010.

increases in Canadian house prices have been relatively moderate since 2010, the truth is that the national average hides from view some very large rates of increase in certain cities. Since 2010 house prices in Toronto, for example, have grown at twice the national average. Given the size of that housing market and similarly fast-growing local housing markets elsewhere, a dramatic fall in prices could have wide-spread effects. For this reason, since 2010 the federal government has introduced a number of changes in mortgage lending rules meant to ensure home buyers do not take on bigger mortgages than they can afford. While these measures seem to have slowed the rate of housing price increases on average (see Figure 7.1), there remain local markets where prices continue to rise rapidly.

7.3 THE DEMAND FOR MONEY

The **demand for money** is the quantity of monetary assets, such as cash and chequing accounts, that people choose to hold in their portfolios. Choosing how much money to demand is, therefore, a part of the broader portfolio allocation decision. In general, the demand for money—like the demand for any other asset—will depend on the expected return, risk, liquidity, and time to maturity of money and of other assets.

In practice, two features of money are particularly important. First, money is the most liquid asset. This liquidity is the primary benefit of holding money.[8] Second, money pays a low return (indeed, currency pays a zero nominal return). The low return earned by money, relative to other assets, is the major cost of holding money. People's demand for money is determined by how they trade off their need for liquidity against the cost of a lower return.

In this section, we look at how some key macroeconomic variables affect the demand for money. Although we primarily consider the aggregate, or total, demand for money, the same economic arguments apply to individual money demands. This relation is to be expected, as the aggregate demand for money is the sum of all individual money demands.

The macroeconomic variables that have the greatest effects on money demand are the price level, real income, and interest rates. Higher prices or incomes increase people's need for liquidity and, thus, raise the demand for money. Interest rates affect money demand through the expected return channel: The higher the interest rate on money, the more money people will demand. However, the higher the interest rate paid on alternative assets to money, the more people will want to switch from money to those alternative assets.

THE PRICE LEVEL

The higher the general level of prices, the more dollars people need to conduct transactions and, thus, the more dollars people will want to hold. For example, 70 years ago, the price level in Canada was about one-tenth of its level today; as your grandfather will tell you, in 1945, a good restaurant meal cost a dollar. Because less money was needed for transactions, the number of dollars your grandfather held in the form of currency or chequing accounts—his nominal demand for money—was probably much smaller than the amount of money you hold today. The general conclusion is that a higher price level, by raising the need for liquidity,

---

[8] Money also has low risk, but many alternative assets (such as short-term government bonds) are no riskier than money and pay a higher return.

increases the nominal demand for money. In fact, because prices are 10 times higher today than they were in 1945, an identical transaction takes 10 times as many dollars today as it did back then. Thus, everything else being equal, the nominal demand for money is *proportional* to the price level.

REAL INCOME

The more transactions that individuals or businesses conduct, the more liquidity they need and the greater is their demand for money. An important factor determining the number of transactions is real income. For example, a large, high-volume supermarket has to deal with a larger number of customers and suppliers and pay more employees than does a corner grocery. Similarly, a high-income individual makes more and larger purchases than a low-income individual. Because higher real income means more transactions and a greater need for liquidity, the amount of money demanded should increase when real income increases.

Unlike the response of money demand to changes in the price level, the increase in money demand need not be proportional to an increase in real income. Actually, a 1% increase in real income usually leads to less than a 1% increase in money demand. One reason why money demand grows more slowly than income is that higher-income individuals and firms typically use their money more efficiently. For example, a high-income individual may open a special cash management account in which money not needed for current transactions is automatically invested in nonmonetary assets paying a higher return. Because of minimum-balance requirements and fees, such an account might not be worthwhile for a lower-income individual.

Another reason why money demand grows more slowly than income is that nations' financial sophistication tends to increase as national income grows. In poor countries, people may hold much of their savings in the form of money, for lack of anything better; in richer countries, people have many attractive alternatives to money. Money substitutes, such as credit cards, also become more common as a country becomes richer, again leading to aggregate money demand growing more slowly than income.

INTEREST RATES

The theory of portfolio allocation implies that with risk and liquidity held constant, the demand for money depends on the expected returns of both money and alternative, nonmonetary assets. An increase in the expected return on money increases the demand for money, and an increase in the expected return on alternative assets causes holders of wealth to switch from money to higher-return alternatives, thus lowering the demand for money.

For example, suppose that of your total wealth of $10000, you have $8000 in government bonds earning 8% interest and $2000 in an interest-bearing chequing account earning 3%. You are willing to hold the bank account at a lower return because of the liquidity it provides. But if the interest rate on bonds rises to 10%, and the bank account interest rate remains unchanged, you may decide to switch $1000 from the bank account into bonds. In making this switch, you reduce your holding of money (your money demand) from $2000 to $1000. Effectively, you have chosen to trade some liquidity for the higher return offered by bonds.

Similarly, if the interest rate paid on money rises, holders of wealth will choose to hold more money. In the example, if the bank account begins paying 5% instead of 3%, with bonds still at 8%, you may sell $1000 of your bonds, lowering your holdings of bonds to $7000 and increasing your bank balance to $3000. The sacrifice in return associated with holding money is less than before, so you increase your bank account balance and enjoy the flexibility and other benefits of extra liquidity. Thus, a higher interest rate on money makes the demand for money rise.

In principle, the interest rate on each of the many alternatives to money should affect money demand. However, as previously noted, the many interest rates in the economy generally tend to move up and down together. For the purposes of macroeconomic analysis, therefore, assuming that there is just one nominal interest rate, i, that measures the nominal return on nonmonetary assets is simpler and not too misleading. The nominal interest rate i minus the expected inflation rate π^e gives the expected real interest rate r that is relevant to saving and investment decisions, as discussed in Chapter 4.

Also, in reality, various interest rates are paid on money. For example, currency pays zero interest, but different types of chequable accounts pay varying rates. Again for simplicity, let's assume that there is just one nominal interest rate for money, i^m. The key conclusions are that an increase in the interest rate on nonmonetary assets, i, reduces the amount of money demanded, and an increase in the interest rate on money, i^m, raises the amount of money demanded.

THE MONEY DEMAND FUNCTION

We express the effects of the price level, real income, and interest rates on money as

$$M^d = P \times L(Y, i), \tag{7.1}$$

where

$\quad M^d$ = the aggregate demand for money, in nominal terms;

$\quad P$ = the price level;

$\quad Y$ = real income or output;

$\quad i$ = the nominal interest rate earned by alternative, nonmonetary assets;

$\quad L$ = a function relating money demand to real income and the nominal interest rate.

Equation (7.1) holds that nominal money demand M^d is proportional to the price level P. Hence, if the price level P doubles (and real income and interest rates do not change), nominal money demand M^d will also double, reflecting the fact that twice as much money is needed to conduct the same real transactions. Equation (7.1) also indicates that for any price level P, money demand depends (through the function L) on real income Y and the nominal interest rate on nonmonetary assets i. An increase in real income Y raises the demand for liquidity and, thus, increases money demand. An increase in the nominal interest rate i makes nonmonetary assets more attractive, which reduces money demand.

We could have included the nominal interest rate on money, i^m, in Eq. (7.1) because an increase in the interest rate on money makes people more willing to hold it, and therefore increases money demand. Historically, however, since the nominal interest rate on money has varied much less than the nominal interest rate on nonmonetary assets (for example, currency and a portion of chequing accounts have always paid zero interest), it has been ignored by many statistical studies of Eq. (7.1). Thus, for simplicity, we do not explicitly include i^m in the equation.

An equivalent way of writing the demand for money expresses the nominal interest rate i in terms of the expected real interest rate and the expected rate of inflation. Recall from Eq. (2.13) that the expected real interest rate r equals the nominal interest rate i minus the expected rate of inflation π^e. Therefore, the nominal interest rate i equals $r + \pi^e$. Substituting $r + \pi^e$ for i in Eq. (7.1) yields

$$M^d = PL(Y, r + \pi^e). \tag{7.2}$$

Equation (7.2) shows that for any expected rate of inflation π^e, an increase in the real interest rate increases the nominal interest rate and reduces the demand for money. Similarly, for any real interest rate, an increase in the expected rate of inflation increases the nominal interest rate and reduces the demand for money.

Nominal money demand M^d measures the demand for money in terms of dollars (or yen, or euros). But, sometimes, measuring money demand in real terms is more convenient. If we divide both sides of Eq. (7.2) by the price level P, we get

$$\frac{M^d}{P} = L(Y, r + \pi^e). \tag{7.3}$$

The expression on the left-hand side of Eq. (7.3), M^d/P, is called real money demand or, sometimes, the demand for real balances. Real money demand is the amount of money demanded in terms of the goods it can buy. Equation (7.3) states that real money demand M^d/P depends on real income (or output) Y and on the nominal interest rate, which is the sum of the real interest rate r and expected inflation π^e. The function L that relates real money demand to output and interest rates in Eq. (7.3) is called the **money demand function**.

OTHER FACTORS AFFECTING MONEY DEMAND

The money demand function in Eq. (7.3) captures the main macroeconomic determinants of money demand, but some other factors should be mentioned. Besides the nominal interest rate on money, which we have already discussed, additional factors influencing money demand include wealth, risk, liquidity of alternative assets, and payment technologies. Summary table 9 contains a comprehensive list of variables that affect the demand for money.

Wealth

When wealth increases, part of the extra wealth may be held as money, increasing total money demand. However, with income and the level of transactions held constant, a holder of wealth has little incentive to keep extra wealth in money rather than in higher-return alternative assets. Thus, the effect of an increase in wealth on money demand is likely to be small.

Risk

Money usually pays a fixed nominal interest rate (zero in the case of cash), so holding money itself isn't usually risky. However, if the risk of alternative assets, such as stocks and real estate, increases greatly, people may demand safer assets, including money. Thus, increased riskiness in the economy may increase money demand.

However, money does not always carry a low risk. In a period of erratic inflation, even if the nominal return on money is fixed, the real return on money (the nominal return minus inflation) may become quite uncertain, making money risky. Money demand then will fall as people switch to inflation hedges (assets whose real returns are less likely to be affected by erratic inflation), such as gold, consumer durable goods, and real estate.

SUMMARY 9

MACROECONOMIC DETERMINANTS OF THE DEMAND FOR MONEY

ALL ELSE EQUAL, AN INCREASE IN	CAUSES MONEY DEMAND TO	REASON
Price level, P	Rise proportionally	A doubling of the price level doubles the number of dollars needed for transactions.
Real income, Y	Rise less than proportionally	Higher real income implies more transactions and thus a greater demand for liquidity.
Real interest rate, r	Fall	A higher real interest rate means a higher return on alternative assets and thus a switch away from money.
Real interest rate, π^e	Fall	Higher expected inflation means a higher return on alternative assets and thus a switch away from money.
Nominal interest rate on money, i^m	Rise	A higher return on money makes people more willing to hold money.
Wealth	Rise	Part of an increase in wealth may be held in the form of money.
Risk	Rise, if risk of alternative assets increases	Higher risk of alternative assets makes money more attractive.
	Fall, if risk of money increases	Higher risk of money makes it less attractive.
Liquidity of alternative assets	Fall	Higher liquidity of alternative assets makes these assets more attractive.
Efficiency of payments technologies	Fall	People can operate with less money.

Liquidity of Alternative Assets

The more quickly and easily alternative assets can be converted into cash, the less need there is to hold money. In recent years, the joint impact of deregulation, competition, and innovation in financial markets has made alternatives to money more liquid. We have mentioned individual cash management accounts whose introduction allowed individuals to switch wealth easily between high-return assets, such as stocks, and more liquid forms. As alternative assets become more liquid, the demand for money declines.

PAYMENT TECHNOLOGIES

A last factor affecting money demand is the technology available for making and receiving payments. For example, the introduction of credit cards allowed people to make transactions without money—at least until the end of the month, when a cheque must be written to pay the credit card bill. Automated teller machines (ATMs) have probably reduced the demand for cash because people know that they can obtain cash quickly whenever they need it. Other innovations like direct payment systems (debit cards) are also undoubtedly reducing the demand for cash. Ultimately, we may live in a "cashless society," in which almost all payments will be made through immediately accessible computerized accounting systems and the demand for traditional forms of money will be close to zero.

ELASTICITIES OF MONEY DEMAND

The theory of portfolio allocation helps economists identify factors that should affect the aggregate demand for money. However, for many purposes—such as forecasting and quantitative analyses of the economy—economists need to know not just which factors affect money demand but also how strong the various effects are. This information can be obtained only through statistical analysis of the data.

Over the past three decades, economists have performed hundreds of statistical studies of the money demand function. The results of these studies are often expressed in terms of elasticities, which measure the change in money demand resulting from changes in factors affecting the demand for money. Specifically, the **income elasticity of money demand** is the percentage change in money demand resulting from a 1% increase in real income. Thus, for example, if the income elasticity of money demand is 2/3, a 3% increase in real income will increase money demand by 2% (2/3 × 3% = 2%). Similarly, the **interest elasticity of money demand** is the percentage change in money demand resulting from a 1% increase in the interest rate.

When we work with the interest elasticity of money demand, some care is needed to avoid a potential pitfall. To illustrate, suppose that the interest rate increases from 5% per year to 6% per year. To describe this increase in the interest rate as a 1% increase in the interest rate is tempting (but incorrect). In fact, it is a 20% increase in the interest rate, because 6 is 20% larger than 5.[9] If the interest elasticity of money demand is −0.1, for example, an increase in the interest rate from 5% to 6% reduces money demand by 2% (−0.1 × 20% = −2%). Note that if the interest elasticity of money demand is negative, as in this example, an increase in the interest rate reduces money demand.

What are the actual values of the income elasticity and interest elasticity of money demand? Although the many statistical studies of money demand provide a range of answers, some common results emerge. First, there is widespread evidence that the income elasticity of money demand is positive. Most studies suggest a value of about 0.5. A positive income elasticity of money demand implies that money demand rises when income rises, as predicted by our theory. An income elasticity of money demand smaller than 1 implies that money demand rises less than proportionally with income. Earlier in the chapter, we discussed some reasons why the demand for money might be expected to grow more slowly than income as an individual or nation becomes richer.

Second, for the interest elasticity of money demand, most estimates suggest of a value of about −0.3. A negative value for the interest elasticity of money demand implies that when interest rates on nonmonetary assets rise, people reduce their holdings of money, again as predicted by the theory.

Finally, many studies have confirmed empirically that the nominal demand for money is proportional to the price level. Again, this result is consistent with the theory, as reflected in the money demand equation, Eq. (7.3).

[9] The change from 5% to 6% can be described as "a 1 *percentage point* increase," or as "a 20 *percent* increase," or as a "100 *basis point* increase."

VELOCITY AND THE QUANTITY THEORY OF MONEY

A concept related to money demand, which at times is used in discussions of monetary policy, is velocity. It measures how often the money stock "turns over" each period. Specifically, **velocity** is nominal GDP (the price level P times real output Y) divided by the nominal money stock M. If we let V represent velocity,

$$V = \frac{\text{nominal GDP}}{\text{nominal money stock}} = \frac{PY}{M}. \tag{7.4}$$

If velocity rises, each dollar of the money stock is being used in a greater dollar volume of transactions in each period, if we assume that the volume of transactions is proportional to GDP. Figure 7.2 shows the M1+ and M2 velocities for Canada during the period 1975–2016. The concept of velocity comes from one of the earliest theories of money demand, the **quantity theory of money**.[10] The quantity theory of money asserts that real money demand is proportional to real income, or

$$\frac{M^d}{P} = kY, \tag{7.5}$$

where M^d/P is real money demand, Y is real income, and k is a constant. In Eq. (7.5), the real money demand function $L(Y, r + \pi^e)$ takes the simple form kY. This way of writing money demand is based on the strong assumption that velocity is a constant, $1/k$, and does not depend on income or interest rates.[11]

Is velocity actually a constant? As Figure 7.2 shows, M1+ velocity is clearly not a constant: It rose steadily during the late 1970s, then became more volatile in the 1980s, before declining more or less steadily since then. Financial innovations played a role in

FIGURE 7.2

VELOCITY OF M1+ AND M2, 1975–2016

M1+ velocity is nominal GDP divided by M1+, and M2 velocity is nominal GDP divided by M2. The velocity of M1+ increased in the late 1970s before falling sharply in the early 1980s. Since then it has fallen more or less continuously. M2 velocity has been more stable than M1+ velocity, but it has been unpredictable over short time periods.

Source: Adapted from Statistics Canada CANSIM 2016. This does not constitute an endorsement by Statistics Canada of this product.

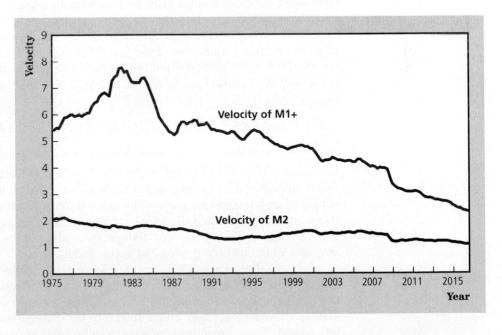

[10] The quantity theory of money was developed by several classical economists, notably Irving Fisher, in the late 19th and early 20th centuries. A famous statement of the theory is contained in Fisher's book *The Purchasing Power of Money*, New York: Macmillan, 1911.

[11] To derive velocity under the quantity theory, we must assume that nominal money demand M^d equals the actual money stock M, an assumption that we justify later in the chapter. Under this assumption, you should verify that $V = 1/k$.

slowing the growth of M1+ velocity in the 1980s. As discussed, the popularity of new interest-bearing chequing accounts during this period raised the demand for M1+ at any level of GDP and thereby lowered its velocity. But, in addition, the quantity theory's assumption that interest rates do not affect money demand—an assumption contradicted by most empirical studies—probably contributed to a fall in the velocity of M1+. That is, lower interest rates on nonmonetary assets in the 1990s and 2000s increased people's willingness to hold low-interest or zero-interest money, which raised the demand for M1+ at any level of GDP and thus reduced M1+ velocity.

M2 velocity, also shown in Figure 7.2, is more stable. It shows a gradual downward trend over the period 1975–1993 before levelling off. However, even M2 velocity has been somewhat unpredictable over short periods, and most economists would be reluctant to treat M2 velocity as a constant. During the late 1990s, for example, the velocity of M2 increased slightly before taking a noticeable fall in 2008 during the financial crisis. Figure 7.2 identifies a similar fall in the velocity of M1+ at that time. Velocity fell during this period as people shifted their wealth back into cash and bank accounts and out of stocks and mutual funds.

7.4 ASSET MARKET EQUILIBRIUM

Recall that the asset market is actually a set of markets, in which real and financial assets are traded. The demand for any asset (say, government bonds) is the quantity of the asset that holders of wealth want in their portfolios. The demand for each asset depends on its expected return, risk, and liquidity relative to other assets. The supply of each asset is the quantity of that asset that is available. At any particular time, the supplies of individual assets are typically fixed, although over time asset supplies change (the government may issue more bonds, firms may issue new shares, more gold may be mined, and so on).

The asset market is in equilibrium when the quantity of each asset that holders of wealth demand equals the (fixed) available supply of that asset. In this section, we examine asset market equilibrium, focusing on the role of money. We then show how asset market equilibrium is linked to the price level.

ASSET MARKET EQUILIBRIUM: AN AGGREGATION ASSUMPTION

In analyzing the labour market in Chapter 3 and the goods market in Chapter 4, we relied on aggregation to keep things manageable. That is, instead of looking at the supply of and demand for each of the many different types of labour and goods in the economy, we studied the supply of and demand for both labour and goods in general. Aggregating in this way allowed us to analyze the behaviour of the economy as a whole without getting lost in the details.

Because there are many different types of assets, aggregation is equally necessary for studying the asset market. Thus, we adopt an aggregation assumption for the asset market that economists often make for macroeconomic analysis: We assume that all assets may be grouped into two categories, money and nonmonetary assets. Money includes assets that can be used in payment, such as currency and chequing accounts. All money is assumed to have the same risk and liquidity and to pay the same nominal interest rate, i^m. The fixed nominal supply of money is M. Nonmonetary assets include all assets other than money, such as stocks, bonds, land, and so on. All nonmonetary assets are assumed to have the same risk and liquidity and to pay a nominal interest rate of $i = r + \pi^e$, where r is the expected real interest rate and π^e is the expected rate of inflation. The fixed nominal supply of nonmonetary assets is NM.

Although the assumption that assets can be aggregated into two types ignores many interesting differences among assets, it greatly simplifies our analysis and has proved to be very useful. One immediate benefit of making this assumption is that if we allow for only two types of assets, *asset market equilibrium reduces to the condition that the quantity of money supplied equals the quantity of money demanded.*

To demonstrate this point, let's look at the portfolio allocation decision of an individual named Ed. Ed has a fixed amount of wealth that he allocates between money and nonmonetary assets. If m^d is the nominal amount of money and nm^d is the nominal amount of nonmonetary assets that Ed wants to hold, the sum of Ed's desired money holdings and his desired holdings of nonmonetary assets must be his total wealth, or

$$m^d + nm^d = \text{Ed's total nominal wealth.}$$

This equation has to be true for every holder of wealth in the economy.

Suppose that we sum this equation across all holders of wealth in the economy. Then, the sum of all individual money demands m^d equals the aggregate demand for money M^d. The sum of all individual demands for nonmonetary assets is the aggregate demand for nonmonetary assets, NM^d. Finally, adding nominal wealth for all holders of wealth gives the aggregate nominal wealth of the economy, or

$$M^d + NM^d = \text{aggregate nominal wealth.} \tag{7.6}$$

Equation (7.6) states that the total demand for money in the economy plus the total demand for nonmonetary assets must equal the economy's total nominal wealth.

Next, we relate the total supplies of money and nonmonetary assets to aggregate wealth. Because money and nonmonetary assets are the only assets in the economy, aggregate nominal wealth equals the supply of money M plus the supply of nonmonetary assets NM, or

$$M + NM = \text{aggregate nominal wealth.} \tag{7.7}$$

Finally, we subtract Eq. (7.7) from Eq. (7.6) to obtain

$$(M^d - M) + (NM^d - NM) = 0. \tag{7.8}$$

The term $M^d - M$ in Eq. (7.8) is the *excess demand for money*, or the amount by which the total amount of money demanded exceeds the money supply. Similarly, the term $NM^d - NM$ in Eq. (7.8) is the *excess demand for nonmonetary assets*.

Now, suppose that the demand for money M^d equals the money supply M so that the excess demand for money $M^d - M$ is zero. Equation (7.8) shows that if $M^d - M$ is zero, $NM^d - NM$ must also be zero; that is, if the amounts of money supplied and demanded are equal, the amounts of nonmonetary assets supplied and demanded also must be equal. By definition, if quantities supplied and demanded are equal for each type of asset, the asset market is in equilibrium.

If we make the simplifying assumption that assets can be lumped into monetary and nonmonetary categories, the asset market is in equilibrium only if the quantity of money supplied equals the quantity of money demanded. This result is convenient because it means that in studying asset market equilibrium, we only have to look at the supply of and demand for money and can ignore nonmonetary assets. As long as the amounts of money supplied and demanded are equal, the entire asset market will be in equilibrium.

THE ASSET MARKET EQUILIBRIUM CONDITION

Equilibrium in the asset market occurs when the quantity of money supplied equals the quantity of money demanded. This condition is valid whether money supply and demand are expressed in nominal terms or real terms. We work with this condition in real terms, or

$$\frac{M}{P} = L(Y, r + \pi^e). \tag{7.9}$$

The left-hand side of Eq. (7.9) is the nominal supply of money M divided by the price level P, which is the supply of money measured in real terms. The right-hand side of the equation is the same as the real demand for money M^d/P, as in Eq. (7.3). Equation (7.9), which states that the real quantity of money supplied equals the real quantity of money demanded, is called the asset market equilibrium condition.

The asset market equilibrium condition involves five variables: the nominal money supply M, the price level P, real income Y, the real interest rate r, and the expected rate of inflation π^e. The nominal money supply M is determined by the central bank through its open-market operations. For now, we treat the expected rate of inflation π^e as fixed (we return to the determination of expected inflation later in the chapter). That leaves three variables in the asset market equilibrium condition whose values we have not yet specified: output Y, the real interest rate r, and the price level P.

In this part of the book, we have made the assumption that the economy is at full employment or, equivalently, that all markets are in equilibrium. Both classical and Keynesian economists agree that the full-employment assumption is reasonable for analyzing the long-term behaviour of the economy. If we continue to assume full employment,[12] we can use the analysis from previous chapters to describe how output and the real interest rate are determined. Recall from Chapter 3 that if the labour market is in equilibrium—with employment at its full-employment level—output equals full-employment output Y. Chapter 4 showed that in a closed economy, for any level of output, the real interest rate must take the value that makes desired national saving and desired investment equal (the goods market equilibrium condition). Chapter 5 demonstrated that in open economies, for any level of real output, the real interest rate is determined in world financial markets and any imbalance between desired national saving and desired national investment is bridged by foreign borrowing or foreign lending (the goods market equilibrium in an open economy).

With the values of output and the real interest rate established by equilibrium in the labour and goods markets, the only variable left to be determined by the asset market equilibrium condition is the price level P. To emphasize that the price level is the variable determined by asset market equilibrium, we multiply both sides of Eq. (7.9) by P and divide both sides by real money demand, $L(Y, r + \pi^e)$, to obtain

$$P = \frac{M}{L(Y, r + \pi^e)}. \tag{7.10}$$

According to Eq. (7.10), the economy's price level P equals the ratio of the nominal money supply M to the real demand for money $L(Y, r + \pi^e)$. For given

---

[12] We relax this assumption in Part III when we discuss short-run economic fluctuations.

values of real output Y, the real interest rate r, and the expected rate of inflation π^e, the real demand for money $L(Y, r + \pi^e)$ is fixed. Thus, Eq. (7.10) states that the price level is proportional to the nominal money supply. A doubling of the nominal money supply M, for instance, would double the price level P, with other factors held constant. The existence of a close link between the price level and the money supply in an economy is one of the oldest and most reliable conclusions about macroeconomic behaviour, having been recognized in some form for hundreds if not thousands of years. We discuss the empirical support for this link in Section 7.5.

What forces lead the price level to its equilibrium value, Eq. (7.10)? A complete description of how the price level adjusts to its equilibrium value involves an analysis of the goods market as well as the asset market; we leave this task until Chapter 9, where we discuss the links among the three main markets of the economy in more detail. Briefly, in Chapter 9, we show that an increase in the money supply leads people to increase their nominal spending on goods and services; this increased nominal demand for output leads prices to rise. Prices continue to rise until people are content to hold the increased nominal quantity of money in their portfolios, satisfying the asset market equilibrium condition (rewritten as Eq. 7.10).

7.5 MONEY GROWTH AND INFLATION

In Section 7.4, we established that when the markets for labour, goods, and assets are all in equilibrium, the price level P is proportional to the nominal money supply M. However, the price level itself is generally of less concern to policymakers and the public than is the rate of inflation, or the percentage rate of increase of the price level. In this section, we extend our analysis of the price level to show how inflation is determined. We conclude that the inflation rate, which is the growth rate of the price level, is closely related to the growth rate of the nominal money supply.

To obtain an equation for the rate of inflation in a full employment economy, we set the growth rate of the left-hand side of Eq. (7.10) equal to the growth rate of its right-hand side to obtain

$$\frac{\Delta P}{P} = \frac{\Delta M}{M} - \frac{\Delta L(Y, r + \pi^e)}{L(Y, r + \pi^e)} \qquad (7.11)$$

where the symbol Δ indicates the change in a variable from one year to the next. The left-hand side of Eq. (7.11) is the growth rate of the price level, $\Delta P/P$, which is the same as the inflation rate π. The right-hand side of Eq. (7.11) expresses the growth rate of the ratio on the right-hand side of Eq. (7.10) as the growth rate of the numerator, M, minus the growth rate of the denominator, $L(Y, r + \pi^e)$. (Appendix Section A.7 provides some useful formulas for calculating growth rates.) Equation (7.11) shows that if the asset market is in equilibrium, *the rate of inflation equals the growth rate of the nominal money supply minus the growth rate of real money demand.*

Equation (7.11) highlights the point that the rate of inflation is closely related to the rate of growth of the nominal money supply. However, to use Eq. (7.11) to predict the behaviour of inflation, we must also know how quickly real money demand is growing. The money demand function, Eq. (7.3), focused on two macroeconomic variables with significant effects on real money demand: income (or output) Y and the nominal interest rate $r + \pi^e$. We show later in this section that in a long-run equilibrium with a constant growth rate of money, the nominal interest rate will be constant. Therefore, here we look only at growth in income as a source of growth in real money demand.

Earlier, we defined the income elasticity of money demand to be the percentage change in money demand resulting from a 1% increase in real income. If $\Delta Y/Y$ is the percentage change in real income from one year to the next and η_Y is the income elasticity of money demand, $\eta_Y \Delta Y/Y$ is the resulting increase in the real demand for money, with other factors affecting money demand held constant. Substituting π for $\Delta P/P$ and $\eta_Y \Delta Y/Y$ for the growth rate of real money demand in Eq. (7.11) yields

$$\pi = \frac{\Delta M}{M} - \eta_Y \frac{\Delta Y}{Y}. \qquad (7.12)$$

Equation (7.12) is a useful simple expression for the rate of inflation. According to Eq. (7.12), the rate of inflation equals the growth rate of the nominal money supply minus an adjustment for the growth rate of real money demand arising from growth in real output. For example, suppose that nominal money supply growth is 10% per year, real income is growing by 3% per year, and the income elasticity of money demand is 2/3. Then, Eq. (7.12) predicts that the inflation rate will be 10% − (2/3)(3%), or 8% per year.

THE EXPECTED INFLATION RATE AND THE NOMINAL INTEREST RATE

In our earlier discussion of asset market equilibrium, we made the assumption that the expected inflation rate is fixed. For a given real interest rate r (which is determined by the goods market equilibrium condition), if the expected inflation rate π^e is fixed, so is the nominal interest rate, at $r + \pi^e$. We close the chapter with a brief look at the factors that determine the expected inflation rate and the nominal interest rate.

What should holders of wealth and others expect the inflation rate to be in the future? As we demonstrated, Eq. (7.12), which relates inflation to the growth rates of the nominal money supply and real income, is useful for predicting inflation. For expected values of money growth (based, for example, on plans announced by the central bank) and real income growth, as well as an estimate of the income elasticity of money demand, Eq. (7.12) can be used to calculate the expected inflation rate. Suppose that people in a particular country expect their nation's money supply to grow much more rapidly over the next two years because the government is committed to large military expenditures and can pay for these expenditures only by printing money. In this case, Eq. (7.12) shows that people should expect much higher inflation rates in the future.

The inflation prediction equation, Eq. (7.12), is particularly easy to apply when the growth rates of the nominal money supply and real income are constant over time. In this case, the expected growth rates of the nominal money supply and real income equal their current growth rates, and (from Eq. 7.12) the expected inflation rate equals the current inflation rate (assuming no change in the income elasticity of money demand). In practice, the current inflation rate often approximates the expected inflation rate, as long as people do not expect money or income growth to change too much in the near future.

The public's expected inflation rate is not directly observable. (As explained in A Closer Look 7.1, the Bank of Canada employs a number of methods to gain insight into inflationary expectations.) However, an observable economic variable that is strongly affected by expected inflation is the nominal interest rate. At any real interest rate r, which is determined by the goods market equilibrium condition that desired national saving equals desired investment, the nominal interest rate $r + \pi^e$ changes one-for-one with changes in the expected inflation rate π^e. Thus, policy actions (such as rapid expansion of the money supply) that cause people to fear future increases in inflation should cause nominal interest rates to rise, all else being equal.

But, as already noted, if people do not expect large changes in the growth rates of the money supply or real income, expected inflation will not be much different from current inflation. In this case, nominal interest rates and current inflation rates should move together. If current inflation is high, for example, expected inflation is also likely to be high; but high expected inflation also causes nominal interest rates to be high, all else being equal.

The historical relationship between nominal interest rates and inflation is illustrated by Figure 7.3, which shows the nominal interest rate on one- to three-year Government of Canada bonds and the annual inflation rate measured by the CPI in Canada from the first quarter of 1960 to the fourth quarter of 2016. The nominal interest rate and the inflation rate have tended to move together, rising during the

A CLOSER LOOK 7.1

MEASURING INFLATION EXPECTATIONS

We noted in Chapter 2 that the expected real interest rate r is the correct interest rate to use for studying most types of economic decisions. This was emphasized again in Chapters 4 and 5, where we saw that the expected real interest rate is an important consideration for decisions related to consumption, saving, and investment. In this chapter we have learned that because the expected real interest rate r equals the nominal rate i minus the expected rate of inflation π^e, the demand for money can be equivalently expressed as a function of the nominal interest rate or as the sum of the expected real interest rate and expected inflation. Thus, Eqs. (7.1) and (7.2) are equivalent statements about the demand for money.

The importance of the expected real interest rate for so many key economic relationships is awkward, given that, as we first noted in Chapter 2, it is not a variable that economists measure with any great deal of accuracy. This problem of measurement arises because although it is straightforward to observe the nominal interest rate i, inflation expectations π^e are not directly observable.

Undaunted, economists at the Bank of Canada have developed a number of methods to gain insights into both inflationary expectations and the expected real interest rate. One approach is to simply ask people what their expectations are for inflation. The answers to these surveys are reported on the Bank of Canada's website at *www.bank-banque-canada.ca*.

A second way in which the Bank of Canada gains insight into inflation expectations is to compare the nominal yields on two different types of Government of Canada bonds. One is a conventional long-term bond. Owners of conventional bonds know in advance the bond's nominal yield to maturity. They do not, however, know in advance what will be the bond's real yield to maturity because that depends on the rate of inflation experienced during the time the bond is owned. The other type of bond is a real return bond. Owners of real return bonds know in advance the bond's real yield to maturity. The nominal yield to maturity varies with changes in the rate of inflation in such a way as to yield a constant real yield. By subtracting the variable nominal yield on the real return bond from the fixed nominal yield on the conventional bond, the Bank can therefore obtain a measure of inflation expectations.

Figure 7.4 shows the Bank of Canada's calculation of the difference in interest rates on real return and conventional bonds. The graph suggests that following a rapid fall beginning in August 2008 and ending in July 2009, inflation expectations increased quickly back to where they were in 2008. The graph also identifies the Bank of Canada's target band for inflation; the Bank's goal is to keep inflation between 1% and 3%. Although expectations of inflation have been kept within the target band, in 1999, 2004, and 2009 they threatened to break through the target band. Each time, the Bank of Canada was able to use monetary policy to moderate inflation expectations and move them back toward the middle of its target band.

FIGURE 7.3

INFLATION AND THE NOMINAL
INTEREST RATE IN CANADA,
1960–2016

The figure shows the nominal interest rate on one- to three-year federal government bonds and the
annual rate of inflation as measured by the CPI. The nominal
interest rate tends to move
together with inflation, although
there are periods, such as the early
1980s and mid-1990s, when the
two variables diverge.

Source: Adapted from Statistics
Canada, 2016. This does not constitute
an endorsement by Statistics Canada of
this product.

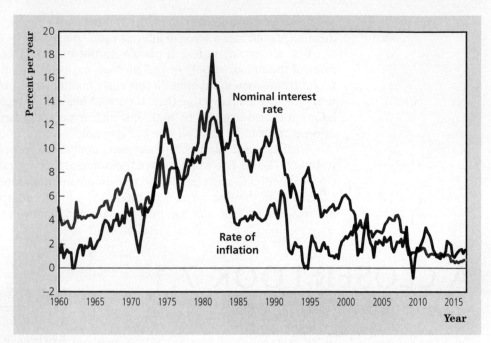

1960s and 1970s and then falling sharply after reaching a peak in 1981. However, movements in the inflation rate are not perfectly matched by movements in the nominal interest rate because the real interest rate has not been constant over this period. In particular, during the late 1970s and early 1980s, the rise in the nominal interest rate was much greater than the rise in the inflation rate, reflecting an increase in the real interest rate from a negative value in the mid-1970s to much higher, positive values in the 1980s. (See Figure 2.2, p. 41, for a graph of the real interest rate.)

FIGURE 7.4

A MEASURE OF INFLATION
EXPECTATIONS

The figure shows monthly data on
the difference in nominal yields
paid to owners of two types of
Government of Canada bonds: a
long-term conventional bond and a
real return bond. This difference
provides an estimate of inflation
expectations. By this estimate,
inflation expectations fell quickly
during the late 1990s but have
been increasing slowly since.

Source: Bank of Canada.

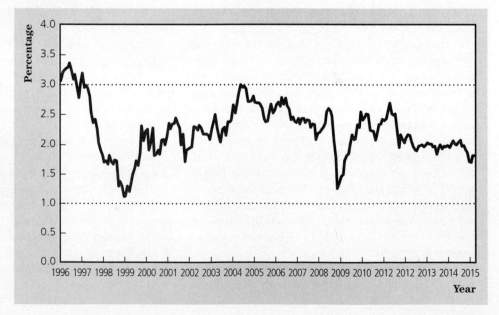

CHAPTER SUMMARY

1. Money is the set of assets that are widely used and accepted as payment, such as currency and chequing accounts. Money functions as a medium of exchange, a unit of account, and a store of value.

2. The supply of money is influenced by the central bank—the Bank of Canada. The central bank's official measures of money are called the monetary aggregates. M1+, which is made up primarily of currency and chequing accounts, and M2, which includes a broader set of monetary assets, are the monetary aggregates that are most widely watched.

3. A portfolio allocation decision is made by a holder of wealth when determining which assets and how much of each asset to hold. The three characteristics of assets that most affect their desirability are expected return, risk, and liquidity.

4. Money demand is the total amount of money that people choose to hold in their portfolios. The principal macroeconomic variables that affect money demand are the price level, real income, and interest rates. Nominal money demand is proportional to the price level. Higher real income increases the number of transactions and, thus, raises real money demand. A higher interest rate on alternative, nonmonetary assets lowers real money demand by making the alternative assets more attractive than money. The money demand function measures the relationship between real money demand and these macroeconomic variables.

5. Velocity is the ratio of nominal GDP to the nominal money stock. The quantity theory of money is an early theory of money demand that assumes that velocity is constant so that money demand is proportional to income. Historically, M2 velocity has been more stable than M1+ velocity, although even M2 velocity is not constant.

6. Under the simplifying assumption that assets can be grouped into two categories—money and nonmonetary assets—the asset market is in equilibrium if the quantity of money supplied equals the quantity of money demanded. When all markets are in equilibrium (the economy is at full employment), the level of output is determined by equilibrium in the labour market, the real interest rate is determined by equilibrium in the goods market, and the price level is determined by equilibrium in the asset market. The equilibrium price level is proportional to the nominal money supply.

7. When all markets are in equilibrium, the inflation rate equals the growth rate of the nominal money supply minus the growth rate of real money demand. The growth rate of real money demand, in turn, depends primarily on the real income growth rate. Expected inflation depends on expected growth rates of the nominal money supply and real income. For a given real interest rate, the nominal interest rate responds one-for-one to changes in expected inflation.

KEY TERMS

demand for money, p. 211
expectations theory of the term structure, p. 205
expected returns, p. 204
income elasticity of money demand, p. 216
interest elasticity of money demand, p. 216
liquidity, p. 204
M1+, p. 201
M2, p. 202
M3, p. 202
medium of exchange, p. 200
monetary aggregates, p. 201
money, p. 199
money demand function, p. 214
money supply, p. 202
open-market operations, p. 203
portfolio allocation decision, p. 204
quantity theory of money, p. 217
risk, p. 204
store of value, p. 201
term premium, p. 206
time to maturity, p. 205
unit of account, p. 200
velocity, p. 217

KEY EQUATIONS

$$\frac{M^d}{P} = L(Y, r + \pi^e) \qquad (7.3)$$

According to the money demand function, the real quantity of money demanded, M^d/P, depends on output and the nominal interest rate on alternative, nonmonetary assets. An increase in output, Y, raises the number of transactions people make and, thus, raises the demand for money. An increase in the nominal interest rate on nonmonetary assets, i (which equals the real interest rate, r, plus the expected rate of inflation, π^e) raises the attractiveness of alternative assets and, thus, reduces the demand for money.

$$V = \frac{\text{nominal GDP}}{\text{nominal money stock}} = \frac{PY}{M} \qquad (7.4)$$

Velocity V is nominal GDP, or P times Y, divided by the nominal money stock, M. Velocity is assumed to be constant by the quantity theory of money.

$$\frac{M}{P} = L(Y, r + \pi^e) \qquad (7.9)$$

The asset market equilibrium condition states that the real supply of money, M/P, and the real demand for money, $L(Y, r + \pi^e)$, are equal.

$$\pi = \frac{\Delta M}{M} - \eta_Y \frac{\Delta Y}{Y} \qquad (7.12)$$

The inflation rate, π, equals the growth rate of the nominal money supply, $\Delta M/M$, minus the growth rate of real money demand. The growth rate of real money demand equals the income elasticity of money demand, η_Y, times the growth rate of real income or output, $\Delta Y/Y$.

REVIEW QUESTIONS

1. Define *money*. How does the economist's use of this term differ from its everyday meaning?
2. What are the three functions of money? How does each function contribute to a more smoothly operating economy?
3. Who determines the country's money supply? Explain how the money supply could be expanded or reduced in an economy in which all money is in the form of currency.
4. What are the three characteristics of assets that are most important to holders of wealth? How does money compare with other assets for each characteristic?
5. List and discuss the macroeconomic variables that affect the aggregate demand for money.

6. Define *velocity*. Discuss the role of velocity in the quantity theory of money.
7. Why is equilibrium in the asset market described by the condition that real money supply equals real money demand? What is the aggregation assumption that is needed to allow ignoring the markets for other assets?
8. What is the relationship between the price level and the nominal money supply when all markets are in equilibrium? What is the relationship between inflation and the nominal money supply?
9. Give an example of a factor that would increase the public's expected rate of inflation. All else being equal, how would this increase in the expected inflation rate affect interest rates?

NUMERICAL PROBLEMS

1. Money demand in an economy in which no interest is paid on money is

$$\frac{M^d}{P} = 5000 + 0.2Y + 1000i.$$

   a. You know that $P = 100$, $Y = 1000$, and $i = 0.10$. Find real money demand, nominal money demand, and velocity.
   b. The price level doubles from $P = 100$ to $P = 200$. Find real money demand, nominal money demand, and velocity.
   c. Starting from the values of the variables given in part (a) and assuming that the money demand function as written holds, determine how velocity is affected by an increase in real income, by an increase in the nominal interest rate, and by an increase in the price level.
2. Mr. Midas has wealth of $100 000 that he invests entirely in money (a chequing account) and government bonds. Mr. Midas instructs his broker to invest $50 000 in bonds, plus $5000 more in bonds for every percentage point that the interest rate on bonds exceeds the interest rate on his chequing account.
   a. Write an algebraic formula that gives Mr. Midas's demand for money as a function of bond and chequing account interest rates.
   b. Write an algebraic formula that gives Mr. Midas's demand for bonds. What is the sum of his demand for money and his demand for bonds?
   c. Suppose that all holders of wealth in the economy are identical to Mr. Midas. Fixed asset supplies per person are $80 000 of bonds and $20 000 of chequing accounts. Chequing accounts pay no interest.

What is the interest rate on bonds in asset market equilibrium?

3. Assume that the quantity theory of money holds and that velocity is constant at 5.0. Output is fixed at its full-employment value of 10 000, and the price level is 2.0.
   a. Determine the real demand for money and the nominal demand for money.
   b. In this same economy, the government fixes the nominal money supply at 5000. With output fixed at its full-employment level and with the assumption that prices are flexible, what will be the new price level? What happens to the price level if the nominal money supply rises to 6000?

4. Consider an economy with a constant nominal money supply, a constant level of real output $Y = 100$, and a constant real interest rate $r = 0.10$. Suppose that the income elasticity of money demand is 0.5 and the interest elasticity of money demand is -0.1.
   a. By what percentage does the equilibrium price level differ from its initial value if output increases to $Y = 106$ (and r remains at 0.10)? (*Hint:* Use Eq. 7.11.)
   b. By what percentage does the equilibrium price level differ from its initial value if the real interest rate increases to $r = 0.11$ (and Y remains at 100)?
   c. Suppose that the real interest rate increases to $r = 0.11$. What would real output have to be in order for the equilibrium price level to remain at its initial value?

5. Suppose that the real money demand function is

$$L(Y, r + \pi^e) = \frac{0.01Y}{(r + \pi^e)},$$

where Y is real output, r is the real interest rate, and π^e is the expected rate of inflation. Real output is constant over time at $Y = 150$. The real interest rate is fixed in the goods market at $r = 0.05$ per year.
   a. Suppose that the nominal money supply is growing at the rate of 10% per year and that this growth rate is expected to persist forever. Currently, the nominal money supply is $M = 300$. What are the values of the real money supply and the current price level? (*Hint:* What is the value of the expected inflation rate that enters the money demand function?)
   b. Suppose that the nominal money supply is $M = 300$. The central bank announces that from now on, the nominal money supply is going to grow at the rate of 5% per year. If everyone believes this announcement, and if all markets are in equilibrium, what are the values of the real money supply and the current price level? Explain the effects on

the real money supply and the current price level of a slowdown in the rate of money growth.

6. The income elasticity of money demand is 2/3 and the interest elasticity of money demand is -0.1. Real income is expected to grow by 4.5% over the next year, and the real interest rate is expected to remain constant over the next year. The rate of inflation has been zero for several years.
   a. If the central bank wants zero inflation over the next year, then what growth rate of the nominal money supply should it choose?
   b. By how much will velocity change over the next year if the central bank follows the policy that achieves zero inflation?

ANALYTICAL PROBLEMS

1. All else being equal, how would each of the following affect the demand for M1+? The demand for M2? Explain.
   a. The maximum number of cheques per month that can be written on money market mutual funds is raised from 3 to 30.
   b. Banks begin to pay interest on current accounts held by firms.
   c. The stock market crashes, and further sharp declines in the market are widely feared.
   d. Banks introduce overdraft protection, under which funds are automatically transferred from savings to chequing as needed to cover cheques.
   e. A crackdown reduces the illegal drug trade (which is carried out largely in currency).

2. Figure 7.2 (p. 220) shows that before the 1990s, M1+ velocity generally rose over time. Suggest some explanations for this upward trend.

3. Assume that prices and wages adjust rapidly so that the markets for labour, goods, and assets are always in equilibrium. What are the effects of each of the following on output, the real interest rate, and the current price level?
   a. A temporary increase in government purchases.
   b. A reduction in expected inflation.
   c. A temporary increase in labour supply.
   d. An increase in the interest rate paid on money.

4. As explained in the text, economists commonly make an aggregation assumption that supposes there are only two forms in which to hold wealth: money and nonmonetary assets. The demand for money depends positively on the level of real income. How is the demand for nonmonetary assets affected by the level of income? Explain.

Chapter 8
Business Cycles

Since the Industrial Revolution, the economies of Canada and many other countries have grown tremendously. That growth has transformed economies and greatly improved living standards. Yet, even in prosperous countries, economic expansion has been periodically interrupted by episodes of declining production, income, and spending, and rising unemployment. Sometimes—fortunately, not very often—these episodes have been severe and prolonged. But whether brief or more extended, declines in economic activity have been followed almost invariably by a resumption of economic growth.

This repeated sequence of economic expansion giving way to temporary decline followed by recovery is known as the *business cycle*. The business cycle is a central concern in macroeconomics because business cycle fluctuations—the ups and downs in overall economic activity—are felt throughout the economy. When the economy is growing strongly, prosperity is shared by most of the country's industries, their workers, and owners of capital. When the economy weakens, many sectors of the economy experience declining sales and production, and the number of unemployed workers increases. Because the effects of business cycles are so widespread, and because economic downturns can cause great hardship, economists have tried to find the causes of these episodes and to determine what, if anything, can be done to counteract them. The two basic questions—(1) what causes business cycles, and (2) how policymakers should respond to cyclical fluctuations—are the main concern of Part III of this book.

The answers to these two questions remain highly controversial. Much of this controversy involves the proponents of the classical and Keynesian approaches to macroeconomics, introduced in Chapter 1. In brief, classical economists view business cycles as generally representing the economy's best response to disturbances in production or spending. Thus, classical economists do not see much, if any, need for government action to counteract these fluctuations. In contrast, Keynesian economists argue that because wages and prices adjust slowly, disturbances in production or spending may drive the economy away from its most desirable level of output and employment for long periods of time. According to the Keynesian view, there may, therefore, be a role for government to intervene and try to smooth business cycle fluctuations.

We explore the debate between classicals and Keynesians, and the implications of that debate for economic analysis and macroeconomic policy, in Chapters 9–12.

This chapter provides essential background for that discussion by presenting the basic features of the business cycle. We begin with a definition and a brief history of the business cycle in Canada. We then turn to a more detailed discussion of business cycle characteristics, or "business cycle facts." We conclude the chapter with a brief preview of the alternative approaches to the analysis of business cycles.

8.1 WHAT IS A BUSINESS CYCLE?

Economists have measured and studied business cycles for more than a century. Figure 8.1 provides a stylized description of a business cycle.

The dashed line shows the average, or normal, growth path of aggregate economic activity, and the solid curve shows the rises and falls of actual business activity. The period of time during which aggregate economic activity is falling is a **contraction** or **recession**. If the recession is particularly severe, it becomes a **depression**. After reaching the low point of the contraction, the **trough**, economic activity begins to increase. The period of time during which aggregate economic activity grows is an **expansion** or a **boom**. After reaching the high point of the expansion, the **peak**, aggregate economic activity begins to decline again. The entire sequence of decline followed by recovery, measured from peak to peak or trough to trough, is a **business cycle**.

Figure 8.1 suggests that business cycles are purely temporary deviations from the economy's long-run growth path. However, part of the output losses and gains that occur during a business cycle may become permanent. The degree to which gains and losses associated with a particular recession become permanent is difficult to ascertain and depends on careful measurement and statistical analysis. This issue is continually revisited by economists because it has important implications for understanding the effect of short-term business cycle fluctuations on long-term living standards.

Peaks and troughs in the business cycle are known collectively as **turning points**. One goal of business cycle research is to identify when turning points

FIGURE 8.1

A BUSINESS CYCLE

The solid curve graphs the behaviour of aggregate economic activity over a typical business cycle. The dashed line shows the economy's normal growth path. During a contraction, aggregate economic activity falls until it reaches a trough, *T*. The trough is followed by an expansion during which economic activity increases until it reaches a peak, *P*. A complete cycle is measured from peak to peak or trough to trough.

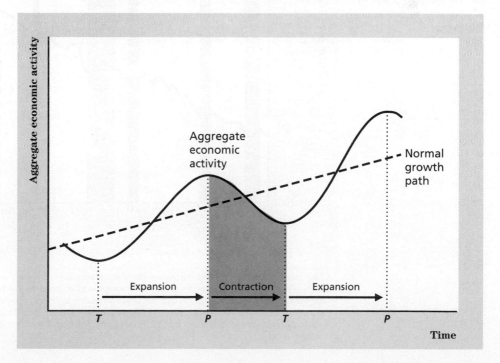

occur. Aggregate economic activity is not measured directly by any single variable, so there is no simple formula that tells economists when a peak or trough has been reached.[1] The precise dating of turning points usually comes well after a peak or trough occurs, so these judgments are more useful for historical analysis of business cycles than as a guide to current policymaking.

The duration of a complete business cycle can vary greatly, from about a year to more than a decade, and predicting it is extremely difficult. However, once a recession begins, the economy tends to keep contracting for a period of time, perhaps for a year or more. Similarly, an expansion, once begun, usually lasts awhile. This tendency for declines in economic activity to be followed by further declines, and for growth in economic activity to be followed by more growth, is called **persistence**. Because movements in economic activity have some persistence, economic forecasters are always on the lookout for turning points, which are likely to indicate a change in the direction of economic activity.

8.2 THE CANADIAN BUSINESS CYCLE: THE HISTORICAL RECORD

Figure 8.2 presents data on real GDP per person in Canada over the period 1870–2015.[2] As explained in Chapter 2, real GDP, also called constant-dollar GDP, measures the physical volume of an economy's final production using the prices of

FIGURE 8.2

REAL OUTPUT PER CAPITA, 1870–2015

The figure shows the value of real output per capita in Canada since 1870. The data are presented using a logarithmic scale. The two deepest recessions in Canada's history occurred in 1920–1921 and 1929–1933.

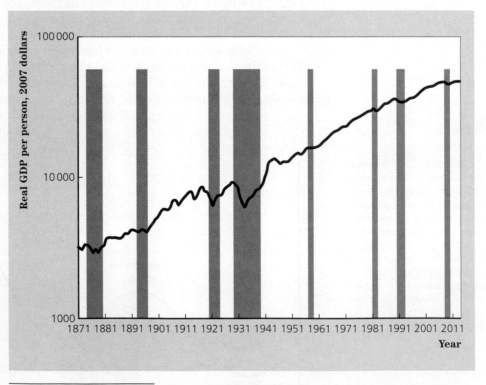

---

[1] A conventional definition used by the media—that a recession has occurred when there are two consecutive quarters of negative real GDP growth—is not widely accepted by economists. The reason why economists tend not to like this definition is that real GDP is only one of many possible indicators of economic activity.

[2] Figure 8.2 presents the data using a logarithmic, or ratio, scale. Equally spaced increments on the vertical axis identify equal proportional differences in the data being graphed. The slope of the line measures the rate of growth in real per capita GDP.

a base year (in this case, the base year is 2007). An increase in real GDP per person means that the average person has greater access to goods and services and thus a higher standard of living. The shaded areas define periods of economic contraction: a period during which the economy is contracting from a peak to a trough.[3] These periods of contraction correspond to the most significant business cycles identified by economic historians and, more recently, by expert members of the C.D. Howe Institute business cycle council.[4]

Figure 8.2 allows us to highlight a number of important features of how real GDP per person, what we consider a reasonable measure of our standard of living, has changed over the past 140 years. Perhaps the most important of these is the fact the line is upward sloping. Since 1870, real GDP per person has increased by an average of 2.1% per year.[5] The model of economic growth presented in Chapter 6 was intended to discuss what factors might slow or speed up this long-run rate of growth. Our focus here, however, is on the business cycle.

The period between Confederation (1867) and World War I (1914–1918) was one of both rapid economic growth and frequent recessions. Economic historians estimate that there were 11 recessions over this period, an average of one every four years. (Recall that for the years prior to 1945, Figure 8.2 identifies only the deepest recessions.) Overall, during this period, the economy suffered nearly as many months of contraction as it did months of expansion. In contrast, since the end of World War II in 1945, the number of months of expansion have outnumbered the number of months of contraction by more than five to one.

Figure 8.2 identifies two major contractions between the two world wars, one in 1920–1921 and another in 1929–1933. As the figure shows, these were the largest contractions experienced in Canada's history. The second of these contractions is known as the Great Depression. After a prosperous decade, at the end of which real GDP per person had finally regained what was lost during the 1920–1921 contraction, the economy suffered a catastrophic depression. Between 1929 and 1933 the unemployment rate rose from about 3% to 20%, with many of those lucky enough to have jobs able to find only part-time employment. The Great Depression ended dramatically with the advent of World War II in 1939. As shown in Figure 8.2, the demand for armaments and other supplies for the war effort caused real output per capita to grow extremely rapidly.

After World War II, instead of falling back into recession as many feared, the Canadian economy began to grow strongly. The recessions experienced in the 1950s and 1960s were of shorter duration and characterized by far less deep falls in output per capita than what had been experienced previously. Following the long stretch of continuous expansion from 1958 to 1981, many economists were speculating that perhaps the business cycle had been "tamed," or even that it was "dead." Evidence to the contrary came with the sharp 1981–1982 recession. That contraction saw the unemployment rate reach 12%, a postwar high. The recovery from that recession was strong, however, and the ensuing expansion lasted until the spring of 1990.

In March 1990, the expansion of more than seven years ended and the economy entered another recession. This recession was longer but shallower than the

---

[3] Thus, the shaded areas in Figure 8.2, and indeed in all the figures that follow, correspond to the shaded area in the stylized representation of a business cycle shown in Figure 8.1.

[4] Canada experienced a great many contractions prior to World War I. To keep Figure 8.2 from being cluttered, we identify only the major contractions prior to 1918.

[5] An implication is that in Canada the average person's standard of living has doubled roughly every 35 years. This calculation uses the "rule of 72," which says that the number of years required for any value to double in size is approximately equal to $72/g$, where g is the annual percentage rate of growth.

1981–1982 recession, and recovery was slow and erratic. Events contributing to the slow and erratic recovery included an ice storm that devastated parts of Ontario, Quebec, and New Brunswick in January 1998 and the terrorist attacks on the United States—Canada's largest trading partner—in September of 2001. Despite these extraordinary events the Canadian economy continued its post-1992 expansion up until January 2008—an expansion lasting just short of 16 years (190 months). This peak was followed by a sharp recession lasting until May 2009. Over those 18 months the unemployment rate increased from 5.9% to 8.6% and real output per capita fell by 3.8%. Clearly, the business cycle is still with us, but equally clearly, the depths of recessions after the war were proving to be far less than what was experienced prior to World War II.

HAVE BUSINESS CYCLES BECOME LESS SEVERE?

The evidence presented in Figure 8.2 makes a strong case for believing that business cycles have generally become less severe.

What accounts for this reduction in the volatility in the economy? Researchers James Stock, of Harvard University, and Mark Watson, of Princeton University, have found that, for the U.S. data they studied, better monetary policy is responsible for about 20%–30% of the reduction in output volatility, but that the largest contributor—40%–50%—was attributable to some unknown form of good luck resulting in smaller shocks to the economy.[6] Since the Stock and Watson paper was published in 2002, much additional research has been undertaken, with mixed results. Although the reasons for the moderation in business cycles have not been definitively nailed down, there is no doubt, as one can see Figure 8.2, that volatility in the economy has fallen a great deal since the early 1980s.

8.3 BUSINESS CYCLE FACTS

Within many countries, the behaviour of a range of economic variables tends to repeat itself from cycle to cycle. Although no two business cycles are identical, all (or most) cycles have features in common. In this section we study the common features of Canadian business cycles over the past half-century.

Knowing these business cycle facts is useful for interpreting economic data and evaluating the state of the economy. In addition, they provide guidance and discipline for developing economic theories of the business cycle. When we discuss alternative theories of the business cycle in Chapters 11 and 12, we evaluate the theories principally by determining how well they account for business cycle facts. To be successful, a theory of the business cycle must explain the cyclical behaviour of not just a few variables, such as output and employment, but a wide range of key economic variables.

THE CYCLICAL BEHAVIOUR OF ECONOMIC VARIABLES: DIRECTION AND TIMING

Two characteristics of the cyclical behaviour of macroeconomic variables are important to our discussion of the business cycle facts. The first is the direction in

---

[6] "Has the Business Cycle Changed and Why?" *NBER Macroeconomics Annual 2002*, Cambridge, MA: MIT Press, 2002, pp. 159–218.

which a macroeconomic variable moves, relative to the direction of aggregate economic activity. An economic variable that moves in the same direction as aggregate economic activity (up in expansions, down in contractions) is **procyclical**. A variable that moves oppositely to aggregate economic activity (up in contractions, down in expansions) is **countercyclical**. Variables that do not display a clear pattern over the business cycle are **acyclical**.

The second characteristic is the timing of the variable's turning points (peaks and troughs) relative to the turning points of the business cycle. An economic variable is a **leading variable** if it tends to move in advance of aggregate economic activity. In other words, the peaks and troughs in a leading variable occur before the corresponding peaks and troughs in the business cycle. A **coincident variable** is one whose peaks and troughs occur at about the same time as the corresponding business cycle peaks and troughs. Finally, a **lagging variable** is one whose peaks and troughs tend to occur later than the corresponding peaks and troughs in the business cycle.

In some cases, the cyclical timing of a variable is obvious from a graph of its behaviour over the course of several business cycles; in other cases, elaborate statistical techniques are needed to determine timing. The fact that some economic variables consistently lead the business cycle suggests that they might be used to forecast the future course of the economy. This is the idea behind indexes of leading indicators published by organizations such as the Conference Board of Canada. Unfortunately, such indexes have not proved to be infallible predictors of recession. The inability of leading indicators to forecast recessions (or their tendency to forecast recessions that do not occur) may simply mean that recessions are often unusual events, caused by large, unpredictable shocks, such as disruptions in the world oil supply, outbreak of disease, and extreme weather. If so, then the pursuit of the perfect index of leading indicators may prove to be frustrating.

Let's now examine the cyclical behaviour of some key macroeconomic variables. We showed the historical behaviour of real output per capita in Figure 8.2. That figure covered a very long time period and was based on annual data. To provide a better view of short-run cyclical behaviour, we now look at quarterly or monthly data describing a much shorter period of time. The direction and timing of the variables considered are presented in Summary table 10.

PRODUCTION

Because the level of production is a basic indicator of aggregate economic activity, peaks and troughs in production tend to occur at about the same time as peaks and troughs in aggregate economic activity. Thus, production is a coincident and procyclical variable.

Although almost all types of production rise in expansions and fall in recessions, the cyclical sensitivity of production in some sectors of the economy is greater than in others. Industries that produce relatively durable, or long-lasting, goods—houses, consumer durables (refrigerators, cars, washing machines), or capital goods (drill presses, computers, factories)—respond strongly to the business cycle, producing at high rates during expansions and at much lower rates during recessions. In contrast, industries that produce relatively nondurable or short-lived goods (foods, paper products) or services (education, insurance) are less sensitive to the business cycle.

SUMMARY 10

THE CYCLICAL BEHAVIOUR OF KEY MACROECONOMIC VARIABLES (THE BUSINESS CYCLE FACTS)

VARIABLE	DIRECTION	TIMING
Production		
Industrial production	Procyclical	Coincident
Durable goods industries are more volatile than nondurable goods and services.		
Expenditure		
Consumption	Procyclical	Coincident
Business fixed investment	Procyclical	Coincident
Inventory investment	Procyclical	Leading
Imports	Procyclical	Coincident
Exports	—	—
Investment is more volatile than consumption.		
Labour Market Variables		
Employment	Procyclical	Coincident
Unemployment	Countercyclical	Coincident
Average labour productivity	Procyclical	Leading
Real wage	Acyclical	—
Money Growth and Inflation		
Money growth	Procyclical	Leading
Inflation	Procyclical	Lagging
Financial Variables		
Stock prices	Procyclical	Leading
Nominal interest rates	Procyclical	Lagging
Real interest rates	Acyclical	—

EXPENDITURE

For components of expenditure, as for types of production, durability is the key to determining sensitivity to the business cycle. Figure 8.3 shows the cyclical behaviour of consumption expenditures on durable goods, services, and nondurable goods, and it shows expenditures on investment in fixed capital. All of these expenditures are measured in real terms. Investment in fixed capital is primarily spending on durable goods. Investment consists of business fixed investment (structures and equipment) and residential investment and is strongly procyclical; note, for example, the dramatic fall in real investment during the 2008–2009 recession. In contrast, consumption expenditures are much smoother. Within the three categories of consumption, consumption expenditures on durable goods (cars, furniture, appliances, and so on) are more strongly cyclical than consumption expenditures on nondurable goods or consumption of services. With respect to timing, consumption and investment are generally coincident with the business cycle, although individual components of fixed investment vary in their cyclical timing.

FIGURE 8.3

CYCLICAL BEHAVIOUR OF
CONSUMPTION AND
INVESTMENT

Both consumption and investment
are procyclical. However, investment is more sensitive than consumption to the business cycle,
reflecting the fact that durable
goods are a larger part of investment spending than they are of
consumption spending.

Source: Statistics Canada, 2016.
Reproduced and distributed on an
"as is" basis with the permission
of Statistics Canada.

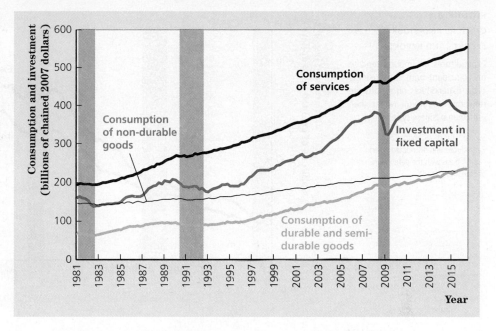

One component of spending that seems to follow its own rules is inventory
investment, shown in Figure 8.4. Inventory investment is procyclical and leading.
Even though goods kept in inventory need not be durable, inventory investment is
also very volatile. Although, on average, inventory investment is a small part (about
1%) of total spending, sharp declines in inventory investment represented a large
part of the total decline in spending in some recessions, most notably those of 1981–
1982, 1990–1992, and 2008–2009. The sense in which inventory investment follows
its own rules is that it often displays large fluctuations that are not associated with
business cycle peaks and troughs, as during the expansion that began in 1992.

FIGURE 8.4

CYCLICAL BEHAVIOUR OF
CHANGES IN BUSINESS
INVENTORIES

Inventory investment, or changes
in business inventories, is procyclical and leading but also extremely
volatile. For example, between
1992 and 2007, inventory investment fluctuated sharply despite the
fact that the economy was continually in expansion.

Source: Statistics Canada, 2016.
Reproduced and distributed on an
"as is" basis with the permission
of Statistics Canada.

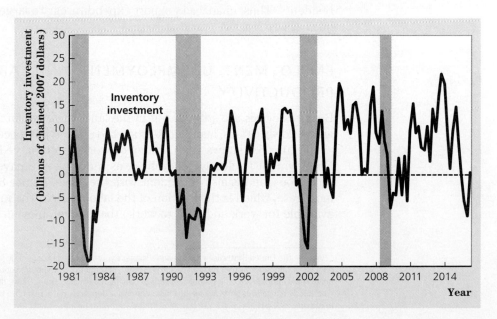

FIGURE 8.5

CYCLICAL BEHAVIOUR OF
EXPORTS AND IMPORTS

Expenditures on imports tend to
be coincident with the business
cycle. Expenditures on exports are
reflective of foreign rather than
Canadian business cycles.

Source: Statistics Canada, 2016.
Reproduced and distributed on an
"as is" basis with the permission
of Statistics Canada.

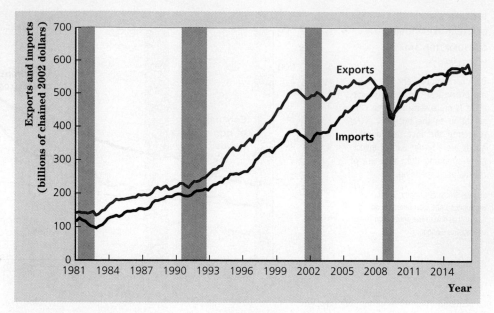

In an economy oriented toward international trade, exports and imports are important components of aggregate expenditure. Figure 8.5 shows the real value of Canadian exports and imports since 1981. As we discuss more fully in Chapter 10, expenditures by Canadians on imported goods are determined in large part by their level of income: A higher income is associated with a higher level of spending on goods and services, some of which are imported. We expect, then, expenditures on imported goods and services to moderate, or fall, during recessions and to grow during expansions.

Import expenditures are generally deemed to be procyclical and coincident with the business cycle. Expenditures on Canadian-produced goods purchased by non-residents—exports—are determined in large part by the incomes of non-residents. Thus, changes in export expenditures are largely a reflection of foreign business cycles, not Canada's.[7]

EMPLOYMENT, UNEMPLOYMENT, AND LABOUR PRODUCTIVITY

Business cycles are strongly felt in the labour market. In a recession, employment grows slowly or falls, many workers are laid off, and jobs become more difficult to find.

Figure 8.6 shows the number of workers employed in Canada since 1976. Employment is clearly procyclical, as more people have jobs in booms than in recessions, and is also coincident with the cycle. Figure 8.7 shows the unemployment rate, which is the fraction of the labour force (the number of people who are available for work and want to work) that is unemployed. The unemployment rate

---

[7] Because the United States is by far Canada's largest export market, an economic upturn or downturn in that economy has a significant impact on Canada's exports and, potentially, on Canada's economy. This means that exports may be, in some circumstances, a leading indicator of Canadian business cycles. As we discuss more fully in Chapter 10, whether a change in exports is a leading indicator or not depends on the response of the exchange rate to the change in exports.

FIGURE 8.6

CYCLICAL BEHAVIOUR OF EMPLOYMENT

Employment is procyclical and coincident with the business cycle.

Source: Statistics Canada, 2016. Reproduced and distributed on an "as is" basis with the permission of Statistics Canada.

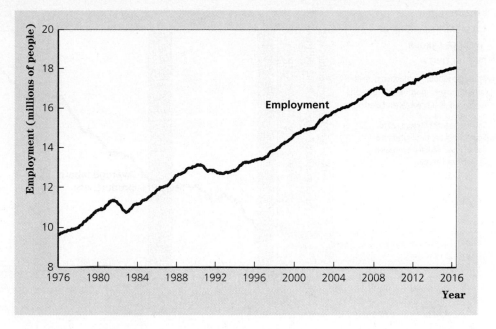

is strongly countercyclical, rising sharply in contractions but falling more slowly in expansions. Figure 8.7 illustrates a somewhat unusual aspect of the 1990–1992 recession: The unemployment rate continued to climb for several months after the recession's trough was reached. The figure also provides evidence of how closely Canada came to experiencing a recession in 2001. Although the unemployment rate increased sharply in 2001, this was either not large enough or the effect on other economic variables not strong enough for the economy to have been judged to have fallen into recession.

FIGURE 8.7

CYCLICAL BEHAVIOUR OF THE UNEMPLOYMENT RATE

The unemployment rate is counter-cyclical and very sensitive to the business cycle. It rises rapidly in contractions but falls more slowly in expansions.

Source: Adapted from 1966–1975: *Canadian Economic Observer, Statistical Summary*; 1976–2006: Statistics Canada CANSIM II database, series v2062815.

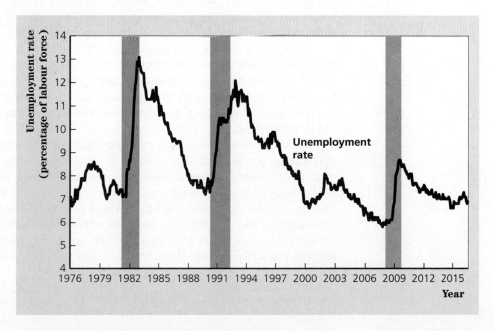

FIGURE 8.8

CYCLICAL BEHAVIOUR OF
AVERAGE LABOUR
PRODUCTIVITY

Average labour productivity, measured as real output per person
employed, is procyclical and leading.

Source: Statistics Canada, 2016.
Reproduced and distributed on an
"as is" basis with the permission
of Statistics Canada.

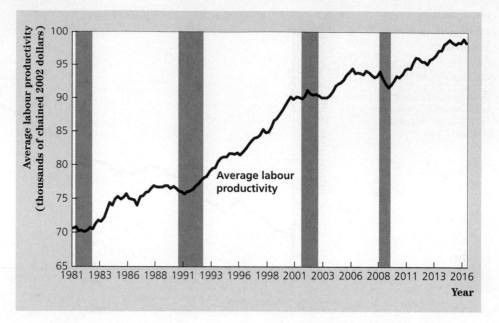

Another significant labour market variable is average labour productivity. As discussed in Chapter 1, average labour productivity is output per unit of labour input. Figure 8.8 shows average labour productivity measured as total real output in the Canadian economy divided by the total number of employed people who produced that output. Average labour productivity tends to be procyclical: In booms workers produce more output during each hour of work than they do in recessions.[8] Also, average labour productivity tends to lead the business cycle.

One important labour market variable we haven't shown is the real wage. Recall from Chapter 3 that the real wage is the compensation received by workers per unit of time (such as an hour or a week) measured in real, or purchasing-power, terms. The real wage is an especially important variable in the study of business cycles because it's one of the main determinants of the amount of labour supplied by workers and demanded by firms.

Generally speaking, two types of studies attempt to characterize the cyclical behaviour of real wages. One examines the average real wage for the economy as a whole. In these studies, the wage is usually measured as the total real compensation paid to all workers in the economy divided by the total number of hours worked. In Canada, the real wage measured in this way is acyclical or perhaps mildly procyclical.

However, some economists point out that the economywide average real wage may not be a good indicator of the real wage received by the typical worker. An example illustrates the potential problem. Imagine that an economy consisted of two employed workers, each earning $9 per hour, and one unemployed worker. Clearly, the average wage paid to workers in this economy is $9 per hour. Now, suppose that this economy expands, with the result that the two employed workers get raises to $10 per hour and that the previously unemployed worker finds a job that pays $7 per hour. If all three workers work the same number of hours, the

---

[8] The Application in Chapter 3, "The Production Function and Productivity Growth in Canada" (p. 49), made the point that total factor productivity A also tends to be procyclical.

economywide average wage is the same as before: ($10 + $10 + $7)/3, or $9 per hour. Thus, although all three workers are earning more in the expansion than they did before, the economywide average wage has not changed. The reason is that the increase in the employed individuals' wages has been offset by a change in the composition of the workforce, which now includes a relatively low-wage worker who was not working before the expansion.

To eliminate effects of changing labour force composition on the measured real wage, the second type of study attempts to measure the cyclical behaviour of the real wages of specific individual workers. Unfortunately, this type of study suffers from a lack of good data on individual wages and from a number of technical statistical problems. A study by Jean Farès, of the Bank of Canada, and Thomas Lemieux, of the University of British Columbia, attempted to respond to these issues by constructing a new data set that adjusted wages by industry, by province, and by both employee and job characteristics.[9] Using these data, they show that the real wages of specific workers are clearly procyclical. They conclude that the failure of previous studies to adjust for changes in the composition of the workforce had made real wages appear less procyclical than is in fact the case. The results of this study notwithstanding, definitive conclusions about the cyclicality of real wages remain elusive.

MONEY GROWTH

Another variable whose cyclical behaviour is somewhat controversial is the money supply. Figure 8.9 shows the behaviour since 1968 of the growth in the M2 measure of the money supply.[10] As we discuss more in later chapters, the rate of growth in the money supply responds to economic conditions but is also a policy

FIGURE 8.9

CYCLICAL BEHAVIOUR OF NOMINAL MONEY GROWTH AND INFLATION

Nominal money growth, here measured as the six-month moving average of monthly growth rates in M2 (expressed in annual rates), is volatile. The efforts of the central bank to influence the economy by changing the rate of money growth during periods of recession is clearly seen in the figure.

Source: Statistics Canada, 2016. Reproduced and distributed on an "as is" basis with the permission of Statistics Canada.

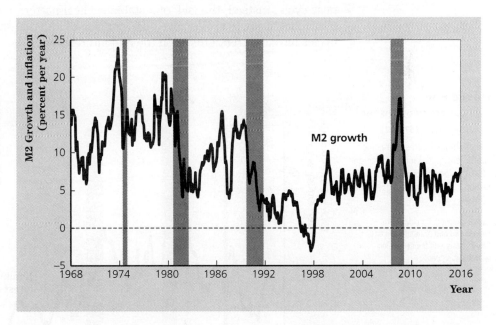

---

[9] "Downward Nominal-Wage Rigidity: A Critical Assessment and Some New Evidence for Canada," in *Price Stability and the Long-Run Target for Monetary Policy*, Proceedings of a seminar held by the Bank of Canada, June 2000.

[10] See Table 7.1 (p. 202) for a definition of M2. To reduce the effect of high month-to-month volatility in money growth, Figure 8.9 presents a six-month moving average of money growth rates; that is, the reported growth rate in each month is actually the average of the growth rate in the current month and in the previous five months.

instrument used by the Bank of Canada to influence the economy. This makes it difficult to determine whether money growth is pro- or countercyclical. In Figure 8.9 we see the 1981–1982 and the 1990–1992 recessions were associated with dramatic slowdowns in money growth while the opposite was true in the 2008–2009 recession. The first two episodes are associated with well-known efforts by the Bank of Canada to reduce inflation with a monetary contraction. The equally dramatic expansion in money growth in 2008–2009 illustrates the Bank of Canada's effort to add financial liquidity into an economy in which private sources of financial liquidity had all but disappeared.

FINANCIAL VARIABLES

Financial variables are another class of economic variables that are sensitive to the cycle. For example, stock prices are generally procyclical (stock prices rise in good economic times) and leading (stock prices usually fall in advance of a recession).

Nominal interest rates are procyclical and lagging. The nominal interest rate shown in Figure 8.10 is the rate on three-month corporate paper. However, other interest rates, such as the prime rate (charged by banks to their best customers) and the rates on Treasury bills, are also procyclical and lagging.

The real interest rate does not have an obvious cyclical pattern. For instance, the real interest rate was actually negative during the 1974–1975 recession but was high during the 1981–1982 and 1990–1992 recessions. (Annual values of the real interest rate are shown in Figure 2.2, p. 41.) The acyclicality of the real interest rate does not necessarily mean that its movements are unimportant over the business cycle. Instead, the lack of a stable cyclical pattern may reflect the facts that individual business cycles have different causes and that these different sources of cycles have different effects on the real interest rate.

FIGURE 8.10

CYCLICAL BEHAVIOUR OF THE NOMINAL INTEREST RATE

The nominal interest rate, measured here as the interest rate on 90-day corporate paper, is procyclical and has recently lagged the business cycle.

Source: Statistics Canada, 2016. Reproduced and distributed on an "as is" basis with the permission of Statistics Canada.

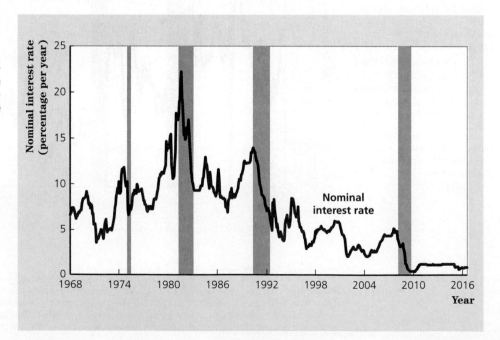

8.4 BUSINESS CYCLE ANALYSIS: A PREVIEW

The business cycle facts presented in this chapter would be useful even if we took them no further. For example, being familiar with the typical cyclical patterns of key macroeconomic variables helps forecasters project the course of the economy. Knowing the facts about cycles is also important for businesspeople making investment and hiring decisions and for financial investors trying to choose portfolios that provide the desired combinations of risk and return. However, macroeconomists are interested not only in *what* happens during business cycles but also in *why* it happens. This desire to understand cycles is not just idle intellectual curiosity. For example, as we demonstrate in Chapters 9–12, the advice that macroeconomists give to policymakers about how to respond to a recession depends on what they think is causing the recession. Thus, with the business cycle facts as background, in the rest of Part III we describe the primary alternative explanations of business cycle fluctuations, as well as policy recommendations based on these explanations.

In general, theories of the business cycle have two main components. The first is a description of the types of factors that have major impacts on the economy— wars, new inventions, weather, disease, and changes in government policy are examples. Economists often refer to these (typically unpredictable) forces hitting the economy as *shocks*. The other component of a business cycle theory is a *model* of how the economy responds to the various shocks. Think of the economy as a car moving down a poorly maintained highway: The shocks can be thought of as the potholes and bumps in the road; the model describes how the components of the car (its tires and shock absorbers) act to smooth out or amplify the effects of the shocks on the passengers.

The two principal business cycle theories that we discuss in this book are the *classical* and the *Keynesian* theories. Fortunately, to present and discuss these two theories we do not have to develop two completely different models. Instead, both can be considered within a general framework called the *aggregate demand–aggregate supply*, or *AD–AS*, *model*.

Building and using the *AD–AS* model to better understand business cycles is our goal over the next four chapters. We develop this understanding using a step-by-step process. We begin, with Chapter 9, by introducing the *IS–LM–FE* model. Understanding the *IS–LM–FE* model is an essential first step as it forms the foundation of our understanding of aggregate demand (*AD*). In Chapter 10 we extend the *IS–LM–FE* model to account for international trade and the international flow of financial capital. By the end of Chapter 10, therefore, we will have developed a firm understanding of the aggregate demand relationship.

Our presentation of the model of *IS–LM–FE* relies on an important assumption about how households and firms expect future events to unfold. Thus, in Chapters 9 and 10 we assume that what households and firms expect to see and experience in the future is not affected by what they see and are experiencing today. This is a restrictive assumption. Most people, reading about an impending war, hearing of a soon-to-be negotiated trade deal, or being told of the consequences of future government policy choices for their pensions or tax bills, change their behaviour today in anticipation of the implications of those future events.

In Chapters 11 and 12 we turn our attention to dealing with the implications of taking into account people's expectations about the future. This requires that we develop models of aggregate supply (*AS*). The model of aggregate supply favoured by classical economists is presented first, in Chapter 11, and then it is brought together with the model of aggregate demand to enable us to present the classical economist's model of *AD–AS*. Then, in Chapter 12, we present the model of aggregate supply developed by Keynesian economists and join it to the model of aggregate demand to present the model of *AD–AS* favoured by Keynesians. Our goal throughout is to use the same framework of analysis to discuss how classical versus Keynesian economists explain the business cycle facts described in this chapter.

Chapter Summary

1. A business cycle consists of a period of declining aggregate economic activity (a contraction or recession) followed by a period of rising economic activity (an expansion or a boom). The low point of the contraction is called the trough, and the high point of the expansion is called the peak. Business cycles have been observed in market economies since the beginning of industrialization.

2. Many economic variables have regular and predictable patterns of behaviour over the course of the cycle. We refer to the typical cyclical patterns of key macroeconomic variables as the "business cycle facts."

3. The fluctuations in aggregate economic activity that constitute business cycles are recurrent, having been observed again and again in industrialized market economies. However, they are not periodic, in that they do not occur at regular or predictable intervals. Business cycle fluctuations are also persistent, which means that once a recession or expansion begins, it usually lasts for a while.

4. Economists believe that the Canadian economy before 1929 had longer recessions and more cyclical volatility than the post–World War II economy. The Great Depression that began in 1929 and did not end until the onset of World War II was the most severe cyclical decline in Canadian history. Moderation of the business cycle after World War II led to premature pronouncements that the cycle was "dead." However, the Canadian economy suffered severe recessions in 1981–1982, 1990–1992, and 2008–2009.

5. The direction of a variable relative to the business cycle can be procyclical, countercyclical, or acyclical. A procyclical variable moves in the same direction as aggregate economic activity, rising in booms and falling in recessions. A countercyclical variable moves oppositely to aggregate economic activity, falling in booms and rising in recessions. An acyclical variable has no clear cyclical pattern.

6. The timing of a variable relative to the business cycle may be coincident, leading, or lagging. A coincident variable's peaks and troughs occur at about the same time as peaks and troughs in aggregate economic activity. Peaks and troughs in a leading variable come before and peaks and troughs in a lagging variable come after the corresponding peaks and troughs in aggregate economic activity.

7. The cyclical direction and timing of major macroeconomic variables—the business cycle facts—are described in Summary table 10 (p. 234). In brief, production, consumption, and investment are procyclical and coincident. Investment is much more volatile over the business cycle than consumption is. Employment and average labour productivity are procyclical, but the unemployment rate is countercyclical. Money and stock prices are procyclical and lead the cycle. Inflation and nominal interest rates are procyclical and lagging. The real interest rate is acyclical.

8. A theory of business cycles consists of (1) a description of shocks that affect the economy and (2) a model that describes how the economy responds to these shocks. In this chapter we have provided a description of the shocks that affect the economy. In the next four

chapters we develop macroeconomic theories that attempt to explain why those shocks affect the economy in the way they do and what, if anything, policymakers might do to mitigate the negative effects of those shocks.

KEY TERMS

acyclical, p. 233
boom, p. 229
business cycle, p. 229
coincident variable, p. 233
contraction, p. 229
countercyclical, p. 233
depression, p. 229
expansion, p. 229
lagging variable, p. 233
leading variable, p. 233
peak, p. 229
persistence, p. 230
procyclical, p. 233
recession, p. 229
trough, p. 229
turning points, p. 229

REVIEW QUESTIONS

1. Draw a diagram showing the phases and turning points of a business cycle. Using the diagram, illustrate the concepts of recurrence and persistence.
2. What is the evidence for the view that the Canadian business cycle has become less severe over time?

Why is the question of whether the cycle has moderated over time an important one?
3. What terms are used to describe the way a variable moves when economic activity is rising or falling? What terms are used to describe the timing of cyclical changes in economic variables?
4. If you knew that the economy was falling into a recession, what would you expect to happen to production during the next few quarters? to investment? to average labour productivity? to the unemployment rate?
5. How is the fact that some economic variables are known to lead the cycle used in macroeconomic forecasting?
6. What are the two components of a theory of business cycles?

ANALYTICAL PROBLEMS

1. Consumer expenditures on durable goods, such as cars and furniture, as well as purchases of new houses, fall much more than expenditures on nondurable goods and services during recessions. Why do you think that is?
2. Output, total hours worked, and average labour productivity are all procyclical. Which variable, output or total hours worked, increases by a larger percentage in expansions and falls by a larger percentage in recessions? (*Hint:* Average labour productivity = output ÷ total hours worked so that the percentage change in average labour productivity equals the percentage change in output minus the percentage change in total hours worked.)

Chapter 9

The *IS–LM–FE* Model:
A General Framework for
Macroeconomic Analysis

The main goal of Chapter 8 was to describe business cycles by presenting the business cycle facts. This and the following three chapters explain business cycles and how policymakers should respond to them. First, we must develop a macroeconomic model that we can use to analyze cyclical fluctuations and the effects of policy changes on the economy. By examining the labour market in Chapter 3, the goods market in Chapters 4 and 5, and the asset market in Chapter 7, we have already identified the three components of a complete macroeconomic model. Now we put these three components together into a single framework that allows us to analyze them simultaneously. This chapter, and its open-economy partner Chapter 10, consolidate our previous analyses to provide the theoretical structure for the rest of the book.

The core of the macroeconomic model developed in this chapter is the *IS–LM* model. (As we discuss later, this name originates in two of its basic equilibrium conditions: investment, *I*, must equal saving, *S*; and money demanded, *L*, must equal money supplied, *M*.) The *IS–LM* model was developed in 1937 by Nobel laureate Sir John Hicks,[1] who intended it as a graphical representation of the ideas presented by Keynes in his famous 1936 book, *The General Theory of Employment, Interest, and Money*. Reflecting John Maynard Keynes's belief that wages and prices do not adjust quickly to clear markets (see Section 1.3), in his original *IS–LM* model Hicks assumed that the price level was fixed. A key adjustment to the *IS–LM* model introduced since Hicks is the relaxation of his assumption of a fixed price level. Allowing the price level to change requires that we add a third element, what we call the full equilibrium (*FE*) condition. This consideration, which we describe in detail in Section 9.1, produces, when added to the *IS–LM* model, a new model called *IS–LM–FE*. The *IS–LM–FE* model has been widely applied in analyses of cyclical fluctuations, macroeconomic policymaking, and forecasting.

Because of its origins, the *IS–LM* model is commonly identified with the Keynesian approach to business cycle analysis. Classical economists—who believe that wages and prices move rapidly to clear markets—would reject Hicks's original *IS–LM* model as a complete description of the economy because of his assumption that the price

---

[1] Hicks outlined the *IS–LM* framework in an article entitled "Mr. Keynes and the Classics: A Suggested Interpretation," *Econometrica*, April 1937, pp. 137–159.

level is fixed. However, the conventional *IS–LM* model is readily adapted to allow for rapidly adjusting wages and prices by the addition of the *FE* condition. Thus, the *IS–LM* framework, although originally developed by Keynesians, may also be used to present and discuss the classical approach to business cycle analysis.

Using the *IS–LM–FE* model as a framework for both classical and Keynesian analyses has several practical benefits: First, using a single model for both classical and Keynesian analyses avoids the need to learn two different models. Second, utilizing a single framework emphasizes the large areas of agreement between the Keynesian and classical approaches while showing clearly how the two approaches differ. Moreover, because versions of the *IS–LM–FE* model (and its concepts and terminology) are so often applied in analyses of the economy and macroeconomic policy, studying this framework will help you understand and participate more fully in current economic debates.

Economists use three approaches when analyzing an economic model: graphical, numerical, and algebraic. In this chapter we rely on a graphical approach. Appendix 9.A examines the *IS–LM* model—the version of our *IS–LM–FE* model with the assumption of fixed prices—with the help of a numerical exercise. Appendix 9.B presents the same analysis, but in algebraic form. If you have difficulty understanding why the curves used in the graphical analysis have the slopes they do or why they shift, or have difficulty conceptualizing how one might solve for values of the interest rate, GDP, or other variables, you may find these appendices helpful.

To keep things as simple as possible, in this chapter we assume that the economy is closed. In Chapter 10, we show how to extend the *IS–LM–FE* model to allow for a foreign sector. Keeping things as simple as possible is also our motivation for assuming, in both this chapter and in Chapter 10, that what households and firms expect to see and experience in the future is not affected by what they see and are experiencing today. We have touched upon this issue a few times in earlier chapters. We return to this issue in Chapters 11 and 12, where we show how the way in which people and firms think about the future plays an important role in determining macroeconomic outcomes.

9.1 THE *FE* LINE: EQUILIBRIUM IN THE LABOUR MARKET

In previous chapters, we discussed the three main markets of the economy: the labour market, the goods market, and the asset market. We also identified some of the links among these markets, but now we want to be more precise about how they fit into a complete macroeconomic system.

Let's turn first to the labour market and recall from Chapter 3 the concepts of the full-employment level of employment and full-employment output. The *full-employment level of employment* $\overline{N}$ is the equilibrium level of employment reached after wages and prices have fully adjusted so that the quantity of labour supplied equals the quantity of labour demanded. *Full-employment output* $\overline{Y}$ is the amount of output produced when employment is at its full-employment level, given the current level of the capital stock and the production function. Algebraically, full-employment output $\overline{Y}$ equals $AF(K,\overline{N})$, where K is the capital stock, A is productivity, and F is the production function (see Eq. 3.4, p. 77).

Our ultimate goal is a diagram that has the real interest rate on the vertical axis and output on the horizontal axis. In such a diagram, equilibrium in the labour market is represented by the **full-employment line**, or *FE*, in Figure 9.1.

FIGURE 9.1

THE *FE* LINE

The full-employment (*FE*) line represents labour market equilibrium. When the labour market is in equilibrium, employment equals its full-employment level $\overline{N}$ and output equals its full-employment level $\overline{Y}$, regardless of the value of the real interest rate. Thus, the *FE* line is vertical at $Y = \overline{Y}$.

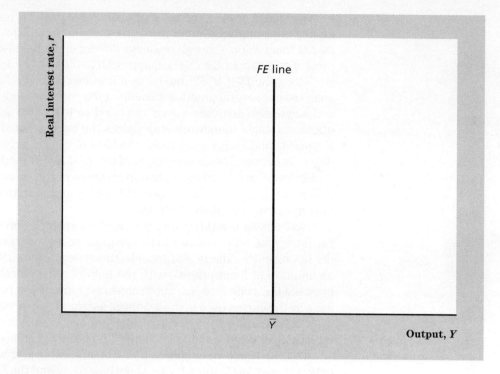

The *FE* line is vertical at $Y = \overline{Y}$ because when the labour market is in equilibrium, output equals its full-employment level, regardless of the interest rate.[2]

FACTORS THAT SHIFT THE *FE* LINE

The full-employment level of output is determined by the full-employment level of employment and the current levels of capital and productivity. Any change that affects the full-employment level of output $\overline{Y}$ will cause the *FE* line to shift. Recall that full-employment output $\overline{Y}$ increases—and, thus, the *FE* line shifts to the right— when the labour supply increases (which raises equilibrium employment $\overline{N}$), when the capital stock increases, or when there is a beneficial supply shock. Similarly, a drop in the labour supply or capital stock, or an adverse supply shock, lowers full-employment output $\overline{Y}$ and shifts the *FE* line to the left. Summary table 11 lists the factors that shift the *FE* line.

It's important to emphasize the assumption we're making in this chapter and the next: that what households and firms expect to see and experience in the future is not affected by what they see and are experiencing today. In Chapters 11 and 12 we relax this assumption and show how some of the macroeconomic responses we describe in this chapter are changed once our assumption about how households and firms think about the future is modified. In Chapter 11, for example, we'll see that classical economists argue that increases in government purchases cause the *FE* line to shift to the right.

---

[2] As we discussed in Chapter 4, a change in the real interest rate affects the desired capital stock of firms. We assume that it takes considerable time for firms to fully adjust to changes in their desired capital stocks. Thus, steel firms do not build new blast furnaces and utilities do not construct new hydroelectric dams overnight. For this reason, while the real interest rate affects investment, and thus the amount of capital that firms will have in the *future*, it does not affect the size of the *current* capital stock and hence does not affect current output.

SUMMARY 11   FACTORS THAT SHIFT THE FULL-EMPLOYMENT (*FE*) LINE

ALL ELSE EQUAL, A(N)	SHIFTS THE *FE* LINE	REASON
Beneficial supply shock	Right	**1.** More output can be produced for the same amount of capital and labour. **2.** If the *MPN* rises, labour demand increases and raises employment. Full-employment output increases for both reasons.
Increase in labour supply	Right	Equilibrium employment rises, raising full-employment output.
Increase in the capital stock	Right	More output can be produced with the same amount of labour. In addition, increased capital may increase the *MPN*, which increases labour demand and equilibrium employment.

9.2 THE *IS* CURVE: EQUILIBRIUM IN THE GOODS MARKET

The second of the three markets in our model is the goods market. Recall from Chapter 4 that the goods market is in equilibrium when desired investment and desired national saving are equal or, equivalently, when the aggregate quantity of goods supplied equals the aggregate quantity of goods demanded. In Chapter 4, we demonstrated that adjustments in the real interest rate (the rate at which the real value or purchasing power of an asset increases over time) help bring about equilibrium in the goods market.

In a diagram with the real interest rate on the vertical axis and real output on the horizontal axis, equilibrium in the goods market is described by a curve called the **IS curve**. Specifically, for any level of output (or income) Y, the *IS* curve shows the real interest rate r for which the goods market is in equilibrium. The *IS* curve is so named because at all points on the curve, desired investment, I^d, equals desired national saving, S^d.

Figure 9.2 shows the derivation of the *IS* curve from the saving–investment diagram introduced in Chapter 4 and used extensively in Chapters 4 and 5 (see Chapter 4 Key Diagram 3, p. 125). Figure 9.2(a) shows the saving–investment diagram drawn for two randomly chosen levels of output, 400 and 500. Corresponding to each level is a saving curve, with the value of output indicated in parentheses next to it. Each saving curve slopes upward because an increase in the real interest rate causes households to increase their desired level of saving. An increase in current output (income) leads to more desired saving at any real interest rate, so the saving curve S for $Y = 500$ lies to the right of the saving curve S for $Y = 400$.

Figure 9.2(a) also shows an investment curve. Recall from Chapter 4 that the investment curve slopes downward because an increase in the real interest rate increases the user cost of capital, which reduces the desired capital stock and hence desired investment. Desired investment is not affected by current output, so the investment curve is the same whether $Y = 400$ or $Y = 500$.

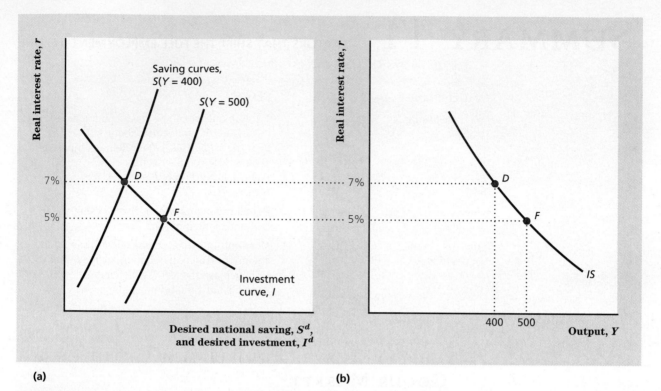

(a)   **(b)**

FIGURE 9.2

DERIVING THE *IS* CURVE

(a) The graph shows the goods market equilibrium for two different levels of output: 400 and 500 (the output corresponding to each saving curve is indicated in parentheses next to the curve). Higher levels of output (income) increase desired national saving and shift the saving curve to the right. When output is 400, the real interest rate that clears the goods market is 7% (point *D*). When output is 500, the market-clearing interest rate is 5% (point *F*).

(b) For each level of output the *IS* curve shows the corresponding real interest rate that clears the goods market. Thus, each point on the *IS* curve corresponds to an equilibrium point in the goods market. As in (a), when output is 400, the real interest rate that clears the goods market is 7% (point *D*); when output is 500, the market-clearing interest rate is 5% (point *F*). Because higher output raises saving and leads to a lower market-clearing interest rate, the *IS* curve slopes downward.

Each level of output implies a different market-clearing real interest rate. When output is 400, goods market equilibrium is at point D and the market-clearing real interest rate is 7%. When output is 500, goods market equilibrium occurs at point F and the market-clearing real interest rate is 5%.

Figure 9.2(b) shows the IS curve for this economy, with output on the horizontal axis and the real interest rate on the vertical axis. For any level of output, the IS curve shows the real interest rate that clears the goods market. Thus, $Y = 400$ and $r = 7\%$ at point D on the IS curve. (Note that point D in Figure 9.2(b) corresponds to point D in Figure 9.2(a).) Similarly, when output is 500, the real interest rate that clears the goods market is 5%. This combination of output and the real interest rate occurs at point F on the IS curve in Figure 9.2(b); it corresponds to point F in Figure 9.2(a). In general, because a rise in output increases national desired saving, thereby reducing the real interest rate that clears the goods market, the IS curve slopes downward.

The slope of the IS curve may also be interpreted in terms of the alternative (but equivalent) version of the goods market equilibrium condition, which states that in equilibrium the aggregate quantity of goods demanded must equal the aggregate quantity of goods supplied. To illustrate, suppose that the economy is initially at point F in Figure 9.2(b). The aggregate quantities of goods supplied and demanded are equal at point F, because F lies on the IS curve, which means that the goods market is in equilibrium at that point.[3] Now, let's conduct a thought experiment[4] and suppose that for some reason the real interest rate rises from 5% to 7%. Recall from Chapter 4 that an increase in the real interest rate reduces both desired consumption C^d (because people desire to save more when the real interest rate rises) and desired investment I^d, thereby reducing the aggregate quantity of goods demanded. If output Y remained at its initial level of 500, the increase in the real interest rate would imply that more goods were being supplied than demanded. For the goods market to reach equilibrium at the higher real interest rate, the quantity of goods supplied has to fall. At point D in Figure 9.2(b), output has fallen enough (from 500 to 400) that the quantities of goods supplied and demanded are equal, and the goods market has returned to equilibrium.[5]

Again, the result of our thought experiment is that, all else equal, an increase in the real interest rate requires a fall in real output in order to maintain goods market equilibrium, so the IS curve slopes downward.[6]

FACTORS THAT SHIFT THE *IS* CURVE

For any level of output, the IS curve shows the real interest rate needed to clear the goods market. With output held constant, any economic disturbance or policy change that changes the value of the goods-market-clearing real interest rate will cause the IS curve to shift. More specifically, *for constant output, any change in the economy that reduces desired national saving relative to desired investment will increase the real interest rate that clears the goods market and, thus, shift the IS curve up and to the right*. Similarly, for constant output, changes that increase desired saving relative to desired investment, thereby reducing the market-clearing real interest rate, shift the IS curve down and to the left. Factors that shift the IS curve are described in Summary table 12 (p. 251).

We can use a change in current government purchases to illustrate IS curve shifts in general. The effects of a temporary increase in government purchases on the IS curve are shown in Figure 9.3. Figure 9.3(a) shows the saving–investment diagram, with an initial saving curve S^1 and an initial investment curve I. The S^1 curve represents saving when output (income) is fixed at $Y = 450$. Figure 9.3(b) shows the initial IS curve, IS^1. The initial goods market equilibrium when output Y

---

[3] We have just shown that desired national saving equals desired investment at point F, or $S^d = I^d$. Substituting the definition of desired national saving, $Y - C^d - G$, for S^d in the condition that desired national saving equals desired investment shows also that $Y = C^d + I^d + G$ at F.
[4] Recall that in a *thought experiment* we imagine we can change just one variable while holding all others constant. In this particular experiment, we imagine a change in the real interest rate without detailing why the interest rate in fact changed. There are many possibilities why the interest rate might change, and some of these would have their own effect on real output. To isolate the effect of just the change in the interest rate, we imagine the interest rate changes without changes in other economic variables.
[5] Although a drop in output Y obviously reduces the quantity of goods supplied, it also reduces the quantity of goods demanded. The reason is that a drop in output is also a drop in income, which reduces desired consumption. However, although a drop in output of one dollar reduces the supply of output by one dollar, a drop in income of one dollar reduces desired consumption C^d by less than one dollar (that is, the marginal propensity to consume, defined in Chapter 4, is less than 1). Thus, a drop in output Y reduces goods supplied more than goods demanded and therefore reduces the excess supply of goods.
[6] Note the careful wording of this sentence. Given the restrictive nature of our thought experiment, you should *not* understand the result of the experiment as being that increases in interest rates are always to be associated with contractions in output. You will see a contrary result in the next section.

equals 450 is represented by point E in both (a) and (b). At E, the initial market-clearing real interest rate is 6%.

Now, suppose that the government increases its current purchases of goods, G. Desired investment at any level of the real interest rate is not affected by the increase in government purchases, so the investment curve does not shift. However, as discussed in Chapter 4, a temporary increase in government purchases reduces desired national saving, $Y - C^d - G$ (see Summary table 5, p. 106), so the saving curve shifts to the left from S^1 to S^2 in Figure 9.3(a). As a result of the reduction in desired national saving, the real interest rate that clears the goods market when output equals 450 increases from 6% to 7% (point F in Figure 9.3(a)).

The effect on the IS curve is shown in Figure 9.3(b). With output constant at 450, the real interest rate that clears the goods market increases from 6% to 7%, as shown by the shift from point E to point F. The new IS curve, IS^2, passes through F and lies above and to the right of the initial IS curve, IS^1. Thus, a temporary increase in government purchases shifts the IS curve up and to the right.

So far, our discussion of IS curve shifts has focused on the goods market equilibrium condition that desired national saving must equal desired investment. However, factors that shift the IS curve may also be described in terms of the

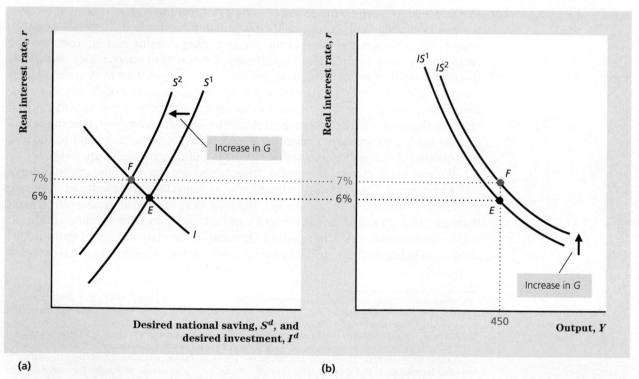

(a)   **(b)**

FIGURE 9.3

EFFECT ON THE *IS* CURVE OF A TEMPORARY INCREASE IN GOVERNMENT PURCHASES

(a) The saving–investment diagram shows the effects of a temporary increase in government purchases, G, with output Y constant at 450. The increase in G reduces desired national saving and shifts the saving curve to the left, from S^1 to S^2. The goods market equilibrium point moves from point E to point F, and the real interest rate rises from 6% to 7%.

(b) The increase in G raises the real interest rate that clears the goods market for any level of output. Thus, the IS curve shifts up and to the right, from IS^1 to IS^2. In this example, with output held constant at 450, an increase in government purchases raises the real interest rate that clears the goods market from 6% (point E) to 7% (point F).

alternative (but equivalent) goods market equilibrium condition—that the aggregate quantities of goods demanded and supplied are equal. In particular, for a given level of output, *any change that increases the aggregate demand for goods shifts the IS curve up and to the right.* This rule works because for the initial level of output, an increase in the aggregate demand for goods causes the quantity of goods demanded to exceed the quantity supplied. Goods market equilibrium can be restored at the same level of output by an increase in the real interest rate, which reduces desired consumption C^d and desired investment I^d. For any level of output, an increase in aggregate demand for goods raises the real interest rate that clears the goods market, so we conclude that an increase in the aggregate demand for goods shifts the *IS* curve up and to the right.

To illustrate this alternative way of thinking about *IS* curve shifts, we again use the example of a temporary increase in government purchases. Note that an increase in government purchases, G, directly raises the demand for goods, $C^d + I^d + G$, leading to an excess demand for goods at the initial level of output. The excess demand for goods can be eliminated and goods market equilibrium at the initial level of output restored by an increase in the real interest rate, which reduces C^d and I^d. Because a higher real interest rate is required for goods market equilibrium when government purchases increase, an increase in G causes the *IS* curve to shift up and to the right.

Although we have used the example of a temporary change in government expenditures to illustrate shifts in the *IS* curve, it is important to stress that

SUMMARY 12   FACTORS THAT SHIFT THE *IS* CURVE

ALL ELSE EQUAL, AN INCREASE IN	SHIFTS THE *IS* CURVE	REASON
Expected future output	Up and to the right	Desired saving falls (desired consumption rises), raising the real interest rate that clears the goods market.
Wealth	Up and to the right	Desired saving falls (desired consumption rises), raising the real interest rate that clears the goods market.
Government purchases, G	Up and to the right	Desired saving falls (demand for goods rises), raising the real interest rate that clears the goods market.
Taxes, T	No change or down and to the left	No change, if consumers take into account an offsetting future tax cut and do not change consumption (Ricardian equivalence); down, if consumers do not take into account a future tax cut and reduce desired consumption, increasing desired national saving and lowering the real interest rate that clears the goods market.
Expected future marginal product of capital, MPK^f	Up and to the right	Desired investment increases, raising the real interest rate that clears the goods market.
Effective tax rate on capital	Down and to the left	Desired investment falls, lowering the real interest rate that clears the goods market.

changes in government policy variables are not the sole, or even the primary, source of *IS* curve shifts. Many events not originating with changes in government policy affect the position of the *IS* curve. Keynes, for example, stressed the role of what he called *animal spirits* in affecting the economy. By this he meant to describe waves of pessimism and optimism that might affect consumption and investment decisions. This idea is captured in Summary table 12 by the effects on the position of the *IS* curve of an increase (or decrease) in expected future output. Thus, a wave of optimism might cause firms and households to expect higher future output. If so, this will result in the *IS* curve shifting up. Similarly, by affecting household wealth, dramatic movements in the stock market will also cause the *IS* curve to shift. This influence is also described in Summary table 12.

9.3 THE *LM* CURVE: ASSET MARKET EQUILIBRIUM

The third and final market in our macroeconomic model is the asset market, presented in Chapter 7. The asset market is in equilibrium when the quantities of assets demanded by holders of wealth for their portfolios equal the supplies of those assets in the economy. In reality, there are many different assets, both real (houses, consumer durables, office buildings) and financial (chequing accounts, government bonds). Recall, however, that we aggregated all assets into two categories—money and nonmonetary assets. We assumed that the nominal supply of money is M and that money pays a fixed nominal interest rate i^m. Similarly, we assumed that the nominal supply of nonmonetary assets is NM and that these assets pay a nominal interest rate i and (given expected inflation π^e) an expected real interest rate r.

With this aggregation assumption, we showed that the asset market equilibrium condition reduces to the requirement that the quantities of money supplied and demanded be equal. In this section, we show that asset market equilibrium can be represented by the *LM* curve. However, in order to discuss how the asset market comes into equilibrium—a task that we did not complete in Chapter 7—we first introduce an important relationship used every day by traders in financial markets: the relationship between the *price* of a nonmonetary asset and the *interest rate* on that asset.

THE INTEREST RATE AND THE PRICE OF A NONMONETARY ASSET

The price of a nonmonetary asset, such as a government bond, is what a buyer has to pay for it. Its price is closely related to the interest rate that it pays (sometimes called its *yield*). To illustrate this relationship with an example, let's consider a bond that matures in one year. At maturity, we assume, the bondholder will redeem it and receive $10 000; the bond does not pay any interest before it matures.[7] Suppose that this bond can now be purchased for $9615. At this price, over the coming year the bond will increase in value by $385 ($10 000 − $9615), or approximately 4% of its current price of $9615. Therefore, the nominal interest rate on the bond, or its yield, is 4% per year.

[7] A bond that does not pay any interest before maturity is called a *discount bond* or a *zero-coupon bond*.

Now, suppose that for some reason the current price of a $10 000 bond that matures in one year drops to $9524. The increase in the bond's value over the next year will be $476 ($10 000 − $9524), or approximately 5% of the purchase price of $9524. Therefore, when the current price of the bond falls to $9524, the nominal interest rate on the bond increases to 5% per year. More generally, given the promised schedule of repayments of a bond or other nonmonetary asset, the higher the price of the asset, the lower the nominal interest rate the asset pays. Thus, a media report that in yesterday's trading the bond market "strengthened" (bond prices rose) is equivalent to saying that nominal interest rates fell.

We have just indicated why the price of a nonmonetary asset and its nominal interest rate are negatively related to each other. For a given expected rate of inflation π^e, movements in the nominal interest rate are matched by equal movements in the real interest rate, so the price of a nonmonetary asset and its real interest rate are also inversely related. This relationship is a key to deriving the *LM* curve and explaining how the asset market comes into equilibrium.

THE EQUALITY OF MONEY DEMANDED AND MONEY SUPPLIED

To derive the *LM* curve, which represents asset market equilibrium, recall again that the asset market is in equilibrium only if the quantity of money demanded equals the currently available money supply. We depict the equality of money supplied and demanded using the money supply–money demand diagram, shown in Figure 9.4(a). The real interest rate is on the vertical axis and money, measured in real terms, is on the horizontal axis.[8] The *MS* line shows the economy's real money supply, M/P. For simplicity, we may suppose that the central bank sets the nominal money supply M.[9] Thus, for a given price level P, the real money supply M/P is a fixed number and the *MS* line is vertical. For example, if $M = 200$ and $P = 2$, the *MS* line is vertical at $M/P = 100$.

Real money demand at two different levels of income Y is shown by the two *MD* curves in Figure 9.4(a). Recall from Chapter 7 that a higher real interest rate r increases the relative attractiveness of nonmonetary assets and causes holders of wealth to demand less money. Thus, the money demand curves slope downward. The money demand curve *MD* for $Y = 400$ shows the real demand for money when output is 400; similarly, the *MD* curve for $Y = 500$ shows the real demand for money when output is 500. Because an increase in income increases the amount of money demanded at any real interest rate, the money demand curve for $Y = 500$ is farther to the right than the money demand curve for $Y = 400$.

Graphically, asset market equilibrium occurs at the intersection of the money supply and money demand curves, where the real quantities of money supplied and demanded are equal. For example, when output is 400 so that the money demand curve is *MD* ($Y = 400$), the money demand and money supply curves intersect at point *A* in Figure 9.4(a). The real interest rate at *A* is 3%. Thus, when output is 400, the real interest rate that clears the asset market (equalizes the quantities of money supplied and demanded) is 3%. At a real interest rate of 3% and an output of 400, the real quantity of money demanded

---

[8] Asset market equilibrium may be expressed as either nominal money supplied equals nominal money demanded, or as real money supplied equals real money demanded. As in Chapter 7, we work with the condition expressed in real terms.

[9] Chapter 14 describes the tools of Canadian monetary policy.

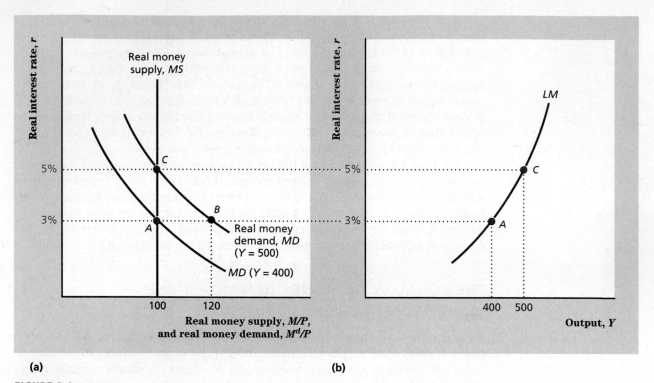

(a)   **(b)**

FIGURE 9.4

DERIVING THE *LM* CURVE

(a) The curves show real money demand and real money supply. Real money supply is fixed at 100. When output is 400, the real money demand curve is *MD* (*Y* = 400); the real interest rate that clears the asset market is 3% (point *A*). When output is 500, more money is demanded at the same real interest rate, so the real money demand curve shifts to the right to *MD* (*Y* = 500). In this case, the real interest rate that clears the asset market is 5% (point *C*).

(b) The graph shows the corresponding *LM* curve. For each level of output, the *LM* curve shows the real interest rate that clears the asset market. Thus, when output is 400, the *LM* curve shows that the real interest rate that clears the goods market is 3% (point *A*). When output is 500, the *LM* curve shows a market-clearing real interest rate of 5% (point *C*). Because higher output raises money demand, and thus raises the real interest rate that clears the asset market, the *LM* curve slopes upward.

by holders of wealth is 100, which equals the real money supply made available by the central bank.

What happens to the asset market equilibrium if output rises from 400 to 500? People need to conduct more transactions, so their real money demand increases at any real interest rate. As a result, the money demand curve shifts up and to the right, to *MD* for *Y* = 500. If the real interest rate remained at 3%, the real quantity of money demanded would exceed the real money supply. At point *B* in Figure 9.4(a), the real quantity of money demanded is 120, which is greater than the real money supply of 100. To restore equality of money demanded and supplied and, thus, bring the asset market back into equilibrium, the real interest rate must rise to 5%. When the real interest rate is 5%, the real quantity of money demanded declines to 100, which is equal to the fixed real money supply (point *C* in Figure 9.4(a)).

How does an increase in the real interest rate eliminate the excess demand for money, and what causes this increase in the real interest rate? Recall that the prices of nonmonetary assets and the interest rates they pay are negatively related. At the initial real interest rate of 3%, the increase in output from 400 to 500 causes people to demand more money (the *MD* curve shifts up and to the right in Figure 9.4(a)). To satisfy their desire to hold more money, people will try to sell some of their nonmonetary assets for money. But when people rush to sell a portion of their nonmonetary assets, the prices of these assets will fall, which will cause the real interest rates on these assets to rise. Thus, it is the public's attempt to increase its holdings of money by selling nonmonetary assets that causes the real interest rate to rise.

Because the real supply of money in the economy is fixed, the public, as a whole, cannot increase the amount of money it holds. As long as people attempt to do so by selling nonmonetary assets, the real interest rate will continue to rise. But the increase in the real interest rate paid by nonmonetary assets makes those assets more attractive relative to money, reducing the real quantity of money demanded (here the movement is *along* the *MD* curve for $Y = 500$, from point B to point C in Figure 9.4(a)). The real interest rate will rise until the real quantity of money demanded again equals the fixed supply of money and restores asset market equilibrium. The new asset market equilibrium is at C, where the real interest rate has risen from 3% to 5%.

The preceding example shows that when output rises, increasing real money demand, a higher real interest rate is needed to maintain equilibrium in the asset market. In general, the relationship between output and the real interest rate that clears the asset market is expressed graphically by the **LM curve**. For any level of output, the *LM* curve shows the real interest rate for which the asset market is in equilibrium, with equal quantities of money supplied and demanded. The term *LM* comes from the asset market equilibrium condition that the real quantity of money demanded, as determined by the real money demand function L, must equal the real money supply M/P.

The *LM* curve corresponding to our numerical example is shown in Figure 9.4(b), with the real interest rate r on the vertical axis and output Y on the horizontal axis. Points A and C lie on the *LM* curve. At A, which corresponds to point A in the money supply–money demand diagram of Figure 9.4(a), output Y is 400, and the real interest rate r is 3%. Because A lies on the *LM* curve, when output is 400, the real interest rate that clears the asset market is 3%. Similarly, because C lies on the *LM* curve, when output is 500, the real interest rate that equalizes money supplied and demanded is 5%; this output–real interest rate combination corresponds to the asset market equilibrium at point C in Figure 9.4(a).

Figure 9.4(b) illustrates the general point that the *LM* curve always slopes upward from left to right. It does so because increases in output, by raising money demand, also raise the real interest rate on nonmonetary assets needed to clear the asset market.

FACTORS THAT SHIFT THE *LM* CURVE

In deriving the *LM* curve, we varied output but held constant other factors, such as the price level, that affect the real interest rate that clears the asset market. Changes in any of these other factors will cause the *LM* curve to shift. In particular, for constant output, *any change that reduces real money supply relative to real money demand will increase the real interest rate that clears the asset market and cause the* LM *curve to shift up and to the left.* Similarly, for constant output, anything that raises real money supply relative to real money demand will reduce the real interest rate that clears the asset market and shift the *LM* curve down and to the right. Here, we discuss in general terms how changes in real money supply or demand affect the *LM* curve. Summary table 13 describes the factors that shift the *LM* curve.

SUMMARY 13 FACTORS THAT SHIFT THE *LM* CURVE

ALL ELSE EQUAL, AN INCREASE IN	SHIFTS THE *LM* CURVE	REASON
Nominal money supply, M	Down and to the right	Real money supply increases, lowering the real interest rate that clears the asset market (equates money supplied and money demanded).
Price level, P	Up and to the left	Real money supply falls, raising the real interest rate that clears the asset market.
Expected inflation, π^e	Down and to the right	Demand for money falls, lowering the real interest rate that clears the asset market.
Nominal interest rate on money, i^m	Up and to the left	Demand for money increases, raising the real interest rate that clears the asset market.

In addition, for constant output, any factor that increases real money demand raises the real interest rate that clears the asset market and shifts the *LM* curve up and to the left. Other factors that increase real money demand (see Summary table 9, p. 215) include

■ an increase in wealth;
■ an increase in the risk of alternative assets relative to the risk of holding money;
■ a decline in the liquidity of alternative assets; and
■ a decline in the efficiency of payment technologies.

Changes in the Real Money Supply

An increase in the real money supply M/P will reduce the real interest rate that clears the asset market and shift the *LM* curve down and to the right. Figure 9.5 illustrates this point and extends our previous numerical example.

Figure 9.5(a) contains the money supply–money demand diagram. Initially, suppose that the real money supply M/P is 100 and output is 400, so the money demand curve is MD ($Y = 400$). Then, equilibrium in the asset market occurs at point A with a market-clearing real interest rate of 3%. The *LM* curve corresponding to the real money supply of 100 is shown as LM ($M/P = 100$) in Figure 9.5(b). At point A on this *LM* curve, as at point A in the money supply–money demand diagram in Figure 9.5(a), output is 400 and the real interest rate is 3%. Because A lies on the initial *LM* curve, when output is 400 and the money supply is 100, the real interest rate that clears the asset market is 3%.

Now, suppose that with output constant at 400, the real money supply rises from 100 to 120. This increase in the real money supply causes the vertical money supply curve to shift to the right, from MS^1 to MS^2 in Figure 9.5(a). The asset market equilibrium point is now point D, where, with output remaining at 400, the market-clearing real interest rate has fallen to 2%.

Why has the real interest rate that clears the asset market fallen? At the initial real interest rate of 3%, there is an excess supply of money—that is, holders of wealth have more money in their portfolios than they want to hold, and consequently, they have a smaller share of their wealth than they would like in nonmonetary assets. To eliminate this imbalance in their portfolios, holders of wealth will want to use some of their money to buy nonmonetary assets. However, when

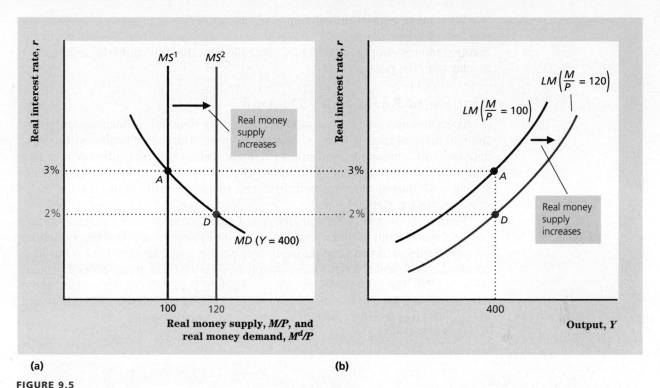

(a)   **(b)**

FIGURE 9.5

AN INCREASE IN THE REAL MONEY SUPPLY SHIFTS THE *LM* CURVE DOWN AND TO THE RIGHT

(a) An increase in the real supply of money shifts the money supply curve to the right, from MS^1 to MS^2. For a constant level of output, the real interest rate that clears the asset market falls. If output is fixed at 400, for example, the money demand curve is MD ($Y = 400$) and the real interest rate that clears the asset market falls from 3% (point A) to 2% (point D).

(b) The graph shows the effect of the increase in real money supply on the *LM* curve. For any level of output, the increase in the real money supply causes the real interest rate that clears the asset market to fall. So, for example, when output is 400, the increase in the real money supply causes the real interest rate that clears the asset market to fall from 3% (point A) to 2% (point D). Thus, the *LM* curve shifts down and to the right, from *LM* for $M/P = 100$ to *LM* for $M/P = 120$.

holders of wealth as a group try to purchase nonmonetary assets, the price of non-monetary assets is bid up and hence the real interest rate paid on these assets declines. As the real interest rate falls, nonmonetary assets become less attractive relative to money. The real interest rate continues to fall until it reaches 2% at point *D* in Figure 9.5(a), where the excess supply of money and the excess demand for nonmonetary assets are eliminated and the asset market is back in equilibrium.

The effect of the increase in real money supply on the *LM* curve is illustrated in Figure 9.5(b). With output constant at 400, the increase in the real money supply lowers the real interest rate that clears the asset market, from 3% to 2%. Thus, point *D*, where $Y = 400$ and $r = 2\%$, is now a point of asset market equilibrium, and point *A* no longer is. More generally, for any given level of output, an increase in the real money supply lowers the real interest rate that clears the asset market. Therefore, the entire *LM* curve shifts down and to the right. The new *LM* curve, *LM* for $M/P = 120$, passes through the new equilibrium point *D* and lies below the old *LM* curve, *LM* for $M/P = 100$.

Thus, with fixed output, an increase in the real money supply lowers the real interest rate that clears the asset market and causes the *LM* curve to shift down and to the right. A similar analysis would show that a drop in the real money supply causes the *LM* curve to shift up and to the left.

What might cause the real money supply to increase? In general, because the real money supply equals M/P, the real money supply will increase whenever the nominal money supply M, which is controlled by the central bank, grows more quickly than the price level P.

Changes in Real Money Demand

A change in any variable that affects real money demand, other than output or the real interest rate, will also shift the LM curve. More specifically, with output constant, an increase in real money demand raises the real interest rate that clears the asset market and, thus, shifts the LM curve up and to the left. Analogously, with output constant, a drop in real money demand shifts the LM curve down and to the right.

Figure 9.6 shows a graphical analysis of an increase in money demand similar to that for a change in money supply shown in Figure 9.5. As before, the money supply–money demand diagram is shown on the left, Figure 9.6(a). Output is constant at 400, and the real money supply again is 100. The initial money demand curve is MD^1. The initial asset market equilibrium point is at A, where the money demand curve MD^1 and the money supply curve MS intersect. At initial equilibrium, point A, the real interest rate that clears the asset market is 3%.

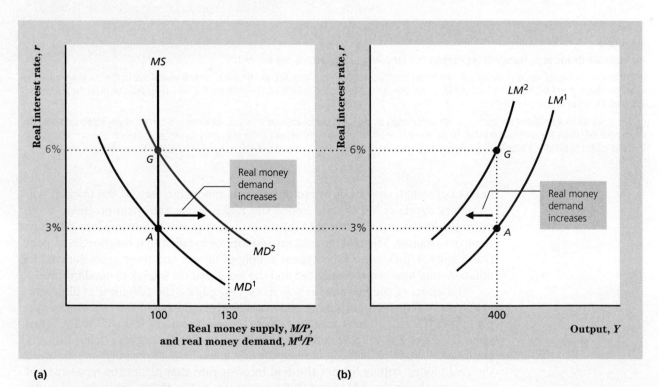

(a)   **(b)**

FIGURE 9.6

AN INCREASE IN REAL MONEY DEMAND SHIFTS THE *LM* CURVE UP AND TO THE LEFT

(a) With output constant at 400 and the real money supply at 100, an increase in the interest rate paid on money raises real money demand. The money demand curve shifts up and to the right, from MD^1 to MD^2, and the real interest rate that clears the asset market rises from 3% (point A) to 6% (point G).

(b) The graph shows the effect of the increase in real money demand on the LM curve. When output is 400, the increase in real money demand raises the real interest rate that clears the asset market from 3% (point A) to 6% (point G). More generally, for any level of output, the increase in real money demand raises the real interest rate that clears the asset market. Thus, the LM curve shifts up and to the left, from LM^1 to LM^2.

Now, suppose that for a fixed level of output, a change occurs in the economy that increases real money demand. For example, if banks decided to increase the interest rate paid on money, i^m, the public would want to hold more money at the same levels of output and the real interest rate. Graphically, the increase in money demand shifts the money demand curve up and to the right, from MD^1 to MD^2 in Figure 9.6(a). At the initial real interest rate of 3% the real quantity of money demanded is 130, which exceeds the available supply of 100; so, 3% is no longer the value of the real interest rate that clears the asset market.

How will the real interest rate that clears the asset market change after the increase in money demand? If holders of wealth want to hold more money, they will exchange nonmonetary assets for money. Increased sales of nonmonetary assets will drive down their price and, thus, raise the real interest rate they pay. The real interest rate will rise, reducing the attractiveness of holding money, until the public is satisfied to hold the available real money supply (100). The real interest rate rises from its initial value of 3% at A to 6% at G.

Figure 9.6(b) shows the effect of the increase in money demand on the *LM* curve. The initial *LM* curve, LM^1, passes through point A, showing that when output is 400 the real interest rate that clears the asset market is 3%. (Point A in Figure 9.6(b) corresponds to point A in Figure 9.6(a).) Following the increase in money demand, with output fixed at 400, the market-clearing real interest rate rises to 6%. Thus, the new *LM* curve must pass through point G (corresponding to point G in Figure 9.6(a)), where $Y = 400$ and $r = 6\%$. The new *LM* curve, LM^2, is higher than LM^1 because the real interest rate that clears the asset market is now higher for any level of output.

9.4 GENERAL EQUILIBRIUM IN THE COMPLETE *IS–LM–FE* MODEL

The next step is to put the labour market, the goods market, and the asset market together and examine the equilibrium of the economy as a whole. A situation in which all markets in an economy are simultaneously in equilibrium is called a **general equilibrium**. Figure 9.7 shows the complete *IS–LM–FE* model, illustrating how the general equilibrium of the economy is determined. The figure shows

- the full-employment, or *FE*, line, along which the labour market is in equilibrium;
- the *IS* curve, along which the goods market is in equilibrium; and
- the *LM* curve, along which the asset market is in equilibrium.

The three curves intersect at point E, indicating that all three markets are in equilibrium at that point. Therefore, E represents a general equilibrium, and because it is the only point that lies on all three curves, it represents the only general equilibrium for this economy.

Although point E obviously is a general equilibrium point, it is not so clear what forces, if any, act to bring the economy to that point. To put it another way, although the *IS* curve and *FE* line must intersect somewhere, we have not explained why the *LM* curve must pass through that same point. In Section 9.5 we discuss the economic forces that lead the economy to general equilibrium. There we show that (1) the general equilibrium of the economy always occurs at the intersection of the *IS* curve and the *FE* line; and (2) adjustments of the price level cause the *LM* curve to shift until it passes through the general equilibrium point

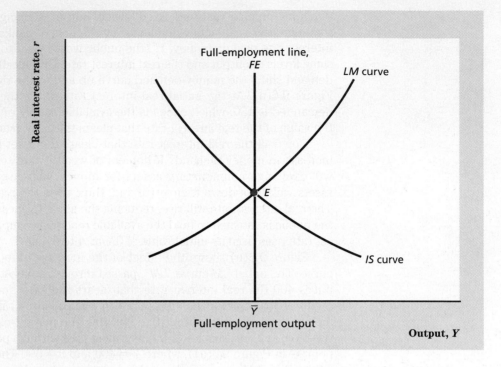

defined by the intersection of the *IS* curve and the *FE* line. Before discussing the details of this adjustment process, however, let's consider an example that illustrates the use of the complete *IS–LM–FE* model.

APPLYING THE *IS–LM–FE* FRAMEWORK: A TEMPORARY ADVERSE SUPPLY SHOCK

An economic shock relevant to business cycle analysis is an adverse supply shock. Specifically, suppose that (because of bad weather or a temporary increase in oil prices) the productivity parameter *A* in the production function drops temporarily.[10] We can use the *IS–LM–FE* model to analyze the effects of this shock on the general equilibrium of the economy and the general equilibrium values of such economic variables as the real wage, employment, output, the real interest rate, the price level, consumption, and investment.

Suppose that the economy is initially in general equilibrium at point *E* in Figure 9.8(a), where the initial *FE* line, FE^1, *IS* curve, and *LM* curve, LM^1, for this economy intersect. To determine the effects of a temporary supply shock on the general equilibrium of this economy, we must consider how the temporary drop in productivity *A* affects the positions of the *FE* line and the *IS* and *LM* curves.

The *FE* line describes equilibrium in the labour market. Hence, to find the effect of the supply shock on the *FE* line, we must start by looking at how the shock affects labour supply and labour demand. In Chapter 3, we demonstrated that an adverse supply shock reduces the marginal product of labour and, thus, shifts the labour demand curve down (see Figure 3.9, p. 72). Because the supply

---

[10] Recall that the production function, Eq. (3.1), is $Y = AF(K, N)$, so a drop in *A* reduces the amount of output that can be produced for any quantities of capital *K* and labour *N*.

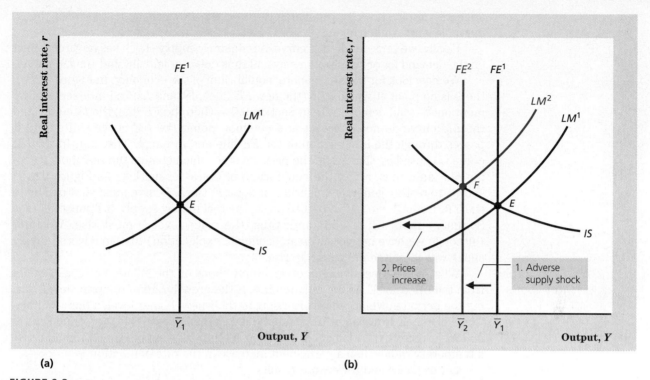

(a)   **(b)**

FIGURE 9.8

EFFECTS OF A TEMPORARY ADVERSE SUPPLY SHOCK

(a) Initially, the economy is in general equilibrium at point E, with output at its full-employment level $\overline{Y}_1$.

(b) A temporary adverse supply shock reduces full-employment output from $\overline{Y}_1$ to $\overline{Y}_2$ and shifts the *FE* line to the left from FF^1 to FE^2. The new general equilibrium is represented by point F, where FE^2 intersects the unchanged *IS* curve. The price level increases and shifts the *LM* curve up and to the left, from LM^1 to LM^2, until it passes through F. At the new general equilibrium point, F, output is lower, the real interest rate is higher, and the price level is higher than at the original general equilibrium point, E.

shock is temporary, we assume that it does not affect workers' wealth or expected future wages and so does not affect labour supply. As a result of the decline in labour demand, the equilibrium values of the real wage and employment, $\overline{N}$, fall. The *FE* line shifts only to the degree that full-employment output $\overline{Y}$ changes. Does $\overline{Y}$ change? Yes. Recall from Chapter 3 that an adverse supply shock reduces full-employment output $\overline{Y}$, which equals $AF(K, \overline{N})$, for two reasons: (1) as we just mentioned, the supply shock reduces the equilibrium level of employment $\overline{N}$, which lowers the amount of output that can be produced; and (2) the drop in productivity A directly reduces the amount of output produced by any combination of capital and labour. The reduction in $\overline{Y}$ is represented by a shift to the left of the *FE* line, from FE^1 to FE^2 in Figure 9.8(b).

Now, consider the effects of the temporary adverse supply shock on the *IS* curve. Recall that we derived the *IS* curve by changing the level of current output in the saving–investment diagram (see Figure 9.2, p. 248) and finding for each level of current output the real interest rate for which desired saving equals desired investment. A *temporary* adverse supply shock reduces current output but does not change any other factor affecting desired saving or investment (such as wealth, expected future income, or the future marginal product of capital). Therefore, a temporary supply shock is just the sort of change in current output that we used to trace out the *IS* curve. We conclude that a temporary adverse supply shock is a movement *along* the *IS* curve, *not a shift* of the *IS* curve, leaving it unchanged.[11]

Finally, we consider the *LM* curve. A temporary supply shock has no direct effect on the demand for or supply of money and thus does not initially shift the *LM* curve.

We now look for the new general equilibrium of the economy. In Figure 9.8(b), there is no point at which FE^2 (the new *FE* line), *IS*, and LM^1 all intersect. As we mentioned—and demonstrate in Section 9.5—when the *FE* line, the *IS* curve, and the *LM* curve do not intersect at a common point, the *LM* curve shifts until it passes through the intersection of the *FE* line and *IS* curve. This shift in the *LM* curve is caused by changes in the price level P, which change the real money supply M/P and, thus, affect the equilibrium of the asset market. As Figure 9.8(b) shows, to restore general equilibrium at point F, the *LM* curve must shift up and to the left, from LM^1 to LM^2. For it to do so, the real money supply M/P must fall (see Summary table 13, p. 256) and, thus, the price level P must rise. We infer (although we have not yet given an economic explanation) that an adverse supply shock will cause the price level to rise.

What is the effect of a temporary supply shock on the inflation rate, as distinct from the price level? As the inflation rate is the growth rate of the price level, during the period in which prices are rising to their new, higher level, a burst of inflation will occur. However, after the price level stabilizes at its higher value (and is no longer rising), inflation subsides. Thus, a temporary supply shock should cause a temporary rather than a permanent increase in the rate of inflation.

Let us pause and review our results.

1. As we have already shown in Chapter 3, a temporary adverse supply shock lowers the equilibrium values of the real wage and employment.

2. Comparing the new general equilibrium, point F, to the old general equilibrium, point E, in Figure 9.8(b), we see that the supply shock lowers output and raises the real interest rate.

3. The supply shock raises the price level and causes a temporary burst in inflation.

4. Because in the new general equilibrium the real interest rate is higher and output is lower, consumption must be lower than before the supply shock. The higher real interest rate also implies that investment must be lower after the shock.

In the Application "Oil Price Shocks Revisited" we see how well our model explains the historical behaviour of the economy.

APPLICATION

OIL PRICE SHOCKS REVISITED

In Chapter 3, we pointed out that an increase in the price of oil is an example of an adverse supply shock, and we looked at the effects of the 1973–1974 and 1979–1980 oil price shocks on the Canadian economy (see the Application "Output, Employment, and the Real Wage During Oil Price Shocks," p. 72). The theory's predictions—that adverse supply shocks reduce output, employment,

---

[11] Analytical Problem 2 at the end of the chapter examines the effect of a permanent adverse supply shock and identifies factors that shift the *IS* curve in that case.

and the real wage—were confirmed for those two episodes. Our analysis using the complete *IS–LM–FE* model is consistent with that earlier discussion. However, it adds the predictions that following an oil price shock, consumption and investment decline, inflation increases, and the real interest rate rises. How well do these predictions match up with what was observed during those periods?

Figure 8.5 (p. 236) shows that real consumption expenditures on durable goods[12] and real investment spending both fell after these oil price shocks. During 1974, real consumption expenditures on durable goods fell 6.6% and real investment expenditures fell 4.8%. Following the onset of the recession in the first quarter of 1980, real consumption expenditures on durable goods fell by 6.1%, and real investment expenditures fell by 3.5% in just one quarter. Inflation also behaved as predicted by our analysis, surging temporarily in 1973–1974 and again in 1979–1980 (see Figure 7.3, p. 224). Our analysis using the *IS–LM–FE* model is therefore consistent with observations of how key macroeconomic variables changed in response to the adverse supply shocks brought about by large increases in the price of oil in the 1970s.

9.5 PRICE ADJUSTMENT AND THE ATTAINMENT OF GENERAL EQUILIBRIUM

We now explain the economic forces that lead prices to change and shift the *LM* curve until it passes through the intersection of the *IS* curve and the *FE* line. In discussing the role of price adjustments in bringing the economy back to general equilibrium, we also show the basic difference between the two main approaches to business cycle analysis: classical and Keynesian.

To illustrate the adjustment process, we first use the complete *IS–LM–FE* model to consider what happens to the economy if the nominal money supply increases. This analysis allows us to discuss monetary policy (the control of the money supply) and to introduce some ongoing controversies about the effects of monetary policy on the economy. We then use the complete *IS–LM–FE* model to consider how the economy responds to a fiscal expansion caused by an increase in government purchases. That analysis will allow us to discuss fiscal policy (changes in government purchases and changes in tax rates) and its effects on the economy.

THE EFFECTS OF A MONETARY EXPANSION

Suppose that the central bank decides to raise the nominal money supply M by 10%. For now, we hold the price level P constant so that the real money supply M/P also increases by 10%. What effects will this monetary expansion have on the economy? Figure 9.9 helps us answer this question with the complete *IS–LM–FE* model.

The three parts of Figure 9.9 show the sequence of events involved in the analysis. For simplicity, suppose that the economy is initially in general equilibrium, so that in Figure 9.9(a), the *IS* curve, the *FE* line, and the initial *LM*

---

[12] We focus on consumption expenditures on durable goods because, as we noted in Chapter 8, these expenditures are the most sensitive to changes in the real interest rate. Since the oil price shocks increase the real interest rate and lower income, their effect should be most pronounced on durable goods consumption.

FIGURE 9.9

EFFECTS OF A MONETARY EXPANSION

(a) The economy is in general equilibrium at point E. Output equals the full-employment level of 1000, the real interest rate is 5%, and the price level is 100.

(b) With the price level fixed, a 10% increase in the nominal money supply M raises the real money supply M/P and shifts the LM curve down and to the right, from LM^1 to LM^2. At point F, the intersection of the IS curve and the new LM curve, LM^2, the real interest rate has fallen to 3%, which raises the aggregate demand for goods. If firms produce extra output to meet the increase in aggregate demand, output rises to 1200 (higher than full-employment output of 1000).

(c) Because aggregate demand exceeds full-employment output at point F, firms raise prices. A 10% rise in P, from 100 to 110, restores the real money supply to its original level and shifts the LM curve back to its original position at LM^1. This returns the economy to point E, where output again is at its full-employment level of 1000, but the price level has risen 10%, from 100 to 110.

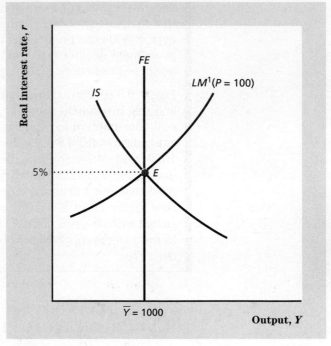

(a)

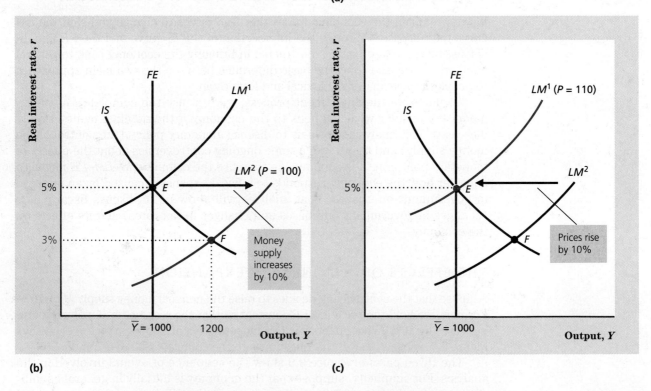

(b)   (c)

curve, LM^1, all pass through the general equilibrium point, E. At E, output equals its full-employment value of 1000, and the real interest rate is 5%. Both the IS and LM curves pass through E, so we know that 5% is the market-clearing real interest rate in both the goods and asset markets. For the moment, the price level, P, is fixed at its initial level of 100.

The 10% increase in the real supply of money M/P does not shift the IS curve or the FE line because with output and the real interest rate held constant, a change in M/P does not affect desired national saving, desired investment, labour demand, labour supply, or productivity. However, Figure 9.5 (p. 257) showed that an increase in the real money supply does shift the LM curve down and to the right, which we show here as a shift of the LM curve from LM^1 to LM^2, in Figure 9.9(b). The LM curve shifts down and to the right because at any level of output, an increase in the money supply lowers the real interest rate needed to clear the asset market.

Note that after the LM curve has shifted down to LM^2, there is no point in Figure 9.9(b) at which all three curves intersect. In other words, the goods market, the labour market, and the asset market are no longer in equilibrium simultaneously. We now must make some assumptions about how the economy behaves when it is not in general equilibrium.

Of the three markets in the model, the asset market (represented by the LM curve) undoubtedly adjusts the most quickly because financial markets can respond within minutes to changes in economic conditions. The labour market (the FE line) is probably the slowest to adjust because the process of matching workers and jobs takes time and wages may be renegotiated only periodically. The adjustment speed of the goods market (IS curve) is probably somewhere in the middle. We assume that when the economy is not in general equilibrium, the asset market and the goods market are in equilibrium *so that output and the real interest rate are given by the intersection of the IS and LM curves*. Note that when the economy is not in general equilibrium the IS–LM intersection does not lie on the FE line, so the labour market is not in equilibrium.

Immediately after the increase in the nominal money supply, therefore, the economy is out of general equilibrium with the level of output and the real interest rate represented by point F in Figure 9.9(b), where the new LM curve, LM^2, intersects the IS curve. At F, output (1200) is higher and the real interest rate (3%) is lower than at the original general equilibrium, point E. We refer to F, the point at which the economy comes to rest before any adjustment occurs in the price level, as the *short-run equilibrium point*. Note that although we refer to F as a short-run equilibrium point, we must keep in mind that only the asset and goods markets are in equilibrium there—the labour market is not.[13]

In economic terms, why does the increase in the money supply shift the economy to point F? The sequence of events can be described as follows: After the increase in the money supply, holders of wealth are holding more money in their portfolios than they desire at the initial values of output and the real interest rate. To bring their portfolios back into balance, they will try to use their excess money to buy nonmonetary assets. However, as holders of wealth bid for nonmonetary assets, they put upward pressure on the price of those assets, which reduces their interest rate. Thus, after an increase in the money supply, wealth-holders' attempts to achieve their desired mix of money and nonmonetary assets cause the interest rate to fall.

---

[13] It is also important to remember that, as a matter of simplification, we are assuming in this chapter and the next that the price level is fixed in the short run. Thus, in this chapter it is accurate to say that the short-run equilibrium occurs prior to *any* change in the price level. More generally, however, we will allow the price level to change in the short run. We explain this adjustment in Chapters 11 and 12. In those chapters the short-run equilibrium will occur prior to the *full* adjustment in the price level required to bring the labour market into equilibrium. In both this chapter and the next, it is always the case that only the asset and goods markets are in equilibrium in the short run—the labour market is not.

The drop in the real interest rate is not the end of the story, however. Because the lower real interest rate increases the demand by households for consumption, C^d, and the demand by firms for investment, I^d, the aggregate demand for goods rises. Here, we make a fundamental assumption, to which we will return shortly: When demanders increase their spending on goods, firms are willing (at least temporarily) to produce enough to meet the extra demand for their output. After the decline in the real interest rate raises the aggregate demand for goods, therefore, we assume that firms respond by increasing production, leading to higher output at the short-run equilibrium point, F.

To summarize, with the price level constant, an increase in the nominal money supply takes the economy to the short-run equilibrium point, F, in Figure 9.9(b), at which the real interest rate is lower and output is higher than at the initial general equilibrium point, E. We made two assumptions: (1) when the economy is not in general equilibrium, the economy's short-run equilibrium occurs at the intersection of the IS and LM curves; and (2) when the aggregate demand for goods rises, firms are willing (at least temporarily) to produce enough extra output to meet the expanded demand.

The Adjustment of the Price Level

So far, we have simply taken the price level P as fixed. In reality, prices respond to conditions of supply and demand in the economy. The price level P refers to the price of output (goods), so to think about how prices are likely to adjust in this example, let's reconsider the effects of the increase in the money supply on the goods market.

In Figure 9.9(b), the short-run equilibrium point, F, lies on the IS curve, implying that the goods market is in equilibrium at that point with equal aggregate quantities of goods supplied and demanded. Recall our assumption that firms are willing to meet any increases in aggregate demand by producing more. In that sense, then, the aggregate quantity of goods supplied equals the aggregate quantity of goods demanded. However, in another sense, the goods market is *not* in equilibrium at point F. The problem is that in order to meet the aggregate demand for goods at F, firms have to produce more output than their full-employment level of output $\overline{Y}$. Full-employment output $\overline{Y}$ is the level of output that maximizes firms' profits because that level of output corresponds to the profit-maximizing level of employment (Chapter 3). Therefore, in meeting the higher level of aggregate demand, firms are producing more output than they want to. In the sense that, at point F, the production of goods by firms is *not* the level of output that maximizes their profits, the goods market is not truly in equilibrium.

At point F the aggregate demand for goods exceeds firms' desired supply of output $\overline{Y}$, so we can expect that at some point firms will begin raising their prices, causing the price level P to rise. With the nominal money supply M set by the central bank, an increase in the price level P lowers the real money supply M/P, which, in turn, causes the LM curve to shift up and to the left. Indeed, as long as the aggregate quantity of goods demanded exceeds what firms want to supply, prices will keep rising. Thus, the LM curve will keep shifting up and to the left until the aggregate quantity of goods demanded equals full-employment output. Aggregate demand equals full-employment output only when the LM curve has returned to its initial position, LM^1 in Figure 9.9(c), where it passes through the original general equilibrium point, E. At E, all three markets of the economy again are in equilibrium, with output at its full-employment level.

Compare Figure 9.9(c) with the initial situation in Figure 9.9(a) and note that after the adjustment of the price level, the 10% increase in the nominal money supply has had no effect on output or the real interest rate. Employment is also unchanged from its initial value, as the economy has returned to its original level of output. However, as a result of the 10% increase in the nominal money supply, the price level is 10% higher (so that $P = 110$). How do we know that the price level changes by exactly 10%? To return the *LM* curve to its original position, the increase in the price level had to return the real money supply M/P to its original value. Because the nominal money supply M was raised by 10%, to return M/P to its original value the price level P had to rise by 10% as well. Thus, the change in the nominal money supply causes the price level to change proportionally. This result is the same result obtained in Chapter 7 (see Eq. 7.10, p. 220), where we assumed that all markets are in equilibrium.

Note that because in general equilibrium the price level has risen by 10% but real economic variables are unaffected, all nominal economic variables must also rise by 10%. In particular, for the real wage to have the same value after prices have risen by 10% as it did before, the nominal wage must rise by 10%. Thus, the return of the economy to general equilibrium requires adjustment of the nominal wage (the price of labour) as well as the price of goods.

Our explanation of how the price level adjusts in the *IS–LM–FE* model is straightforward. Defining $\overline{Y}$ as the full-employment level of output, the price level P rises whenever the observed level of output (Y) exceeds $\overline{Y}$. Similarly, the price level P falls whenever the observed level of output (Y) is less than $\overline{Y}$.

Recall that in Section 9.4, when we discussed the effects of a temporary adverse supply shock with the aid of Figure 9.8, we inferred a change in the price level without offering an economic explanation of why that change would occur.

A CLOSER LOOK 9.1

TREND MONEY GROWTH AND INFLATION

In Figure 9.9, we analyzed the effects of a one-time 10% increase in the nominal money supply, followed by a one-time 10% adjustment in the price level. In reality, in most countries, the money supply and the price level grow continuously. Our framework easily handles this situation. Suppose that in some country, both the nominal money supply M and the price level P are growing steadily at 7% per year, which implies that the real money supply M/P is constant. The *LM* curve depends on the real money supply M/P, so in this situation the *LM* curve will not shift, even though the nominal money supply and prices are rising.

Now, suppose that for one year, the money supply of this country is increased an additional 3%—for a total of 10%—while prices rise 7%. Then the real money supply M/P grows by 3% (10% − 7%), and the *LM* curve shifts down and to the right. Similarly, if for one year the nominal money supply increased by only 4%, with

inflation still at 7% per year, the *LM* curve would shift up, reflecting the 3% drop (−3% = 4% − 7%) in the real money supply.

This example illustrates that changes in M or P *relative to the expected or trend rate of growth of money and inflation* (7% in this example) shift the *LM* curve. Thus, when we analyze the effects of "an increase in the money supply," we have in mind an increase in the money supply relative to the expected, or trend, rate of money growth (for example, a rise from 7% to 10% growth for one year); by a "decrease in the money supply," we mean a drop relative to a trend rate (such as a decline from 7% to 4% growth in money). Similarly, if we say something like "the price level falls to restore general equilibrium," we do not necessarily mean that the price level literally falls, but only that it rises by less than its trend or expected rate of growth would suggest.

We now have that explanation. In Figure 9.8 the adverse supply shock caused full-employment output to fall from $\overline{Y}_1$ to $\overline{Y}_2$ and so caused the *FE* line to shift from FE^1 to FE^2. With short-run equilibrium at point E, output was greater than what was now the full-employment level of output, $\overline{Y}_2$. The price level would therefore eventually increase, and in doing so reduce the real money supply. The result is a shift of the *LM* relationship from LM^1 to LM^2 and a re-establishment of full equilibrium at point F.

THE EFFECTS OF A FISCAL EXPANSION

Now suppose the government chooses to increase the level of government purchases. What effects will this fiscal expansion have on the economy? We use Figure 9.10, where the complete *IS–LM–FE* model is described, to answer this question. As we did with our examination of a monetary expansion, we use Figure 9.10 to show the sequence of events involved in this analysis. We show first how the economy responds in the short-run when we hold the price level, P, constant and then relax that assumption to show how the economy eventually adjusts back into a general equilibrium.

We begin with Figure 9.10(a), where we show the economy in general equilibrium at point E. The *IS*, *LM*, and *FE* lines all intersect at full-employment level of output $\overline{Y}$, which we assume has a value of 1000. The real interest rate is 5%, and we assume the price level P has a value of 100.

The increase in government purchases shifts the *IS* curve from IS^1 to IS^2. We assume the central bank does nothing in response, and so does not change the nominal money supply M. Since for the moment we are also holding the price level P constant, there is no change in the real money supply M/P and so no change in the position of the *LM* curve.

With the shift of the *IS* curve, there is no point in Figure 9.10(b) at which all three markets intersect. In other words, the economy is no longer in general equilibrium. Recalling our assumption that of the three markets in the *IS–LM–FE* model, the labour market (represented by the *FE* curve) is the slowest to adjust, we assume that when the economy is not in general equilibrium, the asset market and the goods market are nonetheless in equilibrium. In terms of Figure 9.10(b), we are at point F where, although the goods and asset markets are in equilibrium, the labour market is not. This is the short-run equilibrium point. At point F, both output (1200) and the real interest rate (6%) are higher than at the original general equilibrium, point E.

In economic terms, we adjusted from point E to point F as a consequence of two influences. The first is the **multiplier effect**. This arises because the increase in government purchases in the form of, say, increased construction of new roads expands the demand for goods and so increases the number of transactions in the economy. The increase in transactions provides additional income to, for example, those whom the government hired to construct new roads. Those people in turn spend their new income on goods and services provided by others who, of course, now also enjoy an increase in income. In this way the impact of the initial increase in government purchases is multiplied a number of times over.[14]

---

[14] The multiplier effect eventually peters out because at each stage some fraction of new income is saved, and this reduces the amount of additional income that is used to purchase goods from the next person. The size of the multiplier effect depends on the marginal propensity to save: the fraction of additional income that people choose to save rather than spend. The larger the marginal propensity to save, the smaller the multiplier effect.

FIGURE 9.10

EFFECTS OF A FISCAL EXPANSION

(a) The economy is in general equilibrium at point *E*. Output equals the full-employment level of 1000, the real interest rate is 5%, and the price level is 100.

(b) An increase in government spending shifts the *IS* curve up and to the right from IS^1 to IS^2. At point *F*, the intersection of the *LM* curve and the new *IS* curve, IS^2, the real interest rate has increased to 6%, which reduces private investment, partially offsetting the increase in aggregate demand caused by the increase in government spending. If firms produce extra output to meet the net increase in aggregate demand, output rises to 1200 and is now higher than full-employment output.

(c) Because aggregate demand exceeds full-employment output, the price level rises from 100 to 105. The increase in the price level reduces the real money supply and shifts the *LM* curve to *LM* (*P* = 105). This returns the economy to general equilibrium at point *G*. Output has returned to full-employment output of 1000, the price level has risen, and the real interest rate has increased.

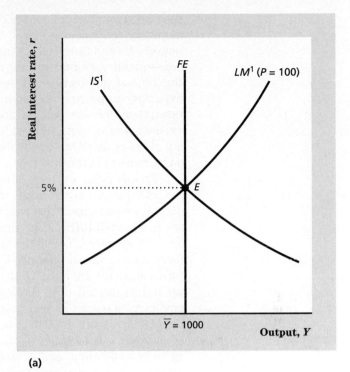

(a)

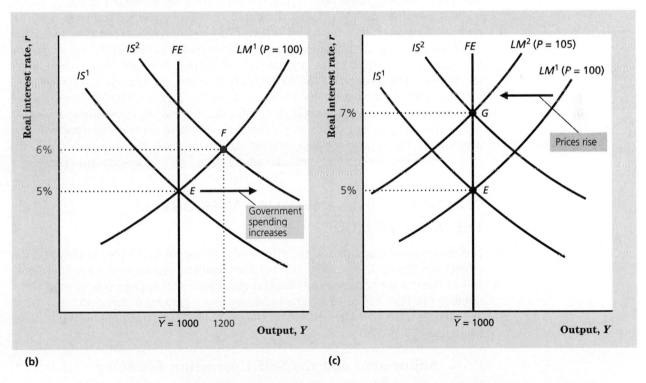

(b)   **(c)**

The other influence affecting the adjustment from point *E* to point *F* is the **crowding out effect**. The increase in new spending caused by the increase in government purchases implies more transactions, and this in turn requires that households hold more of their financial wealth in the form of money. If the central bank has not increased the supply of money, then households and firms can satisfy their need for greater liquidity only by reallocating their financial wealth from non-monetary to monetary assets. This reallocation of financial wealth requires that households and firms sell nonmonetary assets, which causes their price to fall and, consequently, the real interest rate to increase. Thus, as we see in Figure 9.10(b), the interest rate increases from, in this example, 5%–6%. Now firms find it more expensive to borrow, and so investment spending falls. The increase in interest rates, then, "crowds out" private sector investment that would otherwise cause an expansion of output. The net influence of the multiplier effect and the crowding out effect is, as shown by the movement from point E to point F in Figure 9.10(b), an increase in output.

To this point we have simply taken the price level P as fixed. However, as described above, when in the short-run output is different from full-employment output, we can expect that at some point firms will change their prices. Since, as we see in Figure 9.10(b), short-run output is above full equilibrium output, the price level P begins to rise. With the nominal money supply M held constant by the central bank, an increase in the price level P lowers the real money supply M/P, which, in turn, causes the LM curve to shift up and to the left. The LM curve will keep shifting up and to the left until the aggregate quantity of goods demanded equals full-employment output $\overline{Y}$. Aggregate demand equals full-employment output only when the LM curve has shifted to position LM^2, as shown in Figure 9.10(c). A new general equilibrium is established at point G, where all three markets of the economy are again in equilibrium. At G, output has returned to its full-employment level $\overline{Y}$, the interest rate has increased to 7%, and the price level has increased to 105.

Compare Figure 9.10(c) with the initial situation described in Figure 9.10(a), and note that after the adjustment of the price level, output has returned to its full-employment level. Employment is also unchanged from its initial value, as the economy has returned to its original level of output. Nominal wages, then, must increase by the amount of the price level P. Since we assume the price level increased by 5%, it must be that nominal wages also increased by 5% so as to leave the real wage unchanged. Finally, note that the increase in government spending has, in the end, crowded out an equivalent amount of private consumption and investment. By causing the real interest rate to increase, the increase in government purchases permanently crowds out consumption and investment spending.

CLASSICAL VERSUS KEYNESIAN VERSIONS OF THE *IS–LM–FE* MODEL

Our diagrammatic analyses of the effects of a change in the money supply and the effects of a change in government purchases highlights two questions that are central to the debate between the classical and Keynesian approaches to macroeconomics: (1) How rapidly does the economy reach general equilibrium? (2) What are the effects of monetary policy on the economy? Let's examine both questions using the *IS–LM–FE* model.

Price Adjustment and the Self-Correcting Economy

In our analyses of the effects of a monetary expansion and the effects of an increase in government purchases, we showed that the economy is brought into general equilibrium by adjustment of the price level. In graphical terms, if the intersection of the *IS* and *LM* curves lies to the right of the *FE* line—so that the aggregate quantity of goods demanded exceeds full-employment output, as in Figures 9.9(b) and

9.10(b)—the price level will rise. The increase in P shifts the LM curve up and to the left, reducing the quantity of goods demanded, until all three curves intersect at the general equilibrium point, as in Figures 9.9(c) and 9.10(c). Similarly, if the $IS–LM$ intersection lies to the left of the full-employment line—so that desired spending on goods is below firms' profit-maximizing level of output—firms will cut prices. A decrease in the price level raises the real money supply and shifts the LM curve down and to the right until all three curves again intersect, returning the economy to general equilibrium.

There is little controversy about the idea that after some sort of economic disturbance, price level adjustments will eventually restore the economy to general equilibrium. However, the speed at which this process takes place is a much-debated issue in macroeconomics. Under the classical assumption that prices are flexible, the adjustment process is rapid. When prices are flexible, the economy is effectively self-correcting, automatically returning to full employment after a shock moves it away from general equilibrium. Indeed, if firms respond to increased demand by raising prices rather than by temporarily producing more (as we earlier assumed), the adjustment process would be almost immediate.

According to the opposing Keynesian view, however, sluggish adjustment of prices (and of wages, the price of labour) might prevent general equilibrium from being attained for a much longer period, perhaps even several years. While the economy is not in general equilibrium, Keynesians argue, output is determined by the level of aggregate demand, represented by the intersection of the IS and LM curves; the economy is not on the FE line, and the labour market is not in equilibrium. This assumption of sluggish price adjustment, and the consequent disequilibrium in the labour market, distinguishes the Keynesian version of the $IS–LM–FE$ model from the classical version.

It is useful at this point to look ahead to an issue we will address more fully in Chapters 11 and 12: macroeconomic stabilization policy. The list of factors that shift the IS and LM curves, presented in Summary tables 12 and 13 (pp. 251 and 256), is a long one, and only some of these are under the direct control of fiscal and monetary policymakers. We have noted how many shifts in the IS and LM curves arise due to unexpected shocks and due to events that cause households and firms to alter their expectations about the future. We have also discussed how shocks can affect the position of the FE line (these are listed in Summary table 11, p. 247). We have noted, for example, how unexpected changes in oil prices, which emanate from outside of Canada, have in the past proven to have important impacts on the economy. Unexpected shifts in the IS, LM, and FE curves are the source of business cycles—output fluctuations in the normal growth path of the economy. *Stabilization policy* refers to the use of fiscal and monetary policy to shift the positions of the IS and LM curves so as to offset the effects of such shocks and so reduce the size of fluctuations in the economy.

Our discussion of price adjustments and the self-correcting economy suggests that not all economists will judge stabilization policies to be useful. Those economists who believe prices are very flexible believe the economy adjusts quickly to changes that take it away from general equilibrium. Thus, adherents of the classical model believe there is no need for stabilization policies; the economy is quickly self-correcting. Adherents of the Keynesian model, on the other hand, stress that prices can be slow to adjust to changes in the economy and so the economy can remain in disequilibrium for an extended period of time. Many Keynesians argue that rather than allow households and firms to suffer the consequences of a prolonged disequilibrium, policymakers ought to use the levers of fiscal and monetary policy to shift *IS* and *LM* curves in a way that returns the economy to general equilibrium more quickly. We return to this debate in Chapters 11 and 12, but it is useful to note here that the source of disagreement over the use of stabilization policy is based on a central source of disagreement among macroeconomists: How fast do prices adjust?

Monetary Neutrality

Closely related to the issue of how fast the economy reaches general equilibrium is the question of how a change in the nominal money supply affects the economy. We showed that after the economy reaches its general equilibrium, an increase in the nominal money supply has no effect on real variables, such as output, employment, or the real interest rate, but raises the price level. Economists say that there is **monetary neutrality**, or simply that money is neutral, if a change in the nominal money supply changes the price level proportionally but has no effect on real variables. Our analysis shows that after the complete adjustment of prices, money is neutral in the *IS–LM–FE* model.

The practical relevance of monetary neutrality is much debated by classicals and Keynesians. The basic issue again is the speed of price adjustment. In the classical view, a monetary expansion is rapidly transmitted into prices and has, at most, a transitory effect on real variables; that is, the economy moves quickly from the situation shown in Figures 9.9(a) and 9.10(a) to the situation shown in Figures 9.9(c) and 9.10(c), spending little time in the positions shown in Figures 9.9(b) and 9.10(b). Keynesians agree that money is neutral after prices fully adjust, but they believe that because of slow price adjustments, the economy may spend considerable time in the short-run equilibriums identified in Figures 9.9(b) and 9.10(b).

In brief, Keynesians believe in monetary neutrality in the long run (after prices adjust) but not in the short run. Classicals are more accepting of the view that money is neutral even in the relatively short run. We return to the issue of monetary neutrality when we develop the classical and Keynesian models of the business cycle in more detail in Chapters 11 and 12.

9.6 THE AGGREGATE DEMAND CURVE

The *IS–LM–FE* model introduced in this chapter is a complete model representing the general equilibrium of the economy. It is one of the key diagrams of macroeconomic analysis. However, a key ingredient missing from the *IS–LM–FE* model is an understanding of the importance of the way in which households and firms form expectations about the future. Recall that in this chapter we assumed that households and firms believe that what they expect to see and experience in the future is the same as what they see and are experiencing today. There are many times, however, when households and firms will expect the future to look different from today. Announcements of tax cuts, concerns about impending international conflicts, and the possibility of new trade agreements are examples of events that may cause households and firms to change their outlook for the future.

To deal with these possibilities, we need to develop our next key diagram of macroeconomic analysis: the *AD–AS* model. In this section we use the *IS–LM–FE* model to develop one half of that next model; the aggregate demand (*AD*) relationship. In particular, we will learn why the graph of the aggregate demand (*AD*) relationship has the shape it does, and what makes that relationship shift position. We will then put this discussion on hold until we develop, in Chapters 11 and 12, the other half of the *AD–AS* model, namely, the aggregate supply (*AS*) relationship. At that point we will put *AD* and *AS* together.

At that point we will have two complete models of economy. Why have both? The reason is that depending on the issue being addressed, one way of representing the economy may be more convenient than the other. The *IS–LM–FE* model relates the real interest rate to output, and the *AD–AS* model relates the price level to output. Thus, the *IS–LM–FE* model is more useful for examining the effect of various shocks on the real interest rate and on variables, such as saving and investment, that depend on the real interest rate. In Chapter 10, for example, when we discuss international borrowing and lending in open economies, the behaviour of the real interest rate is crucial, and so in that chapter we emphasize the *IS–LM–FE* approach. However, for issues related to the price level, or inflation, use of the *AD– AS* model is more convenient. For example, we rely on the *AD–AS* framework in Chapter 13 when we describe the relationship between inflation and unemployment.

DERIVING THE AGGREGATE DEMAND CURVE

The **aggregate demand curve** shows the relation between the aggregate quantity of goods demanded, $C^d + I^d + G$, and the price level, P. The aggregate demand curve slopes downward, as does the demand curve for a single product (apples, for example). Despite the superficial similarity between the *AD* curve and the demand curve for a specific good, however, there is an important difference between these two types of curves. The demand curve for apples relates the demand for apples to the price of apples *relative to the prices of other goods*. In contrast, the *AD* curve relates the aggregate quantity of output demanded to the *general price level*. If the prices of all goods increase by 10%, the price level, P, also increases by 10%, even though all relative prices of goods remain unchanged. Nevertheless, the increase in the price level reduces the aggregate quantity of goods demanded.

The reason that an increase in the price level, P, reduces the aggregate quantity of output demanded is illustrated in Figure 9.11. Recall that for a *given price level*, the aggregate quantity of output that households, firms, and the government choose to demand is the point at which the *IS* curve and the *LM* curve intersect. Suppose that the nominal money supply is M and that the initial price level is P_1. Then the real money supply is M/P_1, and the initial *LM* curve is LM^1 in Figure 9.11(a). The *IS* and LM^1 curves intersect at point *E*, where the amount of output that households, firms, and the government want to buy is Y_1. Thus, we conclude that when the price level is P_1, the aggregate amount of output demanded is Y_1.

Now, suppose that the price level increases to P_2. With a nominal money supply of M, this increase in the price level reduces the real money supply from M/P_1 to M/P_2. Recall (Summary table 13, p. 256) that a decrease in the real money supply shifts the *LM* curve up and to the left, to LM^2. The *IS* and LM^2 curves intersect at point *F*, where the aggregate quantity of output demanded is Y_2. Thus, the increase in the price level from P_1 to P_2 reduces the aggregate quantity of output demanded from Y_1 to Y_2.

This negative relation between the price level and the aggregate quantity of output demanded is shown as the downward-sloping *AD* curve in Figure 9.11(b). Points *E* and *F* in Figure 9.11(b) correspond to points *E* and *F* in Figure 9.11(a). The *AD* curve slopes downward because an increase in the price level reduces the real money supply, which shifts the *LM* curve up and to the left; the reduction in the real money supply increases the real interest rate, which reduces the demand for goods by households and firms.

FIGURE 9.11

DERIVATION OF THE

AGGREGATE DEMAND CURVE

For a given price level, the aggregate quantity of output demanded is determined where the IS and LM curves intersect. If the price level, P, is P_1 and the initial LM curve is LM^1, the initial aggregate quantity of output demanded is Y_1, corresponding to point E in both (a) and (b). To derive the aggregate demand curve, we examine what happens to the quantity of output demanded when the price level changes.

(a) An increase in the price level from P_1 to P_2 reduces the real money supply and shifts the LM curve up and to the left, from LM^1 to LM^2. Therefore, the aggregate quantity of output demanded, represented by the intersection of the IS and LM curves, falls from Y_1 to Y_2.

(b) The increase in the price level from P_1 to P_2 reduces the aggregate quantity of output demanded from Y_1 to Y_2, so the aggregate demand curve slopes downward.

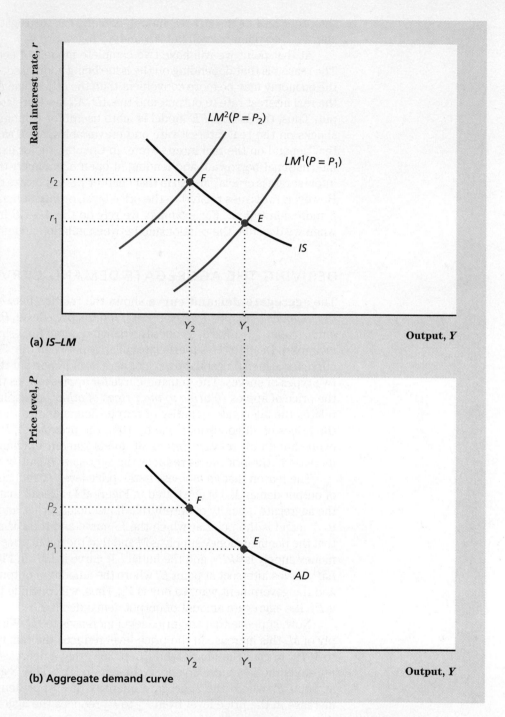

(a) *IS–LM*

(b) **Aggregate demand curve**

Factors That Shift the Aggregate Demand Curve

The AD curve relates the aggregate quantity of output demanded to the price level. For a constant price level, any factor that changes the aggregate demand for output will cause the AD curve to shift, with increases in aggregate demand shifting the AD curve up and to the right and decreases in aggregate demand shifting it down and to the left. Aggregate demand is determined by the intersection of

SUMMARY 14   FACTORS THAT SHIFT THE *AD* CURVE

For a constant price level, any factor that shifts the intersection of the *IS* and *LM* curves to the right increases aggregate output demanded and shifts the *AD* curve up and to the right.

Factors that shift the *IS* curve up and to the right, and thus shift the *AD* curve up and to the right (see Summary table 12, p. 251), include:

- an increase in expected future output;
- an increase in wealth;
- an increase in government purchases, *G*;
- a reduction in taxes, *T*, assuming no Ricardian equivalence (meaning that, as explained in Chapter 4, tax cuts do not affect desired consumption and thus desired national saving) so that consumers respond by raising desired consumption;
- an increase in the expected future *MPK*; and
- a reduction in the effective tax rate on capital.

Factors that shift the *LM* curve down and to the right, and thus shift the *AD* curve up and to the right (see Summary table 13, p. 256), include

- an increase in the nominal money supply, *M*;
- a rise in expected inflation, π^e;
- a decrease in the nominal interest rate on money, i^m; and
- any other change that reduces the real demand for money.

the *IS* and *LM* curves, so we can also say that, holding the price level constant, any factor that causes the intersection of the *IS* curve and the *LM* curve to shift to the right raises aggregate demand and shifts the *AD* curve up and to the right. Similarly, for a constant price level, any factor that causes the intersection of the *IS* and *LM* curves to shift to the left shifts the *AD* curve down and to the left.

In the previous section, Section 9.5, we considered two factors that shift the *AD* curve up and to the right: a monetary expansion and an increase in government spending. We examined these events using the *IS–LM–FE* model. Now let's briefly consider these events again, but this time let's show how they affect the position of the *AD* curve.

The effect of a monetary expansion on the position of the *AD* curve is illustrated in Figure 9.12. The position of the initial *LM* curve, LM^1, is determined in part by the price level, which we assume is at level P_1. This *LM* curve intersects the *IS* curve at point *E* in Figure 9.12(a), so the initial aggregate quantity of output demanded is Y_1. As shown earlier, an increase in the nominal money supply *M* when the price level is held constant shifts the *LM* curve down and to the right to LM^2. A short-run equilibrium occurs at the intersection of *IS* and LM^2 at point *F* and the aggregate quantity of output demanded increases from Y_1 to Y_2.

The shift in the *AD* curve resulting from the monetary expansion is shown in Figure 9.12(b). The increase in the aggregate quantity of output demanded at price level P_1 is shown by the movement from point *E* to point *F*. The entire *AD* curve shifts up and to the right, from AD^1 to AD^2, because the aggregate quantity of output demand increases at every price level.

A temporary increase in government purchases, which we considered earlier in Figure 9.10, has a similar effect on the position of the *AD* curve. The effect of the increase in government purchases on the *AD* curve is illustrated in Figure 9.13.

FIGURE 9.12

THE EFFECT OF A MONETARY EXPANSION ON THE AGGREGATE DEMAND CURVE

(a) An increase in the money supply shifts the *LM* curve down and to the right, from LM^1 to LM^2. At price level P_1, the aggregate quantity of output demanded increases from Y_1 to Y_2, as shown by the shift of the *IS–LM* intersection from point *E* to point *F*.

(b) Because the aggregate quantity of output demanded rises at any price level, the *AD* curve shifts to the right. Points *E* and *F* in part (b) correspond to points *E* and *F* in part (a).

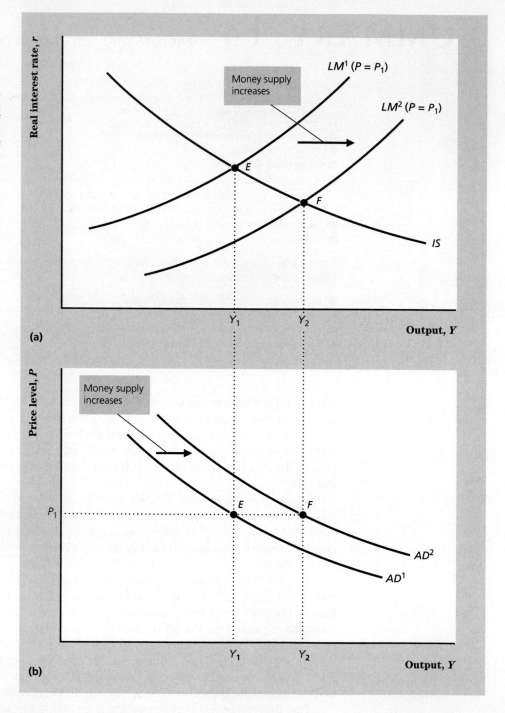

The initial *IS* curve, IS^1, intersects the *LM* curve at point *E* in Figure 9.13(a) so that the initial aggregate quantity of output demanded is Y_1. As we have shown, a temporary increase in government purchases shifts the *IS* curve up and to the right to IS^2. With the price level held constant at its initial value of P_1, the intersection of the *IS* and *LM* curves moves to point *F* so that the aggregate quantity of output demanded increases from Y_1 to Y_2.

FIGURE 9.13

THE EFFECT OF AN INCREASE IN GOVERNMENT PURCHASES ON THE AGGREGATE DEMAND CURVE

(a) An increase in government purchases shifts the *IS* curve up and to the right, from IS^1 to IS^2. At price level P_1, the aggregate quantity of output demanded increases from Y_1 to Y_2, as shown by the shift of the *IS–LM* intersection from point *E* to point *F*.

(b) Because the aggregate quantity of output demanded rises at any price level, the *AD* curve shifts to the right. Points *E* and *F* in part (b) correspond to points *E* and *F* in part (a).

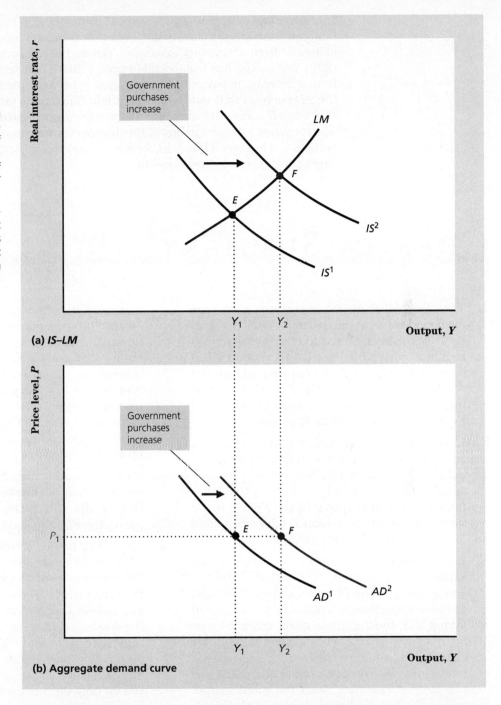

(a) IS–LM

(b) Aggregate demand curve

The shift of the *AD* curve resulting from the increase in government purchases is shown in Figure 9.13(b). The increase in the aggregate quantity of output demanded at price level P_1 is shown by the movement from point *E* to point *F*. Because the increase in government purchases raises the aggregate quantity of output demanded at any price level, the entire *AD* curve shifts up and to the right, from AD^1 to AD^2. Other factors that shift the *AD* curve are listed in Summary table 14, and an algebraic derivation of the *AD* curve is presented in Appendix 9.B.

These two examples of the causes of shifts in the *AD* curve illustrate an important point. An expansionary policy, whether from an increase in government purchases or from a monetary expansion, causes the *AD* curve to shift up and to the right. You should feel comfortable proving that a contractionary policy, whether from a decrease in government purchases or from a monetary contraction, causes the *AD* curve to shift down and to the left. Since monetary and fiscal policy both shift the *AD* curve, they are often referred to as **aggregate demand policies**. We will deepen our understanding of the macroeconomic impact of aggregate demand policies in Chapters 11 and 12, where we also develop our understanding of the aggregate supply (*AS*) relationship.

CHAPTER SUMMARY

1. The *IS–LM–FE* model represents the three main markets of the economy—the labour market, the goods market, and the asset market—simultaneously, in a diagram that has the real interest rate on the vertical axis and output on the horizontal axis. The *IS–LM–FE* model may be used to illustrate both classical and Keynesian analyses of the economy.

2. In the *IS–LM–FE* model, equilibrium in the labour market is represented graphically by the full-employment, or *FE*, line, which is vertical at full-employment output. Factors that raise full-employment output shift the *FE* line to the right, and factors that reduce full-employment output shift the *FE* line to the left.

3. For any level of output, the *IS* curve shows the value of the real interest rate that clears the goods market. The *IS* curve slopes downward because higher output leads to more desired saving and, thus, a lower goods-market-clearing real interest rate. For constant output, any change that reduces desired national saving relative to desired investment increases the real interest rate that clears the goods market and shifts the *IS* curve up and to the right. Equivalently, for constant output, any change that increases the aggregate demand for goods increases the real interest rate that clears the goods market and shifts the *IS* curve up and to the right.

4. For any level of output, the *LM* curve identifies the real interest rate that equates the quantities of money supplied and demanded and, thus, clears the asset market. The *LM* curve slopes upward because an increase in output raises money demand, implying that a higher real interest rate is needed to clear the asset market. With output fixed, any change that reduces the money supply relative to money demand increases the real interest rate that clears the asset market and causes the *LM* curve to shift up and to the left.

5. General equilibrium in the macroeconomy occurs when all markets are in equilibrium. Graphically, this is the point at which the *IS* curve, the *FE* line, and the *LM* curve intersect.

6. The labour market, represented by the *FE* line, is slower to move into equilibrium than either the goods market (represented by *IS*) or the financial market (represented by *LM*). Keynesians believe that a short-run equilibrium where the goods and financial markets are in equilibrium (and so *IS* and *LM* intersect) can persist for possibly long periods of time. Classical economists believe these equilibriums can, at best, last for only short periods of time.

7. When the economy is not in general equilibrium and output Y exceeds full equilibrium output $\overline{Y}$, firms are willing (at least temporarily) to produce enough extra output to meet the expanded demand without raising prices. When the economy is not in general equilibrium and output Y is less than full equilibrium output $\overline{Y}$, firms are willing (at least temporarily) to produce less

output without reducing prices. Eventually, however, price-level adjustments push the economy toward general equilibrium. Specifically, changes in the price level, P, change the real money supply, M/P, which causes the LM curve to shift until it passes through the point at which the FE line and the IS curve intersect.

8. A temporary adverse supply shock causes the general equilibrium levels of the real wage, employment, output, consumption, and investment to fall, and the general equilibrium levels of the real interest rate and price level to increase.

9. A change in the money supply is neutral if it leads to a proportional change in the price level but does not affect real variables. In the *IS–LM–FE* model, money is neutral after prices have adjusted and the economy has returned to general equilibrium.

10. The aggregate demand (AD) curve relates the aggregate quantity of output demanded—the level of output at the intersection of the IS and LM curves—to the price level. An increase in the price level reduces the real money supply and shifts the LM curve up and to the left, thereby reducing the aggregate quantity of output demanded. Because an increase in the price level reduces the aggregate quantity of goods demanded, the aggregate demand curve slopes downward. Factors that increase the aggregate quantity of output demanded at a given price level, such as increases in government purchases or the money supply, shift the AD curve up and to the right.

11. Classical macroeconomists argue that prices and wages adjust rapidly in response to changes in supply or demand. This argument implies that following shocks or changes in policy, the economy quickly reaches its general equilibrium, represented by the *IS–LM–FE* intersection. In contrast, Keynesian macroeconomists argue that prices and wages adjust slowly enough that the economy can remain away from its general equilibrium (long-run equilibrium) for a prolonged period of time. Keynesians agree with classicals, however, in that eventually prices and wages fully adjust so that the economy reaches its general equilibrium.

12. Classicals and Keynesians agree that money is neutral in the long run, after the economy has reached its general equilibrium. Because classicals believe that long-run equilibrium is reached quickly, they dismiss the short-run equilibrium in which money is not neutral as essentially irrelevant. Keynesians, who believe that it may take several years for the economy to reach general equilibrium, ascribe much more importance to the short-run period in which money is not neutral.

KEY DIAGRAM 7

The *IS–LM–FE* Model

The *IS–LM–FE* model shows general equilibrium in the goods, asset, and labour markets. It can be used to analyze the effects of economic shocks on output, the real interest rate, the price level, and other macroeconomic variables.

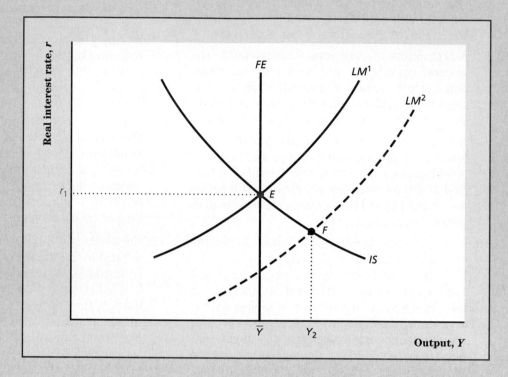

DIAGRAM ELEMENTS

- The real interest rate, r, is on the vertical axis, and output, Y, is on the horizontal axis.

- The full-employment line, *FE*, is vertical at full-employment output. Full-employment output, $\overline{Y}$, is the level of output that firms supply when wages and prices have fully adjusted, so employment is at its full-employment level, $\overline{N}$. Full-employment output is determined by the equation $Y = AF(K,\overline{N})$.

- For any level of output Y, the *IS* curve gives the real interest rate r that clears the goods market—or, in other words, the rate that equalizes desired national saving, S^d, and desired investment, I^d. Because higher output raises desired saving and lowers the real interest rate that clears the goods market, the *IS* curve slopes downward. Equivalently, the *IS* curve gives combinations of output Y and the real interest rate r that equalize the aggregate

quantities of goods supplied and demanded, $Y = C^d + I^d + G$.

- For given values of the price level and output, the *LM* curve gives the real interest rate that clears the asset market, making the real money supply, M/P, and the real quantity of money demanded, $L(Y, r + \pi^e)$, equal. Because an increase in income raises real money demand, which raises the real interest rate that clears the asset market, the *LM* curve slopes upward.

FACTORS THAT SHIFT THE CURVES

- Any factor that raises full-employment output shifts the *FE* line to the right. See Summary table 11 (p. 247).

- For constant output, any change that reduces desired national saving relative to desired investment increases the real interest rate that clears the goods market and shifts the *IS* curve up and to the right. Equivalently, any change that increases the aggregate demand for goods at a specific level of income raises the real interest rate that clears the goods market and shifts the *IS* curve up and to the right. See Summary table 12 (p. 251).

- For constant output, any change that reduces real money supply relative to real money demand increases the real interest rate that clears the asset market and shifts the *LM* curve up and to the left. See Summary table 13 (p. 256).

ANALYSIS

- If we assume that the *LM* curve is LM^1, the economy is in general equilibrium at point E, which lies on all three curves. At E, the labour market (*FE* line), the goods market (*IS* curve), and the asset market (*LM* curve) are all in equilibrium. At E, output equals full-employment output, $\overline{Y}$; and the real interest rate, r_1, clears both the goods and asset markets.

- If we assume that the *LM* curve is LM^2, the *FE* line and *IS* and *LM* curves do not all intersect, and the economy is out of general equilibrium. We assume that when the economy is out of general equilibrium, the short-run equilibrium of the economy occurs at the intersection of the *IS* and *LM* curves (point F), where the goods and asset markets are in equilibrium but the labour market is not. If we further assume that (at least temporarily) firms produce enough output to meet the increased aggregate demand at F, in short-run equilibrium the economy's output is Y_2.

- At the short-run equilibrium point, F, output Y_2 is greater than firms' profit-maximizing level of output, $\overline{Y}$. Because aggregate demand at F exceeds what firms want to produce, they raise prices. An increase in the price level P lowers the real money supply M/P and shifts the *LM* curve up to LM^1, and general equilibrium is reached at E. At E, output again equals full-employment output, $\overline{Y}$. Similarly, if the short-run equilibrium had been to the left of the *FE* line, declines in the price level P would have shifted the *LM* curve to the right and restored general equilibrium at E.

- According to classical economists, the price adjustment process quickly restores the economy to general equilibrium at point E, so the economy spends little or no time away from full employment at point F. Keynesians argue that prices and wages are slow to adjust, so the economy may remain at the short-run equilibrium point, F, with output different from $\overline{Y}$, for an extended period of time.

KEY DIAGRAM 8

The Aggregate Demand Curve

DIAGRAM ELEMENTS

- The price level, P, is on the vertical axis, and the level of output, Y, is on the horizontal axis.

- The aggregate demand (*AD*) curve shows the aggregate quantity of output demanded at each price level. The aggregate amount of output demanded is determined by the intersection of the *IS* and *LM* curves (see Figure 9.10, p. 269). An increase in the price level, P, reduces the real money supply, shifting the *LM* curve up and to the left, and reduces the aggregate quantity of output demanded. Thus, the *AD* curve slopes downward.

FACTORS THAT SHIFT THE CURVES

- The aggregate quantity of output demanded is determined by the intersection of the *IS* and the *LM* curves. At a constant price level, any factor that shifts the *IS–LM* intersection to the right increases the aggregate quantity of goods demanded and, thus, also shifts the *AD* curve up

The *AD* curve is an alternative representation of the *IS–LM* model. It shows, at a given price level, the equilibrium level of output determined in the *IS–LM* model. A monetary expansion or an increase in government purchases both cause the aggregate quantity of output to increase at a given price level. Since these two events both cause the *AD* curve to shift up and to the right, they are often referred to as aggregate demand policies.

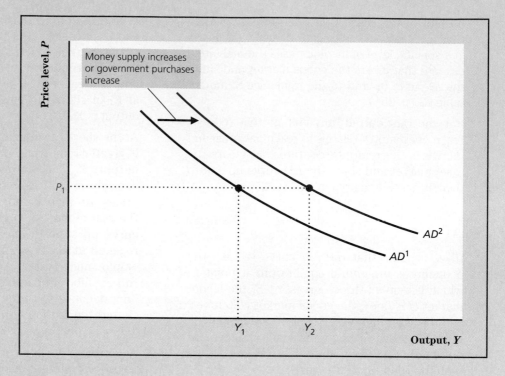

and to the right. Factors that shift the *AD* curve are listed in Summary table 14 (p. 275).

• Shocks that shift the *AD* curve up or to the right include an increase in government purchases and an expansion of the money supply. Expansionary fiscal and monetary policies therefore have the same effect on the position of the *AD* curve, and for that reason are often referred to as aggregate demand policies.

KEY TERMS

aggregate demand curve, p. 273
aggregate demand policies, p. 278
crowding out effect, p. 269
full-employment line, p. 245
general equilibrium, p. 259
IS curve, p. 247
LM curve, p. 255
monetary neutrality, p. 272
multiplier effect, p. 268

REVIEW QUESTIONS

1. What determines the position of the *FE* line? Give two examples of changes in the economy that would shift the *FE* line to the right.
2. What relationship does the *IS* curve capture? Derive the *IS* curve graphically and show why it slopes as it does. Give two examples of changes in the economy that would cause the *IS* curve to shift down and to the left.
3. What relationship does the *LM* curve capture? Derive the *LM* curve graphically and show why it slopes as it does. Give two examples of changes in the economy that would cause the *LM* curve to shift down and to the right.
4. For constant output, if real money supply exceeds the real quantity of money demanded, what will happen to the real interest rate that clears the asset market? In describing the adjustment of the real interest rate, use the relationship that exists between the price of a non-monetary asset and the interest rate that it pays.
5. Define general equilibrium, and show the general equilibrium point in the *IS–LM–FE* diagram. If the economy is not in general equilibrium, what determines output and the real interest rate? What economic forces act to bring the economy back to general equilibrium?

6. Define *monetary neutrality*. Show that after prices adjust completely, money is neutral in the *IS–LM–FE* model. What are the classical and Keynesian views about whether money is neutral in the short run? in the long run?

7. What two variables are related by the aggregate demand (*AD*) curve? Why does the *AD* curve slope downward? Give two examples of changes in the economy that shift the *AD* curve to the right and explain why the shifts occur.

NUMERICAL PROBLEMS

1. Desired consumption and investment are

$$C^d = 360 - 200r + 0.10Y;$$
$$I^d = 120 - 400r.$$

As usual, Y is output and r is the real interest rate. Government purchases G are 120.

a. Find an equation relating desired national saving S^d to r and Y.

b. What value of the real interest rate clears the goods market when $Y = 600$? Use both forms of the goods market equilibrium condition. What value of the real interest rate clears the goods market when $Y = 640$? Graph the *IS* curve.

c. Government purchases rise to 132. How does this increase change the equation for national saving in part (a)? What value of the real interest rate clears the goods market when $Y = 600$? Use both forms of the goods market equilibrium condition. How is the *IS* curve affected by the increase in G?

2. In a particular economy, the real money demand function is

$$\frac{M^d}{P} = 200 + 0.2Y - 2000i.$$

Assume that $M = 300$, $P = 2.0$, and $\pi^e = 0.05$.

a. What is the real interest rate r that clears the asset market when $Y = 500$? when $Y = 600$? Graph the *LM* curve.

b. Repeat part (a) for $M = 360$. How does the *LM* curve in this case compare with the *LM* curve in part (a)?

c. Use $M = 300$ again and repeat part (a) for $\pi^e = 0.04$. Compare the *LM* curve in this case with the one in part (a).

3. An economy has full-employment output of 1000. Desired consumption and desired investment are

$$C^d = 200 + 0.8(Y - T) - 500r;$$
$$I^d = 200 - 500r.$$

Government purchases are 196 and taxes are

$$T = 20 + 0.25Y.$$

Money demand is

$$\frac{M^d}{P} = 0.5Y - 250(r + \pi^e),$$

where the expected rate of inflation $\pi^e = 0.10$. The nominal supply of money $M = 9890$.

a. What are the general equilibrium values of the real interest rate, price level, consumption, and investment?

b. Suppose that government purchases are increased to $G = 216$. What are the new general equilibrium values of the real interest rate, the price level, consumption, and investment?

4. The production function in an economy is

$$Y = A(5N - 0.0025N^2),$$

where A is productivity. With this production function, the marginal product of labour is

$$MPN = 5A - 0.005AN.$$

Suppose that $A = 2$. The labour supply curve is

$$NS = 55 + 10(1 - t)w,$$

where NS is the amount of labour supplied, w is the real wage, and t is the tax rate, which is 0.5. Desired consumption and investment are

$$C^d = 300 = 0.8(Y - T) - 200r;$$
$$I^d = 258.5 - 250r.$$

Taxes and government purchases are

$$T = 20 + 0.5Y;$$
$$G = 50.$$

Money demand is

$$\frac{M^d}{P} = 0.5Y - 250(r + \pi^e)$$

The expected rate of inflation π^e is 0.02, and the nominal money supply M is 9150.

a. What are the general equilibrium levels of the real wage, employment, and output?

b. For any level of output Y, find an equation that gives the real interest rate r that clears the goods market; this equation describes the *IS* curve. (*Hint:* Write the goods market equilibrium condition and solve for r in terms of Y and other variables.) What are the general equilibrium values of the real interest rate, consumption, and investment?

c. For any level of output Y, find an equation that gives the real interest rate that clears the asset market; this equation describes the LM curve. (*Hint:* As in part (b), write the appropriate equilibrium condition and solve for r in terms of Y and other variables.) What is the general equilibrium value of the price level?

d. Suppose that government purchases increase to $G = 72.5$. Now what are the general equilibrium values of the real wage, employment, output, the real interest rate, consumption, investment, and the price level?

5. (Appendix 9.B) This question asks you to use the formulas in Appendix 9.B to find the general equilibrium values of variables for the economy described in Numerical Problem 4. Assume that $G = 50$.

   a. Use the data from Numerical Problem 4 to find the numerical values of the parameters $A, f_1, f_2, n_0, n_w, c_0, c_Y, c_r, t_0, t, i_0, i_r, \ell_0, \ell_Y,$ and ℓ_r defined in Appendix 9.B.

   b. Substitute the values of these behavioural parameters into the relevant equations in Appendix 9.B to compute the general equilibrium values of the real wage, employment, output, the real interest rate, and the price level.

   c. Assume that government purchases G increase to 72.5, and repeat part (b).

6. Consider the following economy:

Desired consumption	$C^d = 1275 + 0.5(Y - T) - 200r$
Desired investment	$I^d = 900 - 200r$
Real money demand	$L = 0.5Y - 200i$
Full-employment output	$\overline{Y} = 4600$
Expected inflation	$\pi^e = 0$

   a. Suppose that $T = G = 450$ and that $M = 9000$. Find an equation describing the IS curve. (*Hint:* Set desired national saving and desired investment equal, and solve for the relationship between r and Y, given P.) Finally, find an equation for the aggregate demand curve. (*Hint:* Use the IS and LM equations to find a relationship between Y and P.) What are the equilibrium values of output, consumption, investment, the real interest rate, and the price level?

   b. Suppose that $T = G = 450$ and that $M = 4500$. What is the equation for the aggregate demand curve now? What are the equilibrium values of output, consumption, investment, the real interest rate, and the price level? Assume that full-employment output $\overline{Y}$ is fixed.

   c. Repeat part (b) for $T = G = 330$ and $M = 9000$.

ANALYTICAL PROBLEMS

1. Use the $IS–LM–FE$ model to determine the effects of each of the following on the general equilibrium values of the real wage, employment, output, the real interest rate, consumption, investment, and the price level.

   a. A reduction in the effective tax rate on capital that increases desired investment.

   b. The expected rate of inflation rises.

   c. An influx of working-age immigrants increases labour supply (ignore any other possible effects of increased population).

   d. The introduction of automated teller machines reduces the demand for money.

2. Use the $IS–LM–FE$ model to analyze the general equilibrium effects of a permanent increase in the price of oil (a permanent adverse supply shock) on current output, employment, the real wage, national saving, consumption, investment, the real interest rate, and the price level. Assume that besides reducing the current productivity of capital and labour, the permanent supply shock lowers both the expected future MPK and households' expected future incomes. Show that if the real interest rate rises at all, it will rise less than in the case of a temporary supply shock that has an equal effect on current output.

3. Suppose that the price level is fixed in the short run so that the economy does not reach general equilibrium immediately after a change in the economy. For each of the following changes, what are the short-run effects on the real interest rate and output? Assume that when the economy is in disequilibrium, only the labour market is out of equilibrium; assume also that for a short period firms are willing to produce enough output to meet the aggregate demand for output.

   a. A decrease in the expected rate of inflation.

   b. An increase in consumer optimism that increases desired consumption at each level of income and the real interest rate.

   c. An increase in government purchases.

   d. An increase in lump-sum taxes, with no change in government purchases (consider both the case in which Ricardian equivalence holds and the case in which it does not).

   e. A scientific breakthrough increases the expected future MPK.

4. (Appendix 9.B) In some macroeconomic models, desired investment depends on the current level of output as well as on the real interest rate. One possible reason why desired investment may depend on output is that when current production and sales are

high, firms may expect continued strong demand for their products in the future, which leads them to want to expand capacity.

Algebraically, we can allow for a link between desired investment and current output by replacing Eq. (9.B.10) with

$$I^d = i_0 - i_r\, r + i_Y Y,$$

where i_Y is a positive number. Use this alternative equation for desired investment to derive the algebraic expressions for the general equilibrium values of employment, the real wage, output, the real interest rate, and the price level.

5. (Appendix 9.B) Recall from Chapter 7 that an increase in i^m, the nominal interest rate on money, increases the demand for money. To capture that effect, let's replace Eq. (9.B.17) with

$$\frac{M^d}{P} = i_0 + \ell_Y Y = \ell_r(r + \pi^e - i^m).$$

How does this modification change the solutions for the general equilibrium values of the variables discussed in Appendix 9.B, including employment, the real wage, output, the real interest rate, and the price level?

APPENDIX 9.A

A WORKED-OUT NUMERICAL EXERCISE FOR SOLVING THE IS–LM MODEL

In this chapter we have learned that in the *IS–LM–FE* model, short-run equilibriums occur at the intersection of the *IS* and the *LM* curves. In what follows we provide an exercise that shows you how to (1) derive numerical equations of *IS* and *LM*, (2) use those equations to solve for equilibrium values of the interest rate and output, and (3) derive an aggregate demand (*AD*) curve.

We begin by presenting equations describing relationships that we have been developing up to this point in the text. Equations (1)–(3) describe relationships examined in Chapter 4, where we discussed the household's decision regarding its desired level of consumption expenditures (C^d), the firm's decision about desired investment expenditures (I^d), and the concept of the goods market equilibrium. To these we have added an equation describing the amount of tax revenue collected (*T*) to be positively related to income (*Y*), and we have assumed a fixed amount of spending on government purchases (*G*). Equations (6)–(9) describe relationships examined in Chapter 7, where we discussed the asset market. In the asset market, the real demand for money (*L*) must equal the real supply of money (*M/P*), and we define the demand for money to be a function of income and the nominal interest rate (*i*). The relationship between the nominal interest rate, the real interest rate (*r*), and the expected rate of inflation (π^e) is defined in Eq. (9). The nominal money supply (*M*) is assumed to have a fixed value. Finally, we will assume that the price level (*P*) is fixed with a value of 120, the expected rate of inflation is fixed at a value of 0.05, and the full equilibrium level of output $\overline{Y}$ is fixed at a value of 2500.

(1) $Y = C^d + I^d + G$

(2) $C^d = 300 + 0.75(Y - T) - 300r$

(3) $I^d = 200 - 200r$

(4) $T = 100 + 0.2Y$

(5) $G = 600$

(6) $M/P = L$

(7) $L = 0.5Y - 500i$

(8) $M = 133\,200$

(9) $i = r + \pi^e$

With this information, we can solve for the values that all the variables in our model economy take on in *IS–LM* equilibrium. As we describe the arithmetic of these solutions, you will find it useful to sketch diagrams of *IS* and *LM* and fill in the values of variables as we discover them. By doing so you will better understand the logic of the steps we describe.

Find the Equation of the IS *Curve*: Equation (1) describes the goods market equilibrium condition, namely, that the sum of all desired expenditures must equal aggregate income. To find the *IS* curve we substitute Eqs. (2)–(5) into the goods market equilibrium condition. The result of these substitutions can be solved for an *IS* curve as an equation for *r* in terms of *Y* or as an equation of *Y* in terms of *r*. You should be able to confirm these two solutions to be $r = 2.05 - 0.0008Y$ and $Y = 2562.5 - 1250r$. These two equations are equivalent; one is simply a rearrangement of the other. They both describe an *IS* curve, and so both describe those combinations of *r* and *Y* that satisfy the goods market equilibrium condition.

Find the Equation of the LM *Curve*: Equation (6) describes the asset market equilibrium condition, namely, that the real supply for money must equal the real demand for money. To find the *LM* curve we substitute Eqs. (7)–(9) into the asset market equilibrium condition. As was the case with *IS*, the result of these substitutions can be solved for an *LM* curve as an equation for r in terms of Y or as an equation of Y in terms of r. You should be able to confirm these two solutions to be $r = 0.001Y - 0.05 - 266.4/P$ and $Y = 1000r + 50 + 266400/P$. These two equations are equivalent; one is simply a rearrangement of the other. They both describe an *LM* curve, and so both describe those combinations of r and Y that satisfy the asset market equilibrium condition. Note that our two versions of the *LM* curve are written in terms of the price level P. Thus, just as we describe in this chapter, changes in the value of the price level cause the *LM* curve to shift position.

Find Short-Run Equilibrium Values: In the short-run we know that $P = 120$. By substituting this value into our solutions for the *LM* curve, we identify where the *LM* curve is positioned in the short run. Thus in the short run, our two versions of the *LM* curve become $r = 0.001Y - 2.27$ and $Y = 1000r + 2270$. Short-run equilibrium occurs where $IS = LM$. If we equate the version of *IS* describing r in terms of Y to the version of *LM* describing r in terms of Y, we can solve for the short-run equilibrium value of Y. You should be able to confirm that the result is $Y = 2400$. Similarly, if we equate the version of *IS* describing Y in terms of r to the version of *LM* describing Y in terms of r, we can solve for the short-run equilibrium value of r. You should be able to confirm that the result is $r = 0.13$. Using these equilibrium values of r and Y, it is now a simple matter to return to Eqs. (1)–(9) and solve for the short-run equilibrium values of i, C^d, I^d, T, and L.

Find the AD Curve: The *AD* curve shows short-run equilibrium values of output Y for various values of the price level P. We have already derived an *IS* curve showing values of r in terms of values of Y and an *LM* curve showing values of r in terms of values of Y and P. Using those versions of *IS* and *LM* and setting them equal, we solve for Y in terms of P. This is an *AD* curve. You should confirm that the equation of the *AD* curve is $Y = 1166.67 + 148000/P$. By substituting any value for the price level P into this equation, you can solve for the short-run equilibrium value of output Y. For example, if we substitute $P = 120$ into the equation, we solve for $Y = 2400$; the same solution we found above.

Find Long-Run Equilibrium Values: Finally, we can use our equation of the *AD* curve to solve for the long-run or general equilibrium values of macroeconomic variables. We are told that the full equilibrium level of output $\overline{Y}$ is fixed at a value of 2500. Substituting this value into the equation for the *AD* curve, we can solve for the long-run equilibrium value of the price level P to be 111. Using these values, it is straightforward to use Eqs. (1)–(9) to solve for the general equilibrium values of i, C^d, I^d, T, and L.

APPENDIX 9.B

ALGEBRAIC VERSION OF THE *IS–LM–FE* MODEL

In this appendix, we present an algebraic version of the *IS–LM–FE* model. We begin with the labour market and derive an algebraic expression of the *FE* line. We use that expression to discuss reasons for the *FE* line to shift and so for full equilibrium output $\overline{Y}$ to increase or decrease. We then turn to the goods and the asset markets to derive algebraic expressions of *IS* and *LM*. We use those expressions to solve for an expression defining the full equilibrium value of the real interest rate r and an expression for full equilibrium value of the price level P. Finally, we derive an expression for the aggregate demand (*AD*) curve.

THE LABOUR MARKET

The demand for labour is based on the marginal product of labour, as determined by the production function. Recall from Chapter 3 (Eq. 3.1) that the production function can be written as $Y = AF(K, N)$, where Y is output, K is the capital stock, N is labour input, and A is productivity. Holding the capital stock K fixed, we can write the production function with output Y as a function only of labour input N and productivity A. A useful specific production function is

$$Y = A(f_1 N - \frac{1}{2} f_2 N^2), \tag{9.B.1}$$

where f_1 and f_2 are positive numbers.

The marginal product of labour, *MPN*, is the slope of the production function. The slope of the production function in Eq. (9.B.1) at any level of employment N equals[15] $A(f_1 - f_2 N)$, so the marginal product of labour is

$$MPN = A(f_1 - f_2 N). \tag{9.B.2}$$

Firms hire labour to the point at which the marginal product of labour equals the real wage. Thus, the relation between the real wage w and the amount of labour demanded *ND* is

$$w = A(f_1 - f_2 ND). \tag{9.B.3}$$

The supply of labour is an increasing function of the current, after-tax real wage. If t is the tax rate on wage income (we assume that $0 < t < 1$) so that $(1 - t)w$ is the after-tax real wage, a simple form of the labour supply curve is

$$NS = n_0 + n_w(1 - t)w, \tag{9.B.4}$$

where *NS* is the amount of labour supplied, and n_0 and n_w are positive numbers. Factors other than the after-tax real wage that affect labour supply, such as wealth or the working-age population, are captured by the constant term n_0 in Eq. (9.B.4).

---

[15] Students who know calculus can derive the slope of the production function by taking the derivative of Eq. (9.B.1) with respect to N.

Equilibrium in the Labour Market

In equilibrium, the amounts of labour demanded *ND* and supplied *NS* are equal; their common value is the full-employment level of employment $\overline{N}$. If we substitute $\overline{N}$ for *NS* and *ND* in Eqs. (9.B.3) and (9.B.4), we have two linear equations in the two variables $\overline{N}$ and w. Solving these equations for w and $\overline{N}$ yields[16]

$$w = A\left[\frac{f_1 - f_2 n_0}{1 + (1 - t)Af_2 n_w}\right] \tag{9.B.5}$$

and

$$\overline{N} = \frac{n_0 + (1 - t)Af_1 n_w}{1 + (1 - t)Af_2 n_w}. \tag{9.B.6}$$

Using the full-employment level of employment $\overline{N}$ in Eq. (9.B.6), we obtain the full-employment level of output $\overline{Y}$ by substituting $\overline{N}$ into the production function in Eq. (9.B.1):

$$\overline{Y} = A\left[f_1 \overline{N} - \frac{1}{2}f_2 \overline{N}^2\right], FE \text{ line.} \tag{9.B.7}$$

The value of full-employment output in Eq. (9.B.7) is the horizontal intercept of the *FE* line.

We can use these equations to analyze the effects on the labour market of changes in productivity and in labour supply. First, consider an increase in productivity A. Equation (9.B.5) shows that an increase in A leads to an increase in the equilibrium real wage (an increase in A raises the ratio $A/[1 + (1 - t)Af_2 n_w]$). Although not directly evident from Eq. (9.B.6), an increase in A also increases $\overline{N}$.[17] To see why, note first that an increase in A does not affect the labour supply curve, Eq. (9.B.4). Second, an increase in A raises the real wage. Hence the implication is that an increase in A raises the equilibrium amount of labour supplied and, thus, also the full-employment level of employment $\overline{N}$. Because an increase in A raises $\overline{N}$, it must also raise full-employment output $\overline{Y}$ (see Eq. 9.B.7) and shift the *FE* line to the right.

Now, consider an increase in the amount of labour supplied at each level of the after-tax real wage, represented algebraically as an increase in n_0 in Eq. (9.B.4). Equations (9.B.5) and (9.B.6) show that an increase in n_0 reduces the equilibrium real wage and increases employment $\overline{N}$. Because an increase in labour supply raises $\overline{N}$, it also raises full-employment output $\overline{Y}$ and shifts the *FE* line to the right.

THE GOODS MARKET

To find equilibrium in the goods market, we start with equations describing desired consumption and desired investment. Desired consumption is

$$C^d = c_0 + c_Y(Y - T) - c_r r, \tag{9.B.8}$$

---

[16] We assume that the constants f_1, f_2, and n_0 are such that $f_1 - f_2 n_0 > 0$. This assumption is needed to guarantee that the marginal product of labour and the equilibrium real wage are positive.

[17] Students who know calculus can compute the derivative of $\overline{N}$ with respect to A in Eq. (9.B.6) and will find that the sign of this derivative is positive only if $f_1 - f_2 n_0 > 0$. As we have assumed that $f_1 - f_2 n_0 > 0$ (see preceding footnote), an increase in A does indeed increase $\overline{N}$.

where $Y - T$ is disposable income (income Y minus taxes T), r is the real interest rate, and c_0, c_Y, and c_r are positive numbers. The number c_Y in Eq. (9.B.8) is the marginal propensity to consume, as defined in Chapter 4; because people consume only part of an increase in disposable income, saving the rest, a reasonable assumption is that $0 < c_Y < 1$. According to Eq. (9.B.8), an increase in disposable income causes desired consumption to increase, and an increase in the real interest rate causes desired consumption to fall (and desired saving to rise). Other factors that affect desired consumption, such as wealth or expected future income, are included in the constant term c_0.[18]

Taxes in Eq. (9.B.8) are

$$T = t_0 + tY, \tag{9.B.9}$$

where t is the tax rate on income (the same tax rate that is levied on wages) and t_0 is a lump-sum tax. As mentioned earlier, $0 < t < 1$, so an increase in income Y increases total taxes T and also increases disposable income $Y - T$.

Desired investment is

$$I^d = i_0 - i_r r, \tag{9.B.10}$$

where i_0 and i_r are positive numbers. Equation (9.B.10) indicates that desired investment falls when the real interest rate rises. Other factors affecting desired investment, such as the expected future marginal product of capital, are included in the constant term i_0.

Equilibrium in the Goods Market

The goods market equilibrium condition in a closed economy is given by Eq. (4.7), which we repeat here:

$$Y = C^d + I^d + G. \tag{9.B.11}$$

Equation (9.B.11) is equivalent to the goods market equilibrium condition, $S^d = I^d$, which could be used equally well here.

If we substitute the equations for desired consumption (Eq. 9.B.8, with taxes T as given by Eq. 9.B.9) and desired investment (Eq. 9.B.10) into the goods market equilibrium condition (Eq. 9.B.11), we get

$$Y = c_0 + c_Y(Y - t_0 - tY) - c_r r + i_0 - i_r r + G. \tag{9.B.12}$$

Collecting the terms that multiply Y on the left-hand side yields

$$[1 - (1 - t)c_Y]Y = c_0 + i_0 + G - c_Y t_0 - (c_r + i_r)r. \tag{9.B.13}$$

Equation (9.B.13) relates output Y to the real interest rate r that clears the goods market. This relationship between Y and r defines the *IS* curve. Because the *IS* curve is graphed with r on the vertical axis and Y on the horizontal axis,

---

[18] Because an increase in taxes T reduces desired consumption in Eq. (9.B.8), this formulation of desired consumption appears, at first glance, to be inconsistent with the Ricardian equivalence proposition discussed in Chapter 4. However, essential to the idea of Ricardian equivalence is that consumers expect an increase in current taxes T to be accompanied by lower taxes in the future. This decrease in expected future taxes would increase desired consumption, which would be captured in Eq. (9.B.8) as an increase in c_0. According to the Ricardian equivalence proposition, after an increase in T with no change in current or planned government purchases, an increase in c_0 would exactly offset the reduction in $c_Y(Y - T)$ so that desired consumption would be unchanged.

we rewrite Eq. (9.B.13) with r on the left-hand side and Y on the right-hand side. Solving Eq. (9.B.13) for r gives us an equation for the *IS* curve:

$$r = \alpha_{IS} - \beta_{IS}Y. \tag{9.B.14}$$

In Eq. (9.B.14), α_{IS} and β_{IS} are positive numbers defined as

$$\alpha_{IS} = \frac{c_0 + t_0 + G - c_Y t_0}{c_r + i_r} \tag{9.B.15}$$

and

$$\beta_{IS} = \frac{1 - (1 - t)c_Y}{c_r + i_r}. \tag{9.B.16}$$

Equation (9.B.14) yields the graph of the *IS* curve. In Eq. (9.B.14), the coefficient of Y, or $-\beta_{IS}$, is the slope of the *IS* curve; because this slope is negative, the *IS* curve slopes downward. Changes in the constant term α_{IS} in Eq. (9.B.14), which is defined in Eq. (9.B.15), shift the *IS* curve. Anything that increases α_{IS}—such as (1) an increase in consumer optimism that increases desired consumption by increasing c_0; (2) an increase in the expected future marginal product of capital MPK^f that raises desired investment by raising i_0; or (3) an increase in government purchases G—shifts the *IS* curve up. Similarly, anything that decreases α_{IS} shifts the *IS* curve down and to the left.

THE ASSET MARKET

In general, the real demand for money depends on real income Y and on the nominal interest rate on nonmonetary assets i, which in turn equals the expected real interest rate r plus the expected rate of inflation π^e. We assume that the money demand function takes the form

$$\frac{M^d}{P} = \ell_0 + \ell_Y Y - \ell_r(r + \pi^e), \tag{9.B.17}$$

where M^d is the nominal demand for money, P is the price level, and ℓ_0, ℓ_Y, and ℓ_r are positive numbers. The constant term ℓ_0 includes factors other than output and the interest rate that affect money demand, such as the liquidity of alternative assets. The real supply of money equals the nominal supply of money M, which is determined by the central bank, divided by the price level P.

Equilibrium in the Asset Market

As we demonstrated in Chapter 7, if we assume that there are only two types of assets (money and nonmonetary assets), the asset market is in equilibrium when the real quantity of money demanded equals the real money supply M/P. Using the money demand function in Eq. (9.B.17), we write the asset market equilibrium condition as

$$\frac{M}{P} = \ell_0 + \ell_Y Y - \ell_r(r + \pi^e). \tag{9.B.18}$$

For fixed levels of the nominal money supply M, price level P, and expected rate of inflation π^e, Eq. (9.B.18) relates output Y and the real interest rate r that clears the asset market. Thus, Eq. (9.B.18) defines the *LM* curve. To get Eq. (9.B.18) into a form that is easier to interpret graphically, we rewrite the equation with r alone on the left-hand side. The result is an equation of the *LM* curve:

$$r = \alpha_{LM} - \left(\frac{1}{\ell_r}\right)\left(\frac{M}{P}\right) + \beta_{LM}Y \qquad (9.B.19)$$

where

$$\alpha_{LM} = \left(\frac{\ell_0}{\ell_r}\right) - \pi^e \qquad (9.B.20)$$

and

$$\beta_{LM} = \left(\frac{\ell_Y}{\ell_r}\right). \qquad (9.B.21)$$

The graph of Eq. (9.B.19) is the *LM* curve. In Eq. (9.B.19), the coefficient of Y, or β_{LM}, is the slope of the *LM* curve; because this coefficient is positive, the *LM* curve slopes upward. Variables that change the intercept of the equation in Eq. (9.B.19), $\alpha_{LM} - (1/\ell_r)(M/P)$, shift the *LM* curve. An increase in the real money supply M/P reduces this intercept and, thus, shifts the *LM* curve down and to the right. An increase in the expected rate of inflation π^e reduces α_{LM} and shifts the *LM* curve down. An increase in real money demand arising from (for example) reduced liquidity of alternative assets raises ℓ_0, which raises ℓ_{LM} and shifts the *LM* curve up and to the left.

GENERAL EQUILIBRIUM IN THE *IS–LM–FE* MODEL

From the supply and demand relationships and equilibrium conditions in each market, we can calculate the general equilibrium values for the most important macroeconomic variables. We have already solved for the general equilibrium levels of the real wage, employment, and output in the labour market: the real wage is given by Eq. (9.B.5); employment equals its full-employment level $\overline{N}$, given by Eq. (9.B.6); and, in general equilibrium, output equals its full-employment level $\overline{Y}$, as given by Eq. (9.B.7).

Turning to the goods market, we obtain the general equilibrium real interest rate by substituting $\overline{Y}$ for Y in Eq. (9.B.14):

$$r = \alpha_{IS} - \beta_{IS}\overline{Y}. \qquad (9.B.22)$$

Having output $\overline{Y}$ and the real interest rate r (determined by Eq. Eq. 9.B.22), we use Eqs. (9.B.9), (9.B.8), and (9.B.10) to find the general equilibrium values of taxes T, consumption C, and investment I, respectively.

The final important macroeconomic variable whose equilibrium value needs to be determined is the price level P. To find the equilibrium price level, we work with the asset market equilibrium condition, Eq. (9.B.18). In Eq. (9.B.18), we substitute full-employment output $\overline{Y}$ for Y and use Eq. (9.B.22) to substitute the equilibrium value of the real interest rate for r. Solving Eq. (9.B.18) for the price level gives

$$P = \frac{M}{\ell_0 + \ell_Y\overline{Y} - \ell_r(\alpha_{IS} - \beta_{IS}\overline{Y} + \pi^e)}. \qquad (9.B.23)$$

Equation (9.B.23) confirms that the equilibrium price level P is proportional to the nominal money supply M.

We can use these equations to analyze the effects of an adverse productivity shock on the general equilibrium, as in the text. We have already shown that an increase in the productivity parameter A increases the equilibrium real wage, the full-employment level of employment, and the full-employment level of output. Thus, an adverse productivity shock (a reduction in A) reduces the general equilibrium levels of the real wage, employment, and output. Equation (9.B.22) indicates that an adverse productivity shock, because it reduces $\overline{Y}$, must increase the equilibrium real interest rate. Lower output and a higher real interest rate imply that both consumption and investment must decline (Eqs. 9.B.8 and 9.B.10). Finally, the decrease in $\overline{Y}$ resulting from an adverse productivity shock reduces the denominator of the right-hand side of Eq. (9.B.23), so the price level P must rise. All these results are the same as those found by graphical analysis.

THE AGGREGATE DEMAND CURVE

Aggregate output demanded at any price level, P, is the amount of output corresponding to the intersection of the IS and LM curves. We find the value of Y at the intersection of the IS and LM curves by setting the right-hand sides of Eqs. (9.B.14) and (9.B.19) equal and solving for Y:

$$Y = \frac{\alpha_{IS} - \alpha_{LM} + \left(\dfrac{1}{\ell_r}\right)\left(\dfrac{M}{P}\right)}{(\beta_{IS} + \beta_{LM})}. \tag{9.B.24}$$

Equation (9.B.24) is the aggregate demand curve. For constant nominal money supply, M, Eq. (9.B.24) shows that the aggregate quantity of goods demanded, Y, is a decreasing function of the price level, P, so that the AD curve slopes downward. Note that the numerator of the right-hand side of Eq. (9.B.24) is the intercept of the IS curve minus the intercept of the LM curve. Thus, for a constant price level, any change that shifts the IS curve up (such as an increase in government purchases) or shifts the LM curve down (such as an increase in the nominal money supply) increases aggregate output demanded and shifts the AD curve up and to the right.

Chapter 10

Exchange Rates, Business Cycles, and Macroeconomic Policy in the Open Economy

In Chapter 9 we focused on a closed economy, or one that does not interact with other economies. For some purposes, ignoring the foreign sector simplifies the analysis. But the reality is that today, more than ever, we live in a highly interdependent world economic system.

There are two primary aspects of the interdependence of the world's economies. The first is international trade in goods and services, which has increased steadily in volume since World War II. Today, firms produce goods and services with an eye on domestic *and* foreign markets, and they obtain many raw materials from distant sources. Expanded international trade has increased productivity by allowing economies to specialize in producing the goods and services best suited to their natural and human resources. However, expanded trade also implies that national economies are more dependent on what happens in other countries. For example, because Canada sells so much of its output to the United States, a U.S. recession or macroeconomic policy change may affect the Canadian economy as well. Thus, during 2009 when the U.S. economy was in recession, Canadian exports to the United States fell by 25%, and this contributed to a contraction in Canada's GDP.

The second is the worldwide integration of financial markets, which allows borrowers to obtain funds and savers to look for their best lending opportunities almost anywhere in the world, not just in their own countries. By allowing savings to flow to the highest-return uses, regardless of where savers and investors happen to live, the integration of world financial markets increases worldwide productivity, as does the development of an integrated world trading system. However financial market linkages, like trade linkages, increase the sensitivity of individual economies to developments abroad. For example, because of closely connected financial markets, macroeconomic policies that change the real interest rate in one country may affect real interest rates and economic activity in other countries. Thus, when U.S. financial markets fell into turmoil as a result of the subprime mortgage crisis in 2008–2009 (see "The U.S. Housing Crisis and Its Aftermath" in Chapter 7, p. 208), real interest rates increased not only in the United States but also in Canada and other countries around the world.

In this chapter, we build on earlier analyses of the open economy (Chapter 5) and cyclical fluctuations (Chapters 8 and 9) to examine the macroeconomic implications of trading and financial links among countries. We are particularly concerned in this chapter with how economic openness affects fiscal and monetary policies and how macroeconomic policy changes affect the economies of a country's trading partners. We begin our discussion by introducing two new variables that play central roles in the international economy: the nominal exchange rate and the real exchange rate.

10.1 EXCHANGE RATES

In discussing exchange rates, we must distinguish between nominal and real exchange rates. Briefly stated, the nominal exchange rate is the answer to the question: How many units of a foreign *currency* can I get in exchange for one unit of my domestic *currency*? The real exchange rate is the answer to the question: How many units of the foreign *good* can I get in exchange for one unit of my domestic *good*?

NOMINAL EXCHANGE RATES

Most countries have their own national currencies: the Canadian and U.S. dollars, the Japanese yen, and the British pound sterling are but a few well-known currencies. The exceptions include countries that belong to the European Monetary Union, which have a common currency, the euro, as well as some Latin American countries, such as Ecuador and Panama, that use the U.S. dollar. If someone in one country (or area with a common currency) wants to buy goods, services, or assets from someone in another country, normally she'll first have to exchange her country's currency for that of her trading partner's country.

The rate at which two currencies can be traded is the nominal exchange rate between the two currencies. For example, if the nominal exchange rate between the Canadian dollar and the Japanese yen is 78 yen per dollar, a dollar can buy 78 yen (ignoring transaction fees) in the **foreign exchange market**, which is the market for international currencies. Equivalently, 78 yen can buy one dollar in the foreign exchange market. More precisely, the **nominal exchange rate** between two currencies, e_{nom}, is the number of units of foreign currency that can be purchased with one unit of the domestic currency. For residents of Canada, the domestic currency is the Canadian dollar, and the nominal exchange rate between the Canadian dollar and the Japanese yen is expressed as $e_{nom} = 78$ yen per dollar. The nominal exchange rate is often simply called the **exchange rate**, so whenever someone mentions the exchange rate without specifying real or nominal, the reference is taken to mean the *nominal* exchange rate.

The dollar–yen exchange rate is not constant. The Canadian dollar might trade for 78 yen one day, but the next day it might rise in value to 80 yen or fall in value to 76 yen. Such changes in the exchange rate are normal under a flexible-exchange-rate system, the type of system in which many of the world's major currencies (including the Canadian dollar and the yen) are currently traded. In a **flexible-exchange-rate system**, or **floating-exchange-rate system**, exchange rates are not officially fixed but rather determined by conditions of supply and demand in the foreign exchange market. Under a flexible-exchange-rate system, exchange rates move continuously and respond quickly to any economic or political news that might influence the supplies and demands for various currencies. A Closer Look 10.1 discusses exchange rate data.

A CLOSER LOOK 10.1

THE EFFECTIVE EXCHANGE RATE

We have noted that there is a nominal exchange rate between every two currencies. There is an exchange rate between the Canadian dollar and the Japanese yen, an exchange rate between the European euro and the Mexican peso, and so on. An excellent source for finding the values of the hundreds of exchange rates in the world is the Bank of Canada's website, www.bankofcanada.ca/rates/exchange.

In Canada, we tend to pay particular attention to the nominal exchange rate between the Canadian and U.S. dollars for the simple reason that the majority of Canada's international trade in goods and services takes place with the United States. Of course, not all Canadian exports go to the United States and not all imports come from the United States; Canadians trade with firms and individuals in many other countries as well. For example, trade with China is becoming increasingly important to Canadians, with the result that more and more Canadians are taking an interest in the exchange rate between the Canadian dollar and the Chinese yuan.

To gain some appreciation for the importance to Canadian exporters and importers of changes in the nominal exchange rates between the Canadian dollar and the currencies of all those countries that trade with Canada, the Bank of Canada calculates the Canadian-dollar effective exchange rate index (CERI). The CERI is a weighted average of nominal exchange rates for the Canadian dollar against the currencies of Canada's six largest trading partners: the United States, the European Union, Japan, China, Mexico, and the United Kingdom. The weights used in the calculation of this average reflect the size of Canada's trade in goods, services, and non-energy commodities with each of these trading partners. The CERI is an index, which means that it measures this weighted average of nominal exchange

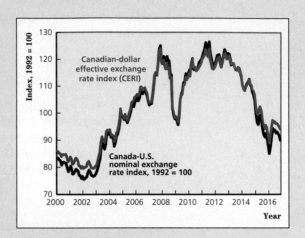

rates relative to what that average was in a base year; in this case, the base year is 1992. Data on the CERI are available from the Bank of Canada's website at www.bank-banque-canada.ca.

The figure plots values of the CERI and values of the Canada–U.S. nominal exchange rate, both measured relative to their 1992 base-year value. While there are times when the two indexes move wider apart and closer together, for the most part the CERI and the Canada–U.S. exchange rate move in tandem. This is not surprising, of course, because most of Canada's trade is with the United States. Indeed, in calculating the CERI the Bank of Canada assumes that 76% of Canada's trade is with the United States.

In the rest of this chapter our discussion of exchange rates will tend to emphasize the Canada–U.S. exchange rate. Although it would make sense to recognize that Canada trades with countries other than the United States, and so use a measure like the CERI, the figure shows that our emphasis on the Canada–U.S. exchange rate is a simplification that is not seriously at odds with what the CERI reports.

The values of currencies have not always been determined by a flexible-exchange-rate system. In the past, some type of **fixed-exchange-rate system**, under which exchange rates were set at officially determined levels, often operated. Usually, these official rates were maintained by the commitment of nations' central banks to buy and sell their own currencies at the fixed exchange rate. For example, under the international gold standard system that operated in the late 1800s and early 1900s, the central bank of each country maintained the value of its currency in terms of gold by agreeing to buy or sell gold in exchange for currency at a fixed rate of exchange. The gold standard was suspended during World War I, was temporarily restored in the late 1920s, and then collapsed during the economic and financial crises of the 1930s.

A more recent example of a fixed-exchange-rate system was the Bretton Woods system, named after the town in New Hampshire where the 1944 conference establishing the system was held. Under the Bretton Woods system, the values of various currencies were fixed in terms of the U.S. dollar, and the value of the dollar was set at $35 per ounce of gold. The Bretton Woods system functioned until the early 1970s. Since the breakdown of the Bretton Woods system, no fixed-exchange-rate system has encompassed all the world's major currencies.

Although no worldwide system of fixed exchange rates currently exists, fixed exchange rates have not disappeared entirely. Many individual countries, especially smaller ones, attempt to fix their exchange rates against a major currency. For example, several African countries tie their currencies to the euro, and Argentina until recently used a system under which its currency, the peso, traded one-for-one with the U.S. dollar. By fixing their exchange rates to a major currency, these countries hope to stabilize their own currencies and reduce the sharp swings in import and export prices that may result from exchange rate fluctuations. We discuss fixed exchange rates in Section 10.6.

REAL EXCHANGE RATES

The nominal exchange rate does not tell you all you need to know about the purchasing power of a currency. If you were told, for example, that the nominal exchange rate between the Canadian dollar and the Japanese yen is 78 yen per dollar, but you didn't know anything else about the Canadian or Japanese economies, you might be tempted to conclude that someone from Vancouver could visit Tokyo very cheaply—after all, 78 yen for just one dollar seems like a good deal. But even at 78 yen per dollar, Japan is an expensive place to visit. The reason is that although one dollar can buy a lot of yen, it also takes a lot of yen (hundreds or thousands) to buy everyday goods in Japan.

Suppose, for example, that you want to compare the price of hamburgers in Tokyo and Vancouver. Knowing that the exchange rate is 78 yen per dollar doesn't help much. But if you also know that a hamburger costs three dollars in Vancouver and 312 yen in Tokyo, you can compare the price of a hamburger in the two cities by asking how many dollars are needed to buy a hamburger in Japan. Because a hamburger costs 312 yen in Tokyo, and 78 yen cost one dollar, the price of a hamburger in Tokyo is four dollars (calculated by dividing the price of a Japanese hamburger, ¥312, by ¥78/$1, to obtain $4 per hamburger). The price of a Canadian hamburger relative to a Japanese hamburger is, therefore, ($3 per Canadian hamburger)/($4 per Japanese hamburger) = 0.75 Japanese hamburgers per Canadian hamburger. The Japanese hamburger is expensive in the sense that (in this example) one Canadian hamburger equals only three-quarters of a Japanese hamburger.

The price of domestic goods relative to foreign goods—equivalently, the number of foreign goods someone gets in exchange for one domestic good—is called the **real exchange rate**. In the hamburger example, the real exchange rate between Canada and Japan is 0.75 Japanese hamburgers per Canadian hamburger.

In general, the real exchange rate is related to the nominal exchange rate and to prices in both countries. To write this relation, we use the following symbols:

e_{nom} = the nominal exchange rate
(78 yen per dollar);

P_{For} = the price of foreign goods, measured in the foreign currency
(312 yen per Japanese hamburger);

P = the price of domestic goods, measured in the domestic currency
(3 dollars per Canadian hamburger).

The real exchange rate e is the number of units of foreign goods (Japanese hamburgers) that can be obtained in exchange for one unit of the domestic good (Canadian hamburgers). The general formula for the real exchange rate is

$$e = \frac{e_{\text{nom}}P}{P_{\text{For}}}$$

$$= \frac{(\text{¥}78/\$1)(\$3/\text{Canadian hamburger})}{\text{¥}312/\text{Japanese hamburger}}$$

$$= 0.75 \text{ Japanese hamburgers per Canadian hamburger.} \qquad (10.1)$$

In defining the real exchange rate as the number of foreign goods that can be obtained for each domestic good, we assume that each country produces a single, unique good. (Think of France producing only bottles of wine and Saudi Arabia producing only barrels of oil; then the French real exchange rate with respect to Saudi Arabia is the number of barrels of oil that can be purchased for one bottle of wine.) The assumption that each country produces a single good (which is different from the good produced by any other country) simplifies the theoretical analysis in this chapter.[1]

Of course, in reality, countries produce thousands of different goods, so real exchange rates must be based on price indexes (such as the GDP deflator or the CPI) to measure P and P_{For}. Thus, the real exchange rate isn't actually the rate of exchange between two specific goods, but rather the rate of exchange between a typical basket of goods in one country and a typical basket of goods in the other country. Each of these baskets contains some goods that are not traded internationally. Changes in the real exchange rate over time indicate that, on average, the goods of the country whose real exchange rate is rising are becoming more expensive relative to the goods of the other country.

APPRECIATION AND DEPRECIATION

When the nominal exchange rate e_{nom} falls so that, say, a dollar buys fewer units of foreign currency, we say that the dollar has undergone a **nominal depreciation**. This is the same as saying that the dollar has become "weaker." If the dollar's nominal exchange rate e_{nom} rises, then the dollar has had a **nominal appreciation**. When the dollar appreciates, it can buy more units of foreign currency and, thus,

---

[1] The assumption that different countries produce different goods is a change from Chapter 5, where we implicitly assumed that all countries produce an identical good that can be used for all purposes (consumption, investment, and so on). The assumption that all countries produce the same good implied that, in the analysis of that chapter, the real exchange rate was always equal to 1.

SUMMARY 15
TERMINOLOGY FOR CHANGES IN EXCHANGE RATES

TYPE OF EXCHANGE RATE SYSTEM	EXCHANGE RATE INCREASES (CURRENCY STRENGTHENS)	EXCHANGE RATE DECREASES (CURRENCY WEAKENS)
Flexible exchange rates	Appreciation	Depreciation
Fixed exchange rates	Revaluation	Devaluation

has become "stronger."[2] The terms *appreciation* and *depreciation* are associated with flexible exchange rates. Under a fixed-exchange-rate system, in which exchange rates are changed only by official government action, different terms are used. Instead of a depreciation, a weakening of the currency is called a **devaluation**. A strengthening of the currency under fixed exchange rates is called a **revaluation** rather than an appreciation. These terms are listed for convenience in Summary table 15.

An increase in the real exchange rate e is called a **real appreciation**. With a real appreciation, the same quantity of domestic goods can be traded for more of the foreign good than before because e, the price of domestic goods relative to the price of foreign goods, has risen. A drop in the real exchange rate, which decreases the quantity of foreign goods that can be purchased with the same quantity of domestic goods, is called a **real depreciation**.

PURCHASING POWER PARITY

How are nominal exchange rates and real exchange rates related? A simple hypothetical case that allows us to think about this question occurs when all countries produce the same good (or same set of goods) and goods are freely traded among countries. In this case, we would expect that in the absence of transportation costs and after accounting for the exchange rate, the price of any good should be the same regardless of where it is sold. If so, the real exchange rate, e, is unity. If $e = 1$, we can use Eq. (10.1) to write

$$P = \frac{P_{\text{For}}}{e_{\text{nom}}}. \tag{10.2}$$

Equation (10.2) says that the price of the domestic good must equal the price of the same good sold in a foreign country when the price of the foreign good is expressed in terms of the domestic currency. (To express the foreign price in terms of the domestic currency, divide by the exchange rate.) The idea that similar foreign and domestic goods, or baskets of goods, should have the same price in terms of the same currency is called **purchasing power parity** (PPP). Equivalently, as

[2] You will sometimes see the exchange rate defined as the number of units of domestic currency per unit of foreign currency, which is the reciprocal of how we have defined it. For example, the exchange rate between the British pound sterling and the Canadian dollar is typically quoted in this form (for example, $2.50 per pound). Under this alternative definition, an appreciation of the dollar corresponds to a fall in the nominal exchange rate. The two ways of defining the exchange rate are equally valid, as long as consistency is maintained. We have chosen to define the exchange rate as the number of units of foreign currency per unit of home currency because it's easier to remember that an appreciation (when the value of the dollar goes up) is associated with a rise in the exchange rate.

implied by Eq. (10.2), purchasing power parity says that the nominal exchange rate should equal the foreign price level divided by the domestic price level, so that

$$e_{\text{nom}} = \frac{P_{\text{For}}}{P}.$$

There is some empirical evidence that PPP holds in the very long run, but (as A Closer Look 10.2 suggests) over shorter periods, PPP does not describe exchange rate behaviour very well. The failure of PPP in the short to medium run occurs for various reasons. For example, countries may produce very different baskets of goods and services, not the same goods as assumed for PPP; some types of goods, and most services, are not internationally traded; and transportation costs and legal barriers to trade may prevent the prices of traded goods and services from being equalized in different countries.

To find a relationship between real and nominal exchange rates that holds more generally, we can use the definition of the real exchange rate in Eq. (10.1), $e = e_{\text{nom}} P/P_{\text{For}}$, to calculate $\Delta e/e$, the percentage change in the real exchange rate. Because the real exchange rate is expressed as a ratio, its percentage change equals the percentage change in the numerator minus the percentage change in the denominator.[3] The percentage change in the

A CLOSER LOOK 10.2

McParity

If PPP holds, similar goods purchased in different countries should cost about the same when their prices are expressed in a common currency—say, U.S. dollars. As a test of this hypothesis, *The Economist* magazine has long recorded the prices of Big Mac hamburgers in different countries. The table shows dollar prices of Big Macs in selected countries as reported in *The Economist*'s July 21, 2016, issue.

Big Macs aren't exactly the same product the world over. For example, in Italy, ketchup costs about 50 cents extra, instead of being included in the price as in the United States and Canada. Nevertheless, the prices suggest that PPP holds only approximately at best for Big Macs. Big Mac prices range from a low of US$1.82 in South Africa to a high of US$7.51 in Norway.

Even though PPP fails to hold exactly, Big Mac prices in different countries still might be expected to come gradually closer together. Such a convergence could occur, for example, if the currencies in countries in which Big Macs are relatively expensive depreciated relative to the currencies of the countries in which Big Macs are cheap. Such a calculation would suggest that the Norwegian krone and the Swiss franc are likely to depreciate in value relative to the U.S. dollar (because Big Macs are most expensive in those countries). In contrast, the Big Mac index suggests that all of the other currencies in our list may appreciate.

Country	U.S.-Dollar Price of a Big Mac
United States	$5.04
Brazil	4.78
Britain	3.94
Canada	4.60
China	2.79
Euro area	4.21
Japan	3.74
Norway	5.51
South Africa	2.10
Switzerland	6.59

---

[3] Section A.7 of the Appendix describes how to calculate growth rates of products and ratios.

numerator of the expression for the real exchange rate[4] is $\Delta e_{nom}/e_{nom} + \Delta P/P$, and the percentage change in the denominator is $\Delta P_{For}/P_{For}$. Thus, the percentage change in the real exchange rate is

$$\frac{\Delta e}{e} = \frac{\Delta e_{nom}}{e_{nom}} + \frac{\Delta P}{P} - \frac{\Delta P_{For}}{P_{For}}.$$

In the preceding equation, the term $\Delta P/P$, the percentage change in the domestic price level, is the same as the domestic rate of inflation π, and the term $\Delta P_{For}/P_{For}$, the percentage change in the foreign price level, is the same as the foreign rate of inflation π_{For}. Making these substitutions and rearranging the equation, we rewrite this equation as

$$\frac{\Delta e_{nom}}{e_{nom}} = \frac{\Delta e}{e} + \pi_{For} - \pi. \tag{10.3}$$

Equation (10.3) is purely definitional and, thus, must always be satisfied. It states that the rate of the nominal exchange rate appreciation $\Delta e_{nom}/e_{nom}$ equals the rate of real exchange rate appreciation $\Delta e/e$ plus the excess of foreign inflation over domestic inflation, $\pi_{For} - \pi$. Hence two factors contribute to strengthening a currency (a nominal appreciation): (1) an increase in the relative price of a country's exports (a real appreciation), which might occur if, for example, foreign demand for those exports rises; and (2) a rate of domestic inflation, π, lower than that of the country's trading partners, π_{For}.

It is worth noting that a special case of Eq. (10.3) occurs when the real exchange rate is constant. This would be so if PPP holds, in which case $e = 1$ and of course $\Delta e/e = 0$. In this case, Eq. (10.3) gives us

$$\frac{\Delta e_{nom}}{e_{nom}} = \pi_{For} - \pi.$$

In this case, the equation above expresses a relationship called relative purchasing power parity. According to **relative purchasing power parity**, the rate of appreciation of the nominal exchange rate equals the foreign inflation rate minus the domestic inflation rate. Relative purchasing power parity usually works well for high-inflation countries because in those countries, changes in relative inflation rates are usually much larger than changes in the real exchange rate.

For low-inflation countries, such as Canada, relative purchasing power parity is not a good guide. Changes in the nominal exchange rate in Canada are not usually matched by changes in Canadian inflation, at least in the short run. Equation (10.3) shows that if a nominal depreciation, say, is not accompanied by much domestic inflation (relative to foreign inflation), then there will also be a real depreciation. In that case, the nominal and real exchange rates will tend to move together.

THE REAL EXCHANGE RATE AND NET EXPORTS

We have defined the real exchange rate, but so far we have not indicated why it is important in macroeconomic analysis. One reason why policymakers and the public should care about the real exchange rate is that it represents the rate at which domestic goods and services can be traded for those produced abroad. An increase

---

[4] This result is obtained by using the rule that the percentage change in a product XY is the percentage change in X plus the percentage change in Y. See Appendix, Section A.7.

in the real exchange rate is good for a country in the sense that its citizens are able to obtain more foreign goods and services in exchange for a given amount of domestic production.

A second reason is that the real exchange rate affects a country's net exports, or exports less imports. Changes in net exports, in turn, have a direct impact on the domestic industries that produce for export or that compete with imported goods in the domestic market. In addition, as we discuss later in the chapter, changes in net exports affect a country's overall level of economic activity and are a primary channel through which business cycle disturbances and macroeconomic policy changes are transmitted internationally.

What is the link between the real exchange rate and net exports? A basic determinant of the demand for any good or service—say, coffee or taxi rides—is the price of that good or service relative to alternatives. If the price of coffee is too high, some people will switch to tea; if taxi fares rise, more people will take the bus. Similarly, the real exchange rate—the price of domestic goods relative to foreign goods—helps determine the demand for domestic goods both in home and foreign markets.

Suppose that the real exchange rate is high such that a unit of the domestic good can buy relatively many units of the foreign good. For example, let's say that a domestically produced car costs twice as much as a comparable foreign car (both prices are measured in terms of the same currency). Domestic residents will then find that foreign cars are less expensive than domestic cars, so (all else being equal) their demand for imported autos will be high. Foreign residents, in contrast, will find that the domestic country's cars are more expensive than their own, so they'll want to purchase relatively few of the domestic country's exports. With few cars being sold abroad and many cars being imported, the country's net exports of cars will be low, probably even negative.

Conversely, suppose that the real exchange rate is low; for example, imagine that a domestically produced automobile costs only half what a comparable foreign car costs. Then, all else being equal, the domestic country will be able to export relatively large quantities of cars and will import relatively few so that its net exports of cars will be high.

The general conclusion, then, is that *the higher the real exchange rate is, the lower a country's net exports will be*, holding constant other factors affecting export and import demand. The reason for this result is the same reason that higher prices reduce the amount of coffee people drink or the number of taxi rides they take. Because the real exchange rate is the relative price of a country's goods and services, an increase in the real exchange rate induces both foreigners and domestic residents to consume less domestic production and more goods and services produced abroad, which lowers net exports.

10.2 How Exchange Rates Are Determined: A Supply-and-Demand Analysis

In flexible-exchange-rate systems, exchange rates change constantly. In fixed-exchange-rate systems, by definition, exchange rates are stable most of the time; but even under a fixed-rate system, large devaluations or revaluations are not uncommon. Exchange-rate changes are notoriously difficult to explain. What economic forces cause a nation's exchange rate to rise or fall? In this section, we address this question by using supply and demand to analyze the determination of exchange rates in a flexible-exchange-rate system (we return to fixed exchange rates in Section 10.6).

For clarity, our supply-and-demand analysis focuses on the nominal exchange rate rather than on the real exchange rate. However, recall from Eq. (10.1) that for given levels of domestic and foreign prices, the real exchange rate and the nominal exchange rate are proportional. Because we hold price levels constant in this section, *all our conclusions about the nominal exchange rate apply equally to the real exchange rate.*

The nominal exchange rate e_{nom} is the value of a currency, say, the Canadian dollar. The value of the dollar, like that of any asset, is determined by supply and demand in the relevant market. For dollars, the relevant market is the foreign exchange market, where banks and currency traders continuously trade dollars for other currencies.

Figure 10.1 shows the supply of and demand for dollars. The horizontal axis of the diagram measures the quantity of dollars supplied or demanded, and the vertical axis measures the value of the dollar in terms of other currencies, or the nominal exchange rate e_{nom}. The supply curve for dollars, S, shows the number of dollars that people want to supply to the foreign exchange market at each "price" (nominal exchange rate). To supply dollars to the foreign exchange market means to offer to exchange dollars for some other currency. When the dollar's value in terms of other currencies is high, people are more willing to supply dollars to the market; thus, the supply curve slopes upward. Similarly, the demand curve for dollars, D, shows the quantity of dollars that people want to buy in the foreign exchange market at each exchange rate. When the dollar is more expensive in terms of other currencies, people demand fewer dollars, so the demand curve slopes downward. The equilibrium value of the dollar at point E is e_{nom}^1, the exchange rate at which the quantity of dollars supplied and the quantity of dollars demanded are equal.

FIGURE 10.1

THE SUPPLY OF AND DEMAND FOR THE CANADIAN DOLLAR

The figure shows the determination of the value of the dollar in the foreign exchange market. The supply curve for dollars, S, indicates the number of dollars that people are willing to sell in the foreign exchange market at each value of the Canadian nominal exchange rate e_{nom}. The demand curve for dollars, D, shows the number of dollars that people want to buy at each nominal exchange rate. At equilibrium, point E, the value of the dollar, e_{nom}^1, is the nominal exchange rate at which the quantity of dollars supplied equals the quantity of dollars demanded.

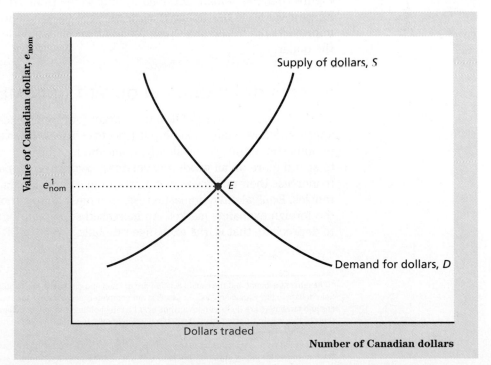

Figure 10.1 aids in understanding the forces that determine the value of the dollar, or any other currency. To go any further, though, we must ask why people decide to demand or supply dollars. Unlike apples or haircuts, dollars are not demanded because people value them in themselves; rather, people value dollars because of what they can buy. Specifically, foreign individuals or firms demand dollars in the foreign exchange market for two reasons:

1. to be able to buy Canadian goods and services (Canadian exports), and

2. to be able to buy Canadian real and financial assets (Canadian capital inflows).

Note that the two types of transactions for which foreigners need dollars (to purchase Canadian exports and Canadian assets) correspond to the two components of the balance of payments accounts: the current account and the capital account.[5]

Similarly, Canadians supply dollars to the foreign exchange market, thereby acquiring foreign currencies, for two reasons:

1. to be able to buy foreign goods and services (Canadian imports), and

2. to be able to buy real and financial assets in foreign countries (Canadian capital outflows).

Thus, factors that increase foreigners' demand for Canadian exports and assets will also increase the foreign-exchange-market demand for dollars, raising the dollar exchange rate. Likewise, the value of the dollar will rise if Canadians' demand for foreign goods and assets declines, so Canadians will supply fewer dollars to the foreign exchange market.

As an example, suppose that Canadian goods improve in quality such that foreigners demand more of them. This increase in the demand for Canadian exports would translate into an increase in the demand for Canadian dollars. In Figure 10.2, the demand for dollars shifts to the right, from D^1 to D^2, and the equilibrium value of the dollar rises from e^1_{nom} to e^2_{nom}. All else being equal, then, improvements in the quality of Canadian goods would lead to an appreciation of the dollar.

EFFECTS OF CHANGES IN OUTPUT (INCOME)

With this understanding of how the market for foreign exchange works, it is easy to appreciate how changes in output (income) affect the exchange rate. An increase in domestic output (equivalently, domestic income) Y causes consumers to want to spend more on all goods and services, *including imports*. Recall that in order to increase their purchases of imports, domestic residents must obtain foreign currencies. Equivalently, domestic residents must supply more domestic currency to the foreign exchange market. An increased supply of domestic currency causes it to depreciate, that is, the exchange rate falls.[6]

---

[5] The current account and the capital account are defined and discussed in Chapter 5. The idea that foreigners must hold dollars to buy Canadian goods or assets is not completely accurate because many transactions between Canadians and foreigners are done without anyone ever literally holding a supply of dollars or the foreign currency. Nevertheless, this way of thinking about the determination of exchange rates is fairly simple and gives the same answers as would a more complex analysis.

[6] We hold the price level constant in this exercise, so our conclusion that an increase in domestic income results in the exchange rate falling applies to the real, as well as nominal, exchange rate.

FIGURE 10.2

THE EFFECT OF INCREASED EXPORT QUALITY ON THE VALUE OF THE DOLLAR

An increase in the quality of Canadian exports raises foreigners' demands for Canadian goods and, hence, their demand for Canadian dollars, which are needed to buy Canadian goods. The demand curve for dollars shifts, from D^1 to D^2, raising the value of the dollar (the nominal exchange rate) from e^1_{nom} to e^2_{nom}.

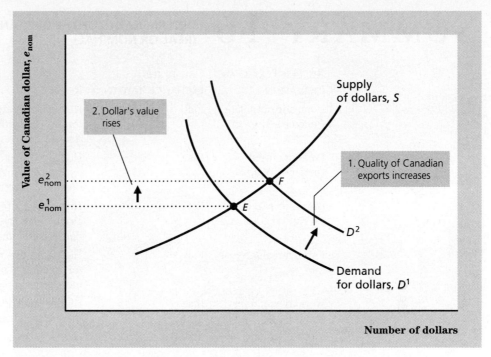

We can also analyze the effects of an increase in the real output of the country's trading partners, Y_{For} (foreign output or income). An increase in Y_{For} leads foreign consumers to increase their spending on all goods and services, including the exports of the domestic country. Thus, an increase in the income of Germany and Japan, for example, would increase those countries' demand for Canadian exports and raise Canadian net exports. The increase in foreign demand for Canadian goods would also increase foreigners' demand for Canadian dollars, raising the value of the dollar. Note that the effects of changes in foreign income are the opposite of the effects of changes in domestic income.

EFFECTS OF CHANGES IN REAL INTEREST RATES

A second key macroeconomic variable to be considered is the real interest rate. Imagine that the domestic country's real interest rate r rises, with other factors (including the foreign real interest rate) held constant. In this case, the country's real and financial assets will become more attractive to foreign savers seeking the highest return on their funds. Because domestic currency can be used to buy domestic assets, a rise in the domestic real interest rate also increases the demand for domestic currency. An increased demand for domestic currency, in turn, leads to exchange rate appreciation.

A rise in the domestic real interest rate r has no *direct* effect on net exports, but it does have an *indirect* effect through the exchange rate. An increase in r raises the exchange rate so that domestic exports become more expensive and imports from abroad become cheaper. Thus, other factors being constant, an increase in r reduces the domestic country's net exports.

The effects of a change in the foreign real interest rate, r_{For}, are the opposite of the effects of a change in the domestic real interest rate. If the foreign real

SUMMARY 16 DETERMINANTS OF THE EXCHANGE RATE (REAL OR NOMINAL)

ALL ELSE EQUAL, AN INCREASE IN	CAUSES THE EXCHANGE RATE TO	REASON
Domestic output (income), Y	Fall	Higher domestic output raises demand for imports and increases supply of domestic currency.
Foreign output (income), Y_{For}	Rise	Higher foreign output raises demand for exports and increases demand for domestic currency.
Domestic real interest rate, r	Rise	Higher real interest rate makes domestic assets more attractive and increases demand for domestic currency.
Foreign real interest rate, r_{For}	Fall	Higher foreign real interest rate makes foreign assets more attractive and increases supply of domestic currency.
World demand for domestic goods	Rise	Higher demand for domestic goods increases demand for domestic currency.

interest rate rises, for example, foreign assets will become more attractive to domestic savers. To get the foreign currency needed to buy foreign assets, domestic savers will supply domestic currency to the foreign exchange market. The increased supply of domestic currency will lead to a depreciation of the exchange rate. The depreciation of the exchange rate caused by the rise in r_{For}, in turn, raises the domestic country's net exports.

Summary tables 16 and 17 list the effects of the various macroeconomic factors on the exchange rate and net exports.

SUMMARY 17 DETERMINANTS OF NET EXPORTS

ALL ELSE EQUAL, AN INCREASE IN	CAUSES NET EXPORTS TO	REASON
Domestic output (income), Y	Fall	Higher domestic output raises demand for imports.
Foreign output (income), Y_{For}	Rise	Higher foreign output raises foreign demand for exports.
Domestic real interest rate, r	Fall	Higher real interest rate raises the real exchange rate and makes domestic goods more expensive relative to foreign goods.
Foreign real interest rate, r_{For}	Rise	Higher foreign real interest rate lowers the real exchange rate and makes domestic goods cheaper relative to foreign goods.
World demand for domestic goods	Rise	Higher demand for domestic goods directly increases net exports.

10.3 THE INTERNATIONAL ASSET MARKET: INTEREST RATE PARITY

Exchange rates play an important role in the international economy by establishing relative prices of goods produced domestically and abroad. Interest rates play a similar role in determining the price of internationally traded financial assets. In the international economy, savers have access to financial assets sold in all countries and borrowers can sell their assets to savers anywhere in the world.[7] This presents opportunities that neither would have if the world were closed to the free flow of financial capital across national boundaries. Savers are now presented with new opportunities for increasing the return on their savings by having access to financial assets sold anywhere in the world. Borrowers now have access to a much larger pool of savings and hence have far greater opportunities to find funding for investments they find profitable. In this section we examine the role of exchange rates in determining the relative prices of internationally traded financial assets.

RETURNS ON DOMESTIC AND FOREIGN ASSETS

In an open economy, savers have the opportunity to purchase financial assets sold by foreign borrowers as well as those sold by domestic borrowers. Thus a Canadian saver might purchase a bond offered for sale by a Canadian government or corporation or purchase a bond offered for sale by a foreign government or corporation. What factors should Canadian savers take into consideration when choosing whether to purchase a domestic as opposed to a foreign asset?

Imagine that you want to purchase a $10 000 financial asset and that you want to hold that asset for one year. Suppose you've limited your choice to either Canadian government bonds or German government bonds. Canadian government bonds are denominated in dollars and pay a nominal interest rate of 8% for one year (that is, $i = 0.08$). German government bonds, which are denominated in euros, pay a nominal interest rate of 6% for one year (that is, $i_{\text{For}} = 0.06$). The two financial assets have comparable liquidity and risk of default, and we will ignore transaction costs and differences in how interest income might be taxed should it be earned at home versus abroad. If you want to maximize your financial return, which bond should you buy?

At first glance, the answer seems obvious: Buy the Canadian government bonds because they offer a higher interest rate. But this answer might not be right. The correct answer depends on what you think is going to happen to the exchange rate between the Canadian dollar and the euro over the next year, the length of time you hold the bond. To understand why, let's compare the financial return on purchasing the Canadian government bonds with the financial return on purchasing the German government bonds.

The financial return on the Canadian government bonds is easy to calculate. At a nominal interest rate of 8%, the bond will earn $800 in interest and will be worth $10 800 in one year. The financial return on the German government bonds is a little more difficult to calculate. This is so because purchasing the German bonds

---

[7] Well, almost. Not all countries allow for the free movement of financial capital. Some countries have at times imposed capital controls that inhibit the free access to domestic capital markets by foreigners. Chile imposed such controls between 1991 and 1998, and Malaysia did so in 1998. Throughout this chapter we assume that financial capital is freely mobile across national boundaries.

first involves purchasing euros in order to buy the German bond. When the German bond matures a year from now, the principal and interest is paid in euros. To compare the total return on the German government bonds with that earned on the Canadian government bonds, those euros must be converted back to dollars. The exchange rate at which this last transaction will take place a year from now will, of course, not be known until then. To compare the total financial return earned on the two bonds therefore requires that you form an expectation of what you believe will be the exchange rate one year from now.

Table 10.1 illustrates the calculations required to determine the financial return on the German government bonds. Let's assume that the current value of the nominal exchange rate e_{nom} is 0.7 euros per dollar and that the exchange rate is expected to depreciate by 3% over the coming year, meaning that the expected future value of the nominal exchange rate e_{nom}^f is 0.679 euros per dollar (0.679 is 97% of 0.7). Converting \$10 000 to euros at an exchange rate of 0.7 euros per dollar yields 7000 euros (Step 1 in Table 10.1), which are used to buy the German government bonds. At a 6% nominal interest rate, the German bonds earn 420 euros in interest and are worth 7420 euros at the end of one year (Step 2). Finally, converting 7420 euros to dollars at 0.679 euros per dollar (the exchange rate that you expect to observe one year from now) yields \$10 928 (Step 3)—which is higher than the \$10 800 that would be obtained from purchasing the Canadian government bonds! Thus the German government bonds have a higher expected rate of return in this case, even though they pay a lower nominal interest rate.

The German bonds have a higher expected rate of return in this example because, relative to the Canadian bonds, the German bonds have *two* sources of return. The first source is the nominal interest rate paid on the bonds ($i_{For} = 0.06$). The second source of return is the expected appreciation of the euro relative to the dollar (which is equivalent to an expected depreciation of the dollar relative to

TABLE 10.1

Calculating the Gross Nominal Rate of Return for a Foreign Asset

Example

Today: $e_{nom} = 0.7$ euros/dollar $i_{For} = 0.06$ Future: $e_{nom}^f = 0.679$ euros/dollar

Step 1	**Step 2**	**Step 3**
Convert home currency to foreign currency $\$10\,000 \to 7000$ euros	Earn interest on foreign bond $\to 7420$ euros	Convert foreign currency to home currency $\to \$10\,928$

General Case

Today   Future

Step 1	**Step 2**	**Step 3**
Convert home currency to foreign currency 1 unit of home currency $\to$ e_{nom} units of foreign currency	Earn interest on foreign bond $\to (1 + i_{For})e_{nom}$ units of foreign currency	Convert foreign currency to home currency $\to [(1 + i_{For})e_{nom}]/e_{nom}^f$ units of home currency

the euro and hence an expected depreciation in the exchange rate). At the end of the year, when you convert the 7420 euros you receive in principal and interest from the redemption of the German bonds, the value of a euro in terms of dollars is 3% higher than at the beginning of the year, when you converted dollars to euros. This second source of return gives a boost to the expected return from purchasing the German bonds that is not available from purchasing the Canadian bonds.

The bottom section of Table 10.1 generalizes the calculations described in the top section. One unit of home currency will buy e_{nom} units of foreign currency (Step 1), which can be used to purchase foreign bonds at a nominal interest rate of i_{For} to yield $(1 + i_{For})e_{nom}$ units of foreign currency at the end of a year (Step 2). Converting the $(1 + i_{For})e_{nom}$ units of foreign currency to home currency yields $(1 + i_{For})e_{nom}/e^f_{nom}$ units of home currency at the end of the year (Step 3). Thus, the gross nominal rate of return from the purchase of the foreign bond is

$$\text{expected gross nominal rate of return on foreign bond} = (1 + i_{For})\frac{e_{nom}}{e^f_{nom}}. \qquad (10.4)$$

Substituting the values we assumed in the example presented in the top portion of Table 10.1, you will find the expected gross nominal rate of return on the German bond to be 1.0928, just as we previously calculated.

Equation (10.4) is an exact expression for the gross nominal rate of return. A simple approximation ($\approx$) to the gross nominal rate of return is

$$\text{approximate expected gross nominal rate of return on foreign bond} \approx 1 + i_{For} - \frac{\Delta e_{nom}}{e_{nom}}. \qquad (10.5)$$

In our example of the German government bonds with $i_{For} = 0.06$ and $\Delta e_{nom}/e_{nom} = -0.03$, Eq. (10.5) indicates that the expected gross nominal rate of return from the purchase of the German bonds is approximately 1.09, which is very close to the exact value of 1.0928. The approximation in Eq. (10.5) permits easy calculation of the expected gross nominal return, generally without using pencil and paper (or a calculator). The other virtue of this approximation is that it makes clear the two sources of expected return from holding the German government bonds: the interest on the bonds i_{For}, and the expected nominal appreciation of the euro relative to the dollar over the course of the year, $-\Delta e_{nom}/e_{nom}$. It is useful to note from Eq. (10.5) that if you do not expect there to be a change in the nominal exchange rate, so that $\Delta e_{nom}/e_{nom} = 0$, then the second source of return from holding foreign bonds disappears. There is now only one source of return on the foreign bond—the nominal interest rate paid on those bonds. As a result, the gross rates of return on the domestic and the foreign bonds are simply $1 + i$ and $1 + i_{For}$, respectively, and the decision of whether to buy one or the other involves an easy comparison of nominal interest rates i and i_{For}.

INTEREST RATE PARITY

In our example, the expected gross nominal rate of return on the German government bonds exceeded the gross nominal rate of return on the Canadian government bonds. However, if both types of bonds have the same liquidity and risk of default, and if we ignore transactions costs and differences in how interest income might be taxed should it be earned at home versus abroad (these are all assumptions we made in our example), then this difference in rates of return would not persist for long. If savers are free to choose between German and Canadian bonds, they will choose the German bonds as long as they offer a higher expected gross nominal rate of return than Canadian bonds. But if savers choose German bonds in preference to Canadian bonds, the rate of return on German bonds will fall. This is so for the reason we discussed in Section 9.3 of the previous chapter: If savers increase the demand for a bond, then the price of that bond rises and the nominal interest rate that asset pays falls. In a similar way, if savers choose to buy fewer Canadian bonds, then the price of those bonds will fall and the nominal interest rate those assets pay rises. In this way, we expect to see the interest rate paid on German bonds i_{For} fall and the interest rate paid on Canadian bonds i increase. By this process, expected gross nominal rates of return adjust until such time as they are equal. Financial-asset traders known as **arbitragers** earn a living spotting differences in expected gross nominal rates of return and then buying and selling assets as appropriate to realize a profit. As a result of the actions of arbitragers, differences in expected gross rates of return do not persist.

In general, when the international asset market is in equilibrium, the gross nominal rates of return to domestic and foreign assets of comparable risk and liquidity must be the same. This equilibrium condition can be written as

$$\frac{e_{nom}}{e_{nom}^f}(1 + i_{For}) = 1 + i, \tag{10.6}$$

where the left side is the expected gross nominal rate of return on the foreign bond (Eq. 10.4) and the right side is the gross nominal rate of return on the domestic bond. The equilibrium condition in Eq. (10.6) is the **nominal interest rate parity condition**, which says that the nominal returns on foreign and domestic financial assets with equal risk and liquidity, when measured in a common currency, must be the same. With the approximation in Eq. (10.5), the nominal interest rate parity condition can also be expressed more simply as $i_{For} - \Delta e_{nom}/e_{nom} \approx i$. According to this approximate formula for nominal interest rate parity, the domestic interest rate i must be equal to the foreign interest rate i_{For} less the expected rate of appreciation of the exchange rate ($\Delta e_{nom}/e_{nom}$). From both of these expressions we can see that if the future value of the nominal exchange rate is expected to remain the same as its current value, then nominal interest rate parity reduces to a condition requiring that in equilibrium

$$i = i_{For}. \tag{10.7}$$

Interest rate parity can also be expressed in terms of real interest rates and real exchange rates. Not surprisingly, this relationship is called the **real interest rate parity condition**. This condition says that the international asset market is in equilibrium when

$$\frac{e}{e^f}(1 + r_{For}) = 1 + r, \tag{10.8}$$

where r_{For} is the foreign real interest rate, r is the domestic real interest rate, and e and e^f are the current and expected future values of the real exchange rate. The real interest rate parity condition, Eq. (10.8), is identical to the nominal interest rate parity condition, Eq. (10.6), except that the nominal interest and exchange rates in Eq. (10.6) are replaced by real interest and exchange rates in Eq. (10.8). Similarly to what we found in our discussion of nominal interest rate parity, if the future value of the real exchange rate is expected to remain the same as it is currently, then the real interest rate parity condition reduces to a requirement that

$$r = r_{For}. \tag{10.9}$$

Interest rate parity conditions suggest that unless financial markets expect large exchange rate appreciations or depreciations, domestic and foreign interest rates will move in tandem. An increase (decrease) in one will lead to a similarly sized increase (decrease) in the other. It is useful to recall our discussion in Chapter 5 where it was first emphasized that domestic and foreign interest rates tend to move in tandem. In that chapter, Figure 5.1 (p. 141) presented a graph showing Canadian and U.S. interest rates rising and falling together. In the discussion of that graph, we emphasized that differences in default risk, in transaction costs, and in how interest income might be taxed at home versus abroad were reasons why domestic and foreign interest rates might differ. In this section we have ignored those considerations in order to focus on another reason why domestic and foreign interest rates might differ: concerns domestic savers might have that the value of exchange rates could change during the time they own a foreign financial asset. We have learned that any event that might cause a domestic saver to believe exchange rates might change in the future will affect the size of the difference in domestic versus foreign interest rates.

APPLICATION

EXPLAINING THE MOVEMENTS IN CANADIAN AND U.S. INTEREST RATES

How does our discussion of interest rate parity help us explain the relative movements in Canadian and U.S. interest rates presented in Figure 5.1? A possible explanation that fits the facts is that between 1975 and 1995, when Canadian interest rates increased relative to U.S. rates, the debts of Canadian governments were large and growing relative to those in the United States. The relative growth in Canadian government debt came about because Canadian governments were increasing spending more quickly than were governments in the United States and despite the fact that Canadian governments were increasing taxes more quickly than were governments in the United States. In this fiscal environment, it would not be surprising to find savers coming to the conclusion that the Canadian government debts would continue to grow relative to those in the United States. If so, savers might sensibly conclude that Canada would have difficulty keeping inflation low relative to that in the United States in the face of the increase in Canadian aggregate demand coming from government budgets. Recalling Eq. (10.3), if savers believed the rate of inflation in Canada, π, was likely to increase, then, all else being equal, they would have expected a nominal exchange rate depreciation. Referring to the equation that approximates interest rate parity, $i_{For} - \Delta e_{nom}/e_{nom} \approx i$, we see that an expected exchange rate depreciation would cause the domestic interest rate, i, to increase relative to foreign rates i_{For}.[8] Looking ahead, there are reasons to believe that the experience of 1975–1995 will be repeated—but this time in the opposite direction. That is, in that earlier period Canadian interest rates increased relative to U.S. rates due to

---

[8] During the 1970s and 1980s, savers might also have demanded that they receive a higher interest rate from Canadian bonds than did U.S. borrowers (a risk premium) to compensate them for the increased relative risk that Canada might default. Threats to Canada's political future resulting from the election of separatist governments in Quebec during this period would also have caused savers to demand a risk premium. Since 1995 the risk premium demanded of Canadian borrowers may have fallen as the separatist threat has abated and Canadian governments have reduced their levels of debt. We return to the issue of government deficits and debt in Chapter 15.

increases in the debts of Canadian governments versus the debt of the U.S. government. Most economists would agree that in the aftermath of the 2008–2009 financial crisis and in consideration of the comments made President Trump the debt of the U.S. government is expected to increase quite rapidly, whereas the increase in the debts of Canadian governments will be more muted. In the near future, then, savers might sensibly conclude that it will now be the United States that will have difficulty keeping inflation low relative to inflation in Canada. In that case, Eq. (10.6) suggests Canada's domestic interest rate, i, will decrease relative to foreign rates, i_{For}.

In the remainder of this chapter we will assume that exchange rates are not expected to change. We will also continue to ignore transaction costs, default risk, and tax treatments that might cause domestic and foreign interest rates to differ. Thus we will assume $r = r_{For}$ in what follows. This assumption simplifies our examination of macroeconomic policy in a small open economy. After examining the results of our model, given our assumption about the formation of exchange rate expectations, we will return to this issue and try to offer some insights into how the results of the model change under alternative assumptions.

10.4 THE *IS–LM–FE* MODEL FOR AN OPEN ECONOMY

Now we are ready to see how considerations of international trade and the international flow of financial capital affect our understanding of the business cycle. To do so, we extend the *IS–LM–FE* model to allow for trade and lending among nations.

Recall that the components of the *IS–LM* model are the *IS* curve, which describes goods market equilibrium; the *LM* curve, which describes asset market equilibrium; and the *FE* line, which describes labour market equilibrium. Nothing discussed in this chapter affects our analysis of the supply of or demand for money; so, in developing the open-economy *IS–LM* model, we use the same *LM* curve that we used for the closed-economy model. Similarly, the labour market and the production function are not directly affected by international factors, so the *FE* line is also unchanged.[9]

However, because net exports are part of the demand for goods, we have to modify the *IS* curve in order to describe the open economy. Our focus in this section, then, is on the *IS* curve. In particular, we will make three main points about the *IS* curve in the open economy:

1. Although the open-economy *IS* curve is derived somewhat differently than the closed-economy *IS* curve, it is a downward-sloping relationship between output and the real interest rate, just as the closed-economy *IS* curve is.

2. All factors that shift the *IS* curve in the closed economy shift the *IS* curve in the open economy in the same way.

---

[9] A case in which the *FE* line does depend on international considerations arises when some raw materials (such as oil) are imported. In this book, we have modelled oil price shocks as productivity shocks, which captures the main domestic macroeconomic effects. A full analysis that includes all the international aspects of an oil price shock is complex, so we do not present it here.

3. In an open economy, factors that change net exports also shift the *IS* curve. Specifically, for given values of domestic output and the domestic real interest rate, factors that raise a country's net exports shift the open-economy *IS* curve up; and factors that lower a country's net exports shift the *IS* curve down.

In making these three points, we will follow the method familiar to us from Chapter 9. That is, we perform *thought experiments* in which we consider the *IS* relationship in isolation from the rest of the open-economy model. Thus, we will hold the money supply and the exchange rate constant but allow the interest rate and the level of output to change. In this way we will see how the shape and position of the *IS* curve is affected by open-economy considerations. Armed with this understanding, in the next section we put all that we have learned into the structure of a complete macroeconomic model. In that model we will allow the *IS* and *LM* relationships to influence one another and we will impose the requirement that the domestic interest rate equal the foreign interest rate.

THE OPEN-ECONOMY *IS* CURVE

For any level of output, the *IS* curve gives the real interest rate that brings the goods market into equilibrium. In a closed economy, the goods market equilibrium condition is that desired national saving S^d must equal desired investment I^d, or $S^d - I^d = 0$. In an open economy, as we showed in Chapter 5, the goods market equilibrium condition is that desired saving S^d must equal desired investment I^d plus net exports NX. Writing the goods market equilibrium condition for an open economy, we have

$$S^d - I^d = NX. \qquad (10.10)$$

To interpret Eq. (10.10), recall that $S^d - I^d$, the excess of national saving over investment, is the amount that domestic residents desire to lend abroad. Recall also that net exports NX (which, if net factor payments are zero, is the same as the current account balance) equals the amount that foreigners want to borrow from domestic savers. Thus, Eq. (10.10) indicates that for the goods market to be in equilibrium, desired foreign lending must equal desired foreign borrowing. An equivalent way to write the goods market equilibrium condition is as follows:

$$Y = C^d + I^d + G + NX. \qquad (10.11)$$

We obtained Eq. (10.11) from Eq. (10.10) by replacing desired saving, S^d, with its definition, $Y - C^d - G$, and rearranging. Equation (10.11) states that the goods market is in equilibrium when the supply of goods, Y, equals the demand for goods, $C^d + I^d + G + NX$. Note that in an open economy, the total demand for goods includes spending on net exports.

Figure 10.3 illustrates goods market equilibrium in an open economy. The horizontal axis measures desired saving minus desired investment, $S^d - I^d$, and net exports, NX. Note that the horizontal axis includes both positive and negative values. The vertical axis measures the domestic real interest rate, r.

The upward-sloping curve, $S - I$, shows the difference between desired national saving and desired investment for each value of the real interest rate r. This curve slopes upward because with output held constant, an increase in the real interest rate raises desired national saving and reduces desired investment, raising the country's desired foreign lending.

FIGURE 10.3

GOODS MARKET EQUILIBRIUM
IN AN OPEN ECONOMY

The upward-sloping curve shows desired saving S^d less desired investment I^d. This curve slopes upward because a higher domestic real interest rate increases the excess of desired saving over desired investment. The NX curve relates net exports to the domestic real interest rate. This curve slopes downward because a higher domestic real interest rate causes the real exchange rate to rise, reducing net exports. Goods market equilibrium occurs at point E, where the excess of desired saving over desired investment equals net exports (equivalently, where desired lending abroad equals desired borrowing by foreigners). The real interest rate that clears the goods market is r_1.

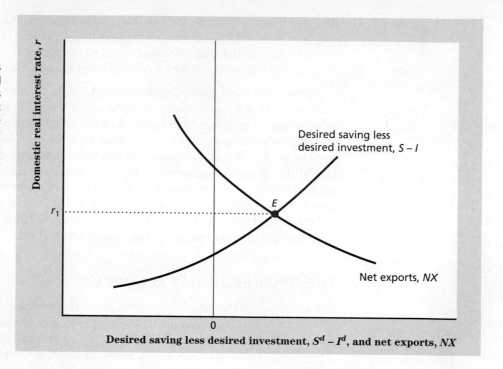

The downward-sloping curve in Figure 10.3, NX, shows the relationship between the country's net exports and the domestic real interest rate, other factors held constant. As discussed in Section 10.2, a rise in the real interest rate raises the exchange rate, which, in turn, reduces net exports (see Summary table 17, p. 306). Hence the NX curve slopes downward.

Goods market equilibrium requires that the excess of desired saving over desired investment equal net exports (Eq. 10.10). This condition is satisfied at the intersection of the $S - I$ and NX curves at point E. Thus, the domestic real interest rate that clears the goods market is the interest rate at E, or r_1.

To derive the open-economy IS curve, we need to know what happens to the real interest rate that clears the goods market when the current level of domestic output rises (Figure 10.4). Suppose that domestic output initially equals Y_1 and that goods market equilibrium is at point E, with a real interest rate of r_1. Now, suppose that output rises to Y_2. An increase in current output raises desired national saving but does not affect desired investment, so the excess of desired saving over desired investment rises at any real interest rate. Thus, the curve measuring the excess of desired saving over desired investment shifts to the right, from $(S-I)^1$ to $(S-I)^2$ in Figure 10.4(a).

What about the NX curve? An increase in domestic income causes domestic consumers to spend more on imported goods, which (other factors held constant) reduces net exports (see Summary table 17). Thus, when output rises from Y_1 to Y_2, net exports fall, and the NX curve shifts to the left, from NX^1 to NX^2.

After the increase in output from Y_1 to Y_2, the new goods market equilibrium is at point F in Figure 10.4(a), with the real interest rate at r_2. The IS curve in Figure 10.4(b) shows that when output equals Y_1, the real interest rate that clears the goods market is r_1; and that when output equals Y_2, the real interest rate that clears the goods market is r_2. Because higher current output lowers the real interest rate that clears the goods market, the open-economy IS curve slopes downward, as for a closed economy.

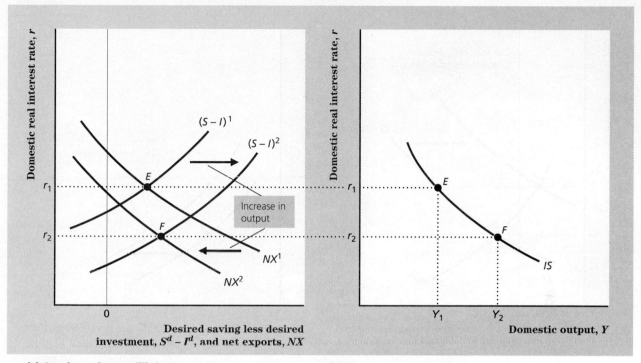

(a) Goods market equilibrium　　　　**(b) Open-economy *IS* curve**

FIGURE 10.4

DERIVATION OF THE *IS* CURVE IN AN OPEN ECONOMY

The initial equilibrium in the goods market is represented by point E in both (a) and (b).

(a) At point E, domestic output is Y_1 and the domestic real interest rate is r_1. An increase in domestic output from Y_1 to Y_2 raises desired national saving at each real interest rate and does not affect desired investment. Therefore, the $S - I$ curve shifts to the right, from $(S - I)^1$ to $(S - I)^2$. The increase in output also raises domestic spending on imports, reducing net exports and causing the NX curve to shift to the left, from NX^1 to NX^2. At the new equilibrium point, F, the real interest rate is r_2.

(b) Because an increase in output from Y_1 to Y_2 lowers the real interest rate that clears the goods market from r_1 to r_2, the IS curve slopes downward.

FACTORS THAT SHIFT THE OPEN-ECONOMY *IS* CURVE

As in a closed economy, in an open economy any factor that raises the real interest rate that clears the goods market at a constant level of output shifts the IS curve up. This point is illustrated in Figure 10.5, which shows the effects on the open-economy IS curve of a temporary increase in government purchases. With output held constant at Y_1, the initial equilibrium is at point E, where the real interest rate is r_1. A temporary increase in government purchases lowers desired national saving at every level of output and the real interest rate. Thus, the $S - I$ curve shifts to the left, from $(S - I)^1$ to $(S - I)^2$, as shown in Figure 10.5(a). The new goods market equilibrium is at point F, where the real interest rate is r_2.

Figure 10.5(b) shows the effect on the IS curve. For output Y_1, the increase in government purchases raises the real interest rate that clears the goods market from r_1 to r_2. Thus, the IS curve shifts up and to the right, from IS^1 to IS^2.

In general, any factor that shifts the closed-economy IS curve up does so by reducing desired national saving relative to desired investment. Because a change that reduces desired national saving relative to desired investment shifts the $S - I$ curve to the left (Figure 10.5(a)), such a change also shifts the open-economy IS curve up.

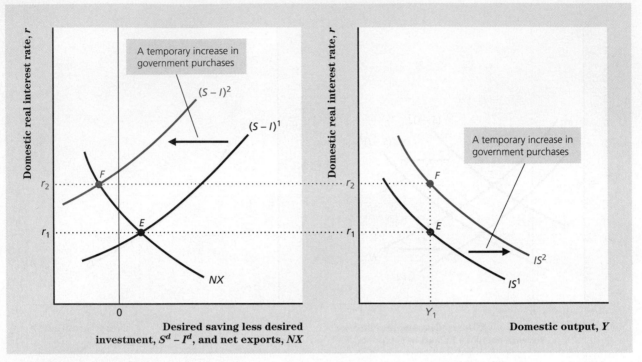

(a) Goods market equilibrium   **(b) Open-economy *IS* curve**

FIGURE 10.5

EFFECT OF AN INCREASE IN GOVERNMENT PURCHASES ON THE OPEN-ECONOMY *IS* CURVE

Initial equilibrium is at point E, where output is Y_1 and the real interest rate is r_1, in both (a) and (b).

(a) A temporary increase in government purchases lowers desired national saving at every level of output and raises the real interest rate. Thus, the $S - I$ curve shifts to the left, from $(S - I)^1$ to $(S - I)^2$.

(b) For output Y_1, the real interest rate that clears the goods market is now r_2, at point F in both (a) and (b). Because the real interest rate that clears the goods market has risen, the *IS* curve shifts up and to the right, from IS^1 to IS^2.

In addition to the standard factors that shift the *IS* curve in a closed economy, some new factors affect the position of the *IS* curve in an open economy. In particular, anything that raises a country's net exports, given domestic output and the domestic real interest rate, will shift the open-economy *IS* curve up. This point is illustrated in Figure 10.6.

At the initial equilibrium point, E, in both Figure 10.6(a) and (b), domestic output is Y_1 and the domestic real interest rate is r_1. Now, suppose that some change raises the country's net exports at any level of domestic output and the domestic real interest rate. This increase in net exports is shown as a shift to the right of the *NX* curve in Figure 10.6(a), from NX^1 to NX^2. At the new goods market equilibrium point, F, the real interest rate has risen to r_2. Because the real interest rate that clears the goods market has risen for constant output, the *IS* curve shifts up and to the right, as shown in Figure 10.6(b), from IS^1 to IS^2.

What might cause a country's net exports to rise, for any given domestic output and domestic real interest rate? We have discussed three possibilities at various points in this chapter: an increase in foreign output, an increase in the foreign real interest rate, and a shift in world demand toward the domestic country's goods (see Summary table 17, p. 306).

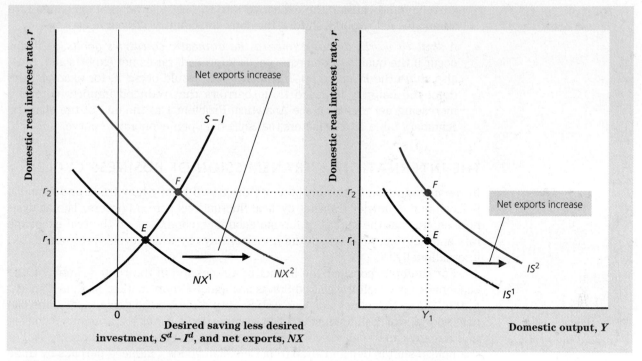

(a) Goods market equilibrium

(b) Open-economy *IS* curve

FIGURE 10.6

EFFECT OF AN INCREASE IN NET EXPORTS ON THE OPEN-ECONOMY *IS* CURVE

In both (a) and (b), at the initial equilibrium point, *E*, output is Y_1 and the real interest rate that clears the goods market is r_1.

(a) If some change raises the country's net exports at any given domestic output and domestic real interest rate, the *NX* curve shifts to the right, from NX^1 to NX^2.

(b) For output Y_1, the real interest rate that clears the goods market has risen from r_1 to r_2, at point *F* in both (a) and (b). Thus, the *IS* curve shifts up and to the right, from IS^1 to IS^2.

- *An increase in foreign output*, Y_{For}, increases purchases of the domestic country's goods by foreigners, directly raising the domestic country's net exports and shifting the *IS* curve up.

- *An increase in the foreign real interest rate*, r_{For}, makes foreign assets relatively more attractive to domestic savers, increasing the supply of domestic

SUMMARY 18   INTERNATIONAL FACTORS THAT SHIFT THE *IS* CURVE

ALL ELSE EQUAL, AN INCREASE IN	SHIFTS THE *IS* CURVE	REASON
Foreign output, Y_{For}	Up	Higher foreign output raises demand for home country exports.
Foreign real interest rate, r_{For}	Up	Higher foreign real interest rate lowers the real exchange rate and raises net exports.
Demand for domestic goods relative to foreign goods	Up	Higher demand for domestic goods raises net exports.

currency and causing the exchange rate to fall. A lower real exchange rate stimulates net exports, shifting the domestic country's *IS* curve up.

- *A shift in world demand toward the domestic country's goods*, as might occur if the quality of domestic goods improved, raises net exports and, thus, also shifts the *IS* curve up. A similar effect would occur if, for example, the domestic country imposed trade barriers that reduced imports (thereby increasing net exports); see Analytical Problem 1 at the end of the chapter. Summary table 18 lists factors that shift the open-economy *IS* curve.

THE INTERNATIONAL TRANSMISSION OF BUSINESS CYCLES

In the introduction to this chapter, we discussed briefly how trade and financial links among countries transmit cyclical fluctuations across borders. The analysis here shows that the impact of foreign economic conditions on the real exchange rate and net exports is one of the principal ways by which cycles are transmitted internationally.

For example, consider the impact of a recession in the United States on the economies for which the United States is a major export market, such as Canada. In the *IS–LM–FE* model a decline in U.S. output lowers the demand for Canadian net exports, which shifts the Canadian *IS* curve down. Similarly, a country's domestic economy can be sensitive to shifts in international tastes for various goods. For example, a shift in demand away from Canadian goods—induced perhaps by trade restrictions against Canadian products—would also shift the Canadian *IS* curve down. How the Canadian economy adjusts to changes in foreign economic conditions is one of the subjects we address in the following section.

10.5 MACROECONOMIC POLICY IN A SMALL OPEN ECONOMY WITH FLEXIBLE EXCHANGE RATES

We are now ready to use our model of an open economy to show how shocks to economic variables affect equilibrium in the economy. An important result from our analysis will be to show that some of the conclusions we came to when examining the closed economy version of the *IS–LM–FE* model will change once we extend the model to allow for trade and lending among nations. In order to identify the role of exchange rates and international capital movements in explaining these changes, we present a model based on the same fundamental assumptions we made in Chapter 9 when examining the closed economy version of the *IS–LM–FE* model. In particular, we continue to assume that what households and firms expect to see and experience in the future is not affected by what they see and are experiencing today. We also continue to assume that of the three markets in our model, the labour market, described by the *FE* line, is the slowest to adjust. This assumption means that when the economy is not in general equilibrium, the asset market and the goods market are nonetheless in equilibrium. Finally, just as we did in Chapter 9 when discussing these events in a closed economy, we begin all of our explanations from a position of general equilibrium. In this general equilibrium the *IS* curve (describing equilibrium in the goods market), the *LM* curve (describing equilibrium in the financial market), and the *FE* line (describing equilibrium in the labour market) all intersect at the same values of r and Y.

An important difference from the closed economy model is that in general equilibrium the domestic interest rate r will be constrained by the real interest rate parity condition to equal the foreign real interest rate r_{For} in general equilibrium. As discussed, this reflects our assumption that international savers do not expect either the real or the nominal exchange rate to change.[10]

A primary reason for developing the *IS–LM–FE* model of the open economy is to determine how borrowing and trading links among countries affect fiscal and monetary policies. Understanding these effects is important because, as we saw in Section 10.4, a country's domestic economy can be sensitive to shifts in international tastes for various goods and to changes in foreign income and interest rates. In this way, business cycles can be transmitted from one country to the next. An important question to be answered in this section is this: To what extent are domestic fiscal and monetary policies useful for offsetting the effects of international shocks affecting the domestic economy?

In this section, we study an open economy that is small in the sense that it cannot affect macroeconomic variables in other countries. This means that what happens in this economy has no impact on foreign interest rates r_{For}, foreign price levels P_{For}, or foreign levels of real output Y_{For}. The open economy model that makes all of these assumptions, as well as the assumption that real interest rate parity is observed in general equilibrium, is known as the Mundell–Fleming model.

Robert Mundell, a Canadian, was awarded the Nobel Prize in Economics in 1999, in large part for his development of this model. In this section, we assume a flexible exchange rate. In Section 10.6 we turn our attention to the case of fixed exchange rates.

A FISCAL EXPANSION

To consider the effects of fiscal policy in a small open economy—in an economy like Canada's—let's look at a temporary increase in domestic government purchases. Figure 10.7 shows the *IS–LM–FE* diagram for a small open economy. The initial equilibrium is at point E at the full-employment level of output $\overline{Y}$ and at the foreign interest rate r_{For}. The domestic interest rate, r, is equal to the foreign interest rate, r_{For}, because of our assumption that real interest rate parity is observed in general equilibrium.

An increase in government purchases shifts the *IS* curve up and to the right from IS^1 to IS^2.[11] The domestic interest rate now moves temporarily above the foreign interest rate to where IS^2 intersects LM^1. If this were a closed economy, the story would be over for the period of the short run when the price level is fixed. We would conclude that in the short run the fiscal expansion had the effect of increasing both output and the interest rate. In the closed economy, the increase in the interest rate means that the fiscal expansion has *crowded out* private sector investment, making the fiscal expansion less effective than it would otherwise have been.

[10] Assuming that the expected rate of change in the real exchange rate is zero is mainly a convenience. What's important is assuming that the expected future value of the real exchange rate is unaffected by what households and firms see and experience today.
[11] Classical economists argue that the increase in government purchases affects the size of the full-employment level of output and so shifts the *FE* line. The mechanism is that households expect their future taxes to be higher to pay for the increase in government spending, and that this will lead to an increase in labour supply. We discuss this mechanism in detail in Chapter 11. In this chapter we assume that what households and firms expect to see and experience in the future is not affected by what they see and are experiencing today, and so the link between fiscal policy and the *FE* line is broken.

FIGURE 10.7

AN INCREASE IN GOVERNMENT PURCHASES IN A SMALL OPEN ECONOMY WITH FLEXIBLE EXCHANGE RATES

An increase in government purchases shifts the *IS* curve up and to the right, from IS^1 to IS^2. There results a temporary increase in the domestic interest rate above the foreign interest rate. As a consequence, the exchange rate appreciates, causing net exports to fall. IS^2 must return to IS^1 because only here does the exchange rate appreciation stop. There is no price level response unless the exchange rate is slow to respond to the temporary increase in the domestic interest rate. For this reason, the Keynesian short run, the Keynesian long run, and the classical model all generate the same result—general equilibrium remains at point *E*.

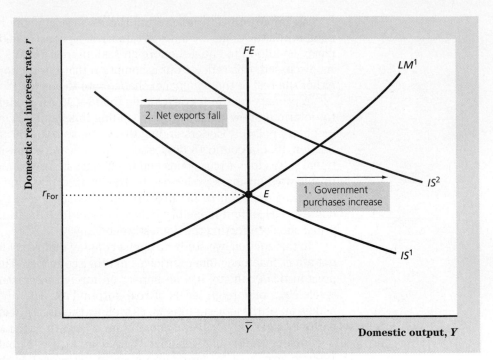

In a small open economy, however, this cannot be the end of the story even during the short-run period when the price level has yet to change.

With the domestic interest rate above the foreign interest rate, there exist arbitrage opportunities. Canadian financial assets are now paying a higher interest rate than foreign assets, causing the demand for Canadian financial assets to increase. When savers take advantage of these arbitrage opportunities, there is a capital inflow into Canada. Because those foreigners who seek to purchase Canadian financial assets must purchase dollars in order to do so, the Canadian dollar appreciates in value. An appreciation in the dollar makes Canadian exports more expensive and imported goods cheaper. For this reason, net exports fall, causing the *IS* curve to shift to the left. The *IS* curve must continue to shift to the left for as long as $r > r_{For}$, that is, for as long as arbitrage opportunities exist. As long as arbitrage opportunities exist, financial traders will continue to purchase Canadian financial assets and the Canadian dollars needed to make these purchases. Thus, the exchange rate will continue to rise and net exports will fall. The process can end only when the *IS* curve has shifted to the left all the way back to position IS^1 where once again $r = r_{For}$. In terms of our diagram, then, we begin at point *E*, move temporarily to the right, and then return to point *E*. Thus, the Mundell–Fleming model has the surprising implication that fiscal policy is ineffective at changing domestic output when there is a flexible exchange rate, even during that period when the price level is fixed.

While an expansionary fiscal policy is ineffective at changing domestic output, that's not to say it doesn't have other important macroeconomic effects. Our model predicts that a fiscal expansion will cause the exchange rate to appreciate and net exports to fall. This effect is referred to as **net export crowding out**. Thus, the increase in government purchases reduces net exports dollar-for-dollar, leaving output unchanged. Finally, unless the adjustment of the exchange rate to the increase in the domestic interest rate rising above the foreign rate is sluggish, there is no reason to expect an increase in output and hence no reason to expect an increase in the price level. This is why we see no change in the position of the LM curve. The Keynesian and classical models, which differ over assumptions about the speed at which the price level adjusts, therefore generate the same results in this case because there is no change in the price level.

A MONETARY EXPANSION

Now let's consider the effect of monetary policy in this model. In particular, what would be the impact on the economy of a monetary expansion? Figure 10.8 shows the IS–LM–FE diagram for a small open economy. Once again, we begin in equilibrium at point E at the full-employment level of output $\overline{Y}$ and at an interest rate r that is equal to the foreign interest rate r_{For}.

A monetary expansion is represented by the shift of the LM curve down and to the right, from LM^1 to LM^2. The domestic interest rate now moves temporarily below the foreign interest rate to where LM^2 intersects IS^1. If this were a closed economy, the story would be over for the period of the short run when the price level is fixed. We would conclude that the monetary expansion had the effect of increasing output but decreasing the interest rate. In the closed economy, the decrease in the interest rate is the source of an increase in output; the lower interest rate spurs new investment spending and hence an expansion of output. In a small open economy, however, this cannot be the end of the story.

With the domestic interest rate below the foreign interest rate, arbitrage opportunities exist. Canadian financial assets are now paying a lower interest rate than foreign assets, causing the demand for Canadian financial assets to decrease. When

FIGURE 10.8

A MONETARY EXPANSION IN A SMALL OPEN ECONOMY WITH FLEXIBLE EXCHANGE RATES

A monetary expansion shifts the LM curve down and to the right, from LM^1 to LM^2. In the Keynesian short run, there results a temporary decrease in the domestic interest rate below the foreign interest rate. As a consequence, the exchange rate depreciates, causing net exports to increase and causing the IS curve to shift up and to the right from IS^1 to IS^2. The curves IS^2 and LM^2 must intersect at point F, where the domestic and foreign interest rates are equal. In the Keynesian long run, the domestic price level increases. This causes LM^2 to shift up and to the left and causes the domestic interest rate to increase temporarily above the foreign interest rate. The currency appreciates, causing a fall in net exports. Both IS^2 and LM^2 return to their original positions at point E. In the classical model, equilibrium remains at point E throughout because of the rapid adjustment of the price level.

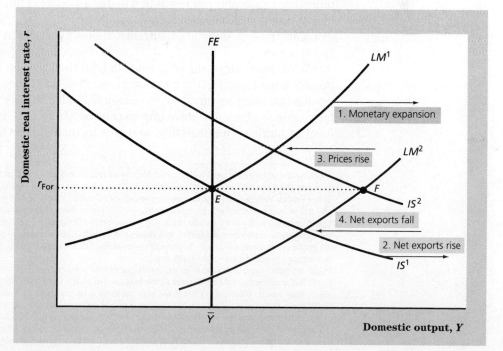

savers take advantage of these arbitrage opportunities, there is a capital outflow from Canada. Because those foreigners who seek to sell Canadian financial assets must sell dollars in order to do so, the Canadian dollar depreciates in value. Depreciation makes Canadian exports less expensive and imported goods more expensive, causing net exports to increase. The increase in net exports causes the IS curve to shift up and to the right. The IS curve must continue to shift in this way for as long as $r < r_{For}$, that is, for as long as arbitrage opportunities exist. For the period when arbitrage opportunities exist, financial traders will continue to sell Canadian financial assets and Canadian dollars in the foreign exchange market. Thus, the exchange rate will continue to fall and net exports rise. The process can end only when the IS curve has shifted to position IS^2, where once again $r = r_{For}$, at point F.

Point F is a short-run equilibrium because we have not yet allowed the price level P to change. With a fixed price level, the Keynesian version of the model thus concludes that a monetary expansion causes an expansion of output, depreciation in the exchange rate, and an increase in net exports.[12] In the long run, however, when enough time has passed for the price level to adjust, the Keynesian model predicts further adjustments. With output now above the full-employment level, the domestic price level increases. As it does so, the LM curve shifts up and to the left and in so doing causes the domestic interest rate to rise above the foreign interest rate. Now all that went before begins to unravel. That is, since Canadian financial assets are now paying a higher rate of interest than foreign assets, there is a capital inflow into Canada. The price of Canadian financial assets increases and the purchases of dollars required for foreigners to buy these assets cause the dollar to appreciate. Now Canadian exports are becoming more expensive and imports cheaper, causing net exports to fall. As this happens, the IS curve shifts to the left. The leftward movements of IS and LM must continue until they return to their initial positions, IS^1 and LM^1, for only here, at point E, is it the case that the domestic interest rate r is equal to the foreign interest rate r_{For} and there no longer exist arbitrage opportunities. In the long run, then, the Keynesian model predicts that a monetary expansion will result in a higher price level but no change in output, no change in the real interest rate, no change in net exports, and no change in the real exchange rate.[13] Monetary neutrality, therefore, holds in the Keynesian model in the long run.

While monetary neutrality holds only in the long run in the Keynesian model, it holds immediately in the classical model. The difference is due to the more rapid price adjustment assumed by the classical model. The shift to the right of the LM curve due to the initial monetary expansion (from LM^1 to LM^2) causes the price level to increase immediately, and this in turn shifts the LM curve back to its

---

[12] During the adjustment to point F domestic income increases, and we know that an increase in domestic income increases the domestic demand for imports. Thus, net exports *decrease* for this reason. However, the depreciation makes exports cheaper and imports more expensive, causing net exports to *increase*. Given these competing effects, why did we conclude that net exports have necessarily increased during the adjustment from point E to point F? Theory does not indicate for certain which way net exports will change. Nevertheless, most empirical evidence suggests that the second effect dominates. In a small open economy, net exports are more responsive to changes in the exchange rate than to changes in domestic income. Overall, then, in the short run a country's net exports will increase as a result of a monetary expansion.

[13] The monetary expansion causes the real exchange rate to depreciate in the short run (when the price level is fixed) but appreciate during adjustment to the long run (when the price level adjusts). How do we know the two changes are exactly offsetting so that in the long run there is no change in the real exchange rate? In this exercise, the IS curve shifts due to changes in net exports. Since IS returns to its original position, it must be the case that net exports don't change in the long run (as we concluded). Since net exports are a function of the real exchange rate, the foreign interest rate, and output, and since the latter two variables haven't changed, then the real exchange rate must also not have changed.

original position. As a result, there is no change in output, no change in the real exchange rate, and no change in net exports. As usual there is no short-run equilibrium in the classical model, only a speedy adjustment between general equilibriums. In this case, assuming a rapid adjustment to the price level, the old and the new general equilibrium are both at point E.

Although changes in the money supply cannot affect the *real* exchange rate in the long run, they do affect the *nominal* exchange rate by changing the domestic price level. (This is one case where the responses of the real and nominal exchange rates to a change in macroeconomic conditions differ.) As we have shown, the long-run neutrality of money implies that a 10% increase in the nominal money supply will increase the domestic price level by 10%. Recall (Eq. 10.1, p. 298) that the nominal exchange rate e_{nom} equals eP_{For}/P, where e is the real exchange rate, P_{For} is the foreign price level, and P is the domestic price level. Because the real exchange rate e and the foreign price level P_{For} are unchanged in the long run by a domestic monetary expansion, the 10% increase in the domestic price level P lowers the nominal exchange rate e_{nom} by (approximately) 10%. Thus, a monetary expansion increases the domestic price level and reduces the nominal exchange rate (depreciation) by the same percentage as the increase in the money supply.

We leave it to the reader to derive the results of fiscal and monetary contractions with a flexible exchange rate. When these results are worked through and compared with the results of the fiscal and monetary expansions presented above, the following general conclusions become apparent. Fiscal policy changes have limited effect in a small open economy with a flexible exchange rate. This is so because fiscal policies cause changes in the exchange rate, which move net exports in a direction that works against the original fiscal policy. As a result, shifts in the *IS* curve caused by fiscal policy changes are undone by *IS* shifts in the opposite direction resulting from changes in the exchange rate. Fiscal policies, then, have no effect on real variables. This is true whether we consider the Keynesian or the classical model, and it is true in both the Keynesian short run and long run. Monetary policy, on the other hand, has a potent effect on output in the Keynesian short run. It does so because moving the domestic interest rate temporarily above or below the foreign interest rate causes a change in the exchange rate, which shifts the *IS* curve in the same direction as the shift in the *LM* curve. In this way, monetary policy causes output to change by more than it would in a closed economy. In the Keynesian long run, these movements are reversed and monetary neutrality holds. In the classical model, monetary policy has no effect on output due to that model assuming a much faster response of prices.

10.6 Fixed Exchange Rates

Canada has had a flexible nominal exchange rate since 1970, and the Canadian dollar also floated in the 1950s. From 1962 to 1970, the dollar was fixed in value relative to the U.S. dollar.[14] Although Canada has not had a fixed nominal exchange rate for nearly 40 years, fixed-exchange-rate systems—in which nominal exchange rates are officially set by international agreement—have been important historically and are still used by many countries. Let's now consider fixed-exchange-rate

---

[14] Over that period, the Canadian dollar was fixed at US$0.925. See James Powell, *A History of the Canadian Dollar*, Bank of Canada, 1999, for an interesting and informative history of exchange rate policy in Canada. An electronic copy of this short book is available from the Bank of Canada website, www.bankofcanada.ca/wp-content/uploads/2010/07/dollar_book.pdf.

systems and address two questions: (1) How does the use of a fixed-exchange-rate system affect an economy and macroeconomic policy? (2) Ultimately, which is the better system: flexible or fixed exchange rates?

FIXING THE EXCHANGE RATE

In contrast to flexible-exchange-rate systems—where exchange rates are determined by supply and demand in foreign exchange markets—in a fixed-exchange-rate system, the value of the nominal exchange rate is officially set by the government, perhaps in consultation or agreement with other countries.[15]

A potential problem with fixed-exchange-rate systems is that the value of the exchange rate set by the government may not be the exchange rate determined by the supply of and demand for currency. Figure 10.9 shows a situation in which the official exchange rate, e_{nom}, is higher than the **fundamental value of the exchange rate**, e^1_{nom}, or the value that would be determined by free market forces without government intervention. When an exchange rate is higher than its fundamental value, it is an **overvalued exchange rate** (often referred to as an *overvalued currency*).

How can a country deal with a situation in which its official exchange rate is different from the fundamental value of its exchange rate? There are several possible strategies: First, the country can simply change the official value of its exchange rate so that it equals, or is close to, its fundamental value. For example, in the case of overvaluation shown in Figure 10.9, the country could simply devalue (lower) its nominal fixed exchange rate from e_{nom} to e^1_{nom}. However, although occasional devaluations or revaluations can be expected under

FIGURE 10.9

AN OVERVALUED EXCHANGE RATE

The figure shows a situation in which the officially fixed nominal exchange rate, $\bar{e}_{nom}$, is higher than the fundamental value of the exchange rate, e^1_{nom}, as determined by supply and demand in the foreign exchange market. In this situation, the exchange rate is said to be overvalued. The country's central bank can maintain the exchange rate at the official rate by using its reserves to purchase its own currency in the foreign exchange market, in the amount of AB in each period. This loss of reserves is also referred to as the country's balance of payments deficit.

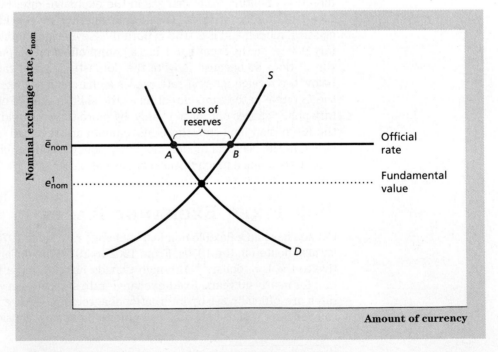

---

[15] In some fixed-exchange-rate systems, the exchange rate is allowed to fluctuate within a narrow, prespecified band. For simplicity, we shall assume in this section that the exchange rate is fixed at a single value.

fixed-exchange-rate systems, if a country continuously adjusts its exchange rate it might as well switch to a flexible-rate system.

Second, the government could restrict international transactions—for example, by limiting or taxing imports or capital outflows. Such policies reduce the supply of the domestic currency to the foreign exchange market, thus raising the fundamental value of the exchange rate toward its fixed value. Some countries go even further and prohibit people from trading the domestic currency for foreign currencies without government approval; a currency that cannot be freely traded for other currencies is said to be an **inconvertible currency**. However, direct government intervention in international transactions has many economic costs, including reduced access to foreign goods and credit.

Third, the government itself may become a demander or supplier of its currency in the foreign exchange market, an approach used by most of the industrialized countries having fixed exchange rates. For example, in the case of overvaluation shown in Figure 10.9, the supply of the country's currency to the foreign exchange market (point B) exceeds private demand for the currency (point A) at the official exchange rate by the amount AB. To maintain the value of the currency at the official rate, the government could buy back its own currency in the amount AB in each period.

Usually, these currency purchases are made by the nation's central bank using official reserve assets. Recall that official reserve assets are assets other than domestic money or securities that can be used to make international payments (examples are gold, foreign bank deposits, or special assets created by international agencies, such as the International Monetary Fund). During the gold standard period, for example, gold was the basic form of official reserve asset, and central banks offered to exchange gold for their own currencies at a fixed price. If Figure 10.9 represented a gold standard country, AB would represent the amount of gold the central bank would have to use to buy back its currency in each period to equalize the quantities of its currency supplied and demanded at the official exchange rate. Recall also that the decline in a country's official reserve assets during a year equals its *balance of payments deficit*. Thus, amount AB measures the reserves the central bank must use to support the currency and corresponds to the country's balance of payments deficit.

Although a central bank can maintain an overvalued exchange rate for a time by offering to buy back its own currency at a fixed price, it cannot do so forever because it has only a limited supply of official reserve assets. During the gold standard period, for example, central banks did not own unlimited amounts of gold. Attempting to support an overvalued currency for a long period of time would have exhausted a central bank's limited gold reserves, leaving the country no choice but to devalue its currency.

A central bank's attempts to support an overvalued currency can be ended quickly and dramatically by a speculative run. A **speculative run** occurs when financial investors begin to believe that an overvalued currency may soon be devalued, reducing the value of assets denominated in that currency relative to assets denominated in other currencies. To avoid losses, financial investors frantically sell assets denominated in the overvalued currency. The panicky sales of domestic assets associated with a speculative run on a currency shift the supply curve for that currency sharply to the right (Figure 10.10), increasing the gap between the quantities supplied and demanded of the currency from amount AB to amount AC. This widening gap increases the rate at which the central bank has to spend its official reserve assets to maintain the overvalued exchange rate, speeding devaluation and confirming the financial investors' expectations.

FIGURE 10.10

A SPECULATIVE RUN ON AN OVERVALUED CURRENCY

Initially, the supply curve of the domestic currency is S^1 and, to maintain the fixed exchange rate, the central bank must use amount AB of its reserves each period to purchase its own currency in the foreign exchange market. A speculative run occurs when holders of domestic assets begin to fear a devaluation, which would reduce the values of their assets (measured in terms of foreign currency). Panicky sales of domestic-currency assets lead to more domestic currency being supplied to the foreign exchange market, which shifts the supply curve of the domestic currency to the right, from S^1 to S^2. The central bank must now purchase its currency and lose reserves in the amount AC. This more rapid loss of reserves may force the central bank to stop supporting the overvalued currency and to devalue it, confirming the market's expectations.

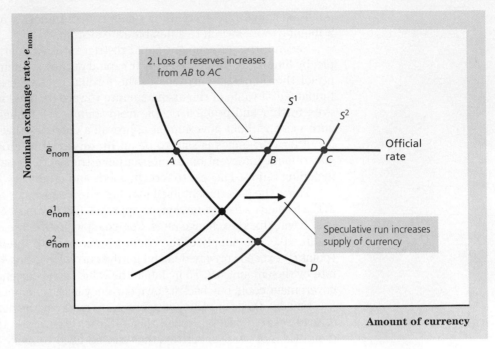

Such a speculative run occurred in December 1994 on the Mexican peso. A capital outflow necessitated a 15% devaluation of the peso against the U.S. dollar and eventually led the Mexican authorities to allow the peso to float and depreciate further. Speculative runs or attacks also occurred during the East Asian crisis that began in 1997 and in Argentina in January 2002. Figure 10.11 shows daily exchange rates from May 1997 through April 1998 for Indonesia, Singapore, the Philippines, Taiwan, South Korea, and Malaysia. During the speculative runs and subsequent floats, several of these currencies depreciated by more than 50%.

Without strong restrictions on international trade and finance (themselves economically costly), we conclude that an overvalued exchange rate is not sustainable for long. If the exchange rate is overvalued, the country must either devalue its currency or make some policy change to raise the fundamental value of the exchange rate. We show in the next section that the basic tool for changing the fundamental value of the exchange rate is monetary policy.

We have focused on overvaluation, but an exchange rate could also be undervalued. As illustrated in Figure 10.12, an **undervalued exchange rate** (or undervalued currency) exists if the officially fixed value is less than the value determined by supply and demand in the foreign exchange market. In this case, instead of buying its own currency, the central bank sells its currency to the foreign exchange market and accumulates reserves in the amount AB each period. With no limit to the quantity of reserve assets (gold, for example) a central bank could accumulate, an undervalued exchange rate could apparently be maintained indefinitely. However, a country with an undervalued exchange rate can accumulate reserves only at the expense of trading partners who have overvalued exchange rates and are, therefore, losing reserves. Because the country's trading partners cannot continue to lose reserves indefinitely, eventually they will put political pressure on the country to bring the fundamental value of its exchange rate back in line with the official rate.

FIGURE 10.11

CURRENCY VALUES IN THE EAST ASIAN CRISIS

The figure shows daily values for six East Asian exchange rates, from May 1, 1997, to April 30, 1998. Rates are in U.S. dollars and apply to the Indonesian rupiah, Malaysian ringgit, Philippine peso, Singapore dollar, Taiwanese dollar, and South Korean won. The exchange rates are scaled so that they are equal to 1.0 in May 1997. These sharp depreciations reflect speculative runs or attacks.

Source: Based on statistics accessed from Pacific Exchange Rate Service, http://fx.sauder.ubc.ca.

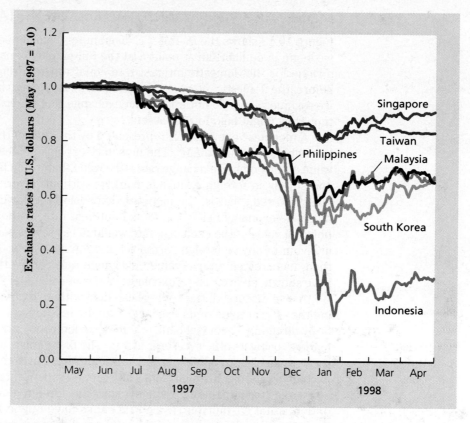

In the next section we consider a small open economy with a fixed nominal exchange rate. We assume that the value of the nominal exchange rate is at its fundamental value. Thus, the exchange rate is neither overvalued nor undervalued and foreign exchange markets clear at the current value of the fixed exchange rate. What is the implication for monetary policy of maintaining a fixed exchange rate?

FIGURE 10.12

AN UNDERVALUED EXCHANGE RATE

The exchange rate is undervalued when the officially determined nominal exchange rate, $\bar{e}_{nom}$, is less than the fundamental value of the exchange rate as determined by supply and demand in the foreign exchange market, e^1_{nom}. To maintain the exchange rate at its official level, the central bank must supply its own currency to the foreign exchange market in the amount AB each period, thereby accumulating foreign reserves.

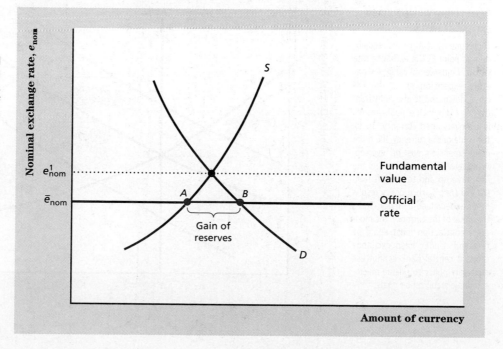

MONETARY POLICY AND THE FIXED EXCHANGE RATE

Figure 10.13 shows the *IS–LM–FE* diagram for a small open economy. Once again, we begin in equilibrium at point *E* at the full-employment level of output $\overline{Y}$ and at a value for the domestic interest rate equal to the foreign interest rate r_{For}. As before, the domestic interest rate r is equal to the foreign interest rate r_{For} because we assume savers do not expect the exchange rate to change during the period of time they might hold foreign assets.

A monetary expansion is represented by the shift of the *LM* curve down and to the right, from LM^1 to LM^2. The monetary expansion means that the fundamental value of the nominal exchange rate—the value that would be determined by demand and supply in foreign exchange markets without government intervention—has been lowered. That is, the monetary expansion has lowered interest rates in the domestic economy below the foreign interest rate. Without government intervention, the value of the exchange rate would fall as savers sold the domestic currency in favour of buying foreign currencies and foreign assets. The monetary expansion, then, has created an overvalued exchange rate (or overvalued currency). As we have shown, an overvalued exchange rate is not sustainable.

As we discussed, the country can deal with an overvalued currency by lowering the official value of its exchange rate, by restricting international transactions, or by directing its central bank to purchase domestic currency in foreign exchange markets using its official reserve assets. The first choice, a revaluation, might make sense as an occasional policy, but continuous use raises the question of why a fixed exchange rate has been chosen. The second response, capital controls, has many economic costs, including reduced access to foreign goods and credit. The third option is not sustainable, as central banks have only a limited supply of official reserve assets. At some point, then, the monetary expansion must be reversed. In terms of our diagram, reversing the monetary expansion causes the *LM* curve to return to position LM^1.

FIGURE 10.13

MONETARY POLICY IN A SMALL OPEN ECONOMY WITH FIXED EXCHANGE FATES

The economy is in general equilibrium at point *E*. The exchange rate is at its fundamental value. A monetary expansion shifts the *LM* curve down and to the right from LM^1 to LM^2. Such a policy results in an overvalued currency. To fix the value of the currency, the monetary expansion must be reversed. A monetary contraction shifts the *LM* curve up and to the left from LM^1 to LM^3. Such a policy results in an undervalued currency. To fix the value of the currency, the monetary contraction must again be reversed. Under fixed exchange rates, a central bank cannot use monetary policy to pursue macroeconomic stabilization goals.

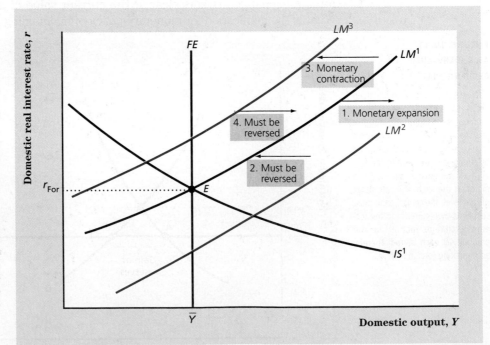

In a similar manner, a monetary contraction creates an undervalued exchange rate. In this case, the LM curve shifts up and to the left from LM^1 to LM^3. Without intervention, the value of the exchange rate would increase as savers, seeking to purchase domestic financial assets paying interest rates above the foreign rate, purchased the domestic currency. As we discussed, an undervalued currency is also not sustainable; the central bank can maintain the exchange rate only by selling domestic currency in foreign exchange markets and forever accumulating foreign exchange reserves. Eventually, the monetary contraction must be reversed and the LM curve shifted back to its original position.

Figure 10.14 illustrates the relationship between the nominal exchange rate and the money supply in a country with a fixed exchange rate.[16] The downward-sloping curve shows the relationship of the money supply to the fundamental value of the nominal exchange rate. This curve slopes downward because, other factors being equal, an increase in the money supply reduces the fundamental value of the nominal exchange rate. The horizontal line in Figure 10.14 is the officially determined exchange rate. The value of M_1 on the horizontal axis is the money supply that equalizes the fundamental value of the exchange rate and its officially fixed value. If the money supply is more than M_1, the country has an overvaluation problem (the fundamental value of the exchange rate is below the official value), and if the money supply is less than M_1 the country has an undervaluation problem.

Figure 10.14 suggests that in a fixed-exchange-rate system, individual countries are typically *not* free to expand their money supplies in order to try to raise output and employment. Instead, the money supply is governed by the condition that the official and fundamental values of the exchange rate be the same. If the

FIGURE 10.14

DETERMINATION OF THE MONEY SUPPLY UNDER FIXED EXCHANGE RATES

The downward-sloping fundamental value curve shows that a higher domestic money supply causes a lower fundamental value of the exchange rate. The horizontal line shows the officially fixed nominal exchange rate. Only when the country's money supply equals M_1 does the fundamental value of the exchange rate equal the official rate. If the central bank increased the money supply above M_1, the exchange rate would become overvalued. A money supply below M_1 would result in an undervalued currency.

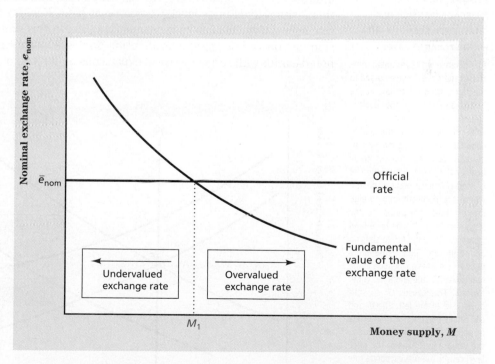

[16] The country's money supply is the amount of money in circulation domestically, as in previous chapters. It is not the supply of currency to foreign exchange markets, which depends only on domestic residents' demands for foreign goods and assets.

country represented in Figure 10.14 wanted to expand its money supply to fight a recession, for example, it could do so only by creating an overvaluation problem (most likely leading to a future devaluation) or by devaluing its currency immediately. *Under fixed exchange rates, then, a central bank cannot use monetary policy to pursue macroeconomic stabilization goals.*

FISCAL POLICY AND THE FIXED EXCHANGE RATE

Figure 10.15 shows the *IS–LM–FE* diagram for a small open economy. Once again, we begin in equilibrium at point E at the full-employment level of output $\overline{Y}$ and at the foreign interest rate r_{For}.

A fiscal expansion is represented by the shift of the *IS* curve up and to the right, from IS^1 to IS^2. The fiscal expansion means that the fundamental value of the nominal exchange rate—the value that would be determined by demand and supply in foreign exchange markets without government intervention—has been increased. That is, the fiscal expansion has increased interest rates in the domestic economy above the foreign interest rate. Without government intervention, the value of the exchange rate would rise as savers purchased the domestic currency so as to enable them to purchase domestic financial assets. All else being equal, then, the fiscal expansion would create an undervalued exchange rate.

As Figure 10.14 indicates, the solution to an undervalued exchange rate is a domestic monetary expansion. In terms of Figure 10.15, the central bank must accommodate the fiscal expansion with a monetary expansion that shifts LM^1 to LM^2. In this way, the domestic interest rate r is kept from rising above the foreign interest rate r_{For} and causing the exchange rate undervaluation. In the short run, then, with a fixed price level, we end up at point F with $r = r_{\text{For}}$ and the exchange rate successfully held at its fundamental value. In this time frame the fiscal expansion has proved successful at affecting domestic output and employment. As we noted earlier with respect to fiscal expansions under a flexible exchange rate, a fiscal

FIGURE 10.15

A FISCAL EXPANSION IN A SMALL OPEN ECONOMY WITH FIXED EXCHANGE RATES

An increase in government purchases shifts the *IS* curve up and to the right, from IS^1 to IS^2. In the Keynesian short run, the result is an undervalued currency. To fix the value of the currency, the central bank must expand the money supply and thus shift the *LM* curve from LM^1 to LM^2. Intersection of IS^2 and LM^2 must occur at point F where the domestic and foreign interest rates are equal. In the Keynesian long run, the price level increases, causing LM^2 to shift up and to the left. The increase in the price level causes an increase in the real exchange rate and a fall in net exports. This causes IS^2 to shift down and to the left. The *IS* and *LM* curves must return to intersect at point E. In the classical model, the rapid adjustment of the price level causes the real exchange rate to increase immediately following the increase in government purchases, leaving the positions of *IS* and *LM* unaffected.

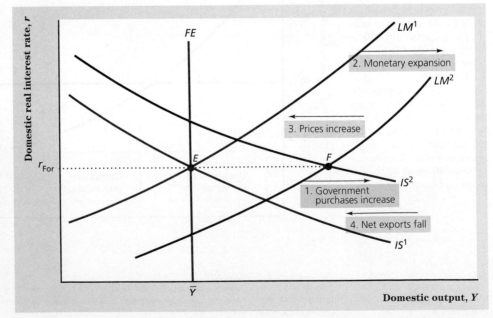

expansion with a fixed exchange rate results in *net export crowding out*. We know this to be true because there has been no change in the real exchange rate that might affect net exports. (Recall Eq. 10.1, p. 298, and the fact that e_{nom}, P, and P_{For} are fixed by our assumptions of a fixed nominal exchange rate and the short run. The real exchange rate e must therefore be unchanged as well.) Since domestic income has increased, imports have also increased and this causes net exports to fall.

With a fixed price level, the Keynesian version of the model thus concludes that a fiscal expansion causes an expansion of output and an increase in net exports. Fiscal policy is successful, of course, because to maintain the fixed exchange rate the central bank must accommodate the fiscal expansion with a monetary expansion. With both fiscal and monetary policy in expansion mode, it is perhaps not surprising that output increases.

In the long run, however, when enough time has passed for the price level to adjust, the Keynesian model predicts further adjustments. With output now above the full-employment level, the domestic price level increases. As it does so, all that went before begins to unravel. From Eq. (10.1),

$$e = \frac{e_{nom}P}{P_{For}}$$

with e_{nom} and P_{For} both fixed, the increase in the domestic price level P causes the real exchange rate e to increase as well. As it does so, net exports fall and this causes the *IS* curve to shift down and to the left. The two curves, *IS* and *LM,* are now both moving to the left. To prevent any under- or overvaluation of the nominal exchange rate that might arise should one of these curves move more quickly than the other, the domestic central bank must again be prepared to introduce changes in the money supply.[17] In this way the two curves adjust back to their original positions, IS^1 and LM^1, and the economy adjusts from point F back to point E. In the Keynesian long run, then, the fiscal expansion has no impact on output. Although the nominal exchange rate e_{nom} has been held fixed, the real exchange rate e has increased in step with the increase in the domestic price level P. Net exports, then, have been crowded out dollar-for-dollar by the fiscal expansion.

In the classical model, the price level increases immediately in response to the fiscal expansion. From Eq. (10.1), this means the real exchange rate also increases immediately. As a result, net exports are immediately crowded out by the fiscal expansion and output remains unchanged at its full-employment level.

We again leave it to the reader to derive the results of fiscal and monetary *contractions* with a fixed exchange rate. When these results are worked through and compared with the results from the fiscal and monetary expansions presented above, the following general conclusions become apparent. Monetary policy is an ineffective tool for adjusting domestic output and employment under a fixed exchange rate. This is so because the money supply is governed by the condition that the official and fundamental values of the exchange rate must be the same. As a result, central banks cannot use monetary policy to pursue macroeconomic goals while also maintaining fixed exchange rates. This conclusion is warranted whether we consider the Keynesian or the classical model, and it is true in both the Keynesian short run and long run. Fiscal policy, on the other hand, is an effective tool for

[17] The speed with which the *LM* curve shifts due to increases in the price level depends on how quickly prices change, while the speed with which the *IS* curve shifts reflects the responsiveness of net exports to the increase in the real exchange rate. It is likely, then, that the *LM* curve will shift to the left in response to changes in the price level by a larger or smaller amount than the *IS* curve shifts to the left, due to the increase in the real exchange rate.

adjusting domestic output and employment, at least during the Keynesian short run. This is so because to fix the nominal exchange rate, the central bank must accommodate fiscal policy changes by shifting the *LM* curve in the same direction as fiscal policy shifts the *IS* curve. In the Keynesian long run, however, fiscal policy has no effect on output. In the classical model, due to the immediate response of the price level, fiscal policy has no effect on output.

10.7 CHOOSING AN EXCHANGE RATE SYSTEM

Fixed- and flexible-exchange-rate systems each have strengths and weaknesses. How should a government choose which system to adopt? In what follows, we discuss some issues that are important for making the choice.

FIXED VERSUS FLEXIBLE EXCHANGE RATES

Proponents of fixed-exchange-rate systems stress two major benefits. First, relative to a situation in which exchange rates fluctuate continuously, stable exchange rates make trading goods and assets among countries easier and less costly. Thus, a system of fixed rates may promote economic and financial integration and improve economic efficiency. Second, fixed exchange rates may improve monetary policy "discipline," in the sense that countries with fixed exchange rates are typically less able to carry out highly expansionary monetary policies; the result may be lower inflation in the long run. For these reasons, even countries that have floating exchange rates frequently use monetary policy to influence the value of their currency. Their central banks also intervene directly in the foreign exchange market by buying and selling foreign currencies. The resulting hybrid is sometimes called a *managed float* or a *dirty float*.

The other side of the monetary discipline argument is that fixed exchange rates take away a country's ability to use monetary policy flexibly to deal with recessions.[18] This inability is particularly serious if the different countries in the fixed-exchange-rate system have different policy goals and face different types of economic shocks. Disagreements among countries in a fixed-exchange-rate system about the conduct of monetary policy may even lead to the breakdown of the system.

A helpful way to think of the choice of an exchange rate system is in terms of the **open-economy trilemma**. In selecting a system, a country can choose only two of the following three features: (1) a fixed exchange rate to promote trade; (2) free international movements of capital; and (3) autonomy for domestic monetary policy. For example, a country can retain some independence in monetary policy while maintaining a fixed exchange rate only if it uses taxes or controls to limit capital flows. Or a country can choose a fixed exchange rate and allow capital mobility if it devotes monetary policy to the goal of maintaining the exchange rate.

Which system is better depends on the circumstances. Fixed exchange rates (or even a common currency) among a group of countries are useful when large benefits can be gained from increased trade and integration and when the countries in the system coordinate their monetary policies closely. Countries that value the ability to use monetary policy independently—perhaps because they face different macroeconomic shocks than other countries or hold different views about the relative costs of recessions and inflation—should retain a floating exchange rate.

---

[18] Keynesians consider this a cost, but classicals do not.

APPLICATION

PROVINCIAL FISCAL POLICIES

In Canada, provincial governments control, in aggregate, roughly one-half of all government spending and taxes. The government of the province of Ontario alone controls roughly 20% of all government spending and taxation in Canada. The Ontario government, then, is capable of exerting a sizable influence on the Canadian economy via its provincial budget. What does our model suggest would be the effects of an expansionary fiscal policy by the government of the province of Ontario?

Let's consider first what happens if Canada maintains flexible exchange rates. An expansionary fiscal policy by Ontario would shift Canada's *IS* curve to the right.[19] The resulting currency appreciation would cause Canada's net exports to fall, causing Canada's *IS* curve to move back to its original position. In the end, Canada's output is unaffected by Ontario's expansionary fiscal policy; the expansionary fiscal policy simply crowds out net exports. But what is the effect in Ontario versus the rest of Canada? The expansionary effect of the fiscal policy is concentrated in Ontario, but the contraction in output caused by the exchange rate appreciation is felt in all provinces and territories.[20] As a result, output increases in Ontario by the amount it falls in all other provinces and territories. In this case, then, Ontario's expansionary fiscal policy is effective at causing output to expand in Ontario but only at the price of reduced output in the other provinces and territories.

How would the results differ if Canada maintained fixed exchange rates? Once again, the expansionary fiscal policy by Ontario shifts Canada's *IS* curve to the right. This time, however, the Bank of Canada must increase the domestic money supply in order to prevent a currency undervaluation. The result, as we have discussed previously, is that Canada's output increases due to the combined effects of the expansionary fiscal policy and the expansion of the money supply. This time all provinces and territories experience an expansion of provincial output because all experience the effects of the monetary expansion. Ontario's fiscal policy is again effective at increasing output in Ontario, but this time it does not come at the price of reduced output in the other jurisdictions.

What do these results tell us about the wisdom of provincially based fiscal policies? One is tempted to conclude that provincial fiscal policies should be discouraged when flexible exchange rates are adopted, since, under flexible exchange rates, a fiscal policy by one province achieves its objective of affecting output only by changing output in the opposite direction in other provinces and territories. However, this so-called beggar-thy-neighbour outcome may be an attractive feature under some circumstances. Suppose, for example, that the business cycle in Ontario is out of phase with the business cycle in the other provinces. Thus, when Ontario is in

---

[19] While an expansionary fiscal policy by any province will have this effect, the size of the shift in Canada's *IS* curve will be in proportion to the size of the provincial government's fiscal policy. Whereas Ontario's provincial government budget is large enough to exert a noticeable influence on aggregate (federal + provincial) government spending and taxation in Canada, this will not, for example, be true for the provincial budget of the government of Prince Edward Island, nor for any of the other provinces, with the possible exception of Quebec.

[20] Those provinces that export goods to Ontario will realize an increase in net exports due to Ontario's expansionary fiscal policy. It turns out, however, that this influence is dominated by the effect of the appreciation in the exchange rate causing provincial net exports to fall. That result, and those in the remainder of this Application, are discussed in William Scarth, "Provincial Stabilization Policy: Coordination Issues," in H. Grubel, D. Purvis, and W. Scarth, eds., *Limits to Government*, C. D. Howe Institute, 1992.

recession the economies of the rest of Canada is booming, and vice versa. In this case, Ontario's expansionary fiscal policy has two beneficial effects: It expands output in recessionary Ontario and it contracts output in the rest of the country where there are inflationary pressures. An assessment of the wisdom of provincial fiscal policies when flexible exchange rates are adopted, therefore, depends on the extent to which provincial business cycles are in phase. It would also depend on a good deal of policy coordination between provincial governments, something that has not to this point been a hallmark of Canadian provincial politics.

CURRENCY UNIONS

An alternative to fixing exchange rates is for a group of countries to form a **currency union**, under which they agree to share a common currency. Members of a currency union also typically cooperate economically and politically.

An effective currency union usually requires more than just cooperation of national central banks. For a currency union to work, the common monetary policy must be controlled by a single institution. Because countries are typically reluctant to give up their own currency and monetary policies, currency unions have been rare. However, if politically feasible, a currency union has at least two advantages over fixed exchange rates. First, the costs of trading goods and assets among countries are even lower with a single currency than under fixed exchange rates. Second, if national currencies are eliminated in favour of the common currency, speculative attacks on the national currencies no longer can occur.[21]

However, a currency union shares the major disadvantage of a fixed-exchange-rate system. It requires all its members to share a common monetary policy. Thus, if one member of a currency union is in a recession while another is concerned about inflation, the common monetary policy cannot deal with both countries' problems simultaneously. In contrast, under flexible exchange rates, each country could set its own monetary policy independently.

THE SELF-CORRECTING SMALL OPEN ECONOMY

In an open economy, the possibilities for unexpected events to affect the domestic economy grow simply because changes in exports, imports, and the demand for foreign financial assets can all influence the economy, whereas they cannot do so in a closed economy. Thus, as we discussed in Section 10.4, unexpected changes in foreign output, foreign interest rates, and changes in preference for foreign versus domestic goods are additional sources of unexpected IS curve shifts that are not present in a closed economy. In a small open economy, then, one is tempted to conclude that with a greater number of sources of unexpected events to push the economy out of general equilibrium, the need for stabilization policies is greater than in a closed economy. What we have discovered, however, is that this conclusion is not necessarily warranted. The reason is that in a small open economy there exist self-correcting mechanisms, in addition to the price level, not found in a closed economy.

---

[21] Some economists argue that fixed-exchange-rate systems are not viable for this reason, so that the choice is between flexible exchange rates and a currency union.

Under a flexible exchange rate, any unexpected event that shifts the *IS* curve produces an automatic self-correcting adjustment by way of an exchange rate adjustment. Thus, an unexpected fall in net exports that causes the *IS* curve to shift to the left causes a depreciation of the exchange rate. In response to the depreciation, there occurs an increase in net exports that produces a shift in the *IS* curve back to the right. Similarly, an unexpected event that causes the *IS* curve to shift to the right causes an appreciation of the exchange rate, a decrease in net exports, and a shift in the *IS* curve back to the left. Thus, while relative to a closed economy a small open economy is subject to additional sources of unexpected events that affect exports and imports, these new sources of unexpected shifts in the *IS* curve are balanced by the availability of an additional self-correcting mechanism, the flexible exchange rate.

Interestingly, then, while the Mundell–Fleming model has the implication that fiscal policy is ineffective at changing domestic output when there is a flexible exchange rate even during that period when the price level is fixed, this bit of seemingly bad news for those who support the use of fiscal policy for stabilization purposes has a silver lining. While it is true that fiscal policy has no impact on real output, it is also true that unexpected events that shift the *IS* curve have no impact on real output. Thus, many unexpected shocks to the economy that require a stabilization policy response in a closed economy require no stabilization policy response in an open economy.

Unfortunately, under a flexible exchange rate, unexpected events that cause shifts in the *LM* curve produce an automatic response from the exchange rate that is destabilizing in the sense of causing output to adjust further from general equilibrium than would be the case in a closed economy.[22] An unexpected event that shifts the *LM* curve to the left causes an exchange rate appreciation and hence a fall in net exports. The leftward shift of the *LM* curve is thus accompanied by a leftward shift in the *IS* curve and a larger fall in output than would be observed in a closed economy. The self-correcting price level response required to bring the economy back into general equilibrium must therefore be greater than what would have been required in a closed economy. Once again the Mundell–Fleming model presents results that cut both ways. The fact that monetary policy is effective at changing output in the Mundell–Fleming model, while good news for those who favour the use of monetary policy for stabilization purposes, is bad news in that it means unexpected events that shift the *LM* curve have a magnified impact on output.

With a fixed exchange rate, we have found that unexpected events that shift the *IS* curve have their impact on output magnified by the automatic response of the domestic money supply. Thus, an unexpected event that shifts the *IS* curve to the left requires a monetary contraction in order to prevent the exchange rate from being overvalued. With both the *IS* and the *LM* curves shifting to the left, the impact on output of the initial *IS* shift is magnified and the self-correcting price level response required to bring the economy back into general equilibrium must be greater than that which would have been required in a closed economy. Thus, while the effectiveness of fiscal policy as a tool of stabilization policy is enhanced by the adoption of a fixed exchange rate, as usual there is no free lunch; it is also the case that unexpected events influencing the position of the *IS* curve have a larger impact on output as well.

---

[22] As we noted in Section 10.4, nothing discussed in this chapter affects our analysis of the supply of or demand for money. Thus, open economy considerations do not add to the list of unexpected events that might cause a shift in the *LM* curve.

Finally, we have found that with a fixed exchange rate, unexpected events that shift the *LM* curve are immediately counteracted by an automatic self-correcting adjustment by way of the money supply. Thus, an unexpected shift to the left of the *LM* curve requires that the domestic central bank expand the money supply so as to prevent an undervalued currency. This response prevents any change in output. Those who are disappointed by the inability of monetary policy to influence output and employment are therefore consoled by the fact that unexpected events that shift the *LM* curve have no impact on output either.

APPLICATION

MACROECONOMIC POLICY RESPONSES TO THE 2008–2009 FINANCIAL CRISIS

In light of what we have learned in this chapter, how would we evaluate the fiscal and monetary policy responses of Canadian policymakers to the 2008–2009 financial crisis and recession? We have learned that in a small open economy with a flexible exchange rate such as Canada, fiscal policy is a largely ineffective response to a recession. Despite this, in early 2009 the Canadian government introduced a significant expansion in government spending. We have also learned that in an economy such as Canada's monetary policy is a very effective response to recession. The Bank of Canada did, in fact, take significant steps to provide a monetary stimulus. So, did monetary policy get it right and did fiscal policy get it wrong?

As we noted in Chapter 7 ("The U.S. Housing Crisis and Its Aftermath," p. 208), the 2008–2009 financial crisis originated in the U.S. mortgage and financial markets. Uncertainty about the viability of sub-prime mortgages and other so-called "exotic" financial assets resulted in a freeze in world credit markets. The fall in financial market liquidity can be represented in our model as a shift to the left in *LM* curves in the United States and, due to close international financial linkages, around the world.

In this way the financial crisis exposed Canada and the world economy to two major shocks. One shock was due to the fact that the fall in financial market liquidity around the world pushed up world interest rates. In terms of the small open economy model we use to describe Canada, the financial crisis pushed r_{For} higher and the *LM* curve to the left, resulting in a fall in output below the full-employment $(\overline{Y})$ level. The other shock was a dramatic slowdown in the economy of the United States—the major export market for Canada and many other countries. Again in terms of the small open economy model, the *IS* curve was also pushed to the left, causing an even further fall in output below full employment.

On the assumption that frozen credit markets would thaw, falling interest rates and prices would eventually enable world economies to adjust back to full employment. Falling prices would move *LM* curves back to the right and cause interest rates to fall. The recovery in the U.S. economy would restore exports in countries trading with the United States and so shift *IS* curves back to the right. One might argue—depending whether one were a Keynesian or a classical—that this would be a fast or a slow response, but eventually full employment would return.

But in 2008–2009, there was nothing to guarantee that credit markets would thaw and so enable this adjustment. Major financial firms were failing and the lack of credit was causing bankruptcies of both small and large firms—including what to that point was the largest car company in the world, General Motors. It appeared that financial markets would take a very long time to recover and that the recession would therefore be deep and prolonged. Many analysts drew comparisons to the Great Depression of the 1930s.

Out of that concern, central banks around the world coordinated their efforts to increase money supplies and so shift *LM* curves down and to the right. Governments similarly coordinated their efforts to expand their spending and shift *IS* curves up and to the right. In this way world interest rates fell back toward precrisis levels, and the world economy began to adjust back toward full equilibrium.

It is difficult to take issue with the Bank of Canada's response to the financial crisis and the recession that followed. The crisis emanated from financial markets, and the response of central banks to add liquidity to the world financial system is widely regarded as having been appropriate. The Bank of Canada's efforts to ensure the viability of Canadian financial institutions—and the security of Canadians' savings—were consistent with an expansionary monetary policy of the sort we have described in this chapter as being an effective response to recession.[23]

What of the Canadian government's fiscal policy response? We have learned that in a small open economy with a flexible exchange rate like Canada, fiscal policy is a largely ineffective response to a recession. It is interesting that the first response of the Canadian government to the onset of recession was for a muted fiscal policy response—a response that would seem to be consistent with our evaluation of the ineffectiveness of fiscal policy as a response to recession. Two things changed the government's mind. First, the muted response proved politically unpopular.[24] Second, it was increasingly apparent that the recession was worldwide in scope, requiring an internationally coordinated response. For both these reasons the Canadian government introduced a significant increase in spending in 2009 and so responded to the recession with an expansionary fiscal policy that coincided with similar efforts in the rest of the world. Because this effort was part of a worldwide fiscal policy expansion, the crowding out of net exports due to an appreciation of the exchange rate that would normally constrain the effect of fiscal policy on output was not so significant. That is, with all countries stimulating their economies, there was less reason to expect that any one currency would appreciate relative to others and so affect net exports. Because Canadian fiscal policy was introduced in coordination with similar efforts in other countries, it likely proved more effective at moving the economy back toward full employment than otherwise would have been the case.

MORE ADVANCED MODELS OF THE OPEN ECONOMY

Relative to the closed economy, consideration of the open economy is considerably complicated by having to deal with exchange rates, exports, imports, and the need to distinguish between domestic and foreign variables. In this chapter we have tried to take you toward an initial understanding of open economy macroeconomics. In this introduction to that field, we have made some strong assumptions to help us along the way. We have, for example, made the assumption that savers, when considering whether to purchase foreign or domestic financial assets,

[23] We will examine the Bank of Canada's response to the financial crisis more closely in Chapter 14.
[24] Indeed, at least in part to address accusations that it was not doing enough to respond to the recession, the government was required to take extraordinary steps to avoid losing power.

assumed that exchange rates would not change during the period of time when they might hold foreign assets. That assumption is consistent with the assumption we have made here and earlier in Chapter 9: that what households and firms expect to see and experience in the future is not affected by what they see and are experiencing today. In more advanced models of the open economy allowance is made for the possibility that savers might anticipate changes in the exchange rate given news they have learned about current policy changes. Indeed, savers might anticipate future currency appreciations and depreciations by selling or buying foreign financial assets possibly even ahead of the actual implementation of new government policies. We will investigate issues like these in the next two chapters, though we will return to the assumption of a closed economy in order to do so. Although we won't be returning to the open economy model to prove it, most of the broad conclusions drawn from our closed economy analysis apply equally well to the case of a small open economy.

CHAPTER SUMMARY

1. The nominal exchange rate is the number of units of foreign currency that can be obtained for one unit of domestic currency. The real exchange rate is the number of units of foreign goods that can be obtained for one unit of the domestic good. The idea that similar foreign and domestic goods should have the same prices in terms of the same currency is called purchasing power parity (PPP).

2. There are two major types of exchange rate systems: flexible- or floating-exchange-rate systems, in which the value of the nominal exchange rate is determined by market forces; and fixed-exchange-rate systems, in which the value of the exchange rate is officially set by a government or group of governments. In a flexible-exchange-rate system, an exchange rate increase is called an appreciation, and an exchange rate decrease is called a depreciation.

3. The real exchange rate is important because it affects net exports, or exports minus imports. With other factors held constant, a decline in the real exchange rate makes domestic goods cheaper relative to foreign goods, and thus tends to increase net exports.

4. In a flexible-exchange-rate system, the value of the (nominal) exchange rate is determined by supply and demand in the foreign exchange market. Foreigners demand the domestic currency to buy domestic goods and assets. Domestic residents supply the domestic currency to obtain the foreign currency needed to buy foreign goods and assets.

5. With other factors held constant, an increase in domestic output leads domestic residents to demand more imports, reducing the country's net exports and depreciating its exchange rate. An increase in the domestic real interest rate makes domestic assets more attractive, increasing the demand for the domestic currency and appreciating the exchange rate; the higher exchange rate, in turn, reduces net exports. The effects of changes in foreign output and the foreign real interest rate on the domestic country's net exports and exchange rate are the opposite of the effects of changes in domestic output and the domestic real interest rate.

6. In open economies and with freely mobile financial capital, savers have the opportunity to purchase financial assets from foreign as well as domestic borrowers. When judging whether to purchase domestic or foreign financial assets, savers must compare more than interest rates. This is so because to buy foreign assets requires

that they purchase foreign currency, and when the asset matures they must then sell that currency. If the value of the currency changes during the time the foreign asset is held, the rate of return on that investment is affected. The decision of whether to purchase a foreign asset thus requires that savers form an expectation about future movements in the exchange rate. Interest rate parity is a condition that states that the gross expected return on a bond issued by a foreign borrower will be the same as the gross expected return on a bond issued by a domestic borrower. If this condition does not hold, arbitragers will buy and sell domestic and foreign assets until interest rates adjust to make it so. In this chapter, we assume real interest rate parity is satisfied and that savers do not expect the exchange rate to change. These two assumptions mean that the domestic interest rate r will always adjust until it is equal to the foreign interest rate r_{For}.

7. The *IS–LM–FE* model for an open economy is similar to that for the closed economy. A principal difference is that in the open-economy model, factors (other than output or the real interest rate) that increase a country's net exports cause the *IS* curve to shift up. Among the factors that increase net exports are a rise in foreign output, an increase in the foreign real interest rate, and a shift in world demand toward the domestic country's goods. Economic shocks or policy changes are transmitted from one country to another by changes in net exports that lead to *IS* curve shifts.

8. In a small open economy with flexible exchange rates, a fiscal expansion has no effect on domestic output even during the Keynesian short run of fixed prices. A fiscal expansion causes an exchange rate appreciation, which causes net exports to fall. The exchange rate must appreciate enough to cause net exports to fall sufficiently to completely offset the effects of the fiscal expansion on domestic output. Only then will the domestic interest rate r again equal the foreign interest rate r_{For} and the appreciation stop. In general, any fiscal policy has limited effect because fiscal policies cause changes in the exchange rate, which move net exports in a direction that works against the original fiscal policy. As a result, shifts in the *IS* curve caused

by fiscal policy changes are undone by *IS* shifts in the opposite direction resulting from changes in the exchange rate.

9. In a small open economy with flexible exchange rates, changes in the money supply have a potent effect on domestic output. A monetary expansion causes an exchange rate depreciation, which causes net exports to increase. The exchange rate must depreciate enough to cause net exports to increase sufficiently to cause the domestic interest rate r to again equal the foreign interest rate r_{For} and cause the depreciation to stop. In the Keynesian short-run period, monetary policy therefore has a potent effect on output. In the Keynesian long run, and in the classical model, money is neutral.

10. In a fixed-exchange-rate system, nominal exchange rates are officially determined. If the officially determined exchange rate is greater than the fundamental value of the exchange rate as determined by supply and demand in the foreign exchange market, the exchange rate is said to be overvalued. The central bank can maintain the exchange rate at an overvalued level for a time by using official reserves (such as gold or foreign-currency bank deposits) to buy its own currency in the foreign exchange market. A country that tries to maintain an overvalued exchange rate for too long will run out of reserves and be forced to devalue its currency. If financial investors expect a devaluation, they may sell large quantities of domestic assets (a speculative run). A speculative run increases the supply of the domestic currency in the foreign exchange market and increases the rate at which the central bank must pay out its reserves.

11. In a small open economy with fixed exchange rates, a fiscal expansion has a potent effect on domestic output during the Keynesian short run of fixed prices. This is so because to fix the nominal exchange rate, the central bank must accommodate fiscal policy changes by shifting the *LM* curve in the same direction as fiscal policy shifts the *IS* curve. In the Keynesian long run and in the classical model, fiscal policy has no effect on output due to the response of the price level.

12. In a small open economy with fixed exchange rates, the domestic central bank cannot use

monetary policy to influence domestic output. This is so because the money supply is governed by the condition that the official and fundamental values of the exchange rate be the same. As a result, central banks cannot use monetary policy to pursue macroeconomic goals while also maintaining fixed exchange rates.

13. The advantages of a fixed-exchange-rate system are that it may promote economic and financial integration among countries and that it imposes discipline on the monetary policies of individual countries. A fixed-exchange-rate system will not work well if member countries have different macroeconomic policy goals or face different macroeconomic disturbances and, thus, are unable or unwilling to coordinate their monetary policies.

14. An open economy is subject to unexpected events that are not experienced by closed economies. Unexpected changes in foreign incomes, foreign interest rates, and the tastes of foreigners for domestically produced goods are examples. All such unexpected events cause the *IS* curve to shift. Some measure of protection from unexpected events is afforded by a flexible exchange rate. In particular, while fiscal policy has no impact on domestic output, it is also the case that unexpected events unique to the open economy also have no impact. Unfortunately, unexpected events that cause shifts in the *LM* curve (these will be the same in open and closed economies) have a magnified impact on output in an open economy with flexible exchange rates.

15. In an open economy with fixed exchange rates, fiscal policy is effective at affecting domestic output. Unfortunately, it is also the case that those open economy events that cause unexpected shifts in the *IS* curve have a similarly large effect on domestic output. Thus, while fiscal policy is effective, it is needed more often to stabilize the economy in the face of unexpected events. While monetary policy is unable to influence domestic output, this is also true of unexpected events that shift the *LM* curve.

KEY DIAGRAM 9

The *IS–LM–FE* Model of a Small Open Economy

The *IS–LM–FE* model shows general equilibrium in the goods, asset, and labour markets. In the small open-economy version of the *IS–LM–FE* model, full equilibrium occurs at the foreign real interest rate, an interest rate determined by the world demand and supply for funds. The model can be used to analyze the effects of foreign and domestic economic shocks on output, the real interest rate, the price level, and other macroeconomic variables. The exchange rate is assumed to be flexible, reflecting the choice of nearly all central banks, including the Bank of Canada

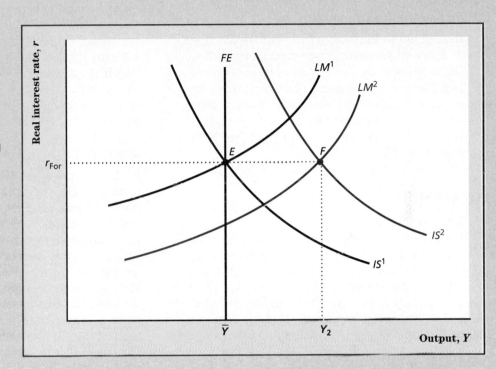

DIAGRAM ELEMENTS

- The real interest rate, r, is on the vertical axis and the level of output, Y, is on the horizontal axis.

- The full-employment (*FE*) line is vertical at full-employment output. Full-employment output, $\overline{Y}$, is the level of output that firms supply when wages and prices have fully adjusted, so employment is at its full-employment level, $\overline{N}$. Full-employment output is determined by the equation $Y = AF(K, \overline{N})$.

- For any level of output Y, the *IS* curve in a small open economy gives the real interest rate r that clears the goods market—in other words, the rate that equalizes the difference between desired national saving S^d and desired investment I^d to the value of net exports NX. Equivalently, the *IS* curve gives combinations of real

output Y and the real interest rate r that equalize the aggregate quantities of goods supplied and demanded, $Y = C^d + I^d + G$.

- For given values of the price level and output, the *LM* curve gives the real interest rate that clears the asset market, making the real money supply, M/P, and the real quantity of money demanded, $L(Y, r + \pi^e)$, equal. Because an increase in income raises real money demand, which raises the real interest rate that clears the asset market, the *LM* curve slopes upward.

FACTORS THAT SHIFT THE CURVES

- Any factor that raises full-employment output shifts the *FE* line to the right. These are the same factors that shift the *FE* line in a closed economy (see Summary table 11, p. 247).

- For constant output, any change that reduces real money supply relative to real money demand increases the real interest rate that clears the asset market and shifts the LM curve up and to the left. These are the same factors that shift the LM curve in a closed economy (see Summary table 12 on p. 251).

- In addition to the factors that shift the IS curve in a closed economy, some new factors affect the position of the IS curve in an open economy. In particular, anything that raises a country's net exports, for given domestic output and a given domestic real interest rate, will shift the open-economy IS curve up and to the right (see Summary table 13 on p. 256).

ANALYSIS

- If we assume that the LM curve is LM^1 and the IS curve is IS^1, the economy is in general equilibrium at point E, which lies at the intersection of all three curves. At E, the labour market (FE line), the goods market (IS curve), and the asset market (LM curve) are all in equilibrium. At E, output equals full employment and the domestic real interest rate, r_1, is equal to the foreign real interest rate, r_{For}.

- A shift up and to the right of the IS curve, from IS^1 to IS^2—whether arising from an expansionary fiscal policy or an exogenous shock to the position of the IS curve—causes a temporary increase in the domestic interest rate above the foreign interest rate. This causes the exchange rate to appreciate, which in turn reduces net exports. The fall in net exports causes IS^2 to shift back toward its original position. This movement continues until the domestic value of the real interest rate is equal to the foreign real interest rate. The IS curve, then, must return to position IS^1 to re-establish full equilibrium at point E. Because the exchange rate responds quickly to the increase in the domestic real interest rate above the foreign real interest rate, these IS movements also occur quickly. As a result,

there is no change in output and so no change in the domestic price level. The classical and the Keynesian model predict the same result.

- A shift down and to the right of the LM curve, from LM^1 to LM^2—whether arising from an expansionary monetary policy or an exogenous shock to the position of the LM curve—causes a temporary decrease in the domestic real interest rate r below the foreign real interest rate r_{For}. In the classical model, the resulting increase in output above the full-employment level causes the domestic price level to quickly rise and so shifts the LM curve up and to the left, from LM^2 back to LM^1. Full equilibrium is re-established at point E with $r = r_{For}$ and $Y = \overline{Y}$.

- In the Keynesian model, domestic prices adjust more slowly. The temporary decrease in the domestic real interest rate below the foreign real interest rate caused by the shift of LM^1 to LM^2 causes the exchange rate to depreciate, which in turn increases net exports. The increase in net exports causes the IS curve to shift up and to the right. This movement causes the domestic real interest rate to rise, and this must continue until it equals the foreign real interest rate. The IS curve must shift from IS^1 to IS^2 where it intersects LM^2 at point F, where $r = r_{For}$ and output is Y_2. Since output is above full-employment output, the domestic price level increases, which causes the real money supply to fall and the LM curve to shift up and to the left, back toward its original position.

This movement causes the domestic real interest rate to rise above the foreign real interest rate, the exchange rate to appreciate, and net exports to fall. The IS curve shifts down and to the left, back toward its original position. The IS and the LM curves must return to IS^1 and LM^1 where they intersect the FE line at point E. Full equilibrium is re-established at point E with $r = r_{For}$ and $Y = \overline{Y}$. In the Keynesian model, depending on the speed with which prices adjust, output may differ from full-employment output for an extended period.

KEY TERMS

arbitragers, p. 310
currency union, p. 334
devaluation, p. 299
exchange rate, p. 295
fixed-exchange-rate system, p. 296
flexible-exchange-rate system, p. 295
floating-exchange-rate system, p. 295
foreign exchange market, p. 295
fundamental value of the exchange rate, p. 324
inconvertible currency, p. 325
net export crowding out, p. 320
nominal appreciation, p. 298
nominal depreciation, p. 298
nominal exchange rate, p. 295
nominal interest rate parity condition, p. 310
open-economy trilemma, p. 332
overvalued exchange rate, p. 324
purchasing power parity, p. 299
real appreciation, p. 299
real depreciation, p. 299
real exchange rate, p. 297
real interest rate parity condition, p. 310
relative purchasing power parity, p. 301
revaluation, p. 299
speculative run, p. 325
undervalued exchange rate, p. 326

KEY EQUATIONS

$$e = \frac{e_{nom}P}{P_{For}} \qquad (10.1)$$

The real exchange rate, e, or the number of foreign goods that can be obtained for one domestic good, is defined in terms of the nominal exchange rate e_{nom} (the amount of foreign currency that can be obtained for one unit of domestic currency), the domestic price level P, and the foreign price level P_{For}.

$$\frac{\Delta e_{nom}}{e_{nom}} = \frac{\Delta e}{e} + \pi_{For} - \pi \qquad (10.3)$$

The percentage change in the nominal exchange rate, $\Delta e_{nom}/e_{nom}$, equals the percentage change in the real exchange rate, $\Delta e/e$, plus the excess of the foreign rate of inflation over the domestic rate of inflation, $\pi_{For} - \pi$.

$$S^d - I^d = NX \qquad (10.10)$$

In an open economy, goods market equilibrium (the *IS* curve) requires that the excess of desired national saving

over desired investment equal net exports. Equation (10.10) is equivalent to the condition that output, Y, must equal the aggregate demand for goods, $C^d + I^d + G + NX$, Eq. (10.11).

REVIEW QUESTIONS

1. Define *nominal exchange rate* and *real exchange rate*. How are changes in the real exchange rate and the nominal exchange rate related?

2. What are the two main types of exchange rate systems? Currently, which type of system determines the values of the Canadian dollar and major currencies, such as the yen, pound, euro, and the U.S. dollar?

3. Define *purchasing power parity* or PPP. Does PPP work well empirically? Explain.

4. For a given real exchange rate, how are a country's net exports affected by an increase in domestic income? an increase in foreign income? How does an increase in the domestic real interest rate affect the real exchange rate and net exports? Explain.

5. Why do foreigners demand dollars in the foreign exchange market? Why do Canadians supply dollars to the foreign exchange market? Give two examples of changes that would lead to an increased demand for dollars and two examples of changes that would lead to an increased supply of dollars in the foreign exchange market.

6. How is the *IS* curve in a small open economy affected by an increase in its major trading partner's income? by an increase in foreign interest rates?

7. Restricting your attention to the Keynesian short run, how are net exports affected by an expansionary fiscal policy under flexible exchange rates? under fixed exchange rates?

8. Assuming flexible exchange rates, what effects does expansionary monetary policy have on the nominal exchange rate in the short run? in the long run?

9. When the exchange rate is flexible, fiscal policy has no impact on domestic output in either the short run or the long run. Explain.

10. What is the fundamental value of a currency? What does saying that a currency is overvalued mean? Why is an overvalued currency a problem? What can a country do about an overvalued currency?

11. Why is a country limited in changing its money supply under a fixed-exchange-rate system?

12. What is the open-economy trilemma? Explain why each element in the trilemma might be desirable and why the three elements are incompatible.

NUMERICAL PROBLEMS

1. West Bubble makes ordinary soap bars that are sold for 5 guilders each. East Bubble makes deluxe soap bars that are sold for 100 florins each. The real exchange rate between West and East Bubble is two ordinary soap bars per deluxe soap bar.

   a. What is the nominal exchange rate between the two countries?

   b. During the following year, West Bubble has 10% domestic inflation and East Bubble has 20% domestic inflation. Two ordinary soap bars are still traded for a deluxe soap bar. At the end of the year, what has happened to the nominal exchange rate? Which country has had a nominal appreciation? Which has had a nominal depreciation?

2. On January 26, 2000, the nominal interest rate paid on a three-month federal government Treasury bill was 5.340% in the United States and 5.034% in Canada. At those interest rates, international bond traders were indifferent between holding Canadian as opposed to U.S. Treasury bills.

   a. Did the financial market expect the Canada–U.S. exchange rate to appreciate or depreciate?

   b. On that date, one Canadian dollar could be purchased for 0.69046 U.S. dollars. What did the market expect the exchange rate to be in three months?

   c. Three months later, on April 26, 2000, when the Treasury bills matured, one Canadian dollar could be purchased for 0.67613 U.S. dollars. Had a Canadian saver purchased the U.S. government Treasury bill back on January 26, what rate of return would he or she have earned?

3. Consider the following classical economy:

Desired consumption	$C^d = 300 + 0.5Y - 200r$
Desired investment	$I^d = 200 - 300r$
Government purchases	$G = 100$
Net exports	$NX = 150 - 0.1Y - 0.5e$
Real exchange rate	$e = 20 + 600r$
Full-employment output	$\overline{Y} = 900$

   In this economy, the real interest rate does not deviate from the foreign interest rate.

   a. What are the equilibrium values of the real interest rate, the real exchange rate, consumption, investment, and net exports?

   b. Now, suppose that full-employment output increases to 940. What are the equilibrium values of the real interest rate, the real exchange rate, consumption, investment, and net exports?

   c. Suppose that full-employment output remains at 940 and that government purchases increase to 132. What are the equilibrium values of the real interest rate, the real exchange rate, consumption, investment, and net exports?

4. Consider the following Keynesian economy:

Desired consumption	$C^d = 200 + 0.6(Y - T) - 200r$
Desired investment	$I^d = 300 - 300r$
Taxes	$T = 20 + 0.2Y$
Government purchases	$G = 152$
Net exports	$NX = 150 - 0.08Y - 500r$
Money demand	$L = 0.5Y - 200r$
Money supply	$M = 924$
Full-employment output	$\overline{Y} = 1000$

   In this economy, the real interest rate does not deviate from the foreign interest rate.

   a. What are the general equilibrium (that is, long-run) values of output, the real interest rate, consumption, investment, net exports, and the price level?

   b. Starting from full employment, government purchases are increased by 60, to 212. What are the effects of this change on output, the real interest rate, consumption, investment, and net exports in the short run?

   c. Using the same information as provided in part (b), in the long run what would happen to the nominal money supply, the price level, and the real money supply?

5. Consider the following Keynesian small open economy:

   $$C^d = 200 + 0.69Y$$
   $$I^d = 80 - 1000r$$
   $$G = 20$$
   $$NX = 85 - 0.09Y - e$$
   $$e = 90$$
   $$M = 115$$
   $$L = 0.5Y - 200r$$
   $$\overline{Y} = 300$$

   In this economy, the real interest rate does not deviate from the foreign interest rate.

   a. Assuming this economy is in general equilibrium, what is the value of the interest rate r?

   b. Assuming fixed nominal exchange rates and a fixed domestic price level, what is the effect on domestic output if the foreign interest rate increases by 0.05? What is the size of the nominal money supply in the new short-run equilibrium?

c. Assuming flexible exchange rates and a fixed domestic price level, what is the effect on domestic output if the foreign interest rate increases by 0.05? What is the value of the real exchange rate in the new short-run equilibrium?

d. In the long run, how does the domestic price level respond to an increase in the foreign interest rate?

ANALYTICAL PROBLEMS

1. Legislators often call for protectionist measures to preserve domestic employment. The purpose of this question is to evaluate the wisdom of legislation passed by domestic legislators to reduce domestic imports.

a. Assuming flexible exchange rates, and assuming a fixed price level, what are the effects of the import restrictions on domestic output, the real exchange rate, exports, imports, and net exports in the short run?

b. How is your answer to part (a) affected by allowing the domestic price level to adjust?

c. Assuming fixed exchange rates now, and assuming a fixed price level, what are the effects of the import restrictions on domestic output, the real exchange rate, exports, imports, and net exports?

d. How is your answer to part (c) affected when you allow the domestic price level to adjust?

2. Small open economies are subject to the whims of foreign legislators when they choose to use protectionist measures to protect employment in their countries. The purpose of this question is to evaluate the economic effects of legislation passed by foreign legislators. Assume that legislators in Country B pass legislation designed to restrict the size of imports from Country A.

a. Assuming flexible exchange rates and a fixed price level, what are the effects of the import restrictions on output, the real exchange rate, exports, imports, and net exports in Country A?

b. How is your answer to part (a) affected by allowing the domestic price level to adjust?

c. Assuming fixed exchange rates now, and assuming a fixed price level, what are the effects of the import restrictions on output, the real exchange rate, exports, imports, and net exports in Country A?

d. How is your answer to part (c) affected by allowing the domestic price level to adjust?

3. Country X's major trading partner is Country Y, a large open economy. The economy of Country Y is sufficiently large that it determines the world interest rate. (Thus the world interest rate is determined by the intersection of Country Y's *IS* and *LM* curves.) Country X, on the other hand, is economically small so that the interest rate in Country X does not deviate from the world interest rate. Changes in Country X have no effect on Country Y.

a. Assuming flexible exchange rates and a fixed price level, what are the effects on Country X of a monetary expansion in Country Y?

b. Assuming flexible exchange rates and a fixed price level, what are the effects on Country X of a fiscal expansion in Country Y?

4. Using an *IS–LM–FE* diagram as an aid, show the effect on a small open economy of a permanent increase in the full-employment level of output. Assume flexible exchange rates and assume that the domestic interest rate does not deviate from the foreign interest rate. Explain what happens to output, the price level, net exports, the nominal exchange rate, and the real exchange rate.

APPENDIX 10.A

AN ALGEBRAIC VERSION OF THE OPEN-ECONOMY *IS–LM–FE* MODEL

In what follows we provide an algebraic version of the small open economy version of the *IS–LM–FE* model. Just as we found in Chapter 9 when we examined the closed economy version of this model, short-run equilibriums in the open economy model occur at the intersection of the *IS* and the *LM* curves. In this appendix we use algebraic versions of *IS* and *LM* to derive expressions describing short-run equilibriums in the small open economy.

The *LM* curve and the *FE* line are unchanged from our closed economy analysis. Recall that the *LM* curve represents the asset market equilibrium condition. From Appendix 9.B it is given by

$$\frac{M}{P} = \ell_0 + \ell_Y Y - \ell_r (r + \pi^e), \tag{9.B.18}$$

where M is the nominal money supply, P is the price level, r is the domestic real interest rate, and π^e is the expected rate of domestic price inflation. As discussed in Appendix 9.B, ℓ_Y and ℓ_r are positive numbers measuring the sensitivity of money demand to changes in income Y and the nominal interest rate paid on nonmonetary assets $r + \pi^e$, respectively. The constant term ℓ_0 includes other factors that affect money demand. It will prove useful to rewrite Eq. (9.B.18) by moving the term involving Y to the left side and all other terms to the right side,

$$\ell_Y Y = [\ell_r \pi^e - \ell_0] + \frac{M}{P} + \ell_r r,$$

and then dividing both sides by ℓ_Y so that

$$Y = \gamma + \left(\frac{1}{P\ell_Y}\right)M + \left(\frac{\ell_r}{\ell_Y}\right)r, \tag{10.A.1}$$

where γ, defined as

$$\gamma = \left[\frac{\ell_r \pi^e - \ell_0}{\ell_Y}\right],$$

is a collection of terms we will hold constant. We will return to Eq. (10.A.1) later in this appendix, but before doing so we turn our attention to the goods market equilibrium condition, the *IS* curve.

The *IS* curve in an open economy is basically the same as that in a closed economy, with the exception that net exports are now an additional source of demand for domestic output. To derive the *IS* curve for the open economy, we begin with the equations describing desired consumption and desired investment, Eqs. (9.B.8) and (9.B.10):

$$C^d = c_0 + c_Y [Y - (t_0 + tY)] - c_r r, \tag{10.A.2}$$

$$I^d = i_0 - i_r r. \tag{10.A.3}$$

Equation (10.A.2) shows that desired consumption depends positively on disposable income, $Y - T$, and negatively on the real interest rate, r. (In Eq. (10.A.2) we used Eq. (9.B.9) to substitute for taxes, T.) Equation (10.A.3) states that desired investment depends negatively on the real interest rate r. Other factors influencing desired consumption and desired investment are included in the constant terms c_0 and i_0, respectively.

In an open economy, net exports are also a source of demand for domestic output. We learned in the text that net exports depend negatively on the real exchange rate e but that the real exchange rate changes ultimately as a result of changes in foreign output Y_{For}, foreign real interest rate r_{For}, domestic demand Y, and changes in domestic interest rates r. (Review Summary tables 16 and 17, p. 306, if you need a reminder.) We therefore assume that net exports are

$$NX = x_0 - x_Y Y + x_{YF} Y_{\text{For}} - x_r r + x_r r_{\text{For}}$$

or, collecting together the last two terms,

$$NX = x_0 - x_Y Y + x_{YF} Y_{\text{For}} - x_r(r - r_{\text{For}}), \qquad (10.A.4)$$

where x_Y, x_{YF}, and x_r are positive numbers measuring the sensitivity of net exports to changes in Y, Y_{For}, and r and r_{For}, respectively. All other influences that might affect the size of net exports, such as the qualities of domestic and foreign goods, are reflected in the constant term x_0. According to Eq. (10.A.4), a country's net exports depend negatively on domestic income Y (increased domestic income raises spending on imports) and positively on foreign income Y_{For} (increased foreign income raises spending on exports). Net exports also depend negatively on the domestic real interest rate r (a higher real interest rate raises the real exchange rate, making domestic goods relatively more expensive) and positively on the foreign real interest rate r_{For} (a higher real foreign interest rate lowers the domestic country's real exchange rate). We assume that net exports are equally sensitive to changes in r as they are to changes in r_{For} (though in the opposite direction).

The goods market equilibrium condition for an open economy, Eq. (5.5), is

$$Y = C^d + I^d + G + NX. \qquad (10.A.5)$$

The alternative version of the open-economy goods market equilibrium condition, $S^d = I^d + NX$, which is emphasized in the text, could be used equally well.

If we substitute the equations for desired consumption, Eq. (10.A.2), desired investment, Eq. (10.A.3), and net exports, Eq. (10.A.4), we get

$$Y = c_0 + c_Y(Y - t_0 - tY) - c_r r + i_0 r - i_r r + G + x_0 - x_Y Y + x_{YF} Y_{\text{For}} - x_r(r - r_{\text{For}}). \qquad (10.A.6)$$

Collecting the terms that multiply r on the left-hand side yields

$$[c_r + i_r + x_r]r = c_0 - [1 - c_Y(1-t) + x_Y]Y - c_Y t_0 + i_0 + G + x_0 + x_{YF} Y_{\text{For}} + x_r r_{\text{For}}. \qquad (10.A.7)$$

To put Eq. (10.A.7) in a form that is easier to interpret graphically, we divide both sides by the term $[c_r + i_r + x_r]$. The result is an equation of the open-economy IS curve

$$r = \alpha'_{IS} - \beta'_{IS}Y. \qquad (10.A.8)$$

Here, α'_{IS} and β'_{IS} are positive numbers defined as

$$\alpha'_{IS} = \frac{c_0 - c_Y t_0 + i_0 + G + x_0 + x_{YF} Y_{For} + x_r r_{For}}{c_r + i_r + x_r} \qquad (10.A.9)$$

and

$$\beta'_{IS} = \frac{1 - (1 - t)c_Y + x_Y}{c_r + i_r + x_r}. \qquad (10.A.10)$$

If there are no net exports, so that $x_0 = x_Y = x_{YF} = 0$, the coefficients α'_{IS} and β'_{IS} reduce to the coefficients of the closed-economy IS curve, α_{IS} and β_{IS} (compare Eqs. 10.A.9 and 10.A.10 with Eqs. 9.B.15 and 9.B.16, p. 291).

We can use the open-economy IS curve equation, Eq. (10.A.8), to confirm the three points made about the curve in the text. First, it slopes downward (the slope of the IS curve is $-\beta'_{IS}$, which is negative). Second, any factor that shifts the closed-economy IS curve also shifts the open-economy IS curve (any factor that changes the intercept α_{IS} also changes the intercept α'_{IS} in the same direction). Finally, for a given output and real interest rate, any factor that increases net exports shifts the open-economy IS curve up. That is, an increase in Y_{For} or r_{For}, or some other change that increases the demand for net exports as reflected in an increase in x_0, raises the intercept term α'_{IS} and thus shifts the IS curve up.

FISCAL AND MONETARY POLICY IN THE ALGEBRAIC MODEL: FLEXIBLE EXCHANGE RATES

In Sections 10.5 and 10.6 of the text, we examined the effects of fiscal and monetary policies on the small open economy. We examined these results for the case of flexible exchange rates and again for the case of fixed exchange rates. In what follows, we show how these results can be derived from our algebraic version of the model. Let's begin by assuming flexible exchange rates.

As we explained in the text, the version of the small open-economy model we have chosen to examine is one in which the domestic interest rate r is always equal to the foreign interest rate r_{For}. What restrictions on our algebraic model must we impose to examine this version of the small open-economy model? One way of answering this is to take another look at Eq. (10.A.4).

Equation (10.A.4) shows the relationships that exist between net exports, domestic and foreign output, and domestic and foreign interest rates. Suppose we rearrange the terms by putting the $x_r(r - r_{For})$ term on the left side and the NX term on the right side. After dividing both sides by x_r the result is

$$(r - r_{For}) = \frac{x_0 - x_Y Y + x_{YF} Y_{For} + NX}{x_r}. \qquad (10.A.11)$$

Equation (10.A.11) shows that the assumption that domestic and foreign interest rates be equal requires that we assume the value of x_r to be very large. (Any number, when divided by a very large number, approaches a value of zero.) As x_r grows ever larger, the difference between r and r_{For} shrinks until it disappears; they become equal. What have we assumed when we set the value of x_r to be very large?

In our discussion of interest rate parity in Section 10.3, we explained how traders in financial assets, arbitragers, earn a living spotting differences in gross rates of return earned on financial assets offered for sale in different countries. By buying and selling assets as appropriate, they realize a profit, and as a result of their actions arbitragers cause differences in gross rates of return to be eliminated. Recalling Eq. (10.8), arbitragers, then, ensure that $(e/e^f)(1 + r_{For}) = 1 + r$, where e and e_f are the current and expected future values of the real exchange rate, respectively. If we assume that savers do not expect changes in real exchange rates, then arbitragers ensure that differences in real interest rates will be eliminated so that eventually $r = r_{For}$. The size of x_r reflects the speed with which the actions of arbitragers cause differences in gross rates of return to disappear. If we assume a large value for x_r, then we assume that differences in gross rates of return disappear very quickly. This, then, is the assumption we made in the text when we imposed the condition that $r = r_{For}$ even during the Keynesian short-run period.

What does this assumption of a large value for x_r imply for our model? From Eq. (10.A.10), we see that a large value of x_r means $\beta'_{IS} = 0$. From Eq. (10.A.9), we see that a large value of x_r means $\alpha'_{IS} = r_{For}$.[25] The equation representing the *IS* curve, then, becomes

$$r = r_{For}. \tag{10.A.12}$$

Our macroeconomic model now consists of Eq. (10.A.12), the *IS* curve, and Eq. (10.A.1), the *LM* curve,

$$Y = \gamma + \left(\frac{1}{P\ell_Y}\right)M + \left(\frac{\ell_r}{\ell_Y}\right)r. \tag{10.A.1}$$

Substituting Eq. (10.A.12) into Eq. (10.A.1), we have an equation describing the value of output Y given by the intersection of the *IS* and the *LM* curves in the open-economy *IS–LM* model:

$$Y = \gamma + \left(\frac{1}{P\ell_Y}\right)M + \left(\frac{\ell_r}{\ell_Y}\right)r_{For}. \tag{10.A.13}$$

We observe from this result that changes in fiscal policy variables, the level of government spending on goods and services G or changes in tax rates t_0 or t, have no effect on domestic output Y. This is just as we concluded in the text. An expansionary fiscal policy causes a currency appreciation that in turn reduces net exports NX. Thus expansionary fiscal policy crowds out net exports, leaving domestic output unaffected. We also observe from Eq. (10.A.13) that a monetary expansion results in an increase in domestic output. This too is just as we concluded in the text. A monetary expansion causes a currency depreciation that in turn increases net exports and hence causes domestic income to increase. Finally, it is worth noting two results not discussed in the text. The first is the fact that an increase in the foreign interest rate r_{For} causes domestic output to increase. The logic of this result is that an increase in the foreign interest rate r_{For} above the value of the domestic interest rate r results in a currency

---

[25] To see this is true, divide every term in the numerator and every term in the denominator by x_r. Now let x_r take on a very large value.

depreciation, an expansion of net exports, and hence an increase in domestic income. The second is that a change in foreign income Y_{For} has no effect on domestic income Y. The logic of this result is that an expansion of foreign income increases domestic exports, but this in turn causes a currency appreciation that reduces net exports. In the end, domestic income is left unchanged.

FISCAL AND MONETARY POLICY IN THE ALGEBRAIC MODEL: FIXED EXCHANGE RATES

Now let's consider how the algebraic version of our model is affected by assuming fixed exchange rates. Two important changes must be made. First, as we discussed in the text, under fixed exchange rates the central bank must be prepared to change the domestic money supply whenever an exchange rate over- or undervaluation is threatened. This means that our equation of the LM curve (Eq. 9.B.18, p. 291) does nothing more than tell us, for alternative values of domestic output Y and the nominal interest rate on nonmonetary assets $r + \pi^e$, how the domestic central bank must change the domestic money supply. We can, then, ignore this relationship. Second, we need to adjust our equation defining net exports (Eq. 10.A.4, p. 347). In our earlier discussion of that equation, we explained that changes in the domestic real interest rate r and the foreign real interest rate r_{For} affected net exports NX only via their influence on the real exchange rate. If the exchange rate is fixed, this means that changes in r and r_{For} have no influence on NX. For this reason we need to modify our net export equation so that it becomes

$$Y = c_0 + c_Y(Y - t_0 - tY) - c_r r + i_0 - i_r r + G + x_0 - x_Y Y + x_{YF} Y_{\text{For}}.$$
(10.A.14)

If we substitute this new equation for net exports (Eq. 10.A.14), and the equations for desired consumption (Eq. 10.A.2, p. 346) and desired investment (Eq. 10.A.3, p. 346) into the goods market equilibrium condition (Eq. 10.A.5, p. 347), we get

$$Y = c_0 + c_Y(Y - t_0 - tY) + c_r r + i_0 - i_r r + G + x_0 - x_Y Y + x_{YF} Y_{\text{For}}.$$
(10.A.15)

Imposing on this equation our assumption of $r = r_{\text{For}}$ and collecting all terms that multiply Y on the left-hand side, we have

$$[1 - c_Y(1 - t) + x_Y]Y = c_0 + i_0 + x_0 - c_Y t_0 - (c_r + i_r)r_{\text{For}} + G + x_{YF}Y_{\text{For}}.$$

Dividing both sides by $[1 - c_r(1 - t) + x_r^Y]$, we have an equation describing the equilibrium value of domestic output Y in the open-economy IS–LM model with a fixed exchange rate:

$$Y = \frac{c_0 + i_0 + x_0 - c_Y t_0 - (c_r + i_r)r_{\text{For}} + G + x_{YF}Y_{\text{For}}}{[1 - c_Y(1 - t) + x_Y]}.$$
(10.A.16)

We observe from this result that changes in the monetary policy variable M have no effect on domestic output Y. This is just as we concluded in the text. A monetary expansion, for example, results in a currency overvaluation and hence requires a monetary contraction to resolve it. We also observe that fiscal policy variables, the level of government spending on goods and services G or changes in tax rates t_0 or t, have potent effects on domestic output. Again, this is just as we concluded in the text. A fiscal expansion produces a currency undervaluation that demands the central bank cause a monetary expansion. With both fiscal and monetary variables moving in the same direction, it is not surprising that fiscal policy has a potent effect on domestic output. Opposite to what we found under a flexible exchange rate, here we find that a change in foreign income Y_{For} has an effect on domestic income. The logic is that the expansion of foreign income results in an increase in domestic net exports, which in turn threatens a currency undervaluation. To prevent this, the central bank must increase the domestic money supply, thereby adding to the positive impact on domestic income brought about by the increase in foreign income. Finally, we observe from Eq. (10.A.16) that an increase in the foreign interest rate r_{For} causes a contraction in domestic output Y. This is opposite to what we found with a flexible exchange rate. The explanation is that the increase in the foreign interest rate above the value of the domestic interest rate results in a threatened currency overvaluation. This demands that the domestic central bank contract the domestic money supply in response, and this in turn contracts domestic income.

Chapter 11

Classical Business Cycle Analysis: Market-Clearing Macroeconomics

Economists generally agree about the basic business cycle facts outlined in Chapter 8. They know that economic growth is not necessarily smooth and that occasionally there are periods of recession in which output declines and unemployment rises. They know that recessions are typically followed by periods of recovery, in which the economy grows more strongly than normal. And they also know a great deal about how other macroeconomic variables—such as productivity, interest rates, and inflation—behave during recessions.

Recall that recessions and booms in the economy raise two basic questions: (1) What are the underlying economic causes of these business cycles? (2) What, if anything, should government policymakers do about them? Unfortunately, economists agree less about the answers to these two questions than about the basic business cycle facts.

The main disagreements about the causes and cures of recessions are between two broad groups of macroeconomists, the classicals and the Keynesians. As discussed first in Chapter 1 and again in Chapter 9, classicals and Keynesians—although agreeing on many points—differ primarily in their views on how rapidly prices and wages adjust to restore general equilibrium after an economic shock. Classical macroeconomists assume that prices and wages adjust quickly to equate quantities supplied and demanded in each market; as a result, they argue, a market economy is largely "self-correcting," with a strong tendency to return to general equilibrium on its own when it is disturbed by an economic shock or a change in public policy. Keynesians usually agree that prices and wages *eventually* change as needed to clear markets; however, they believe that *in the short run* price and wage adjustment is likely to be incomplete. That is, in the short run, quantities supplied and demanded need not be equal and the economy may remain out of general equilibrium. Although this difference in views may seem purely theoretical, it has a practical implication: Because Keynesians are skeptical about the economy's ability to reach equilibrium rapidly on its own, they are more inclined than are classicals to recommend that the government act to raise output and employment during recessions and to moderate economic growth during booms.

In Chapters 9 and 10, our discussion of the effects of shocks on the economy, and the possible policy responses to those shocks, was framed within an assumption that what households and firms expect to see and experience in the future is not affected by what they see and experience today. This is a restrictive assumption. We might expect, for example, that international tensions threatening war in the future may influence trade decisions today. Similarly, news of growing levels of government debt may cause households to expect to pay higher taxes in the future and so increase their savings or their work effort today.

In this chapter and the next, we relax that assumption. Taking account of expectations of future events will require a more sophisticated description of how households and firms decide to respond to price changes than we have used to this point. In Chapters 9 and 10 we used a simple description of this decision on the part of firms; for a period of time, firms will passively expand or contract output without changing prices but will eventually respond by increasing (decreasing) prices should output exceed (fall below) full-employment output $\overline{Y}$.[1] In this chapter and the next we will introduce a more sophisticated description of macroeconomic price-setting behaviour, one that takes into account how households and firms expect future events to unfold. This description, what economists know as the theory of aggregate supply (AS), will be joined with the theory of aggregate demand (AD) developed in Chapter 9 to give us the model of AD–AS, another of the key diagrams of macroeconomic analysis.

In this chapter we focus on describing how adherents of the classical model describe business cycles. We begin with a description of real business cycle theory and how it can be used to explain the business cycle facts presented in Chapter 8. A high degree of price flexibility is a hallmark of that model. Confronting the real business cycle model with evidence suggesting that money is non-neutral leads us to a description of the aggregate supply relationship deemed appropriate by classical economists. That model of aggregate supply will then be joined with the model of aggregate demand to provide a summary of the classical approach to understanding the business cycle.

11.1 BUSINESS CYCLES IN THE CLASSICAL MODEL

We have identified two basic questions of business cycle analysis: What causes business cycles? What can (or should) be done about them? Let's examine the classical answers to these questions, beginning with what causes business cycles.

THE REAL BUSINESS CYCLE THEORY

In general, a complete theory of the business cycle must have two components. The first component is a description of the types of shocks or disturbances believed to affect the economy the most. Examples of economic disturbances emphasized by various theories of the business cycle include supply shocks, changes in monetary or fiscal policy, and changes in consumer spending. The second component is a model that describes how key macroeconomic variables, such as output, employment, and prices, respond to economic shocks. The model preferred by classical economists is the market-clearing version of the *IS–LM–FE* model or some similar

---

[1] Classical economists judge this period of time to be very short, whereas Keynesians believe it may be considerably longer.

framework. However, the issue of which shocks are crucial in driving cyclical fluctuations remains.

An influential group of classical macroeconomists developed a theory that takes a strong stand on the sources of shocks that cause cyclical fluctuations. This theory, the **real business cycle theory** (or RBC theory), argues that real shocks to the economy are the primary cause of business cycles.[2] **Real shocks** are disturbances to the "real side" of the economy, such as shocks that affect the production function, the size of the labour force, the real quantity of government purchases, and the spending and saving decisions of consumers. Economists contrast real shocks with **nominal shocks**, or shocks to money supply or money demand. In terms of the *IS–LM–FE* model, real shocks directly affect only the *IS* curve or the *FE* line, whereas nominal shocks directly affect only the *LM* curve.

Although many types of real shocks could contribute to the business cycle, RBC theorists give the largest role to production function shocks—what we have called supply shocks and what the RBC theorists usually refer to as **productivity shocks**. Productivity shocks include the development of new products or production methods, the introduction of new management techniques, changes in the quality of capital or labour, changes in the availability of raw materials or energy, unusually good or unusually bad weather, changes in government regulations affecting production, and any other factor affecting productivity. According to RBC theorists, most economic booms result from beneficial productivity shocks, and most recessions are caused by adverse productivity shocks.

The Recessionary Impact of an Adverse Productivity Shock

Does the RBC theorists' idea that adverse productivity shocks lead to recessions (and, similarly, that beneficial productivity shocks lead to booms) make sense? We examined the theoretical effects on the economy of a temporary adverse productivity shock in Chapters 3 and 9.[3] In Chapter 3, we showed that an adverse productivity shock (or supply shock), such as an increase in the price of oil, reduces the marginal product of labour (*MPN*) and the demand for labour at any real wage. As a result, the equilibrium values of the real wage and employment both fall (see Figure 3.9, p. 72). The equilibrium level of output (the full-employment level of output $\overline{Y}$) also falls, both because equilibrium employment declines and because the adverse productivity shock reduces the amount of output that can be produced by any amount of capital and labour.

We later used the complete *IS–LM–FE* model (see Figure 9.8, p. 261) to explore the general equilibrium effects of a temporary adverse productivity shock. We confirmed our earlier conclusion that an adverse productivity shock lowers the general equilibrium levels of the real wage, employment, and output. In addition, we showed that an adverse productivity shock raises the real interest rate, depresses consumption and investment, and raises the price level.

---

[2] For a more detailed introduction to real business cycles, see Charles Plosser, "Understanding Real Business Cycles," *Journal of Economic Perspectives*, Summer 1989, pp. 51–78; and Robert G. King and Sergio Rebelo, "Resuscitating Real Business Cycles," in J. Taylor and M. Woodford, eds., *Handbook of Macroeconomics*, Elsevier, 1999. The original research is described by Finn E. Kydland and Edward C. Prescott, "Time to Build and Aggregate Fluctuations," *Econometrica*, November 1982, pp. 1345–1370; and John B. Long and Charles I. Plosser, "Real Business Cycles," *Journal of Political Economy*, February 1983, pp. 36–69. Kydland and Prescott won the 2004 Nobel Prize in Economics in part for their contributions to the development of real business cycle theory.
[3] RBC theorists analyze permanent as well as temporary productivity shocks; we focus on temporary shocks because they are the slightly easier case.

Broadly, then, our earlier analyses of the effects of an adverse productivity shock support the RBC theorists' claim that such shocks are recessionary in that they lead to declines in output. Similar analyses show that a beneficial productivity shock leads to a rise in output (a boom). Note that in the RBC approach, output declines in recessions and rises in booms because the general equilibrium (or full-employment) level of output has changed and because rapid price adjustment ensures that actual output always equals full-employment output. As classical economists, RBC theorists would reject the Keynesian view (discussed in Chapter 12) that recessions and booms are periods of disequilibrium, during which actual output is below or above its general equilibrium level for a protracted period of time.

Real Business Cycle Theory and the Business Cycle Facts

Although the RBC theory—which combines the classical, or market-clearing, version of the *IS–LM–FE* model with the assumption that productivity shocks are the dominant form of economic disturbance—is relatively simple, it is consistent with many of the basic business cycle facts. First, under the assumption that the economy is continuously buffeted by productivity shocks, the RBC approach predicts recurrent fluctuations in aggregate output, which actually occur. Second, the RBC theory correctly predicts that employment will move procyclically—that is, in the same direction as output. Third, supporters of RBC theory claim that the prediction of the model suggesting that the real wages will be higher during booms than during recessions (procyclical real wages) is consistent with business cycle facts. However, as we discussed in Chapter 8, definitive conclusions about the cyclicality of real wages remain elusive.

A fourth business cycle fact explained by the RBC theory is that average labour productivity is procyclical; that is, output per worker is higher during booms than during recessions. This fact is consistent with the RBC theorists' assumption that booms are periods of beneficial productivity shocks, which tend to raise labour productivity, whereas recessions are the results of adverse productivity shocks, which tend to reduce labour productivity. The RBC theorists point out that without productivity shocks—allowing the production function to remain stable over time—average labour productivity would not be procyclical. With no productivity shocks, the expansion of employment that occurs during booms would tend to reduce average labour productivity because of the principle of diminishing marginal productivity of labour. Similarly, without productivity shocks, recessions would be periods of relatively higher labour productivity instead of lower productivity, as observed. Thus, RBC theorists regard the procyclical nature of average labour productivity as strong evidence supporting their approach.

A business cycle fact that does *not* seem to be consistent with the simple RBC theory is that inflation tends to slow during or immediately after a recession. The theory predicts that an adverse productivity shock will both cause a recession and increase the general price level. Thus, according to the RBC approach, periods of recession should also be periods of inflation, contrary to the business cycle fact.

Some RBC theorists have responded by taking issue with the conventional view that inflation is procyclical. They recognize that while the standard view that the price level and inflation are procyclical (they increase when output increases) does seem to hold before World War II, and especially during the Great Depression, this was a period when the economy had a different structure and was subject to different types of shocks than the more recent economy. Since World War II, large adverse supply shocks have caused the price level to rise while output fell. Most notably, inflation surged during the recessions that followed the adverse oil price shocks of 1973–1974 and 1979–1980, an observation consistent with the RBC theory. The issue of the cyclical behaviour of prices remains controversial, however.[4]

APPLICATION

CALIBRATING THE BUSINESS CYCLE

If we put aside the debate about price level behaviour, the RBC theory can account for some of the business cycle facts, including the procyclical behaviour of employment and productivity. However, RBC theorists argue that an adequate theory of the business cycle should be *quantitative* as well as *qualitative*. In other words, in addition to predicting generally how key macroeconomic variables move throughout the business cycle, the theory should predict numerically the size of economic fluctuations and the strength of relationships among the variables.

To examine the quantitative implications of their theories, RBC theorists developed a method called *calibration*. The idea is to work out a detailed numerical example of a more general theory. The results are then compared with observations to see whether model and reality broadly agree.

The first step in calibration is to write a simple classical model of the economy—such as the classical version of the *IS–LM–FE* model—except that specific functions replace general functions. For example, instead of representing the production function in general terms as

$$Y = AF(K, N),$$

the person doing the calibration uses a specific algebraic form for the production function, such as[5]

$$Y = AK^a N^{1-a},$$

where a is a number between 0 and 1. Similarly, specific functions are used to describe the behaviour of consumers and workers.

In the second step, the specific functions chosen are made even more specific by expressing them in numerical terms. For example, for $a = 0.3$, the production function becomes

$$Y = AK^{0.3} N^{0.7}.$$

In the same way, specific numbers are assigned to the functions describing the behaviour of consumers and workers. Where do these numbers come from? Generally, they are *not* estimated from macroeconomic data but are based on other sources. For example, the numbers assigned to the functions in the model may come from previous studies of the production function or of the saving behaviour of individuals and families.

The third step, which must be carried out on a computer, is to find out how the numerically specified model behaves when it is hit by random shocks, such as

[4] Another RBC response to this criticism is to note that in reality the money supply is not literally fixed, as we assumed in our analysis of the effects of a productivity shock in Chapter 9. To the extent that the money supply declines in recessions, the tendency for prices to rise will be less.

[5] This production function is the Cobb–Douglas production function (see Chapter 3). As we noted, although it is relatively simple, it fits data quite well.

productivity shocks. The shocks are created on the computer with a random number generator, with the size and persistence of the shocks (unlike the numbers assigned to the specific functions) being chosen to fit the actual macroeconomic data. For these shocks, the computer tracks the behaviour of the model over many periods and reports the implied behaviour of key macroeconomic variables, such as output, employment, consumption, and investment. The results are then compared with the behaviour of the actual economy to determine how well the model fits reality.

One of the developers of RBC theory, Edward Prescott[6] of the University of Minnesota, performed an early and influential calibration exercise. Prescott used a model similar to the RBC model we present here, the main difference being that our version of the RBC model is essentially a two-period model (the present and the future), and Prescott's model allowed for many periods. The results of Prescott's computer simulations are shown in Figures 11.1 and 11.2.

Figure 11.1 compares the actually observed volatilities of six macroeconomic variables, as calculated from post–World War II U.S. data, with the volatilities predicted by Prescott's calibrated RBC model.[7] Prescott set the size of the random productivity shocks in his simulations so that the volatility of GNP in his model would match the actual volatility in U.S. GNP.[8] That choice explains why the actual

FIGURE 11.1

ACTUAL VERSUS SIMULATED VOLATILITIES OF KEY MACROECONOMIC VARIABLES

The figure compares the actual volatilities of key macroeconomic variables observed in post–World War II U.S. data with the volatilities of the same variables predicted by computer simulations of Edward Prescott's calibrated RBC model. Prescott set the size of the random productivity shocks in his simulations so that the simulated volatility of GNP would match the actually observed volatility of GNP exactly. For these random productivity shocks, the simulated volatilities of the other five macroeconomic variables (with the possible exception of consumption) match the observed volatilities fairly well.

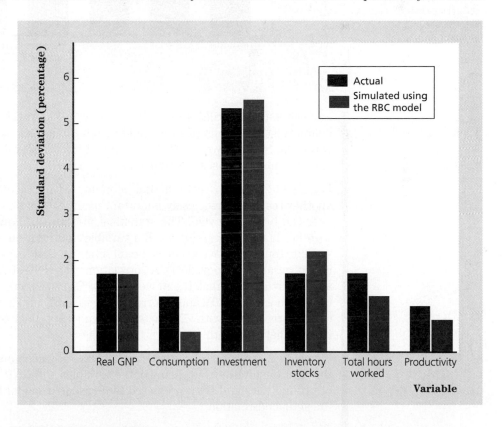

---

[6] "Theory Ahead of Business Cycle Measurement," *Carnegie-Rochester Conference Series on Public Policy*, Volume 25, Autumn 1986, pp. 11–39. Reprinted in *Quarterly Review*, Federal Reserve Bank of Minneapolis, Fall 1986, pp. 9–22.

[7] The measure of volatility used is called the *standard deviation*. The higher the standard deviation, the more volatile the variable being measured.

[8] At the time of Prescott's study, the national income and product accounts of the United States focused on GNP rather than GDP, so Prescott also focused on GNP.

FIGURE 11.2

ACTUAL VERSUS SIMULATED CORRELATIONS OF KEY MACROECONOMIC VARIABLES WITH GNP

How closely a variable moves with GNP over the business cycle is measured by its correlation with GNP, with higher correlations implying a closer relationship. The figure compares the correlations of key variables with GNP that were actually observed in the post–World War II U.S. economy with the correlations predicted by computer simulations of Prescott's calibrated RBC model. Except for productivity, whose predicted correlation with GNP is too high, the simulations predicted correlations of macroeconomic variables with GNP that closely resemble the actual correlations of these variables with GNP.

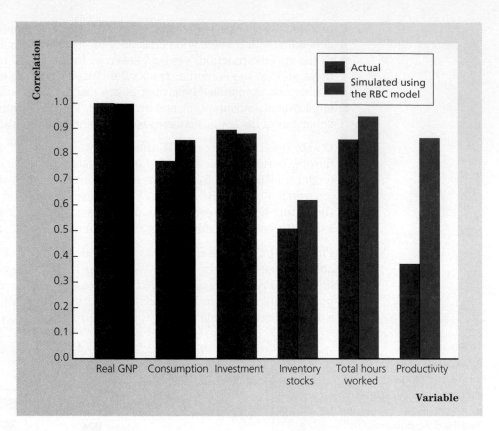

and simulated volatilities of GNP are equal in Figure 11.1. But he did nothing to guarantee that the simulation would match the actual volatilities of the other five variables. Note, however, that the simulated and actual volatilities for the other variables in most cases are quite close.

Figure 11.2 compares the actual economy with Prescott's calibrated model in another respect: how closely important macroeconomic variables move with GNP over the business cycle. The statistical measure of how closely variables move together is called *correlation*. If a variable's correlation with GNP is positive, the variable tends to move in the same direction as GNP over the business cycle (that is, the variable is procyclical). A correlation with GNP of 1.0 indicates that the variable's movements track the movements of GNP perfectly (thus, the correlation of GNP with itself is 1.0), and a correlation with GNP of 0 indicates no relationship to GNP. Correlations with GNP between 0 and 1.0 reflect relationships with GNP of intermediate strength.

Figure 11.2 shows that Prescott's model generally accounts well for the strength of the relationships between some of the variables and GNP, although the correlation of productivity and GNP predicted by Prescott's model is noticeably larger than the actual correlation.

The degree to which relatively simple calibrated RBC models can match the actual data is impressive. In addition, the results of calibration exercises help guide further development of the model. For example, the version of the RBC model discussed here has been modified to improve the match between the actual and predicted correlations of productivity with GNP.

Are Productivity Shocks the Only Source of Recessions?

Although RBC theorists agree, in principle, that many types of real shocks buffet the economy, in practice much of their work rests on the assumption that productivity shocks are the dominant, or even the only, source of recessions. Many economists, including both classicals and Keynesians, have criticized this assumption as being unrealistic. For example, some economists challenged the RBC theorists to identify the specific productivity shocks that they believe caused each of the recessions since World War II. The critics argue that except for the oil price shocks of 1973, 1979, and 1990, and the tech revolution of the late 1990s, historical examples of economywide productivity shocks are virtually nonexistent.

An interesting RBC response to this argument is that, in principle, economywide fluctuations could also be caused by the cumulative effects of a series of small productivity shocks. Moreover, the effects of shocks can persist as the economy adjusts to them.

To illustrate the point that small shocks can cause large fluctuations, Figure 11.3 shows the results of a computer simulation of productivity shocks and the associated behaviour of output for a simplified RBC model. In this simple RBC model, the change in output from one month to the next has two parts: (1) a fixed part that arises from normal technical progress or from a normal increase in population and employment; and (2) an unpredictable part that reflects a random shock to productivity during the current month.[9] The random, computer-generated productivity shocks are shown at the bottom of Figure 11.3, and the implied

FIGURE 11.3

SMALL SHOCKS AND LARGE CYCLES

A computer simulation of a simple RBC model is used to find the relationship between computer-generated random productivity shocks (shown at the bottom of the figure) and aggregate output (shown in the middle of the figure). Even though all the productivity shocks are small, the simulation produces large cyclical fluctuations in aggregate output. Thus, large productivity shocks are not necessary to generate large cyclical fluctuations.

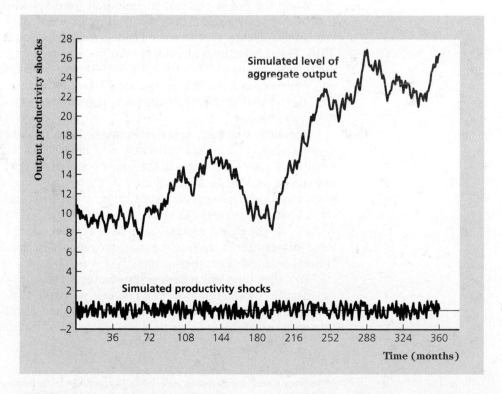

---

[9] Specifically, the model is $Y_t = Y_{t-1} + 0.01 + e_t$, where Y_t is output in month t, Y_{t-1} is output in the previous month, and e_t is the random productivity shock in month t. The productivity shocks are randomly chosen numbers between -1.0 and 1.0. A similar example is given in Numerical Problem 6 at the end of this chapter.

behaviour of output is displayed above them. Although none of the individual shocks is large, the cumulative effect of the shocks causes large fluctuations in output that look something like business cycles. Hence business cycles may be the result of productivity shocks, even though identifying specific, large shocks is difficult.

Does the Solow Residual Measure Technology Shocks?

Because productivity shocks are the primary source of business cycle fluctuations in RBC models, RBC theorists have attempted to measure the size of these shocks. The most common measure of productivity shocks is known as the **Solow residual**, which is an empirical measure of total factor productivity, A. The Solow residual is named after the originator of modern growth theory, Robert Solow, who used this measure in the 1950s.[10]

Recall from Chapter 3 that to measure total factor productivity A, we need data on output, Y, and the inputs of capital, K, and labour, N. In addition, we need to use a specific algebraic form for the production function, such as $Y = AK^a N^{1-a}$. We then compute the value of the productivity parameter, A, also known as the Solow residual, as

$$\text{Solow residual} = \frac{Y}{K^a N^{1-a}} = A. \tag{11.1}$$

The Solow residual is called a "residual" because it is the part of output that cannot be directly explained by measured capital and labour inputs.

When the Solow residual is computed from actual data, using Eq. (11.1), it turns out to be strongly procyclical, rising in economic expansions and falling in recessions. Figure 11.4 shows Canadian values of Solow residuals from 1961 to 2015. The shaded areas identify years of recession. Note that the residuals fell during the recessions of 1981–1982, 1990–1991, and 2008–2009, and increased during economic expansions. This procyclical behaviour is consistent with the premise of RBC theory that cyclical fluctuations in aggregate output are driven largely by productivity shocks.

Recently, however, some economists have questioned whether the Solow residual should be interpreted solely as a measure of technology, as RBC proponents tend to do. If changes in the Solow residual reflect only changes in the technologies available to an economy, it should be unrelated to such factors as government purchases or monetary policy that do not directly affect scientific and technological progress (at least in the short run). However, statistical studies reveal that the Solow residual is, in fact, correlated with such factors as government expenditures, suggesting that movements in the Solow residual may also reflect the impacts of other factors.[11]

To understand why measured productivity can vary, even if the actual technology used in production does not change, we need to recognize that capital and labour are sometimes used more intensively than at other times and that more intensive use of inputs leads to higher output. For instance, a printing press used

---

[10] "Technical Change and the Aggregate Production Function," *Review of Economics and Statistics*, 1957, pp. 312–320. In Chapter 6, we described Solow's contributions to growth theory.

[11] Changes in technology might well be correlated with changes in government spending on research and development (R&D). However, the Solow residual is also highly correlated with non–R&D government spending and with lags too short to be accounted for by the effects of spending on the rate of invention.

FIGURE 11.4

CANADIAN SOLOW RESIDUALS,

1961–2015

Solow residuals are constructed from annual output, employment, and capital series, with $a = 0.3$. Calling it total factor productivity, we previously calculated the Solow residual in Table 3.1 (p. 50). The shaded areas identify recession years. Note that the Solow residual is procyclical and leads the cycle.

Sources: See Table 3.1.

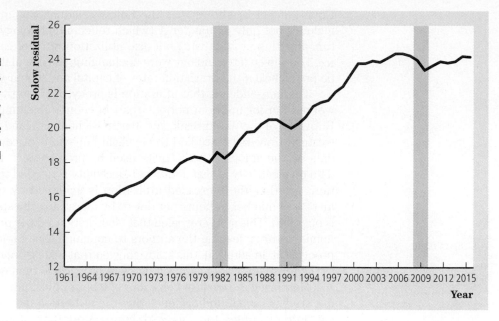

full time contributes more to production than an otherwise identical printing press used half the time. Similarly, workers working quickly (for example, restaurant workers during a busy lunch hour) will produce more output and revenue than the same number of workers working more slowly (the same restaurant workers during the afternoon lull). To capture the idea that capital and labour resources can be used more or less intensively at different times, we define the *utilization rate of capital*, u_K, and the *utilization rate of labour*, u_N. The utilization rate of a factor measures the intensity at which it is being used. For example, the utilization rate of capital for the printing press running full time would be twice as high as for the printing press used half the time; similarly, the utilization rate of labour is higher in the restaurant during lunch hour. The actual usage of the capital stock in production, which we call *capital services*, equals the utilization rate of capital times the stock of capital, or $u_K K$. Capital services are a more accurate measure of the contribution of the capital stock to output than is the level of capital itself because the definition of capital services adjusts for the intensity at which capital is used. Similarly, we define *labour services* to be the utilization rate of labour times the number of workers (or hours) employed by the firm, or $u_N N$. Thus, the labour services received by an employer are higher when the same number of workers are working hard and fast than when they are working slowly (that is, the utilization of labour is higher).

Recognizing that capital services and labour services go into the production of output, we rewrite the production function as

$$Y = AF(u_K K, u_N N) = A(u_K K)^a (u_N N)^{1-a}, \tag{11.2}$$

where we have replaced the capital stock, K, with capital services, $u_K K$, and labour, N, with labour services, $u_N N$. Now we can use the production function in Eq. (11.2) to substitute for Y in Eq. (11.1) to obtain an expression for the Solow residual that incorporates utilization rates for capital and labour:

$$\text{Solow residual} = \frac{A(u_K K)^a (u_N N)^{1-a}}{K^a N^{1-a}} = A u_K{}^a u_N{}^{1-a}. \tag{11.3}$$

Equation (11.3) shows that the Solow residual, as conventionally measured, includes not only parameter A (which reflects technology and perhaps other factors affecting productivity) but also utilization rates of capital and labour u_K and u_N. Thus, even if technology were unchanging, the calculated Solow residual would be procyclical if the utilization rates of capital and labour were procyclical.

There is evidence that utilization is procyclical (so that capital and labour are worked harder in boom periods than in economic slumps). For example, Craig Burnside, of the World Bank, and Martin Eichenbaum and Sergio Rebelo, of Northwestern University, studied the cyclical behaviour of capital utilization by using data on the amount of electricity used by producers.[12] Their rationale for using data on electricity is that additional electricity is needed to increase capital utilization, whether the increased utilization is achieved by operating capital for an increased number of hours per day or by increasing the speed at which the capital is operated. This study revealed that electricity used per unit of capital rises in economic upturns, leading the authors to conclude that capital utilization is strongly procyclical. In addition, this study showed that a measure of technology, analogous to the term A in Eq. (11.2), is much less procyclical than is the Solow residual.

Measuring the cyclical behaviour of labour utilization is more difficult, but various studies have found evidence that the utilization rate of labour is also procyclical. For example, Jon Fay and James Medoff,[13] of Harvard University, sent questionnaires to large manufacturing enterprises, asking about employment and production during the most recent downturn experienced at each plant. Fay and Medoff found that during a downturn, the average plant surveyed cut production by 31% and cut its total use of blue-collar hours to 23% below the normal level. Plant managers estimated that total hours could have been reduced by an additional 6% of the normal level without further reducing output. Of the 6% of normal hours, about half (3% of normal hours) were typically assigned to various types of useful work, including equipment maintenance and overhaul, painting, cleaning, reworking output, and training. The remaining 3% of normal hours were assigned to "make-work" and other unproductive activities. These numbers suggest that firms utilize labour less intensively during recessions.

The tendency to use workers less intensively in recessions than in expansions has been referred to as labour hoarding. **Labour hoarding** occurs when, due to the costs of firing and hiring workers, firms retain some workers in a recession that they would otherwise lay off. Firms keep these workers on the payroll to avoid costs of laying off workers and then rehiring them or hiring and training new workers when the economy revives. Hoarded labour either works less hard during the recession (there is less to do) or is put to work doing tasks, such as maintaining equipment, that are not measured as part of the firm's output. When the economy revives, the hoarded labour goes back to working in the normal way. In much the same way, it may not pay the restaurant owner to send her workers home between the lunch and dinner rush hours, with the result that restaurant workers are less productive during the slow afternoon period. This lower rate of productivity during recessions (or during the afternoon slow period in the restaurant) does not reflect changes in the available technology, but only changes in the rate at which firms utilize capital and labour. Hence we should be cautious about interpreting cyclical changes in the Solow residual (equivalently, total factor productivity, A) as solely reflecting changes in technology.

[12] "Capital Utilization and Returns to Scale," in B. Bernanke and J. Rotemberg, eds., *NBER Macroeconomics Annual*, 1995.
[13] "Labor and Output Over the Business Cycle," *American Economic Review*, September 1985, pp. 638–655.

Although changes in technology or the utilization rates of capital and labour might cause aggregate cyclical fluctuation, history suggests that shocks other than productivity shocks also affect the economy; wars are but one obvious example. Thus, many classical economists favour a broader definition of classical business cycle theory that allows for both productivity and other types of shocks to have an impact on the economy. Because the models they use allow for shocks other than "real" productivity shocks, the models are not called RBC models but rather dynamic, stochastic, general equilibrium (DSGE) models, as they model behaviour over time (dynamic), allow for shocks to the economy (stochastic), and are based on general equilibrium concepts.

The macroeconomic effects of shocks other than productivity shocks can be analyzed with the classical *IS–LM–FE* model. Let's use it to examine the effects of a fiscal policy shock.

FISCAL POLICY SHOCKS IN THE CLASSICAL MODEL

Another type of shock that can be a source of business cycle fluctuations in the classical model is a change in fiscal policy, such as an increase or decrease in real government purchases of goods and services.[14] This claim is seemingly at odds with the classical assumption that prices adjust quickly to ensure output Y is equal to full-employment output $\overline{Y}$. Recalling our discussion of the *IS–LM–FE* model in Chapter 9, an increase in government spending shifts the *IS* curve up and to the right, causing output to expand. Classical economists believe this elicits a speedy response in the form of a higher price level P, which in turn shifts the *LM* curve up and to the left. In this way general equilibrium is re-established at the original level of full-employment output. Classical economists argue, however, that an increase in government purchases will not only shift the *IS* curve but may also shift the *FE* line to the right. If so, an increase in government purchases causes full-employment output $\overline{Y}$ to increase.

The mechanism by which fiscal policy might shift the *FE* line and so affect real output in the classical model is through the possible effect that a change in government purchases has on wealth. If government increases the share of the nation's output that it takes for public spending, then people may feel their wealth has been reduced. If so, then, as discussed in Chapter 3, the decrease in wealth leads workers to increase their labour supply because someone who is poorer can afford less leisure.[15] As a sketch of the simple labour demand and supply diagram shows, an increase in the supply of labour increases the equilibrium level of employment $\overline{N}$ and, consequently, the full-employment level of output $\overline{Y}$.

---

[14] Another example of a change in fiscal policy is a change in the structure of the system of taxation without any change in government purchases. All economists recognize that different types of taxes affect people's incentives to work, save, and invest differently. A change in the structure of the tax system—a switch from income to consumption taxes, for example—may therefore affect the position of the *FE* line and so full-employment output. We have not emphasized this connection in our examination of the business cycle in part because these effects are complicated and depend on the nature of the tax, the type of income or revenue that is taxed, and so on. In addition, fiscal policies intended to dampen the business cycle focus on temporary changes to the total amount of taxes collected (as opposed to changes to the structure of the tax system), and so we have emphasized the impact of temporary tax changes on the aggregate demand (*AD*) curve. Classical economists accept the Ricardian equivalence proposition, and so would not expect changes in the amount of taxes collected without an accompanying change in government purchases to have much effect on the economy.

[15] In Chapter 3 we noted that a change in wealth produces a pure income effect. Just as winning a lottery is expected to increase the consumption of leisure and so reduce the supply of labour, a fall in wealth will result in less leisure being chosen and so a greater supply of labour.

This result is useful for classical economists because it helps their model fit the data. In particular, it suggests that government purchases are procyclical with real output and government purchases moving in the same direction, something we noted previously is observed in the data. The result also means that, because of diminishing marginal productivity of labour, the increase in employment that accompanies an increase in government purchases results in a decline in average labour productivity. This prediction is particularly important because, as we reported in Figure 11.2 (p. 358), a weakness of the RBC model that considers only productivity shocks is that it predicts that average labour productivity and GNP should be highly correlated while the data suggest they are not. If shocks to government purchases are positively correlated with GNP and negatively correlated with average labour productivity, then a classical model containing both productivity shocks and shocks to government purchases can better match the empirical evidence of GNP and average labour productivity being only weakly correlated.

For this to be useful as an explanation for the weak correlation between GNP and the average labour productivity in the data, classical economists must be comfortable with the claim that an increase in government purchases lowers the wealth of individuals and so causes them to increase their supply of labour. This can be a difficult connection to make. For example, if new government spending is on exactly the same goods and services households would have bought had they not funded the new government purchases with new taxes, then clearly there is no impact on household wealth; the exact same goods are purchased by government that would have otherwise been purchased by households. Of course, this is unlikely; we usually ask governments to add our tax payments with those of others to maintain things like a police force, a system of courts, and a road system, things we as individuals desire but may find difficult to build and maintain without collective effort. Examples like these suggest that an increase in government purchases may provide direct benefits to households and firms that *increase*, rather than decrease, private wealth. Other examples of government spending, however, may not provide the same level of comfort to those believing government purchases provide direct benefits to households and firms. Those who believe significant amounts of government spending are wasteful would argue that increases in government purchases clearly decrease private wealth and so encourage an increase in labour supply.

Should Fiscal Policy Be Used to Dampen the Cycle?

Our analysis shows that changes in government purchases may have real effects on the economy. Potentially, then, changes in fiscal policy could be used to offset cyclical fluctuations and stabilize output and employment; for example, the government could increase its purchases during recessions. This observation leads to the second of the two questions posed in the introduction to the chapter: Should policymakers use fiscal policy to smooth business cycle fluctuations?

Classical economists generally oppose attempts to dampen cyclical fluctuations in the economy. This skepticism about the value of active anti-recessionary policies is rooted in the belief of classical economists that since rapid price responses ensure that markets always clear—so that the economy is always in general equilibrium—there are no inefficiencies for policymakers to fix. In the classical model, a fall in full-employment output is an optimal response to an adverse productivity shock. While an increase in government purchases may cause full-employment output to increase, this possibility is associated with a fall in household wealth. In the classical model, then, government's effort to reverse the effects of an adverse productivity shock simply makes people worse off. Classical economists conclude that government purchases should be increased only if the benefits of the expanded government program exceed the cost to taxpayers. They apply this criterion for useful government spending—that the benefits should exceed the costs—whether the economy is in recession or not.

UNEMPLOYMENT IN THE CLASSICAL MODEL

A major weakness of the classical model is that it does not explain why unemployment rises during business downturns. Indeed, in the simple classical, or supply-and-demand, model of the labour market, unemployment is literally zero: Anyone who wants to work can find a job at the market-clearing wage. Of course, in reality, unemployment is never zero. Furthermore, the sharp increases in unemployment that occur during recessions are a principal reason that policymakers and the public are so concerned about economic downturns.

Classical economists are perfectly aware of this issue, and they have developed more sophisticated versions of the classical business cycle model to account for unemployment. The main modification they make to the simple supply-and-demand model of the labour market is to drop the model's implicit assumption that all workers and jobs are the same. Rather than all being the same, workers in the real world have different abilities, skills, and interests, among other things; jobs entail different skill requirements, work environments, locations, and other characteristics. Because workers and jobs both vary in so many ways, matching workers to jobs is not instantaneous and free but rather time consuming and costly. The fact that someone who has lost a job or has just entered the labour force must spend time and effort to find a new job helps explain why there are always some unemployed people.

Some classical economists suggest that differences among workers and among jobs explain not only why the unemployment rate is always greater than zero but also why unemployment rises so sharply in recessions. They argue that productivity shocks and other macroeconomic disturbances that cause recessions also often increase the degree of mismatch between workers and firms.[16] Thus, a major adverse productivity shock might affect the various industries and regions within a country differently, with jobs being destroyed in some sectors but new opportunities emerging in others. An oil price shock, for example, would eliminate jobs in energy-intensive industries but create new opportunities in industries that supply energy or are light energy users.

Following such a shock, workers in industries and regions where labour demand has fallen will be induced to search elsewhere for jobs, which raises the frictional component of unemployment. Some of these workers will find that their skills do not match the requirements of industries with growing labour demand; these workers may become chronically unemployed, raising structural or long-term unemployment.[17] With many unemployed workers looking for jobs, and because creating new jobs takes a while, the time necessary to find a new job is likely to increase. For all these reasons, an adverse productivity shock may raise

---

[16] This idea was proposed in David Lilien, "Sectoral Shifts and Cyclical Unemployment," *Journal of Political Economy*, August 1982, pp. 777–793.

[17] See Chapter 3 for definitions and discussion of frictional and structural unemployment.

unemployment as well as reduce output and employment. Note that this predicted rise in frictional and structural unemployment during recessions is the same as an increase in the natural rate of unemployment (the sum of frictional and structural unemployment rates).

What is the evidence of worker–job mismatch and unemployment? To examine this issue, we start with evidence on just how much potential exists for worker–job mismatch. A recent study by the IMF examined job creation and destruction in six sectors of the Canadian economy over the period 1993–2004,[18] concluding that in those six sectors job destruction averaged about 9% of all existing jobs each year, while the annual rate of job creation was equal to about 11% of existing jobs. Thus, on average over this period, the net addition of new jobs was 2% per year. The study also showed that the rates of job creation and destruction vary across provinces. For example, over the period 1993–2004 the rate of job destruction in Alberta was about 11% per year while the rate of job creation was almost 14% per year. The comparable figures for Ontario were 9% (job destruction) and 10% (job creation). This evidence suggests that a great deal of "churning" of jobs and workers occurs in the economy. Much of this churning reflects the closing of old plants and the opening of new ones within the same industry. But it also reflects the growth of some industries (such as the rapid growth in oil sands production in Alberta) relative to others (such as the relatively slow growth of manufacturing in Ontario).

Modifying the classical model to allow for unemployment doesn't change the classical view that fiscal policy should not be actively used to combat recessions. Classical economists point out that raising the aggregate demand for goods (by increasing government purchases, for example) doesn't directly address the problem of unemployment arising from the mismatch that exists at the microeconomic level between workers and jobs. A better approach, in the classical view, is to eliminate barriers to labour market adjustment, such as regulations that raise businesses' costs of employing additional workers.

11.2 Money in the Classical Model

So far, we have focused on real shocks to the economy, such as productivity shocks and changes in government purchases. However, many macroeconomists believe that nominal shocks—shocks to money supply and money demand—also affect the business cycle. In the rest of the chapter, we discuss the role of money and monetary policy in the classical approach to the business cycle.

MONETARY POLICY AND THE ECONOMY

Monetary policy refers to the central bank's decisions about how much money to supply to the economy (see Chapter 7). Recall that the central bank (the Bank of Canada in Canada) can affect the money supply through open-market operations, in which it sells government bonds to the public in exchange for money (to reduce the money supply) or uses newly created money to buy bonds from the public (to increase the money supply). Other ways the central bank has for changing the money supply are discussed in detail in Chapter 14.

---

[18] See Ravi Balakrishnan, "Canadian Firm and Job Dynamics," *IMF Working Paper*, February 2008.

In Chapter 9, we examined the effects of changes in the money supply using the *IS–LM–FE* model (see Figure 9.9, p. 264). We found that after prices fully adjust, changes in the money supply are neutral: A change in the nominal money supply M causes the price level P to change proportionally, but a change in the money supply has no effect on real variables, such as output, employment, or the real interest rate. Our analysis left open the possibility that a change in the money supply would affect real variables, such as output, in the short run before prices had a chance to adjust. However, because classical economists believe that the price adjustment process is rapid, they view the period of time during which the price level is fixed—and money is not neutral—to be too short to matter. That is, for practical purposes, they view money as neutral for any relevant time horizon.

MONETARY NON-NEUTRALITY AND REVERSE CAUSATION

The prediction that money is neutral is a striking result of the classical model, but it seems inconsistent with the business cycle fact that money is a leading, procyclical variable. If an expansion of the money supply has no effect, why are expansions of the money supply typically followed by increased rates of economic activity? And, similarly, why are reductions in the money supply often followed by recessions?

Some classical economists have responded to these questions by pointing out that although increases in the money supply tend to precede expansions in output, this fact does not necessarily prove that economic expansions are caused by those increases. After all, just because people put snow tires on their cars before winter begins does not mean that winter is caused by putting on snow tires. Rather, people put snow tires on their cars because they know that winter is coming.

Many classical economists, including RBC theorists in particular, argue that the link between money growth and economic expansion is like the link between putting on snow tires and the onset of winter, a relationship they call reverse causation. Specifically, **reverse causation** means that expected future increases in output cause increases in the current money supply and that expected future decreases in output cause decreases in the current money supply, rather than the other way around. Reverse causation explains how money could be a procyclical and leading variable, even if the classical model is correct and changes in the money supply are neutral and have no real effects.

Reverse causation might arise in one of several ways. One possibility (which you are asked to explore in more detail in Analytical Problem 4 at the end of the chapter) is based on the idea that money demand depends on expected future output as well as current output. Suppose that a firm's managers expect business to pick up considerably in the next few quarters. To prepare for this expected increase in output, the firm may need to increase its current transactions (for example, to purchase raw materials, hire workers, and so on), and thus, it will demand more money now. If many firms do so, the aggregate demand for money may rise in advance of the actual increase in output.

Now, suppose that the Bank of Canada observes this increase in the demand for money. If the Bank does nothing, leaving the money supply unchanged, the increase in money demand will cause the equilibrium value of the price level to fall. As one of the Bank's objectives is stable prices, it will not like this outcome; to keep prices stable, instead of doing nothing, the Bank should provide enough extra money to the economy to meet the higher money demand. But if the Bank does so,

A CLOSER LOOK 11.1

MONEY AND ECONOMIC ACTIVITY AT CHRISTMASTIME

According to the reverse causation argument, the association of higher-than-normal money growth with economic booms and lower-than-normal money growth with recessions occurs because money growth responds to changes in output, not because money growth causes changes in output. An example of reverse causation is provided by the behaviour of money and economic activity at Christmastime, as shown in the accompanying table.

In Canada, both the money supply and retail sales grow rapidly in December. Clearly, the sharp increase in December retail sales (measured in real terms) results from Christmas gift buying and not from the December increase in the money supply. Thus, at Christmastime, higher economic activity must cause a higher money supply, rather than vice versa. Where does the extra money come from? The Bank of Canada regularly increases the money supply in December to meet the demands of merchants and shoppers for more money.

The existence of reverse causation from output to money in December does not rule out monetary non-neutrality, but it does mean that we have to be cautious in interpreting the positive association between money and output over the course of the business cycle. This association could arise because of monetary non-neutrality, reverse causation, or both. The relationship between money and economic activity at Christmastime shows that reverse causation does in fact occur and can be important.

Month	Growth of Money Supply	Growth of Real Retail Sales
November	1.4%	0.0%
December	3.3	23.0
January	−2.1	−39.1
February	−1.0	−6.4

Note: Growth rates are measured month to month.
Sources: Calculated using data on retail sales, measured in constant (2002) dollars (CANSIM II series v52367096) and data on the nominal money supply, M1 (CANSIM II series v37258). Both series are for 1997–2015 and are not seasonally adjusted. Statistics Canada, 2016.

the money supply will rise in advance of the increase in output, consistent with the business cycle fact—even though money is neutral.

Undoubtedly, reverse causation explains at least some of the tendency of money to lead output (see A Closer Look 11.1, "Money and Economic Activity at Christmastime," for a seasonal example). However, this explanation does not rule out the possibility that changes in the money supply also sometimes cause changes in output so that money is non-neutral. That is, a combination of reverse causation and monetary non-neutrality could account for the procyclical behaviour of money.

THE NON-NEUTRALITY OF MONEY: ADDITIONAL EVIDENCE

Because of reverse causation, the leading and procyclical behaviour of money cannot by itself establish that money is non-neutral. To settle the issue of whether money is neutral, we need additional evidence. One useful source is a historical analysis of monetary policy. For example, for the United States, the classic study is Milton Friedman and Anna J. Schwartz's *A Monetary History of the United States, 1867–1960*.[19] Using a variety of sources, including Federal Reserve policy statements and the journals and correspondence of monetary policymakers, Friedman and Schwartz carefully described and analyzed the causes of money supply fluctuations and the interrelation of money and other economic variables:

[19] Milton Friedman and Anna J. Schwartz's, *A Monetary History of the United States*, 1867–1960, Princeton University Press for NBER, 1963.

Throughout the near-century examined in detail, we have found that:

1. Changes in the behaviour of the money stock have been closely associated with changes in economic activity, [nominal] income, and prices.

2. The interrelation between monetary and economic change has been highly stable.

3. Monetary changes have often had an independent origin; they have not been simply a reflection of changes in economic activity. (p. 368)

The first two conclusions restate the basic business cycle fact that money is procyclical. The third conclusion states that reverse causation cannot explain the entire relationship between money and real income or output. Friedman and Schwartz focused on historical episodes in which changes in the supply of money were not (they argued) responses to macroeconomic conditions but instead resulted from other factors, such as gold discoveries (which affected money supplies under the gold standard), changes in monetary institutions, or changes in the leadership of the Federal Reserve. In the majority of these cases, "independent" changes in money growth were followed by changes in the same direction in real output. This evidence suggests that money is not neutral.

Christina Romer and David Romer,[20] of the University of California at Berkeley, have reviewed and updated the Friedman–Schwartz analysis. Although they disputed some of Friedman and Schwartz's interpretations, they generally agreed with the conclusion that money is not neutral. In particular, they argued that since 1960 half a dozen additional episodes of monetary non-neutrality have occurred in the United States. In Canada, many economists have attributed the depth of the 1990–1992 recession to restrictive monetary policy on the part of the Bank of Canada. More recently, the financial crisis that struck the world economy beginning in 2007 would seem to offer rather strong evidence of monetary non-neutrality. That crisis, which we earlier noted caused a fall in financial market liquidity akin to a fall in the money supply, is widely regarded as having precipitated a near-global recession. What's more, the coordinated response of central banks to expand the money supply is generally acknowledged to have been effective at averting an even deeper and prolonged contraction. Because of episodes like these (and similar experiences in other countries), most economists now believe that money is not neutral. If we accept that evidence, contrary to the prediction of the classical model, we are left with two choices: Either we must adopt a different framework for macroeconomic analysis or we must modify the classical model. In Section 11.3, we take the second approach and consider how monetary non-neutrality can be explained in a classical model.

11.3 THE MISPERCEPTIONS THEORY AND THE NON-NEUTRALITY OF MONEY

According to the classical model, prices do not remain fixed for any substantial length of time; for any relevant time horizon, output Y is equal to full-employment output $\overline{Y}$. In the IS–LM–FE model, the fact that the FE line is vertical and price responses are fast means that the effect of an LM shift caused by a change in the

---

[20] "Does Monetary Policy Matter? A New Test in the Spirit of Friedman and Schwartz," in Olivier Blanchard and Stanley Fischer, eds., NBER *Macroeconomics Annual*, Cambridge, Mass.: M.I.T. Press, 1989.

money supply M is to change only the price level P with no change in real output. Thus, money is neutral in the classical model.

For money to be non-neutral, a change in the money supply must somehow cause output to change. In this section, we extend the classical model to incorporate the assumption that producers have imperfect information about the general price level, and thus sometimes misinterpret changes in it as changes in the relative prices of the goods they produce. We demonstrate that the assumption that producers may misperceive the aggregate price level—the *misperceptions theory*— implies that real output may be sensitive to unexpected changes in prices. Thus, even though prices may adjust instantaneously, if monetary policy induces a misperception about what is happening to prices, then money is non-neutral for the period of time during which the misperception persists.

The misperceptions theory was originally proposed by Nobel laureate Milton Friedman and then rigorously formulated by another Nobel laureate, Robert E. Lucas, Jr., of the University of Chicago.[21] According to the **misperceptions theory**, *the aggregate quantity of output supplied rises above the full-employment level, $\overline{Y}$, when the aggregate price level, P, is higher than expected.*

To understand the misperceptions theory, let's think about an individual producer of a particular good, say, bread. For simplicity, consider a bakery owned and operated by one person, a baker. The baker devotes all his labour to making bread and earns all his income from selling bread. Thus, the price of bread is effectively the baker's nominal wage, and the price of bread relative to the general price level is the baker's real wage. When the relative price of bread increases, the baker responds to this increase in his current real wage by working more and producing more bread. Similarly, when the price of bread falls relative to the other prices in the economy, the baker's current real wage falls and he decreases the amount of bread he produces.

But how does an individual baker know whether the relative price of bread has changed? To calculate the relative price of bread, the baker needs to know both the nominal price of bread and the general price level. The baker knows the nominal price of bread because he sells bread every day and observes the price directly. However, the baker is probably not as well informed about the general price level because he observes the prices of the many goods and services he might want to buy less frequently than he observes the price of bread. Thus, in calculating the relative price of bread, the baker cannot use the actual current price level. The best he can do is use his previously formed expectation of the current price level to estimate the actual price level.

Suppose that before he observes the current market price of bread, the baker expected an overall inflation rate of 5%. How will he react if he then observes that the price of bread increases by 5%? The baker reasons as follows: I expected the overall rate of inflation to be 5%, and now I know that the price of bread has increased by 5%. This 5% increase in the price of bread is consistent with what I had expected. My best estimate is that all prices increased by 5%, and thus, I think the relative price of bread is unchanged. There is no reason to change my output.

The baker's logic applies equally to suppliers of output in the aggregate. Suppose that all suppliers expected the nominal price level to increase by 5% and that, in fact, all prices do increase by 5%. Then each supplier will estimate that his or

[21] See Friedman, "The Role of Monetary Policy," *American Economic Review*, March 1968, pp. 1–17. Lucas's formalization of Friedman was first presented in Lucas's article, "Expectations and the Neutrality of Money," *Journal of Economic Theory*, April 1972, pp. 103–124.

her relative price has not changed and will not change output. Hence, if expected inflation is 5%, an actual increase in prices of 5% will not affect aggregate output.

For a change in the nominal price of bread to affect the quantity of bread produced, the increase in the nominal price of bread must differ from the expected increase in the general price level. For example, suppose that the baker expected the general price level to increase by 5% but then observes that the price of bread rises by 8%. The baker then estimates that the relative price of bread has increased so that the real wage earned from baking is higher. In response to the perceived increase in the relative price, the baker increases the production of bread.

Again, the same logic applies to the economy in the aggregate. Suppose that everyone expects the general price level to increase by 5%, but instead it actually increases by 8%, with the prices of all goods increasing by 8%. Now all producers will estimate that the relative prices of the goods they make have increased, and hence the production of all goods will increase. Thus, a greater-than-expected increase of the price level will tend to raise output. Similarly, if the price level actually increases by only 2% when all producers expected a 5% increase, producers will think that the relative prices of their own goods have declined; in response, all suppliers reduce their output.

Thus, according to the misperceptions theory, the amount of output that producers choose to supply depends on the actual general price level as compared with the expected general price level. When the price level exceeds what was expected, producers are fooled into thinking that the relative prices of their own goods have risen, and they increase their output. Similarly, when the price level is lower than expected, producers believe that the relative prices of their goods have fallen, and they reduce their output. For a period of time, then, the baker in our example, and producers and workers in general, operate under a misperception that results in a distortion of their labour and production output levels; during this period they are neither maximizing utility nor maximizing profit.

This relation between output and prices is captured by the equation

$$Y = \overline{Y} + b(P - P^e), \tag{11.4}$$

where b is a positive number that describes how strongly output responds when the actual price level exceeds the expected price level.[22] Equation (11.4) summarizes the misperceptions theory by showing that output Y exceeds full-employment output $\overline{Y}$ when the price level P exceeds the expected price level P^e.

Equation (11.4) describes an **aggregate supply curve** (*AS*). An aggregate supply curve shows the relation between the aggregate quantity of goods produced Y and the price level P. We graph the aggregate supply curve described by Eq. (11.4) in Figure 11.5. The figure is drawn for the assumptions that the full-employment level of output is $\overline{Y}$ and that the public expects the price level will be P_0. Thus, in Figure 11.5, $P^e = P_0$. Point E helps us locate the aggregate supply curve. At E, we assume that the actual price level P equals the expected price level P^e so that (from Eq. 11.4) the amount of output supplied Y equals full-employment output $\overline{Y}$. The aggregate supply curve is sloped, illustrating that according to the misperceptions theory, if the actual price level proves to be different from the expected price level, then output will be different from the full-employment level. If, for example, the actual price level turns out to be P_1 then, from Eq. (11.4),

---

[22] How strongly output responds when the actual price level exceeds the expected price level (the size of b) depends on the slopes of labour demand and supply curves and the slope of the production function relating how changes in employment translate into changes in output.

The misperceptions theory holds that for a given value of the expected price level P^e, an increase in the actual price level P fools producers into increasing output. This relationship between output and the price level is shown by the short-run aggregate supply curve $SRAS$. The $SRAS$ in the figure is drawn for the assumption that the expected price level is P_0. If the actual price level is equal to the expected value, output is equal to $\overline{Y}$. This is point E. If the actual price level has a value such as P_1, and is thus greater than the expected value, then output is greater than $\overline{Y}$. This is point A. If the actual price level has a value such as P_2, and is thus less than the expected value, then output is less than $\overline{Y}$. This is point B. In the long run, the expected price level equals the actual price level so that output equals $\overline{Y}$. Thus, the long-run aggregate supply curve $LRAS$ is vertical at $Y = \overline{Y}$.

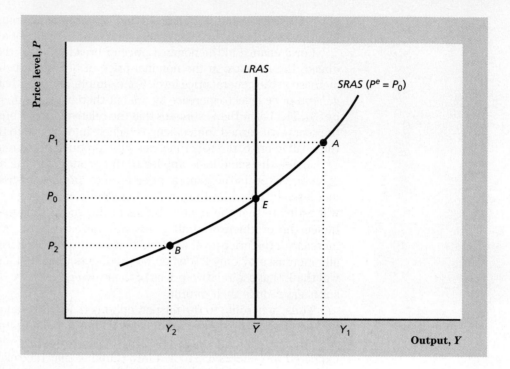

$Y_1 = \overline{Y} + b(P_1 - P_0)$. Assuming, as in Figure 11.5, that $P_1 > P_0$, then $Y_1 > \overline{Y}$ (this is shown as point A in the diagram). If, on the other hand, we assume the actual price level turns out to be P_2, then from Eq. (11.4), $Y_2 = \overline{Y} + b(P_2 - P_0)$. Since $P_2 < P_0$, then $Y_2 < \overline{Y}$ (this is shown as point B in the diagram). If we label the amount by which the actual price level differs from the expected price level as ΔP and the amount by which output differs from the full-employment level by ΔY, then these two examples each show that $\Delta Y = b\Delta P$. Rearranging this expression, we see the slope of the aggregate supply curve can be expressed as $\Delta P/\Delta Y = 1/b$. Thus, the aggregate supply curve is steep if b is small and is relatively flat if b is large.

The aggregate supply curve in Figure 11.6 is called the **short-run aggregate supply curve** ($SRAS$) because it applies only to the period of time when firms and individuals are operating at levels that do not maximize profit and utility. The $SRAS$ therefore shows only a temporary position. Eventually firms and individuals will adjust away from these positions and to positions shown by the $LRAS$ curve. The labelling of the curve in Figure 11.5 as $SRAS$ ($P^e = P_0$) is a reminder that the curve is drawn under the assumption that the expected price level is P_0. It therefore shows the amount of output firms are willing to produce at various price levels, given that they expected the price level to be P_0. In the long run, people learn what is actually happening to prices. As illustrated by Eq. (11.4), when in the long run the expected price level P^e adjusts to equal the actual price level P, then output returns to the full-employment level. In the long run, then, the supply of output will not depend on the price level and the **long-run aggregate supply curve** ($LRAS$) will be vertical at full-employment output $\overline{Y}$.[23]

[23] Since, like the FE line, the $LRAS$ curve is vertical at full-employment level of output $\overline{Y}$, any change in an economic variable that shifts the FE line to the right (left) will also shift the $LRAS$ curve to the right (left). See Summary table 11, Factors That Shift the Full-Employment (FE) Line (p. 255), for a list of factors that shift the $LRAS$ curve.

FIGURE 11.6

THE AGGREGATE SUPPLY
CURVE WITH ALTERNATIVE
EXPECTATIONS OF THE PRICE
LEVEL

$SRAS^0$ represents the short-run
aggregate supply curve that results
when individuals and firms expect
the price level to be P_0. When the
observed price level is equal to
what was expected, output equals
the full equilibrium level. For this
reason, $SRAS^0$ must intersect the
long-run aggregate supply (LRAS)
curve at price level P_0. $SRAS^1$ and
$SRAS^2$ represent short-run aggregate supply curves that result when
individuals and firms expect the
price level to be P_1 and P_2, respectively. The position of the $SRAS$
curve is determined by the
expected price level.

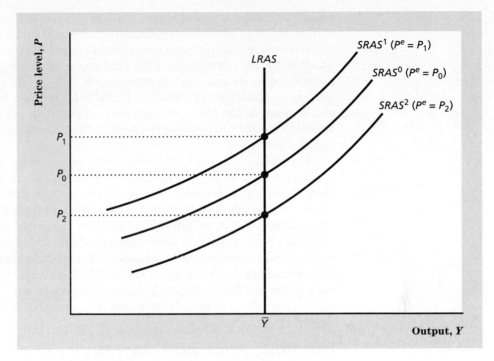

Figure 11.5 is a key diagram of macroeconomic analysis because it summarizes the implications of classical economists' beliefs about how output can vary
from its full-employment level. The diagram is important because it enables classical economists to explain how short-run economic expansions and contractions
arise. In Chapter 12 we'll see that this same diagram also summarizes the implications of Keynesian economists' understanding of how output can vary from the
full-employment level. What will be different in that chapter are the reasons
offered for why producers and workers may operate at levels that do not maximize
profit and utility.

The $SRAS$ curve in Figure 11.5 was drawn for a particular value of the expected
price level. There is a different $SRAS$ for every expected price level. Figure 11.6
shows alternative $SRAS$ curves, each based on a different expected price level. The
figure shows that had firms expected the price level to be P_1, the $SRAS$ would intersect the $LRAS$ at price level P_1. Had firms instead expected the price level to be P_2,
the $SRAS$ would intersect the $LRAS$ at price level P_2. In order to satisfy Eq. (11.4),
it must be the case that if the observed price level turns out to be what was expected,
the amount of output supplied must be shown to equal the full-employment output,
$\overline{Y}$. Thus, the $SRAS$ must always intersect the $LRAS$ at the expected price level.

AGGREGATE DEMAND AND AGGREGATE
SUPPLY EQUILIBRIUM

We are now ready to put together the aggregate demand curve (AD) developed at
the end of Chapter 9 with the aggregate supply curves ($SRAS$ and $LRAS$) defined
above. Recall from our discussion at the end of Chapter 9 that the aggregate
demand curve shows, for any price level P, the total quantity of goods and services
Y demanded by households, firms, and governments. Points on the AD curve

represent combinations of P and Y where the goods market (represented by IS) and the financial market (represented by LM) are both in equilibrium. Any change in the economy that increases the aggregate quantity of goods and services demand will shift the AD curve to the right (and any change that decreases the aggregate quantity of goods and services demand will shift the AD curve to the left). These include, as illustrated by Figures 9.12 and 9.13, changes to government purchases and changes to the size of the nominal supply of money. See Summary table 14, Factors That Shift the AD Curve (p. 275), for a complete list of variables that shift the AD curve.

The value of the AD–AS model, and the reason we introduce it rather than continue to rely solely on the IS–LM–FE model, stems from its ability to easily show the effects of relaxing a key assumption we employed in Chapters 9 and 10; namely, the assumption that what households and firms expect to see and experience in the future is not affected by what they see and experience today. We now relax that assumption and allow current events, including the announcements of policymakers, to influence how households and firms make plans with respect to their consumption, investment, and employment choices. The manner in which households and firms form their expectations about what the future may look like is a key ingredient of the AD–AS model. We turn to that issue next.

RATIONAL PRICE EXPECTATIONS

A question we have not yet answered is how the baker, and firms in general, form their expectation of the general price level, P^e. In terms of Figure 11.6, how do firms decide whether they should expect the general price level to be P_0, P_1, or P_2? In answering this question, economists suggest that it is sensible to assume the public calculates what is known as rational expectations. The hypothesis of **rational expectations** states that *the public's forecasts of various economic variables, including the price level, are based on reasoned and intelligent examination of available economic data.*[24] This is a very natural assumption to make: If it is in the best interests of individuals and firms to know relative prices, and if the general price level cannot be known with certainty, then it is sensible to assume that individuals and firms will form an expectation of the general price level based on a reasoned and intelligent examination of available economic data. What is the implication of this assumption?

To form an intelligent expectation of the general price level, firms and individuals are assumed to take into consideration what they observe about the state of the economy and what they have come to understand to be the nature of government economic policy. Figure 11.7 shows the $LRAS$ curve at the full-employment level of output, $\overline{Y}$. Suppose firms and individuals understand that the state of the economy is such that the aggregate demand curve is located at the position denoted AD^e. Firms and individuals might expect the aggregate demand curve to be in this position because of what they know about the state of the economy and because of what they have learned from listening to policymakers. For example, if the government has announced that a large and permanent income tax cut is to be

[24] The idea of rational expectations was first discussed by John F. Muth in his classic 1961 paper, "Rational Expectations and the Theory of Price Movements," *Econometrica*, July 1961, pp. 315–335. However, this idea was not widely used in macroeconomics until the new classical "revolution" of the early 1970s. In A Closer Look 11.2, "Are Price Forecasts Rational?" we discuss statistical studies that examine the question of the extent to which people form such rational price forecasts.

implemented, then it would be sensible for individuals and firms to conclude that this will spur consumption spending. If so, they would expect the aggregate demand curve to be positioned farther to the right than they might have believed had they not been told of the impending tax cut. Similarly, if news reports are full of stories of a stock market crash, we would expect firms and individuals to anticipate that the resulting decrease in wealth might cause investment and consumption spending to fall. In this case, they might anticipate that the aggregate demand curve will be positioned farther to the left than they might have thought in the absence of the news of a stock market crash.

Having formed an expectation of the level of aggregate demand, individuals and firms now need to draw the appropriate inference for the price level. If the aggregate demand curve is expected to be positioned at AD^e, then the only price level they should expect to observe is price level P_0. To see this is true, recall that the *SRAS* curve intersects the *LRAS* curve at the expected price level. Now suppose that rather than P_0, firms and individuals expect the price level to be P_1. If so, the relevant short-run aggregate supply curve is $SRAS^1$ in Figure 11.7. If the aggregate demand curve in fact ends up positioned at AD^e, output and the price level in the short run will be found at the intersection of AD^e and $SRAS^1$. This is point F, with output Y_2 and price level P_2. The expectation that the price level would end up being P_1 has therefore proven to be wrong. If, on the other hand, individuals and firms expect the price level to be P_0, then the relevant short-run aggregate supply curve is $SRAS^0$. Now if the aggregate demand curve in fact ends up positioned at AD^e, output and the price level in the short run will be found at the intersection of AD^e and $SRAS^0$. This is point E, with output and price level P_0. The expectation that the price level would end up being P_0 has now proven to be

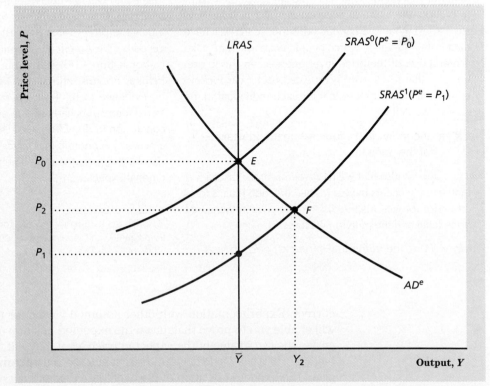

FIGURE 11.7

THE RATIONAL PRICE EXPECTATION

If, based on a reasoned and intelligent examination of available economic data, individuals understand that the state of the economy is such that the aggregate demand curve is located at the position denoted AD^e, then they should expect to observe price level P_0. On the basis of that expectation the short-run aggregate supply curve is $SRAS^0$. If the aggregate demand curve does indeed end up in the position denoted AD^e, expectations are fulfilled. If individuals and firms expect price level P_1, the short-run aggregate supply curve is $SRAS^1$. In this case, if the aggregate demand curve does indeed end up in the expected position AD^e, the expectation proves to be in error: In this case the observed price level is P_2 in the short run. Given the expected position of the aggregate demand curve, price level P_0 is the rational price expectation.

A CLOSER LOOK 11.2

ARE PRICE FORECASTS RATIONAL?

Most classical economists assume that people have rational expectations about future economic variables; that is, people make intelligent use of available information in forecasting variables that affect their economic decisions. The rational expectations assumption has important implications. For example, as we have demonstrated, if monetary non-neutrality is the result of temporary misperceptions of the price level and people have rational expectations about future prices, monetary policy is not able to affect the real economy systematically.

The rational expectations assumption is attractive to economists because it fits well with their presumption that people intelligently pursue their economic self-interests. If people's expectations are not rational, the economic plans that individuals make will not generally be as good as they could be. But the theoretical attractiveness of rational expectations is obviously not enough; economists would like to know whether people really do have rational expectations about important economic variables.

The rational expectations idea can be tested with data from surveys in which people are asked their opinions about the future of the economy. To illustrate how such a test would be conducted, suppose that we have data from a survey in which people were asked to make a prediction of the price level one year in the future. Imagine that this survey is repeated each year for several years. Now suppose that for each individual in the survey, we define

P_t^e = the individual's forecast, made in year $t - 1$, of the price level in year t.

Suppose also that we let P_t represent the price level that actually occurs in year t. Then the individual's forecast error for year t is the difference between the actual price level and the individual's forecast:

$P_t - P_t^e$ = the individual's forecast error in year t.

If people have rational expectations, these forecast errors should be unpredictable random numbers. However, if forecast errors are consistently positive or negative—meaning that people systematically tend to underpredict or overpredict the price level—expectations are not rational. If forecast errors have a systematic pattern—for example, if people tend to overpredict the price level when prices have been rising in the recent past—again, expectations are not rational.

Many statistical studies of price level forecasts made by consumers, journalists, academic economists, and others reject the rational expectations theory. A common finding is that people are too slow to incorporate new information into their forecasts. However, supporters of the rational expectations idea argue that the typical survey respondent isn't likely to think very hard about the forecast she gives to the survey-taker because she has little or no economic stake in the quality of her answer. They argue that a fairer test of rational expectations is to examine the expectations of people who do have a real stake in the quality of their forecasts—namely, professional economic forecasters. Michael Keane and David Runkle,[*] of the Federal Reserve Bank of Minneapolis, studied the U.S. price level forecasts of a panel of professional forecasters who have been surveyed by the American Statistical Association and the National Bureau of Economic Research since 1968. Perhaps not too surprisingly, Keane and Runkle found no evidence to refute the hypothesis that the professional forecasters had rational expectations. A plausible conclusion to draw from the research is that the greater a person's economic incentives to make good forecasts about the future, the more likely that person is to have rational expectations.

---

[*]"Testing the Rationality of Price Forecasts: New Evidence from Panel Data," *American Economic Review*, September 1990, pp. 714–735.

correct. Experimentation with other assumed values for the expected price level will enable you to prove that, given the expected position of the aggregate demand curve, the *only* value of the expected price level that will result in the expectation being accurate is P_0. Price level P_0 is said to be the **rational price expectation**, given the expected position of the aggregate demand curve.

Point E in Figure 11.7 defines a position of general equilibrium. The position of the AD curve reflects the level of planned spending by households, firms, and government, the central bank's plans for the money supply M. The price level is at a value (P_0) that households and firms expect to see in the future given what they understand to be the level of aggregate demand. The nominal wage W is such that the real wage W/P_0 clears the labour market at full-employment output $\overline{N}$, and this in turn means that real output Y is at its full-employment level $\overline{Y}$. The goods market, the financial market, and the labour market are all in equilibrium.

MONETARY POLICY AND THE MISPERCEPTIONS THEORY

Let's now re-examine the neutrality of money in the extended version of the classical model. This framework highlights an important distinction between anticipated and unanticipated changes in the money supply: Unanticipated changes in the nominal money supply have real effects, but anticipated changes are neutral and have no real effects.

Unanticipated Changes in the Money Supply

Suppose that the economy is initially in general equilibrium at point E in Figure 11.8, where AD^1 intersects $SRAS^1$. Here, output equals the full-employment level $\overline{Y}$, and the price level and the expected price level both equal P_1. Suppose that everyone expects the money supply and the price level to remain constant but that the Bank of Canada unexpectedly and without publicity increases the money supply by 10%. A 10% increase in the money supply shifts the AD curve up to AD^2, increasing the price level at each level of output by 10%. Given the expected price level P_1, the $SRAS$ curve remains unchanged, still passing through point E.

FIGURE 11.8

AN UNANTICIPATED INCREASE IN THE MONEY SUPPLY

If we start from the initial equilibrium at point E, an unanticipated 10% increase in the money supply shifts the AD curve up by 10% at each level of output, from AD^1 to AD^2. The short-run equilibrium is located at point F, the intersection of AD^2 and the short-run aggregate supply curve $SRAS^1$, where prices and output are both higher than at point E. Thus, an unanticipated change in the money supply is not neutral in the short run. In the long run, people learn the true price level and the equilibrium shifts to point H, the intersection of AD^2 and the long-run aggregate supply curve $LRAS$. In the long-run equilibrium at H, the price level has risen by 10% but output returns to its full-employment level $\overline{Y}$ so that money is neutral in the long run. As expectations of the price level rise from P_1 to P_3, the $SRAS$ curve also shifts up until it passes through H.

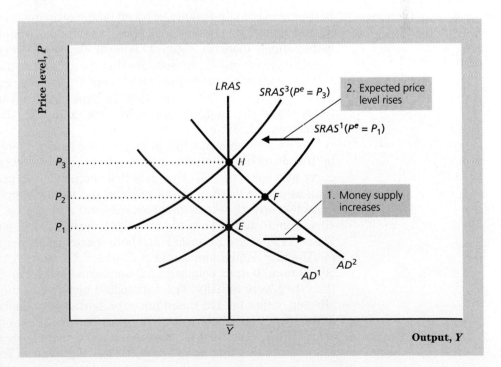

The increase in aggregate demand bids up the price level to the new equilibrium level P_2, where AD^2 intersects $SRAS^1$ (point F). In the new short-run equilibrium at F, the actual price level exceeds the expected price level and output exceeds $\overline{Y}$. Because the increase in the money supply leads to a rise in output, money is not neutral in this analysis.

The reason money is not neutral is that producers are fooled. Each producer misperceives the higher nominal price of his output as an increase in its relative price rather than as an increase in the general price level. Although output increases in the short run, producers are not better off. They end up producing more than they would have if they had known the true relative prices.

The economy cannot stay long at the equilibrium represented by point F because at F the actual price level P_2 is higher than the expected price level P_1. Over time, people obtain information about the true level of prices and adjust their expectations accordingly. The only equilibrium that can be sustained in the long run is one in which people do not permanently underestimate or overestimate the price level, so that the expected price level and the actual price level are equal. Graphically, when people learn the true price level, the relevant aggregate supply curve is the long-run aggregate supply curve $LRAS$, along which P always equals P^e. In Figure 11.8, the long-run equilibrium is point H, the intersection of AD^2 and $LRAS$. At H, output equals its full-employment level $\overline{Y}$, and the price level P_3 is 10% higher than the initial price level P_1. Because everyone now expects the price level to be P_3, a new $SRAS$ curve, $SRAS^3$, passes through H.

Thus, according to the misperceptions theory, an unanticipated increase in the money supply raises output and is not neutral *in the short run*. However, an unanticipated increase in the money supply is neutral in the long run, after people have learned the true price level.

Anticipated Changes in the Money Supply

In the extended classical model based on the misperceptions theory, the effects of an anticipated money supply increase are different from the effects of a surprise money supply increase. Figure 11.9 illustrates the effects of an anticipated money supply increase. Again, we suppose that the initial general equilibrium point is at E, where output equals its full-employment level and the actual and expected price levels both equal P_1. We assume that the Bank of Canada announces that it is going to increase the money supply by 10% and that the public believes this announcement.

As we have shown, a 10% increase in the money supply shifts the AD curve up by 10% at each level of output, from AD^1 to AD^2. However, in this case, the $SRAS$ curve also shifts up. The reason is that the public's expected price level rises as soon as people learn of the increase in the money supply. Suppose that people expect—correctly—that the price level will also rise by 10% so that P^e rises by 10%, from P_1 to P_2. Then the new $SRAS$ curve, $SRAS^2$, passes through point F in Figure 11.9, where Y equals $\overline{Y}$ and both the actual and expected price levels equal P_2. The new equilibrium is also at F, where AD^2 and $SRAS^2$ intersect. At the new equilibrium, output equals its full-employment level and prices are 10% higher than they were initially. The anticipated increase in the money supply has not affected output but has raised prices proportionally. Similarly, an anticipated drop in the money supply would lower prices but not affect output or other real variables. Thus, anticipated changes in the money supply are neutral in the short run as well as in the long run. The reason is that if producers know that increases in the

FIGURE 11.9

AN ANTICIPATED INCREASE IN THE MONEY SUPPLY

The economy is in initial equilibrium at point E when the Bank of Canada publicly announces a 10% increase in the money supply. When the money supply increases, the AD curve shifts upward by 10%, from AD^1 to AD^2. But in addition, because the increase in the money supply is anticipated by the public, the expected price level increases by 10%, from P_1 to P_2. Thus, the short-run aggregate supply curve shifts up from $SRAS^1$ to $SRAS^2$. The new short-run equilibrium, which is the same as the long-run equilibrium, is at point F. At F, output is unchanged at $\overline{Y}$ and the price level is 10% higher than in the initial equilibrium at E. Thus, an anticipated increase in the money supply is neutral in the short run as well as in the long run.

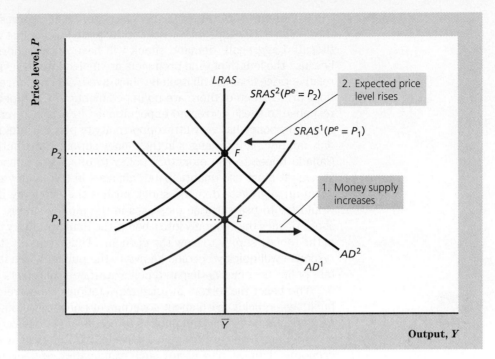

nominal prices of their products are the result of an increase in the money supply and do not reflect a change in relative prices, they will not be fooled into increasing production when prices rise.

RATIONAL EXPECTATIONS AND THE ROLE OF MONETARY POLICY

Our examples of the effects of changes in the money supply discussed in the previous section were strained by the fact that the central bank had no motivation for increasing the money supply. In both Figures 11.8 and 11.9 we began in long-run equilibrium. The bank has no motivation for increasing the money supply when the economy is at full employment. To better understand the role of monetary policy, we must first provide it with a rationale.

The different impact on output of anticipated and unanticipated changes is not limited to changes in aggregate demand resulting from changes in the money supply. Any unanticipated change in aggregate demand will affect output and any anticipated change in aggregate demand will be neutral. Thus, changes in aggregate demand resulting from changed expectations about future output or about future inflation, changes in wealth, changes in factors influencing the demand for money—indeed, changes in any of the long list of factors that shift the aggregate demand curve (these are listed in Summary table 14, p. 275)—will affect output if these changes are unanticipated. By recognizing these additional sources of unanticipated shocks to the position of the aggregate demand curve, have we constructed a case for employing monetary policy as a tool of stabilization policy? That is, can we argue that monetary policy should be used to offset the impact of shocks to aggregate demand?

Adherents of the classical model say no. Their case rests on three points. First, they believe that expectations about the price level adjust quickly. Thus, any unanticipated aggregate demand shock will have only a short-lived effect on output because the length of time producers are fooled into believing that there has been a relative price change will itself be short-lived. Second, once errors in price expectations are corrected, there are no impediments to the rapid adjustment of prices in response to these corrected expectations.[25] For these reasons, then, a corrective monetary policy has very little opportunity to play a useful role. Third, in this model only unanticipated changes in the money supply affect output. Thus, if the Bank of Canada hopes to use monetary policy to offset the impact of aggregate demand shocks, it must use unanticipated changes in the money supply. So, for example, when an aggregate demand shock pushes the economy into recession, the Bank would try to use surprise increases in the money supply to raise output; when a shock pushes the economy into a boom, the Bank would try to use surprise decreases in the money supply to slow the economy. Unfortunately, the pattern of this policy response will quickly become known to the public. When it does, the Bank's monetary policy becomes anticipated policy with neutral effects on real variables.

The belief that errors in price expectations are corrected rapidly and that the public will quickly learn about government policy rests on the assumption of rational expectations—that the public's forecasts of various economic variables, including the price level, are based on reasoned and intelligent examination of available economic data. As part of any such examination of data, firms and individuals are assumed to take into consideration what they observe about the state of the economy and what they have come to understand to be the nature of government economic policy. Aiding them in this effort are private economic forecasters. These people spend a good deal of time and effort trying to forecast macroeconomic variables, such as the money supply and the price level, and their forecasts are well publicized. If the economy changed in a way that caused expectations of the price level to change, forecasters would quickly understand and report this fact. Similarly, if the Bank of Canada began a pattern of raising the money supply in recessions and reducing it in booms, forecasters would also quickly understand and report this fact. As a result, the Bank's efforts to manipulate the money supply in order to offset the impacts of aggregate demand shocks would no longer be unanticipated, and the changes in the money supply would have no effect other than possibly causing instability in the price level. More generally, according to the misperceptions theory, to achieve any systematic change in the behaviour of output, the Bank must conduct monetary policy in a way that systematically fools the public. But there are strong incentives, in financial markets and elsewhere, for people to try to figure out what the Bank is doing. Thus, most economists believe that attempts by central banks to surprise the public in a systematic way cannot be successful.

PROPAGATING THE EFFECTS OF UNANTICIPATED CHANGES IN AGGREGATE DEMAND

The misperceptions theory implies that unanticipated changes in the money supply and other sources of shifts in the aggregate demand curve are non-neutral only because individual producers are temporarily fooled by the change in the price

---

[25] As we will see in Chapter 12, Keynesians dispute this claim. They emphasize the existence of "nominal rigidities" as reasons why, even when expectations are rational, output may remain away from the full-employment level for extended periods of time.

level these shocks cause. However, money supply data are available weekly and price level data are reported monthly. What's more, as we have noted, professional economic forecasters have a strong incentive to identify and correct misperceptions. For these reasons, we ought to expect output to deviate from its full-employment level for only very short periods of time. How, then, can adherents of the misperception model explain the observation reported in Chapter 8 that recessions have typically averaged 14 months and expansions have averaged 72 months? How can they explain such persistent deviations from the full-employment growth path?

To explain how changes in the money supply and other sources of shifts in the aggregate demand curve can have effects on output that last more than a few weeks, classical economists stress the role of propagation mechanisms. A **propagation mechanism** is an aspect of the economy that allows short-lived shocks to have relatively long-term effects on the economy.

An important example of a propagation mechanism is the behaviour of inventories. Consider a manufacturing plant that has both a normal level of monthly sales and a normal amount of finished goods in inventory that it tries to maintain. Suppose that an unanticipated stock market crash occurs and that this decreases aggregate demand. Prices fall below their expected level, and the manufacturing firm is fooled into believing that the relative price of its product has fallen. The firm wishes to reduce output, but because decreasing production sharply in a short period of time is costly, the firm will respond to the decrease in demand partly by producing fewer goods and partly by adding to its inventory of finished goods so that inventory stocks increase above normal levels.

Next month, suppose that everyone learns the true price level. Estimates of the expected price level are adjusted downward, and firms now understand that there has been no change in relative prices. As a result, the manufacturing firm's rate of sales returns to its normal level. Even so, the firm may continue to produce at a less-than-normal rate of production, as it needs to deplete its larger-than-normal inventory stock. The need to deplete inventories built up during an unexpected slowdown in sales illustrates a propagation mechanism that allows a short-lived shock (a stock market crash, in this case) to have a longer-term effect on the economy.

CHAPTER SUMMARY

1. Classical business cycle analysis utilizes the classical *IS–LM–FE* model along with the assumption that wages and prices adjust quickly to bring the economy into general equilibrium.

2. The real business cycle (RBC) theory is a version of the classical theory that emphasizes productivity shocks (shocks to the production function) as the source of business cycle fluctuations. In the classical *IS–LM* model, a temporary decline in productivity reduces the real wage, employment, and output while raising the real interest rate and the price level. The RBC

theory can account for the observed procyclical behaviour of employment, real wages, and labour productivity. However, the prediction of the RBC theory that prices are countercyclical is viewed by some as a failing.

3. The Solow residual is an empirical measure of total factor productivity, A, in the production function. It increases as a result of technical progress that increases the amount of output that can be produced with the same amounts of labour and capital services (inputs). However, the Solow residual also changes as a result of

changes in the utilization rates of capital and labour. The Solow residual is procyclical, at least partly because the utilization rates of capital and labour are procyclical. The procyclical behaviour of the utilization rate of labour may reflect labour hoarding, which occurs when firms continue to employ workers during recessions but use them less intensively or on tasks, such as maintenance, that do not contribute directly to measured output.

4. Classical business cycle analysis allows for other shocks to the economy besides changes in productivity, including changes in fiscal policy. According to the classical *IS–LM–FE* model, an increase in government purchases raises employment, output, the real interest rate, and the price level. Including both fiscal and productivity shocks in the classical model improves its ability to fit the data. Although fiscal policy can affect employment and output, classical economists argue that it should not be used to smooth the business cycle because the invisible hand leads the economy to an efficient outcome without government interference.

5. In the basic classical model (which includes RBC theory), money is neutral, which means that changes in the nominal money supply change the price level proportionally but do not affect real variables, such as output, employment, and the real interest rate.

6. The basic classical model can account for the procyclical and leading behaviour of money if there is reverse causation, that is, if anticipated changes in output lead to changes in the money supply in the same direction. For example, if firms increase their money demand in anticipation of future output increases, and if the central bank (to keep the price level stable) supplies enough extra money to meet the increase in money demand, increases in the money stock precede increases in output. This result holds even though changes in the money stock do not cause subsequent changes in output.

7. Examination of historical monetary policy actions suggests that money is not neutral. More recent experiences, such as the economic slowdown that accompanied the Bank of Canada's pursuit of price stability, also provide evidence for the view that money is not neutral.

8. In order to explain the apparent non-neutrality of money, adherents of the classical model have introduced the misperceptions theory. The misperceptions theory is based on the idea that producers have imprecise information about the current price level. According to the misperceptions theory, the amount of output supplied equals the full-employment level of output $\overline{Y}$ only if the actual price level equals the expected price level. When the price level is higher than expected, suppliers are fooled into thinking that the relative prices of the goods they supply have risen, so they supply a quantity of output that exceeds $\overline{Y}$. Similarly, when the price level is lower than expected, the quantity of output supplied is less than $\overline{Y}$.

9. The short-run aggregate supply curve (*SRAS*) based on the misperceptions theory slopes upward in describing the relation between output and the actual price level, with the expected price level held constant. In the long run, the price level equals the expected price level so that the supply of output equals $\overline{Y}$; thus, the long-run aggregate supply curve (*LRAS*) is a vertical line at the point where output equals $\overline{Y}$. In Chapter 12 we will see that an upward-sloping *SRAS* also summarizes the implications of the way in which Keynesian economists understand how output can vary from the full-employment level. While the explanations that Keynesians offer for the upward slope of the *SRAS* curve will differ from that offered by the misperceptions theory, the shape of the curve and the factors that cause it to shift will be the same.

10. When faced with uncertainty about the future, economists suggest that it is sensible to assume the public will calculate what is known as rational expectations. The hypothesis of rational expectations states that the public's forecasts of various economic variables, including the price level, are based on reasoned and intelligent examination of available economic data. To form an intelligent expectation of economic variables, the public is assumed to take into consideration what they observe about the state of the economy and what they have come to understand to be the nature of government economic policy.

11. The value of the *AD–AS* model, and the reason we introduce it rather than continue to rely

solely on the *IS–LM–FE* model, stems from its ability to easily show the effects of relaxing a key assumption we employed in Chapters 9 and 10; namely, the assumption that what households and firms expect to see and experience in the future is not affected by what they see and experience today. General equilibrium in the *AD–AS* model defines equilibrium values of all macroeconomic variables conditioned on what households and firms expect their values to be in the future.

12. With the upward-sloping *SRAS* curve based on the misperceptions theory, an unanticipated increase in the money supply increases output (and is, thus, non-neutral) in the short run. However, because the long-run aggregate supply curve is vertical, an unanticipated increase in the money supply does not affect output (and

so is neutral) in the long run. An anticipated increase in the money supply causes price expectations to adjust immediately and leads to no misperceptions about the price level; thus, an anticipated increase in the money supply is neutral in both the short and long runs.

13. According to the extended classical model based on the misperceptions theory, only surprise changes in the money supply can affect output. If the public has rational expectations about macroeconomic variables, including the money supply, the Bank of Canada cannot systematically surprise the public because the public will understand and anticipate the Bank's pattern of behaviour. Thus, classical economists argue that the Bank cannot systematically use changes in the money supply to affect output.

KEY DIAGRAM 10

The Upward-Sloping Short-Run Aggregate Supply Curve

The short-run aggregate supply curve shows the amount of output Y that firms are willing to offer for sale in the short run at various observed price levels P. The position of the $SRAS$ is determined by what firms and individuals expected the price level to be at the time they made their output decisions. The $SRAS$ intersects the long-run aggregate supply ($LRAS$) curve at the value of the expected price level P^e.

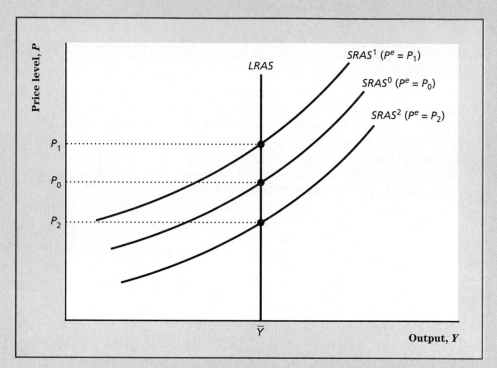

DIAGRAM ELEMENTS

- The actual price level, P, is on the vertical axis and the level of output, Y, is on the horizontal axis.

- The long-run aggregate supply ($LRAS$) curve shows the amount of output firms are willing to offer for sale in the long run, when all prices and wages have adjusted to profit- and utility-maximizing levels and so all markets clear. In the long run, output adjusts to the full-employment level regardless of the price level.

- The short-run aggregate supply ($SRAS$) curve shows the amount of output firms are willing to offer for sale in the short run. The position of the $SRAS$ is determined by the expected price level P^e. The value of P^e is determined by what firms and individuals expected the price level to be at the time they made their output decisions.

FACTORS THAT SHIFT THE CURVES

- The $SRAS$ curve intersects the $LRAS$ curve at the expected price level. As a result, an increase in the expected price level shifts the $SRAS$ up while a decrease in the expected price level shifts the $SRAS$ down.

- Any factor that increases full-employment output shifts both the short-run and the long-run aggregate supply curve to the right. When both curves shift they do so in a way that keeps the $SRAS$ intersecting the $LRAS$ at the expected price level. Factors that increase full-employment output include beneficial supply shocks or an increase in labour supply. An increase in government purchases, because it induces workers to supply more labour, also shifts the short-run and long-run aggregate supply curves to the right in the classical model.

ANALYSIS

- The *LRAS* curve is drawn as a vertical line at the full-employment level of output. In the long run, when all wages and prices adjust to profit- and utility-maximizing levels, the economy adjusts to this level of output regardless of the price level. The *SRAS* shows levels of output that result prior to the time when all wages and prices have adjusted to profit- and utility-maximizing levels. The short run, then, is only a temporary position. Eventually firms and individuals will adjust away from these positions and to positions shown by the *LRAS* curve.

- The *SRAS* can be expressed in equation form as $Y = \overline{Y} + b(P - P^e)$ where b is a positive number. The equation shows that when the observed price level P is equal to the expected price level P^e then output Y will equal the full-employment level. For this reason, the *SRAS* intersects the *LRAS* at the value of the expected price level. The diagram shows three alternative positions of the *SRAS*, each reflecting a different value for the expected price level. All *SRAS* curves show that when the observed price level rises above (falls below) the expected price level, then output rises above (falls below) the full-employment level of output.

- The fact that the observed price level P may differ from the expected price level P^e rests on the assumption that individuals and firms fail to adjust the prices at which they sell their goods and their labour to profit- and utility-maximizing levels. Economists offer a number of explanations for the failure of prices to immediately adjust to these profit- and utility-maximizing levels. Classical economists stress an explanation known as misperceptions theory. In Chapter 12 we will see that Keynesian economists stress other explanations. Although classical and Keynesian economists offer different explanations for why prices and wages fail to immediately adjust to profit- and utility-maximizing levels, both groups use the diagram of the short-run aggregate supply curve.

KEY DIAGRAM 11
The Misperceptions Version of the *AD–AS* Model

The misperceptions version of the *AD–AS* model shows how the aggregate demand for output and the aggregate supply of output interact to determine the price level and output in a classical model in which producers misperceive the aggregate price level.

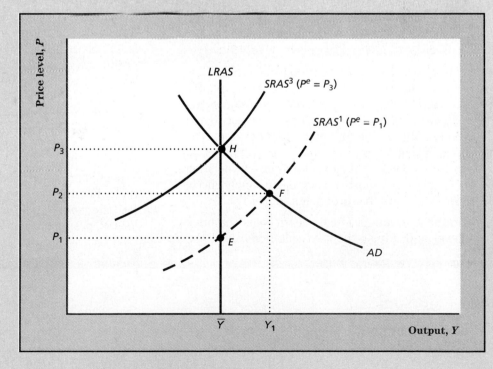

DIAGRAM ELEMENTS

- The actual price level, P, is on the vertical axis, and the level of output, Y, is on the horizontal axis.

- The aggregate demand (*AD*) curve shows the aggregate quantity of output demanded at each price level. It is identical to the *AD* curve in Key Diagram 8 (p. 281). The aggregate amount of output demanded is determined by the intersection of the *IS* and *LM* curves (see Figure 9.10, p. 269). An increase in the price level, P, reduces the real money supply, shifting the *LM* curve up and to the left, and so reduces the aggregate quantity of output demanded. Thus, the *AD* curve slopes downward.

- The misperceptions theory is based on the assumption that producers have imperfect information about the general price level and hence do not know precisely the relative prices of their products. When producers misperceive the price level, an increase in the general price level above the expected price level fools suppliers into thinking that the relative prices of their goods have increased, so all suppliers increase output. The short-run aggregate supply (*SRAS*) curve shows the aggregate quantity of output supplied at each price level, with the expected price level held constant. Because an increase in the price level fools producers into supplying more output, the short-run aggregate supply curve slopes upward, as shown by $SRAS^1$.

- The short-run aggregate supply curve, $SRAS^1$, is drawn so that the expected price level, P^e, equals P_1. When the actual price level equals the expected price level, producers are not fooled and so supply the full-employment level of output, $\overline{Y}$. Therefore, at point E, where the actual price level equals the expected price level (both equal P_1), the short-run aggregate supply curve, $SRAS^1$, shows that producers supply $\overline{Y}$.

- In the long run, producers learn about the price level and adjust their expectations until the actual price level equals the expected price level. Producers then supply the full-employment level of output, $\overline{Y}$, regardless of the price level. Thus, the long-run aggregate supply (*LRAS*) curve is vertical at $Y = \overline{Y}$.

FACTORS THAT SHIFT THE CURVES

- The aggregate quantity of output demanded is determined by the intersection of the *IS* curve and the *LM* curve. At a constant price level, any factor that shifts the *IS–LM* intersection to the right increases the aggregate quantity of goods demanded and, thus, also shifts the *AD* curve to the right. Factors that shift the *AD* curve are listed in Summary table 14 (p. 275).

- Any factor that increases full-employment output, $\overline{Y}$, shifts both the short-run and the long-run aggregate supply curves to the right.

- An increase in the expected price level shifts the short-run aggregate supply curve up.

ANALYSIS

- The short-run equilibrium is at the intersection of the *AD* curve and the *SRAS* curve. For example, if the expected price level is P_1, the *SRAS* curve is $SRAS^1$, and the short-run equilibrium is at point F. At F, output, Y_1, is higher than the full-employment level, $\overline{Y}$, and the price level, P_2, is higher than the expected price level, P_1. As producers obtain information about the price level, the expected price level is revised upward, which shifts the *SRAS* curve up. The long-run equilibrium is at point H, where the long-run aggregate supply (*LRAS*) curve intersects the *AD* curve. In the long run, (1) output equals $\overline{Y}$, and (2) the actual price level equals the expected price level (both equal P_3). In the long run, when the expected price level has risen to P_3, the short-run aggregate supply curve, $SRAS^3$, passes through H.

KEY TERMS

aggregate supply curve, p. 371
labour hoarding, p. 362
long-run aggregate supply curve, p. 372
misperceptions theory, p. 370
nominal shocks, p. 354
productivity shocks, p. 354
propagation mechanism, p. 381
rational expectations, p. 374
rational price expectation, p. 376
real business cycle theory, p. 354
real shocks, p. 354
reverse causation, p. 367
short-run aggregate supply curve, p. 372
Solow residual, p. 360

KEY EQUATION

$$Y = \overline{Y} + b(P - P^e) \qquad (11.4)$$

The short-run aggregate supply curve, based on the misperceptions theory, indicates that the aggregate amount of output supplied, Y, equals full-employment output, $\overline{Y}$, when the price level, P, equals the expected price level, P^e. When the price level is higher than expected $(P > P^e)$, output exceeds $\overline{Y}$; when the price level is lower than expected $(P < P^e)$, output is less than $\overline{Y}$.

REVIEW QUESTIONS

1. What main feature of the classical *IS–LM–FE* model distinguishes it from the Keynesian *IS–LM–FE* model? Why is the distinction of practical importance?
2. What are the two main components of any theory of the business cycle? Describe these two components for the real business cycle theory.
3. Define *real shock* and *nominal shock*. What type of real shock do real business cycle theorists consider the most important source of cyclical fluctuations?
4. What major business cycle facts does the RBC theory explain successfully? Does it explain any business cycle facts less well?
5. What is the Solow residual and how does it behave over the business cycle? What factors cause the Solow residual to change?
6. What effects does an increase in government purchases have on the labour market, according to the classical theory? What effects does it have on output, the real interest rate, and the price level? According to classical economists, should fiscal policy be used to smooth out the business cycle? Why, or why not?

7. In the context of the relationship between the money supply and real economic activity, what is meant by reverse causation? Explain how reverse causation could occur. What business cycle fact is it intended to explain?
8. According to the misperceptions theory, what effect does an increase in the price level have on the amount of output supplied by producers? Explain. Does it matter whether the increase in the price level was expected?
9. What conclusion does the basic classical model (with no misperceptions of the price level) allow about the neutrality or non-neutrality of money? In what ways is this conclusion modified by the extended classical model based on the misperceptions theory?
10. Define *rational expectations*. According to the classical model, what implications do rational expectations have for the ability of the central bank to use monetary policy to smooth business cycles?

NUMERICAL PROBLEMS

1. In a certain economy the production function is

$$Y = A(100N - 0.5N^2),$$

where Y is output, A is productivity, and N is total hours worked. The marginal product of labour associated with this production function is

$$MPN = A(100 - N).$$

Initially, $A = 1.0$, but a beneficial productivity shock raises A to 1.1.

a. The supply of labour is

$$NS = 45 + 0.1w,$$

where w is the real wage. Find the equilibrium levels of output, hours worked, and the real wage before and after the productivity shock. Recall (from Chapter 3) that the *MPN* curve is the same as the labour demand curve, with the real wage replacing the *MPN*.

b. Repeat part (a) if the labour supply is

$$NS = 10 + 0.8w.$$

c. Some studies show that the real wage is only slightly procyclical. Assume for the sake of argument that this finding is correct. Would a calibrated RBC model fit the facts better if the labour supply is relatively insensitive to the real wage, or if it is relatively sensitive? Justify your answer diagrammatically and relate it to your answers to parts (a) and (b).

2. A closed economy is described as follows:

Desired consumption $\quad C^d = 600 + 0.5(Y - T) - 50r$
Desired investment $\quad\quad I^d = 450 - 50r$
Real money demand $\quad\quad L = 0.5Y = 100i$
Full-employment output $\;\bar{Y} = 2210$
Expected inflation $\quad\quad\;\; \pi^e = 0.05$

In this economy, the government always has a balanced budget, so $T = G$, where T is total taxes collected.

a. Suppose that $M = 4320$ and $G = 150$. Use the classical *IS–LM* model to find the equilibrium values of output, the real interest rate, the price level, consumption, and investment. (*Hint:* In the classical model, output always equals its full-employment level.)

b. The money supply rises to 4752. Repeat part (a). Is money neutral?

c. With the money supply back at 4320, government purchases and taxes rise to 190. Repeat part (a). Assume, for simplicity, that $\bar{Y}$ is fixed (unaffected by G). Is fiscal policy neutral in this case? Explain.

3. Consider the following closed economy:

Desired consumption $\quad C^d = 1275 + 0.5(Y - T) - 200r$
Desired investment $\quad\quad I^d = 900 - 200r$
Real money demand $\quad\quad L = 0.5Y - 200i$
Full-employment output $\;\bar{Y} = 4600$
Expected inflation $\quad\quad\;\; \pi^e = 0$

a. Suppose that $T = G = 450$ and that $M = 9000$. Find an equation describing the *IS* curve. (*Hint:* Set desired national saving and desired investment equal, and solve for the relationship between r and Y.) Find an equation describing the *LM* curve. (*Hint:* Set real money supply and real money demand equal, and again solve for the relationship between r and Y, given P.) Finally, find an equation for the aggregate demand curve. (*Hint:* Use the *IS* and *LM* equations to find a relationship between Y and P.) What are the equilibrium values of output, consumption, investment, the real interest rate, and the price level? Assume that there are no misperceptions about the price level.

b. Suppose that $T = G = 450$ and that $M = 4500$. What is the equation for the aggregate demand curve now? What are the equilibrium values of output, consumption, investment, the real interest rate, and the price level? Assume that full-employment output $\bar{Y}$ is fixed.

c. Repeat part (b) for $T = G = 330$ and $M = 9000$.

4. A closed economy has the following *AD* and *AS* curves:

AD curve $\quad\quad Y = 300 + 30(M/P)$
AS curve $\quad\quad Y = \bar{Y} + 10(P + P^e)$

Here, $\bar{Y} = 500$ and $M = 400$.

a. Suppose that $P^e = 60$. What are the equilibrium values of the price level P and output Y? (*Hint:* The solutions for P in this part and in part (b) are multiples of 10.)

b. An unanticipated increase raises the money supply to $M = 700$. Because the increase is unanticipated, P^e remains at 60. What are the equilibrium values of the price level P and output Y?

c. The Bank of Canada announces that the money supply will be increased to $M = 700$, which the public believes. Now what are the equilibrium values of the price level P, the expected price level P^e, and output Y?

5. Output in an economy is given by the production function $Y = AK^{0.3}N^{0.7}$, where Y is output, A measures productivity, the capital stock K is fixed at 30, and employment N is fixed at 100. Output equals 100 in the year 2011 and equals 105 in 2012.

a. Find the Solow residual in the years 2011 and 2012, and its growth rate between those two years.

b. What is the relationship between the growth in the Solow residual between 2011 and 2012 and the growth in productivity (as measured by the parameter A) in the same years? Assume that the rates of utilization of capital and labour remain unchanged.

c. Repeat part (b) under the assumption that utilization of labour increases by 3% between 2011 and 2012. You will have to modify the production function along the lines of Eq. (11.2).

d. Repeat part (b) under the assumption that the utilization rates of both labour and capital increase by 3% between 2011 and 2012.

6. Try the following experiment: Flip a coin 50 times, keeping track of the results. Think of each "heads" as a small positive shock that increases output by one unit; similarly, think of each "tails" as a small negative shock that reduces output by one unit. Let the initial value of output Y be 50, and graph the level of output over time as it is hit by the "positive" and "negative" shocks (coin flips). For example, if your first four flips are three heads and a tail, output takes the values 51, 52, 53, and 52. After 50 flips, have your small shocks produced any large cycles in output?

7. In a particular economy, the labour force (the sum of employed and unemployed workers) is fixed at 10 million. In this economy, each month 1% of the workers who were employed at the beginning of the month lose their jobs, and 19% of the workers who were unemployed at the beginning of the month find new jobs.
   a. The January unemployment rate is 8%. For the rates of job loss and job finding given, what will the unemployment rate be in February? in March?
   b. In April an adverse productivity shock raises the job loss rate to 3% of those employed. The job loss rate returns to 1% in May, while the job finding rate remains unchanged at 19% throughout. Find the unemployment rate for April, May, June, and July.

ANALYTICAL PROBLEMS

1. The discovery of a new technology increases the expected future marginal product of capital.
   a. Use the classical *IS–LM–FE* model to determine the effect of the increase in the expected future *MPK* on current output, the real interest rate, employment, real wages, consumption, investment, and the price level. Assume that expected future real wages and future incomes are unaffected by the new technology. Assume also that current productivity is unaffected.
   b. Find the effects of the increase in the expected future *MPK* on current output and prices from the *AD–AS* diagram based on the misperceptions theory. What accounts for the difference with part (a)?
2. Use the classical *IS–LM–FE* model to analyze the effects of a permanent increase in government purchases of 100 per year (in real terms). The increase in purchases is financed by a permanent increase in lump-sum taxes of 100 per year.
   a. Begin by finding the effects of the fiscal change on the labour market. How does the effect of the permanent increase in government purchases of 100 compare with the effect of a temporary increase in purchases of 100?
   b. Because the tax increase is permanent, assume that at any constant levels of output and the real interest rate consumers respond by reducing their consumption each period by the full amount of the tax increase. Under this assumption, how does the permanent increase in government purchases affect desired national saving and the *IS* curve?

c. Use the classical *IS–LM–FE* model to find the effects of the permanent increase in government purchases and taxes on output, the real interest rate, and the price level in the current period. What happens if consumers reduce their current consumption by less than 100 at any level of output and the real interest rate?
3. Consider a business cycle theory that combines the classical *IS–LM–FE* model with the assumption that temporary changes in government purchases are the main source of cyclical fluctuations. How well would this theory explain the observed cyclical behaviour of each of the following variables? Give reasons for your answers.
   a. Employment
   b. The real wage
   c. Average labour productivity
   d. Investment
   e. The price level
4. This problem asks you to work out in more detail the example of reverse causation described in the text. Suppose that firms that expect to increase production in the future have to increase their current transactions (for example, they may need to purchase more raw materials). For this reason, current real money demand rises when expected future output rises.
   a. Under the assumption that real money demand depends on expected future output, use the classical *IS–LM–FE* model to find the effects of an increase in expected future output on the current price level. For simplicity, assume that any effects of the increase in expected future output on the labour market or on desired saving and investment are small and can be ignored.
   b. Suppose that the Bank of Canada wants to stabilize the current price level. How will the Bank respond to the increase in expected future output? Explain why the Bank's response is an example of reverse causation.
5. Two countries called East and West agree to unify. The real value of full-employment output in East is 1 trillion widgets, and in West it is 2 trillion widgets. The combined full-employment output of the unified country is expected to be the sum of the two full-employment outputs, or 3 trillion widgets.

   Real money demand in the West is 10% of West's real output and will remain so after unification. In the East, people do not have access to financial instruments, such as stocks and bonds, and so are forced to save in the form of money. As a result, real money demand in the East is 40% of East's real output. However, after unification, Easterners will have access to a full range of financial assets, and thus, their real money demand will drop to 10% of output.

The unified country will use only the West's currency. As part of the unification plan, the West central bank has agreed to print new Western currency and trade it for Eastern currency, which will be destroyed. At the initial price levels, the total real value of the Western currency received by Easterners equals the total real value of the Eastern currency they give up.

Use the classical *IS–LM–FE* model to find the effects on post-unification output and prices of the currency swap. Give a quantitative estimate of the effect on the price level (measured in the Western currency). Qualitatively, does your answer change if you use the *AD–AS* model based on the misperceptions theory? What can West's central bank do to offset the effects of the currency swap on the price level?

6. Starting from a situation with no government spending and no taxes, the government introduces a foreign aid program (in which domestically produced goods are shipped abroad) and pays for it with a temporary 10% tax on current wages. Future wages are untaxed.

What effects will the temporary wage tax have on labour supply? Use the classical *IS–LM–FE* model to find the effects of the fiscal change on output, employment, the (before-tax) real wage, the real interest rate, and the price level.

Chapter 12

Keynesian Business Cycle Analysis: Non–Market-Clearing Macroeconomics

In Chapter 11, we presented the classical, or market-clearing, approach to business cycle analysis. Adherents of the classical model emphasize the rapid adjustment of wages and prices. This assumption raises the question of how classical economists can explain why the economy is not always in full equilibrium and, therefore, why the economy experiences business cycles. One response is the development of a variant of the classical approach, known as the real business cycle (RBC) model. RBC theorists argue that it is real shocks—shocks that affect the full-employment level of output—rather than nominal shocks (to which, they argue, the economy adjusts rapidly) that are the cause of business cycle fluctuations. The emphasis on real shocks is awkward for the classical approach because it suggests that changes in the money supply—a nominal shock—cannot be a source of business cycles. Yet there appears to be ample evidence that monetary shocks do in fact have effects on real output.

Another variant within the classical approach, the misperceptions theory, was developed to explain how nominal shocks may cause business cycle fluctuations even though nominal wages and prices respond quickly. In that approach, changes in nominal prices cause misperceptions about the general price level and so cause firms to be fooled into believing there have been changes in relative prices. Believing relative prices have changed, firms alter their output decisions, causing the economy to move away from the full-employment level of output.

An essential part of the misperceptions theory is an explanation of how expectations of price changes are determined. This explanation is provided by the theory of rational expectations, the idea that the public's forecast of economic variables, like the price level, is based on a reasoned and intelligent examination of available information. Together, the misperceptions theory and the theory of rational expectations provide classical economists with an explanation of how the output response of firms is affected by unexpected changes in the general price level. In Chapter 11 we combined the misperceptions theory and the theory of rational expectations to present the theory of aggregate supply (AS) favoured by classical economists, which, when combined with the theory of aggregate demand (AD) developed in Chapter 9, provided a complete model of AD–AS. An important result predicted by the classical economist's version of the AD–AS model is that only unanticipated shifts in the *AD* curve—including shifts initiated by fiscal and monetary policy changes—have real effects.

Keynesians accept much of the classical model. Like classical economists, Keynesians recognize that real shocks contribute to the business cycle by causing shifts in the full-employment level of output. Keynesians also believe, as classical economists do, that the public's forecast of economic variables, including the price level, is based on a reasoned and intelligent examination of available information. Keynesians, then, accept the theory of rational expectations as a model of how expectations are formed. Keynesians, however, are less optimistic about the ability of free-market economies to respond quickly and efficiently to nominal price shocks. One of the central ideas of the Keynesian approach is that wages and prices are "rigid" or "sticky" and do not adjust quickly to their market-clearing levels.

To classical economists, the idea that wages and prices might be rigid or sticky seems odd. After all, argued the classicals, wages and prices are not simply "given" to the economy but are the results of decisions made by millions of individuals and firms. If excessively high wages are causing unemployment, why don't unemployed workers offer to work for lower wages until firms are willing to hire them? If prices are not at the levels at which quantities supplied equal quantities demanded, why don't firms just change their prices? In effect, classical economists challenged Keynesian economists to incorporate the idea of rigid or sticky wages and prices into a cohesive explanation of the business cycle. That challenge required Keynesians to develop a model of aggregate supply different from the model based on misperceptions used by classical economists.

Keynesian researchers accepted this challenge and developed a number of theories to justify their central idea of rigid or sticky wages and prices. We begin this chapter by presenting the Keynesian idea of **nominal-wage rigidity**. We then show what this idea implies for a model of aggregate supply (*AS*). Finally, we combine the Keynesian model of aggregate supply with the theory of aggregate demand (*AD*) developed in Chapter 9 to provide the Keynesian version of the complete model of *AD–AS*. Using that model, we show how Keynesians answer the two central questions about business cycles, namely: What causes business cycles and what should policymakers do about them?

12.1 NOMINAL-WAGE RIGIDITY

Keynesian analysis of the source of the business cycle stresses the role played by wage and price rigidities in causing shocks to have prolonged effects on real variables such as output and employment. We begin with an explanation of why nominal wages might be slow to adjust ("sticky") to changes in labour demand and supply. As we begin this discussion it will be useful to recall from Chapter 3 that the *nominal* wage is the wage paid by firms to employees measured in today's dollars. The *real* wage, w, equals the nominal wage, W, divided by the price level, P.

THE SHORT-RUN AGGREGATE SUPPLY CURVE WITH LABOUR CONTRACTS

In Canada, most labour contracts specify employment conditions and nominal wages for a period of one to three years into the future. Thus, contracts are signed that commit both sides to a nominal wage before the quantity of labour supplied and demanded is known. Although labour contracts specify the nominal-wage rate, they usually do not specify the total amount of employment. Instead, employers unilaterally decide how many hours will be worked and whether workers will be laid off. A number of points about such contracts need to be emphasized.

First, labour contracts specify the *nominal* as opposed to the *real* wage. This seems odd when we recall our discussion of the labour market in Chapter 3. There we showed labour supply and demand to both be functions of the real wage. An increase in the real wage leads to an increase in the amount of labour supplied by employees and a decrease in the amount of labour demanded by firms. Changes in the nominal wage are important to employees and firms only to the extent that they result in changes in the real wage. Why, then, don't labour contracts specify the real wage to be paid? Second, the contracts specify employment conditions and nominal wages for an extended period. Given the frequency with which unanticipated events affect the economy, why would firms and employees choose to limit their flexibility to respond to these events by changing the wage so infrequently?

The answer to both of these questions relies on the observation that it is costly for employees and firms to negotiate wage settlements. Thus, while there are advantages to renegotiating the wage contract so as to take into account unanticipated labour market developments, negotiations are typically time consuming and expensive. For this reason, contracts typically last for years rather than months. The negotiation of real, as opposed to nominal, wages is also made difficult by the fact that when negotiating the wage contract, the two sides have a different idea of what is the appropriate real wage. Each firm defines the real wage that is relevant to it as the nominal wage it pays its workers relative to the price of its own output. Employees, on the other hand, define the real wage that is relevant to them as the nominal wage they receive relative to the general price level—the average price of the goods and services they purchase with their wages. Even if each firm could convince its employees to tie the real wage to the firm's product price, there are monitoring costs. Suppose, for example, that the firm convinced employees to accept profit-sharing as a form of compensation. Such a contract ties compensation to the performance of the firm in a way similar to defining the real wage relative to the product price. Such a contract, however, requires that employees be willing to accept the firm's calculations of revenues and profits or to set up processes that enable them to monitor the firm's calculations and choices.[1] Employees and firms alike may find it less costly to negotiate relatively simple contracts.

A third, and final, important point to be emphasized about the nature of labour contracts is the fact that they commit both sides to a nominal wage one to three years into the future. Thus, contracts are signed that commit both sides to a nominal wage before the future state of the economy is known. The implication of this is that both sides in the negotiation must form an expectation of what they believe will happen to prices during the period of the contract. In this way they each determine what nominal wage they will need to agree upon in order to give them the real wage they hope will maximize their utility (employees) and profits (firms) during the period of the contract. Keynesians, like classical economists, believe that employees' and firms' forecasts of various economic variables, including the price level, are based on reasoned and intelligent examinations of available economic data. Such examinations of the available economic data will take into consideration

---

[1] Hockey fans will recognize this issue as being part of the long-running dispute between team owners and the NHL Players' Association. Team owners want to tie salaries to revenues but players do not trust the owners' claims of poverty. The costs of negotiating such contracts are illustrated by the hockey season shutdowns in 1992, 2004, and 2012.

what they observe about the state of the economy and what they have come to understand to be the nature of government economic policy. Employees and firms, then, calculate rational price expectations, just as we assumed in Chapter 11. Based on this description of the wage-setting process and this understanding of how forecasts of future prices are determined, Keynesians have developed a theory of aggregate supply.

As a preliminary step to understanding the Keynesian model of aggregate supply based on the idea of nominal-wage rigidity, we refer to Figure 12.1 representing the model of the labour market first described in Chapter 3. Assume that firms and employees form an expectation that the price level P will have the value P^e during the period of the labour contract. Based on that expectation, firms, taking into consideration the marginal productivity of their employees, identify labour demand curve ND as representing the combinations of real wage and employment that will maximize their profits. Similarly, based on their expectation that the price level will have the value P^e during the period of the labour contract, workers determine labour supply curve NS as representing the combinations of real wage and employment that will maximize their utility.

Firms and employees negotiate a contract that says a fixed nominal wage W_0 will be paid for the duration of the agreement. The real-wage firms expect to pay, and the real-wage employees expect to receive, is W_0/P^e. That real wage clears the labour market and establishes a full-employment level of employment $\overline{N}$. This is described by point E in Figure 12.1. As long as the price level that is observed during the period of the nominal-wage contract is equal to what both sides of the wage negotiation expected to observe when they negotiated the contract (P^e), the real wage will clear the labour market and full employment will result. With employment at its full-employment level, real output in the economy will be at its full-employment level $\overline{Y}$.

Suppose that during the term of the contract the price level turns out to be P_1, which is higher than what was expected. Because the nominal wage is fixed at W_0 by the negotiated contract, the real wage will be different from value W_0/P^e, the

FIGURE 12.1

THE LABOUR MARKET WITH A STICKY NOMINAL WAGE

ND and *NS* identify the positions of labour demand and labour supply curves based on what firms and workers expect the price level to be during the period of the nominal-wage contract. If the price expectation proves correct, we obtain point *E* and employment will be at its full employment level $\overline{N}$. If the price level is higher or lower than was expected when the wage contract was signed, employment will differ from $\overline{N}$. In these cases there is disequilibrium in the labour market until such time as the wage contract can be renegotiated.

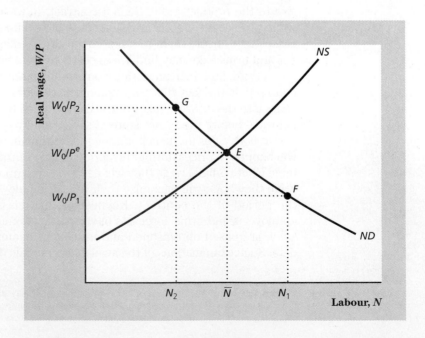

real wage that both firms and employees hoped would be the result of their negotiations over the nominal wage. Since the observed price level (P_1) is higher than what was expected (P^e), then the real wage will be W_0/P_1, which is lower than the market-clearing real wage W_0/P^e. Able to now employ labour at a lower real wage, firms will desire to hire additional workers. In Figure 12.1, point F on the labour demand curve ND identifies the profit-maximizing level of employment for the firm. Employment therefore rises to N_1, above the full-employment level $\overline{N}$, and output Y rises above the full-employment level of output $\overline{Y}$.

Now suppose that during the term of the contract the price level turns out to be P_2, which is lower than what was expected. With the nominal wage fixed at W_0 by the negotiated contract, the real wage, W_0/P_2, will now be higher than the market-clearing real wage W_0/P^e. Firms now find workers to be more expensive than expected and so will desire to reduce the size of their workforce. In Figure 12.1, point G on the labour demand curve ND identifies the profit-maximizing level of employment for the firm. Employment therefore falls to N_2, below the full-employment level $\overline{N}$, and output falls to a level below the full-employment level of output $\overline{Y}$.

As is clear in Figure 12.1, levels of employment identified by points F and G are positions of disequilibrium. At these points labour demand ND does not equal labour supply NS, so that eventually adjustment must occur. In the Keynesian model of sticky nominal wages, this adjustment is delayed until such time as the nominal-wage contract agreed to by firms and employees can be renegotiated. When that happens, the new nominal wage W that will be negotiated will be determined by what firms and workers expect the price level to be during the course of the next contract period. The resulting real wage will clear the labour market at the full-employment level of employment $\overline{N}$ and output will return to full-employment level $\overline{Y}$.

The relation between output supplied and the price level described by the sticky nominal-wage concept is captured by the equation

$$Y = \overline{Y} + b(P - P^e), \tag{12.1}$$

where b is a positive number that describes how strongly output responds when the actual price level exceeds the expected price level. This mathematical representation of the Keynesian model of nominal wage rigidity is the same as that which we described as representing the classical economist's monetary misperceptions theory in Chapter 11 (see Eq. 11.4, p. 371).[2] An important difference is the length of time over which actual output differs from full-employment output. In the monetary misperception model proposed by classical economists, actual output differs from full-employment output for only so long as misperceptions about relative price levels persist. In the nominal-wage rigidity model proposed by Keynesians, actual output will differ from full-employment output for the term of the labour contract, which prevents the nominal wage from adjusting. Thus, even if firms and employees recognize that the price level has changed relative to what they anticipated when they signed the labour contract, the contract would prevent adjustment of the nominal wage until the contract expires.

---

[2] As we noted in Chapter 11, the size of the b term depends on the slopes of labour demand and labour supply curves and the slope of the production function relating changes in employment to changes in output. The size of b also depends on the explanation for output deviating from the full-employment level when there is an unexpected change in the price level. The nominal-wage rigidity explanation implies that b has a larger value than does the misperception explanation.

SRAS represents the short-run aggregate supply curve that is generated by the Keynesian model of nominal-wage rigidity. It is drawn on the assumption that employees and firms have signed a nominal-wage contract on the expectation that the price level they will observe during the contract is P_0. When negotiating the nominal wage, employees and firms seek a nominal wage that clears the labour market at the expected price level. Thus, if the actual price level turns out to be what was expected, output equals the full equilibrium level $\overline{Y}$. For this reason, *SRAS* must intersect the long-run aggregate supply curve (*LRAS*) at price level P_0. If the actual price level is greater (less) than what was expected, the real wage is less (greater) than the market-clearing amount, so that output is greater (less) than $\overline{Y}$.

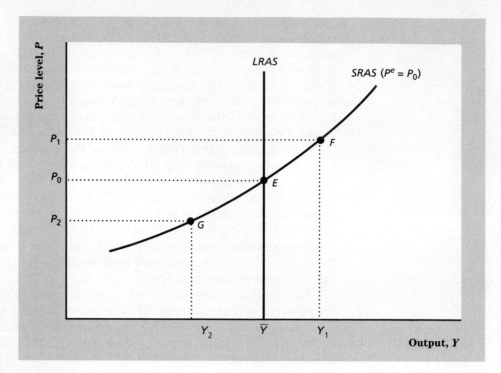

The relation between output supplied and the price level described in equation form by Eq. (12.1) can be equally well represented graphically, as shown in Figure 12.2. In Figure 12.2 we use the same information used to describe Figure 12.1: On the assumption that firms and workers expect to observe price level P_0, the two sides sign nominal-wage contracts that clear the labour market at the full-employment level of employment $\overline{N}$ that, in turn, results in full-employment output $\overline{Y}$. If, during the period of the nominal-wage contract, expectations prove to be correct and the price level is in fact P_0, then output will remain at the full-employment output $\overline{Y}$, as shown by point E. If the price level observed during the period of the contract is higher than expected (P_1), then output will exceed the full-employment level $\overline{Y}$, as shown by point F. On the other hand, if the price level observed during the period of the contract is lower than expected (P_2), then output will fall below the full-employment level $\overline{Y}$, as shown by point G.

Figure 12.2 represents the Keynesian model of aggregate supply. It is interesting that the Keynesian theory of nominal-wage rigidity provides a rationale for sketching the same upward-sloping *SRAS* curve as defended by classical adherents of the misperceptions theory. As we noted in Chapter 11, this is the reason why Figure 12.2, like its counterpart from Chapter 11, Figure 11.6 (p. 373), is a key diagram of macroeconomic analysis.

PRICE EXPECTATIONS AND THE KEYNESIAN SHORT-RUN AGGREGATE SUPPLY CURVE

Just as in the misperceptions theory, in the nominal-wage rigidity theory there is a different *SRAS* for every expected price level. Thus, Figure 11.7 (p. 375) is equally applicable here as in Chapter 11. As noted above, in anticipation of signing a nominal-wage contract, firms and employees form a rational expectation of the level of prices they expect to observe during the period of the contract. The general price level they expect determines the nominal wage they negotiate. If the actual price level turns out to be the price level that was expected, then the actual real wage will be the real wage that clears the labour market. Thus, the *SRAS* must intersect the *LRAS* at the expected price level.

The manner in which labour market participants determine the expected price level is also the same here as described in Chapter 11. For this reason, Figure 11.8 (p. 377) is also as equally applicable here as in Chapter 11. Firms and employees form an expectation of the price level based on reasoned and intelligent examinations of available economic data. Such examinations of the available economic data take into consideration what they observe about the state of the economy and what they have come to understand to be the nature of government economic policy. Employees and firms, then, calculate rational price expectations based on where they expect to observe the location of the aggregate demand curve during the period of the nominal-wage contract. The rational price expectation is determined by the intersection of the *LRAS* and the expected position of the aggregate demand curve, AD^e.

12.2 Monetary and Fiscal Policy in the Keynesian Model

We are now in a position to consider a complete Keynesian model of the business cycle. Like the classical model, the Keynesian model can be expressed in terms of the *IS–LM–FE* diagram, or alternatively, in terms of the *AD–AS* diagram. Rather than describe the Keynesian model in the abstract, we put it to work analyzing the effects of monetary and fiscal policy.

MONETARY POLICY

It will be useful to present the effects of monetary policy using both the *IS–LM–FE* diagram and the *AD–AS* diagram. Figure 12.3 shows both diagrams stacked on top of one another. This stacking is useful because both diagrams present values of output Y on the horizontal axis. Any change in output we show in one diagram must also be shown and explained in the other. In this way, we can show simultaneously the influence of monetary policy on output Y, the price level P, and the real interest rate r.

In drawing Figure 12.3, we have assumed that employees and firms, in anticipation of signing a nominal-wage contract, have formed a rational expectation of the level of prices they expect to observe during the period of the contract. Recall that it is necessary for labour market participants to form such an expectation because the general price level they expect will determine the nominal wage they negotiate. This price level expectation is based on a reasoned and intelligent examination of available economic data and on the knowledge employees and firms have of the state of the economy and what they have come to understand to be the nature of government economic policy. In the diagram, given that the aggregate demand curve is expected to be located at position AD^e, the rational price expectation is P_0. Employees and firms therefore expect to observe price level P_0 during the period of the labour contract. For this reason, the short-run aggregate supply curve intersects the *LRAS* at point E in the *AD–AS* diagram. In panel (a),

FIGURE 12.3

EXPANSIONARY MONETARY POLICY IN THE KEYNESIAN MODEL

The economy begins in full equilibrium at point E in both diagrams. The aggregate demand curve is expected to be in position AD^e and the rational price expectation is P_0. An unanticipated increase in the money supply shifts AD to AD^1, producing a short-run equilibrium at point F. The rise in the price level to P_1 causes a fall in the real wage, and this enables firms to expand employment and output to Y_1. The LM curve shifts from LM^1 to LM^2 as a net result of the increase in the money supply and increase in the price level. The interest rate falls to r_1. The rational price expectation is now P_2, and when wage contracts end, the $SRAS$ adjusts to $SRAS^2$. In the long run, the price level adjusts to P_2 and output returns to $\overline{Y}$. The increase in the price level to P_2 reduces the real money supply and shifts LM^2 back to LM^1. In the long run, the real interest rate is unaffected.

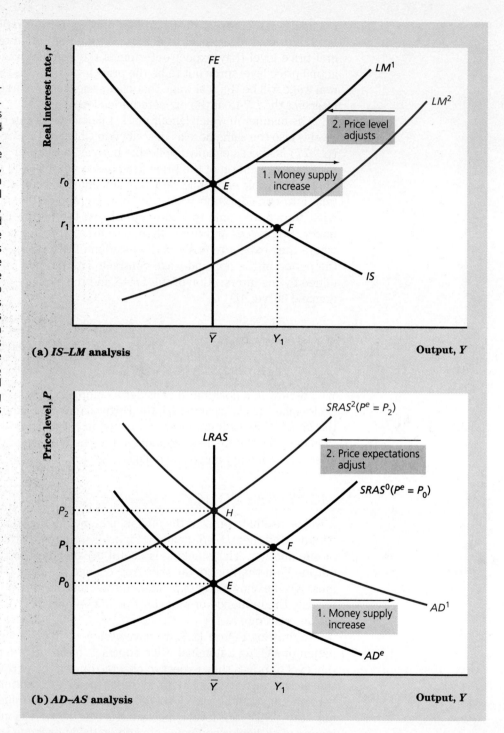

(a) *IS–LM analysis*

(b) *AD–AS analysis*

anticipated levels of consumption, investment, and government spending determine the location of the *IS* curve. The location of the *LM* curve is determined by the expected price level and by the expected size of the money supply. Indeed, the expected positions of the *IS* and *LM* curves in panel (a) of Figure 12.3 are what determine the expected position of *AD* in panel (b). Point *E* represents the initial equilibrium in both panels (a) and (b) of Figure 12.3.

Anticipated Monetary Policy

The first result we can draw from this analysis is that anticipated changes in money supply have no effect on real variables. To see this is true in terms of the diagram, we observe that the position of the LM curve, and hence the position of the AD curve, is determined by the anticipated level of the money supply. That is, we drew the AD curve in the position shown in Figure 12.3 based on the anticipation that the money supply would be such to locate the LM curve where we have drawn it. Whatever the anticipated size of the nominal money supply, labour market participants will identify a rational price expectation such that the anticipated position of AD intersects the $LRAS$ at full-employment output. As long as changes in the nominal money supply are anticipated by firms and employees, therefore, they can have no real effects.

The reasoning behind this result is straightforward. As soon as labour market participants learn of the planned increase in the money supply, their expected price level rises and this affects nominal-wage negotiations. If it is announced, for example, that the money supply will increase by 10%, then employees and firms will expect—correctly—that the price level will also rise by 10%. In anticipation, they negotiate a nominal wage that is 10% higher than it would have been otherwise. There is, then, no change in the real wage and, hence, no change in employment or output. The Keynesian model of sticky nominal wages, therefore, generates the same result as the classical misperception model—anticipated shifts in money supply, while affecting nominal variables such as the price level and nominal wages, have no effect on real variables such as output and employment.

Unanticipated Monetary Policy

Now let's suppose the Bank of Canada has kept secret its intentions to expand the nominal money supply. The unanticipated increase in the nominal money supply causes an unanticipated increase in aggregate demand. The aggregate demand curve is therefore found at AD^1 rather than at AD^e and firms find they can charge a higher price for their output than they anticipated. Because the nominal wage W is fixed by the labour contract, the fact that firms can charge higher prices than they anticipated means that the real wage W/P they pay is lower than expected. Firms respond to the lower real wage by hiring additional employees and hence expanding output. Output increases to Y_1. Short-run equilibrium occurs at point F in panel (b) of Figure 12.3 at price level P_1 and output Y_1.

In the IS–LM–FE diagram, an increase in the money supply shifts the LM curve down and to the right. The position of the LM curve is also affected by the higher than expected price level, moving it up and to the left. The net effect of these two influences is to move the LM curve from LM^1 to LM^2. Because an increase in the money supply does not directly affect the goods or labour markets, the IS curve and the FE line are unaffected. Short-run equilibrium occurs at point F in panel (a) of Figure 12.3 at interest rate r_1 and output Y_1.

Point F is only a short-run equilibrium because the labour market has not yet fully adjusted to the unanticipated monetary policy. The rigidity of the nominal wage is not permanent. Eventually the labour contract expires, and this allows employees and firms to negotiate a new nominal-wage contract. In doing so, they adjust their expectations of the price level. Assuming that they expect the nominal money supply to remain at its current level, they also expect the level of aggregate demand to be as indicated by AD^1. The rational price expectation now becomes P_2. In the labour market, the adjustment to the expected price level and the expiry of the old labour contract means that employees and firms negotiate a new, higher nominal wage. This new nominal wage yields an expected real wage that clears the labour market and returns output to $\overline{Y}$ from Y_1. The newly negotiated nominal wage is expected to produce the same real wage that employees and firms hoped to realize when they signed the old contract. The $SRAS$ shifts from $SRAS^0$ to $SRAS^2$, restoring equilibrium at point H in panel (b) of Figure 12.3. Finally, the increase in the expected price level shifts the LM curve back from LM^2 to LM^1 and restores general equilibrium at point E in panel (a). In the long run, then, monetary policy has no effect on the real interest rate or on output. Only the price level is affected.

Thus, the Keynesian model of nominal-wage rigidity predicts that *money is not neutral in the short run but is neutral in the long run*. In this respect, the predictions of the Keynesian model are the same as those of the extended classical model with misperceptions. In the Keynesian model, short-run wage stickiness prevents the economy from reaching its general equilibrium, but in the long run, prices and wages are flexible, ensuring general equilibrium.

FISCAL POLICY

The Keynesian model was initially developed during the Great Depression as economists struggled to explain the worldwide economic collapse and find policies to help the economy return to normal. The early Keynesians stressed that expansionary fiscal policies—increases in government purchases and/or decreases in taxes—can significantly increase output and employment levels. When, later, economies suffered the negative effects of overheated (booming) economies, Keynesians stressed that fiscal policy could also be used to slow the economy and relieve these pressures by reducing government expenditures and increasing taxes. Let's look at the Keynesians' conclusion that fiscal policy—changes in the size of government purchases and taxes—can be used to affect output and employment.

Anticipated Fiscal Policies

Analogous to our discussion of anticipated monetary policies, an anticipated fiscal policy will cause labour market participants to adjust their expectations of the price level. In anticipation of the effects of the expected fiscal policy, employees and firms negotiate a nominal-wage contract that leaves the real wage unaffected by the anticipated price change. Employees and firms make efforts to correctly anticipate the price level effects of government policy because their goal is to negotiate a nominal wage that produces the market-clearing real wage and, hence, the full-employment level of output. Anticipated fiscal policies, then, have no impact on real variables.

It is noteworthy that this result is different from what is concluded by the classical model. As we discussed in Chapter 11, classical analysis focuses on the fact that increased government purchases require higher current or future taxes to pay for the extra spending. Higher taxes make workers (who are taxpayers) effectively poorer, which induces them to supply more labour. This increase in the labour supply shifts the FE line (in the IS–LM–FE model) and the $LRAS$ (in the AD–AS model) to the right, causing output to rise in the classical model. This response is unaffected by whether or not the fiscal policy is anticipated. The effect of fiscal policy on output is due to its effect on wealth, and, whether the government announces its fiscal policy or keeps it secret, the effect on wealth is the same.

In contrast, in the Keynesian model the effect of fiscal policy on labour supply is not emphasized. Keynesian economists tend to reject the Ricardian equivalence proposition (discussed in Chapter 4), and so emphasize the effect that tax changes and changes in government expenditures have on current consumption as opposed to wealth. For this reason, changes in fiscal policy, whether anticipated or unanticipated, are assumed to have no impact on wealth and, hence, no impact on labour supply or full-employment output.

Unanticipated Fiscal Policies

The Keynesian analysis of how fiscal policy affects the economy is shown in Figure 12.4. It will again prove useful, as in our discussion of monetary policy, to present the effects of fiscal policy using both the *IS–LM* diagram and the *AD–AS* diagram. In this way, we can show simultaneously the influence of fiscal policy on output Y, the price level P, and the real interest rate r.

In drawing Figure 12.4, we have assumed that employees and firms, in anticipation of signing a nominal-wage contract, have formed a rational expectation of the level of prices they expect to observe during the period of the contract. In the diagram, the expected position of the aggregate demand curve, AD^e, reflects the public's judgment, based on a reasoned and intelligent examination of available economic data, of what will be the level of aggregate demand. In the diagram, given that the aggregate demand curve is expected to be located at position AD^e, the rational price expectation is P_0. Employees and firms therefore expect to observe price level P_0 during the period of the labour contract. For this reason, the short-run aggregate supply curve $SRAS^0$ intersects the *LRAS* at point E in panel (b) of Figure 12.4. In panel (a), anticipated levels of consumption, investment, and government spending determine the location of the *IS* curve. The location of the *LM* curve is determined by the expected price level and by the expected size of money supply. Point E represents the initial equilibrium in both panel (a) and panel (b) of Figure 12.4.

A temporary, unanticipated increase in government purchases increases the demand for goods and reduces desired national saving at any level of the real interest rate, so that the *IS* curve shifts up and to the right, from IS^1 to IS^2 (see Summary table 12, p. 251). The unanticipated increase in demand for goods also causes the *AD* curve to be located up and to the right of where the public expected it to be, so that it moves from AD^e to AD^1. Firms find that they can charge higher prices for their output than they had anticipated. Because the nominal wage W is fixed by the labour contract, the fact that firms can charge higher prices than they anticipated means the real wage W/P they pay is lower than expected. Firms respond to the lower real wage by hiring additional employees and hence by expanding output. Output increases to Y_1. Short-run equilibrium occurs at point F in panel (b) at price level P_1 and output Y_1.

In panel (a) of Figure 12.4, the position of the *LM* curve is also affected by the higher-than-expected price level. The increase in price level reduces the real money supply, causing the *LM* curve to shift from LM^1 to LM^2. Because an increase in government spending is assumed not to affect labour supply, the *FE* line is unaffected. Short-run equilibrium occurs at point F at higher interest rate r_1 and higher output Y_1.

Point F is only a short-run equilibrium because the labour market has not yet fully adjusted to the unanticipated fiscal policy. When the labour contract expires, employees and firms negotiate a new nominal-wage contract. In doing so, they

FIGURE 12.4

EXPANSIONARY FISCAL POLICY IN THE KEYNESIAN MODEL

The economy begins in full equilibrium at point E in both diagrams. The aggregate demand curve is expected to be in position AD^e, and the rational price expectation is P_0. An unanticipated increase in government purchases shifts AD to AD^1, producing a short-run equilibrium at point F. The rise in the price level to P_1 causes a fall in the real wage, and this enables firms to expand employment and output to Y_1. In panel (a), the unanticipated increase in government purchases shifts IS^1 to IS^2, and the LM curve shifts from LM^1 to LM^2 as a result of the increase in the price level. The interest rate increases to r_1. The rational price expectation is now P_2, and when wage contracts end, the $SRAS$ adjusts to $SRAS^2$. In the long run, the price level adjusts to P_2 and output returns to $\bar{Y}$. The increase in the price level to P_2 reduces the real money supply still further and shifts LM^2 to LM^3. In the long run, the real interest rate is driven up by an expansionary fiscal policy. The increase in the interest rate crowds out investment and interest-sensitive consumption.

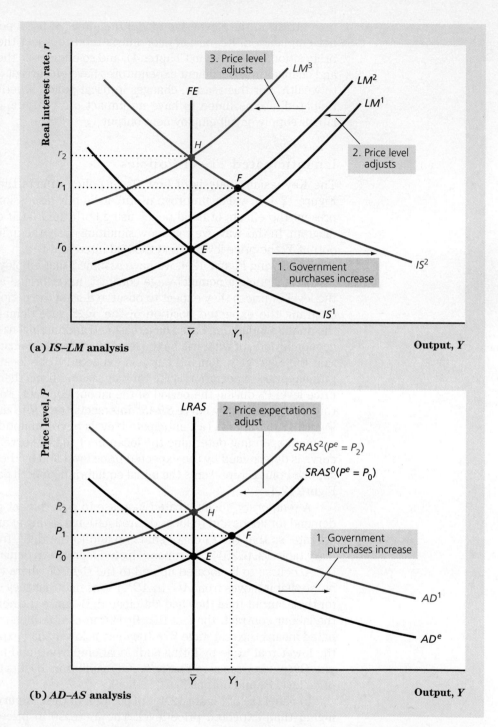

(a) *IS–LM analysis*

(b) *AD–AS analysis*

adjust their expectations of the price level. Assuming that they expect the level of government purchases to remain at current levels, they also expect the level of aggregate demand to remain at AD^1. The rational price expectation now becomes P_2. In the labour market, the adjustment to the expected price level and the expiry of the old labour contract means employees and firms negotiate a new, higher nominal wage. This new nominal wage yields an expected real wage that clears the labour market and returns output to $\overline{Y}$ from Y_1. The newly negotiated wage is expected to produce the same real wage that employees and firms hoped to realize when they signed the old contract. The *SRAS* shifts from $SRAS^0$ to $SRAS^2$, restoring equilibrium at point H in panel (b) of Figure 12.4. The increase in the expected price level shifts the *LM* curve still farther to the left, from LM^2 to LM^3, and restores general equilibrium at point H in panel (a). Thus, while an increase in government purchases causes output to increase in the short run, in the long run it has no impact on output and increases only the price level and the interest rate.

Our example of the effects of an expansionary fiscal policy relied on an unanticipated increase in government purchases, but we could as easily have considered a fiscal policy involving a change in taxes. In the Keynesian model, a tax cut raises desired consumption and shifts the *IS* curve up and to the right in the same way as does an increase in government purchases. Thus, Figure 12.4 can also be used to illustrate the effects of a tax cut. The only difference between a tax cut and an increase in government purchases is that instead of raising the portion of full-employment output devoted to government purchases, a tax cut raises the portion of full-employment output devoted to private consumption.

COMPARING FISCAL AND MONETARY POLICY IN THE KEYNESIAN MODEL

As noted in Chapter 9, fiscal and monetary policies are both referred to as **aggregate demand policies** because they each cause the aggregate demand curve to shift. Their impacts on the economy are also similar: Unanticipated fiscal and monetary policies both affect output and employment in the short run but are neutral in the long run. They differ, however, in the details of how they affect the economy and how they cause output to change.

We refer to a monetary policy that shifts the *LM* curve down and to the right—and, thus, expands output and employment—as an expansionary monetary policy, or "easy" money. Figure 12.3 (p. 398) measures the short-run effects of a policy of easy money by the movement between points E and F. Analogously, a contractionary monetary policy, or "tight" money, is a decrease in the money supply that shifts the *LM* curve up and to the left, contracting output and employment.

Why does easy money expand output in the short run in the Keynesian model? Recall that for holders of wealth to be willing to hold more real money and less in nonmonetary assets, the real interest rate must fall. The lower real interest rate increases both consumption spending (because saving rises) and investment spending. The increase in consumption and investment spending resulting from the monetary policy-induced fall in the interest rate is the source of the increase in aggregate demand (*AD*); the result we illustrated in Chapter 9 with Figure 9.12 (p. 276). With more demand for their output, firms find the price of their outputs bid upward. Because they have contracted to pay a fixed nominal wage, firms find they are paying lower real wages. Thus, firms find it profitable to increase production and expand employment. Noteworthy in this explanation is the key role played by the interest rate. Easy money affects real variables by causing the real interest rate to fall.[3] If changes in the supply of money cannot affect the interest rate, monetary

[3] The effects of monetary policy on the economy that work through changes in the real interest rate are called the **interest rate channel** of monetary policy. We discuss the interest rate channel and other mechanisms by which monetary policy may affect the economy more fully in Chapter 14.

policy cannot affect output. It is also worth noting that the effect of easy money on output depends in part on the slope of *SRAS*, as illustrated in Figure 12.3. The flatter is *SRAS*, the larger the temporary increase in real output.

Analogous to our "easy" and "tight" labels for expansionary and contractionary monetary policy, we can identify a fiscal policy that shifts the *IS* curve up and to the right—and, thus, expands output and employment—as an expansionary, or "easy" fiscal policy, while a fiscal policy that shifts the *IS* curve down and to the left—and, thus, contracts output and employment—as a contractionary, or "tight" fiscal policy. Figure 12.4 (p. 402) measures the short-run effects of an easy fiscal policy by the movement between points *E* and *F*.

Why does an unanticipated easy fiscal policy expand output in the Keynesian model? Recall from our discussion in Chapter 9 that an expansionary fiscal policy exerts two offsetting influences on the economy. Working to expand output is the **multiplier effect**. This arises because an expansionary fiscal policy increases the demand for goods and so increases the number of transactions in the economy. Each transaction provides income to someone else who, in turn, spends their new income on goods and services. In this way the impact of the initial increase in government purchases is multiplied a number of times over.[4] Working in the opposite direction is the **crowding out effect**. The increase in the number of transactions requires that households hold more of their financial wealth in the form of money. If the central bank has not increased the supply of money, then households and firms can satisfy their need for greater liquidity only by reallocating their financial wealth from nonmonetary to monetary assets. This reallocation of financial wealth requires the price of nonmonetary assets to fall and, consequently, the real interest rate to increase. Contrary to easy monetary policy, then, easy fiscal policy is associated with an *increase* in real interest rates. Since higher interest rates decrease both consumption spending (because savings rise) and investment spending, the increase in output due to an easy fiscal policy is reduced by the interest rate response. The net influence of the multiplier effect and the crowding out effect is, as shown in Figure 9.13 (p. 277), an increase in aggregate demand (*AD*).

Just as we described for an easy monetary policy, with more demand for their output, firms find the price of their output is being bid upward. Because they have contracted with employees to pay them a fixed nominal wage, firms find that the real wage they pay has fallen. Thus, firms find it profitable to increase employment and expand output. Once again, the total effect on real output of an expansionary fiscal policy depends in part on the slope of the *SRAS*, as illustrated in Figure 12.4. The flatter the *SRAS*, the larger the temporary effect on output of any shift in aggregate demand (*AD*).

Regardless of the source of the shift in the *AD* curve, the effect on real output is only temporary, as shown in Figures 12.3 and 12.4. This is because in the Keynesian model of sticky nominal wages, when the nominal-wage contract agreed to by firms and employees expires, the new nominal wage that will be negotiated will be determined by what firms and workers expect the price level to be during the course of the next contract period. The resulting real wage will clear the labour market at the full-employment level of employment $\overline{N}$ and output will return to full-employment level $\overline{Y}$.

This comparison of the effects of fiscal and monetary policy in the Keynesian model indicates that either can be used to affect output. Does it matter which is

---

[4] As discussed in Chapter 9, the size of the multiplier effect depends on the marginal propensity to save. The larger the marginal propensity to save, the smaller the multiplier effect.

used? Yes; as our discussion above suggests, there is at least one basic difference between the outcomes of the two policies: Monetary and fiscal policies affect the composition of spending (the amount of output that is devoted to consumption, the amount to investment, and so on) differently. In Figure 12.3 (p. 398), a monetary expansion has no long-run effects on real variables. Output is unaffected and there is no lasting impact on the real interest rate. Thus, consumption and investment spending by the private sector is unaffected in the long run by monetary policy. In Figure 12.4 (p. 402), a fiscal expansion, while having no long-run effects on output, leaves the real interest rate higher and the level of government purchases higher. Because government purchases are higher in the new long-run equilibrium but output is unchanged, the remaining components of spending—private consumption and investment—must be lower. By causing real interest rates to increase, an unanticipated expansionary fiscal policy permanently crowds out consumption and investment spending. In addition, increased government purchases imply higher current or future tax burdens, which also reduce consumption relative to what it would be with monetary expansion.

12.3 CRITICISMS OF THE NOMINAL-WAGE RIGIDITY ASSUMPTION

The Keynesian model we presented in Section 12.2 was based on the idea of nominal-wage rigidity. Many economists object to relying so heavily on the assumption of nominal-wage stickiness to explain business cycles. One objection is that less than a third of the labour force in Canada is unionized and covered by labour contracts. However, many non-union workers receive wages similar to those set in union contracts. For example, although most non-union workers do not have formal wage contracts, they may have "implicit contracts" with their employers, or informal unwritten arrangements for comparable wages.

A second objection is that some labour contracts contain cost-of-living adjustments (COLAs), which tie the nominal wage to the overall price level, as measured, for example, by the consumer price index. COLA clauses allow for the nominal wage to be adjusted automatically to keep up with prices without the need for costly negotiations. If wages are completely indexed to the price level, so that the nominal wage increases by the same percentage as the price level, then the short-run aggregate supply curve is vertical. To show why, let's suppose that the price level increases by 6%. If labour contracts are completely indexed, nominal wages also increase by 6% and the real wage W/P remains unchanged. Because the real wage does not change, firms choose the same levels of employment and output independent of the price level.

However, in most Canadian labour contracts, wages are not completely indexed to prices. In recent years, fewer than half the workers covered by major private-industry bargaining arrangements have had any COLA provisions at all. Those that do have COLA provisions have partial rather than complete indexation. For example, under a contract that calls for 50% indexation, the nominal wage will automatically increase by 50% of the overall rate of increase in prices. Thus, if the price level increases by 6%, the nominal wage increases by 3%. As a result, the real wage falls by 3% (a 3% increase in the nominal wage W minus a 6% increase in the price level P). The reduction in the real wage induces firms to increase employment and production. Thus, with partial indexation, the short-run aggregate supply curve slopes upward.

Why would firms and employees not always negotiate COLA clauses with complete indexation? As we noted earlier, employees and firms have different ideas of what is the appropriate real wage. Firms calculate the real wage as the nominal wage they pay their workers relative to the price of their own output. Employees define the real wage that is relevant to them as the nominal wage they receive relative to the general price level. Unless the rate of increase in the firm's price and the general price level are expected to be the same during the period of the wage contract, partial indexation may be a sensible trade-off between the interests of employees and the interest of the firm.

A third objection is that the nominal-wage rigidity model predicts real wages will be countercyclical. Thus, an increase in aggregate demand, by pushing the price level above that which was expected, and which was the basis of nominal-wage contracts, causes the real wage to fall. Firms expand employment and increase production. The model predicts, then, that the real wage and output will move in opposite directions. This prediction is awkward for Keynesians because, as we noted in Chapter 8, it is difficult to observe a clear negative relationship between the real wage and output as suggested by the nominal-wage rigidity model. Most observers conclude that a careful measurement of the relationship shows that the real wage tends to be either procyclical or acyclical (no clear relationship). The failure of the nominal-wage rigidity model to match this business cycle fact is commonly cited as a serious challenge to the Keynesian model of the business cycle.

One way Keynesians have responded to this challenge is to increase the role in their model for productivity shocks to generate business cycles. As in the RBC model, productivity shocks in the Keynesian model cause cyclical fluctuations that cause the real wage to move procyclically. Thus, a combination of supply shocks (which cause the real wage to move procyclically) and aggregate demand shocks (which cause the real wage to move countercyclically) might average out to a real wage that is either acyclical or mildly procyclical.

A second way Keynesians have responded to the challenge of explaining a procyclical real wage is to offer a different modelling assumption. In particular, they suggest that the key assumption of the classical model, that prices adjust quickly, should be modified. Keynesians suggest that in many parts of the economy, output prices are in fact "sticky" and do not adjust quickly to the changes in economic conditions.

12.4 Price Stickiness

To explain evidence of a procyclical movement of real wages while also explaining how aggregate demand shocks can play an important role in explaining business cycles, Keynesians have developed models of *nominal-price*, as opposed to *nominal-wage*, rigidity. So-called *sticky-price models* have the characteristic that firms, after establishing a price for their output, find it in their best interests not to adjust that price even though there has been a change in demand for their output. If firms choose to produce a larger quantity of output at a given price level, it must be that the demand for labour increased at any real wage. Such shifts in labour demand increase the real wage. In this way, sticky-price models generate the result that the real wage and output move in the same direction; the real wage is procyclical.

Before we look at the reasons why firms might choose to produce a larger quantity of output at a given price level, let's draw the implications of this assumption for the model of the business cycle. Assume two types of firms. Sticky-price firms set a price for their output and commit to sell at that fixed price for some period of time. The price they set is a profit-maximizing one, given what they expect will be the state of the economy during the period over which they have committed to sell their product at the fixed price. They set a fixed price, then, on the basis of an expected price level P^e. If there is an unanticipated increase in aggregate demand so that the actual price level P exceeds the price level they expected to observe (P^e), these firms respond by increasing output. Flexible-price firms, on the other hand, adjust their selling price in response to a change in the demand for their output. The aggregate price level increases due to the choice of flexible-price firms, and output increases due to the choice of fixed-price firms. How much of an unanticipated increase in aggregate demand is absorbed by an increase in the general price level versus an increase in output is dependent on the number of fixed- versus flexible-price firms. An equation describing these responses is

$$Y = \bar{Y} + b(P - P^e), \tag{12.2}$$

where b is a positive number that is related to the fraction of fixed- versus flexible-price firms and to the responsiveness of the output of fixed-price firms to unanticipated changes in price. Equation (12.2) is identical to Eq. (12.1), which summarizes the aggregate supply responses suggested by the sticky-wage model, and to Eq. (11.4), which summarizes the aggregate supply curve in the extended classical model with misperceptions. We conclude, therefore, that sticky-price models generate the same result as those models—that unanticipated aggregate demand shocks affect real output in the short run but are neutral in the long run.

SOURCES OF PRICE STICKINESS: MONOPOLISTIC COMPETITION AND MENU COSTS

It is one thing for Keynesians to say that **price stickiness** can be used as a justification for a positively sloped $SRAS$ and as a way of explaining why the real wage may move procyclically, but Keynesians need to respond to the criticism directed toward the theory by classical economists: Why are prices sticky? In particular, why would profit-maximizing firms find it in their best interests to commit to selling output at a fixed price?

The Keynesian explanation for the existence of price rigidity relies on two main ideas: (1) Most firms actively set the prices of their products rather than taking the prices of their output as given by the market; and (2) when firms change prices, they incur a cost, known as a menu cost.

Monopolistic Competition

Talking about price stickiness in a highly competitive, organized market—such as the market for wheat or the stock exchange—would not make much sense. In these markets, prices adjust rapidly to reflect changes in supply or demand. Principal reasons for price flexibility in these competitive, highly organized markets include standardization of the product being traded (one tonne of wheat, or one share of Tim Hortons stock, is much like any other) and the large number of actual or potential market participants. These two factors make it worthwhile to organize a centralized market (such as the Toronto Stock Exchange) in which prices can react swiftly to changes in supply and demand. These same two factors also promote keen competition among buyers and sellers, which greatly reduces the ability of any individual to affect prices.

Most participants in the wheat market or stock market think of themselves as price takers. A *price taker* is a market participant who takes the market price as given. For example, a small farmer correctly perceives that the market price of wheat is beyond his or her control. In contrast, a *price setter* has some power to set prices.

Markets having fewer participants and less standardized products than the wheat or stock markets may exhibit price-setting rather than price-taking behaviour. For example, consider the market for movies in a medium-sized city. This market may be fairly competitive, with many different movie theatres, each trying to attract customers from other theatres, online streaming, and so on. Although the market for movies is competitive, it is not competitive to the same degree as the wheat market. If a farmer tried to raise the price of a kilogram of his or her wheat by 5¢ above the market price, that farmer would sell no wheat; but a movie theatre that raised its ticket prices by 5¢ above its competitors' prices would not lose all its customers. Because the movie theatre's product is not completely standardized (it is showing a different movie from those in other theatres; its location is better for some people; it has different candy bars in the concession stand, a larger screen, or more comfortable seats, and so on), the theatre has some price-setting discretion. It is a price setter, not a price taker.

Generally, a situation in which all buyers and sellers are price takers (such as the market for wheat) is called **perfect competition**. In contrast, a situation in which there is some competition, but in which a smaller number of sellers and imperfect standardization of the product allow individual producers to act as price setters, is called **monopolistic competition**.

Perfect competition is the model underlying the classical view of price determination, and as we have said, price rigidity or stickiness is extremely unlikely in a perfectly competitive market. Keynesians agree that price rigidity would not occur in a perfectly competitive market but point out that a relatively small part of the economy is perfectly competitive. Keynesians argue that price rigidity is possible, even likely, in a monopolistically competitive market.

To illustrate the issues, let's return to the example of the competing movie theatres. If the market for movie tickets were perfectly competitive, how would tickets be priced? Presumably, there would be some central meeting place where buyers and sellers of tickets would congregate. Market organizers would call out "bids" (prices at which they are willing to buy) and "asks" (prices at which they are willing to sell). Prices would fluctuate continuously as new information hit the market, causing supplies and demands to change. For example, a favourable review would instantly drive up the price of tickets to that movie, but news of a prospective shortage of babysitters would cause all movie ticket prices to fall.

Obviously, though, this is not how movie tickets are priced. Actual pricing by most theatres has the following three characteristics, which are also common to most price-setting markets:

1. Rather than accept the price of movies as completely determined by the market, a movie theatre sets the price of tickets (or a schedule of prices) in nominal terms, and maintains the nominal price for some period of time.

2. At least within some range, the theatre meets the demand that is forthcoming at the fixed nominal price. By "meets the demand," we mean that the theatre will sell as many tickets as people want to buy at its fixed price, to the point that all its seats are filled.

3. The theatre readjusts its price from time to time, generally when its costs or the level of demand changes significantly.

Can this type of pricing behaviour maximize profits? Keynesian theory suggests that it can, if there are costs associated with changing nominal prices and if the market is monopolistically competitive.

Menu Costs and Price Setting

The classic example of a cost of changing prices is the cost that a restaurant faces when it has to reprint its menu to show changes in the prices of its offerings. Hence the cost of changing prices is called a **menu cost**. More general examples of menu costs (which can apply to any kind of firm) include costs of re-marking merchandise, reprinting price lists and catalogues, and informing potential customers. Clearly, if firms incur costs when changing prices, they will change prices less often than they would otherwise, which creates a certain amount of price rigidity.

A potential problem with the menu cost explanation for price rigidity is that these costs seem to be rather small. How, then, can they be responsible for an amount of nominal rigidity that could have macroeconomic significance?

Here is the first point at which the monopolistic competition assumption is important. For a firm in a perfectly competitive market, getting the price "a little bit wrong" has serious consequences: The farmer who prices his or her wheat 5¢ a kilogram above the market price sells no wheat. Therefore, the existence of a menu cost would not prevent the farmer from pricing the product at precisely the correct level. However, the demand for the output of a monopolistically competitive firm responds much less sharply to changes in its price; the movie theatre does not lose many of its customers if its ticket price is 5¢ higher than its competitors'. Thus, as long as the monopolistic competitor's price is in the right general range, the loss of profits from not getting the price exactly right is not too great. If the loss in profits is less than the cost of changing prices—the menu costs—the firm will not change its price.

Over time, the production function and the demand curve the firm faces will undergo a variety of shocks so that eventually the profit-maximizing price for a firm may be significantly different from the preset price. When the profits lost by having the "wrong" price clearly exceed the cost of changing the price, the firm will change its nominal price. Thus, movie theatres periodically raise their ticket and popcorn prices to reflect general inflation and other changes in market conditions.

Empirical Evidence on Price Stickiness

Several studies have examined the degree of rigidity or stickiness in actual prices. Some studies have involved interviewing managers of randomly selected firms about their price behaviour, others have involved tracking prices in the catalogues of firms such as L.L. Bean, and still others have combed the data collected by statistical agencies to produce the consumer price index. Studies involving interviews have concluded that almost half of firms change prices once a year or less, and so suggest that prices are quite sticky.[5] Studies of prices collected by statistical agencies, however, suggest that prices are more flexible than that. For example, a 2004 study by Mark Bils, of the University of Rochester, and Peter Klenow, of Stanford University,[6] found that the average time between price changes among 350 categories of goods (whose prices were record by the Bureau of Labor Statistics for use in calculating the CPI in the United States) was just 4.3 months, suggesting that

---

[5] This evidence comes from a study by Alan Blinder of Princeton University. See his paper "On Sticky Prices: Academic Theories Meet the Real World," in N.G. Mankiw, ed., *Monetary Policy*, Chicago: University of Chicago Press, 1994.

[6] "Some Evidence on the Importance of Sticky Prices," *Journal of Political Economy*, October 2004, pp. 947–985.

prices are quite flexible. However, a recent study by Emi Nakamura and Jon Steinsson,[7] of Columbia University, found that this result is due in part to firms temporarily adjusting prices for sales. Excluding sale prices, they find that the median length of time between price changes more than doubles to 11 months.

Despite the fact that empirical evidence on price stickiness isn't conclusive, Keynesians continue to use the assumption of price stickiness in their models. This is because many price changes are due to shifts in industry and firm-specific demand and supply curves as opposed to changes in economywide aggregate demand. Keynesians argue that it's how firms respond to economywide changes to aggregate demand that matters for understanding how prices restore general equilibrium, not how they respond to industry-specific shocks. For this reason they find the recent research of Jean Boivin of HEC-Montreal, Marc Giannoni of the Federal Reserve Bank of New York, and Ilian Mihov of INSEAD[8] to be persuasive. Those authors show that prices of many goods are very sticky in response to monetary policy shocks but more flexible in response to shocks to supply and demand that affect the relative price of the good compared with other goods. Thus, in our macroeconomic model, the assumption of sticky prices is a useful one, even in the face of the evidence reported by Bils and Klenow.

Another way to study price stickiness is to see whether prices change in response to changes in the exchange rate. For example, when the Canadian dollar depreciates, foreign goods eventually become more expensive for Canadians to buy. Thus, you might expect the retail prices of imported goods in Canada to rise promptly in response to depreciations. However, some studies find that this **pass-through** from the exchange rate to domestic prices is slow or incomplete. Prices do not all adjust fully to the changes in the exchange rate, which suggests that firms are partly absorbing exchange rate changes in changes in their profits.[9]

Export prices might also be expected to adjust when the exchange rate changes. A careful study of this adjustment was undertaken by Lawrence Schembri, of the Bank of Canada, who examined data from the Census of Manufacturers on a Canadian export industry during the period 1973–1985.[10] During this time, the Canadian dollar depreciated on average, which would have lowered the U.S. prices of Canadian exports had prices adjusted fully. Yet firms did not pass on the depreciation to their U.S. customers. Schembri estimated that a 1% depreciation caused U.S. dollar prices to fall by only 0.15% and domestic Canadian prices to rise by only 0.22%. This evidence of incomplete pass-through is an important example of price stickiness.

Meeting the Demand at the Fixed Nominal Price

When prices are sticky, firms react to changes in demand by changing the amount of production rather than by changing prices. According to Keynesians, why are

[7] "Five Facts About Prices: A Reevaluation of Menu Cost Models," *Quarterly Journal of Economics*, November 2008, pp. 1415–1464.
[8] "Sticky Prices and Monetary Policy: Evidence from Disaggregated U.S. Data," *American Economic Review*, March 2009, pp. 350–384.
[9] Between January and November of 2007, the Canadian dollar appreciated by 22% relative to the U.S. dollar, making foreign goods substantially less expensive for Canadians to buy. Thus we might have expected the retail prices of goods imported to Canada to fall promptly. To the dismay of Canadian shoppers, however, there was very little response in retail price levels even after 11 months of a fast-appreciating Canadian dollar. This slow pass-through from the exchange rate to retail prices prompted both the governor of the Bank of Canada and the minister of finance to make comments that suggested consumers should use their buying power to force retailers to lower prices.
[10] "Export Prices and Exchange Rates: An Industry Approach," Chapter 6 in Robert C. Feenstra, ed., *Trade Policies for International Competitiveness*, Chicago: University of Chicago Press and NBER, 1989.

firms willing to meet demand at a fixed nominal price? To answer this question, we again rely on the assumption of monopolistic competition. We have stated that a monopolistically competitive firm can raise its price to some extent without risk of losing all its customers. The profit-maximizing strategy for a monopolistically competitive firm is to charge a price higher than its **marginal cost**, or the cost of producing an additional unit of output. The excess of the price over the marginal cost is the **markup**. For example, if a firm charges a price 15% above its marginal cost, the firm has a markup of 15%. More generally, if the firm charges a constant markup of η over marginal cost, the following markup rule describes its price:

$$P = (1 + \eta)MC, \tag{12.3}$$

where P is the nominal price charged by the firm and MC is the nominal marginal cost.[11]

When the firm sets its price according to Eq. (12.3), it has an idea of how many units will sell. Now suppose that, to the firm's surprise, customers demand several more units than the firm expected to sell at that price. Will it be profitable for the firm to meet the demand at this price?

The answer is "yes." Because the price the firm receives for each extra unit exceeds its cost of producing that extra unit (its marginal cost), the firm's profits increase when it sells additional units at the fixed price. Thus, as long as the marginal cost remains below the fixed price of its product, the firm gladly supplies more units at this fixed price. Furthermore, if the firm is paying an efficiency wage (see Appendix 12.A), it can easily hire more workers to produce the units needed to meet the demand because there is an excess supply of labour.

The macroeconomic importance of firms' meeting demand at the fixed nominal price is that *the economy can produce an amount of output that is not on the full-employment line*. Recall that the *FE* line shows the amount of output that firms would produce after complete adjustment of all wages and prices. However, with nominal-price stickiness, the prices of goods do not adjust rapidly to their general equilibrium values. During the period in which prices have not yet completely adjusted, the amount of output produced need not be on the *FE* line. Instead, as long as marginal cost is below the fixed price, monopolistically competitive firms will produce the level of output demanded.

12.5 THE KEYNESIAN THEORY OF BUSINESS CYCLES AND MACROECONOMIC STABILIZATION

Recall that there are two basic questions about business cycles that a macroeconomic theory should try to answer: (1) What causes recurrent fluctuations in the economy? (2) What, if anything, should policymakers try to do about cycles? We are now ready to give the Keynesian answers to these two questions.

---

[11] Technical note: For a monopolistically competitive firm that faces a demand curve with a constant price elasticity and a fixed wage, the constant-markup rule in Eq. (12.3) will maximize profit. Also, in this case, the labour demand curve is proportional to (rather than equal to) the marginal product of labour curve. Specifically, to maximize profits the firm equates the MPN to $(1 + \eta)w^*$, where w^* is the *efficiency wage*, rather than equating the MPN to w^* itself. This qualification does not affect any conclusions presented in this chapter. The concept of an efficiency wage is discussed in Appendix 12.A.

KEYNESIAN BUSINESS CYCLE THEORY

An explanation of the business cycle requires not only a macroeconomic model but also some assumptions about the types of shocks hitting the economy. For example, RBC theorists believe that productivity shocks, which directly shift the *FE* line, are the most important type of macroeconomic shock.

In contrast to RBC theorists, most Keynesians believe that unanticipated shifts in the position of the aggregate demand curve are a primary source of business cycle fluctuations. This is so because in contrast to RBC theorists, Keynesians believe that wages and prices tend to be sticky. For this reason, shifts in the aggregate demand curve can cause output to deviate from its full-employment level for a prolonged period.

We used Figures 12.3 and 12.4 (pp. 398 and 402) to show the short- and long-run economic effects of unanticipated monetary and fiscal policy changes, respectively. We referred to fiscal and monetary policies as aggregate demand policies because they both cause changes in the position of the aggregate demand curve. These same diagrams, of course, also show the effects of unanticipated changes in any variable that affects aggregate demand. Thus, anything that causes an unanticipated change in the position of the *LM* curve—changes in the supply of money and changes in the demand for money—has the effects illustrated in Figure 12.3. Similarly, anything that causes an unanticipated change in the position of the *IS* curve—changes in fiscal policy variables, changes in desired investment arising from changes in the expected future marginal product of capital (*MPK*),[12] and changes in consumer confidence about the future that affect desired saving—has the effects illustrated in Figure 12.4. In general, changes that result in unanticipated shifts in the aggregate demand curve, whether they originate as shifts in the *IS* curve or the *LM* curve, are known as **aggregate demand shocks**. Their emphasis on aggregate demand shocks as the key explanation for recessions means that Keynesians tend to attribute recessions to "not enough demand" for goods, in contrast to the classical economists who attribute recessions to "not enough supply."

Like the RBC theory, the Keynesian theory of cycles can account for several of the business cycle facts: (1) In response to occasional aggregate demand shocks, the theory predicts recurrent fluctuations in output; (2) the theory correctly implies that employment will fluctuate in the same direction as output; and (3) because it predicts that shocks to the money supply will be non-neutral, the theory is consistent with the business cycle fact that money is procyclical and leading.

A business cycle fact that we previously emphasized (Chapter 8) is that spending on investment goods and other durable goods is strongly procyclical and volatile. This cyclical behaviour of durable goods spending can be explained by the Keynesian theory if shocks to durable goods demand are themselves a main source of cycles. The demand for durable goods would be a source of cyclical fluctuations if, for example, investors frequently reassessed their expectations of the future *MPK*. Another possibility was noted earlier, namely, waves of investor optimism and pessimism, what Keynes called "animal spirits." A rise in the demand for investment goods or consumer durables (at fixed levels of output and the real interest rate) is expansionary because it shifts the *IS* curve up and to the right.

---

[12] A change in the expected future *MPK* might also be thought of as a technological shock because it involves a change in the future production function. However, because a change in the future *MPK* shifts the *IS* curve but does not affect the current *FE* line, Keynesians classify it as an aggregate demand shock.

Investment will also be procyclical in the Keynesian model whenever cycles are caused by fluctuations in the *LM* curve; for example, an increase in the money supply that shifts the *LM* curve down and to the right both increases output and (by reducing the real interest rate) increases investment.

Another important business cycle fact that is consistent with the Keynesian theory is the observation that inflation tends to slow during or just after recessions (inflation is procyclical and lagging). In the Keynesian view, during a recession aggregate output demanded is less than the full-employment level of output. Thus, when firms do adjust their prices, they will be likely to cut them in order to increase their sales. According to the Keynesian model, because demand pressure is low during recessions, inflation will tend to subside when the economy is weak.

Procyclical Labour Productivity and Labour Hoarding

Although the Keynesian model is consistent with many of the business cycle facts, one fact—that labour productivity is procyclical—presents problems for this approach. As we showed in Figure 12.1 (p. 394), in the model of sticky nominal wages an unexpected fall in the price level results in the real wage increasing. Firms respond by reducing employment (in Figure 12.1 we move from point *E* to point *G*), and this in turn results in a temporary fall in output. Remembering that the productivity of labour diminishes with increases in employment, we conclude that in the Keynesian model an unexpected fall in the price level results in a temporary fall in output and an increase in the productivity of labour. Thus, the Keynesian model predicts that average labour productivity is countercyclical, contrary to the business cycle fact.

To explain the procyclical behaviour of average labour productivity, Keynesians modified their models to include labour hoarding.[13] As discussed in Section 11.1, labour hoarding occurs if firms retain, or "hoard," labour in a recession rather than laying off or firing workers. The reason that firms might hoard labour during a recession is to avoid the costs of letting workers go and then having to rehire them or train new workers when the recession ends. Thus, hoarded labour may be used less intensively or be assigned to such activities as training or maintenance. If labour is utilized less intensively during a recession, or workers spend time on such activities as maintenance that do not directly contribute to measured output, then labour productivity may fall during a recession even though the production function is stable. Thus, labour hoarding provides a way of explaining the procyclical behaviour of average labour productivity without assuming that recessions and expansions are caused by productivity shocks.

MACROECONOMIC STABILIZATION

From the Keynesian explanation of why business cycles occur, we turn to the Keynesian view on how policymakers should respond to recessions and booms. Briefly, Keynesians—unlike classical economists—generally favour policy actions to "stabilize" the economy by eliminating large fluctuations in output and employment. Keynesian support of more active policy measures follows from the theory's characterization of business cycle expansions and contractions as periods in which

[13] There also is some evidence that markups decline and labour demand rises in response to demand shocks, which may explain the fact that productivity is procyclical. See Julio J. Rotemberg and Michael Woodford, "Oligopolistic Pricing and the Effects of Aggregate Demand on Economic Activity," *Journal of Political Economy*, December 1992, pp. 1153–1207.

the economy is temporarily away from its general equilibrium. According to Keynesians, recessions are particularly undesirable. As we showed in Figure 12.1, an unexpectedly low price level causes the real wage to increase and results in firms choosing to lay off workers (we move from point E to point G). At the higher real-wage workers want to offer more labour than firms desire to employ, which leads to hardships for the unemployed and to output that is "too low." Keynesians, therefore, argue that average economic well-being would be increased if governments tried to reduce cyclical fluctuations, especially recessions.

The Keynesian analysis of monetary and fiscal policies suggests that these policies can be used to smooth the business cycle. To understand how, consider Figure 12.5. Suppose that the economy is in general equilibrium at point E. The public expects the aggregate demand curve to be in the position AD^e and on this basis has calculated a rational price expectation of price level P_0. On this basis, employees and firms negotiate and commit to nominal-wage contracts, and monopolistically competitive firms establish price lists ("menus") that are costly to change. These responses by firms and individuals establish the position of the short-run aggregate supply curve at $SRAS$ ($P^e = P_0$). Now suppose there occurs an unexpected event that causes the aggregate demand curve to be located at AD^1—a position different from what was expected. This produces a short-run equilibrium at point F and so a fall in output below the full-equilibrium level.

How might policymakers respond to this recession? We consider two possibilities: (1) no change in aggregate demand policies; and (2) an expansionary aggregate demand policy.

- *Scenario 1*: No change in aggregate demand policies. One policy option is to do nothing. With no intervention by policymakers, the economy will eventually correct itself. At point F in Figure 12.5, the price level is below what was anticipated by the public. Firms and employees who committed to nominal-wage contracts anticipating the price level would be P_0 now find that the price level

FIGURE 12.5

RESPONDING TO AGGREGATE DEMAND SHOCKS IN THE KEYNESIAN MODEL

The economy is initially in full equilibrium at point E. The AD curve is expected to remain in position AD^e. From point E the economy is driven into recession at point F by a drop in consumer confidence and spending, which shifts the AD curve to AD^1. Without any action by policymakers (scenario 1), the public will adjust their rational price expectation from P_0 to P_2. When wages and prices are free to adjust, the economy will adjust to point H. If wages and prices are sticky for a prolonged period, this option leaves resources unemployed for a long time. Another option (scenario 2) is to use an expansionary fiscal or monetary policy to shift AD^1 back to position AD^e and so speed up the recovery in output back to the full equilibrium level $\bar{Y}$. Compared with a strategy of doing nothing, expansionary aggregate demand policy helps the economy recover more quickly but leads to a higher price level in the long run.

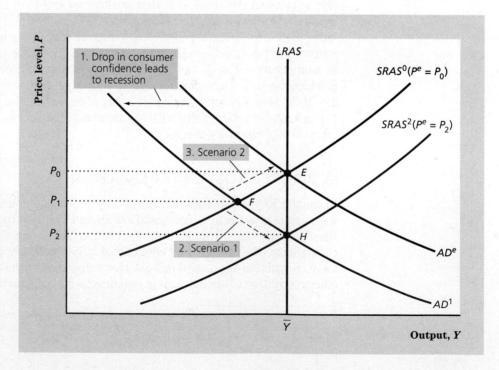

is lower at P_1. The real wage that firms are paying has increased, and firms respond by reducing employment and output. Monopolistically competitive firms find that their prices are too high and that their sales have fallen. They too reduce employment and output. Wage and price rigidities are not permanent, however, and eventually new labour contracts will be negotiated that involve cuts to nominal wages so as to lower the real wage back to the market-clearing level. Similarly, monopolistically competitive firms will eventually find that the profits lost by having the "wrong" price exceed the menu costs of changing the price. When they do, they will adjust their price lists and so recover output. In the long run, the public will adjust its rational price expectation downward from P_0 to P_2, the price level individuals and firms ought to expect, given the position of the aggregate demand curve at AD^1. In Figure 12.5, this change in expectations will shift the $SRAS$ from $SRAS^0$ to $SRAS^2$. In the long run, the economy will adjust to point H and output will return to the full-employment level. A disadvantage of this strategy is that during the (possibly lengthy) price adjustment process, output and employment remain below their full-employment levels.

- *Scenario 2*: An expansionary aggregate demand policy. Instead of waiting for the economy to reach general equilibrium through price adjustment, the Bank of Canada could increase the money supply or governments could cut taxes. Aggregate demand policies such as these could shift the aggregate demand curve from its position at AD^1 back to AD^e, and the economy could adjust to point E. If prices adjust slowly and the fiscal or monetary policy can be implemented quickly, this expansionary aggregate demand policy could move the economy back to full-employment output more quickly than would the policy of doing nothing.

In both scenarios, the economy eventually returns to full employment. However, the use of an expansionary aggregate demand policy (scenario 2) returns the economy to full employment without the need to wait for price adjustment. If wages and prices are sticky for an extended period, so that price adjustment takes a long time, forgoing stabilization policy means allowing real resources—human, financial, and physical—to remain unemployed for an extended period.

Difficulties of Macroeconomic Stabilization Policy

The use of macroeconomic stabilization policy to respond to the recession described above seems like an obvious solution. Unfortunately, even putting aside the debates between classical and Keynesian economists about whether smoothing the business cycle is sensible, actual macroeconomic stabilization has been much less successful than the simple Keynesian theory suggests.

A successful macroeconomic stabilization policy runs into a number of technical problems. First, because they both influence the position of the aggregate demand curve, monetary and fiscal policy must be coordinated. An expansionary fiscal policy introduced at the same time as a contractionary monetary policy may have no influence on the position of the aggregate demand curve. Second, because the ability to measure and analyze the economy is imperfect, gauging how far the economy is from full employment at any particular time is difficult. Third, the precise amount that output will increase in response to a monetary or fiscal expansion is not known. This uncertainty makes assessing how much of a monetary or fiscal change is needed to restore full employment difficult. Fourth, there are often long lags between the time a policy response might be welcome (at the start of a recession, for example) and the time a policy response actually begins to influence the economy. These lags arise because a good deal of data must be collected before policymakers recognize that a policy response is required, the legislative process involved in implementing the policy response can be time consuming, and the full effect of any aggregate demand policy takes many months—perhaps one or two years—to be felt. Finally, in an effort to avoid the issue of there being lags in the implementation of stabilization policies, economists try to forecast future economic conditions and so anticipate when policy actions might be required. Unfortunately, forecasting the future state of the economy is an inexact art at best.

Because of these problems, aggregate demand management has been likened to trying to hit a moving target in a heavy fog. These problems have not persuaded most Keynesians to abandon stabilization policy; however, many Keynesians agree that policymakers should concentrate on fighting major recessions and not try to "fine-tune" the economy by smoothing every bump and wiggle in output and employment.

Beyond the technical problems associated with trying to find the right policies to stabilize the economy, economists also face the practical problem of convincing policymakers to take their advice.

How Large is the Fiscal Policy Multiplier?

Since the financial crisis of 2008–2009, interest rates have remained at very low levels making monetary policy less able to stabilize the economy. The potential for using fiscal policy—changes in government expenditures in particular—to stabilize the economy has therefore gained renewed interest. A lively debate has centred on this renewed interest: Just how large is the government expenditure multiplier? This is important not least because if a government would need to increase its spending by $50 billion in order to expand real output by only $1 billion, taxpayers might fairly complain that this is too large a commitment of their tax dollars for such a small benefit.

In Appendix 12.B we derive an algebraic expression (Eq. 12.B.7) showing what our macroeconomic model predicts to be the change in the value of real output, ΔY, resulting from a change in government spending, ΔG. The ratio of the two measures, $\Delta Y/\Delta G$, is referred to as the *government expenditure multiplier*. The multiplier calculated there is measured on the assumption that the price level and the money supply are held constant. In the Appendix you will see that the size of the government expenditure multiplier depends on the size of the parameters that summarize how households and firms respond to change in the economic environment. Particularly important is the size of the parameters describing the sensitivity of consumption spending and investment spending to changes in the rate of interest. These parameters are important because their size determines the size of the crowding out effect, an influence that diminishes the effectiveness of fiscal policy.

In Figure 12.6, we illustrate the effect of an increase in government expenditures on an economy. The economy is initially in equilibrium at point E when government expenditures are increased causing the aggregate demand curve to shift to the right from position AD^1 to position AD^2. The ΔY in the $\Delta Y/\Delta G$ calculation defined in Appendix 12.B describes the size of the horizontal shift in the AD curve—the distance A to B. The figure shows that once we allow for the price level to vary, the amount by which Y actually changes is less than this; it is measured by the distance A to C. In other words, once we allow the price level to change, the multiplier grows smaller.

FIGURE 12.6

UNDERSTANDING THE SIZE OF THE FISCAL MULTIPLIER

The economy is initially in equilibrium at point A and the goal is to increase the level of output. An increase in government expenditures shifts the aggregate demand curve to the right, from AD^1 to AD^2. The fiscal multiplier derived in Appendix 12.B assumes the price level remains constant at P_0 and so identifies the size of the horizontal distance between points A and B. When we allow the price level to vary, the change in real output from the change in government expenditures is smaller than this; it is measured by the movement from Y_0 to Y_1. A number of factors, including the slope of the $SRAS$ curve, will determine how much output changes for a change in government expenditures.

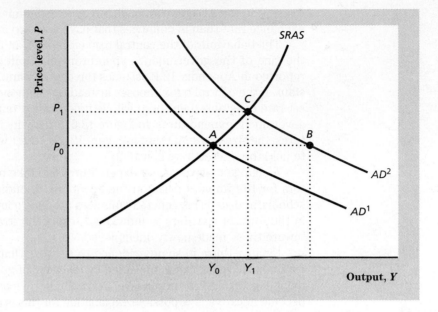

How much smaller the multiplier becomes when the price level is allowed to change depends on the slope of the $SRAS$. The steeper it is, the smaller will be the change in real output resulting from any change in government expenditures.

It is not difficult to imagine that the slope of the $SRAS$ curve is dependent upon economic conditions. During a period of recession, for example, unemployed resources can be re-employed at relatively little cost and with little need to increase input prices. In this case the $SRAS$ is relatively flat and so the multiplier is large. During a boom period, however, adding more output can only be met by reduced output in other sectors or by bidding up input prices. In this case the $SRAS$ is relatively steep and so the multiplier is small.

The suggestion that the government expenditure multiplier is larger during recession is interesting because it means it is largest exactly when expansionary fiscal policy is most needed. This is the conclusion of economists Alan Auerbach and Yuriy Gorodnichenko[14] who find that, in the U.S. economy, the government expenditure multiplier varies between values close to zero during periods of full employment to a value of 1.5 in periods of recession. Thus, during a recession in the United States, a $50 billion increase in government expenditures will result in a $75 billion increase in real output.

Another important consideration is that the size of the multiplier will vary by country. This is true because some countries are more open to international trade than others. In highly open countries, more spending is on imported (foreign produced) goods and so there is less of an impact on domestic output levels. A closely related consideration important for open economies is the choice of exchange rate regime. Thus, as we discussed in Chapter 10, the effect on output of an increase in government expenditures is larger in a country that has adopted a fixed exchange rate than in a country that has adopted a flexible exchange rate. In terms of Figure 12.6, for any increase in government expenditures, the size of

---

[14] "Measuring the Output Responses to Fiscal Policy," *American Economic Journal: Economic Policy*, Volume 4 (2), 2012.

the shift in the AD curve is smaller in open economies that have adopted a flexible exchange rate than in countries that have adopted a fixed exchange rate.

The behaviour of the central bank also plays an important role in determining the size of the government expenditure multiplier. The multiplier calculation reported in Appendix 12.B assumes the central bank holds the money supply constant. If the central bank chooses instead to use monetary policy to keep the interest rate constant, then there will be no crowding out effect from an expansion of government expenditures. In Figure 12.6, for any increase in government expenditures, the size of the AD shift in Figure 12.6 is larger when the central bank chooses to hold the interest rate constant.

A change in government expenditures can take many forms and this also matters for the impact it has on the economy. Spending on infrastructure (roads, schools, and so on) is generally found to produce a larger multiplier than spending in the form of transfers to individuals, especially transfers that are not targeted toward those made newly unemployed.

Finally, there is some evidence to suggest that the size of the government expenditure multiplier is impacted by the level of government debt; once government debt exceeds a certain level the multiplier becomes quite small and may even become negative.[15] A possible explanation for this is that households and firms are more likely to associate an increase in government expenditures with higher tax rates when current debt is high than when it is low.

All of this suggests that the real debate about the size of the multiplier is about the size of the multiplier in a particular situation. It is not a constant; rather, its value will vary depending on all of these considerations and on the economic conditions at the time the policy is implemented. While the debate on this question continues, it seems safe to say that in those economic conditions when stabilization policy is most in need and the central bank provides a supportive monetary policy of maintaining low interest rates, the multiplier associated with a well-designed and targeted government expenditure is much closer to 1 than it is to 2 or 3 or higher. In a small open economy with a flexible exchange rate—such as Canada—the multiplier will be even smaller than this. The implication is that while a $50 billion increase in government expenditures will have an expansionary effect on the economy, it is unlikely to cure all ills in a $2000 billion economy such as Canada's.

SUPPLY SHOCKS IN THE KEYNESIAN MODEL

Until the 1970s, Keynesian business cycle theory focused almost exclusively on aggregate demand shocks as the source of business cycle fluctuations. Although Keynesians would not go so far as to agree with RBC theorists that supply (productivity) shocks are the most important factor in most recessions, they now concede that there have been occasional episodes—the oil price shocks of the 1970s being the leading examples—in which supply shocks have played a primary role in an economic downturn.

Figure 12.7 shows a Keynesian analysis of the effects of a sharp temporary increase in the price of oil (a similar analysis would apply to other supply shocks, such as a drought). As we showed in Chapter 3, if firms respond to an increase in the price of oil by using less energy, the amount of output that can be produced with the same amount of capital and labour falls. Thus, the increase in the price of

FIGURE 12.7

AN OIL PRICE SHOCK

The economy begins in full equilibrium at point E in both diagrams. The aggregate demand curve is expected to be in position AD^e and the rational price expectation is P_0. An increase in the price of oil is an adverse supply shock that reduces full-employment output from $\bar{Y}_1$ to $\bar{Y}_2$. and, thus, shifts the FE line and the $LRAS$ to the left. In the long run, the price level increases to the new rational price expectation, P_1. The increase in the price level reduces the real money supply, causing LM to shift from LM^1 to LM^2 and causing the real interest rate to increase from r_0 to r_1. In the classical model, the adjustment occurs virtually immediately. In the extended classical model, adjustment occurs once firms become aware of the change in the price level. In Keynesian models, adjustment is slower still and must wait until sticky wages and prices adjust.

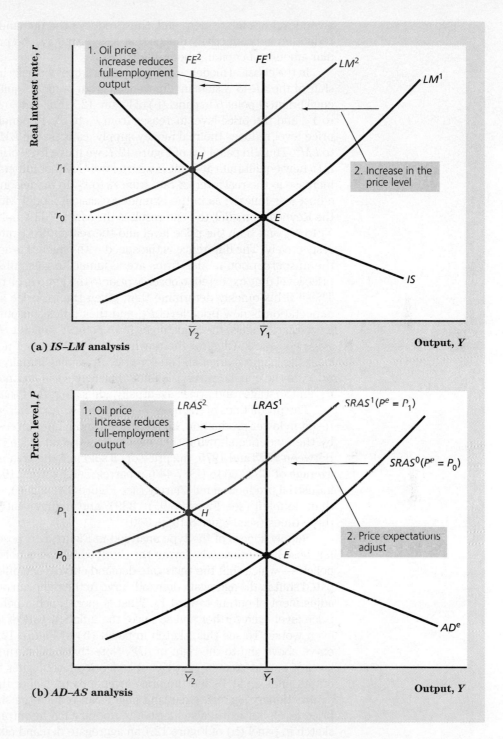

(a) *IS–LM* analysis

(b) *AD–AS* analysis

oil is an adverse supply shock, which reduces the full-employment level of output and shifts the FE line to the left, from FE^1 to FE^2 in panel (a). In panel (b), where we present the AD–AS diagram, the adverse supply shock causes $LRAS$ to shift to the left, from $LRAS^1$ to $LRAS^2$. The shift of the FE line and $LRAS$ reflects two influences. First, the adverse supply shock lowers the marginal product of labour at any given level of employment and, thus, reduces the demand for labour. Second, the reduction in productivity means that less output can be produced with any particular amount of capital, labour, and effort.

In the classical model, wages and prices adjust virtually immediately. The leftward shift of the *LRAS* results in a movement from original equilibrium at point E to new equilibrium at point H in panel (b) of Figure 12.7. Full-employment output falls from $\overline{Y}_1$ to $\overline{Y}_2$, and the price level increases from P_0 to P_1. In panel (a), the increase in the price level reduces the real money supply, causing the LM curve to shift from LM^1 to LM^2. Thus, in panel (a) of Figure 12.7, we move from original equilibrium at point E to new equilibrium at point H with a lower level of full-employment output and an increase in the real interest rate from r_0 to r_1. In models in which wages and prices adjust less quickly, as in the extended classical model with misperceptions and in the Keynesian model, the end result is the same: Full-employment output falls from $\overline{Y}_1$ to $\overline{Y}_2$, and both the price level and the real interest rate increase, to P_1 and r_1, respectively. The difference is the speed with which this adjustment takes place. In the misperception model, firms are assumed to recognize fairly quickly that the price level they expected to observe prior to the jump in oil prices (P_0) has increased. These firms quickly determine that, given the oil price shock, the rational price expectation is now price level P_1, and they adjust output accordingly. Finally, in Keynesian models, the adjustment from point E to point H is slower still. Nominal-wage contracts will slow the downward adjustment of nominal wages needed to clear the labour market and sticky-price firms may initially adjust output more than price. In the end, however, the public calculates the rational price expectation to be P_1, and so wages and prices eventually adjust to reflect that expectation.

The predictions of the model—that a substantial increase in the price of oil will result in lower production, higher prices, and higher interest rates—was borne out by the evidence showing the response to the oil price shock of the mid-1970s. Between 1973 and 1975, the price of oil sold in Canada more than doubled, from an average of US\$3.66 to US\$7.44 per barrel (see Figure 3.10, p. 73). Over this period industrial production fell sharply (see Figure 8.4, p. 235), the rate of inflation more than doubled (see Figure 8.9, p. 239), and nominal interest rates increased by three times (see Figure 8.10, p. 240).[16]

Supply shocks of the type analyzed in Figure 12.7 pose tremendous difficulties for those Keynesians who favour the use of stabilization policies. Fiscal and monetary policies—which shift the aggregate demand curve—can offer little help. An unanticipated shift in the aggregate demand curve to the right can only slow, not prevent, the adjustment of output toward $\overline{Y}_2$. What is more, such a policy will only increase the price level even further and so make the inflation part of the "stagflation" problem even worse. To see this, sketch in panel (b) of Figure 12.7 an aggregate demand curve above and to the right of AD^e. Note that a short-run equilibrium occurs at a level of output greater than $\overline{Y}_2$ but at a price level higher than P_1. In the long run, output ends up at $\overline{Y}_2$ and the price level ends up higher than P_1. An unanticipated contractionary aggregate demand policy can reduce the size of the increase in the price level, but it will also cause a temporary fall in output below $\overline{Y}_2$. To see this, sketch in panel (b) of Figure 12.7 an aggregate demand curve below and to the left of AD^e. Note that a short-run equilibrium occurs at a price level below P_1 but at a level of output even less than $\overline{Y}_2$. In the long run, output ends up at $\overline{Y}_2$ and the

---

[16] Although real interest rates—the nominal interest rate less the expected rate of inflation—are more difficult to measure, investment in fixed capital (see Figure 8.5, p. 236) also declined over this period, which is consistent with an increase in the real interest rate.

price level ends up lower than P_1. Aggregate demand policies, then, seem to offer little respite in the face of the stagflation effects of a large supply shock. Classical economists, on the other hand, identify the fall in output and increase in prices as being the optimal response of firms to a supply shock and, hence, recommend no response from policymakers.

Consideration of the appropriate response to a supply shock initiated by a sharp temporary increase in the price of oil took on new impetus in the fall of 2004 when the price of oil surpassed US$50 per barrel. This marked a 75% increase over the previous 12 months. That shock has ended up being more persistent than many analysts at the time thought it would be. After increasing to US$74 per barrel in July 2006, the price of oil subsided to US$55 early in 2007 before roaring back to over US$95 per barrel in November of that year. The response of policymakers was subdued; they had few serious discussions of aggressive aggregate demand responses. In part, this may have reflected the fact that oil price shocks now have smaller consequences for the Canadian economy than was the case in the 1970s. Recalling our discussion in Chapter 3 (see the Application "Output, Employment, and the Real Wage During Oil Price Shocks," p. 72) we can cite two reasons for optimism. First, in response to the earlier experience with oil price shocks, Canadian firms have become much more energy efficient. Second, the Canadian economy has shifted away from heavy, energy-intensive industries and into knowledge-based industries and services that rely far less heavily on oil as an input. For these reasons, rich countries like Canada use less than half as much oil as they did in 1970 to produce a dollar's worth of real output. In consequence, increases in oil prices have a significantly smaller effect on the position of the *FE* and *LRAS* lines than they did previously.

A CLOSER LOOK 12.1

The Classical–Keynesian Debate and the 2008–2009 Recession

In Chapters 11 and 12, we have compared and contrasted the classical and Keynesian approaches to analyzing the business cycle and to determining stabilization policy. For many years, classical and Keynesian economists pursued research on these issues using very different types of models. As a result, communication between the two groups was difficult.

However, in the past decade some classical economists have been incorporating Keynesian ideas into their models, and some Keynesian economists have been incorporating more classical ideas into their models. As a result, classical and Keynesian economists are now speaking the same language, and so research on macroeconomic ideas is advancing more easily.

One fundamental area of difference between classical and Keynesian economists has always been the degree to which a model incorporated microeconomic foundations. As we discussed in Appendix, classical

economists have tended to emphasize that good models could be developed only by modelling microeconomic foundations, which means showing how households choose labour supply and consumption spending to maximize their own welfare, how firms choose labour demand and investment spending to maximize their own profits, and so on. This modelling approach was based on the assumption that descriptions of how *individual* households and firms make choices could also be used to describe how *aggregations* of households and firms make choices. Keynesian economists, on the other hand, often believed that the attempt to find microeconomic foundations was unlikely to be fruitful because they felt that descriptions of how households and firms make choices in the aggregate need not be precisely described by how they make choices as individuals. Keynesians therefore focused on models based on aggregate relationships rather than those describing individual decision making.

(continued)

Despite the gains that have been made in the past decade, classicals and Keynesians still differ in the fundamental way we have identified throughout this text: Keynesians tend to believe that prices and wages are slow to adjust while classicals think they adjust much faster. Keynesians also tend to have more faith that government policy actions can improve people's welfare while classicals tend to think the opposite—that many government policies make people worse off, especially when it comes to attempts to stabilize the business cycle.

The financial crisis and the recession that it sparked in 2008–2009 has provided more fodder for debate over who is correct about modelling strategy and the advisability of government policy actions. Keynesians emphasize that the financial crisis highlights the fact that the real world is characterized by imperfections—in the form of a weakly regulated financial system and poorly understood financial instruments, for example—that challenge the assumptions deemed appropriate by classical economists of perfect information and readily adaptable households and firms. Responding to the lessons of the 2008–2009 financial crisis and recession, Ricardo Caballero[*] of MIT has emphasized that the complexity of macroeconomic interactions limits the knowledge that can be attained and that assuming households and firms can solve ever more complicated general equilibrium problems stretches what is sensible for economists to assume they are capable of. He therefore argues for macroeconomists to construct models that are more relevant to the real world, even if that means less precise mathematical formulations. Such sentiments give Keynesians reason to feel comfortable with their modelling assumptions and their implications of slow wage and price adjustments, and they applaud the aggressive policy actions taken in 2008–2009 by governments and central banks in response to the crisis, arguing that these actions prevented a deep and lasting contraction.

Classical economists, on the other hand, emphasize that criticisms of recent developments in macroeconomic modelling are overblown. The economic crisis highlighted that a greater effort is required to incorporate insights gained from research into the intricacies of financial markets, not an abandonment of an approach that has advanced the profession's understanding of the economy over the past three decades. For example, Robert Hall[†] of Stanford University suggests a relatively straightforward addition to the macroeconomic model—one that recognizes that uncertainty about the quality of financial instruments adds a "friction" to financial transactions, forcing savers to worry about defaults of the financial institutions that take their wealth as deposits and lend them to firms. Hall notes that most of the time these frictions are tiny, because defaults are rare and the financial system typically operates very smoothly, but when a large shock occurs these frictions suddenly become large and have significant effects on the economy. As for policy, classical economists point to the fact that even after these aggressive policy actions many economies continue to suffer high rates of unemployment—particularly the U.S. economy, where policymakers were particularly aggressive. Classical economists also point to the legacy of these aggressive policy actions—a high level of government debt and potentially higher tax rates in the future—and question whether, in time, individuals will be able to claim that they benefited from government stabilization policy.

---

[*]"Macroeconomics After the Crisis: Time to Deal with the Pretense-of-Knowledge Syndrome," *Journal of Economic Perspectives*, Volume 24, Number 4, Fall 2010, pp. 85–102.
[†]"Why Does the Economy Fall to Pieces After a Financial Crisis?" *Journal of Economic Perspectives*, Volume 24, Number 4, Fall 2010, pp. 3–20.

CHAPTER SUMMARY

1. Keynesians are skeptical that business cycles can be ascribed mainly to real shocks, as claimed by classical economists. They argue that aggregate demand shocks also contribute to business cycles. Keynesians stress the existence of wage and price "stickiness" or "rigidities" as the reasons why aggregate demand fluctuations cause changes in real output.

2. The Keynesian model of nominal-wage rigidity suggests that nominal wages are slow to adjust

to changes in the demand and supply of labour because firms and employees sign nominal-wage contracts. These contracts specify employment conditions and nominal wages for a period of one to three years into the future. Thus contracts are signed that commit both sides to a nominal wage before the quantity of labour supplied and demanded is known. Although labour contracts specify the nominal-wage rate, employers unilaterally decide how many hours will be worked and whether workers will be laid off.

3. Given the need to sign a contract that commits them to a nominal wage W for a number of years into the future, firms and employees must form an expectation of what they believe will be the level of prices P^e in the future. Such price forecasts are necessary to determine what nominal wage they need to agree to in order to obtain the real wage W/P they desire. Employees and firms are assumed to form a rational price expectation that is based on available economic data about the state of the economy and what they have come to understand to be the nature of government economic policy. If the actual price level observed during the period of the nominal-wage contract ends up being what was expected ($P = P^e$), the actual real wage ends up being the real wage desired by both employees and firms. In this case, output is at the full-employment level $\overline{Y}$. If, on the other hand, the actual price level observed during the period of the nominal-wage contract ends up being other than what was expected ($P \neq P^e$), the actual real wage ends up being other than the real wage desired by both employees and firms. In this case, output is different from the full-employment level, $Y \neq \overline{Y}$. Thus, unanticipated changes in aggregate demand, whether the result of unanticipated changes in fiscal and monetary policy or unanticipated changes in other components of aggregate demand, give rise to business cycles by causing the price level to be different from what was expected by employees and firms when they signed nominal-wage contracts.

4. In the Keynesian model, output is determined in the short run at the intersection of the IS and LM curves and the AD and $SRAS$ curves. The economy can be off the FE line and the $LRAS$ because the actual price level differs from what was expected when nominal-wage contracts were signed. In the long run, after the period of nominal-wage contracts has expired, wages are renegotiated. The renegotiated nominal wage is based on an updated rational expectation of the price level and is intended to generate a real wage desired by both employees and firms. In the long run, then, the real wage and employment return to market-clearing levels, and output returns to the full-employment level $\overline{Y}$. The adjustment of the price level causes the LM curve to move to restore general equilibrium with full-employment output in the IS–LM–FE model.

5. Anticipated changes in aggregate demand, whether the result of changes in fiscal and monetary policy or the result of changes in other components of aggregate demand, do not affect output in the Keynesian model. Anticipated changes in aggregate demand are accounted for by firms and employees when negotiating nominal-wage contracts. The contracts they sign take into account the anticipated change in the price level caused by the anticipated change in aggregate demand.

6. In the Keynesian model, an unanticipated increase in the money supply shifts the LM curve down and to the right and shifts the AD curve up and to the right. These shifts raise output, raise the price level above what was expected, and lower the real interest rate in the short run. Thus, unanticipated changes in the money supply are not neutral in the short run. In the long run, however, money is neutral; monetary expansion raises the price level proportionally but has no real effects.

7. In the Keynesian model, an unanticipated increase in government purchases or a cut in taxes shifts the IS and AD curves up and to the right. These shifts raise output, raise the price level above what was expected, and raise the real interest rate in the short run. In the long run, output returns to the full-employment level but the real interest rate increases. Unanticipated fiscal policy is not neutral in the long run because it affects the composition of output among consumption, investment, and government purchases.

8. The Keynesian theory of nominal-wage rigidity has been criticized because it predicts a strong negative relationship between real wages and

output. Thus, the theory predicts that real wages will move countercyclically. This prediction fails to explain the business cycle fact that real wages tend to move procyclically or acyclically. In response to this criticism, Keynesians suggest a theory of price rigidity (or "stickiness") to supplement their theory of wage rigidity.

9. Price stickiness can arise from the profit-maximizing behaviour of monopolistically competitive firms that face menu costs, or costs of changing prices. Such firms are price setters rather than price takers. These firms set a fixed price P based on an expectation of the general price level P^e. If the general price level turns out to be different from what they anticipated, they meet customer demand at their fixed price. Sticky-price firms adjust prices only occasionally, generally when costs or demand have changed significantly. For sticky-price firms, increases in output require increases in the real wage. Thus, the existence of sticky-price firms explains a procyclical real wage.

10. The existence of sticky-price and flexible-price firms produces a *SRAS* relationship equivalent to that resulting from the sticky-wage model. Thus, anticipated and unanticipated aggregate demand shocks have the same effects on output, prices, and the interest rate regardless of which Keynesian theory of stickiness is assumed.

11. Keynesian business cycle theory can account for the procyclical behaviour of employment, money, inflation, and investment. To explain the procyclical behaviour of average labour productivity, Keynesian theory must include the additional assumption that firms hoard labour—that is, they employ more workers than necessary during recessions.

12. Macroeconomic stabilization policy, also called aggregate demand management, is the use of monetary or fiscal policy (or both) to try to eliminate recessions and keep the economy at full employment. Keynesian theory suggests that macroeconomic stabilization is desirable if the period of adjustment back to full employment is prolonged. In cases such as these, argue Keynesians, it is preferable to use stabilization policies to speed up the adjustment back to full employment rather than let economic resources remain unemployed. However, practical problems include the slow speed with which stabilization policies are formulated and implemented and the fact that our ability to measure and analyze the economy is imperfect.

13. Following the oil price shocks of the 1970s, Keynesian theory was modified to allow for supply shocks to affect the economy as well. Supply shocks lead to stagflation (a combination of inflation and recession) and pose great difficulties for those Keynesians who favour the use of stabilization policies.

KEY DIAGRAM 12
The Keynesian Version of the *AD–AS* Model

The Keynesian version of the *AD–AS* model shows how the aggregate demand for output and the aggregate supply of output interact to determine the price level and output in a model in which workers and firms find it in their best interests to adjust prices and wages only occasionally.

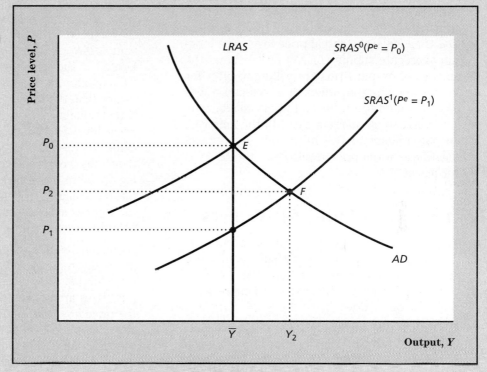

DIAGRAM ELEMENTS

- The actual price level, P, is on the vertical axis and the level of output, Y, is on the horizontal axis.

- The aggregate demand (*AD*) curve shows the aggregate quantity of output demanded at each price level. It is identical to the *AD* curve in previous Key Diagrams. The aggregate amount of output demanded is determined by the intersection of the *IS* and *LM* curves. An increase in the price level P reduces the real money supply, shifting the *LM* curve up and to the left, and so reduces the aggregate quantity of output demanded. Thus, the *AD* curve slopes downward.

- The Keynesian theory of the business cycle is based on the assumption that workers and firms find it preferable to allow their nominal wages and prices to adjust only occasionally. A number of explanations are offered for this behaviour. One, known as nominal-wage rigidity, is based on the observation that workers and firms sign

contracts that obligate workers to accept, and firms to pay, a fixed nominal wage for a certain length of time. These contracts are based on the price level each side expects during the period of the contract. Whatever happens to the actual price level during this period of time has no effect on the negotiated nominal wage; it is fixed. Another explanation for price stickiness is based on assumptions that most firms have some power to set their price at different levels from those charged by other firms in the same industry, and that when firms change prices they incur a cost, known as a menu cost. Keynesians argue that these two assumptions mean that firms will find it optimal to adjust prices only when a substantial change in price is called for.

- The short-run aggregate supply (*SRAS*) curve shows the amount of output firms are willing to offer for sale in the short run. The position of the *SRAS* is determined by the expected price level P^e. The value of P^e is determined by what firms and individuals expected the price level to be at the time they made their decisions about what prices to charge and at the time they agreed to nominal-wage contracts.

- In the long run, workers and firms adjust wages and prices to market-clearing levels, and they adjust their expectations of the price level so that they equal the actual price level. The long-run aggregate supply (*LRAS*) curve shows the amount of output firms are willing to offer for sale in the long run, when all prices and wages have adjusted to profit- and utility-maximizing levels and so all markets clear. In the long run, output adjusts to the full-employment level regardless of the price level. Thus, the *LRAS* is vertical at $Y = \overline{Y}$.

FACTORS THAT SHIFT THE CURVES

- The *SRAS* curve intersects the *LRAS* curve at the expected price level. As a result, an increase in the expected price level shifts the *SRAS* up while a decrease in the expected price level shifts the *SRAS* down.

- Any factor that increases full-employment output shifts both the short-run and the long-run aggregate supply curve to the right. When both curves shift they do so in a way that keeps the *SRAS* intersecting the *LRAS* at the expected price level.

ANALYSIS

- The short-run equilibrium is at the intersection of the *AD* curve and the *SRAS* curve. For example, if, at the time firms and workers signed nominal-wage contracts and firms established what prices they would charge for their output, they expected the price level to be P_1, the relevant *SRAS* curve is $SRAS^1$. If the *AD* curve is located as shown in the diagram, then the short-run equilibrium is at point F. At F, output Y_2 is higher than the full-employment level $\overline{Y}$ and the actual price level P_2 is higher than the expected price level P_1. When nominal-wage contracts come to an end, workers and firms renegotiate their wage contracts based on their understanding of where the actual price level will be in the future. Similarly, price-setting firms re-establish their prices at levels appropriate for where they believe the general price level will be in the future.

- Assuming the *AD* curve remains located as shown in the diagram, the rational price expectation is price level P_0. New wage contracts and new output prices are set based on the expectation that the price level in the future will be P_0. Since the expected price level has increased from P_1 to P_0, the *SRAS* curve shifts up to intersect the *LRAS* at the expected price level P_0. This gives us a long-run equilibrium at point E. In the long run, (1) output equals $\overline{Y}$, and (2) the actual price level equals the expected price level (both equal to P_0).

KEY TERMS

REVIEW QUESTIONS

1. What are the key characteristics of labour contracts in the model of nominal-wage rigidity? What explanation do Keynesians offer for why employees and firms would find it beneficial to sign nominal-wage contracts?

2. Why does signing a nominal-wage contract require that firms and employees calculate a rational price expectation of the price level?

3. What is price stickiness? Why do Keynesians believe that allowing for price stickiness in macroeconomic analysis is important?

4. Define *menu cost*. Why might small menu costs lead to price stickiness in monopolistically competitive markets but not in perfectly competitive markets? Why can a monopolistically competitive firm profitably meet demand at its fixed price when actual demand is greater than the firm anticipated?

5. What does the Keynesian model predict about monetary neutrality (in both the short run and the long run)? Compare the Keynesian predictions about neutrality with those of the basic classical model and the extended classical model with misperceptions.

6. In the Keynesian model, how do increased government purchases affect output and the real interest rate in the short run? In the long run? How do increased government purchases affect the *composition* of output in the long run?

7. Describe two alternative responses available to policymakers when the economy is in recession. What are the advantages and disadvantages of each strategy? Be sure to discuss the effects on employment, the price level, and the composition of output. What are some of the practical difficulties in using macroeconomic stabilization policies to fight recessions?

8. Use the Keynesian model to explain the procyclical behaviour of employment, money, inflation, and investment.

9. What does the Keynesian model predict about the cyclical behaviour of average labour productivity? How does the idea of labour hoarding help bring the prediction of the model into conformity with the business cycle facts?

10. According to the Keynesian analysis, in what two ways does an adverse supply shock reduce output? What problems do supply shocks create for Keynesian stabilization policies?

NUMERICAL PROBLEMS

1. Consider an economy in which all workers are covered by contracts that specify the nominal wage and give the employer the right to choose the amount of employment. The production function is

$$Y = 20\sqrt{N}$$

and the corresponding marginal product of labour is

$$Y = \frac{10}{\sqrt{N}}.$$

Suppose that the nominal wage $W = 20$.

a. Derive an equation that relates the real wage to the amount of labour demanded by firms (the labour demand curve).

b. For the nominal wage of 20, what is the relation between the price level and the amount of labour demanded by firms?

c. What is the relation between the price level and the amount of output supplied by firms? Graph this relation.

   Now suppose that the *IS* and *LM* curves of the economy (the goods market and asset market equilibrium conditions) are described by the following equations:

IS curve	$Y = 120 - 500r$
LM curve	$M/P = 0.5Y - 500r$

d. The money supply M is 300. Use the *IS* and *LM* equations to derive a relation between output Y and the price level P. This relation is the equation for the aggregate demand curve. Graph this relation on the same axis as the relation between the price level and the amount of output supplied by firms (the aggregate supply curve) from part (c).

e. What are the equilibrium values of the price level, output, employment, the real wage, and the real interest rate?

f. Now suppose that the money supply M is 135. What are the equilibrium values of the price level, output, employment, the real wage, and the real interest rate?

2. An economy is described by the following equations:

Desired consumption	$C^d = 130 + 0.5(Y - T) - 500r$
Desired investment	$I^d = 100 - 500r$
Government purchases	$G = 100$
Taxes	$T = 100$
Real money demand	$L = 0.5Y - 1000r$
Money supply	$M = 1320$
Full-employment output	$\overline{Y} = 500$

Assume that expected inflation is zero so that money demand depends directly on the real interest rate. Also assume the *SRAS* is horizontal at the current price level.

a. Write the equations for the *IS* and *LM* curves. (These equations express the relationship between r and Y when the goods and asset markets are in equilibrium.)

b. Calculate the full-employment values of output, the real interest rate, the price level, consumption, and investment.

c. Now suppose that because of investor optimism about the future marginal product of capital, the investment function becomes

$$I^d = 200 - 500r.$$

Assuming that the economy was initially at full employment, what are the new values of output, the real interest rate, the price level, consumption, and investment in the short run? In the long run? Show your results graphically.

3. Consider the following economy:

Desired consumption $C^d = 325 + 0.5(Y - T) - 500r$
Desired investment $I^d = 200 - 500r$
Government purchases $G = 150$
Taxes $T = 150$
Real money demand $L = 0.5Y - 1000r$
Money supply $M = 6000$
Full-employment output $\overline{Y} = 1000$

Assume the *SRAS* is horizontal at the current price level.

a. Calculate the full-employment values of the real interest rate, the price level, consumption, and investment.

b. Now suppose that government purchases are increased to 250, with no change in current taxes. Assuming that the economy was initially at full employment, what are the new values of output, the real interest rate, the price level, consumption, and investment in the short run? In the long run?

c. Repeat part (b) for an increase in the money supply to 7200. Assume that $G = 150$.

4. An economy is described by the following equations:

Desired consumption $C^d = 600 + 0.8(Y - T) - 500r$
Desired investment $I^d = 400 - 500r$
Real money demand $L = 0.5Y - 2000i$, for $i > 0$

Government purchases G and taxes T both equal 1000. The initial price level P equals 2.0, and expected inflation π^e is zero. Full-employment output $\overline{Y}$ is 8000. Notice that the real money demand function above is defined only for positive values of the nominal interest rate. We assume that when the nominal interest rate equals zero, people are willing to hold as much money as the central bank wishes to supply; this assumption implies that the *LM* curve becomes horizontal for zero values of the nominal interest rate.

a. Show that in this economy the requirement that the nominal interest rate must be greater than or equal to zero is not consistent with full employment. Can monetary policy alone restore full employment in this economy? Why or why not?

b. Find a combination of the money supply M and government purchases G that restores full employment while keeping the nominal interest rate at zero. Discuss the relevance of this policy to the case of Japan in the 1990s. Assume that the price level and inflation expectations are unchanged.

5. An open economy is described by the following equations:

Desired consumption $C^d = 120 + 0.5(Y - T) - 200r$
Desired investment $I^d = 120 - 200r$
Net exports $NX = 60 + 0.05Y_{For} - 100r$
Government purchases $G = 100$
Taxes $T = 100$
Real money demand $L = 0.8Y - 200r$
Money supply $M = 10\ 800$
Foreign output $Y_{For} = 1000$
Full-employment output $\overline{Y} = 700$

a. Write the equation for the aggregate demand curve. (*Hint:* Find the equations describing goods market equilibrium and asset market equilibrium. Use these two equations to eliminate the real interest rate. For any given price level, the equation of the aggregate demand curve gives the level of output that satisfies both goods market equilibrium and asset market equilibrium.)

b. Suppose that $P = 18$. What are the short-run values of output, the real interest rate, consumption, net exports, and investment?

c. What are the long-run equilibrium values of output, the real interest rate, consumption, investment, net exports, and the price level?

6. (Appendix 12.A) A firm identifies the following relationship between the real wage it pays and the effort exerted by its workers:

Real Wage	Effort
8	7
10	10
12	15
14	17
16	19
18	20

The marginal product of labour for this firm is

$$MPN = \frac{E(100 - N)}{15},$$

where E is the effort level and N is the number of workers employed. If the firm can pay only one of the six wage levels shown, which should it choose? How many workers will it employ? There are 200 workers in the town where the firm is located, all willing to work at a real wage of 8. Does this change your answer to the first part of this question? If so, how?

7. (Appendix 12.B) Consider the economy described in Numerical Problem 3.

   a. What are the values of α_{IS}, β_{IS}, α_{LM}, β_{LM}, and l_r for this economy? You will have to refer back to Appendix 9.B (p. 288) for definitions of these coefficients.

   b. Suppose that the price level is fixed at $\overline{P} = 15$. What are the short-run equilibrium values of output and the real interest rate?

   c. With the price level still fixed at $\overline{P} = 15$, suppose that government purchases increase from $G = 150$ to $G = 250$. What are the new values of α_{IS} and the short-run equilibrium level of output?

   d. Use Eq. (12.B.7) to compute the size of the change in output that results from a change in government purchases. Use your answer to compute the short-run change in Y resulting from an increase in government purchases from $G = 150$ to $G = 250$. How does your answer here compare with your answer in part (c)?

ANALYTICAL PROBLEMS

1. According to the Keynesian model, what is the effect of each of the following on output, the real interest rate, employment, and the price level? Distinguish between the short run and the long run. In answering this question, use *IS–LM–FE* and *AD–AS* diagrams in the manner of Figures 12.3 and 12.4 (pp. 398 and 402).

   a. Increased tax incentives for investment (the tax breaks for investment are offset by lump-sum tax increases that keep total current tax collections unchanged).

   b. Increased tax incentives for saving (as in part (a), lump-sum tax increases offset the effect on total current tax collections).

   c. A wave of investor pessimism about the future profitability of capital investments.

   d. An increase in consumer confidence, as consumers expect that their incomes will be higher in the future.

2. According to the Keynesian model, what is the effect of each of the following on output, the real interest rate, employment, and the price level? Distinguish

between the short run and the long run. In answering this question, use *IS–LM–FE* and *AD–AS* diagrams in the manner of Figures 12.3 and 12.4.

   a. Financial deregulation allows banks to pay a higher interest rate on chequing accounts.

   b. The introduction of debit cards greatly reduces the amount of money that people need for transactions.

   c. A severe water shortage causes sharp declines in agricultural output and increases in food prices.

   d. A temporary beneficial supply shock affects most of the economy, but no individual firm is affected sufficiently to change its prices in the short run.

3. Suppose that the Bank of Canada has a policy of increasing the money supply when it observes that the economy is in recession. However, suppose that about six months are needed for an increase in the money supply to affect aggregate demand, which is about the same amount of time needed for firms to review and reset their prices and for employees and firms to complete current wage contracts. What effects will the Bank's policy have on output and price stability? Does your answer change if (a) the Bank has some ability to forecast recessions or (b) wage and price adjustment take longer than six months?

4. Classical economists argue that using fiscal policy to fight a recession does not make workers better off. Suppose, however, that the Keynesian model is correct. Relative to a policy of doing nothing, does an increase in government purchases that brings the economy to full employment make workers better off? In answering the question, discuss the effects of the fiscal expansion on the real wage, employment, consumption, and current and future taxes. How does your answer depend on (a) the direct benefits of the government spending program, and (b) the speed with which prices adjust in the absence of fiscal stimulus?

5. (Appendix 12.A) Some labour economists argue that it is useful to think of the labour market as being divided into two sectors: a primary sector, where "good" (high-paying, long-term) jobs are located, and a secondary sector, which has "bad" (low-paying, short-term) jobs. Suppose that the primary sector has a high marginal product of labour and (because effort is costly for firms to monitor) firms pay an efficiency wage. The secondary sector has a low marginal product of labour and no efficiency wage; instead, the real wage in the secondary sector adjusts so that the quantities of labour demanded and supplied are equal in that sector. Workers are alike, and all would prefer

to work in the primary sector. However, workers who cannot find jobs in the primary sector work in the secondary sector.

What are the effects of each of the following on the real wage, employment, and output in both sectors?

a. Expansionary monetary policy increases the demand for primary sector output.

b. Immigration increases the labour force.

c. The effort curve changes so that a higher real wage is needed to elicit the greatest effort per dollar in the primary sector. Effort exerted at the higher real wage is the same as before the change in the effort curve.

d. There is a temporary productivity improvement in the primary sector.

e. There is a temporary productivity improvement in the secondary sector.

APPENDIX 12.A

REAL-WAGE RIGIDITY

In this appendix we discuss the Keynesian notion of **real-wage rigidity**. This is the name Keynesians give to the idea that the real wage moves "too little" to keep the quantity of labour demanded equal to the quantity of labour supplied. Keynesians offer the idea of real-wage rigidity as a response to the claim made by classical economists that in full equilibrium all unemployment arises due to mismatches between workers and jobs (frictional or structural unemployment). Keynesians do not dispute that mismatch is a major source of long-run unemployment, but they are skeptical that it explains all unemployment in general equilibrium.

Keynesians are particularly unwilling to accept the classical idea that recessions are periods of increased mismatch between workers and jobs. If higher unemployment during downturns reflected increased mismatch, Keynesians argue, recessions should be periods of particularly active search by workers for jobs and by firms for new employees. However, surveys suggest that unemployed workers spend relatively little time searching for work (many are simply waiting, hoping to be recalled to their old jobs), and help-wanted advertising and vacancy postings by firms fall rather than rise during recessions. Rather than times of increased worker–job mismatch, Keynesians believe that recessions are periods of generally low demand for both output and workers throughout the economy.

SOME REASONS FOR REAL-WAGE RIGIDITY

For a rigid real wage to be the source of unemployment, the real wage that firms are paying must be higher than the market-clearing real wage, at which quantities of labour supplied and demanded are equal. But if the real wage is higher than necessary to attract workers, why don't firms save labour costs by simply reducing the wage they pay, as suggested by the classical analysis?

Various explanations have been offered for why real wages might be rigid, even in the face of an excess supply of labour. One possibility is that there are legal and institutional factors that keep wages high, such as minimum-wage laws and union contracts. However, most Canadian workers are neither union members nor minimum-wage earners (about 30% are unionized), so these barriers to wage cutting cannot be the main reason for real-wage rigidity. Furthermore, the minimum wage in Canadian provinces is specified in nominal terms so that workers who are paid the minimum wage would have rigid nominal wages rather than rigid real wages. (Union contracts may help explain real-wage rigidity in Western European and other countries in which a high proportion of workers are unionized, and in which nominal wages are typically adjusted for inflation in order to maintain the real wage at its negotiated level.)

Another explanation for why a firm might pay a higher real wage than it "has to" is that this policy might reduce the firm's **turnover costs**, or the costs associated with hiring and training new workers. By paying a high wage, the firm can keep more of its current workers, which saves the firm the cost of hiring and training replacements. Similarly, by developing a reputation for paying well, the firm can assure itself of more and better applicants for any position that it may have to fill.

A third reason why firms might pay real wages above market-clearing levels is that workers who are paid well may have greater incentives to work hard and effectively. If highly paid workers are more productive, the firm may profit from paying its employees well, even though it could attract all the workers it needs at a lower real wage. The idea that a worker's productivity depends on the real wage received and that, therefore, firms may pay wages above the market-clearing level is the essence of the **efficiency wage model**. Because this model of wage determination has played a key role in recent Keynesian analyses and because it has several interesting aspects, we focus on it for the remainder of this appendix.

THE EFFICIENCY WAGE MODEL

If better-paid workers are more productive, firms may gain by paying wages higher than the minimum necessary to attract workers. But why might a worker's productivity depend on the real wage received? The answer has both "carrot" and "stick" aspects.

The *carrot* or positive incentive is based on the idea that workers who feel well treated will work harder and more efficiently. Nobel Laureate George Akerlof,[17] of the University of California at Berkeley, argued that workers who believe that their employer is treating them fairly—say, by paying higher wages than required to retain them and by not cutting wages in slack times—will, in turn, want to treat the employer fairly by doing a good job. Akerlof called this motivation the *gift exchange motive* because it is similar to the one that leads people to exchange gifts.

The *stick* or threat aspect of why a firm would pay a higher wage than necessary has been analyzed in an economic model called the "shirking" model of wage determination.[18] According to the *shirking model*, if a worker is paid only the minimum amount needed to attract her to a particular job, she will not be too concerned about the possibility of being fired if she does not perform well. After all, if the job pays the minimum amount necessary to induce her to take the job, she is not much happier with the job than without the job. In this case, the worker will be more inclined to take it easy at work and shirk her duties, and the employer will have to bear the cost either of the shirking or of paying supervisors to make sure that the work gets done. In contrast, a worker receiving a higher wage will place a greater value on keeping her job (it is not that easy to find another job as good) and will work hard to avoid being fired for shirking.

The gift exchange idea and the shirking model both imply that workers' efforts on the job depend on the real wages they receive. Graphically, the relation between the real wage and the level of effort is shown by the **effort curve** in Figure 12.A.1. The real wage w is measured along the horizontal axis, and the level of effort E is measured along the vertical axis. The effort curve passes through points 0, A, and B. When real wages are higher, workers choose to work harder, for either "carrot" or "stick" reasons; therefore, the effort curve slopes upward. We assume that the effort curve is S-shaped. At the lowest levels of the real wage, workers make hardly any effort, and effort rises only slowly as the

[17] "Labor Contracts as Partial Gift Exchange," *Quarterly Journal of Economics*, November 1982, pp. 543–569.
[18] See Carl Shapiro and Joseph E. Stiglitz, "Equilibrium Unemployment as a Worker Discipline Device," *American Economic Review*, June 1984, pp. 433–444.

FIGURE 12.A.1

DETERMINATION OF THE EFFICIENCY WAGE

The effort curve shows the relation between worker effort, E, and the real-wage workers receive, w. A higher real wage leads to more effort, but above a certain point, higher wages are unable to spur effort much, so the effort curve is S-shaped. For any point on the curve, the amount of effort per dollar of real wage is the slope of the line from the origin to that point. At point A, effort per dollar of real wage is E_A/w_A. The highest level of effort per dollar of real wage is at point B, where the line from the origin is tangent to the curve. The real wage rate at B is the efficiency wage w^*, and the corresponding level of effort is E^*.

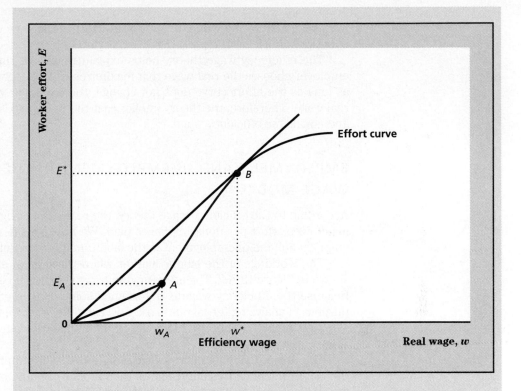

FIGURE 12.A.1

DETERMINATION OF THE EFFICIENCY WAGE

The effort curve shows the relation between worker effort, E, and the real-wage workers receive, w. A higher real wage leads to more effort, but above a certain point, higher wages are unable to spur effort much, so the effort curve is S-shaped. For any point on the curve, the amount of effort per dollar of real wage is the slope of the line from the origin to that point. At point A, effort per dollar of real wage is E_A/w_A. The highest level of effort per dollar of real wage is at point B, where the line from the origin is tangent to the curve. The real wage rate at B is the efficiency wage w^*, and the corresponding level of effort is E^*.

real wage increases. At higher levels of the real wage, effort rises sharply, as shown by the steeply rising portion of the curve. The curve flattens at very high levels of the real wage because there is some maximum level of effort that workers really cannot exceed no matter how motivated they are.

WAGE DETERMINATION IN THE EFFICIENCY WAGE MODEL

The effort curve shows that effort depends on the real wage, but what determines the real wage? To make as much profit as possible, *firms will choose the level of the real wage that gets the most effort from workers for each dollar of real wages paid.* The amount of effort per dollar of real wages equals the amount of effort E divided by the real wage w. The ratio of E to w can be found graphically from Figure 12.A.1. Consider, for example, point A on the effort curve, at which the real wage w_A induces workers to supply effort E_A. The slope of the line from the origin to A equals the height of the curve at point A, E_A, divided by the horizontal distance, w_A. Thus, the slope of the line from the origin to A equals the amount of effort per dollar of real wages at A.

The real wage that achieves the highest effort per dollar of wages is at point B. The slope of the line from the origin to B, which is the amount of effort per dollar of real wage at B, is greater than the slope of the line from the origin to any other point on the curve. In general, to locate the real wage that maximizes effort per dollar of real wage, draw a line from the origin tangent to the effort curve; the real wage at the tangency point maximizes effort per dollar of real wage. We call the real wage that maximizes effort or efficiency per dollar of real wages the **efficiency wage**. In Figure 12.A.1, the efficiency wage is w^*, and the corresponding level of effort is E^*.

The efficiency wage theory helps explain real-wage rigidity. Because the employer chooses the real wage that maximizes effort received per dollar paid, as long as the effort curve does not change, the employer will not change the real wage. Therefore, the theory implies that the real wage is permanently rigid and equals the efficiency wage.

EMPLOYMENT AND UNEMPLOYMENT IN THE EFFICIENCY WAGE MODEL

According to the efficiency wage theory, the real wage is rigid at the level that maximizes effort per dollar of wages paid. We now consider how the levels of employment and unemployment in the labour market are determined.

The workings of the labour market when there is an efficiency wage are shown in Figure 12.A.2. The efficiency wage w^* is indicated by a horizontal line. Because the efficiency wage is determined solely by the effort curve, for the purpose of analyzing the labour market we can take w^* to be fixed. Similarly, we can take the level of effort E^* induced by the efficiency wage w^* as fixed at this stage of the analysis.

The upward-sloping curve is the standard labour supply curve, NS. As in the classical model, this curve shows the number of hours of work that people would like to supply at each level of the real wage.[19]

The downward-sloping curve is the demand curve for labour in the efficiency wage model. Recall from Chapter 3 that the amount of labour demanded by a firm depends on the marginal product of labour, or MPN. Specifically, the labour demand curve is identical to the MPN curve, which, in turn, relates the marginal product of labour MPN to the quantity of labour input N being used. The MPN curve—and hence the labour demand curve—slopes down because of the diminishing marginal productivity of labour.

In the classical model, the marginal product of labour depends only on the production function and the capital stock. A complication of the efficiency wage model is that the amount of output produced by an extra worker (or hour of work) also depends on the worker's effort. Fortunately, as we noted, the efficiency wage w^* and the effort level induced by that wage, E^*, are fixed at this stage of the analysis. Thus, the labour demand curve in Figure 12.A.2, ND^*, reflects the marginal product of labour when worker effort is held fixed at E^*. As in the classical case, an increase in productivity or in the capital stock shifts the labour demand curve ND^* to the right. In addition, any change in the effort curve that led to an increase in the optimal level of effort E^* would raise the MPN, and the labour demand curve ND^* again would shift to the right.

Now, we can put the elements of Figure 12.A.2 together to show how employment is determined. Point A on the labour demand curve ND^* indicates that when the real wage is fixed at w^*, firms want to employ $\overline{N}$ hours of labour. Point B on the labour supply curve indicates that when the real wage is fixed at

[19] For simplicity, we assume that the number of hours of labour that people want to supply does not depend on the effort they must exert while on the job.

When the efficiency wage w^* is paid, the firm's demand for labour is $\overline{N}$. represented by point A. However, the amount of labour that workers want to supply at a real wage of w^* is NS_1. The excess supply of labour equals distance AB. We assume that the efficiency wage w^* is higher than the market-clearing wage w_E that would prevail if the supply of labour equalled the demand for labour at point E.

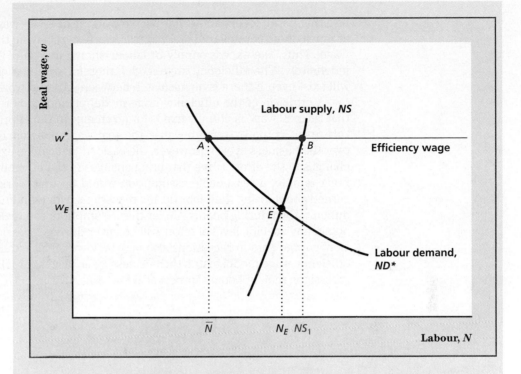

w^*, workers want to supply NS_1 hours of labour, which is greater than the amount demanded by firms. At the efficiency wage, the quantity of labour supplied is greater than the quantity demanded,[20] so the level of employment is determined by the labour demand of firms and hence equals $\overline{N}$. The demand-determined level of employment is labelled $\overline{N}$ because it represents the full employment level of employment for this model; that is, $\overline{N}$ is the level of employment reached after full adjustment of wages and prices. (Note that the value of $\overline{N}$ in the efficiency wage model differs from the full-employment level of employment in the classical model of the labour market, which would correspond to N_E in Figure 12.A.2.) Because the efficiency wage is rigid at w^*, in the absence of shocks the level of employment in this economy remains at $\overline{N}$ indefinitely.

Perhaps the most interesting aspect of Figure 12.A.2. is that it provides a new explanation of unemployment. It shows that even when wages have adjusted as much as they are going to and the economy is technically at "full employment," an excess supply of labour, $NS_1 - \overline{N}$, remains.[21]

Why don't the unemployed bid down the real wage and, thus, gain employment, as they would in the classical model of the labour market? Unlike the classical case, in a labour market with an efficiency wage, the real wage cannot be bid down by people offering to work at lower wages because employers will not

[20] The result that there is an excess supply of labour requires the assumption that the efficiency wage w^* is higher than the real wage that would clear the labour market, shown as w_E in Figure 12.A.2. We always assume that the efficiency wage is higher than the market-clearing wage; if it were not, firms would have to pay the market-clearing wage to attract workers.

[21] Because the unemployment represented by the excess supply of labour persists even when the economy is at full employment, it is considered part of structural unemployment.

hire them. Employers know that people working at lower wages will not put out as much effort per dollar of real wages as workers receiving the higher efficiency wage. Thus, the excess supply of labour shown in Figure 12.A.2. will persist indefinitely. The efficiency wage model, therefore, implies that unemployment will exist even if there is no mismatch between jobs and workers.

A criticism of the efficiency wage model presented here is that it predicts that the real wage is literally fixed (for no change in the effort curve). Of course, this result is too extreme because the real wage does change over time (and over the business cycle). However, the basic model can be extended to allow for changes in the effort curve that bring changes in the efficiency wage over time. For example, a reasonable assumption would be that workers are more concerned about losing their jobs during recessions, when finding a new job is more difficult, than during booms. Under this assumption, the real wage necessary to obtain any specific level of effort will be lower during recessions; hence the efficiency wage paid in recessions also may be lower. This extension may help the efficiency wage model match the business cycle fact that real wages are lower in recessions than in booms (procyclical real wages).

APPENDIX 12.B

AGGREGATE DEMAND POLICIES AND THE POSITION ON THE AGGREGATE DEMAND CURVE

In this chapter, we showed how fiscal policy and monetary policy can be used to shift the aggregate demand curve (AD). In this appendix, we use the algebraic analysis in Appendix 9.B to derive an expression showing the size of the shift in the AD curve that is associated with a change in government purchases G and an expression showing the size of the shift in the AD curve that is associated with a change in the nominal money supply M.

Recall that in Appendix 9.B we derived an expression for the AD curve given by Eq. (9.B.24). We repeat that expression here as Eq. (12.B.1):

$$Y = \frac{\alpha_{IS} - \alpha_{LM} + (1/\ell_r)(M/P)}{\beta_{IS} + \beta_{LM}}. \tag{12.B.1}$$

Also recall, from Appendix 9.B, the following expressions for the terms appearing in Eq. (12.B.1):

$$\alpha_{IS} = \frac{c_0 + i_0 + G - c_Y t_0}{c_r + i_r} \qquad \beta_{IS} = \frac{1 - (1 - t)c_Y}{c_r + i_r}$$

$$\alpha_{LM} = \left(\frac{\ell_0}{\ell_r}\right) - \pi^e \qquad \beta_{LM} = \left(\frac{\ell_Y}{\ell_r}\right). \tag{12.B.2}$$

Let's first consider the effect on aggregate demand of a change in the nominal money supply M. Observe that a change in M has no effect on the value of any of the terms in Eq. (12.B.2). From Eq. (12.B.1), therefore, if the nominal money supply changes by ΔM then the change in output must be:

$$\Delta Y = \frac{(1/\ell_r)(\Delta M/P)}{\beta_{IS} + \beta_{LM}}$$

which can also be rearranged as:

$$\frac{\Delta Y}{\Delta M} = \frac{(1/\ell_r)(1/p)}{\beta_{IS} + \beta_{LM}}. \tag{12.B.3}$$

This expression defines the size of the change in real output resulting from a change in the nominal money supply conditioned on the assumption that the price level P did not change. In other words, this expression measures the size of the horizontal shift in the AD curve caused by a change in the nominal money supply. Since ℓ_r, P, β_{IS}, and β_{LM} are all positive values, then $\Delta Y/\Delta M$ is positive. That is, an increase in the nominal money supply causes an increase in output and so can be represented by a shift to the right in the AD curve.

Now let's consider the effect of a change in government purchases G. Observe from Eq. (12.B.2) that a change in G affects the value of α_{IS} but none of the other terms appearing in Eq. (12.B.1). From Eq. (12.B.1), therefore, the change in output caused by a change in government purchases is equal to:

$$\Delta Y = \frac{\Delta \alpha_{IS}}{\beta_{IS} + \beta_{LM}}. \tag{12.B.4}$$

Since, from the definition of α_{IS} shown in Eq. (12.B.2), $\Delta\alpha_{IS} = \Delta G/(C_r + i_r)$, we can rewrite Eq. (12.B.4) as:

$$\frac{\Delta Y}{\Delta G} = \frac{1}{(\beta_{IS} + \beta_{LM})(c_r + i_r)}.$$

(12.B.5)

This expression defines the size of the change in real output resulting from a change in government purchases conditioned on the assumption that the price level, P, did not change. In other words, this expression measures the size of the horizontal shift in the AD curve caused by a change in the size of government purchases. Since β_{IS}, β_{LM}, C_r, and i_r are all positive values, then $\Delta Y/\Delta G$ is positive. That is, an increase in government purchases causes an increase in output and so can be represented by a shift to the right in the AD curve.

The size of the shifts in the AD curve resulting from a change in the nominal money supply and a change in government purchases may be large or small depending on the specific values of the terms in the expressions contained in Eqs. (12.B.3) and (12.B.5), respectively. To better see this, it is useful to show those two expressions in a different way. To do so, we substitute expressions for β_{IS} and β_{LM} into those calculations. The results are:

$$\frac{\Delta Y}{\Delta M} = \frac{(c_r + i_r)(1/\ell_r P)}{1 - (1 - t)c_Y + (c_r + i_r)(\ell_Y/\ell_r)}$$

(12.B.6)

and

$$\frac{\Delta Y}{\Delta G} = \frac{1}{1 - (1 - t)c_Y + (c_r + i_r)(\ell_Y/\ell_r)}.$$

(12.B.7)

In this chapter we discussed how fiscal and monetary policies have opposite effects on the interest rate. Let's see if our calculations confirm that discussion.

An expansionary monetary policy works to increase output by causing the interest rate to fall, and this encourages investment and consumption spending to increase. The sensitivity of investment spending and consumption spending to changes in the interest rate are measured by the values of i_r and c_r, respectively. If these values are small, then an expansionary monetary policy will have a small influence on output. From Eq. (12.B.6) we see that setting the values of i_r and c_r to zero causes $\Delta Y/\Delta M = 0$. That is, monetary policy is unable to cause a shift in the AD curve if investment and consumption spending are not sensitive to changes in the interest rate. The algebra therefore confirms the discussion in the text.

An expansionary fiscal policy works to increase output *despite* the effect it has on the interest rate. That is, as discussed in this chapter and in Chapter 9, an expansionary fiscal policy "crowds out" interest-sensitive investment and consumption spending. An expansionary fiscal policy will therefore be more effective if the values of i_r and c_r are small. From Eq. (12.B.7) we see that setting the values of i_r and c_r to zero causes $\Delta Y/\Delta G$ to become larger. That is, fiscal policy is able to cause a larger shift in the AD curve when the crowding out effect is absent. Once again the algebra confirms the discussion in the text.

It is important to stress that the calculations in Eqs. (12.B.6) and (12.B.7) represent only the size of the horizontal shift in the AD curve caused by a monetary and a fiscal policy, respectively. That is, these measures assume the price level does not change. The true change in output resulting from a monetary or a fiscal policy will depend on the size of the shift in the AD curve *and* on the slope of the $SRAS$ curve. Because the $SRAS$ is positively sloped, as assumed in the extended classical model and in the Keynesian model, any aggregate demand policy will result in an increase in the price level as well as an increase in output. The steeper the $SRAS$, the smaller will be the effect of any aggregate demand policy on output.

Finally, it is important to emphasize that fluctuations in aggregate demand are not solely, or even mainly, the result of fluctuations in fiscal and monetary policy variables. We are reminded of this by the observation that changes in α_{IS} and α_{LM} (see Eq. 12.B.2) result not only from changes in policy variables like G and t_0 but also from changes in c_0, i_0, and ℓ_0. Thus, Keynes's so-called "animal spirits," which produce waves of pessimism and optimism affecting c_0 and i_0 and shocks to money demand affecting ℓ_0 also give rise to shifts in AD.

Chapter 13

Unemployment and Inflation

In the last several chapters, we focused on the concepts of the business cycle, macroeconomic stabilization, and classical and Keynesian approaches to business cycle analysis. Although these concepts are central to today's macroeconomics, actual policy discussions rarely involve such abstract terms. Policy debates tend to focus on highly publicized economic statistics, such as inflation and unemployment. To make a stronger connection between business cycle theories and policy debates, we now take a closer look at unemployment and inflation, first together and then separately.

Unemployment and inflation—sometimes referred to as the "twin evils" of macroeconomics—are among the most difficult and politically sensitive economic issues that policymakers face. High rates of unemployment and inflation generate intense public concern because their effects are direct and visible: Almost everyone is affected by rising prices, and few workers can be confident that they will never lose their jobs.

Moreover, there is a long-standing idea in macroeconomics that unemployment and inflation are somehow related. In the first part of this chapter, we discuss in some detail the concept of the Phillips curve—an empirical relationship between inflation and unemployment. According to the Phillips curve, inflation tends to be low when unemployment is high and high when unemployment is low. The Phillips curve relationship raises some important questions about how the economy works and how macroeconomic policies should be used.

We then look at unemployment and inflation separately. We examine the costs that each imposes on society and consider the options that policymakers have for dealing with these problems. This chapter begins Part IV of the book, the purpose of which is to explore macroeconomic policymaking in greater detail. Following the discussion of inflation and unemployment in this chapter, Chapter 14 takes a closer look at institutions and debates related to the making of monetary policy, and Chapter 15 provides a similar overview of fiscal policy.

13.1 Unemployment and Inflation: Is There a Trade-Off?

Newspaper editorials and public discussions about economic policy often refer to the "trade-off" between inflation and unemployment. The idea is that to reduce inflation, the economy must tolerate high unemployment, or that to reduce unemployment, more inflation must be accepted. This section examines the idea of an inflation–unemployment trade-off and its implications for macroeconomic policy.

The origin of the idea of a trade-off between inflation and unemployment was a 1958 article by economist A. W. Phillips, of the London School of Economics.[1] Phillips examined 97 years of British data on unemployment and nominal wage growth data; he found that, historically, unemployment tended to be low in years when nominal wages grew rapidly and high in years when nominal wages grew slowly. Economists who built on Phillips's work shifted its focus slightly by looking at the link between unemployment and inflation—that is, the growth rate of prices—rather than the link between unemployment and the growth rate of wages. During the 1960s, many statistical studies examined inflation and unemployment data for numerous countries and time periods, finding, in many cases, a negative relationship between the two variables. This negative empirical relationship between unemployment and inflation is known as the **Phillips curve**.

A striking example of a Phillips curve, shown in Figure 13.1, occurred in Canada during the 1960s. The Canadian economy expanded throughout most of

FIGURE 13.1

THE PHILLIPS CURVE AND THE CANADIAN ECONOMY DURING THE 1960s

During the 1960s, Canadian rates of inflation seemed to lie along a Phillips curve. Inflation rose and unemployment fell fairly steadily during this decade, and policymakers had apparently decided to live with higher inflation in order to reduce unemployment.

Source: Adapted from the following: Unemployment rate: *Historical Statistics of Canada*, Series D233; Inflation rate, 1960–1961: Calculated using GDP deflator, Statistics Canada CANSIM II, series v1997756. This does not constitute an endorsement by Statistics Canada of this product.

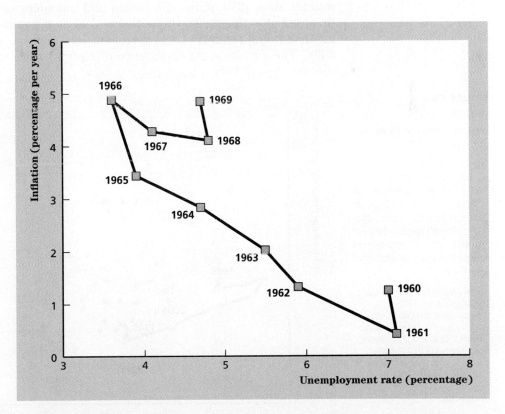

[1] "The Relation Between Unemployment and the Rate of Change of Money Wage Rates in the United Kingdom, 1861–1957," *Economica*, November 1958, pp. 283–299.

the 1960s, with unemployment falling and inflation rising more or less steadily. In Figure 13.1, the inflation rate is measured on the vertical axis, and the unemployment rate is measured on the horizontal axis. Note that years, such as 1961, that had high unemployment also had low inflation, and that years, such as 1966, that had high inflation also had low unemployment. The data produce a clear downward-sloping relation between inflation and unemployment—that is, a Phillips curve. The experience of several countries in the 1960s, which came after Phillips's article had been published and widely disseminated, was viewed by many as a confirmation of his basic finding.

The policy implications of these findings were much debated. Initially, the Phillips curve seemed to offer policymakers a "menu" of combinations of inflation and unemployment from which they could choose. Indeed, during the 1960s, some economists argued that by accepting a modest amount of inflation, macroeconomic policymakers could keep the unemployment rate low indefinitely. This belief seemed to be borne out during the 1960s, when rising inflation was accompanied by falling unemployment.

In the following decades, however, this relationship between inflation and unemployment failed to hold. In Figure 13.2 we add to the data from Figure 13.1 data on inflation and unemployment for the years 1970–2015. Since 1970, unlike the 1960s, there has seemed to be no reliable relationship between unemployment and inflation. The relationship between inflation and unemployment, far from remaining tightly bound within a range of 5 percentage points of inflation and 4 percentage points of unemployment as in the 1960s, went on a four-decade-long wander after 1970. Rates of inflation and unemployment moved to levels not dreamed of in the 1960s. Often, they did so at the same time, as in 1982 when unemployment reached 11% of the labour force and the annual inflation rate was 8.2%. The simultaneous appearance of high inflation and high unemployment

FIGURE 13.2

INFLATION AND UNEMPLOYMENT IN CANADA, 1960–2015

The figure shows the combinations of inflation and unemployment experienced in Canada each year from 1960 to 2015. Unlike the situation during the 1960s, after 1970, the relationship between inflation and unemployment seemed to change from what it had been in the 1960s.

Source: Adapted from the following: Unemployment rate, 1970–1975: *Historical Statistics of Canada*, Series D233; 1976–2015: Statistics Canada CANSIM II, series v2461224; Inflation rate: Calculated using GDP deflator, Statistics Canada CANSIM II, series v1997756. This does not constitute an endorsement by Statistics Canada of this product.

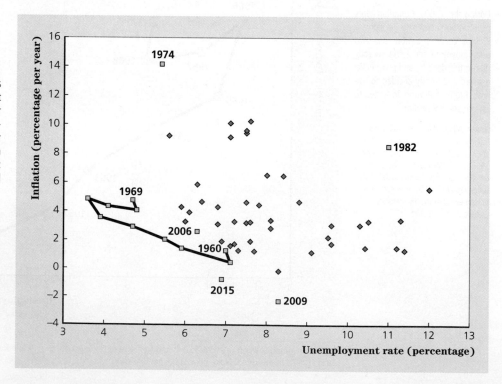

prompted analysts to coin a new phrase to describe this unappetizing set of economic conditions: stagflation. Only in 2006 did rates of inflation and unemployment return to values last seen in the 1960s. In 2015, rates of inflation and unemployment were similar to what they were observed in the early 1960s.

The original empirical results of Phillips and others who extended his work, together with the unexpected experience of the economy after 1970, raise at least three important questions:

- Why was the original Phillips curve relationship between inflation and unemployment frequently observed historically, as in the cases of the United Kingdom in the century before 1958, and Canada, the United States, and elsewhere in the 1960s?

- Why did the simple negative relationship between inflation and unemployment that seemed to exist during the 1960s change after 1970? Was there a systematic relationship between inflation and unemployment in the Canadian economy after 1970?

- Does the Phillips curve actually provide a menu of choices from which policymakers can choose? For example, by electing to maintain a high inflation rate, can policymakers guarantee a *permanently* low rate of unemployment?

Economic theory provides reasonable answers to these questions; in particular, it explains the disappearance of the stable Phillips curve that had been observed during the 1960s. Interestingly, the key economic analysis of the Phillips curve—which predicted that this relationship would not be stable—was done during the 1960s, before the Phillips curve actually proved to be unstable. Thus, we have at least one example of economic theorists predicting an important development in the economy that policymakers and the public did not anticipate.

THE EXPECTATIONS-AUGMENTED PHILLIPS CURVE

Although the Phillips curve seemed to describe adequately the unemployment–inflation relationship in several countries in the 1960s, during the second half of the decade, some economists, notably Milton Friedman,[2] of the University of Chicago, and Edmund Phelps,[3] of Columbia University, questioned the logic of the Phillips curve. Friedman and Phelps argued—purely on the basis of economic theory—that there should not be a stable negative relationship between inflation and unemployment. Instead, a negative relationship should exist between *unanticipated* inflation (the difference between the actual and expected inflation rates) and *cyclical* unemployment (the difference between the actual and natural unemployment rates).[4] Although these distinctions appear to be merely technical, they are crucial in understanding the relationship between the actual rates of inflation and unemployment.

Before discussing the significance of their analyses, we need to explain how Friedman and Phelps arrived at their conclusions. To do so, we use the extended classical model, which includes the misperceptions theory. (Analytical Problem 3

---

[2] "The Role of Monetary Policy," *American Economic Review*, March 1968, pp. 1–17.

[3] "Wage Dynamics and Labor Market Equilibrium," in Edmund Phelps, ed., *Microeconomic Foundations of Employment and Inflation Theory*, New York: W.W. Norton, 1970, pp. 124–166.

[4] In Chapter 3, we defined cyclical unemployment. Recall that the natural rate of unemployment is the unemployment rate that exists when output is at its full-employment level. The natural rate exceeds zero because of frictional and structural unemployment, also defined in Chapter 3.

at the end of this chapter asks you to perform a similar analysis using the Keynesian model.) We proceed in two steps, first considering an economy at full employment with steady, fully anticipated inflation. In this economy, both unanticipated inflation and cyclical unemployment are zero. Second, we consider what happens when aggregate demand growth increases unexpectedly. In this case, both positive unanticipated inflation (inflation greater than expected) and negative cyclical unemployment (actual unemployment lower than the natural rate) occur. This outcome confirms the Friedman–Phelps point that a negative relationship exists between unanticipated inflation and cyclical unemployment.

We develop the first step of this analysis by using the extended classical model to analyze an economy with steady inflation (Figure 13.3). We assume that this economy is in full-employment equilibrium in which the money supply has been growing at 10% per year for many years and is expected to continue to grow at this rate indefinitely. With the money supply growing by 10% per year, the aggregate demand curve shifts up by 10% each year, from AD^1 in year 1 to AD^2 in year 2, and so on. For simplicity, we assume that full-employment output $\overline{Y}$ is constant, but relaxing that assumption would not affect our basic conclusions.

In Figure 13.3, the short-run aggregate supply (SRAS) curve shifts up by 10% each year. Why? Recall our assumption that people form expectations of the price level based on a reasoned and intelligent examination of available economic data. That is, they form a rational price expectation. Given that the money supply has been growing by 10% per year for many years and policymakers have announced their intention to continue with that policy, it is sensible for people to expect the aggregate demand curve to shift up by 10% each year. Thus, in year 2, people expect the aggregate demand curve to be AD^2. The rational price expectation for year 2, then, is price level 110. Given this price expectation for year 2, the short-run aggregate supply curve shifts up to intersect the long-run aggregate supply curve at price level 110.

FIGURE 13.3

ONGOING INFLATION IN THE EXTENDED CLASSICAL MODEL

If the money supply grows by 10% every year, the AD curve shifts up by 10% every year, from AD^1 in year 1 to AD^2 in year 2, and so on. If the money supply has been growing by 10% per year for some time and the rate of inflation has been 10% for some time, the expected rate of inflation is also 10%. Thus, the expected price level also grows by 10% each year, from 100 in year 1 to 110 in year 2, and so on. The 10% annual increase in the expected price level shifts the SRAS curve up by 10% each year, for example, from $SRAS^1$ in year 1 to $SRAS^2$ in year 2. The economy remains in full-employment equilibrium at the intersection of the AD curve and the SRAS curve in each year (point E in year 1 and point F in year 2), with output at $\overline{Y}$, unemployment at the natural rate of unemployment $\overline{u}$, and inflation and expected inflation both at 10% per year.

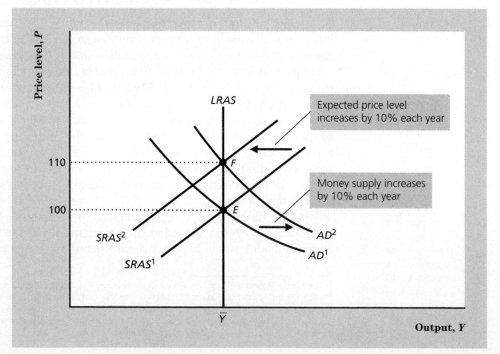

With the growth in the money supply fully anticipated, there are no misperceptions. With no misperceptions, the economy remains at full employment with output at $\overline{Y}$. For example, when the expected price level is 100 in year 1, the $SRAS$ curve is $SRAS^1$. At point E, the price level is 100 (the same as the expected price level) and output is $\overline{Y}$. In year 2, the expected price level is 110, and the $SRAS$ curve is $SRAS^2$. In year 2, equilibrium occurs at point F, again with output of $\overline{Y}$ and equal expected and actual price levels. Each year, both the AD curve and the $SRAS$ curve shift up by 10%, increasing the actual price level and expected price level by 10% and maintaining output at its full-employment level.

What happens to unemployment in this economy? Because output is continuously at its full-employment level $\overline{Y}$, unemployment remains at the natural rate $\overline{u}$. With unemployment at its natural rate, cyclical unemployment is zero. Hence this economy has zero unanticipated inflation and zero cyclical unemployment.

Against this backdrop of 10% monetary growth and 10% inflation, suppose now that in year 2, the money supply grows by 15% rather than by the expected 10% (Figure 13.4). In this case, instead of being 10% higher than AD^1 (as shown by $AD^{2,\,\text{old}}$), the aggregate demand curve in year 2 will be 15% higher than AD^1 (as shown by $AD^{2,\,\text{new}}$). If this increase in the rate of monetary growth is *unanticipated* at the beginning of year 2, the rational price expectation for the price level in year 2 remains at 110, and the short-run aggregate supply curve is $SRAS^2$, as before. The short-run equilibrium in year 2 is at point G, the intersection of the $AD^{2,\,\text{new}}$ and $SRAS^2$ curves. At G, the price level is 113, so the actual rate of inflation in year 2 is 13%. Because the expected rate of inflation was 10%, the 13% inflation rate implies unanticipated inflation of 3% in year 2. Further, because output is above its full-employment level $\overline{Y}$ at G, the actual unemployment rate is below the natural rate and cyclical unemployment is negative.

Why is output above its full-employment level in year 2? Note that in year 2, the 13% rate of inflation is less than the 15% rate of money growth but greater

FIGURE 13.4

UNANTICIPATED INFLATION IN THE EXTENDED CLASSICAL MODEL

If the money supply has been growing by 10% per year for a long time and is expected to continue growing by 10%, the expected price level increases by 10% each year. The 10% increase in the expected price level shifts the $SRAS$ curve up from $SRAS^1$ in year 1 to $SRAS^2$ in year 2. Then, if the money supply actually increases by 15% in year 2 rather than by the expected 10%, the AD curve is $AD^{2,\,\text{new}}$ rather than $AD^{2,\,\text{old}}$. As a result of higher-than-expected money growth, output increases above $\overline{Y}$ in year 2, and the price level increases to 113, at point G. Because the price level rises by 13% rather than the expected 10%, unanticipated inflation is 3% in year 2. This unanticipated inflation is associated with output higher than $\overline{Y}$ and unemployment below the natural rate $\overline{u}$ (negative cyclical unemployment).

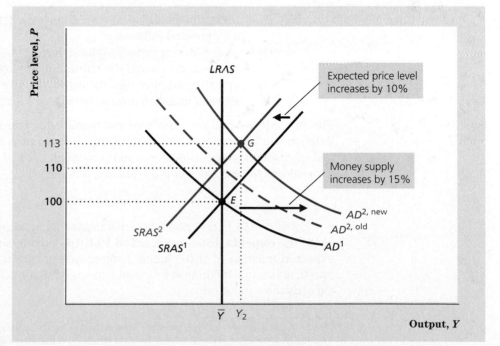

than the 10% expected rate of inflation. Because the price level grows by less than does the nominal money supply in year 2, the real money supply M/P increases, lowering the real interest rate and raising the aggregate quantity of goods demanded above $\overline{Y}$. At the same time, because the price level grows by more than expected, the aggregate quantity of goods supplied is also greater than $\overline{Y}$ as producers are fooled into thinking that the relative prices of their products have increased.

Producers cannot be fooled about price behaviour indefinitely, however. In the long run, producers learn the true price level, the economy returns to full employment, and the inflation rate again equals the expected inflation rate, as in Figure 13.3. In the meantime, however, as long as actual output is higher than full-employment output $\overline{Y}$ and actual unemployment is below the natural rate $\overline{u}$, the actual price level must be higher than the expected price level. Indeed, according to the misperceptions theory, output can be higher than $\overline{Y}$ only when prices are higher than expected (and, therefore, when inflation is also higher than expected).

Thus, in this economy, when the public correctly predicts aggregate demand growth and inflation, unanticipated inflation is zero, actual unemployment equals the natural rate, and cyclical unemployment is zero (see Figure 13.3). However, if aggregate demand growth unexpectedly speeds up, the economy faces a period of positive unanticipated inflation and negative cyclical unemployment (see Figure 13.4). Similarly, an unexpected slowdown in aggregate demand growth could occur, causing the AD curve to rise more slowly than expected; for a time unanticipated inflation would be negative (actual inflation less than expected) and cyclical unemployment would be positive (actual unemployment greater than the natural rate).

The relationship between unanticipated inflation and cyclical unemployment implied by this analysis is

$$\pi - \pi^e = -h(u - \overline{u}),$$

where

$\pi - \pi^e =$ unanticipated inflation (the difference between actual inflation π and expected inflation π^e);

$u - \overline{u} =$ cyclical unemployment (the difference between the actual unemployment rate u and the natural unemployment rate $\overline{u}$);

$h =$ a positive number that measures the strength of the relationship between unanticipated inflation and cyclical unemployment.

The preceding equation expresses mathematically the idea that unanticipated inflation will be positive when cyclical unemployment is negative, negative when cyclical unemployment is positive, and zero when cyclical unemployment is zero.[5] If we add π^e to both sides of the equation, it becomes

$$\pi = \pi^e - h(u - \overline{u}). \tag{13.1}$$

Equation (13.1) describes the expectations-augmented Phillips curve. According to the **expectations-augmented Phillips curve**, actual inflation π exceeds expected inflation π^e if the actual unemployment rate u is less than the natural rate $\overline{u}$; and actual inflation is less than expected inflation if the unemployment rate exceeds the natural rate.

---

[5] The equation also implies that the relationship between unanticipated inflation and cyclical unemployment is linear, but this is for convenience only. The relationship of the two variables might as easily be a curve as a line.

It is worth noting that the size of h, which measures the strength of the relationship between unanticipated inflation and cyclical unemployment, is related to the slope of the short-run aggregate supply ($SRAS$) curve. This is apparent from Figure 13.4: Were the $SRAS$ is flatter, the greater would be the amount by which Y_2 exceeds $\overline{Y}$ and, hence, the greater would be the amount by which the actual unemployment rate would exceed the natural unemployment rate. The close relationship between the Phillips curve and the $SRAS$ is not surprising. They are connected by a common theory of how price expectations are formed and by the production function relating changes in output to changes in employment and unemployment.

THE SHIFTING PHILLIPS CURVE

Let's return to the original Phillips curve, which links the levels of inflation and unemployment in the economy. The insight gained from the Friedman–Phelps analysis is that the relationship illustrated by the Phillips curve depends on the expected rate of inflation and the natural rate of unemployment. If either factor changes, the Phillips curve will shift.

The Phillips curve is traditionally graphed with the rate of inflation, π, on the vertical axis and the unemployment rate, u, on the horizontal axis. To gain a better appreciation of how changes in the expected rate of inflation and the natural rate of unemployment cause the Phillips curve to shift, it is useful to rearrange the equation representing the expectations-augmented Phillips curve, Eq. (13.1), as follows:

$$\pi = (\pi^e + h\overline{u}) - hu. \tag{13.2}$$

The slope of the curve is given by the term $-h$. The terms within brackets define the vertical intercept of a graph of the Phillips curve. From a purely mathematical point of view, then, any change in the values of π^e or $\overline{u}$ will cause the Phillips curve to shift. Let's look at these results more closely.

Changes in the Expected Rate of Inflation

Figure 13.5 shows how a change in the expected inflation rate affects the relationship between inflation and unemployment, according to the Friedman–Phelps theory. The curve PC^1 is the Phillips curve for an expected rate of inflation of 3%. What identifies the expected rate of inflation as 3% along PC^1? Equation (13.1) indicates that when the actual unemployment rate equals the natural rate (6% in this example), the actual inflation rate equals the expected inflation rate. Thus, to determine the expected inflation rate on a Phillips curve, we find the inflation rate at the point where the actual unemployment rate equals the natural rate. For instance, at point A on curve PC^1, the unemployment rate equals the natural rate, and the actual and expected rates of inflation both equal 3%. As long as the expected inflation rate remains at 3% (and the natural unemployment rate remains at 6%), the Phillips curve PC^1 will describe the relationship between inflation and unemployment.

Now, suppose that the expected rate of inflation increases from 3% to 12%. Figure 13.5 shows that this 9 percentage point increase in the expected rate of inflation shifts the Phillips curve up by 9 percentage points at each level of the unemployment rate, from PC^1 to PC^2. When the actual unemployment rate equals the natural rate on PC^2 (at point B), the inflation rate is 12%, confirming that the expected inflation rate is 12% along PC^2. Comparing PC^2 and PC^1 reveals that an increase in the expected inflation rate shifts the Phillips curve relationship between inflation and unemployment up and to the right.

FIGURE 13.5

THE SHIFTING PHILLIPS CURVE:

AN INCREASE IN EXPECTED

INFLATION

The Friedman–Phelps theory implies that there is a different Phillips curve for every expected inflation rate. For example, PC^1 is the Phillips curve when the expected rate of inflation is 3%. To verify this claim, note from Eq. (13.1) that when the actual unemployment rate equals the natural rate $\bar{u}$ (6% here), the actual inflation rate equals the expected inflation rate. At point A, the unemployment rate equals the natural rate and the inflation rate equals 3% on PC^1, so the expected inflation rate is 3% on PC^1. Similarly, at point B on PC^2, where the unemployment rate equals its natural rate, the inflation rate is 12%, so the expected inflation rate is 12% along PC^2. Thus, an increase in the expected inflation rate from 3% to 12% shifts the Phillips curve up and to the right, from PC^1 to PC^2.

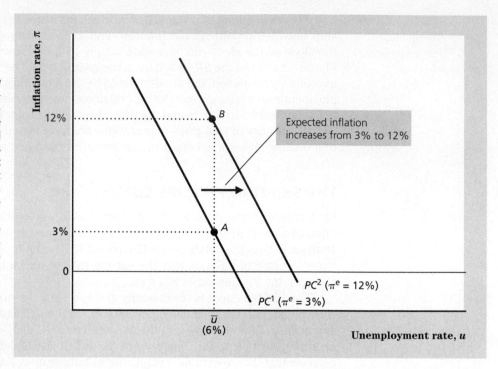

This discussion of how changes in the expected rate of inflation shift the Phillips curve has a close parallel with our discussion in Chapter 11 relating how changes in the expected price level shift the short-run aggregate supply curve (*SRAS*). The two discussions are, in fact, the same except that one speaks to the price level while the other speaks to the rate of inflation. Firms and households desire to correctly anticipate price levels. If they anticipate a change in the price level (inflation) they respond by adjusting their expectations of the price level (the rate of inflation) one-for-one. Such a response shifts the *SRAS* up by the amount of the increase in the expected price level and shifts the Phillips curve up by the amount of the increase in the expected rate of inflation.

Changes in the Natural Rate of Unemployment

The Phillips curve relationship between inflation and unemployment is also shifted by changes in the natural unemployment rate, as illustrated by Figure 13.6. The Phillips curve PC^1 shows a natural unemployment rate at 6% and an expected inflation rate at 3% (PC^1 in Figure 13.6 is the same as PC^1 in Figure 13.5). Now, suppose that the natural unemployment rate increases to 7% but that the expected inflation rate remains unchanged at 3%. As Figure 13.6 shows, the increase in the natural unemployment rate causes the Phillips curve to shift, from PC^1 to PC^3.

To confirm that the natural unemployment rate corresponding to Phillips curve PC^3 in Figure 13.6 is 7%, look at point C on PC^3: At C, where the actual and expected inflation rates are equal, the unemployment rate is 7%. Thus, the natural unemployment rate associated with Phillips curve PC^3 is 7%. This example illustrates that—like an increase in expected inflation—an increase in the natural unemployment rate causes the Phillips curve relationship between inflation and unemployment to shift up and to the right.

FIGURE 13.6

THE SHIFTING PHILLIPS CURVE: AN INCREASE IN THE NATURAL UNEMPLOYMENT RATE

According to the Friedman–Phelps theory, an increase in the natural unemployment rate shifts the Phillips curve up and to the right. At point A on PC^1, the actual inflation rate and the expected inflation rate are equal at 3%, so the natural unemployment rate equals the actual unemployment rate at A, or 6%. Thus, PC^1 is the Phillips curve when the natural unemployment rate is 6% and the expected inflation rate is 3%, as in Figure 13.5. If the natural unemployment rate increases to 7%, with expected inflation unchanged, the Phillips curve shifts to PC^3. At point C on PC^3, both expected and actual inflation equal 3%, so the natural unemployment rate equals the actual unemployment rate at C, or 7%.

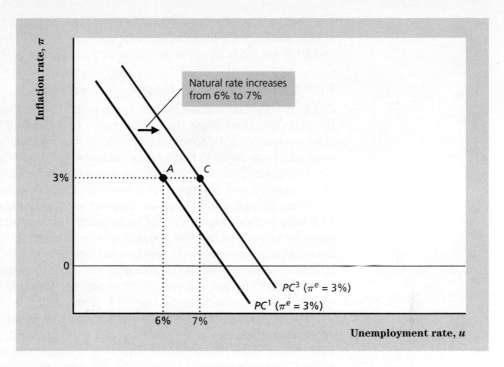

Supply Shocks and the Phillips Curve

The Friedman–Phelps theory holds that changes in either expected inflation or the natural unemployment rate will shift the Phillips curve. One type of economic disturbance that is likely to affect both factors is a supply shock. Recall that an adverse supply shock causes a burst of inflation, which may lead people to expect higher inflation.[6] An adverse supply shock also tends to increase the natural unemployment rate, although the reasons for this effect are different for the classical and Keynesian models.

Recall that from the classical perspective, an adverse supply shock raises the natural rate of unemployment by increasing the degree of mismatch between workers and jobs. For example, an oil price shock eliminates jobs in heavy-energy-using industries but increases employment in energy-providing industries.

In Appendix 12.A we showed that in the Keynesian model, much of the unemployment that exists even when the economy is at the full-employment level is blamed on rigid real wages. In particular, while an adverse supply shock has no effect on the supply of labour,[7] it does reduce the marginal product of labour and, thus, labour demand. With a rigid real wage, the drop in labour demand increases the excess of labour supplied over labour demanded, raising the amount of unemployment that exists when the economy is at full employment. Thus, as in the classical model, the Keynesian model predicts that an adverse supply shock will raise the natural unemployment rate.

Because adverse supply shocks raise both expected inflation and the natural unemployment rate, according to the Friedman–Phelps analysis, they should cause

---

[6] The inflationary impact of a supply shock will be reinforced if, in an attempt to moderate the rise in unemployment caused by the shock, the central bank increases the money supply.

[7] This statement is strictly true only for a temporary adverse supply shock. A permanent adverse supply shock, if it reduces expected future wages, would increase labour supply and thus cause an even larger rise in the natural rate of unemployment.

the Phillips curve to shift up and to the right. Similarly, beneficial supply shocks should shift the Phillips curve down and to the left. Overall, the Phillips curve should be particularly unstable during periods of supply shocks.

The Shifting Phillips Curve in Practice

Our analysis of the shifting Phillips curve (see Figures 13.5 and 13.6) helps answer the basic questions about the Phillips curve raised earlier in the chapter. The first question was: Why did the original Phillips curve relationship between inflation and unemployment apply to many historical cases, including Canada during the 1960s? The Friedman–Phelps analysis shows that a negative relationship between the levels of inflation and unemployment holds *as long as expected inflation and the natural unemployment rate are approximately constant.* As shown in Figure 13.9 later in this chapter (p. 456), the natural unemployment rate changes relatively slowly, and during the 1960s, it was approximately constant. Expected inflation was probably also nearly constant in Canada in the 1960s because at that time, people were used to low and stable inflation and inflation remained low for most of the decade. Thus, not surprisingly, the Canadian inflation and unemployment data for the 1960s seem to lie along a single Phillips curve (see Figure 13.1, p. 441).

The second question was: Why did the simple negative relationship between inflation and unemployment that seemed to exist during the 1960s change after 1970 (see Figure 13.2, p. 442)? The answer suggested by the Friedman–Phelps analysis is that in the period after 1970, the expected inflation rate and the natural unemployment rate varied considerably more than they had in the 1960s, causing the Phillips curve relationship to shift erratically.

Contributing to the shifts of the Phillips curve after 1970 were the two large supply shocks associated with sharp increases in the price of oil that hit the Canadian economy in 1973–1974 and 1979–1980 (see Figure 3.10, p. 73). Recall that adverse supply shocks are likely to increase both expected inflation and the natural rate of unemployment, shifting the Phillips curve up and to the right. Oil prices have occasionally varied considerably since then, most notably when they declined precipitously in 1986 and jumped upward after both wars in Iraq (1991 and 2003). More recently, oil prices more than doubled during 2007 and early 2008 before collapsing late in 2008, and fell again in the fall of 2014 following a long period of high prices. If there is one thing that is certain about oil prices it is that they are uncertain!

Beyond the direct effects of supply shocks, other forces may have increased the variability of expected inflation and the natural unemployment rate after 1970. As we discuss later in the chapter, the natural unemployment rate rose during this period as a result of labour force composition changes, changes in Employment Insurance legislation, and faster structural changes in the economy.

Expected inflation probably varied more after 1970 because actual inflation varied more (see Figure 2.1, p. 37, for the Canadian inflation rate for the period 1945–2015). After being relatively low during the 1950s and 1960s, inflation, driven by monetary and fiscal policies that had probably been over-expansionary for several years, emerged as a problem at the end of the 1960s. The 1970s were a period of high and erratic inflation, the result of the oil price shocks and macroeconomic policies that again were probably too expansionary, especially in the latter part of the decade. In contrast, following the anti-inflationary policies of the Bank of Canada and other central banks from 1979 through 1982, inflation returned to a relatively low level during the 1980s. To the extent that expected inflation followed the path of actual inflation—high and erratic in the 1970s, low in the 1980s—our

FIGURE 13.7

THE EXPECTATIONS-AUGMENTED PHILLIPS CURVE IN CANADA, 1960–2015

The expectations-augmented Phillips curve is a negative relationship between unanticipated inflation and cyclical unemployment. The figure shows this relationship for the years 1960–2015 in Canada. Unanticipated inflation equals actual inflation minus expected inflation, where expected inflation in any year is measured here as the average inflation rate for the preceding two years. Cyclical unemployment for each year is the actual unemployment rate minus an estimate of the natural unemployment rate for that year (see Figure 13.9, p. 456). Note that years in which unanticipated inflation is high are usually years in which cyclical unemployment is low.

Source: Adapted from Statistics Canada Unemployment rate, 1970–1975: *Historical Statistics of Canada*, Series D233; 1976–2015: Statistics Canada CANSIM II, series v2461224; Inflation rate: Calculated using GDP deflator, Statistics Canada CANSIM II, series v1997756. This does not constitute an endorsement by Statistics Canada of this product.

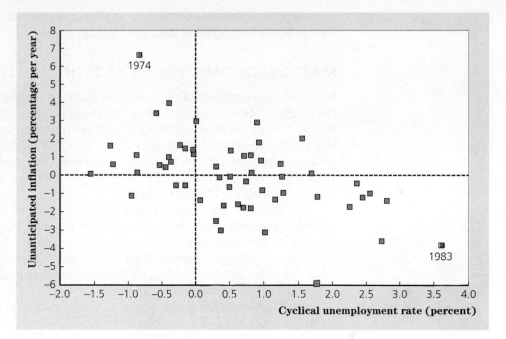

analysis suggests that the Phillips curve relationship between inflation and unemployment would not have been stable over the period.

Does the unstable Phillips curve during the period 1970–2015 imply that there was no systematic relationship between inflation and unemployment during that period? The answer is no. According to the Friedman–Phelps analysis, a negative relationship between *unanticipated* inflation and *cyclical* unemployment should appear in the data, even if expected inflation and the natural unemployment rate are changing. Measures of unanticipated inflation and cyclical unemployment for each year during the period 1960–2015 are shown in Figure 13.7. These measures are approximate because we cannot directly observe either expected inflation (needed to calculate unanticipated inflation) or the natural unemployment rate (needed to find cyclical unemployment). We assumed that expected inflation for each year was the average inflation rate of the previous two years, and we used estimates of the natural unemployment rate presented later in the chapter in Figure 13.9.[8]

Figure 13.7 suggests that despite the instability of the traditional Phillips curve relationship between inflation and unemployment, a negative relationship between unanticipated inflation and cyclical unemployment did exist during the period 1960–2013, as predicted by the Friedman–Phelps analysis. That is, years such as 1983, in which actual inflation was less than expected inflation (so that unanticipated inflation, $\pi - \pi^e$, took on a negative value), were typically associated with periods when actual unemployment was greater than natural unemployment (so that the cyclical unemployment rate, $u - \overline{u}$, was positive). Conversely, years such as 1974, in which actual inflation exceeded expected inflation (so that unanticipated inflation, $\pi - \pi^e$, took on a positive value), were typically associated with

---

[8] The data graphed in Figure 13.7 represent the Phillips curve relationship as represented by the equation $(\pi - \pi^e) = -h(u - \overline{u})$. It is worth repeating a point made in footnote 5 (p. 446), namely, that the equation implies a linear relationship between unanticipated inflation and cyclical unemployment, but this is for convenience only. The relationship of the two variables might as easily be a curve as a line. A line of best fit drawn through these data suggests a value of h equal to 1.0.

periods when actual unemployment was less than natural unemployment (so that the cyclical unemployment rate, $u - \overline{u}$, was negative).

MACROECONOMIC POLICY AND THE PHILLIPS CURVE

We have addressed two of the questions about the Phillips curve raised earlier in the chapter—the questions of why the Phillips curve was observed in historical data and why it seemed to shift after 1970. We must still answer the third question: Can the Phillips curve be thought of as a "menu" of inflation–unemployment combinations from which policymakers can choose? For example, can policymakers reduce the unemployment rate by increasing the rate of inflation (moving up and to the left along the Phillips curve)?

According to the expectations-augmented Phillips curve, unemployment will fall below the natural rate only when inflation is higher than anticipated. Important sources of unanticipated inflation are unanticipated movements in aggregate demand and aggregate supply. Thus the sudden outbreak of war, waves of pessimism, oil price shocks—indeed, all the sources of aggregate demand and supply shocks listed in Summary tables 11 and 14 (pp. 247 and 275)—are potential causes of unanticipated inflation and, hence, potential causes of cyclical unemployment. So the question becomes: Can macroeconomic policy be usefully employed to offset the effects of unanticipated shifts in aggregate demand and aggregate supply?

This is a question we first raised in Chapter 9 and which we discussed in greater detail in Chapters 11 and 12. There, our discussions were in terms of the price level and output, but it can be equally well applied here in terms of inflation and unemployment. In terms of the Phillips curve, shocks to aggregate demand and aggregate supply give rise to unanticipated inflation and, hence, cyclical unemployment. Classical economists stress that the economy is quickly self-correcting. In particular, there are few impediments to price adjustment, and inflation expectations adjust quickly to unanticipated inflation. For these reasons the unemployment rate will deviate from the natural rate for only short periods of time. Stabilization policies, then, have little opportunity to play a useful role.

In contrast, Keynesians contend that stabilization polices can, in fact, play a useful role in offsetting the effects on output and unemployment of unanticipated inflation. They claim this because they believe that although price and inflation expectations adjust quickly, wage and price stickiness prevent prices and inflation from adjusting as quickly as claimed by classical economists. As a consequence, the unemployment rate can deviate from the natural rate for an extended period of time, allowing stabilization policy time to play a useful role. Thus, in response to an unexpected fall in aggregate demand that reduces inflation below what was expected—and so pushes the unemployment rate above the natural rate[9]—policymakers can use an expansionary aggregate demand policy to increase inflation back to levels that were anticipated and used as the basis for nominal-wage contracts and price lists. (While stabilization policy may, thus, have a useful role to play, this is not to say that the effects of policy changes are always easy to predict. A Closer Look 13.1, "The Lucas Critique," explores a general lesson for policymakers based on the shifting Phillips curve.)

---

[9] An unanticipated fall in the rate of inflation means that prices are increasing less quickly than anticipated by firms and employees. In the Keynesian model of nominal-wage rigidity, real wages increase faster than anticipated, causing firms to reduce employment and causing the unemployment rate to exceed the natural rate. In the model of nominal-price rigidity, monopolistically competitive firms find that their posted prices are too high and so reduce output and employment.

A CLOSER LOOK 13.1

THE LUCAS CRITIQUE

Suppose that you observed, in a particular season, that the Winnipeg Blue Bombers of the Canadian Football League punted 100% of the time when faced with third down deep in their own territory. Could you safely conclude, on the basis of this empirical evidence, that the Bombers would punt on third down in their own territory next season? In most cases, you probably could safely make this prediction, even if you did not know anything about football. But what if, during the off-season, the rules were changed to allow five attempts to make a first down? Would you still expect the Bombers to follow historical precedent and punt on third down? Certainly, no one familiar with football would expect them to follow their old strategy, which would be foolish under the new rules. The simple lesson from this example is that when the rules of the game change, people's behaviour also changes.[*]

In an influential article,[†] Robert E. Lucas, Jr., of the University of Chicago, applied this lesson to macroeconomic policymaking. Frequently, in attempting to forecast the effects of a new set of policies, economists and policymakers assume that historical relationships between macroeconomic variables will continue to hold after the new policies are in place. Lucas objected to this assumption, asserting what has become known as the *Lucas critique*. According to the Lucas critique, because new policies change the economic "rules" and, thus, affect economic behaviour, no one can safely assume that historical relationships between variables will hold when policies change.

A good example of the Lucas critique in action is the shifting Phillips curve. Historically, there seemed to be a stable relationship between inflation and unemployment, which led some policymakers to believe that they could permanently reduce unemployment by increasing inflation. However, as we have discussed, when policymakers allowed inflation to rise, the public's inflation expectations also rose. As a result, the Phillips curve shifted and the historical relationship between inflation and unemployment broke down.

The main message of the Lucas critique for economists is that in order to predict the effects of policy changes on the economy, they must understand how economic behaviour will change under the new policies. Understanding the impact of policy changes on behaviour—particularly the introduction of policies that have not been tried before—requires the use of economic theory as well as empirical analysis.

---

[*] The example is based on one from Thomas Sargent, *Rational Expectations and Inflation*, New York: Harper & Row, 1986, pp. 1–2.
[†] "Econometric Policy Evaluation: A Critique," in K. Brunner and A. H. Meltzer, eds., *Carnegie-Rochester Conference Series on Public Policy*, Volume 1, 1976.

THE LONG-RUN PHILLIPS CURVE

Although classical and Keynesian economists disagree about the speed with which prices adjust, and hence disagree about the usefulness of stabilization policies, they agree that in the long run the economy will adjust to a general equilibrium in which expectations of inflation will equal actual inflation ($\pi^e = \pi$). The expectations—augmented Phillips curve (Eq. 13.1, p. 446) implies that when $\pi^e = \pi$, the actual unemployment rate u equals the natural unemployment rate $\bar{u}$. Thus, the actual unemployment rate equals the natural rate in the long run, regardless of the rate of inflation that is maintained.

The long-run relationship of unemployment and inflation is shown by the **long-run Phillips curve**. In the long run, because unemployment equals the natural rate regardless of the inflation rate, the long-run Phillips curve is a vertical line at $u = \bar{u}$, as shown in Figure 13.8.

The vertical long-run Phillips curve is related to the long-run neutrality of money, discussed in Chapters 11 and 12. Classicals and Keynesians agree that

FIGURE 13.8

THE LONG-RUN PHILLIPS CURVE

Because people will not permanently overestimate or underestimate the rate of inflation, in the long run the expected and actual inflation rates are equal and the actual unemployment rate equals the natural unemployment rate. Because in the long run actual unemployment equals the natural rate regardless of the inflation rate, the long-run Phillips curve (*LRPC*) is vertical.

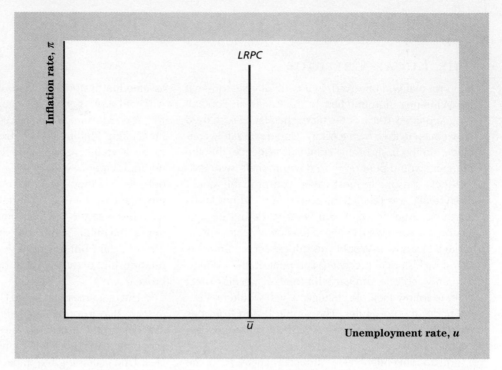

changes in the money supply will have no long-run effects on real variables, including unemployment. The vertical long-run Phillips curve carries the notion of monetary neutrality one step further by indicating that changes in the growth rate of money, which lead to changes in the inflation rate, also have no real effects in the long run.

13.2 THE PROBLEM OF UNEMPLOYMENT

In the rest of the chapter, we look more closely at unemployment and inflation, beginning with unemployment in this section. We start by discussing the costs of unemployment, then consider the factors that determine the long-run unemployment level, and conclude by exploring some ways in which macroeconomic policy can address unemployment.

THE COSTS OF UNEMPLOYMENT

There are two principal costs of unemployment. The first is the loss of output that occurs because fewer people are productively employed. This cost is borne disproportionately by unemployed workers themselves, in terms of the income they lose because they are out of work. However, because the unemployed may stop paying taxes and instead receive unemployment insurance benefits or other government payments, society (in this case, taxpayers) also bears some of the output cost of unemployment.

How big is the output cost of unemployment? One estimate is provided by a relationship between inflation and output sometimes referred to as Okun's law. **Okun's law** is a rule of thumb describing the relationship between changes in the cyclical unemployment rate and changes in real output. It suggests that a 1 percentage point increase in the cyclical unemployment rate reduces real output by approximately 2 percentage points. Thus, if full-employment output is $1000 billion, Okun's law indicates that each percentage point of cyclical unemployment sustained for one year reduces output by $20 billion.

The loss of output predicted by Okun's law reflects not only the direct impact of increased unemployment but also other labour market changes that occur during recessions, such as shorter workweeks, reduced labour force participation, and lower productivity. (Numerical Problem 9 in Chapter 3, p. 89, illustrates these effects.) Thus, the output cost of unemployment estimated by Okun's law is probably too high. Nevertheless, an output loss that was only one-quarter of that predicted by Okun's law would still be a significant cost, particularly if it were borne largely by the relatively poor and disadvantaged members of society.

The other substantial cost of unemployment is the personal or psychological cost faced by unemployed workers and their families. This cost is especially important for workers suffering long spells of unemployment and for the chronically unemployed. Workers without steady employment for long periods lose job skills and self-esteem, and suffer from stress.

The costs of unemployment are real and serious, but two offsetting factors should be noted. First, to the extent that unemployed workers engage in economically productive activities, such as searching for a job or acquiring new skills, the loss of output arising from current unemployment may be compensated for by increased output in the future. In particular, frictional unemployment—the result of workers and firms seeking appropriate matches—raises future productivity and output and, thus, may impose little net economic cost, or even lead to an economic gain.

A second offsetting factor is that unemployed people have more leisure time—to spend with family and friends, work around the house, and so on. However, the benefits of extra leisure time decrease as the amount of leisure increases, and most unemployed workers would not feel that increased leisure was adequate compensation for their lost income.

THE LONG-TERM BEHAVIOUR OF THE UNEMPLOYMENT RATE

Classical and Keynesian economists agree that although the actual unemployment rate may deviate from the natural unemployment rate in the short run, in the long run the actual rate equals the natural rate. Thus, understanding the behaviour of unemployment in all but the short run requires identifying the determinants of the natural rate of unemployment. In Chapter 3, we discussed the reasons for the natural unemployment rate always being greater than zero; here we focus more narrowly on the reasons for changes in the natural rate in recent years in Canada, the United States, and Europe.

The Changing Natural Rate

The natural unemployment rate corresponds to full-employment output. Unfortunately, because we cannot be sure when the economy is at full employment, we cannot directly observe the natural rate and, so, must estimate it. Inevitably, therefore, there is some uncertainty about the value of the natural rate at any particular time. Figure 13.9 shows estimated values of the natural unemployment rate, along with the actual unemployment rate, for the period 1960–2015. Our estimate of the natural rate reflects a number of considerations. First, calculations

FIGURE 13.9

ACTUAL AND NATURAL
UNEMPLOYMENT RATES IN
CANADA

The figure shows the actual unemployment rate and an estimate of the natural rate of unemployment in Canada for the period 1960–2015. The difference between the actual and natural unemployment rates is the cyclical unemployment rate. Note that the natural rate of unemployment rose from the 1960s to the 1980s but has fallen since.

Source: Adapted from Statistics Canada Unemployment rate, 1970–1975: *Historical Statistics of Canada*, Series D233; 1976–2015: Statistics Canada CANSIM II, series v2461224; Inflation rate: Calculated using GDP deflator, Statistics Canada CANSIM II, series v1997756. This does not constitute an endorsement by Statistics Canada of this product.

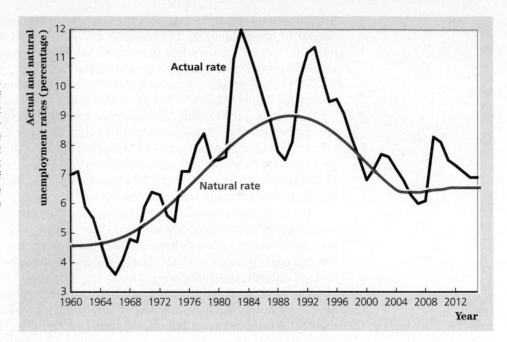

by Andrew Burns,[10] then of the Economic Council of Canada, show that in the mid-1960s the natural rate was roughly 4.5% and that it increased to roughly 8.5% by the mid-1980s. Second, most analysts agree that the natural rate has fallen since the mid- to late 1980s. The fact that our estimate of the natural rate of unemployment for 2006, 6.3%, is the same as the actual unemployment rate is consistent with the Bank of Canada's estimate that the economy was at or near full employment in that year. Similarly, the fact that we show our estimate of the natural unemployment rate moving slightly upward following the recession of 2008–2009 is also consistent with the view of the Bank of Canada.

Giving a fully satisfactory explanation for the rise and fall in the natural rate of unemployment is difficult. Researchers have identified a number of possible explanations:

- *Demographic changes.* The unemployment rate you might expect to experience varies by your age and sex. In particular, workers younger than 25 years have significantly higher unemployment rates than older workers. This reflects the fact that they have relatively fewer skills and less experience than older workers. Until 1990, women experienced higher rates of unemployment than men. This likely reflected the fact that, historically, women have spent more time than men taking care of children and, thus, have had more interruptions in their careers. Moving in and out of the labour force would therefore have involved periods of unemployment for women. Since 1990, the unemployment rate for women has fallen and in fact in most years is now below that for men.[11] These considerations suggest that the composition of the labour force is

---

[10] "The Natural Rate of Unemployment: Canada and the Provinces," in Surendra Gera, ed., *Canadian Unemployment*, Ottawa: Economic Council of Canada, 1991.

[11] In 1976, the average unemployment rate for those aged 25 years and above was 6.5% for women and 4.3% for men. In 2015, these unemployment rates were 5.4% for women and 6.2% for men. The unemployment rate for workers younger than 25 years was 12.4% in 1976 and 13.2% in 2015.

changing to include a larger percentage of groups with higher unemployment rates, which raises the overall unemployment rate. Certainly during the 1960s and 1970s, the fraction of the labour force composed of women and young workers increased, and this event was a likely contributor to a rise in the natural unemployment rate that extended into the 1980s. Since that time, a fall in the fraction of the labour force composed of young workers and the change in the work patterns of women versus men may be contributing to a fall in the natural unemployment rate. While the pattern of these changes is consistent with our estimate of the natural unemployment rate presented in Figure 13.9, most analysts suggest that changes in the composition of the labour force can account for only a small portion of the variation in the natural rate.

- *Technological change.* Another factor that some analysts have suggested may have contributed to the rise in the natural unemployment rate during the 1970s and 1980s was a faster pace of structural change in the economy during that period. Technological changes increase the skill levels that firms demand from workers, reducing the employment opportunities for low-skilled or poorly educated workers (see the Application "Technological Change and Wage Inequality" in Chapter 3, p. 74). Also, during this period some industries grew while others suffered long-term declines; notably, the share of jobs in manufacturing fell while that in services increased. Both changes worsened the problem of mismatch between jobs and workers, raising frictional and structural unemployment and hence the natural rate. This explanation, while perhaps appropriate for explaining the rise in the natural rate in the 1970s and 1980s, seems less able to explain what most economists agree is the fall in the natural unemployment rate since about 1990. If anything, the rate of technological change has increased since the 1980s, and so we might expect an increase in the natural rate, not a decline.

- *Hysteresis.* According to proponents of **hysteresis** (a term taken from physics) theory, a shock to the economy that causes the actual unemployment rate to increase also increases the natural unemployment rate. Why would this be? Some economists suggest that when a high unemployment rate leaves workers idle for a long period of time, their skills deteriorate (or the workers fail to get training in the first place). Lower skill levels increase the mismatch between workers and firms and raise the natural unemployment rate. Other economists stress that high levels of unionization and government regulation restrict the ability of firms to fire workers; because firms know that firing workers is difficult, they are reluctant to hire additional workers unless they are confident that they will not need to reduce their workforces for a long time. A downturn in the economy tends to be more persistent in heavily unionized and regulated economies because firms are cautious about rehiring workers they have laid off or hiring new workers.

   Figure 13.9 would appear to suggest support for the hysteresis theory; our estimate of the natural unemployment rate seems to change in response to changes in the actual unemployment rate. Not all economists would support that conclusion, however, and it is important to remember that the estimate of the natural unemployment rate presented in Figure 13.9 is only that, an estimate.

- *Employment insurance.* Figure 13.10 shows, for the period 1976–2015, the actual unemployment rate in three provinces: Alberta, Ontario, and Nova Scotia. The difference in unemployment rates across these provinces has

FIGURE 13.10

UNEMPLOYMENT RATES BY REGION

The figure shows unemployment rates for selected provinces from 1976 to 2015. The average value of the unemployment rate differs systematically across provinces. Although the changes in the provincial unemployment rates from year to year have a common pattern, there are also movements specific to each province. For example, the unemployment rate in Alberta is particularly sensitive to the price of fossil fuels. Thus, while the 1982 recession increased unemployment rates in all provinces, the added effect of a legislated reduction in the price of oil caused Alberta's unemployment rate to move from well below Ontario's rate to well above. Since the end of energy price controls, the unemployment rate in Alberta has again fallen below that in Ontario. It is interesting to note that the recession of 2008–2009 increased the unemployment rate in Ontario and in Alberta significantly more than in Nova Scotia.

Source: Adapted from Statistics Canada CANSIM II series v2465004, v2466894, and v2463114. This does not constitute an endorsement by Statistics Canada of this product.

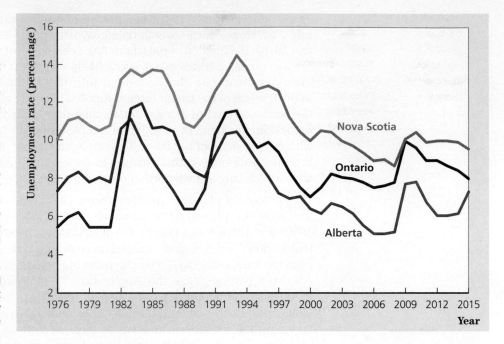

largely persisted over the past 40 years. The unemployment rate in Nova Scotia has exceeded that in Alberta by an average of 4.2 percentage points over that period. Except for a brief period in the 1980s—a time of very low energy prices that benefited Ontario's economy and harmed Alberta's—the unemployment rate in Alberta has remained below that in Ontario by about 2.1 percentage points. What can explain these persistent differences? The fact these differences have persisted for so long suggests they are not due to differences in cyclical unemployment rates but are rather due to differences in natural unemployment rates. Why might some provincial labour markets have higher natural unemployment rates than others? Some economists highlight the role of the federal government's program for providing unemployment insurance, a program that has been known as Employment Insurance, or EI, since 1996.

The generosity of any unemployment insurance program can be measured by three factors:

1. The *replacement ratio*, which measures the size of the unemployment benefit relative to lost wages;

2. The *benefit duration*, which measures the amount of time that an unemployed worker may receive benefits; and

3. *Eligibility requirements*, which specify what a worker must do in order to be eligible to collect benefits.

Eligibility requirements and benefit duration depend on local unemployment rates and so vary by province. In a economic survey of Canada, the OECD[12] created a "disincentive index" based on the three factors measuring the generosity of Canada's EI program. The study reports that, based on its

---

[12] "Economic Survey of Canada 2004," *OECD Economic Surveys*, Volume 24, no. 16, 2004.

design in 2003, the EI program created greater disincentives in some provinces than others for the unemployed to search for jobs or to accept job offers.[13] With respect to the three provinces whose unemployment rates we show in Figure 13.10, the reported disincentive index is highest in Nova Scotia and lowest in Alberta, with Ontario lying in between, suggesting that the EI program has at least some role to play in explaining differences in provincial unemployment rates.

While stressing once again that our estimate of the natural unemployment rate presented in Figure 13.9 is only an estimate, the fact that it rises to a peak around 1990 and falls thereafter suggests that a role is played by the EI program in explaining those movements. This is so because the EI program became significantly more generous in 1971–1972 but has since the early 1990s become much less so. Added to this is the fact that the design of the EI program is such that its provisions are more generous in provinces like Nova Scotia than in provinces like Alberta—a characteristic that would go at least some way toward explaining the persistence in the unemployment rate gap between those provinces. These two points explain why many economists highlight the role of the EI program in movements of the natural unemployment rate.

Because of the prominent role played by the natural rate of unemployment in economic theory, policymakers would like to use measures of the natural rate when they formulate economic policy. In simple terms, if policymakers observe that the actual unemployment rate is above the natural rate, then the intersection of the *AD* and *SRAS* curves must be to the left of the *LRAS* curve. Thus a policymaker might consider using an expansionary monetary or fiscal policy to shift the *AD* curve to the right and so bring the economy back to its full-employment equilibrium. To use the actual unemployment rate as an indicator for setting policy, however, the policymaker needs a good measure of the natural rate of unemployment.

Unfortunately, trying to nail down the value of the natural rate is extremely difficult, and estimates are generally quite imprecise. This is important to emphasize because the implications of basing policy on an imprecise measure of the natural rate can be significant. For example, some researchers have blamed the rise of inflation in the 1970s on the failure of central banks to properly estimate the natural rate. Thinking the natural rate was lower than it in fact was (and, conversely, that the cyclical unemployment rate was higher than it actually was), they pursued an expansionary, and ultimately inflationary, monetary policy even though the economy was at full employment.[14] Uncertainty about precise values of the natural rate has led some researchers to suggest that policymakers might want to be less aggressive in pursuing policy changes that are based on it.[15]

---

[13] The effects of the EI program on unemployment rates can be analyzed at an even finer degree than at the provincial level. Miles Corak and Wen-Hau Chen, researchers at Statistics Canada, show in their paper "Who Benefits from Unemployment Insurance in Canada: Regions, Industries or Individual Firms" *Social Research and Development Corporation Working Paper Series* 03-07, November 2003, that because employees and employers in all industries pay the tax that finances the EI program, but employers and employees in certain industries draw benefits more than in others, there is a cross-subsidy across industries. They report that during the period of their analysis (1986–1996) firms in fishing, forestry, construction, and agricultural industries were consistently (and heavily) subsidized by employers and employees in other industries.

[14] See Athanasios Orphanides and John Williams, "The Decline of Activist Stabilization Policy: Natural Rate Misperceptions, Learning, and Expectations," *Journal of Economic Dynamics and Control*, November 2005, pp. 1927–1950.

[15] See Volker Wieland, "Monetary Policy and Uncertainty About the Natural Unemployment Rate: Brainard-Style Conservatism versus Experimental Activism," *Advances in Macroeconomics*, Volume 6, no. 1, 2006.

POLICIES TO REDUCE THE NATURAL RATE OF UNEMPLOYMENT

Although we call the rate of unemployment toward which the economy gravitates in the long run the "natural" rate of unemployment, we do not mean to imply that it is necessarily desirable or optimal. Many people would argue that for both economic and social reasons, economic policies should be used to try to lower the natural unemployment rate. Although no surefire method for reducing the natural rate exists, our discussion in the preceding section suggests some possible policy actions.

One is to make it easier for workers who have been made unemployed by a shrinking industry to retrain and find re-employment in expanding industries. Thus a case can be made for such policy measures as tax credits, subsidies for training, and relocating unemployed workers. If these measures have their desired effect, the mismatch between workers and jobs would be eliminated more quickly and the natural unemployment rate would fall. Many of the recent modifications to the Employment Insurance program have lain in this direction, and the current program emphasizes, more than it has in the past, the goal of retraining and encouraging unemployed workers to move to where new jobs are being created.

A second potential way of reducing the natural unemployment rate is to minimize the size of payroll taxes that firms pay when employing workers. The cost to a firm of hiring a worker includes not only the wage paid to the worker but also the contributions firms make to paying for Employment Insurance, Worker's Compensation, and the Canada and Quebec Pension Plans. These extra costs paid by the firm are said to drive a "wedge" between the wage received by the worker and the total cost to the firm of hiring that worker. The larger that wedge, the fewer workers firms find it profitable to hire. For this reason economists generally favour efforts to reduce the size of payroll taxes to the minimum level necessary to fund the programs they support.

Finally, economists who emphasize the problem of hysteresis argue that if monetary and fiscal policy are used aggressively to keep unemployment as low as possible—a "high-pressure economy"—the natural rate will be minimized because fewer workers will suffer the prolonged bouts of unemployment that cause them to see their skills deteriorate and so become less attractive to potential employers. Opponents of this suggestion point out that a high-pressure macroeconomic strategy also carries with it the risk of inflation.

13.3 THE PROBLEM OF INFLATION

In the federal election of June 1974, Prime Minister Pierre Trudeau called wage and price controls "a proven disaster looking for a new place to happen." Yet in October 1975, with the inflation rate near 11%, his government announced a three-year program of wage and price controls, to be administered by the Anti-Inflation Board (AIB). What caused the government to undertake this dramatic U-turn, with the associated political costs? During the late 1980s, the Canadian inflation rate hovered near 5%. The Bank of Canada introduced a set of targets for reducing this rate, with the goal of zero inflation. Why did the Bank undertake this policy? In this section, we look at inflation, beginning with a discussion of inflation costs and then turning to the question of what can be done to control inflation.

THE COSTS OF INFLATION

The costs of inflation depend primarily on whether consumers, investors, workers, and firms are able to predict the inflation before it occurs. To illustrate this point, we discuss two extreme cases: an inflation that everyone is able to predict and an inflation that comes as a complete surprise.

Perfectly Anticipated Inflation

Let's first consider the case of an inflation that is perfectly anticipated by the public. Imagine, for example, that everyone knows the inflation rate will be 4% per year. To keep things simple, also assume that there's no change in relative prices, meaning that the prices of all individual goods and services are also rising at the rate of 4% per year.

Why then does a fully anticipated inflation impose any costs? The prices you pay for groceries, movie tickets, and other goods would increase by 4% per year, but so would your nominal wage or the nominal value of the goods or services you produce. Because your nominal income is rising along with prices, your purchasing power isn't hurt by the perfectly anticipated inflation.[16]

What about the money you hold in your savings account? Although inflation reduces the purchasing power of money, perfectly anticipated inflation would not hurt the value of your savings account. The reason is that the nominal interest rate would adjust to offset the drop in the purchasing power of money. For instance, with a zero inflation rate and a nominal interest rate on savings deposits of 3%, the real interest rate is also 3% per year. If inflation rises to a perfectly anticipated rate of 4% per year, an increase in the nominal interest rate to 7% per year will leave the real interest rate unchanged at 3%. Because both savers and banks care only about the real interest rate, when inflation rises to 4% banks should be willing to offer 7% nominal interest, and savers should be willing to accept that nominal return. Thus, neither banks nor savers are hurt by an anticipated increase in inflation.[17]

The suggestion that perfectly anticipated inflation imposes no economic costs is not quite correct: Inflation erodes the value of currency, which leads people to keep less currency on hand—for example, by going to the bank or the automated teller machine to make withdrawals every week instead of twice a month. Similarly, inflation may induce firms to reduce their cash holdings by introducing computerized cash management systems or adding staff to the accounting department. The costs in time and effort incurred by people and firms who are trying to minimize their holdings of cash are called **shoe leather costs**. For modest inflation rates, shoe leather costs are small but not completely trivial. For example, the shoe leather costs of a 10% perfectly anticipated inflation have been estimated to be about 0.3% of GDP, which is about $5 billion per year in Canada.

A second cost of perfectly anticipated inflation arises from menu costs, or the costs of changing nominal prices. When there is inflation and prices are continually rising, sellers of goods and services must use resources to change nominal prices. For instance, mail-order firms have to print and mail catalogues or update their websites frequently to report the increases in prices. Although some firms face

---

[16] It may be true that, psychologically, people think of increases in their wages arising from ongoing inflation as being earned and, thus, "fair," but that increases in the prices they pay because of inflation are "unfair." This is a confusion, although one that may have real political consequences if it causes the public to demand strong action on inflation.

[17] This argument ignores the fact that interest is taxed on a nominal basis. If the after-tax real interest rate is to be kept constant, the nominal interest rate will have to rise by somewhat more than the increase in inflation.

substantial menu costs, for the economy as a whole these costs are probably small. Furthermore, technological progress, such as the introduction of electronic scanners in supermarkets, reduces the cost of changing prices.

While the costs of anticipated inflation are likely positive, researchers have generally found it difficult to quantify or to demonstrate these costs empirically. The benefits of reducing the volatility and unpredictability of inflation are generally believed to be much greater. These benefits are discussed in the next section.

Unanticipated Inflation

Much of the public's aversion to inflation is aversion to unanticipated inflation—inflation that is different from the rate expected. For example, if everyone expects the inflation rate to be 4% per year, but it's actually 6% per year, unanticipated inflation is 2% per year.

What is the effect of 6% inflation if (1) you expected 4% inflation, and (2) your savings account pays 7% interest? When inflation is 6% per year instead of 4% per year, the actual real interest rate on your savings account is only 1% per year (the nominal interest rate of 7% minus the inflation rate of 6%) instead of the 3% per year you expected. By earning a lower actual real interest rate, you lose as a result of the unanticipated inflation. However, your loss is the bank's gain because the bank pays a lower real interest rate than it expected. Note that the roles would have been reversed if the actual inflation rate had been lower than expected; in that case, the real interest rate that you earn, and that the bank has to pay, would be higher than anticipated.

Similarly, suppose that your nominal salary is set in advance. If inflation is higher than expected, the real value of your salary is less than you expected, and your loss is your employer's gain. If inflation is lower than expected, however, you benefit and your employer loses.

These examples show that a primary effect of unanticipated inflation is to transfer wealth from one person or firm to another. People who lend or save at fixed interest rates (creditors) and those with incomes set in nominal terms are hurt by unanticipated inflation, whereas people who borrow at fixed interest rates (debtors) or who must make fixed nominal payments are helped by unanticipated inflation.

For the economy as a whole, a transfer of wealth from one group to another is not a net loss of resources and, hence, does not represent a true cost. However, from the viewpoints of individual people and firms in the economy, the *risk* of gaining or losing wealth as a result of unanticipated inflation is unwelcome. Because most people do not like risk, the possibility of significant gains or losses arising from unexpected inflation makes people feel worse off and, hence, is a cost of unanticipated inflation. Furthermore, any resources that people use in forecasting inflation and trying to protect themselves against the risks of unanticipated inflation represent an additional cost. However, some of these costs of unanticipated inflation can be eliminated by contracts that are indexed to the price level (see A Closer Look 13.2).

Another cost of unanticipated inflation relates to the fact that prices serve as signals in a market economy. For example, if wheat becomes more expensive than corn, that's a signal to consumers to switch from wheat to corn and to farmers to produce more wheat and less corn. However, the prices that act as signals in the economy are *relative* prices, such as the price of wheat relative to the price of corn. Knowing that wheat is so many dollars per tonne doesn't help the consumer and farmer make good economic decisions unless they also know the price of corn.

A CLOSER LOOK 13.2

INDEXED CONTRACTS

In principle, much of the risk of gains and losses associated with unanticipated inflation can be eliminated by using contracts in which payments are indexed to inflation. If a bank wanted to offer a guaranteed 3% real interest rate on savings accounts, for instance, it could index the nominal interest rate to the rate of inflation by offering to pay a nominal interest rate equal to 3% plus whatever the rate of inflation turns out to be. Then, if the actual inflation rate is 6%, the bank would end up paying a nominal interest rate of 9%—giving the depositor the promised 3% real interest rate. Similarly, other financial contracts, such as loans, mortgages, and bonds, can be indexed to protect the real rate of return against unanticipated inflation. Wage payments set by labour contracts can also be indexed to protect workers and employers against unanticipated inflation (we discussed the macroeconomic effects of wage indexation in Appendix 12.A).

How widespread is indexing? Most financial contracts in Canada are not indexed to the rate of inflation, although since 1991, the federal government has offered "real return bonds" that compensate investors for CPI inflation. Payments on some long-term financial contracts (adjustable-rate mortgages, for example) are indexed to nominal interest rates, such as the prime rate charged by banks or the Treasury bill interest rate. Because nominal interest rates move roughly in step with inflation, these long-term financial contracts are to some extent indexed to inflation. Many labour contracts in Canada are indexed to the rate of inflation through provisions called cost-of-living adjustments, or COLAs. They provide for some increase in nominal wages if inflation is higher than expected, but a 1% increase in unanticipated inflation usually results in somewhat less than a 1% adjustment of wages.

In contrast, in countries that have experienced high and unpredictable inflation rates, indexed contracts are common. A case in point is Israel, which had a CPI inflation rate of 445% per year in 1984. At that time, over 80% of liquid financial assets in Israel were indexed; for example, long-term government bonds were indexed to the CPI, and banks offered short-term deposits whose purchasing power was tied to that of the U.S. dollar. However, the fraction of financial assets that were indexed decreased after the Israeli hyperinflation ended in the second half of 1985, and continued to decrease as Israeli inflation fell to single digits.[*]

---

[*] See Stanley Fischer, "Israeli Inflation and Indexation," in J. Williamson, ed., *Inflation and Indexation: Argentina, Brazil, Israel*, Institute for International Economics, 1985, reprinted in Stanley Fischer, *Indexing, Inflation, and Economic Policy*, Cambridge, Mass.: M.I.T. Press, 1986; and Zalman F. Shiffer, "Adjusting to High Inflation: The Israeli Experience," *Federal Reserve Bank of St. Louis Review*, May 1986, pp. 18–29.

When inflation is unanticipated, particularly if it is erratic, people may confuse changes in prices arising from changes in the general price level with changes in prices arising from shifts in the supply of or demand for individual goods. Because the signals provided by prices may be distorted by unanticipated inflation, the market economy works less efficiently. In addition, when there is a great deal of uncertainty about the true inflation rate, people must spend time and effort learning about different prices, by comparison shopping, for example.

The Costs of Hyperinflation

Hyperinflation occurs when the inflation rate is extremely high for a sustained period of time.[18] We mentioned the German hyperinflation of 1922–1923 in Chapter 1, and there are many other examples. During a 12-month period

---

[18] Philip Cagan, in his classic study of hyperinflation ("The Monetary Dynamics of Hyperinflation," in Milton Friedman, ed., *Studies in the Quantity Theory of Money*, Chicago: University of Chicago Press, 1956), defined a hyperinflation as beginning in the month in which the rate of inflation first exceeds 50% per month.

beginning in August 1945, the average rate of inflation in Hungary was 19 800% *per month*.[19] In the more recent hyperinflation in Bolivia, the annual rate of inflation was 1281% in 1984; it soared to 11 750% in 1985 before dropping to 276% in 1986.[20] The costs of inflation during these hyperinflations were much greater than the costs associated with moderate inflation. For example, when prices are increasing at such mind-boggling rates, the incentives to minimize holdings of currency are powerful and the resulting shoe leather costs are enormous. In severe hyperinflations workers are paid much more frequently— perhaps even more than once a day—and they rush out to spend their money (or to convert their money into some other form, such as a foreign currency) before prices rise even further. The time and energy devoted to getting rid of currency as fast as possible wastes resources and disrupts production.

One early casualty of hyperinflations is the government's ability to collect taxes. In a hyperinflation, taxpayers have an incentive to delay paying their taxes as long as possible. Because tax bills are usually set in nominal terms, the longer the taxpayer delays, the less the real value of that obligation is. The real value of taxes collected by the government falls sharply during hyperinflations, with destructive effects on the government's finances and its ability to provide public services.

Finally, the disruptive effect of inflation on market efficiency that we discussed earlier becomes most severe in the case of a hyperinflation. If prices change so often that they cease to be reliable indicators of the supply of and demand for different goods and services, markets cannot allocate resources efficiently.

FIGHTING INFLATION: THE ROLE OF INFLATIONARY EXPECTATIONS

In essence, inflation occurs when the aggregate quantity of goods demanded at any particular price level is rising more quickly than the aggregate quantity of goods supplied at that price level (Figure 13.3, p. 444, illustrates such a situation). Many factors can cause rapid increases in the aggregate quantity of goods demanded relative to the aggregate quantity supplied. Among these sources of inflation are increases in consumption or investment spending, expansionary fiscal policies, and adverse supply shocks. However, as discussed in Chapter 7, in general, the only factor that can create *sustained* rises in aggregate demand and, thus, ongoing inflation is a high rate of money growth.

If rapid money growth is inflationary, why do central banks permit rapid monetary expansion? As mentioned in Chapter 7 (and discussed in more detail in Chapter 15), in developing or war-torn countries governments may not be able to raise enough revenue by taxing or borrowing, so they print money to finance their spending. However, in industrialized countries not engaged in or recovering from a war, governments are usually able to either tax or borrow enough to cover their expenditures. In these countries, rapid money growth is usually the result of past attempts to use expansionary monetary policy to fight recessions without being balanced by tighter monetary policies in periods when output is above the full-employment level.

---

[19] *Ibid.*, Table 1.

[20] See Table 7.3, Juan-Antonio Morales, "Inflation Stabilization in Bolivia," in Michael Bruno, Guido De Tella, Rudiger Dornbusch, and Stanley Fischer, eds., *Inflation Stabilization: The Experience of Israel, Argentina, Brazil, Bolivia, and Mexico*, Cambridge, Mass.: M.I.T. Press, 1988.

Because ongoing inflation is generally the result of rapid money growth, the prescription for stopping inflation appears to be simple: Reduce the rate of money growth. Unfortunately, the process of **disinflation**—the reduction of the inflation rate—by slowing money growth may lead to a serious recession. In terms of the expectations-augmented Phillips curve (Eq. 13.1, p. 446), if macroeconomic policy succeeds in reducing inflation below the expected rate, unemployment will rise above the natural rate. Unemployment will remain above the natural rate until expected inflation falls to the new, lower actual inflation rate.

Is there some way to reduce inflation without incurring serious unemployment costs? The expectations-augmented Phillips curve suggests one possibility: If the public's expected rate of inflation could be lowered as actual inflation was being brought down, unemployment would not have to rise above the natural rate. (You should confirm that in Eq. 13.1, if actual inflation π and expected inflation π^e fall by the same amount, cyclical unemployment $u - \overline{u}$ does not increase.) That is, if expected inflation can be reduced, the original Phillips curve relating inflation and unemployment can be shifted down and to the left, reducing the rate of inflation associated with any level of unemployment.

But how can policymakers reduce the public's inflationary expectations? In the rest of this section, we discuss some suggested approaches for reducing both inflation and inflationary expectations.

Rapid versus Gradual Disinflation

Some classical economists have proposed that disinflation should be implemented quickly by a rapid and decisive reduction in the growth rate of the money supply—a strategy sometimes referred to as **cold turkey**. Because a cold-turkey disinflation is dramatic and highly visible to the public, proponents of this policy argue that it will quickly and substantially reduce inflationary expectations, particularly if the policy is announced well in advance. If expected inflation falls sufficiently, the expectations-augmented Phillips curve implies that the unemployment costs of the disinflation will be minimal.

However, most Keynesian economists disagree with the idea that rapid disinflation can be achieved without significant costs in terms of increased cyclical unemployment. They note that the secret to the success of the cold-turkey approach is the ability of prices to adjust rapidly with expectations. Keynesians stress that because of such factors as menu costs and nominal-wage contracts, several years may be required for prices and wages to adjust to a disinflationary policy; during the adjustment period, cyclical unemployment could be high. Further, Keynesians point out that the cold-turkey strategy may not lower inflation expectations because people may expect the government to abandon the policy if the resulting unemployment reaches politically intolerable levels.

Because they fear the possible unemployment consequences of the cold-turkey strategy, many Keynesians recommend a policy of **gradualism**, or reducing the rate of money growth and inflation gradually over a period of years. Keynesians argue that a gradual approach, which gives prices, wages, and expectations more time to adjust to the disinflation, will raise the unemployment rate by less than the cold-turkey strategy—although the period during which unemployment exceeds the natural rate may be longer. They further argue that because the policy will be viewed as sustainable politically, gradualism may be as effective as the cold-turkey approach at reducing inflationary expectations. The results of one study comparing cold turkey and gradualism are discussed in A Closer Look 13.3.

A CLOSER LOOK 13.3

THE SACRIFICE RATIO

To reduce inflation, tight monetary and fiscal policies must be used to slow the growth rate of aggregate demand. However, if these policies are not perfectly anticipated, they will also cause output and employment to fall below their full-employment levels—at least for a time. This loss of output and jobs is an important cost that must be weighed against the benefits of inflation-reducing policies.

Economists sometimes use the sacrifice ratio to measure the cost of lowering the inflation rate. The **sacrifice ratio** is the amount of output lost when the inflation rate is reduced by 1 percentage point. For example, according to a study by Laurence Ball, of Johns Hopkins University,[*] during the disinflation of the early 1980s, the inflation rate in Canada fell by 7.83 percentage points (from a rate of 11.60% per year to 3.77% per year). For the 16 quarters of this disinflation, Ball estimated the total loss in output caused by inflation—reducing policies to be 18.58% of one year's potential GDP. Dividing the output loss of 18.58% of potential GDP by the 7.83 percentage point reduction in inflation yields a sacrifice ratio of 2.37 for this episode. We can interpret this result as saying that each percentage point by which Canadian inflation was reduced during the early 1980s cost the country 2.37% of a year's potential GDP.

Using quarterly data for nine countries, Ball calculated the sacrifice ratio for 28 disinflations that occurred during the 1960s, 1970s, and 1980s. The accompanying table reports the average sacrifice ratio he found for each country and demonstrates that the output cost of reducing inflation may vary considerably. The average sacrifice ratio ranges from less than 1 in France, the United Kingdom, and Japan to almost 3 in Germany. In other words, reducing inflation in Germany is three times more expensive, in terms of lost output, than it is in those other industrialized countries. What accounts for these differences?

Average Sacrifice Ratios by Country

Australia	1.00
Canada	1.50
France	0.75
Germany	2.92
Italy	1.74
Japan	0.93
Switzerland	1.57
United Kingdom	0.79
United States	2.39

By comparing the characteristics of the different countries in his sample, Ball found that one factor affecting the sacrifice ratio is the flexibility of the labour market. Countries in which wages adjust relatively slowly to changes in labour supply and demand— owing, for example, to heavy government regulation of the labour market—tend to have higher sacrifice ratios. This finding makes sense because countries with inflexible labour markets should take longer to reach long-run equilibrium following an unexpected slowing of the growth of aggregate demand. Ball also found that rapid disinflations tend to have lower sacrifice ratios than do slow disinflations, which is a bit of evidence in favour of the cold-turkey approach rather than of gradualism.

Ball's results are interesting but should be interpreted with some caution. One problem is that determining exactly how much output loss can be attributed to a particular set of anti-inflationary policies is not easy. For example, to calculate the output loss owing to disinflation, we have to estimate the amount of output if there had been no disinflation, which is difficult. If the output loss calculation is wrong, the sacrifice ratio calculation will also be wrong. Such factors as supply shocks, which affect both output and inflation, can also distort the calculation of sacrifice ratios. Thus, at best, the sacrifice ratio is a rough measure of the costs of reducing inflation.

---

[*] "What Determines the Sacrifice Ratio?" in N. Gregory Mankiw, ed., *Monetary Policy*, Chicago: University of Chicago Press, 1994, pp. 155–188.

Wage and Price Controls

Frustrated by the costs and difficulties of reducing inflation by reducing money growth, policymakers in some countries have taken a more direct approach and imposed wage and price controls—legal limits on the ability of firms to raise wages or prices. These controls have sometimes been used in wartime, and peacetime supporters of wage–price controls (or of *incomes policies*, as wage–price controls are also called) argue that by using the force of law to stop price increases the government can "break the back" of inflationary expectations, allowing a disinflation to proceed without serious unemployment consequences.

Critics of price controls make two points. First, price controls are likely to cause shortages. In a free market the ever-changing forces of supply and demand lead to changes in relative prices, with the prices of some products rising more rapidly than the prices of others. If price controls prevent the price of a product from rising to the level at which quantity supplied equals quantity demanded, there will be excess demand for the product, that is, a shortage. These shortages and the disruptions they cause are a major cost of price controls.

Second, critics dispute that wage–price controls have a major effect on the public's inflation expectations. Although controls stop inflation for the moment, because they cause shortages and disrupt the economy they eventually have to be removed. Knowing that the controls are temporary, people may expect even greater inflation in the future.

One factor that may affect expectations of inflation during the period of controls is how the government handles monetary and fiscal policy. If macroeconomic policies allow aggregate demand to continue to grow rapidly, people may expect renewed inflation when the controls are lifted (see Analytical Problem 5 at the end of the chapter). But if controls are accompanied by tight monetary and fiscal policy, the idea that inflation will not resume when controls are lifted is more plausible.

Credibility and Reputation

Classicals and Keynesians agree that for disinflation to be achieved without high unemployment costs, reducing the public's expected inflation rate is important. Perhaps the most important factor determining how quickly expected inflation adjusts is the credibility, or believability, of the government's announced disinflationary policy. How can policymakers improve their credibility with the public? One way is to make a clear and unambiguous announcement of a policy whose purpose is to reduce or maintain the rate of inflation. This is precisely what the governor of the Bank of Canada and the federal minister of finance have done in a series of five announcements beginning in 1991. The latest agreement, recently renewed in 2016 and effective until 2021, aims to maintain inflation within a range (1%–3%), with an average rate of 2% per year. By making a joint declaration, policymakers in charge of monetary and fiscal policy are intending to announce their commitment, to one another and to workers, consumers, and firms, to make every effort to keep inflation under control. This, it is hoped, will encourage households and firms to keep their expectations of inflation low and so make it easier for policymakers to keep actual inflation low.

While declarations of commitment are useful, credibility is ultimately won only when policymakers develop a reputation for carrying through on their promises. This can sometimes require a willingness to weather political storms that arise when an economic shock generates politically motivated "calls to action" even when that action might threaten previously announced commitments. Policymakers who are not elected can typically maintain their policy stances, and hence their credibility, better than those who must face re-election from time to time.

It was just this consideration that prompted the 1997 announcement by the newly elected Labour government of British Prime Minister Tony Blair that, from that time forward, the Bank of England would be operationally independent of elected officials. Economists applauded the announcement as an important step in the direction of increasing the credibility of the British central bank. We explore the relationships among institutional structure, government credibility, and inflation expectations in greater detail in Chapter 14.

CHAPTER SUMMARY

1. Following the famous 1958 article by A. W. Phillips, empirical studies often showed that inflation is high when unemployment is low and low when unemployment is high. This negative empirical relationship between inflation and unemployment is called the Phillips curve. Inflation and unemployment in Canada conformed to the Phillips curve during the 1960s but not during the 1970s and 1980s.

2. Economic theory suggests that, in general, the negative relationship between inflation and unemployment should not be stable. Instead, in an economy in which there are unanticipated changes in the growth rate of aggregate demand, there should be a negative relationship between unanticipated inflation and cyclical unemployment. In particular, when actual and expected inflation are equal (so that unanticipated inflation is zero), the actual unemployment rate will equal the natural unemployment rate (so that cyclical unemployment is zero). This negative relationship between unanticipated inflation and cyclical unemployment is called the expectations-augmented Phillips curve.

3. According to the theory of the expectations-augmented Phillips curve, a stable negative relationship between inflation and unemployment (a Phillips curve) will be observed only if expected inflation and the natural unemployment rate are constant. An increase in expected inflation or an increase in the natural unemployment rate shifts the Phillips curve up and to the right. Adverse supply shocks typically increase both expected inflation and the natural unemployment rate and also shift the Phillips curve up and to the right. Major supply shocks during

the 1970s, a rising natural unemployment rate, and highly variable expected inflation rates explain why the Phillips curve shifted erratically in Canada after about 1970.

4. According to the expectations-augmented Phillips curve, unemployment will fall below the natural rate only when inflation is higher than anticipated. Important sources of unanticipated inflation are unanticipated movements in aggregate demand and aggregate supply arising from waves of pessimism, oil price shocks, and other such unexpected events. Classical economists stress that there are few impediments to price adjustment and that inflation expectations adjust quickly to unanticipated inflation. For these reasons the unemployment rate will deviate from the natural rate for only short periods of time and there is little scope for stabilization policies to play a useful role in trying to offset the effects of unexpected shocks. In contrast, Keynesians believe that although price and inflation expectations adjust quickly, nominal-wage and price stickiness prevent prices and inflation from adjusting as quickly as claimed by classical economists. As a consequence, the unemployment rate can deviate from the natural rate for an extended period of time, allowing stabilization policy time to play a useful role.

5. Classicals and Keynesians agree that in the long run expected and actual inflation rates are equal. Thus, in the long run, the actual unemployment rate equals the natural rate, regardless of the inflation rate. Reflecting the fact that there is no long-run trade-off between inflation and unemployment, the long-run Phillips curve is vertical at the natural unemployment rate.

6. The costs of unemployment include output lost when fewer people are working and the personal or psychological costs for unemployed workers and their families.

7. In the long run, the unemployment rate is determined by the natural unemployment rate. According to some estimates, the natural unemployment rate in Canada rose during the 1970s and 1980s but has since fallen. Explanations for the changes in the natural rate of unemployment include demographic changes in the labour force and technological changes, hysteresis, and changes in the system of unemployment insurance.

8. Policies to reduce the natural unemployment rate include government support for job training and worker relocation and efforts to minimize the size of payroll taxes. Some proponents of the hysteresis theory argue that pushing down the actual unemployment rate by means of expansionary policies (a "high-pressure" economy) will ultimately reduce the natural rate as well.

9. The costs of inflation depend on whether the inflation was anticipated or unanticipated. The costs of anticipated inflation, which (except in extreme inflations) are relatively minor, include shoe leather costs (resources used by individuals and firms to reduce their holdings of currency) and menu costs (costs of changing posted prices during an inflation). Unanticipated inflation causes unpredictable transfers of wealth among individuals and firms. The risk of unpredictable gains and losses, and the resources that people expend in trying to reduce this risk, are costs of unanticipated inflation. Unanticipated inflation may also reduce the efficiency of the market system by making it more difficult for people to observe relative prices.

10. Disinflation is a reduction in the rate of inflation. Attempts to disinflate by slowing money growth will cause cyclical unemployment to rise if actual inflation falls below expected inflation. To reduce the unemployment cost of disinflation, the public's expected inflation rate should be brought down along with the actual inflation rate. Strategies for reducing expected inflation include rapid and decisive reduction in the growth rate of the money supply (the cold-turkey approach), wage and price controls, and taking measures to improve the credibility of government policy announcements.

KEY TERMS

cold turkey, p. 465
disinflation, p. 465
expectations-augmented Phillips curve, p. 446
gradualism, p. 465
hyperinflation, p. 463
hysteresis, p. 457
long-run Phillips curve, p. 453
Okun's law, p. 454
Phillips curve, p. 441
sacrifice ratio, p. 466
shoe leather costs, p. 461

KEY EQUATION

$$\pi = \pi^e - h(u - \overline{u}). \qquad (13.1)$$

The expectations-augmented Phillips curve states that unanticipated inflation, $\pi - \pi^e$, is negatively related to cyclical unemployment, $u - \overline{u}$. The expectations—augmented Phillips curve also implies that inflation, π, is negatively related to unemployment, u, only if the expected inflation rate π^e and the natural unemployment rate $\overline{u}$ are constant. Changes in the expected inflation rate or in the natural unemployment rate cause the relationship between inflation and unemployment—the traditional Phillips curve—to shift.

REVIEW QUESTIONS

1. What is the Phillips curve? Does the Phillips curve relationship hold for Canadian data? Explain.

2. How does the expectations-augmented Phillips curve differ from the traditional Phillips curve? According to the theory of the expectations-augmented Phillips curve, under what conditions should the traditional Phillips curve relationship appear in the data?

3. How do changes in the expected inflation rate account for the behaviour of the Phillips curve in the 1970s, 1980s, and 1990s in Canada? What role do supply shocks play in explaining the behaviour of the Phillips curve in Canada?

4. Is there a role for stabilization policy to alleviate cyclical unemployment? Explain both the classical and Keynesian points of view.

5. Why is the natural unemployment rate an important economic variable? What factors explain the changes in the natural rate over time in Canada, the United States, and Europe? What government policies, if any, might be used to reduce the natural unemployment rate?

6. Give two costs of anticipated inflation and two costs of unanticipated inflation. How is the magnitude of each affected if, instead of a moderate inflation, hyperinflation occurs?

7. What is the greatest potential cost associated with disinflation? How does the responsiveness of the public's inflation expectations affect the size of this potential cost?

8. Discuss at least two strategies for reducing expected inflation rapidly. What are the pros and cons of these strategies?

NUMERICAL PROBLEMS

1. Consider an economy in long-run equilibrium with an inflation rate π of 12% (0.12) per year and a natural unemployment rate $\overline{u}$ of 6% (0.06). The expectations-augmented Phillips curve is

$$\pi = \pi^e - 2(u - \overline{u}).$$

Assume that Okun's law holds so that a 1 percentage point increase in the unemployment rate maintained for one year reduces GDP by 2.0% of full-employment output.

a. Consider a two-year disinflation. In the first year, $\pi = 0.04$ and $\pi^e = 0.08$. In the second year, $\pi = 0.04$ and $\pi^e = 0.04$. In the first year, what is the unemployment rate? By what percentage does output fall short of full-employment output? In the second year, what is the unemployment rate? By what percentage does output fall short of full-employment output?

b. Now consider a four-year disinflation according to the following table:

Year	1	2	3	4
π	0.08	0.04	0.04	0.04
π^e	0.10	0.08	0.06	0.04

What is the unemployment rate in each of the four years? By what percentage does output fall short of full-employment output each year? What is the sacrifice ratio for this disinflation?

2. Consider the following extended classical economy (in which the misperceptions theory holds):

AD	$Y = 300 + 10(M/P)$
SRAS	$Y = \overline{Y} + P - P^e$
Full-employment output	$\overline{Y} = 500$
Natural unemployment rate	$\overline{u} = 0.06$

a. Suppose that the money supply $M = 1000$ and that the expected price level $P^e = 50$. What are the short-run equilibrium values of output Y and the price level P? What are the long-run equilibrium values of these two variables?

b. Now suppose that an unanticipated increase raises the nominal money supply to $M = 1260$. What are the new short-run equilibrium values of output Y and the price level P? What are the new long-run equilibrium values of these two variables? In general, are your results consistent with an expectations-augmented Phillips curve?

3. In a certain economy, the expectations-augmented Phillips curve is

$$\pi = \pi^e - 2(u - \overline{u})$$

and

$$\overline{u} = 0.06.$$

a. Graph the Phillips curve of this economy for an expected inflation rate of 0.10. If the central bank chooses to keep the actual inflation rate at 0.10, what will be the unemployment rate?

b. An aggregate demand shock (resulting from increased government spending) raises expected inflation to 0.12 (the natural unemployment rate is unaffected). Graph the new Phillips curve and compare it with the curve you drew in part (a). What happens to the unemployment rate if the central bank holds actual inflation at 0.10? What happens to the Phillips curve and the unemployment rate if the central bank announces that it will hold inflation at 0.10 after the aggregate demand shock, and this announcement is fully believed by the public?

c. Suppose that a supply shock (a drought) raises expected inflation to 0.12 and raises the natural unemployment rate to 0.08. Repeat part (b).

ANALYTICAL PROBLEMS

1. Suppose that the government institutes a program to help unemployed workers learn new skills, find new jobs, and relocate as necessary to take the new jobs.

a. If this program reduces structural unemployment, what is the effect on the expectations-augmented Phillips curve and the long-run Phillips curve?

b. The government program is expensive, and critics argue that a cheaper way to cut unemployment would be by monetary expansion. Comment.

2. Two extended classical economies (in which the misperceptions theory holds) differ only in one

respect: In economy A money growth and inflation have been low and stable for many years, but in economy B money growth and inflation have fluctuated erratically between very low and very high levels. When producers in economy B observe changes in the prices of the goods they produce, from past experience they usually attribute these changes to fluctuations in the overall price level rather than to changes in the relative prices of their goods.

Will the slope of the short-run aggregate supply curve for economy B be flatter or steeper than the slope of the curve for economy A? What about the slope of the Phillips curve?

3. In this problem, you are asked to show that the expectations-augmented Phillips curve (derived in the text using the extended classical model) can be derived using the Keynesian model.

Consider a Keynesian economy in which full-employment output is constant and in which the nominal money supply has been growing at 10% per year for some time and is expected to keep growing at that rate in the future. To avoid some technical complications, suppose that instead of growing continuously over time, the money supply is increased by 10% each December 31 and then held constant until the next December 31. Monopolistically competitive firms reset their prices on December 31 of each year to the level that they expect will allow them to sell the full-employment level of output during the coming year. Inflation is measured as the percentage change in prices between January 1 and December 31 of each year.

a. Show how the *AD* curve, *SRAS* curve, output, the price level, and the expected price level evolve over time in this economy. What are the values of unanticipated inflation and cyclical unemployment?

b. Now, suppose that on June 30, 2012, the money supply is unexpectedly raised by an additional 5%. However, the central bank announces—and it is believed by firms—that this extra increase in the money supply is a one-time-only increase and that next December 31 the central bank will return to its policy of increasing the money supply by 10%. (Thus, the total increase in the money supply between January 1, 2012, and December 31, 2012, is 15%.) Firms do not change prices until

December 31, as usual, but when they do they respond fully to the new information about money supply growth.

What are the actual and unanticipated inflation rates during 2012? Is cyclical unemployment positive, negative, or zero (on average) during 2012? Relate your results to the expectations-augmented Phillips curve.

4. Some economists have suggested that someday we will live in a "cashless society," in which all businesses (including stores) and banks will be linked to a centralized accounting system. In this system you will be able to pay for purchases directly from your bank account without using cash. What are the costs of anticipated inflation in a cashless society? What are the costs of unanticipated inflation?

5. To fight an ongoing 10% inflation, the government makes raising wages or prices illegal. However, the government continues to increase the money supply (and hence aggregate demand) by 10% per year. The economy starts at full-employment output, which remains constant.

a. Using the Keynesian *AD–AS* framework, show the effects of the government's policies on the economy. Assume that firms meet the demand at the fixed price level.

b. After several years in which the controls have kept prices from rising, the government declares victory over inflation and removes the controls. What happens?

6. How would each of the following changes likely affect the natural unemployment rate?

a. A new law prohibits people from seeking employment before age 18 years.

b. A new Internet service, CareerOwl.ca, makes it easy for people to check on the availability of jobs around the country.

c. The length of time that unemployed workers can receive Employment Insurance doubles.

d. A shift in the public's buying habits greatly expands the demand for sophisticated consumer electronics while reducing the demand for traditional consumer goods and services, such as clothing and restaurant meals.

e. Tight monetary policy, introduced to reduce the inflation rate drives the economy into a recession.

Chapter 14

Monetary Policy and the Bank of Canada

Monetary policy is one of the two principal tools available for affecting macroeconomic behaviour. (The other, fiscal policy, is discussed in Chapter 15.) Monetary policy decisions have widespread implications for the economy. The macroeconomic models that we have presented predict that changes in the money supply will affect nominal variables, such as the price level and the nominal exchange rate. In addition, theories that allow for non-neutrality (including the extended classical theory with misperceptions and the Keynesian theory) imply that in the short run, monetary policy also affects real variables, such as real GDP, the real interest rate, and the unemployment rate. Because monetary policy has such pervasive economic effects, the central bank's announcements and actions are closely monitored by the media, financial market participants, and the general public.

In this chapter we look more closely at monetary policy, concentrating first on the basic question of how the country's money supply is determined. In previous chapters, we have assumed, for simplicity, that the money supply is determined by the central bank. We now demonstrate that although a country's central bank (such as the Bank of Canada) can exert strong influence over the level of the money supply, the money supply is also affected by the banking system's behaviour and the public's decisions.

In the second part of the chapter, we explore this question: How should the central bank conduct monetary policy? Not surprisingly, because of classical and Keynesian differences over the effects of monetary policy and the desirability of trying to smooth the business cycle (Chapters 11 and 12), the question is controversial. Some Keynesians argue that monetary authorities should have considerable latitude to try to offset cyclical fluctuations. Opposing this view, both classical economists and a group of economists called *monetarists* believe that monetary policy should not be left to the discretion of the central bank but, instead, should be governed by simple rules. Although establishing rules for monetary policy might seem to tie policymakers' hands unnecessarily, monetarists and classicals argue that the use of rules would lead to a more stable and less inflationary economy in the long run. After examining the arguments for and against the use of rules, we discuss the effectiveness of rules-based monetary policies in Canada and other countries. We also discuss how the debate about rules is related to questions of how monetary policymaking institutions should be designed. For example, should the central bank be largely independent from the government, or should it be more directly controlled by the federal Parliament and Cabinet?

14.1 PRINCIPLES OF MONEY SUPPLY DETERMINATION

How is the country's money supply determined? So far, we have assumed that the money supply, M, is controlled directly by the central bank. Although this assumption is a useful simplification, it is not literally true. The central bank's control of the money supply is only indirect and depends to some extent on the structure of the economy.

Most generally, three groups affect the money supply: the central bank, depository institutions, and the public.

1. In nearly all countries, the **central bank** is the governmental institution responsible for monetary policy.[1] Examples of central banks are the Bank of Canada, the Federal Reserve System in the United States, the European Central Bank, and the Bank of Japan.

2. **Depository institutions** are privately owned banks, trust companies, credit unions, and caisses populaires that accept deposits from and make loans directly to the public. We refer to depository institutions as banks, for short.

3. The public includes every person or firm (except banks) that holds money, either as currency and coin or as deposits in banks—in other words, virtually the whole private economy outside of the banking system.

Before investigating how these groups interact to set the money supply in a financially complex country, such as Canada, we begin with an example of a primitive agricultural economy, which we call Agricola. Examining the introduction of money and the development of banking in Agricola identifies clearly the factors involved in the determination of the money supply. Additionally, the development of the monetary and banking systems in fictitious Agricola loosely parallels the actual evolution of such systems over the centuries in many countries.

THE MONEY SUPPLY IN AN ALL-CURRENCY ECONOMY

The imaginary country of Agricola is an agricultural nation that produces a variety of fruits, nuts, vegetables, and grains. Initially, Agricola has no money supply, so all trading is done by barter, or the direct trading of goods for goods. Recall, however, that a trading system based on barter is extremely inconvenient (Chapter 7). Under a barter system, a farmer who wants to trade barley for pomegranates must find someone willing to exchange pomegranates for barley, which involves a costly and time-consuming search.

The benevolent leader of Agricola recognizes this inconvenience and decides to create a national money to ease trade among the people. The first step in establishing a national money is to create a government agency called the Agricolan

---

[1] Most industrialized countries established central banks in the 19th century or early 20th century. Prior to the establishment of central banks, national treasury or finance departments were often responsible for currency issue and other matters pertaining to the money supply.

Central Bank. The Central Bank then prints paper certificates[2] and decrees the value of each certificate to be one florin (abbreviated fl), which becomes the national currency of Agricola. The government of Agricola prohibits anyone other than the Agricolan Central Bank from printing these certificates.

To get the florins into general circulation, the Central Bank uses them to buy some real assets from the public. In the agricultural economy of Agricola, real assets are storable agricultural products, such as coconuts, so the Central Bank uses newly printed florins to buy coconuts from the public. Why do people in Agricola willingly surrender valuable coconuts in exchange for paper certificates? In general, people accept paper money in payment for goods, services, or assets because they expect to be able to use it to buy other goods, services, or assets in the future. In other words, people accept paper money because they believe that other people also will accept it. The belief that money has value becomes self-justifying: If most people believe that money has value, then it has value.[3] The government helps convince the public that paper money has value by decreeing that the money is *legal tender*—that is, creditors are required to accept the money in settlement of debts—and by stating its own willingness to accept money from the public in payment of taxes.

Suppose that the people of Agricola accept the new currency and that the Central Bank trades one million florins to the public for one million coconuts. The balance sheet of the Agricolan Central Bank is

Agricolan Central Bank			
ASSETS		LIABILITIES	
Coconuts	1 000 000 fl	Currency	1 000 000 fl

On the left-hand side of the balance sheet are the Central Bank's assets—what it owns or is owed, in this case, the coconuts. On the right-hand side are the bank's liabilities—what it owes to others. Because the florins are technically debt obligations of the Central Bank, they are entered as liabilities on the balance sheet. The liabilities of the Central Bank that are usable as money are called the **monetary base**, or, equivalently, **high-powered money**. The monetary base of Agricola is, thus, one million florins.

Assume that Agricola initially has no banking system. With no banks and hence no bank deposits, the total money supply is the currency held by the public. That is, the paper certificates distributed by the Agricolan Central Bank are used directly as money. Thus, the money supply in Agricola equals one million florins, which, in turn, equals the monetary base (the liabilities of the Agricolan Central Bank). Hence, *in an all-currency economy (one with no bank deposits) the money supply equals the monetary base.*

THE MONEY SUPPLY UNDER FRACTIONAL RESERVE BANKING

As the people of Agricola become financially more sophisticated, a system of private banks emerges. The banks announce their willingness to accept deposits from the public.

[2] In many countries, the actual printing of paper money is done by a separate agency, not by the central bank itself.

[3] Also possible is that no one believes that money has value, which would again be a self-justifying belief because no one would then accept money in payment. In the next section, we will see an example of this outcome in Canadian history.

For the time being, let's assume that because currency is easily lost or stolen, Agricolans want to hold all their money in bank deposits rather than in currency. After the Agricolans deposit all their currency (one million florins) in banks, the combined, or consolidated, balance sheet of all the private banks is

Consolidated Balance Sheet of Private Banks			
ASSETS		LIABILITIES	
Currency	1 000 000 fl	Deposits	1 000 000 fl

The banking system's assets are the one million paper florins in bank vaults. The banking system's liabilities are the deposits, which are the banks' debts or obligations to the public. The balance sheet of the Central Bank remains the same.

Liquid assets held by banks to meet the demands for withdrawals by depositors or to pay the cheques drawn on depositors' accounts are called **bank reserves**. In general, bank reserves comprise currency held by private banks in their vaults and deposits held by private banks at the Central Bank. Here, all bank reserves are held as currency in the banks' vaults. Note that the bank reserves equal total deposits of 1 000 000 fl. This type of banking system is called **100% reserve banking** because bank reserves equal 100% of deposits. Under 100% reserve banking, banks are nothing more than a safekeeping service for the public's currency. Indeed, the only way that banks could cover their expenses and make a profit under 100% reserve banking would be to charge depositors a fee for holding their money for them (that is, to pay negative interest on deposits).

However, one day, an enterprising Agricolan banker notices that the paper florins the bank has accepted from depositors are just sitting idly in neat stacks in the bank's vault. True, a few florins flow out when a depositor writes a cheque to someone who banks elsewhere, or when a depositor switches an account to another bank. However, this outflow is balanced by a roughly equivalent inflow, when the bank's depositors receive cheques drawn on other banks or the bank attracts a depositor away from another bank. The banker calculates that keeping florins in the vault equal to, say, 20% of outstanding deposits would more than cover this random ebb and flow. The remaining 80% of the florins on deposit could be lent to earn interest for the bank!

Under the Agricolan banker's scheme, the reserves held by the bank will equal only a fraction of the bank's outstanding deposits. In this case, the **reserve-deposit ratio**, or reserves divided by deposits, equals 20%. A banking system in which banks hold only a fraction of their deposits in reserve, so that the reserve-deposit ratio is less than one, is called **fractional reserve banking**. Fractional reserve banking is profitable for banks because instead of sitting in the vault earning no interest for the bank, a portion of the funds received from depositors can be used to make interest-earning loans.

All the bankers of Agricola quickly grasp the idea of fractional reserve banking and decide to hold reserves of 20% of deposits and lend the other 80% (800 000 fl) to farmers. The farmers use the loans to buy fertilizer for their farms. The sellers of the fertilizer receive 800 000 fl in payment, and because everyone prefers having bank deposits to holding currency, they deposit the 800 000 fl in the banking system. After these deposits are made all the florins are back in the banks, and the consolidated balance sheet of the banking system is

Consolidated Balance Sheet of Private Banks			
ASSETS		LIABILITIES	
Currency (reserves)	1 000 000 fl	Deposits	1 800 000 fl
Loans to farmers	800 000 fl		
Total	1 800 000 fl	Total	1 800 000 fl

The banks' assets now include the 800 000 fl in loans to farmers (the loans are owed to the banks, so they are assets of the banks). The banks' assets also include one million paper florins: 200 000 fl originally kept in reserve plus the 800 000 fl deposited by the sellers of the fertilizer.

The banks' consolidated liabilities equal 1 800 000 fl in deposits: the 1 000 000 fl in original deposits and the 800 000 fl in new deposits from the fertilizer sellers.

At this point, as the bankers examine their balance sheets, they note that their reserves (holdings of paper florins) are back up to 1 000 000 fl. Their deposits equal 1 800 000 fl. On the basis of the principle that reserves need be only 20% of deposits, their reserves of 1 000 000 fl are too high. The bankers need to hold only 360 000 fl, or 0.20(1 800 000 fl). The other 640 000 fl, or 1 000 000 fl − 360 000 fl, can be lent again to earn more interest.

So, the banks make additional interest-bearing loans in the amount of 640 000 fl. The banks' borrowers use the funds to make purchases. As before, these florins are eventually re-deposited in the banking system. At this point, the consolidated balance sheet of all the banks is

Consolidated Balance Sheet of Private Banks			
ASSETS		LIABILITIES	
Currency (reserves)	1 000 000 fl	Deposits	2 440 000 fl
Loans to farmers	1 440 000 fl		
Total	2 440 000 fl	Total	2 440 000 fl

The assets of the banks now include one million paper florins (the 360 000 fl kept as reserves and the 640 000 fl re-deposited by the public) and 1 440 000 fl in loans (the 800 000 fl of first-round loans and the 640 000 fl of second-round loans). The liabilities are 2 440 000 fl in deposits (the 1 800 000 fl from earlier deposits and the 640 000 fl in new deposits).

The process does not stop here. Checking their balance sheets after this latest round of loans and re-deposits, the bankers find that their reserves (1 000 000 fl) still exceed 20% of their deposits, or 0.20(2 440 000 fl) = 488 000 fl. So, yet another round of loans and re-deposits of loaned funds will occur.

This process of **multiple expansion of loans and deposits**, in which fractional reserve banking increases an economy's loans and deposits, will stop only when the reserves of the banking system equal 20% of its deposits. The reserves of the banks always equal 1 000 000 fl (the entire supply of paper florins) at the end of each round, so the process will stop when total bank deposits equal 1 000 000 fl/0.20, or 5 000 000 fl. At this final point the consolidated balance sheet of the banks is

Consolidated Balance Sheet of Private Banks			
ASSETS		LIABILITIES	
Currency (reserves)	1 000 000 fl	Deposits	5 000 000 fl
Loans to farmers	4 000 000 fl		
Total	5 000 000 fl	Total	5 000 000 fl

At this final stage, the ratio of reserves to deposits equals the ratio desired by banks (20%). No further expansion of loans and deposits can occur after this point because the ratio of reserves to deposits is at its minimum acceptable level. What is the money supply in Agricola at the end of this process? Recall that the public does not hold any currency but, instead, deposits any currency received in the banking system, where it is held in the form of bank reserves. The reserves in the banks' vaults are not available for transactions and, thus, are not counted as money. However, the public *is* holding deposits. Because they are liquid and can be used for transactions, bank deposits are counted as part of the money supply.[4] Indeed, as there is no public holding of currency in Agricola, bank deposits are the money supply. Therefore, the money supply equals 5 000 000 fl, or the total quantity of deposits.

What is the relationship between the money supply and the monetary base with fractional reserve banking and no holding of currency by the public? We use the following variables to answer this question algebraically:

$$M = \text{the money supply;}$$
$$BASE = \text{the monetary base;}$$
$$DEP = \text{total bank deposits;}$$
$$RES = \text{total bank reserves;}$$
$$Res = \text{the banks' desired reserves to total bank deposits} = RES/DEP.$$

With no currency being held by the public, the money supply equals the quantity of bank deposits:

$$M = DEP. \tag{14.1}$$

For any level of deposits DEP, the amount of reserves that banks want to hold is $(res)(DEP)$. At the end of the multiple-expansion process, bank reserves must equal the amount of currency distributed by the Central Bank (the monetary base). Therefore,

$$(res)(DEP) = BASE. \tag{14.2}$$

Solving Eq. (14.2) for deposits yields $DEP = BASE/res$. Because the money supply equals deposits in this example,

$$M = DEP = \frac{BASE}{res}. \tag{14.3}$$

Hence, *in an economy with fractional reserve banking and no currency held by the public, the money supply equals the monetary base divided by the reserve–deposit ratio.* In Agricola, the monetary base is 1 000 000 fl and the reserve–deposit ratio chosen by the banks is 0.20. The money supply is, therefore, 1 000 000 fl/0.20, or 5 000 000 fl, as we have already shown.

The multiple expansion of loans and deposits allows the economy to create a money supply that is much larger than the monetary base. Each unit of monetary base allows $1/res$ units of money to be created, leading to a money supply that is a multiple of the monetary base. Because each unit of monetary base permits creation of several units of money supply, the base is also called *high-powered money.*

---

[4] Recall from Chapter 7 that the most narrowly defined monetary aggregate, M1+, includes demand deposits and other chequable deposits. Slightly less liquid deposits, such as savings deposits and time deposits, are included in broader monetary aggregates.

BANK RUNS

Fractional reserve banking works on the assumption that outflows and inflows of reserves will roughly balance and, in particular, that a large fraction of a bank's depositors will never want to withdraw their funds at the same time. If a large number of depositors attempt to withdraw currency simultaneously (more than 20% of the bank's deposits in Agricola), the bank will run out of reserves and be unable to meet all its depositors' demands for cash.

Historically, in Canada, there were episodes in which rumours circulated that a particular bank had made some bad loans and was at risk of becoming bankrupt. On the principle of "better safe than sorry," the bank's depositors lined up to withdraw their money. From the depositors' perspective, withdrawal avoided the risk that the bank would fail and not be able to pay off depositors in full. A large-scale, panicky withdrawal of deposits from a bank is called a **bank run**. Even if the rumours about the bank's loans proved untrue, a large enough run could exhaust the bank's reserves and force it to close. To stop a run, a bank had to convince customers that it was "sound"—financially solvent—and had plenty of funds available. More recently, the Bank of Canada and federal and provincial regulators (along with deposit insurance) have played roles in preventing bank runs.

THE MONEY SUPPLY WITH BOTH PUBLIC HOLDINGS OF CURRENCY AND FRACTIONAL RESERVE BANKING

In most economies, the public holds some currency (as at first in Agricola), and there is also a fractional reserve banking system (as later in Agricola). Currency in the public's hands and bank deposits may both be used for transactions, so both are forms of money. When the public holds both currency, CU, and bank deposits, DEP, the money supply M is

$$M = CU + DEP. \tag{14.4}$$

In this situation, the monetary base has two uses: Some of the monetary base is held as currency by the public, and the rest is held as reserves by banks. Therefore, the monetary base equals the sum of the two, or

$$BASE = CU + RES. \tag{14.5}$$

The central bank may control the amount of monetary base but does not directly control the money supply. To relate the money supply to the monetary base, we first divide the money supply, Eq. (14.4), by the monetary base, Eq. (14.5), to get

$$\frac{M}{BASE} = \frac{CU + DEP}{CU + RES}. \tag{14.6}$$

Next, we divide both the numerator and the denominator on the right-hand side of Eq. (14.6) by DEP to obtain

$$\frac{M}{BASE} = \frac{(CU/DEP) + 1}{(CU/DEP) + (RES/DEP)}. \tag{14.7}$$

The right-hand side of Eq. (14.7) contains two important ratios. The first is the **currency–deposit ratio** (CU/DEP, or cu), which is the ratio of the currency held by the public to the public's deposits in banks. The currency–deposit ratio is determined by the public and depends on the amount of money the public wants to hold as currency versus the amount it wants to hold as deposits. The public can raise the currency–deposit ratio to any level that it wants by withdrawing currency from banks (which increases currency held and reduces deposits); similarly, by depositing currency in banks, the public can lower the currency–deposit ratio.

The second important ratio on the right-hand side of Eq. (14.7) is the reserve–deposit ratio (RES/DEP, or res), which we have already discussed. The reserve–deposit ratio is determined by banks' decisions about how much of their deposits to lend.[5]

When the process of multiple expansion of loans and deposits is complete, the currency–deposit ratio equals the ratio desired by the public, cu, and the reserve–deposit ratio equals the ratio desired by the banks, res. Substituting cu for CU/DEP and res for RES/DEP in Eq. (14.7) and multiplying both sides of Eq. (14.7) by $BASE$, we obtain

$$M = \left(\frac{cu + 1}{cu + res}\right)BASE. \tag{14.8}$$

Equation (14.8) states that the money supply is a multiple of the monetary base. The relation of the money supply to the monetary base depends on the currency–deposit ratio chosen by the public and the reserve–deposit ratio chosen by banks. The factor $(cu + 1)/(cu + res)$, which is the number of dollars of money supply that can be created from each dollar of monetary base, is called the **money multiplier**. The money multiplier will be greater than 1 as long as res is less than 1 (that is, with fractional reserve banking). Note that if the public holds no currency ($cu = 0$), the money multiplier equals $1/res$, or the same value as that in Agricola when all money was held as bank deposits (Eq. 14.3).

Table 14.1 uses Canadian data to illustrate the money multiplier and the relation among currency, reserves, monetary base, and the money supply. With these data, you can verify that the currency–deposit ratio is 0.1086 and that the reserve–deposit ratio is 0.0374. Thus, the money multiplier, $(cu + 1)/(cu + res)$, equals 7.5930. You can verify this formula by dividing the money supply ($797 779 million) by the monetary base ($105 068 million) to obtain 7.5930.

TABLE 14.1
The Monetary Base, the Money Multiplier, and the Money Supply in Canada

Currency outside banks, CU	$ 78 122 million
Bank reserves, RES	$ 26 946 million
Monetary base, $BASE$ (= $CU + RES$)	$ 105 068 million
Deposits, DEP	$719 657 million
Money supply, M (= $CU + DEP$)	$797 779 million
Reserve–deposit ratio, res (= RES/DEP)	0.0374
Currency–deposit ratio, cu (= CU/DEP)	0.1086
Money multiplier, $(cu + 1)/(cu + res)$	7.5930
Ratio of money supply to base, $M/BASE$	7.5930

Source: Calculated from *Bank of Canada Banking and Financial Statistics*, December 2016. Tables B2 and E1. Deposits are personal and non-personal chequable deposits. Currency outside banks includes coins. Data are for October 2016.

[5] In some countries, but not Canada, government regulations may set minimum levels for banks' reserve–deposit ratios.

It can be shown algebraically that the money multiplier decreases when either the currency–deposit ratio *cu* or the reserve–deposit ratio *res* increases.[6] Recall that the reason the monetary base gets "multiplied" is that under fractional reserve banking, banks use some of the currency received as deposits to make loans to the public. The public can either hold the money it borrows from banks as currency or re-deposit its borrowings in the banking system, but in either case, the result is a higher total money supply than existed before the loans were made. When the reserve–deposit ratio rises, banks lend a smaller fraction of each dollar of deposits, creating less money for the same amount of monetary base; thus, an increase in the reserve–deposit ratio lowers the money multiplier. When the currency–deposit ratio rises, the public puts a smaller fraction of its money in banks, which means that banks have less money to loan. With banks lending less, less money is created from the same amount of monetary base, again reducing the money multiplier.

OPEN-MARKET OPERATIONS

We have shown how the monetary base and the money multiplier determine the money supply. To change the level of the money supply, a central bank must change the amount of monetary base or change the money multiplier. For now, we focus on the most direct and frequently used way of changing the money supply: raising or lowering the monetary base. For any value of the money multiplier, Eq. (14.8) indicates that a change in the monetary base will cause a proportional change in the money supply.

Suppose that the Agricolan Central Bank decides to increase the monetary base by 10%, from 1 000 000 to 1 100 000 fl. How would it actually do so? First, the Central Bank has to print the extra 100 000 fl. Then, it can use the 100 000 new florins to buy assets (coconuts) from the public. After purchasing the additional coconuts, the Agricolan Central Bank's balance sheet is

Agricolan Central Bank			
ASSETS		LIABILITIES	
Coconuts	1 000 000 fl	Currency	1 000 000 fl

By purchasing 100 000 fl of coconuts, the Central Bank puts 100 000 more paper certificates (florins) into circulation. The monetary base, which is the same as the total liabilities of the Central Bank, rises to 1 100 000 fl. If the money multiplier remains unchanged, the money supply also increases by 10%.

Suppose, instead, that the Agricolan Central Bank wanted to reduce the monetary base by 10%. To do so, it would sell 100 000 fl of coconuts to the public for 100 000 fl in currency. The 100 000 fl collected by the Central Bank are retired from circulation. (The retired florins are not treated as assets of the Central Bank; if you paid off a debt and retrieved your IOU, you would not consider the IOU to be an asset.) The Agricolan Central Bank's balance sheet is now

Agricolan Central Bank			
ASSETS		LIABILITIES	
Coconuts	900 000 fl	Currency	900 000 fl

[6] That the money multiplier decreases when *cu* increases is not obvious, as *cu* appears in both the numerator and the denominator of the money multiplier. However, as you can confirm by trying numerical examples or by taking a derivative, an increase in *cu* reduces the money multiplier as long as *res* is less than 1, which must always be the case under fractional reserve banking.

The Agricolan Central Bank's liabilities outstanding (the monetary base) have been reduced to 900 000 fl. With a constant money multiplier, the money supply will fall proportionately.

Recall (Chapter 7) that a purchase of assets by the central bank is called an **open-market purchase**.[7] It increases the monetary base and, thus, the money supply. A sale of assets to the public by the central bank is called an **open-market sale**. It reduces the monetary base and the money supply. Open-market purchases and sales are collectively called open-market operations. Open-market operations are the most direct way for central banks to change their national money supplies.

However, the Bank of Canada has observed that the money multiplier in Canada is rather unstable, and so it has not tried to use base control to precisely influence the money supply. Instead, it has affected the monetary base so as to influence short-term interest rates. In Section 14.2 we discuss the Bank of Canada's methods in detail.

14.2 MONETARY CONTROL IN CANADA

The principles of money supply determination developed in the Agricola example can be applied directly to actual economies by adding a few institutional details. In this section, we link these general principles to monetary institutions in Canada.

THE BANK OF CANADA

The Canadian central bank, the Bank of Canada, was created in 1934 on the basis of a recommendation by a Royal Commission, and was modelled on the Bank of England.

The Bank operated as a private corporation until 1938; it is now a Crown corporation, with headquarters in Ottawa. It is directed by a Board of Directors, which includes the governor, the senior deputy governor, the deputy minister of finance, and 12 part-time directors. The part-time directors are private citizens, appointed for three-year terms. The governor is appointed by the board, with the government's approval, for a renewable seven-year term.

On paper, the Bank seems to be an arm of the government. The governor must make an annual report to the minister of finance; manage the government's debt, its deposits with chartered banks, and its foreign exchange reserves; and consult regularly with the minister. If these consultations do not lead to an agreement on monetary policy, then the government may issue a public directive, with which the Bank must comply.

However, the Bank has much more independence than the Bank of Canada Act might suggest. For example, since the government has ultimate responsibility for monetary policy, it refrains from public criticism of the Bank's actions. While the government may issue a directive to the Bank, it has not done so since the act was amended in 1967 to allow this. It is understood that if a directive were issued the governor might resign, which would severely damage the government's credibility in financial markets.

The government cannot readily influence policy through the Board of Directors either. The directors are appointed on a part-time basis, serve overlapping terms, and are not experts on monetary policy (bankers and economists are not

---

[7] The term *open market* refers to the fact that the central bank's transactions with the public take place in regular asset markets that are open to and used by the public.

allowed to sit on the board). The minutes of board meetings, published in the *Bank of Canada Review*, suggest that the board acts as a rubber stamp. The government can influence the Bank directly by not renewing the governor's appointment when it expires, or it could amend the Bank of Canada Act. In either case, though, it cannot directly control short-term monetary policy.

THE BANK OF CANADA'S BALANCE SHEET

The balance sheet of the Bank of Canada at the end of October 2016 is shown in Table 14.2. The Bank's largest asset by far is its holdings of government securities (bonds). Indeed, the Bank owns nearly 20% of outstanding Treasury bills. It also owns small amounts of other assets and makes loans (advances) to banks, which count as assets for the Bank.

The largest liability of the Bank is notes in circulation ($77 192 million). Some of this is held in private banks but most is held by the public. It makes up the majority of the amount of currency (notes in circulation plus coins) that is held outside of banks; we label it *CU*. The other principal liabilities of the Bank are deposits made by members of the Canadian Payments Association, a cheque-clearing organization of banks. In accepting deposits from banks, the Bank of Canada acts as the "banks' bank." Chartered banks make deposits at the Bank of Canada because it's a convenient way of holding reserves and of settling their accounts with other banks.

These accounts at the Bank of Canada ($515 million), together with currency at banks, sometimes called vault cash ($26 431 million), equal the total reserves of the banking system ($26 946 million), what we call *RES*. Recall from Eq. (14.5) and Table 14.1 that the monetary base equals bank reserves ($26 946 million) plus currency outside banks ($78 122 million), or $105 068 million. The monetary base can be calculated equivalently as the sum of total currency outstanding ($104 553 million) plus bank deposits at the Bank of Canada ($515 million), which again is $105 068 million.

Other liabilities of the Bank of Canada are the deposits there that are owned by foreign central banks and by the federal government.

TABLE 14.2

The Balance Sheet of the Bank of Canada (millions of dollars)

Assets		Liabilities	
Treasury bills	$ 18 331	Notes in circulation	$ 77 192
Other government securities	$ 77 775	Deposits	
Advances to members of the Canadian Payments		Government of Canada	$ 23 570
		Members of the Canadian	
Association	$ 14	Payments Association	$ 515
All other assets	$ 8 018	Other Liabilities	$ 2 862
Total Assets	$104 138	Total Liabilities	$104 138

Addenda

Reserves = bank deposits at Bank of Canada + currency at banks = $26 946 million
Monetary base = currency outside banks + reserves = $105 068 million

Source: Calculated from *Bank of Canada Banking and Financial Statistics*, December 2016, Tables B2 and E1. Deposits are personal and non-personal chequable deposits. Currency outside banks includes coins. Data are for October 2016.

TOOLS OF MONETARY POLICY

Overnight Rates

To understand how the Bank of Canada influences the money supply, first recall that most money in Canada is in the form of demand deposits. Each day, millions of cheques are written on these bank accounts, so balances must be transferred between banks. Suppose that a $100 cheque is written on an account at the National Bank and deposited at the Royal Bank. The same day, an $80 cheque is written on an account at the Royal Bank and deposited at the National Bank. Rather than transferring $100 one way and then $80 the other way, the banks make only the net transfer: $20 from the National Bank to the Royal Bank. To make these transfers, the banks hold balances at the Bank of Canada, called clearing or **settlement balances** (shown in Table 14.2 as deposits of members of the Canadian Payments Association). In Canada, banks are not required to hold reserves at the central bank, but 13 large banks and credit union associations called **direct clearers** do so to settle these net transfers. At the end of the day, in this example, $20 is transferred from the National Bank's account at the Bank of Canada to the Royal Bank's account.

The main system for clearing cheques in Canada is the Large Value Transfer System (LVTS). Financial institutions that clear cheques but do not take part in the LVTS hold accounts with larger banks, which, in turn, hold settlement balances at the Bank of Canada on their behalf.

If a bank finds itself with a larger balance than it needs to meet its settlement obligations, then it can lend some of its balances (reserves) to another bank for one day, charging an interest rate called the **overnight rate**. The Bank of Canada implements monetary policy by influencing this very short-term interest rate. The Bank announces a range or operating band of 0.5 percentage points for the overnight rate on eight preset dates each year (or at other times in unusual circumstances). The centre of this band is the **target overnight rate**, which is the key indicator of the stance of monetary policy.

To ensure that the overnight rate remains within the 0.5 percentage-point band, the Bank is prepared to lend at the interest rate at the top of the band (called the **Bank rate**). This puts a ceiling on the overnight interest rate, for banks would not borrow at a higher rate than the one offered by the Bank of Canada. Conversely, the Bank pays interest on deposits at the rate given by the bottom edge of the band, which places a floor under the overnight rate. In practice, most transactions in the overnight market are between banks, at roughly the target overnight rate. Figure 14.1 shows the operating band for the overnight rate during the period January 1, 2008, to December 31, 2010. This period is chosen to illustrate how the operating band changed during and following the recession that Canada fell into at the beginning of 2008. The Bank responded to the onset of recession by reducing the target overnight rate from 4.25% in January 2008 to just 0.25% by April 2009. The target overnight rate began to increase beginning in June 2010 following the Bank's announcement that the recession appeared to end in mid-2009. The Bank supplemented the significant stimulus that resulted from its cut to the overnight rate with an announcement in April 2009 that it would commit to keeping the target overnight rate at just 0.25% until the second quarter of 2010. At that time the Bank announced as well that the target for the overnight rate would also act as the floor of the operating band, and so the operating band would be narrowed to 0.25 percentage points from its normal 0.50 percentage points. The intention of these two announcements was to convince financial markets that there would be no further cuts to the overnight rate and that the Bank was committed to maintaining its monetary stimulus.

FIGURE 14.1

THE OVERNIGHT RATE AND THE BANK OF CANADA OPERATING BAND, 2008–2010

The solid lines show the lower and upper edges of the Bank of Canada's operating band for the overnight interest rate. The dashed line shows the actual overnight rate. The overnight rate deviates very little from the target overnight rate, which is the centre of the operating band. Note that the Bank of Canada responded strongly to the onset of recession in 2008 by quickly reducing the overnight rate. By mid-2009 the Bank, judging the recession to have ended, began to increase the overnight rate.

Sources: Adapted from Statistics Canada, CANSIM series v39076, 39077, 39079. This does not constitute an endorsement by Statistics Canada of this product.

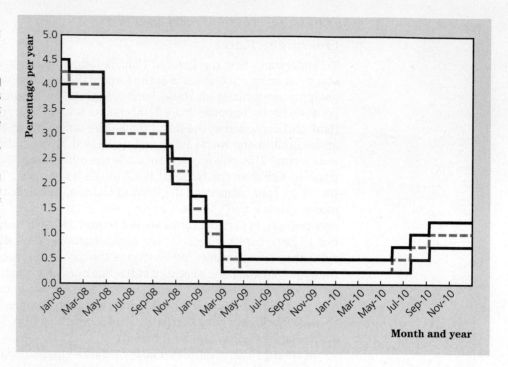

To see how this operating band affects the money supply, let's consider a situation in which the Bank of Canada wishes to loosen monetary policy. Suppose that the Bank announces that it is lowering its target for the overnight interest rate. To bring about this change, the Bank could offer advances to banks at the upper edge of the newly lowered band. Any increase in these advances would show up as an increase in the assets of the Bank, on the left-hand side of its balance sheet (see Table 14.2). A bank accepting an advance would be credited with an increased deposit balance at the Bank of Canada, which would increase the monetary base. Thus, you can think of this as an expansionary monetary policy brought about by a traditional open-market purchase of assets, but one in which the assets are advances to banks. The key feature is that the Bank of Canada announces the target interest rate, then stands ready to offer advances to make that interest rate the market-clearing one.

This increase in the monetary base allows an increase in the money supply. Since reserves are higher, banks expand their own loans and deposits to restore their reserve–deposit ratios. As a result, the money supply rises. Conversely, an increase in the overnight rate leads to a decrease in the money supply. Once again, the money supply and interest rates move in opposite directions, just as we have described from Chapter 9 on, in discussing shifts in the *LM* curve.

In practice, when banks need reserves they most often borrow them from other banks (at the overnight rate) rather than from the Bank of Canada (at the higher Bank rate). However, the Bank of Canada's willingness to lend at the Bank rate serves as a reminder that a central bank exists partly to prevent financial crises (such as bank runs) by serving as a **lender of last resort**. The central bank fulfills this function by standing ready to lend reserves to banks that need cash to meet depositors' demands or settlement needs.

So far, we have described how the Bank of Canada influences the overnight rate and how that rate, in turn, affects the money supply. How does the Bank affect interest rates on bank accounts and mortgages? As we saw in Chapter 4, interest rates on different assets tend to move together. Again, suppose that the Bank of Canada lowers its operating band for the overnight rate. If the overnight rate falls, banks with adequate reserves will choose to invest in some higher-yielding assets rather than holding reserves. But if many banks react this way, then the returns offered on other assets will tend to fall as lenders compete for those investments. Thus, other interest rates will adjust if the change in the overnight rate persists. For example, the prime rate (the loan rate charged by banks to their best customers) adjusts fairly quickly to changes in the overnight rate. Interest rates on mortgages, savings deposits, and guaranteed investment certificates (GICs) also adjust, though with some delays. Figure 14.2 shows the target overnight rate, the prime rate, and the one-year mortgage rate during the period from 1994 to 2016. The stability in all three interest rates since 2011 is a notable departure from what had been experienced in the two decades prior.

Open-Market Operations

Like the Agricola Central Bank, the Bank of Canada can change the money supply through open-market operations. To increase the money supply, for example, the Bank could conduct an open-market purchase, in which it would buy Government of Canada securities (instead of coconuts, as in Agricola) from the public. A purchase of $100 million in securities would increase the Bank's assets by $100 million. To pay for these securities, the Bank would write a cheque on itself, redeemable by a bank either as a deposit at the Bank or as cash. In either case, the monetary base would rise by $100 million. This open-market purchase would lower interest rates and raise the money supply. Because of the money multiplier, an increase in the monetary base translates into a larger increase in the money supply.

FIGURE 14.2

SHORT-TERM INTEREST RATES, 1994–2016

The figure shows monthly averages of the target overnight interest rate, the prime rate, and the interest rate on one-year mortgages during the period 1994–2016. Changes in the target overnight rate lead to similar changes in the interest rates administered by banks on loans and mortgages. This is a key way in which monetary policy influences the economy.

Source: Adapted from Statistics Canada, CANSIM II series v39079, v122495, and v122520. This does not constitute an endorsement by Statistics Canada of this product.

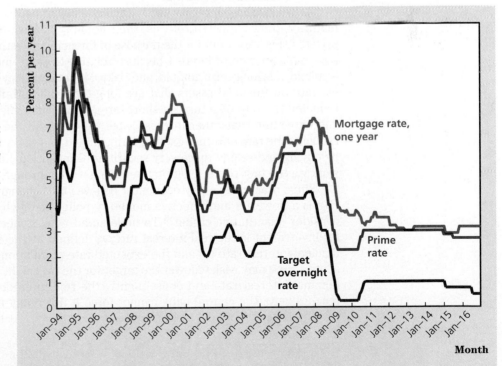

Similarly, to reduce the money supply, the Bank may make an open-market sale. The Bank could sell $100 million of government securities to the public, receiving cheques drawn on banks in exchange. The Bank's assets would fall by $100 million (it owns $100 million less in securities). The Bank would use the $100 million in cheques it receives to eliminate $100 million in deposits of banks so that the monetary base would fall by $100 million. This would tend to raise interest rates and lower the money supply.

Although the Bank of Canada most often implements policy by influencing the overnight rate, it sometimes also uses open-market operations to affect interest rates and the money supply. For example, the Bank might wish to target the value of the overnight interest rate within its operating band. It can do this using transactions called **Special Purchase and Resale Agreements** (SPRAs, sometimes called repos) and **Sale and Repurchase Agreements** (SRAs). In an SPRA transaction, the Bank of Canada buys short-term government securities from banks and investment dealers and then sells them back on the next day. When the Bank buys these securities, it pays for them by adding to the seller's settlement balance. As we have seen, this increase in settlement balances will tend to put downward pressure on the overnight interest rate. SRAs have the opposite effect.

While open-market operations are normally conducted using very short-term government securities, there is no reason the Bank of Canada cannot buy and sell government securities of longer maturity. Thus, if the Bank used 91-day (three-month) Treasury bills in its open-market operations, it could try to influence somewhat longer (three-month) interest rates directly rather than through overnight rates. Under extraordinary circumstances the Bank could buy and sell securities of even longer maturity and could even buy and sell non-government securities. Open-market operations that involve the purchase and sale of government or non-government securities with long terms to maturity have become known as exercises in **quantitative easing**.

As we discussed in Chapter 7, financial instruments differ by their terms to maturity, their expected returns, their liquidity, and their risk of default. When private firms issue debt for the purpose of financing investment, the debt generally pays a higher rate of interest because relative to three-month Treasury bills, for example, it is long-term, illiquid, and risky. Monetary policy can influence the interest rate on financial assets that are long-term, illiquid, and risky either by (1) reducing the rate of return on short-term, liquid, and safe government securities and expecting that other interest rates will move in the same direction; or (2) reducing the rate of return on long-term, illiquid, and risky securities more directly by buying and selling those very securities. Conventional open-market operations work via the first route. Quantitative easing works through the second.

Since practically every economist believes that changing the target overnight rate is a powerful and effective monetary policy tool, why would a central bank consider quantitative easing?[8] To understand why, remember that what matters for investment is the real interest rate, r, defined as the difference between the nominal interest rate (i) and the expected rate of inflation (π). In a recession the central bank may wish to lower the target for the overnight rate so as to reduce the nominal interest rate and consequently the real interest rate. However, once i reaches zero, the central bank cannot force it down any further. This leaves the real interest rate "stuck" at its minimum value of $-\pi$. At this point, conventional

---

[8] For an accessible description and discussion of quantitative easing, see Alan Blinder, "Quantitative Easing: Entrance and Exit Strategies," *Federal Reserve Bank of St. Louis Review*, November/December 2010, Volume 92(6), pp. 465–479.

monetary policy can do no more to stimulate aggregate demand. This is when quantitative easing becomes a useful tool. Although the interest rate on short-term, liquid, and riskless assets (that is, the overnight rate) has fallen to zero, the interest rates on longer-term, illiquid, and risky assets remain high. Lowering those interest rates is the goal of quantitative easing.

During the financial crisis of 2007–2009, many central banks—most notably the U.S. Federal Reserve—used quantitative easing as a way of directly influencing the rates of return on the sorts of securities that private firms rely upon to raise funds for investment. The use of quantitative easing was also encouraged as a way of ensuring the viability of private banks thought to be at risk of collapse. Thus, the U.S. Federal Reserve purchased risky assets with government-issued Treasury bills and in this way took those assets off the books of private banks. Although the Bank of Canada indicated in April 2009 that it was willing to consider the use of quantitative easing if conditions warrant, it had not found it necessary to follow the example of the U.S. Federal Reserve. However, as we discuss in A Closer Look 14.1, while the Bank of Canada did not need to resort to quantitative easing, it nonetheless provided the financial system with a large dose of liquidity when the usual sources dried up.

A CLOSER LOOK 14.1

THE BANK OF CANADA'S RESPONSE TO THE 2007–2009 FINANCIAL CRISIS

While in normal times the Bank of Canada's tools for controlling the money supply are very effective at influencing the state of the economy and keeping it running smoothly, on rare occasions extraordinary steps are required. Such a rare occasion arose as a result of a financial crisis that began in 2007 and had its origins in the U.S. financial system.

In Chapter 7 (Application "The U.S. Housing Crisis and Its Aftermath"), we described how a crisis in the U.S. housing market triggered a series of events that would lead to a crisis in U.S. financial markets, widespread bankruptcies both within and outside the financial sector, a dramatic fall in stock prices, rapidly increasing unemployment rates, and concerns that the world's financial system was about to collapse. We described how most analysts believe that the Canadian financial system avoided the worst of the financial crisis thanks in part to the tighter regulations imposed on Canadian financial institutions by the Bank of Canada and the Office of the Superintendent of Financial Institutions (OSFI).

As well as relying on tighter regulations already in place, the Bank of Canada took a number of extraordinary steps that were designed to calm financial markets and that better enabled the Canadian financial system to weather the financial crisis. For the most part, these steps were designed to address the problem that during the crisis financial institutions were wary of accepting the financial instruments of others. Financial institutions, unsure of their own exposure and the exposure of their trading partners to sub-prime mortgages, mortgage-backed securities (MBSs), and other so-called toxic assets, simply stopped trading with one another. By making available new ways for financial institutions to convert any asset into money—the financial asset all are readily willing to accept—the Bank added liquidity to the financial sector and so kept it running smoothly.

By December 2008, the Bank was providing $41 billion of liquidity support to a far wider range of participants in the financial system than it had ever done previously. Financial conditions improved throughout 2009, and as a consequence the Bank of Canada was able to begin to unwind its measures to increase liquidity. By February 2010, the Bank had reduced its injection of liquidity into the financial system to $23 billion. By early 2010 the financial crisis had subsided and financial conditions improved significantly in Canada and around the world.

As important as these measures proved to be, just as important are the economic principles that the Bank followed when making these decisions.

(continued)

Most importantly, the Bank was careful to design interventions in a way that mitigated the "moral hazard" that is said to arise when someone protected from risk behaves differently from how they would otherwise (for example, having fire insurance might encourage you to play with matches more than you might do in the absence of insurance). When designing its financial market interventions, the Bank minimized the problem of moral hazard by choosing to intervene only when the crisis was severe, to intervene only with temporary measures, and to monitor the response of market participants. In this way it hoped to minimize the incentives market participants might have to change their behaviour and take greater risks than they might otherwise now and in the future.

It is often said that a good crisis is a terrible thing to waste. With that in mind, the Bank of Canada's economists are busy studying the effects of its efforts to increase liquidity during the financial crisis. It is particularly interested in understanding how effective were its efforts to resolve the lack of liquidity, how its efforts may have altered the behaviour of financial market participants, and whether some of these efforts were more successful than others. Finally, the Bank is particularly interested in understanding ways of increasing the resilience of the financial market in the face of future crises. The hope here is that the private sector can in future deal with similar events without the need of the Bank of Canada to intervene.

The Exchange Fund Account

The Bank of Canada also manages the federal government's holdings of various currencies in a separate **exchange fund account**. Table 14.3 reports the composition of the exchange fund account as of December 2016. Over the past nearly two decades, the composition of this fund has undergone significant change. In particular, the fraction of the amount of securities and deposits denominated in U.S. dollars has fallen from 97% in 1996 to just 63% in 2016. This is almost all due to the growing importance of euro-denominated assets in the account. Another important change in the composition of the account is the falling importance of gold. As reported in the table, by the end of 2016 there was no gold held in the exchange fund account. This reflects a decision on the part of the government to hold the exchange fund in the form of assets that yield a predictable rate of return.

The reserves held in the exchange fund account can be used to intervene in the foreign exchange market. But as we saw in Chapter 10, monetary policy and exchange rate policy are really the same thing. To see this more concretely, suppose that U.S. interest rates rise, meaning that the Canadian dollar depreciates as investors demand U.S. dollars in order to buy high-yielding U.S. bonds. The Bank may be concerned that the depreciation will be passed through into domestic inflation, and so it may try to counteract the depreciation.

TABLE 14.3

Exchange Fund Account (millions of U.S. dollars)

Securities and deposits	
Denominated in U.S. dollars	$52 496
Denominated in euros	$14 392
Denominated in pound sterling	$ 5 506
Denominated in yen	$ 555
Gold	$ 0
Other reserve holdings	$10 181
Total	$83 130

Source: Reproduced with the permission of the Department of Finance, 2017 http://www.fin.gc.ca.

One way it can do this is by selling U.S. dollars in exchange for Canadian dollars. This additional demand for Canadian dollars will tend to increase the value of the Canadian dollar. However, the Bank's sale of foreign exchange reserves reduces its assets, just as an open-market sale of government securities does. Thus, the money supply will fall, and interest rates will rise. This is exactly what we showed in Chapter 10: A central bank that tries to target the exchange rate will have to devote domestic monetary policy to this task.

SETTING MONETARY POLICY IN PRACTICE

The *IS–LM–FE* or *AD–AS* analysis of monetary policy suggests that using monetary policy to affect output and prices is a relatively simple matter. All that the Bank of Canada needs to do is change the money supply enough to shift the *LM* curve or the *AD* curve to the desired point. In reality, however, making monetary policy is a complex, ongoing process. Two important practical issues that policymakers have to deal with are the lags in the effects of monetary policy on the economy and uncertainty about the channels through which monetary policy works.

Lags in the Effects of Monetary Policy

If changes in the monetary policy instrument led to immediate changes in output or prices, then using monetary policy to stabilize the economy would be relatively easy. The central bank would simply have to adjust its policy instruments until the economy attained full employment with stable prices. Unfortunately, most empirical evidence suggests that changes in monetary policy take a fairly long time to affect the economy.

The Bank of Canada judges that interest rate changes can take from 18 to 24 months to work their way through the economy and have a significant effect on the target: the rate of inflation. The process of adjustment follows these stages:

- changes in interest rates lead to changes in spending and sales;

- changes in spending and sales lead to changes in production (and employment); and

- changes in production lead to changes in prices and, thus, to changes in inflation.

Each of these stages lags behind the previous one, and the length of the lags can vary.

The long lags in the operation of monetary policy make it very difficult to use this policy instrument with precision.[9] Because of these long lags, the Bank of Canada cannot base its decisions on current levels of output and inflation alone. Instead, it must try to forecast what the economy will be doing six months to two years in the future—and make policy based on those forecasts. Because economic forecasts are often inaccurate, monetary policymaking has sometimes been likened to trying to steer a ship in dense fog.

An illustration of the problems raised by the delayed effects of monetary policy is the recent debate about how aggressive the Bank of Canada should be in reversing its strongly expansionary monetary policy introduced in response to the 2008–2009 recession. As illustrated in Figure 14.1 (p. 491), after a rapid series of

---

[9] Indeed, as we discuss shortly, a group of economists known as monetarists argue that these long lags make monetary policy next to worthless as a tool for stabilizing the economy.

reductions in the target overnight rate beginning early in 2008, the Bank reversed course and began to increase the target overnight rate beginning in June 2010. More increases followed in July and September of 2010. During this time, the unemployment rate remained relatively high (at over 8%) and the rate of inflation, at 1.8% over the past year, did not seem to be threatening the Bank's target for inflation. Critics of the Bank asked why tightening monetary policy was necessary when inflation wasn't currently a problem. The response of the Bank of Canada was that it wasn't responding to current inflation but rather to forecasts of inflation a year or more into the future. The Bank was correct in asserting that, because of lags in the effects of monetary policy, it's necessary to try to anticipate future inflation rather than react only to current inflation. But because of the difficulties in forecasting inflation, there was plenty of room for debate about how tight monetary policy needed to be in order to prevent future inflation.

The Channels of Monetary Policy Transmission

Another practical difficulty faced by monetary policymakers is determining exactly how monetary policy affects the economy. So far, we have determined two primary ways in which monetary policy affects economic activity and prices. First, according to the Keynesian analysis (see Chapter 12), a reduction in the money supply or an increase in the target overnight rate raises all real interest rates, which, in turn, reduces aggregate demand (spending by consumers and firms). Declining aggregate demand leads to falling output and prices, relative to trends. The effects of monetary policy on the economy that work through changes in real interest rates are called the **interest rate channel** of monetary policy.

Second, in open economies, a tightening of monetary policy raises the real exchange rate (see Chapter 10). A higher real exchange rate, by making domestic goods more expensive for foreigners and foreign goods cheaper for domestic residents, reduces the demand for the home country's net exports. All else being equal, this reduced demand for net exports also reduces aggregate demand, depressing output and prices. The effects of monetary policy working through changes in the real exchange rate are called the **exchange rate channel**.

According to some economists, a tightening of monetary policy also works by reducing both the supply of and demand for credit, a mechanism referred to as the **credit channel** of monetary policy. On the supply side of the credit market, according to this theory, tight monetary policy leads to reduced lending by banks. The reason is that, as we showed earlier in this chapter, a tightening of monetary policy reduces bank reserves and, thus, the quantity of customer deposits that banks can accept. With fewer deposits on hand, banks have a smaller quantity of funds available to lend. As banks cut back on their lending, borrowers who depend on banks for credit, such as consumers and small firms, are unable to obtain the credit they need to make planned purchases. The resulting decline in spending depresses aggregate demand and thus economic activity. On the demand side of the credit market, tight monetary policy has the effect of making potential borrowers less "creditworthy" or less eligible for loans. The reason is that high interest rates add to a borrowing firm's interest costs and lower its profitability, making it harder for the firm to obtain loans.

Controversy swirls about the relative importance of these different channels of monetary policy. That, in turn, increases the difficulty that policymakers have in judging how "tight" or "easy" monetary policy is at any particular time. For example, suppose that the Bank of Canada observes that real interest rates are currently high but that the dollar has been falling. Is monetary policy tight or not? It's hard to say, unless we know the relative strengths of the interest rate channel and the exchange rate channel. Similarly, suppose that the real interest rate is low (suggesting an easy monetary policy) but that borrowing and lending have been unusually weak (suggesting a tight monetary policy). Again, the signals are conflicting and the judgment about whether monetary policy is expansionary ("easy") or contractionary ("tight") depends on the relative strength of the different channels.

In discussing the many problems of practical monetary policymaking, we do not mean to suggest that good monetary policy is impossible. Indeed, Canadian monetary policy over the past quarter century has been successful at maintaining low rates of inflation and regulating a relatively stable and well-functioning financial sector. However, this discussion does illustrate why making monetary policy may be described as an art as well as a science.

14.3 THE CONDUCT OF MONETARY POLICY: RULES VERSUS DISCRETION

How should monetary policy be used? On some aspects of this question, there is broad agreement. Most classicals and Keynesians agree that money is neutral in the long run so that changes in money growth affect inflation but not real variables in the long run. Therefore, most would accept that the main long-run goal of monetary policy should be to maintain a low and stable inflation rate. However, there is less agreement about the effects of monetary policy and its appropriate use in the short run (Chapters 11 and 12). Many Keynesians believe that monetary policy can and should be used to smooth the business cycle, but most classicals do not. In this section, we revisit the debate about the appropriate use of monetary policy by addressing a long-standing question in macroeconomics: Should monetary policy be conducted according to fixed rules or at the discretion of the central bank?

The use of rules in monetary policy has been advocated primarily by a group of economists known as monetarists and also by classical macroeconomists. Supporters of **rules** believe that monetary policy should be essentially automatic. In particular, in monetary policy, the central bank should be required to follow a set of simple, pre-specified, and publicly announced rules. Many such rules can be imagined. For example, the Bank of Canada might be instructed to increase the monetary base by 1% each quarter. An alternative rule, which has been used historically, is to require the central bank to conduct monetary policy to keep the price of gold at a predetermined level (this rule was the essence of the gold standard). One might also imagine a rule that permits the Bank of Canada to respond to the state of the economy in some well-specified manner, something we discuss in some detail below.

Although the exact form of the rule chosen isn't crucial, supporters of the rules-based approach emphasize that the monetary rule should be simple; there cannot be dozens of exceptions and conditions. Furthermore, the rule should be stated in terms of variables that the Bank can control directly or nearly directly. Because a central bank can control the monetary base fairly precisely, a pre-specified growth rate for the monetary base is acceptable as a rule. But as the Bank's control over, say, the national unemployment rate is indirect and imperfect, an instruction to the Bank to "keep the unemployment rate at 4%" is not acceptable to advocates of a rules-guided monetary policy.

The opposite of the rules approach, which has been supported by many (though not all) Keynesian economists, is called **discretion**. The idea behind discretion is that the central bank should be free to conduct monetary policy in any way that it believes will advance the ultimate objectives of low and stable inflation, high economic growth, and low unemployment. In particular, the central bank should continuously monitor the economy and, using the advice of economic experts, should change the money supply as needed to best achieve its goals. Because a strategy of discretion involves active responses by the central bank to changes in economic circumstances, such a strategy is sometimes called *activist*.

From this description of rules and discretion, you may have trouble understanding why many economists advocate the use of rules. After all, why should anyone arbitrarily and unnecessarily tie the hands of the central bank? The idea that giving the central bank the option of responding to changing economic conditions is always better than putting monetary policy in a straitjacket dictated by rules is the essence of the Keynesian case for discretion.

This basic argument for discretion is sound, but a strong case may also be made for rules. Next, we discuss the traditional monetarist argument for rules. We then consider a relatively new argument for rules: that the use of rules increases the credibility of the central bank.

THE MONETARIST CASE FOR RULES

Monetarism emphasizes the importance of monetary factors in the macroeconomy. Although monetarists have included numerous outstanding economists, the dominant figure and leader of the group was the late Milton Friedman. For many years, Friedman argued that monetary policy should be conducted by rules, and this idea has become an important part of monetarist doctrine.[10]

The monetarist argument for rules may be broken down into a series of propositions.

> Proposition 1. *Monetary policy has powerful short-run effects on the real economy. In the longer run, however, changes in the money supply have their primary effect on the price level.*

Friedman's research on U.S. monetary history (with Anna Schwartz) provided some of the earliest and best evidence that changes in the money supply can be non-neutral in the short run (Chapter 11). Monetarists believe that fluctuations in the money supply have historically been one of the most significant—if not the most significant—sources of business cycle fluctuations. On long-run neutrality, Friedman (along with Edmund Phelps) was one of the first to argue that because prices eventually adjust to changes in the money supply, the effect of money on real variables can only be temporary (Chapter 13).

> Proposition 2. *Despite the powerful short-run effect of money on the economy, there is little scope for using monetary policy actively to try to smooth business cycles.*

Monetarists back this proposition with several ideas (some of which we discussed in connection with macroeconomic policy more generally in earlier chapters). First, time is needed for the central bank and other agencies to gather and process information about the current state of the economy. These information

---

[10] Friedman's 1959 book, *A Program for Monetary Stability*, New York: Fordham University Press.

lags may make it difficult for the central bank to determine whether the economy is actually in a recession and whether a change in policy is appropriate.

Second, there is considerable uncertainty about how much effect a given change in interest rates or the money supply will have on the economy and how long the effect will take to occur. Monetarists argue that there are *long and variable lags* between monetary policy actions and their economic results. From empirical research, monetarists claim that, on average, monetary changes take about a year to have a significant impact on the economy (that is, the lag is long). Furthermore, the time required for policy to have an effect is unpredictable and variable. As we noted earlier, the Bank of Canada believes monetary policy actions require 18–24 months to influence the rate of inflation.

Third, wage and price adjustment, although not instantaneous, is so fast that by the time the central bank recognizes that the economy is in a recession and increases the money supply, the economy may already be heading out of the recession. If the expansion in the money supply stimulates the economy with a lag of about a year, the stimulus may take effect when output has already recovered and the economy is in a boom. In this case, the monetary expansion will cause the economy to overshoot full employment and cause prices to rise. Thus, the monetary increase, intended to fight the recession may actually be destabilizing (causing more variability of output than there would have been otherwise) as well as inflationary.

> Proposition 3. *Even if there is some scope for using monetary policy to smooth business cycles, the central bank cannot be relied on to do so effectively.*

One reason that monetarists do not trust central banks to manage an activist monetary policy effectively is political. For example, the central bank might be pressured to stimulate the economy during an election year. If timed reasonably well, an election-year monetary expansion could expand output and employment just before voters go to the polls, with the inflationary effects of the policy not being felt until after the incumbents were safely re-elected.

More fundamentally, though, monetarists' skepticism about discretion arises from their interpretation of macroeconomic history. From his work with Anna Schwartz, Friedman concluded that for whatever reason—incompetence, shortsightedness, or bad luck—monetary policy has historically been a greater source of economic instability than stability. The primary example cited by Friedman was the 1929–1933 period in the United States, when the Federal Reserve System (the central bank in the United States, also known as the Fed) was unable or unwilling to stop the money supply from falling by one-third in the wake of widespread runs on U.S. banks. Friedman and Schwartz argued that this monetary contraction was one of the main causes of the Great Depression. Thus, Friedman concluded that eliminating monetary policy as a source of instability would substantially improve macroeconomic performance.

How could the central bank be removed as a source of instability? This question leads to Friedman's policy recommendation, the last proposition:

> Proposition 4. *The central bank should choose a specific monetary aggregate (such as M1 or M2) and commit itself to making that aggregate grow at a fixed percentage rate, year in and year out.*

For monetarists, the crucial step in eliminating the central bank as a source of instability is to get it to give up activist, or discretionary, monetary policy and to commit itself—publicly and in advance—to following some rule. Although the exact choice of a rule is not critical, monetarists believe that a constant-money-growth rule would be a good choice for two reasons. First, the central bank has considerable influence, though not complete control, over the rate of money growth. Thus, if money growth deviated significantly from its target, the central bank could not easily blame the deviation on forces beyond its control. Second, monetarists argue that steady money growth would lead to smaller cyclical fluctuations than the supposedly "countercyclical" monetary policies utilized historically. They conclude that a constant-money-growth rate would provide a "stable monetary background" that would allow economic growth to proceed without concern about monetary instability.

Monetarists do not advocate a sudden shift from discretionary monetary policy to a low, constant rate of money growth. Instead, they envision a transition period in which the Bank of Canada, by gradual, pre-announced steps, would steadily reduce the growth rate of money. Ultimately, the growth rate of the monetary aggregate selected would be consistent with an inflation rate near zero. Importantly, after the constant growth rate has been attained, the Bank would not respond to modest economic downturns by changing money growth but would continue to follow the policy of maintaining a fixed rate of money growth. However, some monetarists appear to leave open the possibility that the monetary rule could be temporarily suspended in the face of major economic crises, such as a depression.

RULES AND CENTRAL BANK CREDIBILITY

Much of the monetarist argument for rules rests on pessimism about the competence or political reliability of central banks. Economists who are more optimistic about the ability of the government to intervene effectively in the economy (which includes many Keynesians) question the monetarist case for rules. A "policy optimist" could argue as follows:

Monetary policy may have performed poorly in the past. However, as time passes, we learn more about the economy and the use of policy gets better. For example, Canadian monetary policy was clearly handled better after World War II than during the Great Depression. Imposing rigid rules just as we are beginning to learn how to use activist policy properly would be foolish. As to the issue of political reliability, that problem affects fiscal policymakers and, indeed, all our branches of government. We just have to trust in the democratic process to ensure that policymakers will take actions that for the most part are in the best interests of the country.

For policy optimists, this reply to the monetarist case for rules seems perfectly satisfactory. During the past two decades, however, a new argument for rules has been developed that applies even if the central bank knows exactly how monetary changes affect the economy and is completely public-spirited. Thus, the new argument for rules is a challenge even to policy optimists. It holds that the use of monetary rules can improve the credibility of the central bank, or the degree to which the public believes central bank announcements about future policy, and that the **credibility** of the central bank influences how well monetary policy works.

One reason why the central bank's credibility matters is that people's expectations of the central bank's actions affect their behaviour. For example, suppose the central bank announces that it intends to maintain a stable price level by maintaining a stable money supply. If firms increase prices and the aggregate price level increases, the real money supply will fall, causing the *LM* curve to shift up and to the left. As a result, output and employment will fall. If firms collectively believe that the central bank will try to fight the drop in output and employment by increasing the nominal money supply—contrary to its stated intentions to maintain a stable money supply—they will go ahead and raise prices. However, if firms collectively believe that the central bank will abide by its stated intention to maintain a stable money supply, they will not increase their prices because they'll realize that the central bank will allow the drop in output and employment to occur and that the firms will have to reduce prices in the future anyway. Thus, if the central bank's statement that it intends to maintain stable prices and money is credible, firms won't raise prices; however, if the central bank's statement lacks credibility, prices will rise.

Rules, Commitment, and Credibility

If a central bank is credible, it can reduce money growth and inflation without incurring high unemployment. But how can a central bank achieve credibility?

One possibility is for the central bank to develop a reputation for carrying out its promises. Suppose that in the preceding example firms raise their prices, fully expecting the Bank to increase the money supply. However, the Bank holds the money supply constant, causing a recession. The next time, the firms may take the Bank's promises more seriously.

The problem with this strategy is that it may involve serious costs while the reputation is being established: The economy suffers a recession while the central bank establishes its reputation. Is there some less costly way to achieve credibility?

Advocates of rules suggest that by forcing the central bank to keep its promises, rules may substitute for reputation in establishing credibility. Suppose that there is an ironclad rule—ideally, enforced by some outside agency—that the Bank must gradually reduce the growth of the money supply. Observing the existence of this rule, the firms might well believe that money supply growth is going to decline no matter what, and price stability can be achieved. Note that if it increases credibility, a rule improves central bank performance, even if the central bank is competent and public-spirited. Hence, this reason for monetary policy rules is different from the monetarists' argument presented earlier.

How do advocates of discretion respond to the credibility argument for rules? Keynesians argue that there may be a trade-off between credibility and flexibility. For a rule to establish credibility, it must be virtually impossible to change—otherwise, no one will believe that the Bank will stick to it. In the extreme, the monetary growth rule would be added as an amendment to the constitution, which could then be changed only at great cost and with long delays. But if a rule is completely unbreakable, what happens (ask the Keynesians) if some unexpected crisis arises—for example, a new depression? In that case, the inability of the Bank to take corrective action—that is, its lack of flexibility—could prove disastrous. Therefore, Keynesians argue, establishing a rule ironclad enough to create credibility for the central bank would, by eliminating policy flexibility, also create unacceptable risks.

THE TAYLOR RULE

Advocates of the use of rules in monetary policy believe that central banks should be required to follow a set of simple, pre-specified, publicly announced rules when setting policy instruments. Nothing in the concept of rules, however, necessarily prohibits a central bank from responding to the state of the economy, as long as these responses are built into the rule itself. An example of a monetary policy rule that allows a central bank to take economic conditions into account is the so-called Taylor rule, introduced by John Taylor[11] of Stanford University. The **Taylor rule** is given by

$$i = \pi + 0.02 + 0.5y + 0.5(\pi - 0.02), \tag{14.9}$$

where

i = the nominal overnight interest rate (the Bank of Canada's policy instrument)

π = the rate of inflation over the previous four quarters

$y = (Y - \bar{Y})\bar{Y}$ = the percentage deviation of output from full-employment output.

The Taylor rule requires that the real overnight rate, $i - \pi$, responds to (1) the difference between output and full-employment output, and (2) the difference between inflation and the Bank's target for inflation, here taken to be 2% or 0.02.

Notice that if the economy is "overheating," with output growing more rapidly than full-employment output ($y > 0$) and inflation above its target ($\pi > 0.02$), the Taylor rule would have the Bank of Canada tighten monetary policy by raising the real overnight interest rate ($i - \pi$) above 2%. Conversely, if the economy shows weakness, with output below its full-employment level ($y < 0$) and inflation below its target ($y < 0.02$), the Taylor rule would have the Bank of Canada reduce the real overnight interest rate ($i - \pi$) below 2%, thereby easing monetary policy. Both responses are consistent with the practice of many central banks. For example, Taylor showed that historically his relatively simple rule describes the actual behaviour of the U.S. Federal Reserve quite accurately.

Unlike some advocates of rules, Taylor has not argued that central banks follow his rule slavishly and mechanically. Rather, he would have his rule serve as a guideline for monetary policy. Deviations from the rule would be permitted when, in the judgment of the policymakers, special circumstances prevailed. Nevertheless, for the idea of a policy rule to have meaning, a central bank would have to commit to following the rule (or staying very close to it) the great majority of the time.

APPLICATION

SHOOTING AT TARGETS

The decade of the 1970s, with its combination of high unemployment and high inflation, led many central banks around the world to wonder whether monetary policy could be handled more effectively. Since then, many have experimented with alternative monetary policy strategies in the hope of improving macroeconomic performance. In response to economists' arguments for the importance of credibility, many of these strategies have involved public announcements by central banks of their goals, accompanied by attempts to convince the public that monetary policymakers were committed to those goals. In this Application we discuss Canada's experience with one such strategy and its flirtation with a new, as yet untried, way of conducting monetary policy.

Since 1990, a number of countries—including Canada, Sweden, the United Kingdom, Spain, Israel, Brazil, and Australia—have adopted an approach to conducting monetary policy called inflation targeting. In Canada, inflation targets were introduced in a joint statement by the Bank of Canada and the federal government in early 1991, with a target for the end of 1992 of 3% for the 12-month increase in the

---

[11] "Discretion versus Policy Rules in Practice," *Carnegie-Rochester Conference Series on Public Policy*, 1993, pp. 195–214.

497

CPI. At the same time, targets for 1994 and 1995 of 2.5% and 2% were announced, with a band of plus or minus 1 percentage point around them. The 1%–3% target range has been renewed at regular intervals since that time, with the latest renewal committing the Bank to this target range until the end of 2016.

When using a strategy of *inflation targeting*, as the name implies, the central bank targets one of its ultimate goals, the rate of inflation, rather than targeting an intermediate variable (such as money growth). A strategy of inflation targeting does not preclude the use of monetary policy to help stabilize output or other macroeconomic variables in the short run. However, by announcing an inflation target, the central bank signals that hitting that target in the longer run is its first priority.[12]

Inflation targeting has advantages and disadvantages. One clear advantage is that it's simple to understand. This is important because, as discussed in Chapters 11 and 12 in particular, households and firms make choices based on expectations about future events, expectations they formulate in part based on what they understand to be the behaviour of policymakers like the Bank of Canada. The more clearly the Bank of Canada explains its intentions, the better Canadian households and firms are able to plan their own choices and maximize their own well-being.

A major disadvantage of inflation targeting is that inflation responds to policy actions only with a long lag. To stay close to the inflation target therefore requires that the Bank take action now to influence inflation 12–18 months from now. Thus, inflation-targeting central banks may miss their targets, losing credibility as a result.

Despite what appears to have been considerable success in conducting monetary policy using an inflation target, the Bank of Canada has in recent years been studying the idea of moving to a different monetary policy rule, one that targets the price level as opposed to the rate of change in the price level (inflation). Why might this be an attractive change in the Bank's monetary policy rule?

The attraction of price-level targeting is that it provides more certainty about the long-term purchasing power of money than does inflation targeting. To understand why, note that the Bank of Canada's inflation target of 2% allows actual inflation to vary within the 1%–3% range. This means that someone making a 25-year investment—in a mortgage, long-term bond, or direct investment in a new factory—must plan for cumulative inflation of as much as 109% (if the actual rate of inflation is always at the upper end of the range) or as little as 28% (if actual inflation is always at the lower end of the range). The price level will have increased from 100 (say) in the first year to anywhere between 128 and 209 by year 25.

Now consider price-level targeting, and suppose that the Bank judges 2% inflation, on average, to be ideal. If the price level is 100 this year, it will ideally be 102 next year, 104.04 in the second year, 106.12 in the third year, and so on. At the end of 25 years, the price level will be 164.06 with certainty. That's the good news. Unfortunately, price-level targeting has a drawback: It requires that the central bank allow the rate of inflation to be variable.

To see this, suppose inflation turns out to be only 1% in year one, pushing the price level from 100 to 101. Under the inflation target the Bank would aim to return to

---

[12] Inflation targeting does not qualify as a policy rule in the strict sense for two reasons. First, it involves targeting a goal variable (inflation), rather than an instrument of policy, such as an interest rate or the monetary base. Second, this approach allows the central bank to exercise some discretion in the short run, as long as it meets the inflation target in the longer run. Advocates of inflation targeting hope that this approach will combine the credibility benefits of a strict rule with the advantage of having some degree of policy discretion.

2% inflation the next year. That would leave the price index at 103.02 in year two, which is lower than the planned path for the price level (104.04 at the end of year two). If the central bank instead targets the price level, then it will make up the lost ground on prices that occurred because of the low rate of inflation (1%) in year one. In year two, then, it will target an increase in the price level from 101 at the end of year one to 104.04 by the end of year two. This puts prices back on the ideal path but requires 3% inflation in year two. Certainty in the price level therefore comes at the cost of uncertainty in the rate of inflation.

If we are simply trading uncertainty in the price level for uncertainty in the rate of inflation, then what, if anything, is to be gained by moving to price-level targeting? One answer is that it provides the central bank with greater flexibility. Suppose, for example, that a housing boom is encouraging excessive mortgage borrowing. The central bank might be hesitant to raise interest rates (to slow the boom) if doing so also pushed inflation below its target. Under price-level targeting, the central bank could raise interest rates and lower inflation as long as it committed to speed inflation at a later date and so make up for lost ground on the long-term price-level target.

The relative merit of price-level as opposed to inflation targeting is by no means settled. An important issue is to what extent households and firms will fully understand what the Bank is trying to do should it adopt price-level targets. Important here is the extent to which they look well ahead and plan their economic choices on the basis of the Bank's announced monetary policies. If they do so, then they will better understand why the Bank must allow the rate of inflation to be variable in order to hit long-run targets for the price level. If, on the other hand, people base their expectations about the future using the recent past as a guide, then they will fail to interpret variations in the rate of inflation as being part of a stable long-term plan. The Bank of Canada continues to study the question of whether it should abandon inflation targets for a price-level target.

OTHER WAYS TO ACHIEVE CENTRAL BANK CREDIBILITY

Besides announcing targets for money growth or inflation, are there other ways to increase the central bank's credibility and, thus, improve the performance of monetary policy? Three possibilities have been suggested: (1) appoint a "tough" central banker, (2) change central bankers' incentives, and (3) increase the central bank's independence.

1. *Appointing a "tough" central banker.* By definition, a credible central bank is one that will be believed by the public when it states its intention to reduce money growth and inflation. One way to increase credibility is for the government to appoint a central bank governor who strongly dislikes inflation and who people believe is willing to accept increased unemployment, if necessary, to bring inflation down. Thus, when U.S. President Jimmy Carter faced a serious inflation problem in 1979, he appointed Paul Volcker—an imposing individual with a strong anti-inflation reputation—to be chair of the Fed. In appointing a "tough" central banker, Carter hoped to convince the financial markets and the public that he was serious about reducing inflation. In Canada, economists agree that an important part of the success the Bank of Canada enjoyed when it introduced a low inflation target in 1991 was the reputation of the Governor of the Bank of Canada, John Crow, as an inflation "hawk."

2. *Changing central bankers' incentives.* A second way to enhance the central bank's credibility is to give its leadership strong incentives to be "tough" on inflation (and to ignore any unemployment costs associated with disinflation). If the incentives are strong enough and are publicly known, people may find the central bank's anti-inflation pronouncements to be credible. An interesting recent example of this approach is a law passed in New Zealand that sets explicit inflation targets for the central bank and provides for the replacement of the head of the central bank if those targets are not met. Inflation has come down significantly in New Zealand, but unemployment has risen. Again, credibility problems have not been completely solved.

3. *Increasing central bank independence.* A third strategy is to increase the independence of the central bank from the other parts of the government—for example, by limiting the legal ability of the legislature to interfere in monetary policy decisions. The rationale is that a more independent central bank will be less subject to short-term political pressures to try to expand output and employment (say, before an election) and will be more strongly committed to maintaining a low long-run inflation rate. Because the public will recognize that an independent central bank is less subject to political pressures, announcements made by the central bank should be more credible.

Considerable evidence supports the idea that independent central banks are more credible. Figure 14.3, taken from a study by Alberto Alesina and Lawrence Summers, of Harvard University,[13] shows the relationship between central bank

FIGURE 14.3

CENTRAL BANK INDEPENDENCE AND INFLATION

The figure compares average inflation to an index of central bank independence from the rest of the government (higher values of the index imply that the central bank is more independent) for each of 16 countries for the period 1955–1988. It shows that countries with more independent central banks have lower average inflation rates.

Source: Based on Alberto Alesina and Lawrence Summers, "Central Bank Independence and Macroeconomic Performance," *Journal of Money, Credit and Banking*, May 1993, pp. 151–162, Table A1 and Figure 1a.

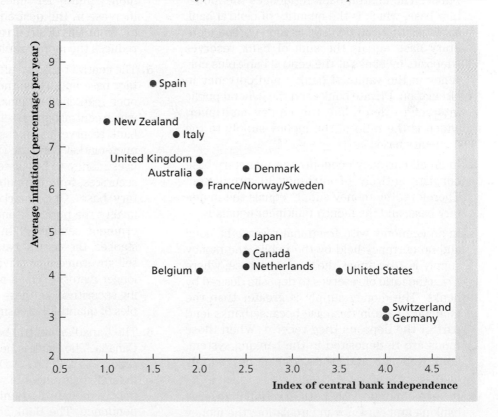

[13] "Central Bank Independence and Macroeconomic Performance," *Journal of Money, Credit and Banking*, May 1993, pp. 151–162.

independence and inflation in 16 industrialized countries. The vertical axis measures average inflation for each country for the period 1955–1988. The horizontal axis shows an index of central bank independence (based on such factors as the ease with which the government can dismiss the head of the central bank or reverse central bank decisions). Countries with relatively independent central banks, such as Germany, Switzerland, and the United States, clearly have lower long-run inflation rates than countries without independent central banks, such as the United Kingdom, New Zealand, Italy, and Spain. A similar figure in the Alesina–Summers study shows that countries with independent central banks do not have higher long-run rates of unemployment. This evidence supports the idea that increased central bank independence raises credibility and, thus, lowers the unemployment cost of keeping inflation low.

Chapter Summary

1. Three groups help determine the money supply: the central bank, private banks, and the general public. The central bank influences the monetary base, which is the quantity of central bank liabilities that can be used as money. The monetary base equals the sum of bank reserves (deposits by banks at the central bank plus currency in the vaults of banks) and currency in circulation. Private banks and the general public interact to determine the money multiplier, which is the ratio of the money supply to the monetary base.

2. In an all-currency economy the monetary base consists entirely of currency in circulation. Therefore, the money supply equals the monetary base, and the money multiplier equals 1.

3. In an economy with fractional reserve banking and no currency held by the public, the money supply is $1/res$ times the monetary base, where res is the ratio of reserves to deposits desired by banks. The money supply is greater than the monetary base in this case because banks lend part of the deposits they receive. When those funds are re-deposited in the banking system, bank deposits and, thus, the money supply increase.

4. In an economy with both fractional reserve banking and currency in circulation, the money multiplier equals $(cu + 1)/(cu + res)$, where cu is the public's desired ratio of currency to deposits. The money supply equals deposits plus currency in circulation and also equals the money multiplier times the monetary base. An increase in the desired currency–deposit ratio cu or in the desired reserve–deposit ratio res reduces the money multiplier.

5. The central bank can affect the size of the monetary base and, thus, the money supply through open-market operations. An open-market sale (in which central bank assets are sold for currency or bank reserves) reduces the monetary base. An open-market purchase (in which the central bank uses money to buy assets, such as government securities, from the public) increases the monetary base. Open-market operations typically involve the purchase and sale of short-term government securities. In extraordinary circumstances, the central bank may choose to buy or sell government or privately issued securities of longer maturity. Open-market operations involving securities like these are referred to as examples of quantitative easing.

6. The Canadian central bank is called the Bank of Canada. The Bank is headed by a governor who reports to a Board of Directors. Ultimately, the federal government is responsible for monetary policy, though the Bank has considerable independence. The Bank serves as a lender of last resort, implements monetary policy, and acts as fiscal agent for the federal government.

7. The Bank of Canada affects the Canadian money supply primarily through changes in the overnight interest rate. Changes in monetary policy are signalled with the target overnight rate, the centre of the operating band for the overnight rate. Open-market operations may also be used to influence interest rates.

8. The channels through which monetary policy has its effects include the interest rate channel, the exchange rate channel, and the credit channel. These channels work with lags, so policy must be based on forecasts of future macroeconomic variables.

9. Monetary policy may be conducted either by rules or by discretion. Under rules, the central bank is required to follow a simple predetermined rule for monetary policy, such as a requirement for constant money growth, and is not allowed to respond to current economic conditions. Under discretion, the central bank is expected to monitor the economy and use monetary policy actively to maintain full employment and to keep inflation low. Discretion for monetary policy is usually favoured by Keynesians, who argue that it gives central banks maximum flexibility to stabilize the economy.

10. Monetarists, following Milton Friedman, argue that because of information problems and lags between the implementation of policy changes and their effects, the scope for using monetary policy to stabilize the economy is small. Furthermore, they argue, central banks cannot be relied on to use active monetary policy wisely and in the public interest. Monetarists advocate a constant-growth-rate rule for the money supply in order to discipline the central bank and keep monetary fluctuations from destabilizing the economy.

11. An additional argument for rules is that they increase central bank credibility. Supporters of rules claim that the use of ironclad rules will cause the public to believe the central bank if it says (for example) that money supply growth will be reduced, with the implication that inflation can be reduced without a large increase in unemployment.

12. Like many other central banks, the Bank of Canada experimented with money-growth targets in the 1970s and 1980s. By and large these experiments proved to be failures. Since 1991, the Bank of Canada has targeted inflation directly, which requires that monetary policy respond to forecasts of future inflation. The Bank of Canada is currently studying the possibility of replacing its policy of inflation targeting with a policy of targeting the price level.

13. Possible alternatives for increasing a central bank's credibility are to appoint a central banker who is "tough" on inflation, to increase central bankers' incentives to reduce inflation, and to increase the central bank's independence from other parts of the government.

KEY TERMS

Bank rate, p. 483
bank reserves, p. 475
bank run, p. 478
central bank, p. 473
credibility, p. 494
credit channel, p. 490
currency–deposit ratio, p. 478
depository institutions, p. 473
direct clearers, p. 483
discretion, p. 491
exchange fund account, p. 488
exchange rate channel, p. 490
fractional reserve banking, p. 475
high-powered money, p. 474
interest rate channel, p. 490
lender of last resort, p. 484
monetarism, p. 492
monetary base, p. 474
money multiplier, p. 479
multiple expansion of loans and deposits, p. 476
100% reserve banking, p. 475
open-market purchase, p. 481
open-market sale, p. 481
overnight rate, p. 483
quantitative easing, p. 486
reserve–deposit ratio, p. 475
rules, p. 491
Sale and Repurchase Agreement, p. 486
settlement balances, p. 483
Special Purchase and Resale Agreement, p. 486
target overnight rate, p. 483
Taylor rule, p. 496

KEY EQUATIONS

$$M = CU + DEP \qquad (14.4)$$

The money supply, M, is the sum of currency in circulation, CU, and deposits held by the public at banks, DEP.

$$BASE = CU + RES \qquad (14.5)$$

The monetary base, or the liabilities of the central bank that are usable as money, equals the sum of currency in circulation, CU, and bank reserves, RES.

$$M = \left(\frac{cu + 1}{cu + res} \right) BASE \qquad (14.8)$$

The money supply, M, equals the monetary base times the money multiplier, $(cu + 1)/(cu + res)$, where cu is the currency–deposit ratio chosen by the public and res is the reserve–deposit ratio chosen by banks.

REVIEW QUESTIONS

1. Define *monetary base*. What is the relationship between the monetary base and the money supply in an all-currency economy?

2. Define *money multiplier*. What is the value of the money multiplier in a system of 100% reserve banking? What is the value of the money multiplier in a system of fractional reserve banking if all money is held in the form of deposits? Why is the money multiplier higher under fractional reserve banking than under 100% reserve banking?

3. Discuss how actions of the public and banks can cause the money multiplier to rise or fall. Does the fact that the public and banks can affect the money multiplier imply that the central bank cannot control the money supply? Why, or why not?

4. How can the Bank of Canada affect bank reserves and overnight interest rates using its operating band for the overnight rate? How do changes in overnight rates affect other interest rates and the money supply?

5. What is the effect on interest rates and the money supply of an open-market purchase of Treasury bills?

6. What are intermediate targets? How do they differ from monetary policy goals? List the two principal types of intermediate targets that the Bank of Canada has used.

7. What are the three channels of monetary policy? Explain each channel briefly.

8. "It is plain to see that discretion is a better way to run monetary policy than following a rule because a policy of discretion gives the central bank the ability to react to news about the economy." What is the monetarist response to the statement? What is the more recent argument for using rules rather than discretion?

9. Has the use of money-growth or inflation targets significantly improved central bank credibility? Besides adopting such targets, what other actions can a country take to increase the credibility of its central bank?

NUMERICAL PROBLEMS

1. The Agricolan monetary base is 1 000 000 florins. The public always holds half its money supply as currency and half as deposits. Banks hold 20% of deposits in the form of reserves. Starting with the initial creation of a monetary base that accompanies the purchase by the central bank of 1 000 000 fl worth of coconuts from the public, show the consolidated balance sheet of the banks after they first receive deposits, after a first round of loans and re-deposits, and after a second round of loans and re-deposits. (*Hint:* Don't forget that the public keeps only half its money in the form of bank deposits.)

   Show the balance sheets of the central bank, the banking system, and the public at the end of the process of multiple expansion of loans and deposits. What is the final value of the money supply?

2. Answer the following:
   a. The money supply is $6 000 000, currency held by the public is $2 000 000, and the reserve–deposit ratio is 0.25. Find deposits, bank reserves, the monetary base, and the money multiplier.
   b. In a different economy, vault cash is $1 000 000, deposits by depository institutions at the central bank are $4 000 000, the monetary base is $10 000 000, and bank deposits are $20 000 000. Find bank reserves, the money supply, and the money multiplier.

3. When the real interest rate increases, banks have an incentive to lend a greater portion of their deposits, which reduces the reserve–deposit ratio. In particular, suppose that

$$res = 0.4 - 2r,$$

where res is the reserve–deposit ratio and r is the real interest rate. The currency–deposit ratio is 0.4, the price level is fixed at 1.0, and the monetary base is 60. The real quantity of money demanded is

$$L(Y, i) = 0.5Y - 10i,$$

where Y is real output and i is the nominal interest rate. Assume that expected inflation is zero so that the nominal interest rate and the real interest rate are equal.

a. If $r = i = 0.10$, what are the reserve–deposit ratio, the money multiplier, and the money supply? For what real output Y does a real interest rate of 0.10 clear the asset market?

b. Repeat part (a) for $r = i = 0.05$.

c. Suppose that the reserve–deposit ratio is fixed at the value you found in part (a) and is not affected by interest rates. If $r = i = 0.05$, for what output Y does the asset market clear in this case?

d. Is the LM curve flatter or steeper when the reserve–deposit ratio depends on the real interest rate rather than when the reserve–deposit ratio is fixed? Explain your answer in economic terms.

ANALYTICAL PROBLEMS

1. How would each of the following affect the Canadian money supply? Explain.

a. Banks decide to hold more reserves as a precaution against bank runs.

b. People withdraw cash from their bank accounts for Christmas shopping.

c. The Bank of Canada sells gold to the public.

d. The introduction of automated teller machines, which allow people to withdraw cash from the bank as needed, makes deposits relatively more convenient.

e. The federal government sells $20 billion of new government bonds to the Bank of Canada. The proceeds of the sale are used to pay government employees.

f. The Bank of Canada sells some of its government securities in Tokyo for yen.

2. Suppose that the central bank strictly followed a rule of keeping the real interest rate at 3% per year. That rate happens to be the real interest rate consistent with the economy's initial general equilibrium. Assume a closed economy.

a. Assume that the economy is hit only by money demand shocks. Under the central bank's rule, how will the money supply respond to money demand shocks? Will the rule make aggregate demand more stable or less stable than it would be if the money supply were constant?

b. Assume that the economy is hit only by IS shocks. Under the central bank's interest-rate rule, how will the money supply behave? Will the interest-rate rule make aggregate demand more stable or less stable than it would be if the money supply were constant? Will the central bank be able to follow its rule in the long run?

c. Assume that the economy is hit only by supply shocks (shocks to the FE line). Repeat part (b).

d. Now assume a small open economy with a flexible exchange rate. Repeat part (a) with this assumption.

e. Still assuming a small open economy with a flexible exchange rate, repeat part (b).

3. Suppose that the Bank of Canada were committed to following the Taylor rule. For each of the following types of shocks, determine whether the use of the Taylor rule would tend to be stabilizing or destabilizing, or would have an ambiguous effect, relative to a policy of leaving the money supply unchanged. Consider the behaviour of both output and inflation.

a. An increase in money demand.

b. A temporary increase in government purchases.

c. An adverse supply shock.

d. A decline in consumer confidence.

e. An increase in export demand.

Chapter 15

Government Spending and Its Financing

At every level of government, fiscal policy—government decisions about how much to spend, on what to spend, and how to finance spending—is of central importance. Politicians and the public understand that the government's fiscal choices have a direct impact on the "bread and butter" issues of how much they pay in taxes and what government benefits and services they receive. Equally important are the effects of fiscal policy on the economy. In recent years, people have become more aware of the macroeconomic effects of fiscal policy as the economic implications of government budget deficits, tax reform, and other aspects of fiscal policy have been extensively debated.

This chapter takes a closer look at fiscal policy and its macroeconomic effects. To provide some background, we begin with definitions and facts about the government's budget. We then discuss some basic fiscal policy issues, including the effects of government spending and taxes on economic activity, the burden of government debt, and the link between budget deficits and inflation.

15.1 THE GOVERNMENT BUDGET: SOME FACTS AND FIGURES

Before getting into the analytical issues of fiscal policy, we first set the stage by describing what definition of government will be represented by the facts and figures we present. We will then discuss three main aspects of the budget: (1) expenditure; (2) tax revenues, or receipts; and (3) the budget deficit or surplus. That discussion reviews and builds on Chapter 2, which introduced basic budget concepts.

DEFINING THE GOVERNMENT SECTOR

The government sector in Canada is defined by four major subsectors: the federal government, provincial and territorial government, local government, and the Canada and Quebec Pension Plans. The definitions of these subsectors are fairly broad. Thus, school boards are included within the local government subsector, and within the provincial and territorial government subsector are included universities and colleges as well as public hospitals. As broad as these definitions are, they exclude what are called "government business enterprises," some of which perform government-like functions. Thus the Bank of Canada is not included in the federal government subsector even though it performs an important governing function. Similarly, many provinces and local governments own utilities whose purpose is to distribute electricity, water, and/or natural gas. These institutions, while performing a function many might consider a government service, are not included in the provincial and territorial government or the local government subsectors. In our discussion that follows we will, unless noted otherwise, be referring to the total government sector, defined as the sum of the federal government, provincial and territorial government, local government, and the Canada and Quebec Pension Plan subsectors.

GOVERNMENT EXPENDITURE

Government expenditure, the total spending by the government during a period of time, is divided into three primary categories: government purchases, transfer payments, and interest payments.

1. *Government purchases* are government spending on currently produced goods and services. Examples are spending on schools, defence, highway repairs, and government workers' salaries.

2. *Transfer payments* are payments made to individuals for which the government does not receive current goods or services in exchange. Examples of transfers include Old Age Security payments, veteran and civil service pensions, foreign aid, Employment Insurance benefits, and social assistance payments. We also include subsidies to businesses in this category. Over 40% of federal transfers go to other levels of government, mainly to provincial governments as equalization payments and for spending on health, postsecondary education, and social assistance payments. Provincial governments in turn make significant transfers to local governments to fund services such as police, public transit, and social services. Intergovernmental transfers constitute an expenditure for the granting government and a revenue for the receiving government. As a result, when we aggregate government sectors into the total government sector, intergovernmental transfers are netted out. The measure of transfer payments reported for the total government sector, then, measures only transfers to households and firms.

3. *Interest payments* are the interest paid to the holders of government bonds, such as Treasury bills or Canada Savings Bonds.

In Canada, total government expenditure (federal, provincial, territorial, and local) is currently about 40% of GDP.

How does the size of government expenditure in Canada compare with what is observed in other countries with similar living standards? Because official accounting rules for measuring the government budget vary widely among countries, the answer is not as straightforward as you might think. Nevertheless, Table 15.1 compares the ratios of government spending to GDP for 16 countries in the Organisation for Economic Co-operation and Development (OECD). The table shows values for three years, 1987, 2000, and 2016, and they are ordered by the size of government in 1987. It's interesting that over a span of nearly

TABLE 15.1

Government Spending in 16 OECD Countries, Percentage of GDP, 1987, 2000, and 2016

Country	1987	2000	2016
Sweden	62.3	55.1	50.2
Netherlands	58.4	44.1	44.3
New Zealand	53.6	38.1	41.8
Ireland	52.0	31.2	32.0
France	51.9	51.6	56.6
Italy	50.8	45.8	50.0
Norway	50.5	42.3	50.8
Finland	48.5	48.4	58.3
Canada	**46.1**	**40.5**	**40.5**
Germany	45.8	45.1	44.3
United Kingdom	43.6	39.1	44.3
Australia	38.9	33.9	35.5
Iceland	37.4	41.9	40.5
United States	37.0	33.4	37.9
Japan	31.5	38.5	40.8
South Korea	17.7	22.4	32.3
Average OECD	40.4	38.4	40.9

Source: Based on *OECD Economic Outlook No. 99, Annex Table 29, Statistical Annex Tables,* June 2016.

30 years, from 1987 to 2016, the level of government spending in Canada adjusted from being significantly above the OECD average to being slightly below. Other notable changes over this period include Ireland and Sweden, both of which significantly reduced the size of government spending, and South Korea and Japan, which did the opposite.

REVENUE

On the revenue side of the government's budget, the main components are tax receipts. There are two principal components of tax receipts: *direct taxes* and *indirect taxes*. Other important sources of revenue are investment income and receipts from the sales of goods and services. The share of government revenue in GDP peaked at 44% of GDP in 1998 but has fallen since. In 2014 government revenue was equal to 38% of GDP.

The largest category of tax receipts is *direct taxes*. What constitutes a direct tax is ambiguous, but in general, a direct tax is one imposed on the taxpayer, who is meant to bear the burden of that tax. Direct taxes consist of taxes paid by individuals (such as personal income taxes, property taxes, and payroll taxes for Employment Insurance and the Canada and Quebec pension plans) and taxes paid by enterprises (such as the corporate income tax). Direct taxes comprise three-quarters of all government revenue.

The second category of revenue is *indirect taxes*. An indirect tax is one that is imposed on a person or enterprise who is expected to pass the burden of the tax on to a different person or enterprise. Thus, indirect taxes include sales taxes (such as provincial sales taxes, the federal GST, and the combined federal/provincial HST), because while such taxes are collected by the merchant, the tax is borne by the consumer in the form of a higher product price. Indirect taxes comprise about 20% of all government revenue.

The revenue gained from the *sale of goods and services* makes up only 3% of total government revenue but is a very important source of revenue for local governments. This revenue is mainly in the form of user fees such as transit fares and parking fees.

The final category of revenue is *investment income*, which includes revenue from loans to Crown corporations, to farmers, and to students, for example. This category of revenue also includes natural resource royalties, a revenue source that is of particular importance to the governments of Alberta, Saskatchewan, British Columbia, and Newfoundland and Labrador.

THE COMPOSITION OF REVENUE AND EXPENDITURE: THE FEDERAL GOVERNMENT VERSUS PROVINCIAL, TERRITORIAL, AND LOCAL GOVERNMENTS

So far our description of government spending and revenue has lumped together federal, provincial, territorial, and local governments, as well as the Canada and Quebec pension plans. For most purposes of macroeconomic analysis, combining all levels of government is the most sensible course. The macroeconomic effect of a new highway-building program, for example, should not depend on whether the new highways are financed from federal, provincial, or local budgets—or from a combination of those budgets. Similarly, the effect on national saving of a budget surplus does not depend on whether the surplus is the result of revenues exceeding expenditures in the federal budget or in the accounts of the Canada Pension Plan.

Nevertheless, it is useful to know that in Canada federal government budgets have a much different composition, on both the expenditure and the revenue sides, from those of provincial, territorial, and local governments. A summary of the major components of both the federal and the combined provincial, territorial, and local government budgets for 2015 is given in Table 15.2 (p. 508). Note in particular the following points:

1. *Goods and services.* Three-quarters of provincial and local spending is for goods and services. In contrast, only a quarter of federal spending is for goods and services. About four-fifths of all government spending on goods and services in Canada is done by provincial, territorial, and local governments.

2. *Transfer payments.* The federal government spends a larger share of its budget on transfer payments to individuals than to other governments. As a group, lower-tier government transfers are almost wholly to individuals and businesses.

3. *Interest payments.* Because of the large quantity of federal government bonds outstanding, interest payments are an important component of federal spending. In 2015 the federal government paid $23.4 billion in interest payments, an amount equal to 8.2% of all federal spending. Interest payments cost provincial/territorial and local governments more—9.2% of total spending—but this varied by province, from a high of 10.6% in Quebec to 1.6% in Alberta.

TABLE 15.2

Federal, Provincial, and Local Government Expenditure and Revenue, 2015

	Federal		Provincial and Local	
	Billions of Dollars	**Percentage of Expenditure**	**Billions of Dollars**	**Percentage of Expenditure**
Expenditure				
Goods and services	70.9	24.7	412.7	77.4
Transfers to persons, businesses, and non-residents	105.1	36.7	70.5	13.2
Transfers to other levels of government	83.6	29.2	0.9	0.2
Interest payments	23.4	8.2	48.9	9.2
Total expenditure	286.4	100.0	533.0	100.0

	Federal		Provincial and Local	
	Billions of Dollars	**Percentage of Revenue**	**Billions of Dollars**	**Percentage of Revenue**
Revenue				
Direct taxes from persons	169.5	60.3	127.6	24.6
Direct taxes from enterprises	38.6	13.7	24.5	4.7
Indirect taxes	56.1	19.9	179.0	34.6
Transfers from other levels of government	0.9	0.3	83.6	16.1
Sales of goods and services	8.3	2.9	65.7	12.7
Investment income*	7.7	2.7	37.3	7.2
Total revenue	281.0	100.0	517.6	100.0
Surplus (revenue minus expenditure; deficit if negative)	−5.4		−15.4	
Primary surplus (surplus minus net interest payments)	−18.0		−33.5	

Source: Adapted from Statistics Canada Cansim Table 3800080. This does not constitute an endorsement by Statistics Canada of this product.

Note: The expenditures and revenues of the Canada and Quebec Pension Plans are excluded from this table. In 2015, the CPP and QPP in aggregate ran a surplus equal to $11.9 billion.

*Investment income includes sales of assets and includes natural resource royalties.

4. *Composition of revenue.* Just over 60% of federal government revenue comes from personal taxes (primarily the federal income tax), while 13.7% of federal revenues are from corporate income taxes. Indirect taxes make up 19.9% of federal revenue but account for nearly 35% of provincial and local revenue. Revenue from the sales of goods and services is a minor revenue source for the federal government (just short of 3% of total revenue), but it is much more important at the combined provincial and local level (nearly 13% of revenue). Nearly 25% of provincial and local revenues come from personal taxes (both income taxes and property taxes). As already mentioned, provincial and local governments also count as revenue the transfers they receive from the federal government. Finally, investment income, which includes revenues from the sale of natural resources like oil and natural gas, is a much more important source of revenue at the provincial than the federal level because in Canada natural resources are deemed to be owned by provincial governments.

SURPLUSES OR DEFICITS

Government expenditure need not equal the sum of tax revenue and investment income in each period. In Chapter 2, we showed that when government revenues exceed expenditures, there is a government budget surplus, and when expenditures exceed revenues, there is a government budget deficit. For ease of reference, we write the definition of the surplus for the total government sector as[1]

$$
\begin{aligned}
\text{surplus} &= \text{revenue} - \text{expenditure} \\
&= (\text{tax revenue}[2]) - (\text{government purchases} + \text{transfers} + \text{interest payments}) \\
&= \text{tax revenue} - \text{government purchases} - \text{transfers} - \text{interest payments} \\
&= T - G - TR - INT
\end{aligned}
\tag{15.1}
$$

A second surplus concept, called the **primary budget surplus**, excludes interest payments from the calculation:

$$
\begin{aligned}
\text{primary surplus} &= \text{revenue} - \text{expenditure} + \text{interest payments} \\
&= \text{tax revenue} - \text{government purchases} - \text{transfers} \\
&= T - G - TR.
\end{aligned}
\tag{15.2}
$$

The primary surplus is the amount by which tax revenue exceeds government purchases and transfers; the primary surplus minus interest payments equals the surplus. Figure 15.1 illustrates the relationship between the two concepts.

---

[1] In Eq. (15.1), "transfers" refer to transfers made to persons, businesses, and non-residents. As noted earlier, by aggregating overall levels of government, intergovernmental transfers—which are an expenditure for one level of government and a revenue for another—net out. Hence, only transfers to individuals and enterprises remain. If we were to write the definition of the surplus for one level of government, expenditures would include intergovernmental transfers paid to other levels of government, and revenues would include intergovernmental transfers received from other levels of government.

[2] As noted in Table 15.2, in government accounts investment income includes the royalties provincial governments receive from the sale of oil and natural gas. For provinces like Alberta, Saskatchewan, and Newfoundland and Labrador, which have large oil and gas sectors, investment income is therefore a significant source of revenue. In Eq. (15.1) we include investment income as part of our definition of tax revenue.

FIGURE 15.1

THE RELATIONSHIP BETWEEN
THE TOTAL BUDGET SURPLUS
AND THE PRIMARY BUDGET
SURPLUS

The standard measure of the total
government budget surplus is the
amount by which revenue exceeds
government expenditure. The primary surplus is the amount by which
revenue exceeds government purchases plus transfers. The primary
budget surplus equals the total budget surplus plus net interest
payments.

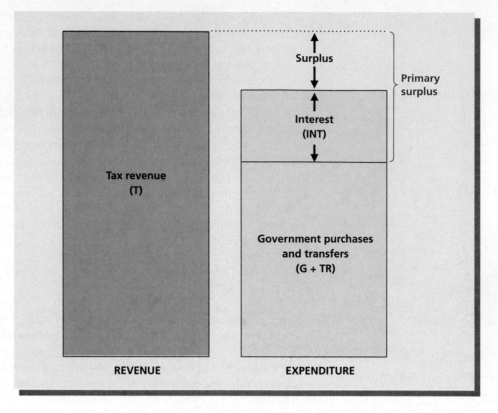

Why have two surplus concepts? The reason is that each answers a different question. The standard or total budget surplus answers the question, How much can the government pay down its debt and still pay for its total expenditure? Similarly, the deficit measures how much the government must borrow to pay for its spending.

The primary surplus answers the question, Can the government afford its *current* programs? If the primary surplus is zero, the government is collecting just enough tax revenue to pay for its current purchases of goods and services and its current social programs (as reflected by transfer payments). If there is a primary surplus, then current tax revenue can pay for more than current government purchases and social programs. Interest payments are ignored in the calculation of the primary surplus or deficit because they represent the cost of past expenditures financed by past borrowing. A useful way of thinking of the primary surplus, then, is that it measures what the budget surplus would be were it not for past borrowing.

In 2015, the primary surplus of the federal government was $18.0 billion. This means that in 2015 the federal government collected $18 billion in revenue more than it spent on government programs and transfers. The fact it ran an overall deficit of $5.4 billion is due to the fact it needed to spend $23.4 billion in interest payments.

An interesting feature of the federal government surplus or deficit—the fact that it varies in size by province and territory—is the subject of A Closer Look 15.1 ("Government Budgets by Province and Territory").

A CLOSER LOOK 15.1

GOVERNMENT BUDGETS BY PROVINCE AND TERRITORY

In Table 15.2 we have grouped all provinces and territories together (as well as grouping provincial/territorial and local governments together). This aggregation sometimes obscures striking differences between provinces and territories in expenditure, revenue, and deficits. Also, we have not looked at the regional allocation of federal government spending and revenue. In general, the federal government may not spend the same amount in a region that it raises there as revenue.

Statistics Canada provides annual data that identify the federal tax revenue and spending in each province and territory. Data for 2014 is presented in the accompanying table.

The table shows the federal government's expenditure and revenue for each territory and province, along with the corresponding entries for provincial and local governments combined, for 2014. You can see that the federal government ran a surplus in four of the provinces and territories and deficits in the others. It ran a particularly large surplus in the province of Alberta and a particularly large deficit in the province of Quebec.* The size of the federal budget surplus or deficit across

provinces reflects differences in the size of federal transfers to provincial governments (particularly the federal program of equalization payments) and differences in average incomes across provinces. Thus, the federal government's surplus with Alberta is due in large part to high incomes in that province relative to the national average. With a progressive income tax rate, this means the average Albertan pays more in taxes than the average Canadian. The federal government's share of oil and gas royalties is also a key contributor to its surplus with Alberta.

In 2014, consolidated provincial/territorial and local governments ran surpluses in 4 of the 10 provinces and in the Northwest Territories/Nunavut. In aggregate, the provincial/territorial and local government sector ran a deficit of $13 512 million in 2014. As you can see from the table, most of this deficit was accrued by governments in Ontario.

---

*These entries do not sum to the federal deficit for 2014 because of data revisions and because of federal expenditure and revenue outside Canada.

Expenditure and Revenue by Level of Government in Each Province and Territory, 2014 (millions of dollars)

	Federal			Provincial, Territorial, and Local		
	Expenditure	Revenue	Surplus	Expenditure	Revenue	Surplus
British Columbia	30106	34840	4734	63971	64023	52
Alberta	23329	47604	24275	71588	72487	899
Saskatchewan	8608	9363	755	20152	20169	17
Manitoba	12116	8378	−3738	21162	19719	−1443
Ontario	99288	107893	8605	210522	198398	−12124
Quebec	62745	48545	−14200	140823	141721	898
New Brunswick	8948	4596	−4352	11207	10043	−1164
Nova Scotia	12535	6177	−6358	14723	14202	−521
Prince Edward Island	1926	819	−1107	2291	2261	−30
Newfoundland and Labrador	5893	4642	−1251	10303	10262	−41
Yukon Territory	1370	327	−1043	1422	1273	−149
NWT and Nunavut	3710	944	−2766	4118	4212	94

Source: Adapted from Statistics Canada, CANSIM II, Table 384-0047. This does not constitute an endorsement by Statistics Canada of this product.

Note: Surplus is defined as revenue minus expenditure. Negative values indicate a deficit.

15.2 GOVERNMENT SPENDING, TAXES, AND THE MACROECONOMY

How does fiscal policy affect the performance of the macroeconomy? Economists emphasize three main ways by which government spending and taxing decisions influence macroeconomic variables, such as output, employment, and prices: (1) aggregate demand, (2) government capital formation, and (3) incentives.

FISCAL POLICY AND AGGREGATE DEMAND

Fiscal policy can affect economic activity by influencing the total amount of spending in the economy, or aggregate demand. Recall that aggregate demand is represented by the intersection of the *IS* and *LM* curves. In either the classical or the Keynesian *IS–LM* model, an increase in government purchases reduces desired national saving and shifts the *IS* curve up and to the right, thereby raising aggregate demand.

Classical and Keynesian economists have different beliefs about the effect of tax changes on aggregate demand. Classicals usually accept the Ricardian equivalence proposition, which says that lump-sum tax changes do not affect desired national saving and, thus, have no impact on the *IS* curve or aggregate demand.[3] Keynesians generally disagree with this conclusion; in the Keynesian view, a cut (for example) in taxes is likely to stimulate desired consumption and reduce desired national saving, thereby shifting the *IS* curve up and to the right and raising aggregate demand.

Classicals and Keynesians also disagree over the question of whether fiscal policy should be used to fight the business cycle. We discussed the nature and source of this disagreement earlier in Chapters 11–13. Classicals generally reject attempts to smooth business cycles, by fiscal policy or by other means, because they believe wages and prices adjust relatively quickly to disturbances that move the economy away from general equilibrium. In contrast, Keynesians generally argue that using fiscal policy to stabilize the economy—for example, by changing tax rates or by changing the level of government spending—is potentially desirable. Keynesians suggest that stabilization policy is potentially useful because they believe wages and prices adjust relatively slowly to disturbances that move the economy away from general equilibrium.

Despite their claims that it is potentially useful as a tool of stabilization policy, Keynesians admit that the use of fiscal policy for this purpose is difficult. A significant problem is *lack of flexibility*. The government's budget has many purposes besides macroeconomic stabilization, such as providing income support for eligible groups, developing the country's infrastructure (roads, bridges, and public buildings), and supplying government services (education and health). Much of government spending is committed years in advance (as in hydroelectric projects) or even decades in advance (as for pensions). Rapidly expanding or contracting total government spending for macroeconomic stabilization purposes is, thus, difficult without either spending wastefully or compromising other fiscal policy goals. Taxes are somewhat easier to change than spending, but the tax laws also have many different goals and may be the result of a fragile political compromise (between levels of government or between political parties) that is not easily altered.

---

[3] We introduced the Ricardian equivalence concept in Chapter 4. We discuss this idea further in Section 15.3.

Compounding the problem of inflexibility is the problem of *long time lags* that result from the slow-moving political process by which fiscal policy is made. This lag makes effective countercyclical use of fiscal policy difficult because, for example, by the time an anti-recession fiscal measure actually has an impact on the economy, the recession might already be over.

Automatic Stabilizers and the Full-Employment Surplus or Deficit

One way to get around the problems of fiscal policy inflexibility and long lags that impede the use of countercyclical fiscal policies is to build automatic stabilizers into the budget. **Automatic stabilizers** are provisions in the budget that cause government spending to rise or taxes to fall automatically—without legislative action—when GDP falls. Similarly, when GDP rises, automatic stabilizers cause spending to fall or taxes to rise without any need for direct legislative action.

A good example of an automatic stabilizer is the federal government's Employment Insurance program. When the economy goes into a recession and unemployment rises, more people receive employment benefits, which are paid automatically without further action by Parliament. Thus, the Employment Insurance component of transfers rises during recessions, making fiscal policy automatically more expansionary.[4]

Quantitatively, the most important automatic stabilizer is the income tax system. When the economy goes into a recession, people's incomes fall, and they pay less income tax. This "automatic tax cut" helps cushion the drop in disposable income and (according to Keynesians) prevents aggregate demand from falling as far as it might otherwise. Likewise, when people's incomes rise during a boom, the government collects more income tax revenue, which helps restrain the increase in aggregate demand. Keynesians argue that this automatic fiscal policy is a major reason for the increased stability of the economy since World War II.

A side effect of automatic stabilizers is that government budget surpluses tend to fall (or deficits rise) in recessions because government spending automatically rises and taxes automatically fall when GDP declines. Similarly, the surplus tends to rise in booms. In order to distinguish changes in the surplus or deficit caused by recessions or booms from changes caused by other factors, some economists advocate the use of a surplus measure called the full-employment surplus or deficit. The **full-employment surplus** or **full-employment deficit** indicates what the government budget balance *would be*—given the tax and spending policies currently in force—if the economy were operating at its full-employment level.[5] The full-employment surplus is also called the cyclically adjusted or *structural surplus*. Because it eliminates the effects of automatic stabilizers, the full-employment surplus measure is affected primarily by changes in fiscal policy reflected in new legislation. In particular, expansionary fiscal changes—such as increases in government spending programs or (in the Keynesian model) reduced tax rates—lower the full-employment surplus, whereas contractionary fiscal changes raise the full-employment surplus. Deriving an estimate

[4] This statement assumes that the Keynesian view is right, so that an increase in transfers—which is equivalent to a reduction in taxes—raises aggregate demand.

[5] In practice, the calculation of full-employment deficits uses the Keynesian assumption that recessions reflect deviations from full employment rather than the classical assumption that (in the absence of misperceptions) recessions reflect changes in full-employment output.

FIGURE 15.2

**FULL-EMPLOYMENT AND
ACTUAL BUDGET SURPLUSES,
1975–2014**

The actual and full-employment
budget surpluses for all levels of
government are shown as a percentage of GDP. The actual budget
surplus (the green bars) was less
than the full-employment surplus
(the black bars) by substantial
amounts during the 1981–1982,
1990–1992, and 2008–2009
recessions, reflecting the importance of automatic stabilizers.

Source: Fiscal Reference Table, October
2015, Table 46 and author's
calculations.

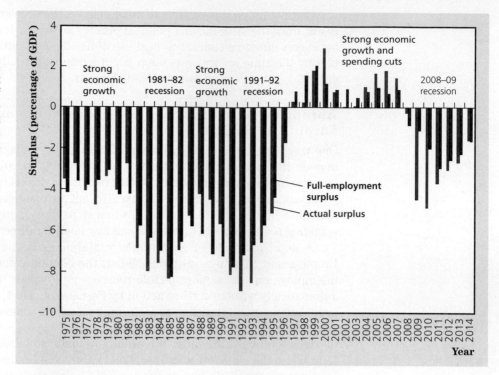

of the full-employment (or structural) surplus requires making assumptions and
applying judgments regarding the sensitivities of revenue and spending to
changes in economic conditions. This leaves the door open for disagreements
over precise values of the structural surplus.

Figure 15.2 shows, for the years 1975–2014, the actual surplus of the total government sector as well as estimates of the structural surplus produced by the federal government's Department of Finance. The figure tells a troubling story over
the period 1975–1996. Although this period was marked by two significant recessions (1981–1982 and 1990–1992), it was also marked by periods of strong economic growth. The influence of automatic stabilizers certainly contributed to the
increase in the size of the overall deficit (that is, they made negative values of
the actual surplus larger in absolute terms) during these recessions, but the figure
shows that even strong economic growth failed to generate budget surpluses.
Thus, during this period government spending and tax rates were set at levels that
would cause the overall government sector to realize large budget deficits
(negative values of the actual surplus) even if the economy were operating at full
employment. This, of course, is exactly what we see in the black bars, showing
the value of the full employment surplus. Not surprisingly, as we discuss below,
Canadian governments accumulated a lot of debt during this period.

As noted earlier, in the mid-1990s governments at all levels responded to the
large deficits run during the 1970s and 1980s by cutting spending. These actions
caused the structural deficit to turn positive. From 1997 to 2007, the combination
of strong economic growth and earlier efforts to cut spending kept the overall surplus in positive territory. The structural balance also remained positive, indicating
that at full employment the government sector in Canada would realize an overall
budget surplus. The 2008–2009 recession had a dramatic effect on the overall

surplus, sending it into a deficit equal in size to 4.5% of GDP in 2009. It is noteworthy that the estimate of the full-employment surplus for 2009 was much smaller in absolute value, at -1.1% of GDP, than the actual surplus. This indicates that, in the view of the Department of Finance, most of the overall deficit in that year was due to the recession causing tax revenues to fall and spending obligations to rise.

GOVERNMENT CAPITAL FORMATION

The health of the economy depends not only on *how much* the government spends but also on *how* it spends its resources. For example, as we discussed in Chapter 6, the quantity and quality of public infrastructure—roads, schools, hospitals, and so on—are potentially important for the rate of economic growth. Thus, the formation of **government capital**—long-lived physical assets owned by the government—is one way that fiscal policy affects the macroeconomy. The government budget affects not only physical capital formation but also human capital formation. At least part of government expenditures on health and education are an investment, in the sense that they will lead to a more productive workforce in the future.

In Canada, the government budget accounting system distinguishes between expenditures on current items, such as the salaries of police officers or agricultural subsidies, and expenditures on capital items, such as the construction of mass transit systems. When the deficit is measured on a current basis, capital spending is not included as part of government spending. The resulting measure in the national accounts is called "saving" and is defined as follows:

$$\begin{aligned} \text{saving} &= S_{\text{govt}} \\ &= T - (G + TR + INT) \\ &= \text{surplus.} \end{aligned} \tag{15.3}$$

In 2015, saving by all levels of government in Canada was $\$-32.7$ billion.[6] When saving is measured in this way, government purchases include only the component of public investment that is needed to maintain the stock of public capital, by offsetting depreciation. This makes sense because depreciation can be thought of as current spending. So, to measure government spending including investment, Statistics Canada subtracts depreciation dK_{govt} from G (so as not to count it twice) and then adds all public investment I_{govt}. The result is called "net lending":

$$\begin{aligned} \text{net lending} &= T - (G + TR + INT - dK_{\text{govt}} + I_{\text{govt}}) \\ &= \text{saving} + dK_{\text{govt}} - I_{\text{govt}}. \end{aligned} \tag{15.4}$$

New investment usually exceeds depreciation, so net lending is less than saving, or the surplus that includes investment spending is less than the surplus based on current spending only. In 2015, net lending was $\$-26.2$ billion.

INCENTIVE EFFECTS OF FISCAL POLICY

The third way in which fiscal policy affects the macroeconomy is by its effects on incentives. Tax policies in particular can affect economic behaviour by changing the financial rewards to various activities. For example, Chapter 4

---

[6] In Table 15.2 we reported that the surplus (saving) of the federal and the provincial/territorial/local sectors summed to $\$-20.8$ billion. The amount of saving reported here is for the total government sector and accounts for the fact that the Canada and Quebec pension plans had savings of $11.9 billion in that year.

showed how tax rates influence the incentives of households to save and of firms to make capital investments.

Average versus Marginal Tax Rates

To analyze the effects of taxes on economic incentives, we need to distinguish between average and marginal tax rates. The **average tax rate** is the total amount of taxes paid by a person (or a firm), divided by the person's before-tax income. The **marginal tax rate** is the fraction of an *additional* dollar of income that must be paid in taxes. For example, suppose that in a particular country, no taxes are levied on the first $10 000 of income, and a 25% tax is levied on all income above $10 000 (see Table 15.3). Under this income tax system, a person with an income of $18 000 pays a tax of $2000. Thus, her average tax rate is 11.1% ($2000 in taxes divided by $18 000 in before-tax income). However, this taxpayer's marginal tax rate is 25% because a $1 increase in her income will increase her taxes by $0.25. Table 15.3 shows that everyone with an income higher than $10 000 faces the same marginal tax rate of 25% but that the average tax rate increases with income.

We can show why the distinction between average and marginal tax rates is important by considering the individual's decision about how much labour to supply. The effects of a tax increase on the amount of labour supplied depend strongly on whether average or marginal taxes are being increased. Economic theory predicts that an increase in the average tax rate, with the marginal tax rate held constant, will *increase* the amount of labour supplied at any (before-tax) real wage. In contrast, the theory predicts that an increase in the marginal tax rate, with the average tax rate held constant, will *decrease* the amount of labour supplied at any real wage.

To explain these conclusions, let's first consider the effects of a change in the average tax rate. Returning to our example from Table 15.3, imagine that the marginal tax rate stays at 25% but that now all income over $8000 (rather than all income over $10 000) is subject to a 25% tax. The taxpayer with an income of $18 000 finds that her tax bill has risen from $2000 to $2500, or 0.25 ($18 000 − $8000), so her average tax rate has risen from 11.1% to 13.9%, or $2500/$18 000. As a result, the taxpayer is $500 poorer. Because she is effectively less wealthy, she will increase the amount of labour she supplies at any real wage (see Summary table 4, p. 70). Hence, an increase in the average tax rate, holding the marginal tax rate fixed, shifts the labour supply curve (in a diagram with the before-tax real wage on the vertical axis) to the right.[7]

TABLE 15.3

Marginal and Average Tax Rates: An Example (total tax = 25% of income over $10 000)

Income	Income − $10 000	Tax	Average Tax Rate	Marginal Tax Rate
$ 18 000	$ 8000	$ 2000	11.1%	25%
50 000	40 000	10 000	20.0%	25%
100 000	90 000	22 500	22.5%	25%

---

[7] In terms of the analysis of Chapter 3, the increase in the average tax rate has a pure income effect on labour supply.

Now consider the effects of an increase in the marginal tax rate, with the average tax rate constant. Suppose that the marginal tax rate on income is raised from 25% to 40% and is accompanied by other changes in the tax law that keep the average tax rate—and, thus, the total amount of taxes paid by the typical taxpayer—the same. To be specific, suppose that the portion of income not subject to tax is increased from $10 000 to $13 000. Then, for the taxpayer earning $18 000, total taxes are $2000, or 0.40($18 000 − $13 000), and the average tax rate of 11.1%, or $2000/$18 000, is the same as it was under the original tax law.

With the average tax rate unchanged, the taxpayer's wealth is unaffected, and so there is no change in labour supply stemming from a change in wealth. However, the increase in the marginal tax rate implies that the taxpayer's after-tax reward for each extra hour worked declines. For example, if her wage is $20 per hour before taxes, at the original marginal tax rate of 25%, her actual take-home pay for each extra hour of work is $15 ($20 minus 25% of $20, or $5, in taxes). At the new marginal tax rate of 40%, the taxpayer's take-home pay for each extra hour of work is only $12 ($20 in before-tax wages minus $8 in taxes). Because extra hours of work no longer carry as much reward in terms of real income earned, at any specific before-tax real wage the taxpayer is likely to work fewer hours and enjoy more leisure instead. Thus, if the average tax rate is held fixed, an increase in the marginal tax rate causes the labour supply curve to shift to the left.[8]

Tax-Induced Distortions and Tax Rate Smoothing

Because taxes affect economic incentives, they change the pattern of economic behaviour. If the invisible hand of free markets is working properly, the pattern of economic activity in the absence of taxes is the most efficient, so changes in behaviour caused by taxes reduce economic welfare. Tax-induced deviations from efficient, free-market outcomes are called **distortions**.[9]

To illustrate the idea of a distortion, let's go back to the example of the worker whose before-tax real wage is $20. Because profit-maximizing employers demand labour up to the point that the marginal product of labour equals the real wage, the real output produced by an extra hour of the worker's labour (her marginal product) is also $20. Now, suppose that the worker is willing to sacrifice leisure to work an extra hour if she receives at least $14 in additional real earnings. Because the value of what the worker can produce in an extra hour of labour exceeds the value that she places on an extra hour of leisure, her working the extra hour is economically efficient.

In an economy without taxes, this efficient outcome occurs because the worker is willing to work the extra hour for the extra $20 in real wages. She would also be willing to work the extra hour if the marginal tax rate on earnings were 25% because at a marginal tax rate of 25%, her after-tax real wage is $15, which exceeds the $14 real-wage minimum that she is willing to accept. However, if the marginal tax rate rises to 40% so that the worker's after-tax wage falls to only $12, she would decide

[8] In terms of the discussion in Chapter 3, a change in the marginal tax rate with no change in the average tax rate has a pure substitution effect on labour supply.

[9] The "if" at the beginning of the previous sentence is, of course, a big if. Markets rarely exist that are free of imperfections. Thus, for example, a monopoly supplier introduces inefficiencies and distortions into the market in which it operates, and these reduce economic welfare. Similarly, production externalities (such as air and water pollution) cause firms to produce inefficient levels of output and so introduce distortions. Externalities and imperfectly competitive markets are examples of market failures. In cases like these, taxes are sometimes used to reduce or eliminate the distortion introduced by the market failure. In the discussion that follows, we consider the effects of taxes on markets that are otherwise free of distortions.

that it's not worth her while to work the extra hour, even though for her to do so would have been economically efficient. The difference between the number of hours the worker would have worked had there been no tax on wages and the number of hours she actually works when there is a tax reflects the distorting effect of the tax. The higher the tax rate is, the greater the distortion is likely to be.

APPLICATION

THE POVERTY TRAP

You may be surprised to learn that some of the highest marginal tax rates are faced by relatively poor Canadians. These high effective marginal tax rates are possible because transfers under several social programs depend on a household's income. As income rises, the benefits may fall (perhaps suddenly at some cut-off point) in order to limit the transfers to high-income earners. A household that earns an additional dollar in wages may lose almost as much in benefits as its income rises above a cut-off point. According to our analysis, these high marginal tax rates (combined with low average tax rates) should act to discourage labour supply. This situation is known as the **poverty trap**.

Figure 15.3 shows the effective marginal tax rate (combined federal and provincial) for a one-earner couple with two children in Ontario in 2000. As income rises along the horizontal axis, eligibility for social assistance, the Canada child tax benefit, the national child benefit (introduced in 1998), and the GST credit declines. As a result, disposable income does not rise as fast as earned income because additional wage earnings are offset by lost benefits and tax credits. The implied marginal tax rates are measured on the vertical axis and, at many income levels, are greater than 70%.

Eliminating the poverty trap is challenging for two reasons. First, defraying the costs that low-income workers face when entering the labour force costs money. Recently, the federal government has enriched the working income supplement to the child tax benefit so that the benefit doesn't drop as rapidly with income. But avoiding disincentive effects without making a transfer universal, and possibly expensive, remains a challenge. Second, removing the trap requires coordination between the federal government, which is responsible for most refundable income-tax credits, and provincial governments, which administer social assistance. An example of such coordination occurred in 1997, when the federal government enriched the child tax benefit while provincial governments simultaneously reduced social assistance payments for children and redirected their spending to programs (such as daycare or school meals) that benefit poor children, whether their parents receive social assistance or not.

Because doing entirely without taxes is not possible, the problem for fiscal policymakers is how to raise needed government revenues while keeping distortions relatively small. Because high tax rates are particularly costly in terms of economic efficiency, economists argue that keeping tax rates roughly constant at a moderate level is preferable to alternating periods of very low and very high tax rates. For example, if the government's spending plans require it to levy a tax rate that over a number of years averages 20%, most economists would advise the

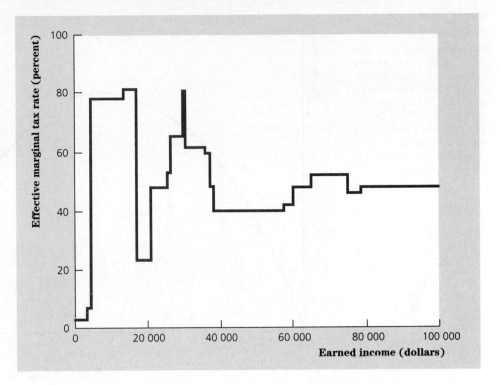

government *not* to set the tax rate at 30% half the time and 10% the other half. The reason is the large distortions that the 30% tax rate would cause in the years that it was effective. A better strategy is to hold the tax rate constant at 20%. A policy of maintaining stable tax rates so as to minimize distortions is called **tax rate smoothing**.

The Laffer Curve

How taxes affect economic incentives is sensitive to the level of taxes itself. This idea is represented in a relationship known as the Laffer curve.

The Laffer curve is named after economist Arthur Laffer, a former advisor to U.S. President Ronald Reagan in the early 1980s. It describes a simple idea: that with either a 0% or a 100% tax rate, government can collect no revenue from that source. This must be true for the 0% tax rate, of course, but we would also expect it to be true with a 100% tax rate because people would not likely be willing to work and earn income if government took it all away. In that case, the tax *base*, the income against which the government applies its tax rate, falls to zero. In between these two extreme values of the tax rate we would expect the government to collect tax revenue. But *changes* in the tax rate may cause tax revenue to rise or fall depending on how close the tax rate was to one extreme value or the other.

Figure 15.4 illustrates these ideas. As the tax rate increases from a low level, say from 15% to 20%, we should not be surprised to observe that the amount of tax revenue collected by the government rises. That is, at low tax rates, a small increase is unlikely to cause a significant change in the effort to earn income and so would not be expected to cause a significant change in the tax base. Thus an increase in the tax rate results in a net increase in tax revenue. At high tax rates, however, any further increase in the rate should be expected to prompt a response from

FIGURE 15.4

THE LAFFER CURVE

As tax rates increase, the tax base tends to shrink. At low tax rates, the government collects more revenue from an increase in the tax rate because the tax base does not shrink very much. At very high tax rates, an additional increase in the rate will cause such a large shrinkage in the tax base that the government collects less revenue.

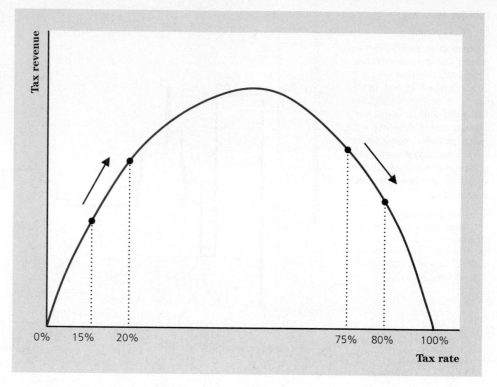

taxpayers to try to avoid paying still more of their income in tax. This might take the form of taxpayers working less, taking a greater effort at tax avoidance by seeking the use of tax "loopholes," or simply moving to jurisdictions with lower tax rates. In all these cases, the size of the tax base shrinks a great deal and so the government, despite applying a higher tax rate, collects less in revenue.

As you may have concluded by now, while the ideas behind the Laffer curve seem sensible, the tricky bit is identifying at what tax rate revenue starts to fall with increases in the tax rate. In particular, are the tax rates currently imposed by governments so high that cutting those rates might actually yield an increase in revenue? In other words, are current tax rates on the downward sloping part of the Laffer curve?

To be on the downward sloping part of the Laffer curve requires that the cost of tax avoidance be less than the tax one might be expected to save as a result of these efforts. For this reason, whether current tax rates put us on the downward sloping part of the Laffer curve depends on the type of tax being considered. Avoiding income taxes by curtailing work effort, for example, is more costly than avoiding taxes owed on capital gains by delaying the sale of stock shares. Where we are on the Laffer curve may also depend on socio-cultural considerations. Thus, a unilingual French speaker may find it difficult to move to avoid high tax rates in Quebec and so may be less able to engage in tax avoidance efforts than, say, a unilingual English speaker in Saskatchewan.

In a recent study, economists Ergete Ferede and Bev Dahlby[10] use Canadian provincial government data to identify where current provincial government

---

[10] "Cutting Provincial Corporate Income Tax Rates to Promote Investment, Employment and Economic Growth," *SPP Communiqué*, Volume 8, Issue 8, March 2016.

corporate income-tax rates are located on the Laffer curve. They find that in 2013, in 5 of 10 provinces corporation income tax rates were so high that lowering the rate would actually increase tax revenues. These provinces (Saskatchewan, New Brunswick, Nova Scotia, Newfoundland and Labrador, and PEI), then, were all on the downward sloping portion of their corporation income tax Laffer curve. For other types of taxes, current tax rates seem to put us on the upward sloping part of the Laffer curve. This does not suggest those tax rates should necessarily be increased. Any tax rate increase creates distortions that may reduce economic welfare. Being on the upward sloping portion of the Laffer curve only suggests that an increase in the tax rate would yield more tax revenue.

15.3 GOVERNMENT DEFICITS AND DEBT

The single number in the federal government's budget that is the focus of most public debate is the size of the budget deficit or surplus. During the 1980s and early 1990s, a series of unprecedentedly large (for peacetime) deficits led to a barrage of claims and counterclaims about the potential impact of big deficits on the economy. Then the emergence of budget surpluses in the late 1990s brought a debate about paying down public debt. In the rest of this chapter, we discuss the government budget deficit or surplus, the government debt, and their effects on the economy.

THE GROWTH OF GOVERNMENT DEBT

There is an important distinction between the government budget surplus or deficit and the government debt (also called the national debt). The government budget surplus or deficit (a flow variable) is the difference between expenditures and tax revenues in any fiscal year. The **government debt** (a stock variable) is the total value of government bonds outstanding at any particular time. (A Closer Look 15.2, "How Large Is the Government Debt?," discusses different ways in which government debt can be measured.) Because the excess of government expenditures over revenues equals the amount of new borrowing that the government must do—that is, the amount of new government debt that it must issue—any year's deficit (measured in dollar, or nominal, terms) equals the change in the debt in that year. We can express the relationship between government debt and the budget deficit by

$$\Delta B = \text{nominal government budget deficit}$$
$$= -(\text{nominal government budget surplus}), \qquad (15.5)$$

where ΔB is the change in the nominal value (or face value) of government bonds outstanding.

It's important to note at this point that the government debt we are speaking of is a net figure. That is, we noted previously that governments pay interest on debts they owe but they also receive interest on funds they have lent to others. The fact that governments both pay and receive interest reflects the fact that they have both financial liabilities (what they owe to others and on which they pay interest) and financial assets (what others owe to the government and on which the government receives interest). When we talk about government debt, we are referring to government net debt—the value of all financial liabilities less the value of all financial assets.

A CLOSER LOOK 15.2

How Large Is the Government Debt?

In Figure 15.5 (p. 524), we present graphs showing the size of the federal and the provincial/territorial government debt as ratios of GDP. To calculate these ratios we must, of course, have known the size of government debt. The question posed in this box, then, seems odd; surely we know the answer! It turns out, however, that there are different ways of measuring government debt and even different ways of conceptualizing what defines government debt. In an effort to understand the significance of these considerations, William Robson,[*] of the C. D. Howe Institute, provides alternative measures of just how big is government debt.

Robson suggests that there are different ways of thinking about government debt, and that these lead us to different ways of measuring it. One way is to think about government debt as an indicator of its ability to meet its interest obligations. From this perspective, it makes sense to measure a government's net debt as the difference between its current financial liabilities (on which it pays interest) and its current financial assets (on which it receives investment income). We present this measure of net debt in Figure 15.5. In his work, Robson fine-tunes these estimates to account for the assets and liabilities of government business enterprises that we have omitted from our definition of the government sector (recall our discussion in Section 15.1) and for some accounting adjustments. His fine tuning decreased the size of the government sector's net debt in 2000 by about $70 billion (or about 10%).

Another way to think about government net debt is to not focus solely on *current* financial assets and liabilities but to also pay attention to longer-term issues pertaining to assets and liabilities. This issue arises because governments often make commitments to future spending without accounting for the cost of financing those obligations. Examples include education spending, the Canada and Quebec pension plans, and the future cost of government-financed health care. A commitment to continue these programs implies a significant future spending obligation for Canada's governments. Of course, Canadians expect to continue to pay taxes to government, and the taxes they pay will increase over time as taxpayers' incomes rise. There is, then, a future revenue stream that governments can look forward to. The question is this: Do these two future financial streams match up? Robson investigates

this issue by calculating the future stream of revenue that will accrue to governments given assumptions about the speed with which tax bases will grow. He then compares this with an estimate of the future spending obligations of governments. He defines as an "unfunded liability" the excess of future spending obligations over future tax revenue. It turns out that Canadian governments have a large unfunded liability exceeding $1 trillion, or roughly 100% of GDP. The implication is that Canadian governments will need to increase tax rates, or hope for a faster rate of economic growth than Robson assumes, in order to meet their future spending obligations. From this perspective, then, government debt in Canada is significantly larger than what we show in Figure 15.5.

An interesting part of Robson's calculations is how levels of government differ in terms of their unfunded liabilities. The federal government's net debt is actually *lower* than the figure we use in producing Figure 15.5. This is mainly because the federal government can look forward to receiving a large amount of deferred taxes in the future. These arise because baby boomers, who purchased large amounts of tax-deferred Registered Retirement Savings Plans (RRSPs) during their working lives, will soon be retiring and paying those deferred taxes. The opposite is true for provincial governments. Large future spending obligations, in the form of higher health-care costs in particular, mean that their unfunded liabilities are very large. Robson calculates that taking these unfunded liabilities into account causes the net debt of the provincial/territorial sector to increase by 40%.

Calculations such as these, which show that the spending obligations of provincial governments are increasing much faster than their revenues—while the opposite is true for the federal government—are behind the claims of those who suggest there is a "fiscal imbalance" between these two levels of government. It is on the basis of such calculations that many analysts, and all provincial premiers, suggest that the federal government needs to lower federal tax rates and so "make room" for provincial governments to increase theirs.

---

[*] "How Big Is the Debt?" in Christopher Ragan and William Watson, eds., *Is the Debt War Over? Dispatches from Canada's Fiscal Frontline*, Montreal: Institute for Research on Public Policy, 2004.

The fact that we will be referring to net debt does not affect the relationship between the budget deficit or surplus and the size of government debt we discussed above. A budget surplus can be used to retire outstanding debt or it can be used to increase financial assets (as might happen if governments used a surplus to increase the size or number of student loans, for example). Whether a surplus is used to retire outstanding debt or to increase financial assets, net debt falls when there is a budget surplus. Similarly, a revenue shortfall (a budget deficit) may require governments to issue new debt or sell some of their financial assets to cover the shortfall. In either case, net debt increases when there is a budget deficit.

In a period of persistently large budget deficits, the nominal value of the government's debt will grow quickly. For example, between 1979 and 1997, federal government debt outstanding increased tenfold in nominal terms, from $59 billion in 1979 to $609 billion in 1997. Even if we remove the effects of inflation and measure debt in real terms, the (real) value of federal government debt outstanding in 1997 was more than four times as large as in 1979. However, 1997 marked the end of the sequence of deficits. In that year, the federal government began to run nominal budget surpluses, which led to reductions in debt.

Because countries with a high GDP have relatively more resources available to pay the principal and interest on the government's bonds, a useful measure of government indebtedness is the quantity of government debt outstanding divided by the GDP, or the **debt–GDP ratio**.[11] Figure 15.5 shows the history of the debt–GDP ratio in Canada. The upper curve shows the federal debt–GDP ratio, while the lower curve shows the debt–GDP ratio for all provincial, territorial, and local levels of government.

A striking feature of Figure 15.5 is the large increase in the debt–GDP ratio that occurred during World War II when the government sold bonds to finance the war effort. By the end of the war the debt–GDP ratio exceeded 100%, implying that the value of government debt outstanding was greater than a year's GDP. Over the following 30 years governments in Canada ran budget surpluses and used the excess of revenue over expenditures to pay down the debt incurred during World War II. That, plus strong growth in GDP, caused the federal debt–GDP ratio to fall steadily. Beginning in 1975, however, the federal government returned to running budget deficits. The shortfall of revenue relative to expenditures was met by borrowing, and the debt–GDP ratio began to climb. By 1996, the federal debt–GDP ratio hit its postwar high of 67%. When combined with the debt of provincial, territorial, and local governments, the combined federal–provincial debt–GDP ratio peaked at 96% in that year. Since that time, the debt–GDP ratio has fallen. In 2016, despite a 4-percentage-point increase resulting from the 2008–2009 recession, the federal debt–GDP ratio had fallen to 30.8%, while that of the aggregated provincial/territorial/local government sector was 28.4%. Using comparable measures of government debt, the ratio of government debt to GDP in Canada in 2012 was significantly lower than it was in the United States, and was the lowest of any country in the G7.[12]

[11] Comparing the size of debt relative to income is also a sensible way of measuring the indebtedness of individuals. Whether we should judge someone with a $20 000 debt to be in financial difficulties depends on whether that person has an income of $5000 or an income of $100 000. The logic of comparing an individual's debt to his or her income is the same logic that inspires economists to compare government debt to GDP.

[12] A comparison of debt–GDP ratios across countries is available from Department of Finance, *Fiscal Reference Tables*, Table 54, October 2015 (www.fin.gc.ca).

FIGURE 15.5

RATIOS OF FEDERAL AND PROVINCIAL NET DEBT TO GDP

The upper curve shows the ratio of federal government net debt to GDP for the period 1926–2016. The lower curve shows the ratio of debt to GDP for provincial, territorial, and local levels of government for the period 1977–2016. The federal debt–GDP ratio was high during the Great Depression, rose dramatically during World War II, then rose again after 1976, peaking in 1996. After an increase due to the 2008–2009 recession, the federal ratio has levelled off. The provincial/territorial/local ratio rose rapidly during the 1980s and 1990s and has increased steadily since 2007.

Sources: Federal net debt is adapted from Statistics Canada, CANSIM series v62698060. Net debt of provincial, territorial, and local governments is adapted from series v62698061.

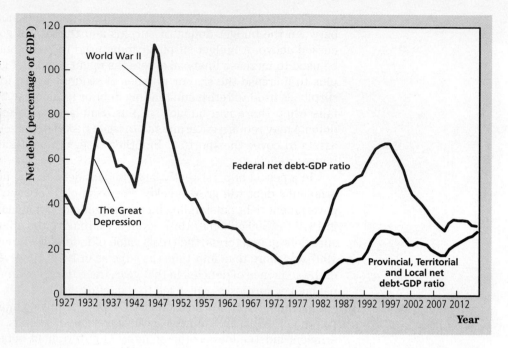

We can describe the change in the debt–GDP ratio from one year to the next by the following formula (derived in Appendix 15 at the end of this chapter):

$$\Delta\left(\frac{B}{Y}\right) = \left(\frac{G + TR - T}{Y}\right) + (i - g)\left(\frac{B_{-1}}{Y}\right), \tag{15.6}$$

where B is the nominal value of government bonds outstanding, B_{-1} is the nominal value of government bonds outstanding in the previous year, Y is GDP, i is the nominal interest rate paid on government bonds, g is the growth rate of GDP, G is government spending on goods and services, TR is government transfers, and T is tax revenue. The difference between government spending on goods and services and transfers on the one hand, and tax revenue on the other, is the primary deficit, $(G + TR - T)$. Finally, the ratio B/Y is the debt–GDP ratio and $\Delta(B/Y)$ is the change in the debt–GDP ratio from one year to the next.

Equation (15.6) emphasizes that two factors cause the debt–GDP ratio to change from one year to the next: (1) a primary deficit and (2) an interest rate on outstanding government debt that exceeds the growth rate of GDP.

Why does Eq. (15.6) make sense? Let's for the moment focus on the first term on the right-hand side, $(G + TR - T)/Y$. This measures the primary deficit as a fraction of GDP. Recall from our earlier discussion that the primary deficit measures what the government's budget balance would be were it not for past revenue and spending choices that resulted in lending and borrowing. It is, then, a measure of what impact current choices with respect to government spending and taxes have on the deficit. This term, then, simply indicates that if current tax and spending choices are such as to produce a primary deficit—so that $(G + TR - T)/Y > 0$— then the government will need to borrow to cover the revenue shortfall and the debt–GDP ratio will increase. If current tax and spending choices are such to produce a primary surplus—so that $(G + TR - T)/Y < 0$—then the government can use the excess of revenue over spending to retire previously issued debt, and the debt–GDP ratio will decrease.

The second term on the right-hand side of Eq. (15.6) indicates that even if the primary deficit is zero, the debt–GDP ratio might increase. The reason it might is that the government must, in the current period, deal with the financial consequences of revenue and spending choices it made in the past. The impact on the current deficit of having accumulated debt in the past is the sum of two considerations. First, if the government has accumulated debt in the past, it must now pay interest to those who hold that debt. The larger the amount of debt accumulated in the past (B_{-1}) is, and the larger the interest rate paid on that debt (i) is, the larger the deficit in the current period (ΔB) will be. The second consideration recognizes that Eq. (15.6) measures the change in the ratio of debt to GDP. Thus, all else being equal, the larger the growth rate of GDP (g) is, the smaller the size of debt relative to the size of GDP will be. The second term on the right-hand side of Eq. (15.6) indicates that whether the debt–GDP ratio increases in the current period depends on how large is the influence on the debt–GDP ratio due to the interest rate relative to the influence on the debt–GDP ratio due to the economic growth rate. If the interest rate is larger than the rate of growth in GDP, the debt–GDP ratio will increase. If the interest rate is smaller than the rate of growth in GDP, the debt–GDP ratio will decrease.

Two interesting economic lessons can be drawn from the simple accounting relationship between the primary deficit, the interest rate paid on outstanding debt, the growth rate of GDP, and the annual change in the debt–GDP ratio described by Eq. (15.6). *First*, the combination of slow economic growth (a low value of g) and a high interest rate payable on government debt (a high value of i) can have serious consequences for debt accumulation. If $i > g$, then the debt–GDP ratio will increase each year in proportion to the size of this difference and in proportion to the size of the previous year's debt. This was exactly the unfortunate combination of economic conditions that described the Canadian economy in the late 1970s and early 1980s, and is part of the reason why government debt–GDP ratios in Canada began an unprecedented (for peacetime) increase between 1975 and 1995 (see Figure 15.5). On the other hand, the combination of rapid economic growth (a high value of g) and a low interest rate payable on government debt (a low value of i) sets the stage for a rapid reduction in the debt–GDP ratio. This was the combination of economic conditions that described the Canadian economy in the 30 years following World War II. It was a period that economist William Robson, of the C. D. Howe Institute,[13] has stressed was unusual in Canada's economic history. The large negative value of the ($i - g$) term enabled Canada's federal government to reduce the debt–GDP ratio from 111% in 1946 to 16% in 1975 without the need for large primary surpluses.

The *second* interesting lesson to be drawn from the accounting relationship described by Eq. (15.6) is that during what is the historically usual case of interest rates being either equal to or greater than economic growth rates, a reduction in the debt–GDP ratio requires primary surpluses (so that $(G + TR - T)/Y < 0$). This requirement was driven home to Canadians in years after 1996. In that year, the debt–GDP ratio hit its postwar peak. To reduce the debt–GDP ratio, Canadian governments introduced budgets containing spending cuts and tax rate increases that combined to produce sizable primary surpluses. In the 14 years between 1996 and 2009, primary surpluses averaged 6.7% of GDP, and these were the main reason for the rapid reductions in the debt–GDP ratio for all governments in Canada over that time span.

---

[13] "Putting Some Gold in the Golden Years: Fixing the Canada Pension Plan," C. D. Howe Institute, *Commentary*, no. 76, January 1996.

The election of a new federal government in 2015 has been accompanied by a promise to increase spending and to pay for that spending with a significant increase in net debt. At the time of this announcement, interest rates and growth rates were both low, suggesting the debt ratio may only grow modestly. If economic conditions change to produce a large positive value to the $(i - g)$ term then strong actions to cut spending and/or raise taxes may again be required to halt a rapid increase in the debt ratio.

THE BURDEN OF THE GOVERNMENT DEBT ON FUTURE GENERATIONS

People often express concern that the billions of dollars of federal and provincial government debt accumulated in recent years will impose a crushing financial burden on their children and grandchildren, who will someday be taxed to pay off these debts. In this view, high rates of government borrowing amount to "robbing the future" to pay for government spending that is too high or taxes that are too low in the present.

This conventional argument ignores the fact that most Canadian government bonds are owned by Canadian citizens. Therefore, although our descendants may someday face heavy taxes to pay the interest and principal of the government debt, these future taxpayers also will inherit the outstanding government bonds and, thus, will be the *recipients* of most of those interest and principal payments. To a substantial degree, we owe the government debt to ourselves, so the debt is not a burden in the same sense that it would be if it were owed entirely to outsiders.

Although the popular view of the burden of the government debt is faulty, economists have pointed out several ways in which the government debt can become a burden on future generations. First, if tax rates have to be raised substantially in the future to pay off the debt, the resulting distortions will cause the economy to function less efficiently and impose costs on future generations.

Budget deficits can also lead to other distortions. Meeting interest obligations severely limits the scope for countercyclical fiscal policy as a stabilization tool and may also lead to reductions in public investment. Some economists also argue that heavily indebted governments face higher interest rates than they otherwise would, which creates further pressure for tax increases and spending reductions.

Second, most people hold small amounts of government bonds (perhaps through pension funds) or no government bonds at all. In the future, people who hold few or no bonds may have to pay higher taxes to pay off the government debt than they receive in interest and principal payments; they may also receive fewer public services. People holding large quantities of bonds may receive more in interest and principal than they pay in increased taxes. Bondholders are richer on average than non-bondholders, so the need to service the government debt might lead to a transfer of resources from the relatively poor to the relatively rich. However, this transfer could be offset by other tax and transfer policies—for example, by raising taxes on high-income people.

The third argument is probably the most significant: Many economists claim that government deficits reduce national saving; that is, when the government runs a deficit, the economy accumulates less domestic capital and fewer foreign assets than it would have if the deficit had been lower. The second effect on domestic consumption is particularly relevant for Canada, which is a small open economy; government deficits most likely lead to current account deficits rather than less domestic capital formation. If this argument is correct, deficits will lower the standard of living for our children and grandchildren, both because they may inherit a smaller capital stock and especially because they will have to pay more interest to foreigners than they otherwise would have. This reduction in the future standard of living would constitute a true burden of the government debt.

David Johnson,[14] of Wilfrid Laurier University, has considered these arguments and weighed the evidence regarding their importance. He has concluded that the accumulation of debt by Canadian governments between 1975 and 1996 resulted in a reduction in Canadians' incomes of between 3% and 10%. To put this loss in perspective, Canada's GDP in 2012 was $1888 billion. Johnson's estimate suggests, then, that the accumulation of debt by Canadian governments cost Canadians between $57 billion and $189 billion.

Crucial to arguments suggesting that a burden is imposed on future generations when governments run budget deficits and accumulate debt is the idea that government deficits reduce national saving. As we have mentioned at several points in this book (notably in Chapter 4), the question of whether budget deficits affect national saving is highly controversial. We devote most of the rest of this section to further discussion of this issue.

BUDGET DEFICITS AND NATIONAL SAVING: RICARDIAN EQUIVALENCE REVISITED

Under what circumstances will an increased government budget deficit cause national saving to fall? Virtually all economists agree that an increase in the deficit caused by a rise in government purchases—say, to fight a war—reduces national saving and imposes a real burden on the economy. However, whether a deficit caused by a cut in current taxes or an increase in current transfers reduces national saving is much less clear. Recall that advocates of Ricardian equivalence argue that tax cuts or increases in transfers will not affect national saving, whereas its opponents disagree.

Ricardian Equivalence: An Example

To illustrate Ricardian equivalence, let's suppose that, holding its current and planned future purchases constant, the government cuts this year's taxes by $100 per person. (Assuming that the tax cut is a lump sum allows us to ignore incentive effects.) What impact will this reduction in taxes have on national saving? In answering this question, we first recall the definition of national saving (Eq. 2.8):

$$S = Y - C - G. \tag{15.7}$$

Equation (15.7) states that national saving S equals output Y less consumption C and government purchases G.[15] If we assume that government purchases G are constant and that output Y is fixed at its full-employment level, we know from Eq. (15.7) that the tax cut will reduce national saving S only if it causes consumption C to rise. Advocates of Ricardian equivalence assert that if current and planned future government purchases are unchanged, a tax cut will not affect consumption and, thus, will not affect national saving.

---

[14] "Does the Debt Matter?" in Christopher Ragan and William Watson, eds., *Is the Debt War Over? Dispatches from Canada's Fiscal Frontline*. Montreal: Institute for Research on Public Policy, 2004.

[15] We assume that net factor payments from abroad, *NFP*, are zero.

Why wouldn't a tax cut that raises after-tax incomes cause people to consume more? The answer is that—if current and planned future government purchases do not change—a tax cut today must be accompanied by an offsetting increase in expected future taxes. To see why, note that if current taxes are reduced by $100 per person, without any change in government purchases, the government must borrow an additional $100 per person by selling bonds. Suppose that the bonds are one-year bonds that pay a real interest rate r. In the following year, when the government repays the principal ($100 per person) and interest ($100 \times r$ per person) on the bonds, it will have to collect an additional $100(1 + r)$ per person in taxes. Thus, when the public learns of the current tax cut of $100 per person, they should also expect their taxes to increase by $100(1 + r)$ per person next year.[16]

Because the current tax cut is balanced by an increase in expected future taxes, it does not make taxpayers any better off in the long run despite raising their current after-tax incomes. Indeed, after the tax cut, *taxpayers' abilities to consume today and in the future are the same as they were originally*. That is, if no one consumes more in response to the tax cut—so that each person saves the entire $100 increase in after-tax income—in the following year, the $100 per person of additional saving will grow to $100(1 + r)$ per person. This additional $100(1 + r)$ per person is precisely the amount needed to pay the extra taxes that will be levied in the future, leaving people able to consume as much in the future as they had originally planned. Because people are not made better off by the tax cut (which must be coupled with a future tax increase), they have no reason to consume more today. Thus, national saving should be unaffected by the lump-sum tax cut, as supporters of Ricardian equivalence claim.

Ricardian Equivalence Across Generations

The argument for Ricardian equivalence rests on the assumption that current government borrowing will be repaid within the lifetimes of people who are living today. In other words, any tax cuts received today are offset by the higher taxes that people must pay later. But what if some of the debt the government is accumulating will be repaid not by the people who receive the tax cut but by their children or grandchildren? In that case, wouldn't people react to a tax cut by consuming more?

Harvard economist Robert Barro[17] has shown that, in theory, Ricardian equivalence may still apply even if the current generation receives the tax cut and future generations bear the burden of repaying the government's debt. To state Barro's argument in its simplest form, let's imagine an economy in which every generation has the same number of people and suppose that the current generation receives a tax cut of $100 per person. With government purchases held constant, this tax cut increases the government's borrowing and outstanding debt by $100 per person. However, people currently living are not taxed to repay this debt; instead, this obligation is deferred until the next generation. To repay the government's increased debt, the next generation's taxes (in real terms) will be raised by $100(1 + R)$ per person, where $1 + R$ is the real value of a dollar borrowed today at the time the debt is repaid.[18]

---

[16] The government might put the tax increase off for two, three, or more years. Nevertheless, the general conclusion that the current tax cut must be offset by future tax increases would be unchanged.

[17] "Are Government Bonds Net Wealth?" *Journal of Political Economy*, November/December 1974, pp. 1095–1117.

[18] For example, if the debt is to be repaid in 30 years and r is the one-year real interest rate, then $(1 + R) = (1 + r)^{30}$.

Seemingly, the current generation of people, who receive the tax cut, should increase their consumption because the reduction in their taxes is not expected to be balanced by an increase in taxes during their lifetimes. However, Barro argued that people in the current generation should not increase their consumption in response to a tax cut if they care about the well-being of the next generation. Of course, people do care about the well-being of their children, as is reflected, in part, in the economic resources devoted to children, including funds spent on children's health and education, gifts, and inheritances.

How does the concern of this generation for the next affect the response of people to a tax cut? A member of the current generation who receives a tax cut—call him Joe—might be inclined to increase his own consumption, all else being equal. But, Barro argues, Joe should realize that for each dollar of tax cut he receives today, his son Joe Junior will have to pay $1 + R$ dollars of extra taxes in the future. Can Joe do anything on his own to help out Joe Junior? The answer is yes. Suppose that instead of consuming his $100 tax cut, Joe saves the $100 and uses the extra savings to increase Joe Junior's inheritance. By the time the next generation is required to pay the government debt, Joe Junior's extra inheritance plus accumulated interest will be $100(1 + R)$, or just enough to cover the increase in Joe Junior's taxes. Thus, by saving his tax cut and adding these savings to his planned bequest, Joe can keep both his own consumption and Joe Junior's consumption the same as they would have been if the tax cut had never occurred.

Furthermore, Barro points out, Joe *should* save all his tax cut for Joe Junior's benefit. Why? If Joe consumes even part of his tax cut, he will not leave enough extra inheritance to allow Joe Junior to pay the expected increase in his taxes, and so Joe Junior will have to consume less than he could have if there had been no tax cut for Joe. However if Joe wanted to increase his own consumption at Joe Junior's expense, he could have done so without changes in the tax laws—for example, by contributing less to Joe Junior's university tuition payments or by planning to leave a smaller inheritance. That Joe did not take these actions shows that he was satisfied with the division of consumption between himself and Joe Junior that he had planned before the tax cut was enacted; there is no reason that the tax cut should cause this original consumption plan to change. Therefore, if Joe and other members of the current generation do not consume more in response to a tax cut, Ricardian equivalence should hold even when debt repayment is deferred to the next generation.

This analysis can be extended to allow for multiple generations and in other ways. These extensions do not change the main point, which is that if taxpayers understand that they are ultimately responsible for the government's debt, they should not change their consumption in response to changes in taxes or transfers that are unaccompanied by changes in planned government purchases. As a result, deficits created by tax cuts should not reduce national saving and, therefore, should not burden future generations.

DEPARTURES FROM RICARDIAN EQUIVALENCE

The arguments for Ricardian equivalence are logically sound, and this idea has greatly influenced economists' thinking about deficits. Although 30 years ago most economists would have taken for granted that a tax cut would substantially increase consumption, today there is much less agreement about this claim. In some countries, Ricardian equivalence seems to have worked quite well, at least at times with declines in government saving offset by increases in private saving. On the other hand, Ricardian equivalence seemed to fail spectacularly in the 1980s in the United States, when high government budget deficits were accompanied by extremely low rates of national saving.

Our judgment is that tax cuts that lead to increased government borrowing probably affect consumption and national saving, although the effect may be small. We base this conclusion on the experiences of Canada during the 1990s and the United States in the 1980s and on the fact that there are some theoretical reasons to expect Ricardian equivalence not to hold exactly. The main arguments against Ricardian equivalence are the possible existence of borrowing constraints, consumers' shortsightedness, the failure of some people to leave bequests, and the non–lump-sum nature of most tax changes.

1. *Borrowing constraints.* Many people would be willing to consume more if they could find lenders who would extend them credit. However, consumers often face limits, known as *borrowing constraints*, on the amounts they can borrow. A person who wants to consume more, but who is unable to borrow to do so, will be eager to take advantage of a tax cut to increase consumption. Thus, the existence of borrowing constraints may cause Ricardian equivalence to fail.

2. *Shortsightedness.* In the view of some economists, many people are short-sighted and do not understand that as taxpayers they are ultimately responsible for the government's debt. For example, some people may determine their consumption by simple "rules of thumb," such as the rule that a family should spend fixed percentages of its current after-tax income on food, clothing, housing, and so on, without regard for how its income is likely to change in the future. If people are shortsighted, they may respond to a tax cut by consuming more, contrary to the prediction of Ricardian equivalence. However, Ricardians could reply that ultra-sophisticated analyses of fiscal policy by consumers are not necessary for Ricardian equivalence to be approximately correct. For example, if people know generally that big government deficits mean future problems for the economy (without knowing exactly why), they may be reluctant to spend from a tax cut that causes the deficit to balloon, consistent with the Ricardian prediction.

3. *Failure to leave bequests.* If people do not leave bequests, perhaps because they do not think about the long-run consequences of tax cuts for their children, they will increase their consumption if their taxes are cut, and Ricardian equivalence will not hold. Some people may not leave bequests because they expect their children to be richer than they are and, thus, not need any bequest. If people continue to hold this belief after they receive a tax cut, they will increase their consumption and again Ricardian equivalence will fail.

4. *Non–lump-sum taxes.* In theory, Ricardian equivalence holds only for lump-sum tax changes, with each person's change in taxes being a fixed amount that does not depend on the person's economic decisions, such as how much to work or save. As we discussed in Section 15.2, when taxes are not lump sum, the level and timing of taxes will affect incentives and, thus, economic behaviour. Thus, non–lump-sum tax cuts will have real effects on the economy, in contrast to the simple Ricardian view.

We emphasize, though, that with non–lump-sum taxes, the incentive effects of a tax cut on consumption and saving behaviour will depend heavily on the tax structure and on which taxes are cut. For example, a temporary cut in sales taxes would likely stimulate consumption, but a reduction in the tax rate on interest earned on savings accounts might increase saving. Thus, we cannot always conclude that just because taxes are not lump sum, a tax cut will increase consumption. That conclusion has to rest primarily on the other three arguments against Ricardian equivalence we presented.

While the logic of the Ricardian view is sound, there are a number of equally compelling reasons to believe there will be significant departures from the economic choices and behaviours predicted by that view. Where one stands on the issue of Ricardian equivalence must, therefore, be determined by the evaluation of the evidence.

15.4 Deficits and Inflation

In this final section of the chapter, we discuss one more concern that has been expressed about government budget deficits: that deficits are inflationary. We show that the principal link between deficits and inflation is that in some circumstances deficits lead to higher rates of growth in the money supply and that high rates of money growth, in turn, cause inflation.

THE DEFICIT AND THE MONEY SUPPLY

Inflation—a rising price level—results when aggregate demand increases more quickly than aggregate supply. In terms of the *AD–AS* framework, suppose that the long-run aggregate supply curve (which reflects the productive capacity of the economy) is fixed. Then, for the price level to rise, the aggregate demand curve must rise over time.

Both the classical and Keynesian models of the economy imply that deficits can cause aggregate demand to rise, leading to an increase in the price level. In both models, a deficit owing to increased government purchases reduces desired national saving, shifting the *IS* curve upward and causing aggregate demand to rise. This increase in aggregate demand causes the price level to rise.[19] If we assume (as Keynesians usually do) that Ricardian equivalence does not hold, a budget deficit resulting from a cut in taxes or an increase in transfers also reduces desired national saving, increases aggregate demand, and raises the price level. Thus, deficits resulting from expansionary fiscal policies (increased spending or reduced taxes) will be associated with inflation.

However, an increase in government purchases or a cut in taxes causes only a one-time increase in aggregate demand. Therefore, although we expect expansionary fiscal policies to lead to a one-time increase in the price level (that is, a temporary burst in inflation), we do not expect an increase in government purchases or a cut in taxes to cause a *sustained* increase in inflation. In general, the only factor that can sustain an increase in aggregate demand, leading to continuing inflation, is sustained growth in the money supply. Indeed, high rates of inflation are almost invariably linked to high rates of national money growth (Chapter 7). The key question therefore is this: Can government budget deficits lead to ongoing increases in the money supply?

The answer is yes. The link is the printing of money to finance government spending when the government cannot (or doesn't want to) finance all of its

---

[19] The classical analysis predicts that an increase in government purchases may also cause aggregate supply to rise, but we have assumed that the supply effect is smaller than the demand effect.

spending by taxes or borrowing from the public. In the extreme case, imagine a government that wants to spend $10 billion (say, on submarines) but has no ability to tax or borrow from the public. One option is for this government to print $10 billion worth of currency and use this currency to pay for the submarines. The revenue that a government raises by printing money is called **seignorage**. Any government with the authority to issue money can use seignorage; governments that do not have the authority to issue money, such as provincial and local governments in Canada, cannot use seignorage.

Actually, governments that want to finance their deficits through seignorage do not simply print new currency but use an indirect procedure. First, the finance department or treasury authorizes government borrowing equal to the amount of the budget deficit ($10 billion in our example), and a corresponding quantity of new government bonds are printed and sold. Thus, the deficit still equals the change in the outstanding government debt (Eq. 15.5, p. 521). However, the new government bonds are not sold to the public. Instead, the finance department asks (or requires) the central bank to purchase the $10 billion in new bonds. The central bank pays for its purchases of new bonds by printing $10 billion in new currency,[20] which it gives to the finance department in exchange for the bonds. This newly issued currency enters general circulation when the government spends it (on the submarines, say). Note that the purchase of bonds by the central bank increases the monetary base by the amount of the purchase (see Chapter 14), as when the central bank purchases government bonds on the open market.

The precise relationship between the size of the deficit and the increase in the monetary base is

$$\text{deficit} = \Delta B = \Delta B^p + \Delta B^{cb} = \Delta B^p + \Delta BASE. \tag{15.8}$$

Equation (15.8) states that the (nominal) government budget deficit equals the total increase in (nominal) government debt outstanding, ΔB, which can be divided into additional government debt held by the public, ΔB^p, and by the central bank, ΔB^{cb}. The increase in government debt held by the central bank, in turn, equals the increase in the monetary base, $\Delta BASE$. The increase in the monetary base equals the amount of seignorage collected by the government.

The final link between the budget deficit and the money supply has to do with the relationship between the money supply and the monetary base. In general, the increase in the money supply M equals the money multiplier times the increase in the monetary base (Eq. 14.8, p. 479). In an all-currency economy, the money supply and the monetary base are the same and the money multiplier is 1. Nothing significant in this discussion depends on the value of the money multiplier, so for simplicity, we focus on an all-currency economy, in which the change in the money supply equals the change in the monetary base. On the basis of this assumption, Eq. (15.8) implies that

$$\text{deficit} = \Delta B = \Delta B^p + \Delta B^{cb} = \Delta B^p + \Delta M, \tag{15.9}$$

where $\Delta BASE = \Delta M$.

Why would governments use seignorage to finance their deficits, knowing that continued money creation ultimately leads to higher inflation? Under normal conditions, developed countries rarely use seignorage. For example, in recent years, the amount of seignorage revenue in Canada has typically been around $2 billion

---

[20] The new money created by the central bank could also be in the form of deposits at the central bank; the ultimate effect is the same.

per year, which is only about 0.7% of federal government expenditure. This is not an amount that threatens the Bank of Canada's ability to keep the rate of inflation within its target range of 1%–3%. Heavy reliance on seignorage usually occurs in war-torn or developing countries, in which military or social conditions dictate levels of government spending well above what the country can raise in taxes or borrow from the public.

CHAPTER SUMMARY

1. Government expenditures are government purchases of goods and services, transfers, and interest payments. To pay for them, the government collects revenue of three main types: direct taxes, indirect taxes, and investment income.

2. The government budget surplus equals government revenue minus expenditure and indicates how much the government can reduce its debt during the year. A deficit (a negative surplus) indicates how much the government must borrow. The primary government budget surplus is the total surplus plus net interest payments. The primary surplus indicates by how much tax revenue exceeds the cost of current programs (measured by current government purchases and transfers) during the year.

3. Fiscal policy affects the economy through its effects on aggregate demand, government capital formation, and incentives.

4. Increases or decreases in government purchases affect aggregate demand by changing desired national saving and shifting the IS curve. If Ricardian equivalence does not hold, as Keynesians usually argue, changes in taxes also affect desired national saving, the IS curve, and aggregate demand. Automatic stabilizers in the government's budget allow spending to rise or taxes to fall automatically in a recession, which helps cushion the drop in aggregate demand during a recession. The full-employment surplus is what the surplus would be—given current government spending programs and tax laws—if the economy were at full employment. Because of automatic stabilizers that increase spending and reduce taxes in recessions, the actual surplus

falls below the full-employment surplus in recessions.

5. Government capital formation contributes to the productive capacity of the economy. Government capital formation includes both investment in physical capital (roads, schools) and investment in human capital (education, health care). Official measures of government investment include only investment in physical capital.

6. The average tax rate is the fraction of total income paid in taxes, and the marginal tax rate is the fraction of an additional dollar of income that must be paid in taxes. Changes in average tax rates and changes in marginal tax rates have different effects on economic behaviour. For example, an increase in the average tax rate (with no change in the marginal tax rate) increases labour supply, but an increase in the marginal tax rate (with no change in the average tax rate) decreases labour supply.

7. Policymakers must be concerned about the fact that taxes induce distortions, or deviations in economic behaviour from that which would have occurred in the absence of taxes. One strategy for minimizing distortions is to hold tax rates approximately constant over time (tax rate smoothing) rather than alternating between high and low tax rates.

8. Governments own financial assets and carry financial liabilities. The government's net debt is the value of its financial liabilities less the value of its financial assets. The government budget deficit, expressed in nominal terms, measures the change in government net debt from the previous year. The change in the debt–GDP ratio from one year to the next depends on the size of the

primary deficit and on the relative magnitudes of the interest rate paid on outstanding debt versus the growth rate of GDP. If the interest rate paid on government debt exceeds the growth rate of GDP, the debt–GDP ratio will, all else being equal, increase from one year to the next. In that situation, increases in the debt–GDP ratio can be halted only if the government introduces primary budget surpluses.

9. Deficits are a burden on future generations if they cause national saving to fall, because lower national saving means that the country will have less capital and fewer foreign assets than it would have had otherwise. Ricardian equivalence indicates that a deficit caused by a tax cut will not affect consumption and, therefore, will not affect national saving. In the Ricardian view, a tax cut does not affect consumption because the increase in consumers' current income arising from the tax cut is offset by the prospect of increased taxes in the future, leaving consumers no better off. In theory, Ricardian equivalence still holds if the government debt is not repaid by the current generation, provided that people care about the well-being of their descendants and, thus, choose not to consume more at their descendants' expense.

10. Ricardian equivalence may not hold—and, thus, tax cuts may affect national saving—if (1) borrowing constraints prevent some people from consuming as much as they want to, (2) people are shortsighted and do not take expected future changes in taxes into account in their planning, (3) people fail to leave bequests, or (4) tax cuts are not lump sum. The empirical evidence on Ricardian equivalence is mixed.

KEY TERMS

automatic stabilizers, 513
average tax rate, 516
debt–GDP ratio, 523
distortions, 517
full-employment deficit, 513
full-employment surplus, 513
government capital, 515
government debt, 521
marginal tax rate, 516
poverty trap, 518
primary budget surplus, 509
seignorage, 532
tax rate smoothing, 519

KEY EQUATIONS

$$\Delta B = \text{nominal deficit}$$
$$= -\text{nominal surplus} \qquad (15.5)$$

The change in the nominal value of the government debt equals the nominal government deficit.

$$\Delta\left(\frac{B}{Y}\right) = \left(\frac{G + TR - T}{Y}\right) + (i - g)\left(\frac{B_{-1}}{Y}\right) \quad (15.6)$$

The change in the debt–GDP ratio from one year to the next depends on the size of the primary deficit relative to the size of GDP, $(G + TR - T)/Y$, and on the size of the difference between the interest rate paid on outstanding government debt and the growth rate of GDP, $(i - g)$.

$$\text{deficit} = \Delta B = \Delta B^p + \Delta B^{cb} = \Delta B^p + \Delta M \quad (15.9)$$

The government budget deficit equals the increase in the stock of government debt outstanding, B, which in turn equals the sum of additional holdings of government debt by the public, B^p, and by the central bank, B^{cb}.

REVIEW QUESTIONS

1. What are the major components of government expenditure? What are the major sources of government revenue? How does the composition of the federal government's expenditure and revenue differ from that of provincial and local governments?
2. Explain the difference between the overall government budget surplus and the primary surplus. Why are two surplus concepts needed?
3. How is government debt related to the government deficit? What factors contribute to a high growth rate of the debt–GDP ratio?
4. What are the three main ways that fiscal policy affects the macroeconomy? Explain briefly how each channel of policy works.
5. Define *automatic stabilizer* and give an example. For proponents of anti-recessionary fiscal policies, what advantage do automatic stabilizers have over other types of taxing and spending policies?
6. Give a numerical example that shows the difference between the average tax rate and the marginal tax rate on a person's income. For a constant before-tax real wage, which type of tax rate most directly affects how wealthy a person feels? Which type of tax rate affects the reward for working an extra hour?

7. Why do economists suggest that tax rates be kept roughly constant over time rather than alternating between high and low levels?

8. In what ways is the government debt a potential burden on future generations? What is the relationship between Ricardian equivalence and the idea that government debt is a burden?

9. Discuss four reasons why the Ricardian equivalence proposition is not likely to hold exactly.

NUMERICAL PROBLEMS

1. The following budget data are for a country having both a federal government and provincial governments:

Federal purchases of goods and services	200
Provincial purchases of goods and services	150
Federal transfer payments to persons	100
Provincial transfer payments to persons	50
Federal-to-provincial transfers	100
Federal tax receipts	500
Provincial tax receipts	100
Interest received from private sector by federal government	10
Interest received from private sector by provincial governments	10
Total federal government debt	1000
Total provincial government debt	0
Federal government debt held by provincial governments	200
Nominal interest rate	10%

Calculate the overall and primary deficits for the federal government, the provincial governments, and the combined governments.

2. Parliament votes a special one-time $1 billion transfer to bail out the buggy whip industry. Tax collections do not change, and no change is planned for at least several years. By how much will this action increase the overall budget surplus and the primary surplus in the year that the transfer is made? in the next year? in the year after that? Assume that the nominal interest rate is constant at 10%.

3. Because of automatic stabilizers, various components of the government's budget depend on the level of output Y. The following are the main components of that budget:

Tax revenues	$1000 + 0.1Y$
Transfers	$800 - 0.05Y$
Government purchases	1800
Interest payments	100

Full-employment output is 10 000. Find the actual budget deficit and the full-employment budget deficit for
   a. $Y = 12\,000$.   **b.** $Y = 10\,000$.   **c.** $Y = 8000$.
In general, how does the relationship between the actual deficit and the full-employment deficit depend on the state of the economy?

4. Suppose that the income tax law exempts income under $8000 from tax, taxes income between $8000 and $20 000 at a 25% rate, and taxes income greater than $20 000 at a 30% rate.
   a. Find the average tax rate and the marginal tax rate for someone earning $16 000 and for someone earning $30 000.
   b. The tax law is changed so that income of less than $6000 is untaxed, income from $6000 to $20 000 is taxed at 20%, and income of more than $20 000 continues to be taxed at 30%. Repeat part (a).
   c. How will the tax law change in part (b) affect the labour supply of the person initially making $16 000? How will it affect the labour supply of the person making $30 000?

5. Suppose that all workers value their leisure at 90 goods per day. The production function relating output per day Y to the number of people working per day N is
$$Y = 250N - 0.5N^2.$$
Corresponding to this production function, the marginal product of labour is
$$MPN = 250 - N.$$
   a. Assume that there are no taxes. What are the equilibrium values of the real wage, employment N, and output Y? (*Hint:* In equilibrium, the real wage will equal both the marginal product of labour and the value of a day's leisure to workers.)
   b. A 25% tax is levied on wages. What are the equilibrium values of the real wage, employment, and output? In terms of lost output, what is the distortion cost of this tax?
   c. Suppose that the tax on wages rises to 50%. What are the equilibrium values of the real wage, employment, and output? In terms of lost output, what is the distortion cost of this higher tax rate? Compare the distortion caused by a 50% tax rate with that caused by a 25% tax rate. Is the distortion caused by a 50% tax rate twice as large, more than twice as large, or less than twice as large as that caused by a 25% tax rate? How does your answer relate to the idea of tax smoothing?

6. Suppose the goal of the government is to balance its total budget. Suppose as well that the interest rate

paid on government debt is 7% and the amount of government debt outstanding is $500 billion. How large must be the primary surplus?

7. Suppose GDP is $1000 billion, the national debt last year was $500 billion, the interest rate paid on government debt is 7%, and GDP is growing by 5% per year.
   a. If the goal of the government is to hold the debt–GDP ratio constant, what must the size of the primary surplus be? What is the size of the total budget surplus in this case?
   b. If the interest rate paid on government debt were 5% and the growth rate of GDP were 7%, what would the primary surplus need to be to maintain a constant debt–GDP ratio? What is the size of the total budget surplus in this case?

8. Evaluate the following claim: To reduce the debt–GDP ratio, governments must maintain primary surpluses.

ANALYTICAL PROBLEMS

1. Why is some provincial government spending paid for by transfers from the federal government instead of having every provincial government pay for its own spending by levying taxes on its residents? What are the advantages and disadvantages of such a system?

2. Access the Department of Finance website at www.fin.gc.ca. Follow the link "Economic and Fiscal Info" to the Fiscal Reference Tables. Open the latest issue of the Fiscal Reference Tables and find the table providing data on actual and cyclically adjusted budget balances for the federal government. Compare these values for the years 1988 and 1998. What does the size of the actual budget balance relative to the size of the cyclically adjusted budget balance imply about the state of the economy in each of those years?

3. Both transfer programs and taxes affect incentives. Consider a program designed to help the poor that promises each aid recipient a minimum income of $10 000. That is, if the recipient earns less than $10 000, the program supplements his or her income by enough to bring it up to $10 000.

   Explain why this program would adversely affect incentives for low-wage recipients. (*Hint:* Show that this program is equivalent to giving the recipient $10 000, then taxing his or her labour income at a high marginal rate.) Describe a transfer program that contains better incentives. Would that program have any disadvantages? If so, what would they be?

4. Show that Eq. (15.6), which describes how the debt–GDP ratio evolves, still holds if the primary budget deficit, the outstanding stock of government bonds, the interest rate, and the growth rate of GDP are all expressed in real, rather than nominal, terms. (*Hint:* Use the growth-rate formulas in the Appendix, Section A.7, to show that the growth rate of nominal GDP equals the growth rate of real GDP plus the inflation rate.)

5. A constitutional amendment has been proposed that would force the federal and provincial governments to balance their budgets each year so that current expenditure would be no greater than revenue. (Several provinces already have laws something like this.) Discuss some advantages and disadvantages of such an amendment. How would a balanced-budget amendment affect the following, if in the absence of such an amendment the government would run a large deficit?
   a. The use of automatic stabilizers.
   b. The government's ability to "smooth" taxes over time.
   c. The government's ability to make capital investments.

APPENDIX 15.A

THE DEBT–GDP RATIO

In this appendix, we derive Eq. (15.6), which shows how the debt–GDP ratio changes in value from one year to the next. We begin with the definition of the budget deficit provided by Eq. (15.5):

$$\Delta B = \text{nominal government budget deficit}$$
$$= -(\text{nominal government budget surplus}). \qquad (15.5)$$

Next, we substitute into this expression the definition of the government budget surplus provided by Eq. (15.1). The result is

$$\Delta B = G + TR - T + INT. \qquad (15.A.1)$$

The interest payment the government makes on its debt in the current fiscal year, INT, is the product of the interest rate owed on that debt, i, and the size of the debt accumulated in past years, B_{-1}. Thus, $INT = iB_{-1}$. It is also useful to note that by definition $\Delta B = B - B_{-1}$. Using these two results, we can rewrite Eq. (15.A.1) as

$$B = G + TR - T + iB_{-1} + B_{-1}. \qquad (15.A.2)$$

Our goal is to describe the change in the debt–GDP ratio from one year to the next. This change can be expressed as

$$\Delta\left(\frac{B}{Y}\right) - \left(\frac{B}{Y}\right) - \left(\frac{B_{-1}}{Y_{-1}}\right). \qquad (15.A.3)$$

We substitute Eq. (15.A.2) into Eq. (15.A.3) to produce

$$\Delta\left(\frac{B}{Y}\right) = \left(\frac{G + TR - T + iB_{-1} + B_{-1}}{Y}\right) - \left(\frac{B_{-1}}{Y_{-1}}\right). \qquad (15.A.4)$$

The size of GDP in the current period, Y, is equal to the size of GDP in the previous period, Y_{-1}, times $(1 + g)$ where g is the rate of growth in GDP from one year to the next. Thus, for example, if GDP grows by 10% per year ($g = 0.10$), and if GDP were equal to $1000 billion last year ($Y_{-1} = 1000$), then GDP this year is 10% higher, or $1100 million. Thus, $Y = (1 + g)Y_{-1}$. Our last step is to replace Y_{-1} in Eq. (15.A.4) with $Y/(1 + g)$:

$$\Delta\left(\frac{B}{Y}\right) = \left(\frac{G + TR - T + iB_{-1} + B_{-1}}{Y}\right) - \left(\frac{B_{-1}(1 + g)}{Y}\right).$$

Now we need only gather together all of the terms involving B_{-1}. The result is Eq. (15.6):

$$\Delta\left(\frac{B}{Y}\right) = \left(\frac{G + TR - T}{Y}\right) + (i - g)\left(\frac{B_{-1}}{Y}\right). \qquad (15.6)$$

Appendix
Some Useful Analytical Tools

This Appendix reviews some basic algebraic and graphical tools that are used in this book.

A.1 FUNCTIONS AND GRAPHS

A function is a relationship among two or more variables in which one variable is defined by the other(s). For an economic illustration of a function, suppose that in a certain firm, each worker employed can produce five units of output per day. Let

N = the number of workers employed by the firm;
Y = total daily output of the firm.

In this example, the relationship of output Y to the number of workers N is

$$Y = 5N. \tag{A.1}$$

Equation (A.1) is an example of a function relating the variable Y to the variable N. Using this function, for any number of workers N, we can calculate the total amount of output Y that the firm can produce each day. For example, if $N = 3$, then $Y = 15$.

Functions can be described graphically as well as algebraically. The graph of the function $Y = 5N$, for values of N between 0 and 16, is shown in Figure A.1. Output Y is shown on the vertical axis, and the number of workers N is shown on the horizontal axis. Points on the line OAB satisfy Eq. (A.1). For example, at point A, $N = 4$ and $Y = 20$, a combination of N and Y that satisfies Eq. (A.1). Similarly, at point B, $N = 12.5$ and $Y = 62.5$, which also satisfies the relationship $Y = 5N$. Note that (at B, for example) the relationship between Y and N allows the variables to have values that are not whole numbers. Allowing fractional values of N and Y is reasonable because workers can work

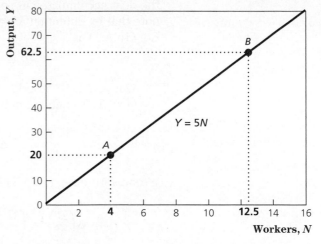

FIGURE A.1

Points on the line OAB satisfy the relationship $Y = 5N$. Because the graph of the function $Y = 5N$ is a straight line, this function is called a linear function.

part time or overtime, and a unit of output may be only partially completed during a day.

Functions, such as $Y = 5N$, whose graph is a straight line, are called *linear functions*. Functions whose graphs are not a line are called *nonlinear*. An example of a *nonlinear* function is

$$Y = 20\sqrt{N}. \tag{A.2}$$

The graph of the nonlinear function $Y = 20\sqrt{N}$ is shown in Figure A.2. All points on the curve satisfy Eq. (A.2). For example, at point C, $N = 4$ and $Y = 20\sqrt{4} = 40$. At point D, $N = 9$ and $Y = 20\sqrt{9} = 60$.

Both examples of functions given so far are exact numerical relationships. We can also write functions in

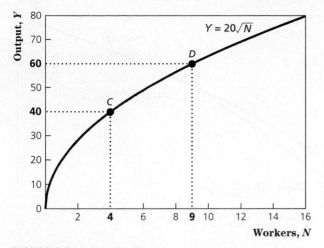

FIGURE A.2

The function $Y = 20\sqrt{N}$, whose graph is shown in this figure, is an example of a nonlinear function.

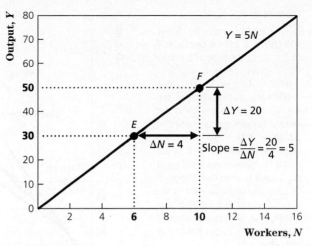

FIGURE A.3

The slope of a function equals the change in the variable on the vertical axis (Y) divided by the change in the variable on the horizontal axis (N). For example, between points E and F, the increase in N, ΔN, equals 4 and the increase in Y, ΔY, equals 20. Therefore, the slope of the function between E and F, $\Delta Y/\Delta N$, equals 5. In general, the slope of a linear function is constant, so the slope of this function between any two points is 5.

more general terms, using letters or symbols. For example, we might write

$$Y = G(N). \tag{A.3}$$

Equation (A.3) states that there is some general relationship between the number of workers N and the amount of output Y, which is represented by a function G. The numerical functions given in Eqs. (A.1) and (A.2) are specific examples of such a general relationship.

A.2 SLOPES OF FUNCTIONS

Suppose that two variables N and Y are related by a function $Y = G(N)$. Generally speaking, if we start from some given combination of N and Y that satisfies the function G, the *slope* of the function G at that point indicates by how much Y changes when N changes by one unit.

To define the slope more precisely, we suppose that the current value of N is a specific number N_1 so that the current value of Y equals $G(N_1)$. Now, consider what happens if N is increased by an amount ΔN (ΔN is read "delta N" or "the change in N"). Output Y depends on N; therefore, if N changes, Y must also change. The value of N is now $N_1 + \Delta N$, so the value of Y after N increases is $G(N_1 + \Delta N)$. The *change* in Y is

$$\Delta Y = G(N_1 + \Delta N) - G(N_1).$$

The slope of the function G, for an increase in N from N_1 to $N_1 + \Delta N$, is

$$\text{slope} = \frac{\Delta Y}{\Delta N} = \frac{G(N_1 + \Delta N) - G(N_1)}{(N_1 + \Delta N) - N_1}. \tag{A.4}$$

Note that if $\Delta N = 1$, the slope equals ΔY, the change in Y.

Figures A.3 and A.4 show graphically how to determine slopes for the two functions discussed in the preceding section. Figure A.3 shows the graph of the function $Y = 5N$ (as in Figure A.1). Suppose that we start from point E in Figure A.3, where $N = 6$ and $Y = 30$. If N is increased by 4 (for example), we move to point F on the graph, where $N = 10$ and $Y = 50$. Between E and F, $\Delta N = 10 - 6 = 4$ and $\Delta Y = 50 - 30 = 20$, so the slope $\Delta Y/\Delta N = 20/4 = 5$.

In general, the slope of a linear function is the same at all points. You can prove this result for the linear function $Y = 5N$ by showing that for any change ΔN, $\Delta Y = 5\Delta N$. So, for this particular linear function, the slope $\Delta Y/\Delta N$ always equals 5, a constant number.

For a nonlinear function, such as $Y = 20\sqrt{N}$, the slope is not constant but depends on both the initial value of N and the size of the change in N. These results are illustrated in Figure A.4, on the next page, which displays the graph of the function $Y = 20\sqrt{N}$ (as in Figure A.2). Suppose that we are initially at point G, where $N = 1$ and $Y = 20$, and we increase N by 8 units. After the increase in N we are at point D, where $N = 9$ and $Y = 20\sqrt{9} = 60$. Between G and D, $\Delta N = 9 - 1 = 8$ and $\Delta Y = 60 - 20 = 40$. Thus, the slope of the function between G and D is $40/8 = 5$. Geometrically, the slope of the function between G and D equals the slope of the straight line between G and D.

Starting once again from point G in Figure A.4, if we instead increase N by 3 units, we come to point C, where $N = 4$ and $Y = 20\sqrt{9} = 40$. In this case $\Delta N = 3$ and $\Delta Y = 40 - 20 = 20$, so the slope between G and C is $20/3 = 6.67$, which is not the same as the slope of 5 that we

FIGURE A.4

Between points G and D, the change in N (ΔN) is 8 and the change in Y (ΔY) is 40, so the slope of the function between points G and D is $\Delta Y/\Delta N = 40/8 = 5$. This slope is the same as the slope of the line GD. Similarly, the slope of the function between points G and C is $\Delta Y/\Delta N = 20/3 = 6.67$. The slope of the line tangent to point G, which equals 10, approximates the slope of the function for very small changes in N. Generally, when we refer to the slope of a nonlinear function at a specific point, we mean the slope of the line tangent to the function at that point.

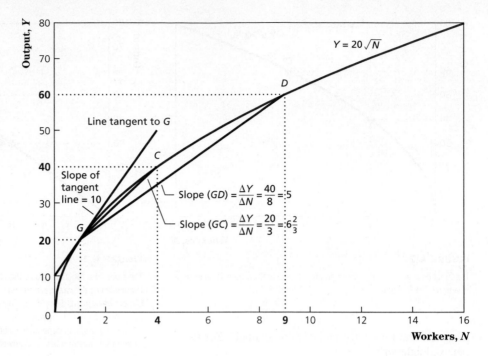

calculated when earlier we increased N by 8 units. Geometrically, the slope of the line between G and C is greater than the slope of the line between G and D; that is, line GC is steeper than line GD.

In Figure A.4, we have also drawn a line that touches but does not cross the graph of the function at point G; this line is *tangent* to the graph of the function at point G. If you start from point G and find the slope of the function for different values of ΔN, you will discover that the smaller the value of ΔN is, the closer the slope will be to the slope of the tangent line. For example, if you compare the slope of line GD (for which $\Delta N = 8$) with the slope of line GC (for which $\Delta N = 3$), you will see that of the two the slope of line GC is closer to the slope of the line tangent to point G. For values of ΔN even smaller than 3, the slope would be still closer to the slope of the tangent line.

These observations lead to an important result: *For small values of ΔN, the slope of a function at any point is closely approximated by the slope of the line tangent to the function at that point.* Unless specified otherwise, in this book, when we refer to the slope of a nonlinear function, we mean the slope of the line tangent to the function at the specified point. Thus, in Figure A.4, the slope of the function at point G means the slope of the line tangent to the function at point G, which happens to be 10.[1]

The numerical example illustrated in Figure A.4 shows that the slope of a nonlinear function depends on the size of the increase in N being considered. The slope of a nonlinear function also depends on the point at which the slope is being measured. In Figure A.4, note that the slope of a line drawn tangent to point D, for example, would be less than the slope of a line drawn tangent to point G. Thus, the slope of this particular function (measured with respect to small changes in N) is greater at G than at D.

A.3 ELASTICITIES

Like slopes, elasticities indicate how much one variable responds when a second variable changes. Suppose, again, that there is a function relating Y to N, so that when N changes, Y changes as well. The *elasticity* of Y with respect to N is defined to be the percentage change in Y, $\Delta Y/Y$, divided by the percentage change in N, $\Delta N/N$. Writing the formula, we have

$$\text{elasticity of } Y \text{ with respect to } N = \frac{\Delta Y/Y}{\Delta N/N}.$$

Because the slope of a function is $\Delta Y/\Delta N$, we can also write the elasticity of Y with respect to N as the slope times (N/Y).

If the elasticity of Y with respect to N is large, a 1% change in N causes a large percentage change in Y. Thus, a large elasticity of Y with respect to N means that Y is very sensitive to changes in N.

---

[1] Showing that the slope of the line tangent to point G equals 10 requires basic calculus. The derivative of the function $Y = 20\sqrt{N}$, which is the same as the slope, is $dY/dN = 10/\sqrt{N}$. Evaluating this derivative at $N = 1$ yields a slope of 10.

A.4 FUNCTIONS OF SEVERAL VARIABLES

A function can relate more than two variables. To continue the example of Section A.1, suppose that the firm's daily output Y depends on both the number of workers N the firm employs and the number of machines (equivalently, the amount of capital) K the firm owns. Specifically, the function relating Y to K and N might be

$$Y = 2\sqrt{K}\sqrt{N}. \qquad (A.5)$$

So, if there are 100 machines and 9 workers, by substituting $K = 100$ and $N = 9$ into Eq. (A.5), we get the output $Y = 2\sqrt{100}\sqrt{9} = 2 \times 10 \times 3 = 60$.

We can also write a function of several variables in general terms using symbols or letters. A general way to write the relationship between output Y and the two inputs, capital K and labour N, is

$$Y = F(K, N).$$

This equation is a slight simplification of a relationship called the production function, which we introduce in Chapter 3.

The graph of a function relating three variables requires three dimensions. As a convenient way to graph such a function on a two-dimensional page, we hold one of the right-hand-side variables constant. To graph the function in Eq. (A.5), for example, we might hold the number of machines K constant at a value of 100. If we substitute 100 for K, Eq. (A.5) becomes

$$Y = 2\sqrt{100}\sqrt{N} = 20\sqrt{N}. \qquad (A.6)$$

With K held constant at 100, Eq. (A.6) is identical to Eq. (A.2). Like Eq. (A.2), Eq. (A.6) is a relationship between Y and N only and thus can be graphed in two dimensions. The graph of Eq. (A.6), shown as the solid curve in Figure A.5, is identical to the graph of Eq. (A.2) in Figure A.2.

A.5 SHIFTS OF A CURVE

Suppose that the relationship of output Y to machines K and workers N is given by Eq. (A.5) and we hold K constant at 100. As in Section A.4, with K held constant at 100, Eq. (A.5) reduces to Eq. (A.6) and the solid curve in Figure A.5 shows the relationship between workers N and output Y. At point C in Figure A.5, for example, $N = 4$ and $Y = 20\sqrt{4} = 40$. At point D, $N = 9$ and $Y = 20\sqrt{9} = 60$.

Now, suppose that the firm purchases additional machines, raising the number of machines K from 100 to 225. If we substitute this new value for K, Eq. (A.5) becomes

$$Y = 2\sqrt{225}\sqrt{N} = 30\sqrt{N}. \qquad (A.7)$$

Equation (A.7) is shown graphically as the dashed curve in Figure A.5. Note that the increase in K has shifted the curve up. Because of the increase in the number of machines, the amount of daily output Y that can be produced for any given number of workers N has risen. For example, initially when N equalled 9, output Y equalled 60 (point D in Figure A.5). After the increase in K, if $N = 9$, then $Y = 30\sqrt{9} = 90$ (point J in Figure A.5).

This example illustrates some important general points about the graphs of functions of several variables.

FIGURE A.5

Suppose that output Y depends on capital K and workers N, according to the function in Eq. (A.5). If we hold K fixed at 100, the relationship between Y and N is shown by the solid curve. If K rises to 225 so that more output can be produced with a given number of workers, the curve showing the relationship between Y and N shifts upward, from the solid curve to the dashed curve. In general, a change in any right-hand-side variable that does not appear on an axis of the graph causes the curve to shift.

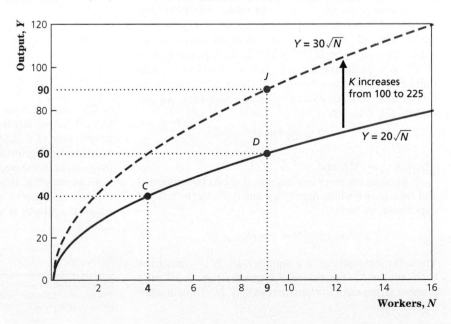

1. To graph a function of several variables in two dimensions, we hold all but one of the right-hand-side variables constant.

2. The one right-hand-side variable that is not held constant (N in this example) appears on the horizontal axis. Changes in this variable do not shift the graph of the function. Instead, changes in the variable on the horizontal axis represent movements along the curve that represents the function.

3. The right-hand-side variables held constant for the purpose of drawing the graph (K in this example) do not appear on either axis of the graph. If the value of one of these variables is changed, the entire curve shifts. In this example, for any number of workers N, the increase in machines K means that more output Y can be produced. Thus, the curve shifts up, from the solid curve to the dashed curve in Figure A.5.

A.6 EXPONENTS

Powers of numbers or variables can be expressed by using superscripts called *exponents*. In the following examples, 2 and 4 are the exponents:

$$5^2 = 5 \times 5, \text{ and } Z^4 = Z \times Z \times Z \times Z.$$

For any numbers Z, a, and b, exponents obey the following rules:

$$Z^a \times Z^b = Z^{a+b}, \text{ and } (Z^a)^b = Z^{ab}.$$

An illustration of the first rule is $5^2 \times 5^3 = (5 \times 5) \times (5 \times 5 \times 5) = 5^5$. An illustration of the second rule is $(5^3)^2 = (5^3) \times (5^3) = (5 \times 5 \times 5) \times (5 \times 5 \times 5) = 5^6$.

Exponents do not have to be whole numbers. For example, $5^{0.5}$ represents the square root of 5. To understand why, note that by the second of the two rules for exponents, $(5^{0.5})^2 = 5^{(0.5)2} = 5^1 = 5$. That is, the square of $5^{0.5}$ is 5. Similarly, for any number Z and any whole number q, $Z^{1/q}$ is the qth root of Z. Thus, $5^{0.25}$ means the fourth root of 5, for example. Using exponents, we can rewrite Eq. (A.5) as

$$Y = 2K^{0.5}N^{0.5},$$

where $K^{0.5} = \sqrt{K}$ and $N^{0.5} = \sqrt{N}$.

In general, consider any number that can be expressed as a ratio of two whole numbers p and q. Using the rules of exponents, we have

$$Z^{p/q} = (Z^p)^{1/q} = q\text{th root of } Z^p.$$

Thus, for example, as 0.7 equals 7/10, $N^{0.7}$ equals the tenth root of N^7. For values of N greater than 1, $N^{0.7}$ is a number larger than the square root of N, $N^{0.5}$, but smaller than N itself.

Exponents also may be zero or negative. In general, the following two relationships hold:

$$Z^0 = 1, \text{ and } Z^{-a} = \frac{1}{Z}.$$

Here is a useful way to relate exponents and elasticities: Suppose that two variables Y and N are related by a function of the form

$$Y = kN^a, \tag{A.8}$$

where a is a number and k can be either a number or a function of variables other than N. Then the elasticity of Y with respect to N (see Section A.3) equals a.[2]

A.7 GROWTH RATE FORMULAS

Let X and Z be any two variables, not necessarily related by a function, that are changing over time. Let $\Delta X/X$ and $\Delta Z/Z$ represent the growth rates (percentage changes) of X and Z, respectively. Then, the following rules provide useful approximations (proofs of the various rules are included for reference):

Rule 1. The growth rate of the product of X and Z equals the growth rate of X plus the growth rate of Z.

Proof. Suppose that X increases by ΔX and Z increases by ΔZ. Then the absolute increase in the product of X and Z is $(X + \Delta X)(Z + \Delta Z) - XZ$, and the growth rate of the product of X and Z is

$$\begin{aligned} \text{growth rate of } (XZ) &= \frac{(X + \Delta X)(Z + \Delta Z) - XZ}{XZ} \\ &= \frac{(\Delta X)Z + (\Delta Z)Z + \Delta X \Delta Z}{XZ} \\ &= \frac{\Delta X}{X} + \frac{\Delta Z}{Z} + \frac{\Delta X \Delta Z}{XZ}. \end{aligned} \tag{A.9}$$

The last term on the right-hand side of Eq. (A.9), $(\Delta X \Delta Z)/XZ$, equals the growth rate of X, $\Delta X/X$, times the growth rate of Z, $\Delta Z/Z$. This term is generally small; for example, if the growth rates of X and Z are both 5% (0.05), the product of the two growth rates is only 0.25% (0.0025). If we assume that this last term is small enough to ignore, Eq. (A.9) indicates that the growth rate of the product XZ equals the growth rate of X, $\Delta X/X$, plus the growth rate of Z, $\Delta Z/Z$.

---

[2] Showing that the elasticity equals the exponent requires basic calculus. The derivate of $Y = kN^a$ is $dY/dN = akN^{a-1} = a(Y/N)$. Thus elasticity $= (dY/dN)/(Y/N) = a$.

Rule 2. The growth rate of the ratio of X to Z is the growth rate of X minus the growth rate of Z.

Proof. Let W be the ratio of X to Z, so $W = X/Z$. Then $X = ZW$. By Rule 1, as X equals the product of Z and W, the growth rate of X equals the growth rate of Z plus the growth rate of W:

$$\frac{\Delta X}{X} = \frac{\Delta Z}{Z} + \frac{\Delta W}{W}.$$

Rearranging this equation to put $\Delta W/W$ on the left-hand side and recalling that $\Delta W/W$ equals the growth rate of (X/Z), we have

$$\text{growth rate of } (X/Z) = \frac{\Delta X}{X} - \frac{\Delta Z}{Z}. \qquad \text{(A.10)}$$

Rule 3. Suppose that Y is a variable that is a function of two other variables X and Z. Then

$$\frac{\Delta Y}{Y} = \eta_{Y,X} \frac{\Delta X}{X} + \eta_{Y,Z} \frac{\Delta Z}{Z}, \qquad \text{(A.11)}$$

where $\eta_{Y,X}$ is the elasticity of Y with respect to X, and $\eta_{Y,Z}$ is the elasticity of Y with respect to Z.

Proof (informal). Suppose that only X changes so that $\Delta Z/Z = 0$. Then Eq. (A.11) boils down to the definition of an elasticity, $\eta_{Y,X} = (\Delta Y/Y)/(\Delta X/X)$, as in Section A.3. Similarly, if only Z changes, Eq. (A.11) becomes $\eta_{Y,Z} = (\Delta Y/Y)/(\Delta Z/Z)$, which is the definition of the elasticity of Y with respect to Z. If both X and Z change, Eq. (A.11) indicates that the overall effect on Y is approximately equal to the sum of the individual effects on Y of the change in X and the change in Z.

Rule 4. The growth rate of X raised to the power a, or X^a, is a times the growth rate of X:

$$\text{growth rate of } (X^a) = a \frac{\Delta X}{X}. \qquad \text{(A.12)}$$

Proof. Let $Y = X^a$. Applying the rule from Eq. (A.8) and setting $k = 1$, we find that the elasticity of Y with respect to X equals a. Therefore, by Eq. (A.11), the growth rate of Y equals a times the growth rate of X. Because $Y = X^a$, the growth rate of Y is the same as the growth rate of X^a, which proves the relationship in Eq. (A.12).

Example: The real interest rate. To apply the growth rate formulas, we derive the equation that relates the real interest rate to the nominal interest rate and the inflation rate, Eq. (2.12).

The real value of any asset, say, a savings account, equals the nominal or dollar value of the asset divided by the price level:

$$\text{real asset value} = \frac{\text{nominal interest rate}}{\text{price level}}. \qquad \text{(A.13)}$$

The real value of an asset is the ratio of the nominal asset value to the price level, so, according to Rule 2, the growth rate of the real asset value is approximately equal to the growth rate of the nominal asset value minus the growth rate of the price level. The growth rate of the real value of an interest-bearing asset equals the real interest rate earned by that asset; the growth rate of the nominal value of an interest-bearing asset is the nominal interest rate for that asset; and the growth rate of the price level is the inflation rate. Therefore, Rule 2 implies the relationship

real interest rate = nominal interest rate − inflation rate,

which is the relationship given in Eq. (2.12) (p. 40).

PROBLEMS

1. Graph the function $Y = 3X + 5$ for $0 \leq X \leq 5$. What is the slope of this function?
2. Graph the function $Y = X^2 + 2$ for $0 \leq X \leq 5$. Starting from the point at which $X = 1$, find the slope of the function for $\Delta X = 1$ and $X = -1$. What is the slope of the line tangent to the function at $X = 1$? (See Problem 3.)
3. For the function $Y = X^2 + 2$, use Eq. (A.4) to write a general expression for the slope. This expression for the slope will depend on the initial value of X, X_1, and on the change in X, ΔX. For values of ΔX sufficiently small that the term $(\Delta X)^2$ can be ignored, show that the slope depends only on the initial value of X, X_1. What is the slope of the function (which is the same as the slope of the tangent line) when $X_1 = 1$?
4. Suppose that the amount of output Y that a firm can produce depends on its amount of capital K and the number of workers employed N, according to the function

$$Y = K^{0.3} N^{0.7}.$$

  a. Suppose that $N = 100$. Give the function that relates Y to K and graph this relationship for $0 \leq K \leq 50$. (You need calculate only enough values of Y to get a rough idea of the shape of the function.)
  b. What happens to the function relating Y and K and to the graph of the relationship if N rises to 200? If N falls to 50? Give an economic interpretation.
  c. For the function relating Y to K and N, find the elasticity of Y with respect to K and the elasticity of Y with respect to N.
5. Use a calculator to find each of the following:
  a. $5^{0.3}$
  b. $5^{0.3} 5^{0.2}$
  c. $(5^{0.25})^2$
  d. $(5^{0.5} 5^{0.3})^2 5^{0.4}$
  e. $5^{0.2}/5^{0.5}$
  f. $5^{-0.5}$

6. Answer the following:

a. Nominal GDP equals real GDP times the GDP deflator (see Section 2.4). Suppose that nominal GDP growth is 12% and real GDP growth is 4%. What is inflation (the rate of growth of the GDP deflator)?

b. The "velocity of money," V, is defined by the equation

$$V = \frac{PY}{M},$$

where P is the price level, Y is real output, and M is the money supply (see Eq. 7.4, p. 217). In a particular year, velocity is constant, money growth is 10%, and inflation (the rate of growth of the price level) is 7%. What is real output growth?

c. Output Y is related to capital K and the number of workers N by the function

$$Y = 10K^{0.3}N^{0.7}.$$

In a particular year, the capital stock grows by 2% and the number of workers grows by 1%. By how much does output grow?

GLOSSARY

(The number in parentheses after the glossary term is the chapter(s) in which that term first appears or is most extensively discussed.)

absorption: (5) total spending by domestic residents, firms, and governments, equal to $C + I + G$. (p. 139)

acyclical: (8) not displaying a regular pattern of behaviour over the business cycle. See *procyclical, countercyclical*. (p. 233)

aggregate demand (*AD*) curve: (9) in a diagram with output on the horizontal axis and the price level on the vertical axis, the downward-sloping relation between the price level and the economywide demand for output. (p. 273)

aggregate demand for labour: (3) the sum of the labour demands of all employers in an economy. (p. 63)

aggregate demand policies: (9, 12) fiscal and monetary policies, both of which cause the aggregate demand curve to shift. (pp. 278, 403)

aggregate demand shocks: (12) shocks to the economy that shift the *IS* curve or the *LM* curve and, thus, affect the aggregate demand for output. (p. 412)

aggregate supply (*AS*) curve: (11) in a diagram with output on the horizontal axis and the price level on the vertical axis, the relation between the price level and the total amount of output that firms supply. (p. 371)

aggregate supply of labour: (3) the sum of the labour supplied by everyone in the economy. (p. 64)

aggregation: (1) the process of adding individual economic variables to obtain economywide totals. (p. 6)

arbitrage: (10) financial-asset traders who earn a living spotting differences in expected gross nominal rates of return and then buying and selling assets as appropriate to realize a profit. (p. 310)

automatic stabilizers: (15) provisions in the government's budget that automatically cause government spending to rise or taxes to fall when GDP falls. (p. 513)

average labour productivity: (1) the amount of output produced per unit of labour input (per worker or per hour of work). (p. 2)

average tax rate: (15) the total amount of taxes paid divided by the taxpayer's income. (p. 516)

balance of payments: (5) the net increase (domestic less foreign) in a country's official reserve assets; also known as the official settlements balance. (p. 135)

balance of payments accounts: (5) the record of a country's international transactions, consisting of the current account and the capital account. (p. 131)

bank rate: (14) the upper edge of the Bank of Canada's operating band for the overnight interest rate; the interest rate on loans from the Bank to direct clearers. (p. 483)

bank reserves: (14) liquid assets held by banks to meet the demands for withdrawals by depositors or to pay the cheques drawn on depositors' accounts. (p. 475)

bank run: (14) a large-scale withdrawal of deposits from a bank, caused by depositors' fear that the bank may go bankrupt and not pay depositors in full. (p. 478)

boom: (8) in a business cycle, the period of time during which aggregate economic activity grows; also known as an expansion. (p. 229)

budget deficit: (2) government expenditure minus government revenue. See *government expenditure, government revenue*. (p. 30)

budget surplus: (2) government revenue minus government expenditure. See *government expenditure, government revenue, government saving*. (p. 30)

business cycle: (8) a decline in aggregate economic activity (a contraction or recession) to a low point (a trough), followed by a recovery of activity (an expansion or boom) to a high point (a peak). A complete business cycle can be measured from peak to peak or from trough to trough. (p. 229)

capital account: (5) the record of a country's international trade in existing assets, either real or financial. (p. 134)

capital account balance: (5) the value of capital inflows (credit items) minus the value of capital outflows (debit items) in a country's capital account. (p. 134)

capital and financial account: (5) the official name for the record of a country's trade in existing assets. (p. 134)

capital good: (2) a good that is produced, is used to produce other goods, and—unlike an intermediate good—is not used up in the same period that it is produced. (p. 23)

capital–labour ratio: (6) the amount of capital per worker, equal to the capital stock divided by the number of workers. (p. 169)

central bank: (14) the governmental institution responsible for monetary policy, such as the Bank of Canada, the Federal Reserve System in the United States, and the Bank of Japan in Japan. (p. 473)

chronically unemployed: (3) workers who are unemployed a large fraction of the time. (p. 81)

closed economy: (1) a national economy that does not have trading or financial relationships with the rest of the world. (p. 4)

coincident variable: (8) a variable with peaks and troughs that occur at about the same time as the corresponding business cycle peaks and troughs. See *lagging variable, leading variable*. (p. 233)

cold turkey: (13) a rapid and decisive reduction in the growth rate of the money supply aimed at reducing the rate of inflation; in contrast to *gradualism*. (p. 465)

comparative statics experiments: (1) experiments conducted by macroeconomists. (p. 9)

consumer price index: (2) a price index calculated as the current cost of a fixed basket of consumer goods divided by the cost of the basket in the base period. (p. 36)

consumption: (2) spending by domestic households on final goods and services. (p. 25)

consumption-smoothing motive: (4) the preference of most people for a relatively constant or stable pattern of consumption over time, as opposed to having high consumption at some times and low consumption at others. (p. 94)

contraction: (8) in a business cycle, the period of time during which aggregate economic activity is falling; also known as a recession. (p. 229)

countercyclical: (8) tending to move in the opposite direction to aggregate economic activity over the business cycle (up in contractions, down in expansions). See *procyclical, acyclical.* (p. 233)

credibility: (14) the degree to which the public believes the central bank's announcements about future policy. (p. 494)

credit channel: (14) the effects of monetary policy on credit supply and credit demand, which affect the economy in addition to effects operating through interest rates and exchange rates. (p. 490)

crowding out effect: (9, 12) the reduction in consumption and investment resulting from the increase in interest rates. (pp. 269, 404)

currency–deposit ratio: (14) the ratio of the currency held by the public to the public's deposits in banks. (p. 478)

currency union: (10) a group of countries that agree to share a common currency. (p. 334)

current account: (5) the record of a country's international trade in currently produced goods and services. (p. 131)

current account balance: (2, 5) payments received from abroad in exchange for currently produced goods and services (including factor services), minus the analogous payments made to foreigners by the domestic economy. (pp. 31, 133)

current transfers: (5) payments made from one country to another that do not correspond to the purchase of any good, service, or asset; examples are foreign aid or gifts by domestic residents to foreigners. (p. 132)

cyclical unemployment: (3) the excess of the actual unemployment rate over the natural rate of unemployment; equivalently, unemployment that occurs when output is below its full-employment level. (p. 82)

debt–GDP ratio: (15) the quantity of government debt outstanding divided by GDP. (p. 523)

deflation: (1) a situation in which the prices of most goods and services are falling over time. (p. 4)

demand for money: (7) the quantity of monetary assets, such as cash and chequing accounts, that people choose to hold in their portfolios. (p. 211)

depository institutions: (14) privately owned banks and other institutions (such as credit unions) that accept deposits from and make loans directly to the public. (p. 473)

depreciation: (4) the amount of capital that wears out during a given period of time. (p. 109)

depression: (8) a particularly severe and prolonged downturn in economic activity. (p. 229)

desired capital stock: (4) the amount of capital that allows a firm to earn the highest possible expected profit. (p. 107)

devaluation: (10) a reduction in the value of a currency by official government action under a fixed-exchange-rate system. (p. 299)

diminishing marginal productivity: (3) a feature of production functions that implies that the more a particular factor of production is used, the less extra output can be gained by increasing the use of that factor still further (with the usage of other factors of production held constant). For example, for a given capital stock, adding an extra worker increases output more when employment is initially low than when it is initially high. (p. 53)

direct clearers: (14) large banks that hold reserves at the Bank of Canada to settle net transfers. (p. 483)

discouraged workers: (3) people who stop searching for jobs because they have become discouraged by lack of success at finding a job; discouraged workers are not included in the official unemployment rate. (p. 80)

discretion: (14) the freedom of the central bank to conduct monetary policy in any way that it believes will advance the ultimate objectives of low and stable inflation, high economic growth, and low unemployment; in contrast to *rules.* (p. 491)

disinflation: (13) a fall in the rate of inflation. (p. 465)

distortions: (15) tax-induced deviations in economic behaviour from the efficient, free market outcome. (p. 517)

duration: (3) the length of time that an unemployment spell lasts. (p. 80)

economic model: (1) a simplified description of some aspect of the economy, usually expressed in mathematical form. (p. 8)

economic theory: (1) a set of ideas about the economy that have been organized in a logical framework. (p. 8)

effective tax rate: (4) a single measure of the tax burden on capital that summarizes the many provisions of the tax code that affect investment. (p. 113)

efficiency wage: (12) the real wage that maximizes worker effort or efficiency per dollar of real wages received. (p. 434)

efficiency wage model: (12) a model of the labour market in which because workers exert more effort when they receive a higher real wage, profit-maximizing employers choose to pay a real wage that is higher than the real wage that clears the labour market; the efficiency wage model can be used to help explain real-wage rigidity and the existence of unemployment. (p. 432)

effort curve: (12) the relation between the level of effort put forth by workers and the real wage; its positive slope indicates that a higher real wage induces workers to exert greater effort. (p. 432)

empirical analysis: (1) a comparison of the implications of an economic theory or model with real-world data. (p. 8)

employment ratio: (3) the fraction of the adult population that is employed. (p. 79)

endogenous growth theory: (6) a new branch of growth theory that tries to explain productivity growth (hence, the growth rate of output) within a model of economic growth. (p. 184)

equilibrium: (1) a situation in which the quantities demanded and supplied in a market or set of markets are equal. (p. 9)

exchange fund account: (14) the federal government's holdings of foreign exchange, managed by the Bank of Canada; purchases and sales of foreign currencies from this account can influence the exchange rate. (p. 488)

exchange rate: (1, 10) the number of units of foreign currency that can be purchased with one unit of the home currency; also known as the nominal exchange rate. (pp. 4, 295)

exchange rate channel: (14) the effects of monetary policy that work through changes in the real exchange rate. (p. 490)

expansion: (8) in a business cycle, the period of time during which aggregate economic activity is rising; also known as a boom. (p. 229)

expectations-augmented Phillips curve: (13) an inverse relation between unanticipated inflation and cyclical unemployment. (p. 446)

expectations theory of the term structure: (7) the idea that investors compare the returns on bonds with differing times to maturity to see which is expected to give them the highest return. (p. 205)

expected after-tax real interest rate: (4) the nominal after-tax rate of return (equal to the nominal interest rate times 1 minus the tax rate) minus the expected rate of inflation; equals the expected increase in the real value of an asset after payment of taxes on interest income. (p. 101)

expected real interest rate: (2) the nominal interest rate minus the expected rate of inflation; equals the expected increase in the real value of an asset. (p. 41)

expected returns: (7) the rates of return on real or financial assets that financial investors expect to earn. (p. 204)

expenditure approach: (2) a procedure for measuring economic activity by adding the amount spent by all purchasers of final goods and services. (p. 19)

export: (1) the selling of goods to other countries. (p. 4)

factors of production: (3) inputs to the production process, such as capital goods, labour, raw materials, and energy. (p. 48)

_FE_ line: (9) see _full-employment line._ (p. 245)

final goods and services: (2) goods and services that are the end products of the production process, in contrast to intermediate goods and services. (p. 22)

financial inflow: (5) a credit (plus) item in a country's financial and capital account that arises when a resident of the country sells an asset to someone in another country. (p. 134)

financial outflow: (5) a debit (minus) item in a country's financial and capital account that arises when a resident of the country buys an asset from abroad. (p. 134)

fiscal policy: (1) policy concerning the level and composition of government spending and taxation. (p. 5)

fixed-exchange-rate system: (10) a system in which exchange rates are set at officially determined levels and are changed only by direct governmental action. (p. 296)

flexible-exchange-rate system: (10) a system in which exchange rates are not officially fixed but are determined by conditions of supply and demand in the foreign exchange market; also known as a _floating-exchange-rate system._ (p. 295)

floating-exchange-rate system: (10) see _flexible-exchange-rate system._ (p. 295)

flow variable: (2) a variable that is measured per unit of time; an example is GDP, which is measured as output per year or quarter. See _stock variable._ (p. 32)

foreign exchange market: (10) the market in which the currencies of different nations are traded. (p. 295)

fractional reserve banking: (14) a banking system in which banks hold reserves equal to a fraction of their deposits so that the reserve–deposit ratio is less than 1. (p. 475)

frictional unemployment: (3) the unemployment that arises as the result of the matching process in which workers search for suitable jobs and firms search for suitable workers. (p. 81)

full-employment deficit: (15) what the government budget deficit would be, given the tax and spending policies currently in force, if the economy were operating at its full-employment level. (p. 513)

full-employment level of employment: (3) the equilibrium level of employment, achieved after wages and prices fully adjust. (p. 71)

full-employment (_FE_) line: (9) a vertical line representing full-employment output in a diagram with output on the horizontal axis and the real interest rate on the vertical axis. (p. 245)

full-employment output: (3) the level of output that firms supply when wages and prices in the economy have fully adjusted to their equilibrium levels. (p. 77)

full-employment surplus: (15) what the government budget surplus would be, given the tax and spending policies currently in place, if the economy were operating at its full-employment level. (p. 513)

fundamental identity of national income accounting: (2) the accounting identity that states that total production, total income, and total expenditure during a given period are equal. (p. 20)

fundamental value of the exchange rate: (10) the value of the exchange rate that would be determined by the forces of supply and demand in the foreign exchange market, in the absence of government intervention. (p. 324)

GDP: (2) see _gross domestic product._ (p. 20)

GDP deflator: (2) a measure of the price level, calculated as the ratio of current nominal GDP to current real GDP. (p. 36)

general equilibrium: (9) a situation in which all markets in an economy are simultaneously in equilibrium. (p. 259)

GNP: (2) see _gross national product._ (p. 23)

Golden Rule capital–labour ratio: (6) the level of the capital–labour ratio that maximizes consumption per worker in the steady state. (p. 173)

government capital: (15) long-lived physical assets owned by the government, such as roads and public schools. (p. 515)

government debt: (15) the total value of government bonds outstanding at any given time. (p. 521)

government expenditure: (2) the government's purchases of goods and services plus transfers and interest payments. (p. 30)

government purchases: (2) spending by the government on currently produced goods and services. (p. 26)

government revenue: (2) taxes and other revenues collected by the government. (p. 30)

government saving: (2) the government's tax receipts minus its expenditure; equal to the government budget surplus. (p. 30)

gradualism: (13) a prescription for disinflation that involves reducing the rate of monetary growth and the rate of inflation gradually over a period of several years; in contrast to _cold turkey._ (p. 465)

gross domestic product (GDP): (2) the market value of final goods and services newly produced within a nation's borders during a fixed period of time. (p. 20)

gross investment: (4) the total purchase or construction of new capital goods. (p. 114)

gross national product (GNP): (2) the market value of final goods and services newly produced by domestically owned factors of production during a fixed period of time. (p. 23)

growth accounting: (6) a method for dividing total output growth into parts attributable to growth of capital, labour, and productivity. (p. 164)

growth accounting equation: (6) the production function written in growth rate form; it states that the growth rate of output is the sum of (1) the growth rate of productivity, (2) the elasticity of output with respect to capital times the growth rate of capital, and (3) the elasticity of output with respect to labour times the growth rate of labour. (p. 163)

high-powered money: (14) the liabilities of the central bank, consisting of bank reserves and currency in circulation, that are usable as money; also known as the *monetary base*. (p. 474)

human capital: (6) the productive knowledge, skills, and training of individuals. (p. 185)

hyperinflation: (13) a situation in which the rate of inflation is extremely high for a sustained period of time; one suggested definition is a 50% or more monthly rate of inflation. (p. 463)

hysteresis: (13) the tendency of the natural rate of unemployment to change in response to the actual unemployment rate, rising if the actual unemployment rate is above the natural rate and falling if the actual unemployment rate is below the natural rate. (p. 457)

import: (1) the buying of goods from other countries. (p. 4)

income approach: (2) a procedure for measuring economic activity by adding all income received, including taxes and after-tax profits. (p. 19)

income effect (of a higher real wage): (3) the tendency of workers to supply less labour in response to an increase in the real wage; arises because an increase in the real wage makes workers wealthier and leads them to want to consume more leisure. (p. 65)

income effect (of the real interest rate on saving): (4) the tendency of savers to consume more and save less in response to an increase in the real interest rate because they are made wealthier; the tendency of borrowers to consume less and save more in response to an increase in the real interest rate because they are made less wealthy. (p. 99)

income elasticity of money demand: (7) the percentage change in money demand resulting from a 1% increase in real income. (p. 216)

income–expenditure identity: (2) the accounting identity that states that total income (product) equals the sum of the four types of expenditure: consumption, investment, government purchases, and net exports. (p. 24)

inconvertible currency: (10) a currency that cannot be traded freely for other currencies, usually because of government-imposed restrictions. (p. 325)

industrial policy: (6) a strategy for economic growth by which the government, using taxes, subsidies, or regulation, attempts to influence the nation's pattern of industrial development. (p. 191)

inflation: (1) a situation in which the prices of most goods and services are rising over time. (p. 4)

inflation tax: (15) the resources raised by the government by issuing money and creating inflation; also known as *seignorage*. (p. 531)

interest elasticity of money demand: (7) the percentage change in money demand resulting from a 1% increase (different from a 1 percentage point increase) in the interest rate. (p. 216)

interest rate: (2) the rate of return promised by a borrower to a lender. (p. 39)

interest rate channel: (12, 14) the effects of monetary policy that work through changes in real interest rates. (pp. 403, 490)

intermediate goods and services: (2) goods and services that are used up in the production of other goods and services in the same period that they themselves were produced; an example is wheat used up in making bread. (p. 21)

inventories: (2) stocks of unsold finished goods, goods in process, and production materials held by firms. (p. 23)

investment: (2) spending for new capital goods, called fixed investment, and increases in firms' inventory holdings, called inventory investment. See *gross investment, net investment.* (p. 26)

invisible hand: (1) the idea (proposed by Adam Smith) that if there are free markets and individuals conduct their economic affairs in their own best interests, the economy as a whole will work well. (p. 11)

IS curve: (9) in a diagram with output on the horizontal axis and the real interest rate on the vertical axis, a downward-sloping curve that shows the value of the real interest rate that clears the goods market for any given value of output. At any point on the *IS* curve, desired national saving equals desired investment (in a closed economy); equivalently, the aggregate quantity of goods demanded equals the aggregate quantity of goods supplied. (p. 247)

labour force: (3) the number of people willing to work, including unemployed people actively searching for work, as well as employed workers. (p. 78)

labour hoarding: (11) a situation that occurs if, because of the costs of firing and hiring workers, firms continue to employ some workers in a recession that they otherwise would have laid off. (p. 362)

lagging variable: (8) a variable with peaks and troughs that tends to occur later than the corresponding peaks and troughs in the business cycle. See *coincident variable, leading variable.* (p. 233)

large open economy: (5) an economy that trades with other economies and is large enough to affect the world real interest rate. (p. 149)

leading variable: (8) a variable with peaks and troughs that tends to occur earlier than the corresponding peaks and troughs in the business cycle. See *coincident variable, lagging variable.* (p. 233)

leisure: (3) all off-the-job activities, including eating, recreation, and working in the yard and on the house. (p. 64)

lender of last resort: (14) the role served by a central bank when it stands ready to lend reserves to banks to avoid bank runs or financial crises. (p. 484)

liquidity: (7) the ease and quickness with which an asset can be exchanged for goods, services, or other assets. (p. 204)

LM curve: (9) in a diagram with output on the horizontal axis and the real interest rate on the vertical axis, an upward-sloping curve that shows the value of the real interest rate that clears the asset market for any given value of output. At any point on the *LM* curve, the quantities of money supplied and demanded are equal. (p. 255)

long-run aggregate supply (LRAS) curve: (11) in a diagram with output on the horizontal axis and the price level on the vertical axis, a vertical line at full-employment output; indicates that in the long run the supply of output does not depend on the price level. (p. 372)

long-run Phillips curve: (13) in a diagram with unemployment on the horizontal axis and inflation on the vertical axis, a vertical line at the natural rate of unemployment; indicates that in the long run, the unemployment rate equals the natural rate, independent of the rate of inflation. (p. 453)

M1+: (7) the most narrowly defined monetary aggregate, made up of currency and travellers' cheques held by the public, demand deposits (personal chequing accounts) at commercial banks, and other chequable deposits. (p. 201)

M2: (7) a monetary aggregate that includes everything in M1+ and a number of other assets that are somewhat less moneylike, such as savings deposits and non-personal notice deposits. (p. 202)

M3: (7) a broad monetary aggregate that includes everything in M2 plus further accounts at banks, such as term deposits of businesses and foreign currency accounts. (p. 202)

macroeconomics: (1) the study of the structure and performance of national economies and of the policies that governments use to try to affect economic performance. (p. 1)

marginal cost: (12) the cost of producing an additional unit of output. (p. 411)

marginal product of capital (*MPK*): (3) the amount of output produced per unit of additional capital. (p. 53)

marginal product of labour (*MPN*): (3) the amount of output produced per unit of additional labour. (p. 54)

marginal propensity to consume (*MPC*): (4) the amount by which desired consumption rises when current output rises by one unit. (p. 95)

marginal revenue product of labour (*MRPN*): (3) the extra revenue obtained by a firm when it employs an additional unit of labour and sells the resulting increase in output; for competitive firms, equal to the price of output times the marginal product of labour. (p. 58)

marginal tax rate: (15) the fraction of an additional dollar of income that must be paid in taxes. (p. 516)

market policy: (6) the extent to which government restricts the free operation of markets. (p. 192)

markup: (12) the difference between the price charged for a good and its marginal cost of production, expressed as a percentage of marginal cost. (p. 141)

medium of exchange: (7) an asset used in making transactions. (p. 200)

menu cost: (12) the cost of changing prices, for example, the cost of printing a new menu or remarking merchandise. (p. 409)

merchandise trade balance: (5) a country's merchandise exports (exports of goods) minus its merchandise imports. (p. 132)

misperceptions theory: (11) predicts that because of producers' inability to observe directly the general price level, the aggregate quantity of output supplied rises above the full-employment level when the aggregate price level is higher than expected; hence the short-run aggregate supply curve is upward-sloping. (p. 370)

monetarism: (14) a school of macroeconomic thought that emphasizes the importance of monetary factors in the macroeconomy, but which opposes the active use of monetary policy to stabilize the economy. (p. 492)

monetary aggregates: (7) the official measures of the money supply, such as M1+ and M2. See *M1+, M2, M3*. (p. 201)

monetary base: (14) the liabilities of the central bank, consisting of bank reserves and currency in circulation, that are usable as money; also known as high-powered money. (p. 474)

monetary neutrality: (9) characterizes an economy in which changes in the nominal money supply change the price level proportionally but have no effect on real variables. The basic classical model predicts neutrality; the classical model with misperceptions and the Keynesian model predict that neutrality holds in the long run but not in the short run. (p. 272)

monetary policy: (1) policies determining the level and rate of growth of the nation's money supply, which are under the control of a government institution known as the central bank (the Bank of Canada in Canada). (p. 5)

money: (7) assets that are widely used and accepted as payment. (p. 199)

money demand function: (7) the function that relates the real demand for money to output and the interest rate paid by nonmonetary assets. (p. 214)

money multiplier: (14) the number of dollars of money supply that can be created from each dollar of monetary base, calculated as the ratio of the money supply to the monetary base. (p. 479)

money supply: (7) the total amount of money available in an economy, consisting of currency in circulation and deposits; also known as the "money stock." (p. 202)

monopolistic competition: (12) a market situation in which some competition exists but in which a relatively small number of sellers and imperfect standardization of the product allow individual producers to act as price setters, rather than as price takers. (p. 408)

multiple expansion of loans and deposits: (14) in a fractional reserve banking system, the process in which banks lend out some of their deposits, the loaned funds are ultimately re-deposited in the banking system, and the new deposits are lent out again; as a result of the multiple-expansion process, the money supply can greatly exceed the monetary base. (p. 476)

multiplier effect: (9, 12) the effect of an increase in government purchases or an expansionary fiscal policy whereby the demand for goods and thus the number of transactions in the economy also increase (pp. 268, 404)

national income accounts: (2) an accounting framework used in measuring current economic activity. (p. 17)

national saving: (2) the saving of the economy as a whole, including both private saving (business and household) and government saving. (p. 30)

national wealth: (2) the total wealth of the residents of a country, consisting of the country's domestic physical assets (such as its stock of capital goods and land) and its net foreign assets. (p. 29)

natural rate of unemployment: (3) the rate of unemployment that exists when the economy's output is at its full-employment level; consists of frictional unemployment and structural unemployment. (p. 82)

neoclassical growth model: (6) a model of economic growth based on capital accumulation and population growth, with a constant savings rate (also called the Solow model). (p. 168)

net export crowding out: (10) the reduction in net exports resulting from an exchange rate appreciation. (p. 320)

net exports: (2) exports of goods and services minus imports of goods and services. (p. 26)

net factor payments from abroad (*NFP*): (2) income paid to domestic factors of production by the rest of the world, minus income paid to foreign factors of production by the domestic economy. (p. 24)

net foreign assets: (2) a country's foreign assets (for example, foreign stocks, bonds, and factories owned by domestic residents) minus its foreign liabilities (domestic physical and financial assets owned by foreigners). (p. 33)

net investment: (4) the change in the capital stock over the year, equal to gross investment minus depreciation of existing capital. (p. 114)

nominal appreciation: (10) an increase in the nominal exchange rate in a flexible-exchange-rate system. (p. 298)

nominal depreciation: (10) a decrease in the nominal exchange rate in a flexible-exchange-rate system. (p. 298)

nominal exchange rate: (10) the number of units of foreign currency that can be purchased with one unit of the home currency; also known as the *exchange rate*. (p. 295)

nominal GDP: (2) the value of an economy's final output measured using current market prices; also known as "current-dollar GDP." (p. 35)

nominal interest rate: (2) the rate at which the nominal value of an interest-bearing asset increases over time; equivalent to the market interest rate. (p. 39)

nominal interest rate parity condition: (10) the condition that the difference between the nominal interest rates in two countries equals the rate at which the currency of the country with the higher interest rate is expected to depreciate. (p. 310)

nominal shocks: (11) shocks to money supply or money demand, which cause the *LM* curve to shift. (p. 354)

nominal variables: (2) variables measured in terms of current market prices. (p. 34)

nominal-wage rigidity: (12) from the Keynesian perspective, the tendency of labour demanders (firms) and labour suppliers (employees) to enter into contracts that fix a nominal wage for the period of that contract. (p. 392)

normative analysis: (1) an analysis of policy that tries to determine whether a certain policy should be used; involves both analysis of the consequences of the policy and value judgments about the desirability of those consequences. See *positive analysis*. (p. 10)

official reserve assets: (5) assets held by central banks, other than domestic money or securities, that can be used in making international payments; examples are gold, foreign bank deposits, and special assets created by the International Monetary Fund. (p. 134)

official settlements balance: (5) the net increase (domestic less foreign) in a country's official reserve assets; also known as the balance of payments. (p. 135)

Okun's law: (13) a rule of thumb that says that output falls by 2.0% for each percentage point increase in the cyclical unemployment rate. (p. 454)

100% reserve banking: (14) a banking system in which banks hold reserves equal to 100% of their deposits. (p. 454)

open economy: (1) a national economy that has significant trading and financial relationships with other national economies. (p. 4)

open-economy trilemma: (10) a constraint on monetary policy in which policymakers can adopt only two of fixed exchange rates, mobility of financial capital, and independent monetary policy. (p. 332)

open-market operations: (7) an open-market purchase or sale of assets by the central bank, used to affect the money supply. See *open-market purchase, open-market sale*. (p. 203)

open-market purchase: (14) a purchase of assets (such as Treasury bills) from the public by the central bank, used to increase the money supply. (p. 481)

open-market sale: (14) a sale of assets (such as Treasury bills) to the public by the central bank, used to reduce the money supply. (p. 481)

overnight rate: (14) the interest rate charged by one direct clearer to another, for settlement balances lent for one day. (p. 483)

overvalued exchange rate: (10) in a fixed-exchange-rate system, an exchange rate that is higher than its fundamental value. See *fundamental value of the exchange rate*. (p. 324)

participation rate: (3) the fraction of adults who are in the labour force. (p. 79)

pass-through: (12) the extent to which a decrease in the nominal exchange rate leads to an increase in domestic prices. (p. 410)

peak: (8) in a business cycle, the point in time when economic activity stops increasing and begins to decline. (p. 229)

perfect competition: (12) a market situation in which there is a standardized good and many buyers and sellers so that all buyers and sellers are price takers. (p. 408)

persistence: (8) the tendency for declines in economic activity to be followed by further declines and for growth in economic activity to be followed by more growth. (p. 230)

Phillips curve: (13) a downward-sloping relationship between the inflation rate and the unemployment rate; theory suggests that a Phillips curve will be observed in the data only in periods in which expected inflation and the natural rate of unemployment are relatively stable. See *expectations-augmented Phillips curve, long-run Phillips curve*. (p. 441)

portfolio allocation decision: (7) a wealth-holder's decision about which assets and how much of each asset to hold. (p. 204)

positive analysis: (1) an analysis of the economic consequences of a policy that does not address the question of whether those consequences are desirable. See *normative analysis*. (p. 10)

poverty trap: (15) a situation in which an increase in labour income reduces eligibility for transfers, which implies high marginal tax rates for low-income earners. (p. 518)

price index: (2) a measure of the average level of prices for some specified set of goods and services, relative to the prices of a specified base period. (p. 36)

price stickiness: (12) in Keynesian theory, the tendency of prices to adjust only slowly to changes in the economy; also known as "price rigidity." (p. 407)

primary budget surplus: (15) a measure of the surplus that excludes government interest payments from total expenditure; equal to the total budget surplus plus net interest payments. (p. 509)

private disposable income: (2) the income of the private sector (households and businesses taken together) after payment of taxes and receipt of transfer payments and interest from the government. (p. 28)

private saving: (2) the saving of the private sector (households and businesses), equal to private disposable income minus consumption. (p. 29)

procyclical: (8) tending to move in the same direction as aggregate economic activity over the business cycle (up in expansions, down in contractions). See *acyclical, countercyclical*. (p. 233)

product approach: (2) a procedure for measuring economic activity by adding the market values of goods and services produced, excluding any goods and services used up in intermediate stages of production; equivalently, by summing the values added of all producers. (p. 18)

production function: (3) a function that shows the amount of output that can be produced (by a firm or by an entire economy) by using any given quantities of capital and labour. (p. 48)

productivity: (3) a measure of the overall effectiveness with which the economy uses capital and labour to produce output; also known as total factor productivity. (p. 47)

productivity shocks: (11) a change in an economy's production function; equivalently, a change in the amount of output that can be produced using given quantities of capital and labour; also known as a *supply shock*. (p. 354)

propagation mechanism: (11) an aspect of the economy, such as the behaviour of inventories, that allows short-lived shocks to have longer-term effects on the economy. (p. 381)

purchasing power parity: (10) the idea that similar domestic and foreign goods, or baskets of goods, should have the same price in terms of the same currency. (p. 299)

quantitative easing: (14) a form of open-market operation that involves the central bank buying or selling government or privately issued assets with long times to maturity. (p. 486)

quantity theory of money: (7) a theory that asserts that nominal money demand is proportional to nominal GDP so that velocity is constant. (p. 217)

rational expectations: (11) expectations about the future values of economic variables that are based on reasoned and intelligent examination of available economic data; although they may make forecast errors, people with rational expectations cannot be systematically surprised by changes in macroeconomic policy or in the economy. (p. 374)

rational price expectation: (11) the price level economic agents expect to observe in the future, given their reasoned and intelligent examination of available economic data. (p. 376)

real appreciation: (10) an increase in the real exchange rate, which increases the quantity of foreign goods that can be purchased with a given quantity of domestic goods. (p. 299)

real business cycle (RBC) theory: (11) a version of the classical theory that assumes that productivity shocks (supply shocks) are the primary source of cyclical fluctuations. (p. 354)

real depreciation: (10) a fall in the real exchange rate, which decreases the quantity of foreign goods that can be purchased with a given quantity of domestic goods. (p. 299)

real exchange rate: (10) the quantity of foreign goods that can be obtained in exchange for one domestic good. (p. 297)

real GDP: (2) the market value of an economy's final output measured in terms of the prices that prevailed during some fixed base period; also known as "constant-dollar GDP." (p. 35)

real interest rate: (2) the rate at which the real value or purchasing power of an interest-bearing asset increases over time; equal to the nominal interest rate minus the rate of inflation. (p. 39)

real interest rate parity condition: (10) the condition that the difference between the real interest rates in two countries equals the rate at which the real exchange rate of the country with the higher real interest rate is expected to fall. (p. 310)

real shocks: (11) disturbances to the "real side" of the economy, such as shocks that affect the production function, the size of the labour force, the real quantity of government purchases, or the spending and saving decisions of consumers; real shocks affect the *IS* curve or the *FE* line. (p. 354)

real variable: (2) a variable measured in terms of the prices of a fixed base year; a measure intended to represent physical quantities produced or used. (p. 35)

real wage: (3) the real value (measured in terms of goods) of what firms must pay per unit of labour input that they employ; equal to the nominal (dollar) wage divided by the price level. (p. 58)

real-wage rigidity: (12) from the Keynesian perspective, the apparent tendency of real wages to move too little over the business cycle to keep the quantity of labour supplied equal to the quantity of labour demanded. (p. 431)

recession: (8) in a business cycle, the period of time during which aggregate economic activity is falling; also known as a contraction. (p. 229)

relative purchasing power parity: (10) the idea that the rate of appreciation of the nominal exchange rate equals the foreign inflation rate minus the domestic inflation rate. (p. 301)

reserve–deposit ratio: (14) the ratio of reserves held by banks to the public's deposits in banks. (p. 475)

revaluation: (10) an increase in the value of a currency by official government action under a fixed-exchange-rate system. (p. 299)

reverse causation: (11) the tendency of expected future changes in output to cause changes in the current money supply in the same direction; used by real business cycle theorists to explain why the money supply leads the cycle. (p. 367)

Ricardian equivalence proposition: (4) the proposition that changes in the government budget deficit caused entirely by changes in (lump-sum) tax collections have no effect on the economy. (p. 105)

risk: (7) the possibility that the actual return received on an asset will be substantially different from the expected return. (p. 204)

rules: (14) a set of simple, pre-specified, and publicly announced guidelines for conducting monetary policy; in contrast to *discretion*. (p. 491)

sacrifice ratio: (13) the amount of output lost when the inflation rate is reduced by one percentage point. (p. 466)

Sale and Repurchase Agreement (SRA): (14) a transaction in which the Bank of Canada sells Treasury bills to banks and investment dealers and then buys them back the next day; it lowers settlement balances and raises the overnight rate. (p. 486)

saving: (2) current income minus spending on current needs. (p. 29)

seignorage: (15) government revenue raised by printing money; also known as the *inflation tax*. (p. 532)

settlement balances: (14) balances held by direct clearers at the Bank of Canada; also called "clearing balances." (p. 483)

shocks: (1) a variable in an economic model whose value is not affected by changes in other variables in the model. (p. 10)

shoe leather costs: (13) the costs incurred in the process of economizing on holdings of cash, for example, in more frequent trips to the bank. (p. 461)

short-run aggregate supply (SRAS) curve: (11) in a diagram with output on the horizontal axis and the price level on the vertical axis, the relationship between the price level and the amount of output that applies in the short run. In the short run, prices remain fixed, and producers produce the quantity demanded at the fixed price level, so the *SRAS* curve is horizontal. In the extended classical model based on the misperceptions theory, the *SRAS* curve slopes upward, as producers are fooled into supplying more output when the price level is higher than expected; the short run in this model is the period of time during which the expected price level remains unchanged. (p. 372)

small open economy: (5) an economy that trades with other economies but is too small to affect the world real interest rate. (p. 139)

Solow residual: (11) an empirical measure of total factor productivity. (p. 360)

Special Purchase and Resale Agreement (SPRA): (14) a transaction in which the Bank of Canada buys Treasury bills from banks and investment dealers and then sells them back the next day; it raises settlement balances and lowers the overnight rate. (p. 486)

speculative run: (10) a situation in which financial investors, fearing the imminent devaluation of a currency in a fixed-exchange-rate system, rush to sell assets denominated in that currency. (p. 325)

statistical discrepancy: (5) an amount added to the sum of the current and capital account balances for this sum to reach its theoretical value of zero. (p. 137)

steady state: (6) a situation in which the economy's output per worker, consumption per worker, and capital stock per worker are constant over time. (p. 170)

stock variable: (2) an economic quantity that is defined at a specific time; examples are wealth or the money supply. See *flow variable*. (p. 32)

store of value: (7) a means of holding wealth over time. (p. 201)

structural unemployment: (3) long-term and chronic unemployment arising from imbalances between the skills and other characteristics of workers in the market and the needs of employers. (p. 82)

substitution effect (of a higher real wage): (3) the tendency of workers to substitute work for leisure in response to a higher real wage. (p. 65)

substitution effect (of the real interest rate on saving): (4) the tendency of consumers to save more, and thereby substitute future consumption for current consumption, in response to a higher reward for saving. (p. 99)

supply shock: (3) a change in an economy's production function, that is, in the amount of output that can be produced by using given quantities of capital and labour; also known as a *productivity shock*. (p. 55)

target overnight rate: (14) the centre of the Bank of Canada's operating band for the overnight interest rate, set through monetary policy. (p. 483)

tax-adjusted user cost of capital: (4) indicates how large the before-tax expected future marginal product of capital must be in order to make a proposed investment profitable; equivalently, the (unadjusted) user cost of capital divided by 1 minus the effective tax rate. (p. 112)

tax rate smoothing: (15) a policy of maintaining stable tax rates over time in order to minimize the distortions created by the tax code. See *distortions*. (p. 519)

Taylor rule: (14) a guideline for monetary policy, it relates the real target overnight rate to the difference between output and full-employment output and the difference between inflation and its target. (p. 496)

term premium: (7) the higher interest rate paid to holders of long-term bonds to compensate them for the added risk compared with short-term bonds, so that the interest rate on long-term bonds exceeds that suggested by the expectations theory of the term structure. (p. 206)

time to maturity: (7) the amount of time until an asset matures and the investors receive their principal. (p. 205)

total factor productivity: (3) a measure of the overall effectiveness with which the economy uses capital and labour to produce output; also known as productivity. (p. 49)

trade deficit: (1) a nation's excess of imports over exports. (p. 4)

trade surplus: (1) a nation's excess of exports over imports. (p. 4)

transfers: (2) payments by the government, excluding payments made in exchange for current goods or services; examples of transfers are Old Age Security benefits, unemployment insurance, and welfare payments. (p. 26)

trough: (8) in a business cycle, the time when economic activity stops falling and begins rising. (p. 229)

turning points: (8) peaks or troughs in the business cycle. (p. 229)

turnover costs: (12) the costs associated with hiring and training new workers. (p. 431)

underground economy: (2) the portion of the economy that includes both legal activities hidden from government record-keepers and illegal activities. (p. 21)

undervalued exchange rate: (10) in a fixed-exchange-rate system, an exchange rate that is lower than its fundamental value. See *fundamental value of the exchange rate*. (p. 326)

unemployment: (1) the number of people who are available for work and actively seeking work but cannot find jobs. (p. 4)

unemployment rate: (3) the fraction of the labour force that is unemployed. (p. 49)

unemployment spell: (3) the period of time that an individual is continuously unemployed. (p. 80)

unit of account: (7) the basic unit for measuring economic value (dollars, for example). (p. 200)

user cost of capital: (4) the expected real cost of using a unit of capital for a specified period of time; equal to the depreciation cost plus the interest cost. (p. 108)

uses-of-saving identity: (2) the accounting identity that states that private saving equals the sum of investment, the government deficit, and the current account balance. (p. 31)

value added: (2) for any producer, the value of output minus the value of purchased inputs. (p. 18)

velocity: (7) the number of times the money stock "turns over" each period; calculated as nominal GDP divided by the nominal money supply. (p. 217)

wealth: (2) the assets minus the liabilities of an individual, firm, or country; also known as "net worth." (p. 29)

world real interest rate: (5) the real interest rate that prevails in the international capital market in which individuals, businesses, and governments borrow and lend across national borders. (p. 139)

Name Index

NOTE: Entries followed by "n" represent footnotes.

SUBJECT INDEX

NOTE: Entries for tables, figures, and notes are followed by "*t*", "*f*", and "*n*" respectively.